In Favour of Govinddevjī

In Favour of Govinddevjī

Historical documents relating to a deity of Vrindaban and Eastern Rajasthan

by

Monika Horstmann

In collaboration with

Heike Bill

INDIRA GANDHI NATIONAL CENTRE FOR THE ARTS
NEW DELHI

MANOHAR
1999

First published 1999

ISBN 81-7304-315-9

Published by
Indira Gandhi National Centre for the Arts
Janpath, New Delhi 110001
in association with
Ajay Kumar Jain for
Manohar Publishers & Distributors
2/6 Ansari Road, Daryaganj
New Delhi 110002

Printed at
Rajkamal Electric Press
B 35/9 G T Karnal Road Indl Area
Delhi 110033

To the memory of

Tarapada Mukherjee

(1928-1990)

Contents

Abbreviations and Symbols

Ā'īn	Abū'l-Fazl 'Allāmī. 1927-49
AME	Habib 1982
b.	(1) *badī*, (2) *bīghā*(s)
BPL	Grierson 1885
ch.	*chaṭāṃk*(s)
CHI V	Dodwell 1929
DCH	*District Census Handbook*, see India 1983
DK	*Dastūr komvār*
GD	Govinddevjī
GJRT	Wilson 1855
HŚS	Śyāmsundardās 1986
KD	Bahura and Singh 1988
MU	Śāh Navāz Khān 1941
Platts	Platts 1884
rev.y.	revenue year
RM	Rādhāmādhavjī
rp.	rupee(s)
RSA	Rajasthan State Archives, Bikaner
RSK	Lāḷas V.S. 2018-35
ś.	*śukla*
s/o	son of
Steingass	Steingass 1892
v.	*viśvā*(s)
VRI	Vrindaban Research Institute
V.S.	Vikrama *saṃvat*
VV	Śyāmaldās 1886
→ *(followed by date)*	calendared document published in this volume
[*date*]	unpublished calendared document
* *(followed by date)*	untraceable calendared document

Foreword

One amongst other objectives of the Indira Gandhi National Centre for the Arts (IGNCA) is to investigate the diverse levels of interaction within a single geographical unit, region. What are the processes by which a particular place acquires significance as a major cultural centre? It becomes the place to which energies converge and from which energies relate; both centripetal and centrifugal movements are evident. While these centres emerge in historical time, they develop into sacred places, what are these confluences of socio-economic political forces, religious movements, which generate artistic expressions? How does overlayering take place over a period of time and why do they continue to hold attention of both those inside and outside the region or the cultural centres? Often a temple or mosque is the physical or notional centre, at other times the whole area acquires a trans-, space and time presence.

One such region is *Vraj* where millions throng to relive the experience of the childhood and beyond of Kṛṣṇa. Each place, hamlet or grove, lane or by-lane evokes the memory of the myth. An annual calendar of rituals and festivities recreates and relives the life of the blue god.

And yet the place is in historical time. Monuments were built at particular times by specific people. There are texts which testify to the self-awareness of the patrons and the community. Alongside are the living repositories of the tradition who transmit the memory of the community orally generation after generation. The temples have a living presence which is renewed, modified and even changed through ritual practices. Which methodological tools of research may be adopted to create a virtual picture of the totality and not the parts, the multi-dimensional dynamics of these places?

The IGNCA has endeavoured to evolve an alternative model for the study of such centres. Both textual and oral sources, primary and secondary, are explored, the layout of the area, the architectural features of the principal monuments and the inscriptional and epigraphical texts are analysed. An audio-visual documentation of the ritual is made, the artistic experience of sculpture, painting, music and dance related to the monument is studied. Finally an attempt is made to integrate the evidence from these diverse sources with a view to reflecting the holistic world view embedded in these places, and the staggering variety of interactions and dialogues which were and continue to take place.

Vraj in the north and Tanjavur in the south were obvious choices for such an undertaking called the *Kṣetra Sampadā* projects of the IGNCA which are now beginning to yield the first results of the research undertaken by a variety of scholars, each a specialist in his or her field. In the case of Tanjavur, a definitive study of the Bṛhadīśvara temple has already appeared. Two volumes on the sculptural schema and the iconography are in the press, a third volume on the inscriptions is under preparation. Concurrently the texts of the *āgamas* are being edited and translated and a fairly extensive documentation of contemporary rituals, hymnology and music and dance traditions has been made. All this is being integrated into a multi-media programme which will enable future research easy access to the material and facilitate comprehension of the complexity.

The Vraj and Nāthadvārā project is even more complex. Many dimensions of space, time and place have to be explored. There is an abundance of textual material, primary, secondary and tertiary. There are historical records, land grants and chronicles; the theologians kept their own records. Besides, there is a large corpus of literary material both theological as also poetic. Equally rich are the oral traditions. Contemporary practices emerge from the past, but also effect and affect it. No single scholar, or any institution could undertake such a task in isolation. Collaboration and multi-disciplinary team work was a necessity.

Fortunately, three institutions and many scholars had been engaged in diverse aspects of the Vraj and the Govindadeva temple in particular.

It was time to hold an international seminar on the Govindadeva temple as a first initial step. The *Caitanya Prema Saṁsthana* and the Indira Gandhi National Centre for the Arts brought together many scholars from different parts of the world to take stock of the work done and to explore the directions of further research. The volume entitled *Govindadeva: A Dialogue in Stone* testified to the complexities to studying the multifaceted and multilayered personality of Vraj through the great Govindadeva temple built in the Mughal period. Its subsequent enigmatic history of the deity travelling to Jaipur is as mysterious as revealing of the cultural movements. Two volumes; one a definitive edition of the *Śri Śri Bhaktīrasāmṛtasindhū* by Rūpa Gosvāmī and another entitled *Evening Blossoms: The Temple Tradition of Sāñjhī in Vṛndāvana* have been published. Alas the editor of the first and the author of the second, Dr. Premlata Sharma and Shrí Asim Krishnadasa passed away before completing other works they had undertaken.

At the international seminar were present amongst other renowned scholars, Prof. Irfan Habib and Prof. Monkia Horstmann. Both of them had been closely associated with the renowned scholar, the late Dr. Tarapada Mukherjee of SOAS, London, and the Vrindavan Research Institute's programme. Prof. Irfan Habib along with Dr. Tarapada Mukherjee has published a series of seminal papers based on the Persian sources, the *farmāns* as land grants and much else. While these revealed the involvement of Akbar and the Mughal court, there was the other group of sources from Rajasthan. Rājā Mānsingh was equally engaged in the enterprise. Dr. Tarapada Mukherjee had collected many documents from the Vaiṣṇava temples. It was left to Prof. Monika Horstmann to fill the void and complete the unfinished work of Dr. Tarapada Mukherjee in the spirit of a true scholar dedicated to continuing the unfinished task. Besides, the documents collected by Dr. Tarapada Mukherjee, Prof. Horstmann investigated the Bikaner Archives and has made full use of these. The result is this welcome monograph.

The documents presented in the volume reflect the relationship of the Kachavāhā dynasty of Eastern Rajasthan (Amber/Jaipur) with the Gauḍīya sect. The first custodian of Govinddevjī was Rūpa Gosvāmī, and the deity's great temple of Vrindavan, as it exists to this day, was erected by the Kachavāhā Rājā Mānsingh. He was a loyal exponent of the Mughal power and, at the same time, a Hindu King, eminently powerful in his own right. His royal architecture reflects this double bind, and so does the history of the temple of Govindadeva and other old Vaiṣṇava temples that were all the objects of both Mughal and Hindu royal patronage.

Mughal patronage is documented by Persian grants to this and other Vaiṣṇava temples and the representatives of various Vaiṣṇava sects. This book deals exclusively with the Kachavāhā grants and other documents, which are related to these grants or deal with the affairs of the custodians of the Govindadeva temple. Prof. Horstmann traces the history of the grants from the middle of the 17th century to the 1950s and thus implicitly establishes an aspect of the relationship between the Kachavāhās and the Gauḍīyas, and even beyond that, between the modern state of Rajasthan and the specific religious sect.

The book thus provides a documentary history of a facet of the politico-religious history of Vraj and Rajasthan. It also provides insight into the character of the special type of its documents and, therefore, is a valuable contribution to the diplomatics of the chancery of Eastern Rajasthan. Prof. Horstmann states that although the focus of the book is mainly on the contents of the documents, she found it necessary to add a chapter (Chapter 2) devoted to their diplomatic and administrative aspects. Though these aspects have been studied carefully from the Persian documents available, they have not received sufficient attention as far as the Rajasthani documents are concerned. A description of the diplomatic conventions and administrative procedures involved goes a long way in understanding the structure of the documents.

This picture of an active collaboration and interaction will be complete only if the vast corpus of oral information gathered by the late Dr. Mukherjee from the Gosvāmīs is also transcribed and published. It will be our endeavor to do this also.

The late Dr. Tarapada Mukherjee to whom Prof. Monika Horstmann dedicates her volume was keenly aware of the nature of the materials and their significance. In an article published in the *IAVRI Bulletin* [No. 8, 1980:16] he said:

> 'These materials should not be seen merely as records of sectarian interest. They are, in fact, community

> records that provide a key to the knowledge of the history of the area. In the absence of community records such as these, the traditional history of India is imperfect and inadequate. The history of India is not the history of the 'seats of power', the true and intimate history of India is the history of the centres of learning, religion and culture. How much do we know of these centres, how much do we care to know of them?
>
> Vrindaban is a city of temples venerated for its association with Kṛṣṇa. Not unjustifiably therefore, one associates Vrindaban with devotion and devotional literature. This association, however, has obscured its historical identity and the materials of its history. We never expected that the ascetics who developed the area would record every step of their movement and preserve those records for the posterity. From these records we know how efficient and strong was the organisation of the sects and how firm was the control of the ascetics over the spiritual and economic life of the community. With an astonishing skill of diplomacy, the ascetics maintained their superiority over the rulers of the country while enjoying support and sympathy from them. Soon after the death of the six Gosvāmīs, the big temples of the Gauḍīya sect accumulated so much land and wealth that each of their custodians attained the status of a zamindar. The history of these zamindars is the history of Vrindaban. It is a history of the development of a mediaeval township which was cosmopolitan, prosperous and self-contained, and above all, a holy place that attracted pilgrims and ascetics of all denominations from all over the country. The rulers fostered its growth and the natives accepted the economic and social supremacy of the migrants without qualms. There were disputes and rivalries among and within the sects but life seems to have been harmonious and peaceful, at least while the six Gosvāmīs were alive. No other mediaeval town in India seems to have such a well defined and well documented history. The materials of its history now being accessible, it is hoped that the final outcome of the project would be a definitive history of Vrindaban. But the materials are yet to be deciphered, studied and interpreted.'

Pertinently he observed that a huge number of documents and materials remain to be deciphered and printed together step by step in order to eventually yield a history of Vrindavan and the political and religious ideologies of the characteristic of Kṛṣṇa devotionalism.

The IGNCA joins Prof. Horstmann in paying tribute to this scholar. It is grateful to her for offering her work for publication to the IGNCA. Shri Srivats Goswami, Director of the Caitanya Prema Saṁsthana has actively collaborated. We are thankful to him. Prof. Irfan Habib read the first draft and made useful suggestions. We are indebted to him.

Dr. Lalit M. Gujral, my colleague in the IGNCA, has painstakingly seen the book through the press. I thank him.

12 April, 1999 KAPILA VATSYAYAN

Preface

This book owes its existence to the late Tarapada Mukherjee who brought together and had photographed the bulk of the documents analysed herein. With respect and warmth, Irfan Habib (1996:131), who knew Mukherjee so much better than I had the privilege to do, has pointed out Mukherjee's achievements in the field of the preservation and study of manuscripts relating to the Bengal Vaiṣṇavas of Braj. When Mukherjee realised that he would succumb to an incurable disease, he requested me to study those of the documents that came from Rajasthan and that he had not yet been able to tackle, even though we were not personally acquainted. In the spring of 1990, he made his last journey but one and visited me in Cologne, where I taught at the time, in order to introduce me to the material and discuss with me the shape of the publication to be brought out. He died in July 1990. I have done my best to carry out his intentions, but I am painfully aware that in the absence of his intimate knowledge of the material and his advice, I have achieved little.

Although the focus of the book is on the contents matter of the documents, I have found it necessary to add a chapter (Chapter 2) devoted to their diplomatic and administrative aspects. Whereas these aspects have been studied carefully for Persian documents from India, they have received very little attention as far as the Rajasthani documents are concerned. However, without a rough idea of the diplomatic conventions and administrative procedures involved, the reader may find the appearance and structure of the documents rather unclear.

In the preparation of this volume I have enjoyed the cooperation of Heike Bill. She has edited and translated the Persian versions of the documents, deciphered the Persian seals, and has provided the chart of *siyāq* numerals in Appendix 5 of Chapter 2. I am grateful to her for her dedicated cooperation.

I also acknowledge with gratitude the forthcomingness which I encountered at the Rajasthan State Archives, especially on the part of their now retired Director, Dr G.N. Sharma. Invaluable help was rendered by Shri Shivcandji Tiwari, Officer in-charge, Old Historical Records, Jaipur section, but for whose intimate knowledge of the largely uncatalogued material I would have failed to trace the relevant papers.

Shri Shrivatsa Goswami, Director of the Sri Caitanya Prema Samsthana, Vrindaban, first suggested to Mukherjee that he seek my cooperation and thus put us in contact. I wish to thank him for this as much as for his encouragement and hospitality, which I have enjoyed many times in the past. I thank Robyn Beeche, also of the Sri Caitanya Prema Samsthana, Vrindaban, for allowing me to use one of her photographs for the jacket illustration.

The first draft of this book was read by Professor Irfan Habib. Like all students of the Mughal period, I am deeply indebted to his scholarship. However, the generosity with which he gave of his time and advice have added in a personal way to the debt that I owe him.

I also gratefully acknowledge the help of my colleague, Clive Bell, who checked the English of the first two chapters of this book; of Heike Ulrich, who prepared the map, and of Ulrike Stark and Silke Bünz, who assisted me in preparing the camera-ready copy.

I am grateful to the Indira Gandhi National Centre for the Arts and in particular to its Academic Director, Dr Kapila Vatsyayan, for accepting this study for publication in the series of the Vraja Nāthadvārā Prakalpa, a long-term project devoted to the study of the sacred region of Vraja which the IGNCA inaugurated under her guidance and in collaboration with the Sri Caitanya Prema Samsthana under its Director, Shri Shrivatsa Goswami. The publication of the book in that series gives me the opportunity to pay my tribute to the spirited guides of the project and to the achievements of the many scholars engaged in it. Dr Lalit M. Gujral, Honorary Adviser, IGNCA, took care of the publication of the book and gave of his expert advice, helpfully and reassuringly. I also acknowledge the cooperation extended to me by Manohar Publishers.

Monika Horstmann

Note on Transcription

For modern Indic words, the transcription used by R.S. McGregor, *The Oxford Hindi-English Dictionary,* Oxford and Delhi, 1993, has been adhered to, apart from the following exceptions. *ṣ* for [kh] and [k͟h] has been retained in words quoted from the documents. The earlier of the documents published make a careful distinction between [bə] and [wə], written व and व़, resp. (ब also occurs, although rarely). Also, य [yə] is found to be subscribed by a diacritical dot in order to distinguish it from [ǰə] and also from the similar grapheme प. The diacritical dots often merge with the vertical strokes of the respective letters, which results in a stroke curved towards the left in its lower part. After the nineteenth century, this scribal distinction became obsolete. Both व/व़ and य/य़ have been rendered by *v* and *y*, respectively.

Words which would be rather associated with Sanskrit have often been transliterated in full. Well-known names have been used without diacritics. This applies to many names of towns and districts. For the lesser known names of tehsils and villages, the diacritics have been retained.

The system of transliteration as it has been adopted here had to do justice to two scripts, the Nāgarī and the Persian. In their standard transliteration, different letters are often represented by identical transliterations. In order to avoid confusion, the Persian transliteration, which occurs less frequently in the book, has been modified as shown in the following table.

آ	ā	ش	ś
ا	a, i, u	ص	s̲
ب	b	ض	z̲
پ	p	ط	t
ت	t	ظ	z
ٹ	ṭ	ع	c
ث	t̲	غ	ġ
ج	j	ف	f
چ	c	ق	q
ح	h̲	ك	k
خ	k̲h̲	گ	g
د	d	ل	l
ڈ	ḍ	م	m
ذ	ẓ	ن	n
ر	r	و	v, ū, o, au
ڑ	ṛ	ہ	h, -a
ز	z	ی	y, ī, e, ai
ژ	ż	iz̲āfa	- i
س	s		

1. INTRODUCTION

The documents edited in this volume relate to the deity Govinddevjī (GD), who resides in Jaipur in Rajasthan, in the temple which bears his name. The temple forms part of the precincts of Jaipur's City Palace. The images of GD and the other deities who form his entourage were installed in that temple as late as in the earlier part of the eighteenth century, but GD's history as the chief deity of a Vaiṣṇava temple started in Vrindaban in the earlier part of the sixteenth century.

GD's image was installed by Rūp Gosvāmī in the temple which he built and consecrated to this deity (Entwistle 1987:147; Nath 1996:161). Rūp Gosvāmī was one of the Six Gosvāmīs, the disciples of Caitanya (1486-1533). Besides Vallabha and his followers, the Caitanya or Gauḍīya sect made the most important contribution to the establishment of devotion to Kṛṣṇa in the Braj country and to its theological underpinnings when that area, which lies around 150 km to the south of Delhi, had been rediscovered as the sacred land of Kṛṣṇa in the 15th century. Rūp Gosvāmī built the first permanent temple for GD around 1535 (Nath 1996:161). He had obtained the image of the deity, according to tradition, in a miraculous way, for the icon is said to have manifested itself and thus been only "discovered" by Rūp.[1] The temple thus belonged to the initial period of the Bengali type of Kṛṣṇa devotion in Braj, and, to this day GD, now in Jaipur, is attended to by brahmin Bengali Caitanyas. The temple which Rūp Gosvāmī built was located at the centre of Vrindaban, the *yogapīṭha*, where the image is said to have manifested itself. Braj is conceived as a tantric cosmic diagram, *yantra*. Its centre is the *yogapīṭha*, which is interpreted as the meeting point of the flute-playing Kṛṣṇa-Govinda and his consort, Rādhā.[2] This place is the nodal point of his creative energy, *yogamāyā*.[3] The Caitanya theology, as it had been developed since the sixteenth century, thus reflected the unique significance of the site of the temple.

---

[1]According to the tradition of the custodians of GD, Rūp discovered the image in Vrindaban at the mound called Gomāṭīlā in 1525 (Roy 1978:161, fn.). Nath (1996:161) thinks that Rūp "discovered" the image of GD in about A.D. 1534. He identifies Gomāṭīlā with the *yogapīṭha*, the place where the first and second (present-day) temple of GD in Vrindaban was erected. He does not, however, mention the source on which his claim is based.

[2]For the tantric origin of the concept, its theological elaboration and its scriptural ramifications, cp. Entwistle 1987:247-52.

[3]Thakur 1996:16 with reference to Kṛṣṇadās Kavirāj's *Govindalīlāmṛta*, 21.28.

In 1565, the temple of GD and other Vaiṣṇava temples were first recorded to have received grants of revenue by Emperor Akbar (Mukherjee and Habib 1988:235-36). GD came to form the chief temple heading a group of Vaiṣṇava temples (*ibid.*:240, §4.6). The grant was made "on the report of" Rājā Bhār Malla, who was the Kachavāhā chief of Amber (r. 1547-73) and who had married his daughter to Akbar. In 1584, Ṭoḍar Mal made a *jāgīr* grant of 100 *bīghās* to Gopāldās, who was officiating priest, *sevak*, of the Madanmohan temple. According to a document of 1565, Gopāldās was also officiant at the GD temple, a position which he is likely to have held in the year 1584, too. In that year, Ṭoḍar Mal "apparently held the area in *jāgīr*" (Mukherjee and Habib 1988: 236). All this shows the considerable involvement of the Mughal court in the affairs of the recently emerged Gauḍīya Vaiṣṇava temples of Braj.

Thus, from an early period, three groups interacted in the affairs of GD, namely, the sect of Caitanya, the Mughal State and the Kachavāhās, the Rajput dynasty of Eastern Rajasthan, who had their residence in Amber until this was shifted to Jaipur in the earlier part of the eighteenth century.

The Kachavāhās ranked high in the nobility of the Mughal Empire. Mānsiṅgh, who was Rājā of Amber from 1589 to 1614 and became the highest ranking Hindu officer of the Mughal court (MU II:48-49), was instrumental in establishing and securing Mughal power in wide tracts of northern India and was governor of Bihar and Bengal from 1588 to 1606 (Sarkar 1984:75-88). "He was sometimes called the *Mirzā Rāja*" (MU II:49), that is, he was given a title which was also conferred by the Mughal emperors upon his successors. This title of *Mirzā*, which is of Timurid origin, symbolically indicated that the Emperor considered its holder equal to a member of his own house (Sarkar 1984:86).

The Kachavāhās extended patronage to Vaiṣṇava and Non-Vaiṣṇava religious institutions alike, but at some point started to develop a closer relationship with the Caitanyas. Allegedly, Bhagavantdās (Bhagavāndās), who was Rājā from 1573 to 1589, had been initiated into the Caitanya sect (Entwistle 1987:160). He is reported to have built the Satī Burj, a tower erected in memory of his mother, at the Viśrām Ghāṭ at Mathura, and he built the Haridev temple at Govardhan. He was Mānsiṅgh's father and may have influenced his son's decision to build a new magnificent temple on the site of the first GD temple of Vrindaban (Asher 1996:216). Mānsiṅgh's temple was probably begun in 1576 and was completed in 1590 (Nath 1996:163). It is the temple that has survived to this day.[4] The link between the Kachavāhās and GD endured from the time of Mānsiṅgh onwards, but it was Jaisiṅgh II who eventually was to make the deity the lord of the palace of Jaipur.

[4]For the most detailed treatment, cp. Case 1996.

The first and the second temple of GD, like other Vaiṣṇava temples of Braj, continued to be supported by imperial grants (Mukherjee and Habib 1988, 1989). In 1633, the Kachavāhās were put in direct charge of GD.

> Shahjahan... took a measure to enhance the Amber family's control over the management of the Govind-dev temple. This was done by his *farman* of 1 Amurdas, 6 R.Y. (24 July 1633). The *farman* cites Akbar's grant of 1598 to the Govind-dev group of temples, but the *zimn* contains Shahjahan's oberservation that "it is not the rule (to make grants) in the name of temples." ... [T]he reason was seemingly put forward only to enable the grant to be transferred to the Amber house, which would then control the temples by controlling a major source of their income. The entire grant of 135 *bighas* was made an *in'am* of Raja Jai Singh.... Thereafter the Mughal administration recognised the control of the temple management to be vested in Raja Jai Singh, who would appoint a person (Radha Kishandas Chakravarti) to supervise worship there.... (Mukherjee and Habib 1989:290).

This would naturally imply that the administration of grants to GD became vested in the Kachavāhā chancery. The deeds which are documented in this volume span the period from 1628 to 1950. These three centuries are marked by three turning points. The first of these occurred in 1633, when the Kachavāhās were put in charge of GD. The second took place in 1669 and the third, which marked the culmination of a development of two and a half decades, in 1739. Around 1669, the images of GD and his consort, Rādhā, and that of Vṛndādevī, the tutelary goddess of Vrindaban, who had a shrine of her own within the GD temple (Thakur 1996:16, fig. 2.68), were removed from Vrindaban and taken to the Kachavāhā territory. The period from 1670 to 1739 is characterized by the gradual transformation of GD from the Lord of Braj's Vrindaban to the Lord of a new Golden Vrindaban, which was located in the vicinity of what was to become Jaipur, and eventually from the Lord of Vrindaban to the Lord of the palace of Jaipur, a Lord who demanded tribute from the entire Jaipur State.[5] This glorious transformation was achieved by Jaisiṅgh II. After Jaisiṅgh's death in 1743, the fortunes of GD came to reflect the political upheaval caused by the waning of the Mughal Empire and the fights mainly of the Marāṭhās and the Rajput princes for both self-assertion and political survival. No conspicuous fresh grants were issued henceforth, although the parties in power renewed existing grants. Non-Kachavāhās also made a couple of grants.

The revenue grants which were made by the Kachavāhās survived into the period when the Jaipur State merged with the State of Rajasthan (30 March 1949). These titles were eventually transformed into an annuity, which the State of Rajasthan pays to the temple of GD.[6]

---

[5] → V.S. 1797, Māgha b. 5.

[6] In 1974 this amounted to 32,063rp. 13a; Roy 1978:27, fn. 49.

The documents thus tell us about the relationship between GD and his princely Kachavāhā patrons of Amber/Jaipur. The way in which they speak to us is restricted in scope and style; for they are limited to economic affairs. The Kachavāhā endowments, moreover, formed only one, though an important, source of temple income.[7] The style of the documents is that appropriate to grants, office notes and other formal papers. The personal and political motives which prompted them normally remain hidden, thereby opening the way to speculation, which must be avoided unless there are known historical facts to guide and discipline it. The documents are hardly self-explanatory, nor do they combine automatically to form a consistent history. This deficiency does not necessarily imply that the GD records must be suspected to have fatal gaps. Rather it reflects the fact that the web of relations connecting Caitanya and other religious institutions with the Kachavāhās has not been studied very much to date. Once this has been done, it will be easier to determine the relative position that GD occupied in the history of Braj and Rajasthan.

Govinddevjī and its management

To speak of GD is to imply several divine images, of whom GD is the chief.[8] GD, the *ṭhākur*, the "Lord", is accompanied by his consort, the *ṭhakurāṇī*, who, in the Indic version of the documents, is never called Rādhā, though in one Persian version her name is given.[9] These two images were the main icons of the GD temple of Vrindaban, that is, the first one, built by Rūp Gosvāmī, and the second one, built by Mānsiṅgh and superseding Rūp's. The image of Rādhā, "who stays on Govinda's left side, was offered to the Lord in V.S. 1690/A.D. 1633, when the King of Uḍīsā, Puruṣottama Deva, son of Pratāparudra, had them married with great pomp" (Bahura 1996:206).[10]

There is yet another image of Kṛṣṇa worshipped in the present-day temple of GD in Jaipur. This is a *tribhaṅgī* (bent-in-three-places) icon which is much smaller than the Govinda image. Allegedly, it was sent by Caitanya himself "through the hands of Kāśīśvara Pāṇḍita, with this message: 'This image is identical with me.'" (Bahura 1996:206). Kāśīśvar, indeed, is said to have been sent to Vrindaban by Caitanya and entrusted with the worship of Govinda.[11] This

---

[7]For the period up to 1725, invaluable details of the economics of Caitanya institutions of Braj have been made available by Habib (1996).

[8]Cp. also Case 1996, frontispiece, for a photograph of the images of GD and his consort, and of the small image of Kṛṣṇa-Caitanya in its left lower corner.

[9]Cp. → A.H. 1102, 21 Rabīʻ I, l. 22. - Bahura (1996:206) reports that Rādhā's image was donated by Rājā Puruṣottamdev of Orissa, son of Pratāprudradev. Nath (1996:161) puts this event in Rūp Gosvāmī's lifetime. Rūp, however, must have died shortly after he entrusted the custodianship of GD to Jīv Gosvāmī, which was in 1568 (Habib 1996:144 *s.v.* Jīv Gosā'in, and 156 *s.v.* Rūp).

[10]No source is given for this claim.

[11]Priyādās, *kavitta* 398, on Nābhādās's *Bhaktamāl*; cp. also Entwistle 1987:149.

image does not figure in the documents authored by the Kachavāhās. Its absence can be established beyond doubt on the strength of lists of donations made to individually named deities. A document of this kind is that of 1670.[12]

In Mānsiṅgh's temple, two more deities were worshipped in shrines of their own, namely, Vṛndādevī and Yogamāyā.[13] When GD and his consort were removed from the temple of Vrindaban, Vṛndādevī accompanied them, but was soon separated from them; for since 1671 or thereabouts she has been kept and worshipped in Kāmāṁ, in a temple where all the three images had stayed together for some time (Entwistle 1987:185, Nath 1996:168). Yogamāyā did not leave Vrindaban, and is still worshipped in a chamber in the basement of the temple. GD and his consort eventually came to be installed in Jaipur in the temple which was consecrated in 1739.[14] The divine consort was, in the course of time, complemented by two images of *sakhīs*, confidantes, who joined the couple in 1727 and 1803, respectively.[15] Bahura (1996:206) reports the name of the first one as Lalitā, which is, however, not given in the documents presently under review.[16]

The management of GD lies in the hands of a custodian, *adhikārī*. He bears the title *Gosvāmī* and is the human representative of the deity, who is a juridic person. The documents are based on this understanding, and it is therefore the deity himself who is understood to be the applicant for, and the recipient of, grants, whereas his consort and the *sakhīs* are not taken to act autonomously. The custodians trace their spiritual genealogy to Rūp Gosvāmī.[17] From the fourth custodian onwards most of them are found to be related by blood or adoption,[18] which ensured that the property of the temple would run in their line. Strictly speaking, however, they were only caretakers and not proprietors of GD's wealth. This distinction may have been obscured at times, but it remained nevertheless essential and fundamentally uncontested. The religious importance of GD enhanced the deity's wealth, and symbolic power and wealth combined gave power to the custodians, who represented the deity on earth.

---

[12]→ A.H. 1080, 12 Ramaẕān.

[13]For architectural details, cp. Thakur 1996.

[14]For which cp. below, p. 25.

[15]→ V.S. 1784, Āśvina b. 11; → V.S. 1860, Māgha b. 2.

[16]Lalitā is one of the standard number of eight *sakhīs*, for which cp. Entwistle 1987:51.

[17]The custodianship of GD was disputed in the time of the second to sixth custodian, for which cp. → A.H. 1038, 2 Śavvāl, commentary.

[18]Cp. chart "The Custodians of the Govinddevjī Temple" with notes, pp. 353-55.

The Mahārājās and Govinddevjī

As a rule, the custodians would themselves select their successors. Custodians could, and a number of them did, in fact, retire from office and entrust the custodianship and their personal property to their successors in the interest of a smooth transition. The new custodian had, however, to be recognized and officially appointed by the Emperor before 1633, and by the Mahārājā thereafter.[19] The temple of GD, as much as other religious estates of similar order, could not be run independently of the authority of the state. The Mahārājā is the temple's *mālik*, its hereditary proprietor, who holds authority also over the land from which the temple receives revenue grants. The *adhikārī*, or the officiants acting under him, the *(ṭahaluvā) pujārī*s, solicit his decision in cases of dispute.[20]

The court ritual links the Mahārājā and GD. Details of this are recorded in the *Dastūr komvār*, the court protocol of Jaipur, and in the manuals of court ritual.[21] Notwithstanding subsequent changes, the rules followed now were supposedly formed in the time of Jaisiṅgh II. The condolence ritual for a deceased *adhikārī* and the investiture of a new custodian of GD required the Mahārājā's presence. If he was a minor, the highest-ranking court official with the retinue of courtiers would act in his stead. The Mahārājā's presence would be symbolised by the royal sword, which his deputy would carry and place on the throne cushion spread for the Mahārājā.[22] Also, the coming and going of the *adhikārī* to and from Jaipur was ceremonially observed by the court. On all these occasions, there took place an exchange of ceremonial gifts, which emphasized the religious authority of the *adhikārī*. For in ritual matters, but only in these, the Mahārājā was inferior, because he received the custodian's *prasād*, consecrated gifts.

The coronation of the Mahārājā required the presence of the *adhikārī*, who, in ritual importance, vied with the Rāmānandīs and other religious dignitaries. Clémentin-Ojha (1997:57) gives the essential details of this relationship, here quoted in translation:

---

[19]Also after 1633, the Imperial Court continued to be the addressee of petitions and complaints on the part of custodians or their contestants, for which cp. Habib 1996. It is not clear from what period onwards the right to appoint custodians and decide issues of similar importance became completely vested in the Kachavāhā Mahārājā.

[20]This is, for example, emphasized in the *mahzarnāma* referred to in fn. 95. There frequently occurs another term, namely, *sevak*, "servant, officiating priest", which often refers to a custodian or future custodian. It is not quite clear in what way exactly a *sevak*'s postion differs from or overlaps with, that of a custodian or future custodian on the one hand and a *pujārī* on the other.

[21]Clémentin-Ojha 1997 quotes the unpublished *Jayasiṃhakalpadruma* and a modern work, *His Highness's household: Jaipur ceremonial procedure, compiled by the Ceremonials Committee under the commands of His Highness the Maharaja Sahib Bahadur,* Jaipur, n.d.

[22]Cp. for example DK 5:326-27. For further details, see also Horstmann 1998.

> [The] history [of the relationship between the Gauḍīya Vaiṣṇavas and the Rāmānandīs] is directly connected with the royal patronage of their respective icons, namely, Govindadeva and Sītārāma. The deities, incorporated in the palace, are crucial to the ruling dynasty, and their human caretakers, who command precious ritual accomplishment, are important persons at the Sarhad (palace quarters - MH). They have free access to the palace and are associated with the great ceremonies of the kingdom and, accordingly, are greatly honoured. Among the Rāmānujī-Rāmānandīs the incumbent of Galta (headquarters of their lineage - MH) ... supervises all ritual ceremonies .... But ... sometimes he is eclipsed by the *adhikārī* (shebait) of Govindadeva, because since the time of Jai Singh II Govindadeva has superseded Sītārāma in the heart of the rulers and in certain ceremonies of the court... [O]n the evening of the coronation he becomes the most prominent Vaiṣṇava of the kingdom: the new Mahārājā first renders obeisance to Govindadeva, then to the tutelary goddesses of his territory and clan and only then presents himself at the temple of Sītārāma (whose officiants are the Rāmānujī-Rāmānandīs - MH).

On the Vijaya-daśamī, however, the Rāmānandīs enjoy precedence over the Gauḍīya Vaiṣṇavas (*ibid.*).

The nobility also observed ritual obligations *vis-à-vis* GD. In 1756, Harsahāy, Mādhavsiṅgh's minister, received the title *Rājā* and a *manṣab* of 5,000. In recognition thereof he first went to pay obeisance to GD, to whom he offered a saffron-coloured suit. Only then did he go to the *sabhānivās*, court, and don the *siropāv*, robe of honour, which had been given to him before by the Mahārājā.[23]

The Kachavāhā Mahārājās maintained firm links with the Vaiṣṇava temples of Braj and of their own patrimonial land as well as in territories obtained otherwise. This, however, must not be taken to imply that they neglected to support other religious institutions. We are not in a position to assess the precedence that GD enjoyed over other institutions. GD's increasing pre-eminence is, however, obvious and will be traced presently, although the basis for doing so in a comparative perspective is sadly missing.

When Mānsiṅgh was at the height of his power, he built the great GD temple of Vrindaban. The Kachavāhā munificence is visible everywhere in Braj. The Kachavāhās' attachment to the sacred land of Kṛṣṇa became, in acts of political and religious symbolism, converted into a visible inventory, and the grants which the family made perpetuated their dynastic presence. GD was the symbol of Kachavāhā glory. If we are looking for the personal religious attachment on the part of a Kachavāhā, it is most of all Jaisiṅgh II, however, who comes in view. He was to

---

[23] DK 3:726-27 for V.S. 1813, Caitra ś. 8.

convert GD into a dynastic symbol by integrating the deity into the new palace of Jaipur, although this was hardly at the expense of other institutions.[24]

The issue of the position of GD gained a dynamic of its own in the course of the contemporary political events. GD was removed from Vrindaban together with his consort and Vṛndādevī when Aurangzeb displayed an increasing intolerance towards the Hindus. The contemporary historian Sāqī Musta'idd Khān (1947:51-52) reported that on 8 April 1669, the Emperor had issued orders to demolish Hindu schools and temples and to restrain the practice of the Hindu religion. In August 1669, the Viśvanāth temple of Banaras was destroyed and later on, the Keśavrāy temple of Mathura (Sharma 1940:131-38). It is certainly debatable whether this happened on the order of the Emperor: for the Viśvanāth temple at least, a contemporary author gives a description which suggests that the cause of the destruction was what in a modern terminology could be called a Hindu-Muslim communal riot (*ibid.*:144, note 12). GD was taken to the Kachavāhā territory, where, after a number of stops, he reached the Kachavāhā residence.[25] This process took nearly 70 years, from around 1670 to 1739. The symbol of Kachavāhā power, thus taken to the patrimonial land of the dynasty, also marked the growing assertiveness of the Rajputs in the face of declining Mughal power, an assertiveness which was expressed also in terms of religion and theology.[26] GD became part of a considerably vaster design of a newly strengthened concept of Hindu kingship. In other words, in relation to Jaisiṅgh II, GD was a symbol of the inextricable unity of personal and political attitudes. After Jaisiṅgh II, GD remained a most important symbol of Kachavāhā kingship, though not the only one, to be sure; for the Kachavāhās, like other Rajput dynasties, pay allegiance also to the Goddess and to their forefather Rām, who, in the form of the couple Sītārām, figures in the seals of the Kachavāhā Mahārājās from Jaisiṅgh II onwards.[27] The devotion to GD forms, therefore, a prime register in which the dynastic self-expression was activated in the proper ritual and political contexts. It was not unique, but it was one without which the aspirations of the Kachavāhā state would not have found expression. It was therefore appropriate that on 15 July 1939, the Home Minister of the Jaipur State, in a rejoinder to the Revenue Minister, pointed out that "this temple enjoyed a unique position and it was necessary to keep up the standard (of *bhog* expenses - MH) maintained up-till-now (*sic!*)", when the Council of State had to cope with the reduced income from the estates of GD, while the *bhog* expenses remained fixed at 24,826rp. 2a.[28]

---

[24]In this connection, cp. the perhaps exceptional grant of 1740, pp. 263-65.

[25]For the itinerary, cp. Nath 1996.

[26]For which cp. Horstmann 1994a and b.

[27]For the seals, cp. pp. 75-76.

[28]RSA. Jaipur, File No 1657-28, "Proceedings of a Meeting of the Council of State, 1 May 1940".

The documents in their major part refer to this income of GD in so far as it serves for the maintenance of worship. This is technically called *bhog*, "sacrificial feeding".[29] The basis of *bhog* has been the grants which have come down from the seventeenth century and thereafter, and which were all drawn from the Kachavāhā territory, either patrimonial land of the dynasty or land aquired later on, especially by Jaisiṅgh II.[30] The Jaipur State and, eventually, the modern State of Rajasthan verified the grants, which will be listed presently.[31] It is from these that the dues the state pays to GD nowadays are derived.[32] These verified grants appear in the chronological order of their first traceable promulgation.[33]

---

[29]For details, cp. p. 35.

[30]Wills 1933 is devoted to this, cp. especially Appendix G; also Gupta 1986, ch. 1.

[31]For their location, cp. the map on p. 352.

[32]The actual annuity is unknown to me. In 1974 it was 32,063rp. 13a.; Roy 1978:27, fn. 49.

[33]Historical events have been benign in allowing us insight into the titles verified. In 1935 Kiśancandra (Kṛṣṇacandra), the custodian of GD, had died and was succeeded by Bholānāth. The fiscal system of Jaipur required that on his succession to the title on a religious or secular estate *(ṭhikānā)*, the new incumbent was liable to pay the *matalbā mātamī* (from Persian *maṭlaba*, "proposition, intention", and *mātamī*, "pertaining to mourning"), a tax levied on the basis of the land-holdings of the estate. GD's new custodian, however, claimed the right to be exempted from the tax, which amounted to 6,846rp.10a. The resulting litigation dragged on; for when Bholānāth died in 1945, also his successor Pradyumnakumār pleaded to be exempted from the tax. In the course of litigation, the titles of GD were sifted and in 1953 and 1959 the State of Rajasthan eventually drafted two reports which listed the titles verified by the state. Cp. RSA. Jaipur, File No 1657-28, 17 January 1953 and 18 March 1959.

In the following, the grants are once again listed alphabetically by place-names:

Bicūṇ	[V.S. 1928, Caitra b. 15 (Bicūṇ)]
Catrapur-vās Khijuryā	→ V.S. 1764, Śrāvaṇa b. 3
Coru	[V.S. 1928, Caitra b. 15 (Coru)]
Dayālpuro	→ V.S. 1774, Jyeṣṭha ś. 15
Gaṅgārāmpuro	*V.S. 1771, Bhādrapada ś. 4
Gaṇolī *alias* Gahnolī	[V.S. 1930, Phālguṇa ś. 4], in continuation of an earlier title on Jaitpuro, which cp. below
Gordhanpuro	→ V.S. 1805, Māgha ś. 1
Govindpuro Baṛo *alias* Govindpuro Bujarg	→ A.H. 1078, 30 Jumādā II
Govindpur-vās Hāthyod *alias* Govindpur Khurd	*V.S. 1792, Pauṣa b. 5
Hathrohī	→ V.S. 1869, Caitra ś. 1
Jāhautā	→ A.H. 1072, 15 Śavvāl/ Āṣāḍha b. 3

Jaisiṅgh I (1621-67)

1662: Jāhautā (→ A.H. 1072, 15 Śavvāl/Āṣāḍha b. 3)

Date unknown: Govindpuro Baṛo/Bujarg (→ A.H. 1078, 30 Jumādā II)

Rāmsiṅgh I (1667-89)

1688: *Catrapur-vās Khijuryā; this grant was for some time replaced by a grant for Jhujhārpur, but later on it reverted to Catrapur-vās Khijuryā (cp. → V.S. 1764, Śrāvaṇa b. 3)

Vijaisiṅgh (1708-171?)

1711: Sālimpur (→ A.H. 1123, 21 Ramaẕān)

Jaitpuro	→ V.S. 1839, Āṣāḍha b. 5 (title on toll-tax); title on *bhog* earlier than V.S. 1939, referred to in → V.S. 1930, Phālguṇa ś. 4; transferred to Gaṇolī and Sahajpur
Jugalpuro Khurd	[rev.y. 1846, Āṣāḍha b. 2]
Kalyāṇpur-vās and Jasodhānand-purā-vās of Syosiṅghpurā	→ V.S. 1860, Māgha b. 2
Kirapārāmpurā-vās of Śrīkisnapuro	→ V.S. 1869, Jyeṣṭha ś. 13
Kūkas	*V.S. 1928, Vaiśākha b. 4 (verified in 1953, but not again in 1959
Maū Khās	[rev.y. 1801/ V.S. 1802, Bhādrapada b. 5]; the document is not listed in the "Calendar of Documents" because it belongs to the Rādhāmādhavjī temple
Nīmlā	*V.S. 1798
Rājsar Phuṭolāv	*V.S. 1776
Rāmsar	→ V.S. 1825, Māgha b. 15
Sahajpur	[V.S. 1930, Phālguṇa ś. 4], but in continuation of an earlier title on Jaitpuro, which cp. above
Sālimpur	→ A.H. 1123, 21 Ramaẕān
Sekhpuro Baṛo	*V.S. 1774, Jyeṣṭha I, ś. 13
Śrīvrīdāvanpurā (267 *bīghās*, 2 *viśvās* land)	→ V.S. 1790, Māgha ś. 4
13 shops in *kasbā* Savāī Jaipur	→ V.S. 1840, Āśvina b. 10

Jaisiṅgh II (1700-43)

1714: Gaṅgārāmpuro (*V.S. 1771, Bhādrapada ś. 4)

1717: Dayālpur (→ V.S. 1774, Jyeṣṭha ś. 15)

1717: Maū Khās (*V.S. 1774, Mārgaśiras ś. 10), originially granted to the Rādhāmādhavjī temple, which was under the authority of GD's custodian

1717: Sekhpuro Baṛo (*V.S. 1774, Jyeṣṭha I, ś. 13)

1719: Rājsar Phuṭolāv (*V.S. 1776)

1734: Śrīvrīdavanpurā[34] (267 *bīghās*, 2 *viśvās*) (→ V.S. 1790, Māgha ś.4)

1735: Govindpur-vās Hāthyod/Govindpur Khurd (*V.S. 1792, Pauṣa b.5)

1741: Nīmlā (*V.S. 1798)

Īśvarsiṅgh (1743-50)

1749: Gordhanpuro (→ V.S. 1805, Māgha ś. 1)

Pratāpsiṅgh (1778-1803)

1783: Jaitpuro (→ V.S. 1839, Āṣāḍha b. 5; title on toll-tax; title on *bhog* earlier than V.S. 1939 and on an unknown date transferred to Gaṇolī and Sahajpur referred to in doc. [V.S. 1930, Phālguṇa ś. 4])

1783: 13 shops in *kasbā* Savāī Jaipur (→ V.S. 1840, Āśvina b. 10)

1789: Jugalpuro Khurd ([rev.y. 1846, Āṣāḍha b. 2])

Jagatsiṅgh (1803-18)

1803: Kalyānpur-vās and Jasodhānandpurā-vās of Syosiṅghpurā (→ V.S. 1860, Māgha b. 2)

1812: Hathrohī (→ V.S. 1869, Caitra ś. 1)

1812: Kirapārāmpur-vās of Śrīkisnapuro (→ V.S. 1869, Jyeṣṭha ś. 13)

Rāmsiṅgh II (1835-80)

Gaṇolī and Sahajpur, for which cp. Jaitpuro in the regnal period of Pratāpsiṅgh

Bicūṇ, Corū and Kūkas: the titles on these were confirmed in Rāmsiṅgh's regnal period; their first promulgation remains unknown

Bakhtāvarsiṅgh, Prince of Alvar (Mahārājā of Alvar: 1791-1815)

1769: Rāmsar (→ V.S. 1825, Māgha b. 15)

---

[34]The name is only given in doc. [V.S, 1928, Caitra b. 15 (aggregate grant)].

This list leads to the conclusion that almost all ancient titles of revenue grants and donations, which owe their existence to the Kachavāhās, survived into this century. The exceptions are the following:

(1) The most prominent grant, the one for *bheṭ* which was first issued in 1740 (→ V.S. 1797, Māgha b. 5),[35] has disappeared, as is also evident from the "Calendar of Documents", where it figures last in 1786 (V.S. 1842, Caitra ś. 8a).

(2) The grant for cattle-pasture (*V.S. 1771, Āśvina b.13), confirmed for the last time in 1751, has disappeared.

(3) The grant in Hathrohī, dated 1771 (→ V.S. 1828, Vaiśākha b.4), has disappeared, though it may have survived through merging with other deeds.[36]

(4) The *inām* of 1804 (→V.S. 1860, Māgha b.7) has disappeared. As a grant benefitting an individual, it did not refer directly to the GD temple. However, as it forms part of the temple records, one would expect it to have played a role among the titles of the temple proper.

(5) All grants of salt, of cash from *parganā*-treasuries and of cash and/or kind allowances for the temple's staff of workers have disappeared. This would be expected, as administrative changes had made these grants obsolete.

(6) The grant referring to the management of the 135 *bīghās* of land, which was originally promulgated by Akbar's *farmān* of 1598/99,[37] no longer figures among the titles. Irrespective of the state that this title may have at present, it falls outside the territorial rights of the State of Rajasthan and is thus beyond its jurisdiction.

The grants in historical perspective

Subsequent to the initial period of GD in Vrindaban, the history of the temple grants is concomitant with that of the deities' exodus from Braj, their gradual approach to Amber, and their establishment and enduring sojourn in Jaipur. The itinerary of GD from its exodus from

[35] Cp. pp. 263-65.
[36] See the "Calendar of Documents" for the date quoted.
[37] Cp. "Calendar of Documents" for doc. → A.H. 1108, 22 [Rabī' II].

Vrindaban to its installation in Jaipur has been studied mainly by Roy (1978), more recently by Nath (1996) and, with the focus on GD's impact on the Kachavāhās, by Bahura (1996). Nath was able to use documents and combined their data with arguments built on the analysis of the development of temple architecture. He made use of the same documents as Bahura, and to a certain extent, these tie up with the documents published here. For Nath and Bahura, who are interested in the itinerary and growing impact of GD, respectively, the analysis of the documents was not a priority, which is why they have quoted only select passages from a few of them. Nath also tried to do justice to local traditions relating to the itinerary of the deities. In the following, the results of Nath's especially rich study will be related to the facts – and the gaps – as they are contained in the documents of this volume.[38]

Jaisiṅgh I (1621-67)

In the deed of 1628 (→ A.H. 1038, 2 Śavvāl), the GD temple was still grouped with a number of other Vaiṣṇava temples. After 1669 (→ A.H. 1078, 30 Jumādā II), this was rather a rare exception.[39] After 1628, the grant is not found to have been reconfirmed.

Jaisiṅgh I laid the foundation of what was to develop into a cluster of charities which were located adjacent to each other in *tapā* Khoh of *parganā* Amber, now in Sanganer Tahsil of Jaipur District. He seems to have been the first to grant GD the revenue of Govindpur(o) (Baṛo/Bujarg), (Great) Govindpur(o), *alias* Raihphoṛā or Rahphoṛā. His grant has not come down to us, but it was confirmed by Rāmsiṅgh I after the death of Jaisiṅgh I in 1667.[40] Govindpur is an *alias*, a programmatic name related to the deity to whom it was endowed, and, indeed, the place was to become the residence of GD, which is first documented in 1707.[41] The temple of Govindpur was abandoned in 1714, when GD was transferred to the new Golden Vrindaban.[42] The adjacent revenue sources, which came to complement the temple's income from Govindpur, were Catrapur-vās Khijuryā and Jhujhārpur, both endowed in the period of Rāmsiṅgh I.[43] Govindpur, a place in the patrimonial land of the Kachavāhās, was thus dedicated to GD a few years before the images were removed from Vrindaban.

---

38 Details which are relevant only or mainly to particular documents have been discussed in the commentaries following the translated documents.

39 For one such exception, cp. Vijaisiṅgh's deed of → A.H. 1123, 21 Ramaẕān. If the custodian of GD was also in charge of another temple and the document referred to both estates, this would naturally also hold good, e.g. → V.S. 1777, Āśvina ś. 14.

40 → A.H. 1078, 30 Jumādā II.

41 → V.S. 1764, Śrāvaṇa b. 3.

42 Cp. below, pp. 19-23.

43 For further details, cp. below, p. 177.

Rāmsiṅgh I (1667-89)

The images were removed from the GD temple of Vrindaban in the regnal period of Rāmsiṅgh. Vrindaban's GD temple was not destroyed on an alleged or actual order of Aurangzeb,[44] although its sanctuary was dismantled and figures on the doorway of the *jagmohan* (the space in front of the inner sanctuary) were defaced. The date of this is unknown. Michell (1996) points out that the sanctuary of the Rādhāvallabh temple of Vrindaban was dismantled, too, but that otherwise both temples show no signs of grave mutilation. The temples of Madanmohan, Gopīnāth and Yugalkiśor were spared, which may suggest that the desecration was aimed at only the chief temples of the Gauḍīya and Rādhāvallabhīya sects. No random iconoclastic raids, allegedly prompted by Aurangzeb, can be concluded to have occurred in Vrindaban. The political climate, however, had grown inclement. Rāmsiṅgh was certainly determined to forestall impending danger. To what extent he may have aimed at resistance against Aurangzeb remains a matter of speculation. He was a high-ranking member of the Mughal nobility and he abided by his commitment to the Emperor, although the mishap of Śivājī's escape from Mughal custody in 1666 could hardly have taken place without his complicity. He had been in charge of this precious rebel prisoner and had turned a blind eye to Śivājī's preparations for flight. Accordingly, Aurangzeb dismissed the young Kachavāhā prince from his *manṣab* and prohibited him from entering the *darbār* (Bhimsen 1972:50). This happened about a year before Rāmsiṅgh succeeded to the throne of Amber.

At any rate, GD as well as several more Vaiṣṇava images were removed from Vrindaban (Entwistle 1987:184-85). GD is reported to have been taken to Kāmāṁ in August 1670.[45] The removal of GD to Kāmāṁ is also corroborated by a document of 1671 (Habib 1996:157). This must be taken to imply the two companion deities, the *ṭhakurāṇī* and Vṛndādevī.[46] Nath (1996:165-68) purports that the images were first taken to Rādhākuṇḍ, about 25 km to the west of Vrindaban, though there exists no written testimony to this effect. For the time being, it is impossible to either espouse or reject the local tradition that GD stayed there. The Gosvāmīs of GD rely on a tradition which mentions a number of halts *en route* to Amber/Jaipur, not all of which are supported by presently available documentary evidence. Nath has tried to bridge this missing documentary basis by an argument based on both architectural considerations and that tradition, which has also been briefly reported by Mukherjee (1980:15):

---

[44]For which cp. pp. 23-24.

[45]This needs to be taken with some caution. Horstmann 1994a:83 refers to an inscription which dates the removal Bhādrapada ś. 12, V.S. 1727/17 August 1670. This information came from an inscription in the possession of the Vrindaban Research Institute and was exhibited in facsimile at the Conference on the Govinda Temple in Vrindaban, Vrindaban, 1991. At that time the author could not copy the inscription and strangely enough it does not appear in Case 1996. Therefore this inscription unfortunately remains unverified.

[46]The silence of the Kachavāhā documents on the image of Kṛṣṇa-Caitanya, for which see pp. 4-5, precludes any further speculation on the fate of this icon before its eventual presence in the present-day temple of Jaipur.

> In the possession of the present custodian of the Govinda temple, Jaipur, there are several thousand *parvānās* issued by the Jaipur kings to the successive custodians of the Govinda temple between 1590 and 1790. In some of them is documented Govindadeva's journey from Vrindaban to Jaipur during Aurangzeb's time. On the way to Jaipur, Govindadeva accompanied by the Custodians and 5 or 6 *Pūjārīs* took temporary shelter in different places, first at Rādhākuṇḍ and afterwards at Kāmban (= Kāmāṁ - MH), Govindapur, Ghāṭī Āmer, and finally in Jainivās where the idol now resides. In each of the places where the idol was temporarily housed, temples were erected and services were established by land grants and endowments from Maharaj Ramsingh who died in 1690 *(sic!)*.

The point is that the documentary evidence restates the case: The grants at the various places were not given to GD because the images had been or were on the point of being taken there, but the images were taken to halts which had been made objects of grants to GD earlier, as is evident from the grants of Govindpur and adjacent villages. The same applies to Kāmāṁ, for GD's relationship with that place antedates 1671 by at least eleven years. As early as 1660, Prince Kīratsiṅgh, who was the younger son of Jaisiṅgh I and in charge of *parganā* Kāmāṁ, had bestowed a grant of garments on the deities. This is reported in a document of that year, which was confirmed in February 1670.[47] In the document of 1670, the "servant" of GD is also mentioned to have appeared personally at court in order to put forth his complaint of outstanding dues of garments for the deities.

Nath submits that GD left Kāmāṁ by 1675 and stayed somewhere else until 1700, and he suggests that the images of GD and Rādhā had been taken to Govindgaṛh in Alvar (1996:169-71). At least for the time around 1690,[48] it must be assumed that the three images stayed together in one place, which one would expect to have been Kāmāṁ, for this is where Vṛndādevī stayed behind when the other two images left for good.

The situation before 1690 remains obscure. A document of 1679[49] mentions only GD and his consort, but not Vṛndādevī, as beneficiaries of a grant for garments for the Phūlḍol festival. Against this, another grant, which is dated December 1690[50], is for garments to all the three deities. This favours the assumption that in 1679, GD and the *ṭhakurāṇī* were kept separately from Vṛndādevī.

---

[47] → A.H. 1071, 10 S̲afar; → A.H. 1080, 12 Ramaẕān, ll. 8-13.

[48] → A.H. 1102, 21 Rabī' I.

[49] → A.H. 1089, 20 Z̲ī'l-ẖijja.

[50] → A.H. 1102, 21 Rabī' I.

For the period after 1690, we are informed that the then custodian, Kṛṣṇacaraṇ, who had left Vrindaban some time between 1689 and 1692 and had made "for the Rājpūt country" because of the Jāṭ disturbances, had gone to Kāmāṁ in 1694 and resided there in 1696, which was the year of his death (Habib 1996:145). One would expect GD's custodian to have wanted to live close to GD, and this would have been Kāmāṅ rather than Alvar. The documentary evidence suggests that Kāmāṁ considered only a provisional sojourn of GD, for in 1690, Govindpur was complemented by the adjacent village of Jhujhārpur to serve as a source of revenue income for GD.[51] This shows that while GD stayed in Kāmāṁ, provisions were made to meet the *bhog* expenses of the Govindpur shrine.

Kṛṣṇacaraṇ's, the custodian's, elder brother and successor, Govindcaraṇ, was, in the year of his succession, confirmed as manager of the 135 *bīghā*s land which Akbar had granted first in 1598/99 to the group of Vaiṣṇava temples headed by GD. In 1633, this grant had been transferred to the Kachavāhās and thence been entrusted to GD.[52] In this book, no documents could be produced for the period from 1697 to 1706. However, Persian documents which were analysed by Habib (1996:138-39) indicate that Govindcaraṇ was able to consolidate his power and wealth during that period and that he also prevailed over claims on the part of the heirs of Jīv Gosvāmī (*ibid.*:136).[53] In 1703, Govindcaraṇ was a resident of Kāmāṁ (*ibid.*:138), which points also to GD's presence.

Nath thinks that between 1700 and 1707, GD was kept in Khavā in *parganā* Jamvā-Rāmgaṛh (1996:172-74), for which no documentary testimony is available and on which some doubt is cast by the above.

Jaisiṅgh II (1700-43)

In 1707, when GD can, at last, be proved to have resided in the temple of Govindpur, the village first assigned to GD by Jaisiṅgh I, Jaisiṅgh II had been chief of Amber for more than seven years. In that year, the revenue grants to GD in Govindpur and its neighbourhood started becoming consolidated. Adjacent to Govindpur there was Catrapur-vās Khijuryā, granted to GD by Rāmsiṅgh, but the locality assigned was shifted variously. For some time, it had been replaced by Jhujhārpur and then been assigned to a Jāṭ, until it was restored to GD, now no longer as a mere village share but in its entirety.[54]

51→ A.H. 1102, 21 Rabīʻ I; → A.H. 1106, 12 Jumādā I; → A.H. 1108, 23 Rabīʻ II.

52→ A.H. 1108, 22 [Rabīʻ] II; for Akbar's *farmān*, cp. Mukherjee and Habib 1989:293, 295. In 1710 the management of this land was transferred to Gopīraman of the Rādhādāmodar temple, for which cp. → V.S. 1767, Mārgaśiras b. 2.

53 After Rūp Gosvāmī's death, Jīv had become custodian of GD which was not as undisputed as it seems. Cp. Horstmann 1996:188.

54→ V.S. 1764, Śrāvaṇa b. 3; → rev.y. 1767, Āśvina b. 5.

The temple of Govindpur is now completely delapidated.

> The Govindpurā temple was situated on the slope of the hill, on a rock, at a much higher level than the village. It has now been completely destroyed except for traces of the ladão ceiling of the jagamohana, and the site is entirely covered by the temple's debris. It appears to have been a very small temple of the mandira type, and was destroyed by landslides rather than by human agency; its situation, though ideal for security, was not architecturally viable. A pratibhū vigraha was established here after the deity's transfer to Kanaka Vṛndāvana (as was done everywhere else), and was under worship until recently. It was apparently only after Independence that the temple collapsed and worship was closed (Nath 1996:174).[55]

Jaisiṅgh II's long regnal period was interrupted by a phase during which his patrimonial land had been confiscated by the Emperor and his younger brother, Vijaisiṅgh, claimed to be the chief of Amber and to some extent was recognized in that position. This phase started around July 1707. It is documented by two grants which were promulgated by Vijaisiṅgh in October 1711, when he had been almost ousted from his short-lived position of power by Jaisiṅgh.[56] The conflict between the two brothers was decided in 1713, when Jaisiṅgh put his brother in confinement (Bhatnagar 1974:87). There Vijaisiṅgh spent the rest of his life until he was put to death by Jaisiṅgh in 1729, after he had been found planning to usurp the throne once again (*ibid.*:217-18).

This affair was linked with the succession of the new Emperor after the death of Aurangzeb in February 1707. In the struggle for succession, Vijaisiṅgh sided with the future Emperor, Bahādur Śāh (r. 1707-12), whereas Jaisiṅgh belonged to the opposition party. It was by no means uncommon that nobles who had sided in the succession contest with the opposition would quickly revert to loyalty once the new Emperor was installed. In the interest of political stability, they were normally confirmed in their positions. However, in 1707, the weakness of the Empire had become visible, and numerous conflicts flared up, which contributed to the widening of the cracks in the imperial edifice. This produced opportunities for dissidence and the open assertion of power on the part of regional chiefs, and put the Emperor under constraints, to which he reacted unusually restrictively. On the intervention of Vijaisiṅgh, the Emperor confiscated the State of Amber and made it *k͟hālis̤a* land, a step announced to Amber in July 1707 and effected in January 1708 (*ibid.*:38). Other recalcitrant Rajput chiefs were treated similarly. In 1708, Ajītsiṅgh of Marwar and Jaisiṅgh II joined with the Mahārāṇā of Mewar,

---

[55] When I visited Govindpur in 1991, I was told by a local brahmin that in the 1950s, he had still seen the temple in a much better state of repair whereas for the last few decades, it had been raided for building material. He also reported that to this day, Govindpur's *pujārī* of GD receives *prasād* from the GD temple of Jaipur.

[56] → A.H. 1123, 19 and 21 Ramaẕān.

and in the same year, the Rajput confederacy repelled an attack by the Mughals. Jaisiṅgh started also negotiations with the Marāṭhās, whose support he sought. At the same time, the Rajput negotiations with the Mughals went on. In 1710, a rapprochement between the Rajputs and the Emperor was worked out. Jaisiṅgh was restored his patrimonial land. Notwithstanding ongoing negotiations with other parties, especially the Marāṭhās, Jaisiṅgh and the Mughals now operated in a relationship of reciprocity. Engulfed in this, Vijaisiṅgh deserted the Mughal camp in April 1711. Six months later, in October, he was still in a position to promulgate deeds under title of *Mirzā Rājā*[57] and in an ostensibly restorative style: in Persian-Rājasthānī bilingual versions and dated according to the Hijrī calendar, both habits which had been discontinued by his brother.

In April 1712, after Bahādur Śāh's death in February, Jaisiṅgh was conferred the titles of *Mirzā Rājā* and *Mahārājā* (*ibid.*:95), and in June, he received that of *Savāī*.[58] In the documents issued thereafter, he made no use of the title *Mirzā Rājā*. This title, which underscored a quasi-kin relationship with the Emperor, would not have tallied with his own image of himself as a ruler. After the death of Bahādur Śāh, the legend of his seal was also changed. From 1716[59] on, the legend no longer paid allegiance to the Emperor, and in 1727, Jaisiṅgh started using a seal, which was adopted also by his successors as the official Kachavāhā seal, in which allegiance is paid to Sītārām. These symbols illustrate that within fifteen years, Jaisiṅgh had created for himself a new identity as a Hindu king responsible only to his Hindu Lord and no longer to the Mughal Emperor.[60]

The years between 1707 and 1711 or so formed a critical phase, from which eventually ensued the consolidation of Jaisiṅgh's position and from which he rose as a chief assertive of his Hindu identity, albeit a loyal noble of the Emperor whose political and military achievements gave rise to great influence and wealth in territory.

At the same time, GD rose to his position of pre-eminence. This was apparent in 1713, which must be considered as the turning point in the relationship between GD and the Kachavāhā house. All that had happened up to the deity's transfer to, and through his sojourn in, Govindpur was prefigured by actions taken by Jaisiṅgh's predecessors. They had provided for the material basis, the *bhog*, upon which GD would be able to draw while residing in Govindpur, notwithstanding the fact that the actual transfer of the deity to that place was carried

[57]For which cp. p. 2.

[58]Bhatnagar 1974:105: July; according to the Vakil Reports (RSA 1974: serial no 220), June.

[59]No documents could be traced for the period between 1713 and 1715. However, there does exist a document dated 1720, which was issued to the militant Rāmānandīs and to which Jaisiṅgh's Persian seal is found to be affixed (I acknowledge gratefully that I was given access to this document by the abbot of Jaipur's Bālānand Pīṭh, Jagadguru Lakṣmaṇānandjī).

[60]For other measures which contributed to this identity, cp. also Horstmann 1994a.

out under Jaisiṅgh II. It is the year 1713 that marks the beginning of GD's transformation from an important deity of the Kachavāhās into the family deity who would one day come to share the Mahārājā's residence and where henceforth two lords would reign, the king and the Lord Supreme. It was in 1713 that GD came to form part of the emerging concept of Hindu kingship as it was henceforth displayed by Jaisiṅgh. Despite the contemporary reports of his attachment to GD (Horstmann 1994a), there is no evidence that Jaisiṅgh was initiated into the Gauḍīya sect. All is rather in favour of the assumption that he saw to a balanced support of the various Vaiṣṇava and other sects, although he is known to have theologically favoured the Gauḍīya views (Horstmann 1994a and b).

In 1713, Jaisiṅgh laid out two gardens which became GD's successive abodes. He first constructed Kanakvṛndāvan, the Golden Vrindaban, which was intended to be Vrindaban transported to Kachavāhā territory, though "more enjoyable than Vrindaban".[61] Kanakvṛndāvan lies to the left of the road from Amber to Jaipur, which was founded in 1727,[62] while Amber lies about 10 km to the north of Jaipur. Kanakvṛndāvan was laid out on the border of the Mānsarovar, also called the Mānsāgar, a water reservoir constructed by Mahārājā Mānsiṅgh (r. 1589-1614). We do not know when exactly the deities were taken to Kanakvṛndāvan and where they were installed. On 7 September 1714, GD was granted the maintenance of servants to look after his habitation.[63] A little later, on 25 September, a cattle pasture adjacent to Mānsarovar was also granted.[64] Pradyumna Kumar Banerjea (Pradyumnakumār Dev), custodian of GD from 1945 to 1997, said that the surviving GD temple at Kanakvṛndāvan, which lies on the northern edge of Kanakvṛndāvan on the spot called Āmer Ghāṭī,[65] "is actually that of Rādhā-Mādhava, while that of Śrī Govindadeva was nearby. The latter, having been removed from Rūpāheḍā,[66] was installed in the Mānasāgara temple, of which the remains, including the 'pillar of glory' (kīrtistambha), ... were visible until a little while ago. The water of the lake rose, threatening the temple, and for that reason Mahārājā Savāī Jaya Siṃha installed Govinda in the Jayanivāsa" (Bahura 1996:205). As for Rādhāmādhavjī, Bahura (1996:207) says,

> It is possible that Śrī Govinda's image was installed in this Ghāṭīvālā temple after having been taken from the temple at Mānasāgara and was then installed in the Jayanivāsa garden, and the Rādhā-Mādhava image might have been installed there, in the Ghāṭīvālā temple, as a representative image. This much is

---

[61]For details, cp. Ātmārām 1979, st. 447-53; Horstmann 1994a:85-86; Bahura 1996:206-06; Nath 1996:175.
[62]Roy 1978:42-44; foundation date Pauṣa b. 1, V.S. 1784/17 November 1727; according to Roy (1978:44) "29th Nov., (New Style) 1727".
[63]Doc. of Bhādrapada ś. 9, V.S. 1771, partly quoted by Bahura (1996:205-06).
[64]*V.S. 1771, Āśvina b. 13; → rev.y. 1801/V.S. 1802, Bhādrapada b. 5 (pasture).
[65]The name means "Āmer slope", that is, the place where the pass to Amber starts ascending.
[66]This is the modern name of Govindpur Baṛo *alias* Raihphoṛā/Rahphoṛā - MH.

> certain, that the latter image had been installed in the Ghāṭīvālā temple before V.S. 1776/A.D. 1719, because by the order of "Āsoja [Āśvina] dark 10 Saṃvat 1776"[67] Savāī Jaya Siṃha sanctioned Rs. 221/- yearly for the clothing of Lord Rādhā-Mādhava. After that, in V.S. 1787/A.D. 1730, the same king issued an order for yearly income of Rs. 4238/13 annas and 6 paise to Śrī Govindadeva and Śrī Rādhā-Mādhava, ...

In the documents of this volume, Rādhāmādhav appears first in 1717, as will be discussed presently.

The second garden was Jainivās. Jainivās is the *omphalos* of Jaipur, because it became the site of the new City Palace.[68] Nowadays Jainivās is the designation of the palace gardens.[69] The image of GD – that is, of GD and his consort – had been taken to Jainivās by 1716, although the exact date of the transfer and the place where the image or images were kept remain unknown. From the fact that on 14 August 1716[70] the servant staff of the deity (gardeners etc.) were granted a food allowance according to an application submitted on 26 May and that this food allowance was stipulated to be provided as long as the deity would reside in Jainivās, it must be assumed that the removal had taken place in the hot season of 1716.

There is no evidence at hand which would explain why GD was transferred to Jainivās. Nath (1996:179-80) discusses the argument that GD was removed from Kanakvṛndāvan because the level of Mānsarovar was rising and an inundation of the temple was feared (a temple of which, *nota bene*, we know only from Pradyumna Kumar Banerjea's report).[71] Nath (1996:179-80) thinks that,

> The argument generally advanced to justify the transfer, that the Kanaka Vṛndāvana temple was inundated, is not convincing. Medieval planners were endowed with considerable common sense, and flooding would not have been a prime concern when they selected the site for the proposed building. The temple at Kanaka Vṛndāvana was situated on the higher slope of the ghāṭī ... at the northern edge of the Māna Sāgara area. ... The temple was securely enclosed and built on a high platform, making the

---

[67]The date does not tally with the calendar of V.S. 1776, which had an intercalary month of Āśvina which would normally be indicated in the deed (note, MH).

[68]The new *qasba* of Savāī Jaipur occupied the locality previously called Chāp kī bāvarī *alias* Jainivās (Gupta 1986:36).

[69]"In front of the main entrance to the Chandra Mahal and to the north lie the palace gardens known as the Jai Newas Gardens.
At the end of the Upper Gardens, or just in the centre of the Upper and Lower Gardens, stands the temple of Shri Govindji, which contains a very famous image of Krishna, and beyond Govindji's temples comes the Nichla Bag or the Lower Gardens" (Showers 1916:20).

[70]→ V.S. 1773, Bhādrapada ś. 8.

[71]For which cp. p. 19.

inundation theory illogical. That some sort of embankment was also built is indicated by Savāī Jaya Siṃha's parvānā of 1714.[72]

Nath's argument holds good for the Kanakvṛndāvan temple that has survived, that is, the one at Āmer Ghāṭī, but not necessarily for its predecessor, which, according to P.K. Banerjea, was situated at a more vulnerable place close to the water reservoir. By 1733, the Mānsarovar had indeed risen, for in that year, GD was granted a piece of land in compensation for the some 267 *bīghās* (more than 160 acres if calculated by Akbar's standard *bīghā*) inundated by the reservoir.[73] Nath (1996:180) rather feels that GD's transfer must be seen in the perspective of the deity's power of legitimizing the Kachavāhā rule,

> There is evidence that the city of Jayapura was built during the fourteen years from 1713 to 1727, when it was formally founded. In these years, the Candra Mahala[74], Govinda Mahala, and Bādala Mahala were completed. (That these buildings were ready for use on the eve of the founding of Jayapura city in 1727 is confirmed by Bakhat Rāma Sāha in his *Buddhi Vilāsa*, which he composed in 1770.) "Govinda Mahala" obviously refers to the Sūrya Mahala, which now houses the temple of Śrī Govindadeva; it is noteworthy that it is named "Mahala" (palace) instead of "Mandira" (temple). This implies that Śrī Govindadeva was now the tutelary deity of the Kachavāhas, virtually given the status of sovereign of the state, and he lived in a palace instead of a mandira. We do not know where the deity's image was housed from 1715 to 1727, but it seems certain that its new home, Govinda Mahala (Sūrya Mahala) was completed and it was installed there before the founding of the city on 18 November A.D. 1727. The transfer of the deity from Kanaka Vṛndāvana to Jayanivāsa thus appears to have been guided by reasons of state, and it is even likely that the founding of the city was delayed until the deity could be consecrated in the present temple. The city of Jayapura was, in fact, dedicated to Śrī Govindadeva, where he was already virājamāna.

This suggestive argument must be taken with a pinch of salt in view of the fact that from November 1719, regular worship for GD was conducted in his new (Āmer Ghāṭī) temple at Kanakvṛndāvan, as will be discussed presently.[75]

---

[72]Nath (1996:183, note 42) specifies this *parvānau* as follows, "Parvānā (ḍhūnaḍhārī) of Savāī Jaya Siṃha II … dated V.S. 1771/A.D. 1714 conferring a perpetual grant for perfumes and *lavājamā* (accoutrement) of the garden (Kanaka Bāgha) for the maintenance of nine *mālīs* (gardeners) and two *darbānas* (gatekeepers), bullocks and cows, on Śrī Govindeva *(sic!)* who had been virājamāna at Kanaka Bāgha Vṛndāvana since V.S. 1770/A.D. 1713". For this deed, cp. also Bahura 1996:205, who quotes from it. The embankment is not mentioned in the passage quoted.

[73]→ V.S. 1790, Māgha ś. 4.

[74]Hybrid spelling throughout the quoted passage.

[75]The early date of the completion of the City Palace is rather incongruent with the fact that Vidyādhar, its architect, was rewarded as late as 1734 for the "speedy construction" of it (Sarkar 1984: 216-17).

While the duration of GD's stay at Jainivās remains unknown, increased support granted to the deity is documented for the year 1717.[76] In August 1719,[77] we find GD about to leave for "Kurorī" (= Karaulī?[78]), and again we do not know if, when and why this happened.[79] 1719 is also the year when GD's history becomes, visibly for us, linked up with that of Rādhāmādhavjī (RM), the deities mentioned by P.K. Banerjea.[80] The history of RM itself is beyond the scope of this study, but out of the three readily available documents on these deities, two, dated 1717 and 1720, respectively, form part of the GD records.[81] The third document belongs to the holdings of the Rajasthan State Archives, Bikaner, and is a *ḍaul* of 1728.[82] The fact that the document made out for RM alone forms part of the GD records, and that GD and RM were given joint grants supports P.K. Banerjea's assertion that the RM temple was under the authority of the custodian of GD. As far as this corpus of documents is concerned, RM appears first in the aforementioned document of 1717, at that time alone and without an indication of the images' residence. On 1 July 1717, it was decided to grant RM a *puni ūdik*, a grant of charitable land, in *parganā* Khoh.[83] It had been stipulated that the land would yield 1,500rp. revenue. However, no suitable land could be allocated for that purpose, so that on 2 December 1717 village Maū Khās, located in *parganā* Hiṇḍaun, was assigned instead. This grant was confirmed in 1751, but in c. 1824/V.S. 1881, the records show it to have been transferred to GD.[84] The document of 1720 confirms a grant which GD and RM had received jointly up to the hot season harvest of 1719/V.S. 1776. It covers expenses for *bhog* and other items which would safeguard the performance of worship and the maintenance of the temple's infrastructure,

---

[76]*V.S. 1774, Jyeṣṭha ś. 13; → V.S. 1774, Jyeṣṭha ś. 15.

[77]→ V.S. 1776, Bhādrapada ś. 6.

[78]My tentative identification with Karaulī was affirmed in March 1996 by Shri Shivcand Tiwari, Officer-in-charge, Old Historical Records, Jaipur section, Rajasthan State Archives, Bikaner, to whom this variant reading was quite familiar from other documents.

[79]The paucity of evidence resists a conclusive interpretation of this and a number of other events of the second decade of the 18th century. It might be expedient not to lose sight also of events which do not surface at all in the documents. Around 1718, Jaisiṅgh sought to settle conflicts between rivalling Vaiṣṇava sects, presumably not so much as an arbitrator but rather as an interested party. After this, he seems to have especially favoured the Caitanyas, as is evident from a treatise commissioned by him and written in 1723 by Kṛṣṇadeva Bhaṭṭācārya, a theologian affiliated to the Madanmohan temple and a recipient of many favours from the Mahārājā (Horstmann 1994b).

[80]Cp. above, p. 19.

[81]One of them refers to RM separately and hence has not been edited in this volume. Its date is Mārgaśiras ś. 10, V.S. 1774/2 December 1717; the other refers to GD and RM jointly, → V.S. 1777, Āśvina ś. 14/4 October 1720.

[82]For documents called *ḍaul*, cp. p. 57 below. The date of this *ḍaul* is rev.y. 1784, Vaiśākha I ś. 15/13 April 1728. It was published by Horstmann (1995) under the wrong assumption that it referred to GD alone. It was made in preparation of a confirmatory *parvānau* of the document of 1720, which is incomplete as to several portions, including the *elevatio*. It is, however, clear from the text of the *ḍaul* of 1728 that the *parvānau* of 1728 referred to both GD and RM. Also RSA. Jaipur, File No 1657-28, 17 December 1952, refers to the *parvānau* of V.S. 1777 and to the joint grantees, namely, GD and RM.

[83]For *puni ūdik*, cp. below, pp. 36-37.

[84]RSA. Jaipur, File No 1657-28, 17 December 1952.

cattle, etc. This proves that GD and RM did, in fact, both reside in Kanakvṛndāvan, though the buildings which they occupied are not mentioned.

On 3 December 1719,[85] a *sanad* was issued which enjoined that work in the GD temple and the construction of a new house for the priest be carried out during the following hot season. The temple is not specified in the *sanad*, but it was only the Kanakvṛndāvan temple that was in need of a new house for the priest; for the old temple of Vrindaban had had one since the sixteenth century, which has survived to this day,[86] whereas by 1719, the Govindpur temple had fallen into disuse. The document also mentions arrears which might have accrued since Kārttika, ś. 3 in the payment of GD's claims, hence a month before the date of the document.[87] All these details combine to suggest that at least during the period between Kārttika ś. 3 and Mārgaśiras ś. 3 of V.S. 1776/November-December 1719, GD must have been present in Kanakvṛndāvan. This is in consonance with the document of 1720 which was made out for GD and RM jointly and mentions a grant for *bhog* etc. in force up to the hot season harvest of V.S. 1776/1719 and to be continued from the winter harvest of V.S. 1777/1720.

This leads to the conclusion that at least for some part of 1719, and definitely from 1720, GD had been present in Kanakvṛndāvan and, furthermore, that the GD temple and the house of its priest were completed by the hot season of 1720. The images of RM were worshipped in an unknown locality at Kanakvṛndāvan but under the authority of GD's custodian.[88]

After the completion and consecration of the temple of Kanakvṛndāvan, there were issued in 1721 and 1725 two *sanad*s which draw our attention once again to the GD temple of Vrindaban. So far, there are no records available which might clarify the fortunes of this temple after the removal of GD and the other two images. The *sanad* of 11 September 1712[89] points to a shrine without an image of GD, for the building is called "the temple of Śrī[GD]jī", that is, the reference is not to GD as impersonated in his icon, but rather to the deity's residence. The *sanad* decrees that arrangements for a new curtain and, if need be, a new canopy be made. In November 1725,[90] a deed on the supply of coal for the deity GD is confirmed. Another confirmation of the same was made in November 1730.[91] In both the *sanad*s referring to coal,

---

85→ V.S. 1776, Mārgaśiras ś. 3.

86For which see Thakur 1996:[18] with fig. 2.16.

87The Yamadvitīyā festival falls on that date.

88 The history of RM beyond their stay in Kanakvṛndāvan has remained unexplored. There is now a RM temple on the south-western side of the Tāl Kaṭorā tank within the precincts of Jaipur's City Palace whose relationship with the images of the 18th century RM temple is not clear; cp. Nath 1996:178.

89→V.S. 1778, Āśvina ś. 1.

90V.S. 1782, Mārgaśiras b. 14.

91→ V.S. 1787, Kārttika ś. 3.

the deity GD himself is made the beneficiary of the charity.This indicates that a substitute image of GD was worshipped in the Vrindaban temple. The deed of 18 June 1729[92] tallies with this. Being an order of Prince Sūrajmal, the Jāṭ heir apparent, it must refer to Jāṭ territory, and this is what Vrindaban was in that period. Hence the deed may be taken to refer to the GD temple of Vrindaban. The two bundles of betel leaves reported in this document to arrive each month at the temple point to ongoing worship. Moreover, the presence of a Gosvāmī taking care of the temple at Vrindaban is testified by a *sanad* of 10 April 1732.[93] These scattered bits of evidence cannot be assembled to form a consistent picture, but they suggest that in the 1720s and early 1730s, worship was conducted in the GD temple of Vrindaban. This conjecture is all the more likely because the Jāṭs, who controlled the region of Mathura and Vrindaban, were patrons of Vaiṣṇava religion and intimately connected with the Kachavāhās (Entwistle 1987:194-95). The Vrindaban temple was under the supervision of the GD temple of the Amber/Jaipur territory, as can be concluded from a letter of June 1782.[94] In this, the *adhikārī* Haṃsdās, obviously the local custodian of the GD temple of Vrindaban, is reported to be unwilling to be employed as manager of Rājā Kiśordās's property in Vrindaban without the permission of the Amber/Jaipur custodian of GD, Kṛṣṇaśaraṇ. Also belonging to the end of the eighteenth or perhaps to the early years of the nineteenth century is an undated *maẖzarnāma* authored by Vaiṣṇava *gosvāmīs* and officiating priests of Vrindaban and addressed to Mahārājā Pratāpsiṅgh. The authors report therein that the *ṭahailvā* (officiating, acting) *pujārīs* of the GD temple of Vrindaban had massively encroached upon the Rāmānandī Tulsīdās's right to conduct worship at the temples of Bālmukundjī and Nṛtyagopāljī.[95]

In the course of time, GD and his consort were joined by two *sakhīs*, that is, images of Rādhā's confidantes.[96] Each of them was granted a daily allowance of 1rp. for *bhog* and garments, which was as much as the daily allowance of GD's custodian. The difference between the "pay-scales" was, however, that the companion deities were granted their allowance on the basis of the religious, lunar year of 354 days, while the human beings received theirs on the basis of the year of 360 days, the working year.[97]

The period starting with the consecration of the new temple of Kanakvṛndāvan is marked by a steep increase in cash revenue grants, namely,

---

92→ V.S. 1786, Āṣāḍha ś. 8.

93→ V.S. 1789, Vaiśākha b. 12.

94→ V.S. 1839, Jyeṣṭha II b. 15.

95 Unpublished document in the possession of the Bālānand Pīṭh, Jaipur (courtesy Jagadguru Lakṣmaṇānandjī).

96 Cp. p. 5 above.

97 For which cp. pp. 71-72.

1719: 4,239rp. 9a. of which 1,956rp. 9a. were granted to GD, while the rest was the share of the Rādhāmādhav temple which was managed by GD's custodian (Rājsar Phuṭolāv, *V.S. 1776; →V.S. 1777, Āśvina ś. 14)

1727: 354 Aurangśāhī rp.[98] (from the Amber treasury, →V.S. 1784, Āśvina b. 11)

1734: revenue realized from 267 *bīghās*, 2 *viśvās* land (*parganā* Savāī Jaipur; →V.S. 1790, Māgha ś. 4)

1735: 1,770rp. (Govindpur-vās Hāthyod, →V.S. 1792, Pauṣa b. 5)

1736: 35rp. 6a. (probably from the *parganā* treasury, *V.S. 1793, Āṣāḍha b. 14)

These added up to more than 4,100rp., exclusive of the unspecified income that the revenue grant of 1734 would provide.

The temple within the precincts of the new palace of Jaipur, at the site called Jainivās, was consecrated in 1739 (Bahura 1996:206). The apogee of Jaisiṅgh II's munificence is represented by the deed of 27 December 1740,[99] when he decreed that there should be collected from each of the holders of titles on revenue and other taxes 1rp. for the maintenance of the GD temple and a quarter rupee as allowance for the Gosvāmī on top of every 1,000rp. revenue and other taxes. The grant was confirmed regularly until April 1786,[100] on this last occasion by the Marāṭhās. With this grant the relationship between the Kachavāhās and the temple assumed a new dimension, for GD was now raised to the status of an object of veneration and financial obligation of the entire state and its office-holders. GD was now no longer merely a family deity of the Kachavāhās but a public religious symbol of the state which was residing in the palace itself. GD was, however, not confined to his residence in Kanakvṛndāvan or, later on, in Jainivās. He is rather reported to have returned from Udaipur (which Udaipur?) in May 1748 and from Vrindaban in September 1741.[101]

Jaisiṅgh, who in the remaining years of his life, is described as having concentrated increasingly on the worship of GD, died in 1743.[102]

From Īśvarsiṅgh (r. 1743-50) to Jagatsiṅgh (r. 1803-18)

The period immediately after Jaisiṅgh II was marked by the internal conflict of the new Mahārājā Īśvarsiṅgh and Prince Mādhavsiṅgh over the succession to the throne of Jaipur, in

[98]In the deed, the amount is not mentioned. It appears, however, in the deed quoted in Bahura 1996: 206-07.

[99]→ V.S. 1997, Māgha b. 5.

[100][V.S. 1842, Caitra ś. 8a and b].

[101]Jyeṣṭha ś. 1, V.S. 1795 and Āśvina b. 14, V.S.. 1798 (DK 8: 49-50).

[102]For Jaisiṅgh's religious life in those years, cp. Bahura 1996:209-10; Asimakrishna Dasa 1996:246; Horstmann 1994a.

which they were both variously allied with the parties engaged in the power contest that ensued with the wane of the Mughal Empire. During the decades to come, these parties, mainly the Marāṭhās, Marwar, and the Mughal army, by invasions, raids, negotiations and short-lived treaties left their mark on Jaipur until it, like the other states of Rajasthan, eventually came under British paramountcy in 1818.

In the period of Īśvarsiṅgh's reign (1743-50), the extant grants were renewed. Of the grant of 1720, which had set the starting-point for the worship of GD at Kanakvṛndāvan,[103] however, there is no trace of confirmation until it re-emerges in 1872[104] and is recognized by the Jaipur State as a rightful claim on the part of the GD temple. The only fresh revenue grant in evidence in that period is that for Gordhanpuro, a village in *parganā* Khaṇḍelā, promulgated by order of the Jaipur court by the Mahārājā of Khaṇḍelā, Vṛndāvandās, who was in fief to Jaipur.[105] This grant, too, was recognized as valid in 1872.[106] Its estimated revenue income was 1,000rp.[107]

Mādhavsiṅgh (r. 1750-68) confirmed existing revenue grants. Immersed in debts, he enters the records by a single, original donation of 700 maunds of salt from Sāmbhar effective from 1751.[108] This was confirmed, and increased by 50 salt maunds, by the Jodhpur State when it obtained control over the salt lake of Sāmbhar.[109] There is a document dated 23 August 1751,[110] in which GD is reported to reside in Kanakvṛndāvan. GD's move out of the city is made plausible in view of the invasion of Jaipur by the Marāṭhās between the end of 1750 and the beginning of 1751, eventful weeks during which Īśvarsiṅgh committed suicide (13 or 14 December 1750) and Mādhavsiṅgh succeeded him (Sarkar 1964, I: 185-91).

In the latter half of the eighteenth century, a number of stray deeds appear, among these two which were issued in 1765 and 1771,[111] respectively, by Rāmsiṅgh, the deposed chief of Marwar, whose realm had been reduced to that part of the salt lake of Sāmbhar which was under Marwar's rule and who made grants of salt to GD.

103*V.S. 1776; → V.S. 1777, Āśvina ś. 14.

104[V.S. 1928, Caitra b. 15 (Rājsar Phuṭolāv).

105Jaisiṅgh II had obtained Khaṇḍelā in *ijāra* in 1725 (Wills 1933:76; Wills 1933: App. G gives the date 1734).

106[V.S. 1928, Caitra b. 15 (Gordhanpuro)].

107As given in a note of 1953. Cp. "Calendar of Documents" for doc. →V.S. 1808, Māgha ś. 1.

108*V.S. 1808.

109→ V.S. 1822, Pauṣa ś. 14 foll.

110→ V.S. 1808, Bhādrapada ś. 13.

111→ V.S. 1822, Pauṣa ś. 14 and → V.S. 1828, Vaiśākha b. 4.

During the minority rule in the regnal period of Mahārājā Pṛthvīsiṅgh (1768-78), only one *parvānau*, namely, the famous one of 1740, was confirmed. One new *parvānau*, which referred to village Hathrohī, is testified to by a *sanad* of 1771.[112]

None of the *parvānaus* confirmed by Pratāpsiṅgh (1778-1803) has come down to us. During his reign, Jaipur was intermittently invaded by the Marāṭhās. In the course of these events, Jaisiṅgh II's famous grant of 1740 was confirmed in 1786 in the name of Mādhorāv Śinde, the Peśvā.[113] The turmoil prevailing in this period is also reflected by the various attempts made between 1786 and 1791 by Gosvāmīs of Vrindaban to sell charities granted by the Kachavāhās.[114] The only fresh *parvānau* from Pratāpsiṅgh's time is the one of September 1783, when GD was granted thirteen shops in the town of Jaipur,[115] a deed recognized as valid in 1950.[116] Important for the history of the GD temple is a *parvānau* in favour of the second *sakhī*, whose image had been installed by Pratāpsiṅgh on 27 April 1803, but for whom he seems not to have issued a grant for *bhog*.[117] Pratāpsiṅgh died in August of that year. The *bhog* grant was only promulgated by his successor Jagatsiṅgh in December of the same year.[118]

Two deeds authored by Prince Bakhtāvarsiṅgh of Alvar in 1792 are noteworthy in the light of Bakhtāvarsiṅgh's subsequent attempts to legitimize the new state of Alvar, which had been founded in 1775, by claiming GD to be the ruling family's deity, a claim not without justification, for the family belongs to a Kachavāhā clan, namely, that of the Narūkās.[119]

During the regnal period of Jagatsiṅgh (1803-18), a number of fresh grants were made, although confirmations of earlier ones are missing. This does not, however, indicate that they lapsed, for they were eventually confirmed as valid by Rāmsiṅgh II, who succeeded to the throne in 1835 (minority rule until 1851). As is evident from his letter of 30 October 1806,[120] the advent of British rule in Vrindaban caused great anxiety to the successor of the recently deceased custodian of GD, Kṛṣṇaśaraṇ. He solicited a bond from Jaipur's minister which would guarantee that the revenue management of the 135 *bīghās* land in Vrindaban, which Akbar had granted to the GD group of temples in 1598/99 and which after their transfer to the Kachavāhās

---

112→ V.S. 1828, Vaiśākha b. 4.

113[V.S. 1842, Caitra ś. 8a and b].

114→ V.S. 1843a and b; V.S. 1848, Bhādrapada b. 7.

115→ V.S. 1840, Āśvina b. 10.

116[V.S. 2006, Phālguṇa b. 7].

117For which cp. pp. 5 and 24.

118→ V.S. 1860, Māgha b. 2.

119For a discussion of this claim and on the alleged sojourn of GD in the Alvar region, see Nath 1996:171-72.

120→ V.S. 1863, Kārttika b. 3.

in 1633 had been managed most of the time by the custodian of GD, would not lapse to the British revenue authority.

Mahārājā Rāmsiṅgh II (minority rule 1835-51, r. 1851-80)

No deeds issued by the agents of Jaisiṅgh III, whose regnal period was one of minority rule,[121] have come down to us, but in the period of Mahārājā Rāmsiṅgh II's reign, GD's grants were confirmed in the years 1871 to 1873. No early confirmatory grants of his reign have been traced to date. Of the extant ones, only one[122] commended itself for publication, because the rest were only available in copies made in the 1930s and thereafter, when GD's titles were verified.[123] Prepared for office use, these copies raise the suspicion that they might have been prepared with less orthographic care than would be desirable for the purpose of an edition, and consequently they have only been called for in the "Calendar of Documents". The single original deed in this edition, which comes from the GD temple archives, shows the effect of the administrative reforms introduced under Rāmsiṅgh, under which the Jaipur State was divided into administrative divisions, called *nizāmat*, which were headed by magistrates who bore the title *nāzim.*[124] From 1867, the state was administered by the "Royal Council".[125]

During the reign of Rāmsiṅgh II, GD's custodian, like other Vaiṣṇavas, was under heavy pressure to comply with Śaiva customs. The Mahārājā had personally embraced Śaivism and he dismissed recusant Vaiṣṇavas, even evicting them from the state. DK reports that in 1866, Rāmsiṅgh had demanded that Gosvāmī Śyāmsundar, the then custodian, wear the Śaiva necklace of *rudrākṣa* beads. As expected, Śyāmsundar objected to this "because it was against his *śāstra*", whereupon the Mahārājā kept him in house arrest and took over the superintendance of the affairs of the GD temple. He transferred the right to worship to one Gosvāmī Līlmaṇī and resumed the villages from which the temple had drawn income for *bhog*. The treasures of the temple were made accessible for consumption so that "then the Gosvāmī started wearing the *rudrākṣa* necklace and the temple was restored to its former state".[126] The confirmation of GD's grants in the years 1871 to 1873 are probably related to this affair. The fact that he had yielded to the Mahārājā's pressure left Śyāmsundar in a dilemma, for he fell into disrepute with his Caitanya confrères, the consequences of which came into the open in 1875 at

---

[121]This was an especially troubled period, for which cp. Vashishtha 1978:20-23, 148-152; also VV 2.2:1520.

[122]→ V.S. 1930, Phālguṇa ś. 4.

[123]Cp. fn. 33 above.

[124]→ V.S. 1930, Phālguṇa ś. 4, ll. 1; Sarkar 1984:354.

[125]→ V.S. Phālguṇa ś. 4, ll. 2-3.

[126]DK 5:539 for the year V.S. 1923. The confirmations of deeds of 1871 to 1873 may or may not have been the first ones after that incident.

a festive event at the temple of Rādhādāmodar in Vrindaban, which was, of course, part of the British imperial territory. In the words of Growse (1882:257),

> The temple of Rádhá Dámodar has a special claim to distinction from the fact that it contains the ashes of Jíva, its founder, as also of his two uncles, the Gosáins Rúpa and Sanátan, the founders of the temple of Govind Deva,[127] ... The joint anniversary is celebrated in the month of Sáwan, when the three shrines are visited by crowds of Bengalis, who, according to custom, make each some small offering. The proceeds used to be divided between the priests of the two temples; but in 1875, the Rádhá Dámodar Mahant made an attempt to engross the whole by excluding to Gobind Deva people from any participation in the ceremony. The plea advanced was that they were renegades from Vaishnavism since the time they had complied with the Jaypur Mahárája's order and marked their foreheads with the three horizontal lines that indicate a votary of Siva. This exclusion was naturally resented by the Gobind Deva Mahant, who claimed the immemorial right of free access to his founder's tomb, and as there seemed cause to anticipate that the two rival factions would come to blows, precautions were taken to suppress all external manifestations whatever, much to the chagrin of the Rádhá Dámodar claimants, who had prepared to signalize their triumph by a display of exceptional magnificence.

The modern State of Rajasthan verified and recognized the grants confirmed by the erstwhile Jaipur State and has thus given continuity to a relationship whose foundation was laid in the end of the sixteenth century by Mahārājā Mānsiṅgh and to which the Mughal Emperors had made a sizeable contribution.

[127]This needs to be corrected: The founder of the GD temple was Rūp Gosvāmī whereas Sanātan Gosvāmī founded the Madanmohan temple.

2. THE DOCUMENTS: DIPLOMATIC AND ADMINISTRATIVE ASPECTS

The deeds that were promulgated by the Kachavāhās in favour of GD were mainly revenue grants. They provided a stable income and, in the course of time, became titles which the temple enjoyed in perpetuity.[1] In addition, the other deeds published here cover donations in cash and kind which were, at least in principle, of a temporary nature.[2] Most of the documents published here were issued by the Kachavāhās, the rest by various other authors, who appeared on the political stage of Rajasthan in the latter part of the eighteenth century.

The fiscal system of the Mughal Empire, of which the Kachavāhā State formed a part, revolved around the institution of *jāgīr,* revenue assignment.[3] These assignments were made out of the land belonging to the state which was called *khālsā* (< Pers. *khāliṣa*). There were various types of *jāgīrs*, of which this volume reflects only one, namely, the *tankhāh jāgīrs* (< Pers. *tankhwāh j.*). These provided salaries in the form of revenue assignments. They were given to civil and military servants, who also had to pay their military contingents out of the *jāgīr*; but they were also bestowed on religious institutions and their representatives for the maintenance of worship and for salary, respectively. *Jāgīrs* represented temporary assignments in principle, but were often quasi-permanent in practice. This implied that the income source of a *jāgīrdār* (*jāgīr*-holder) was liable to change.[4] The revenue assignments entitled the *jāgīr*-holders to collect the revenue by themselves or through their agents, which allowed for a wide margin of profit beyond the revenue assigned. The revenue was called *tan,* derived from *tankhāh. Tan* was the assessed, hence notional revenue, not the actually realized net amount. Basically, the *jāgīrdār*'s income would be calculated on the basis of *tan,* but what he actually received was an amount that was subject to change.[5] It was in the very nature of these assignments that the net income might fall short of the assessed revenue, for the crop yields fluctuated and so would the many other taxes which were comprised in the revenue.[6] If the revenue of an entire village was

---

[1]Cp. also pp. 33-34.

[2]It must be borne in mind that the temple received many more gifts from the Kachavāhās as well as from other sources which are not accounted for in the documents published in this volume. A great number of donations made on particular occasions, such as religious festivals or the visit of the Mahārājā himself or a member of his household or a noble, are recorded in DK 8, the volume which refers to the temples, *ṭhākurdvārā*. Thus, the revenue and sundry grants formed only a fraction of the total income of GD.

[3]The *jāgīr* system has been studied in great detail. For the Mughal state, cp. Habib 1963, for Eastern Rajasthan, Gupta 1986.

[4]Cp. Gupta 1986: 219-20 and Siṅgh 1990: 148.

[5]For the several methods of fixing the net revenue income, cp. presently.

[6]For the various agricultural taxes, cp. Gupta 1986:144-59 and Singh 1990:108-19.

assigned to a single *jāgīrdār*, this was called *tan darobast* (< Pers. *dar-ū-bast*), "entire revenue", or *gāṁv darobast*, "entire village".[7]

The realized revenue was called *hāsil* (< Pers. *hāṣil*, "produce, profit").[8] Synonymously with *hāsil* there occurs the term *upejyau*, namely, in docs. → rev. y. 1801, Bhādrapada b. 5 (Gaṅgārāmpur-vās Khijūryā), l. 17, and → V.S. 1825, Māgha b. 15, l. 4. Like *hāsil*, the term *ūpejyau* means "produce". Also doc. → V.S. 1796, Jyeṣṭha ś. 13, ll. 39-41 is illustrative of the term as being synonymous with *hāsil*. It contains the stipulation that land given as a charity to a certain brahmin should "yield approximately 1rp. per *bīghā*" (*dhartī bīghā 1/- maiṃ hāsil ūnmāṃn rupayā 1/- vapjai*).

For the beneficiary, the crucial question was how the assessed revenue would relate to the amount collected. This was settled if the grant guaranteed him the revenue amount actually to be drawn, which was termed *vasūl*, "drawn, recovered", or *vasūlī*, "recoverable amount"(< Pers. *vaṣūl(ī)*).[9] The meaning is made quite explicit by the phrasing of various documents of rev. y. 1801, Bhādrapada b. 5, for instance, the one referring to Govindpuro, ll. 17 *recto*, 11 *verso*: *tan darobast (maiṃ) ūsūlī rupayā*, "Out of the entire revenue... (the) recoverable amount [of]".[10]

Quite often, the net revenue allowance would cover only a part of the revenue amount assessed. These reductions, introduced by Śāh Jahān (Aziz 1945:52-53), became increasingly common towards the end of the Mughal period. The growing number of *manṣabdārs*, who lived on and maintained their military contingents by *jāgīrs*, had led to a scarcity of *jāgīrs*. The situation was aggravated by the instability of agricultural production in times of war and famine. One way to cope with this was to assign *jāgīrs* with reduced revenue rates, a method which was also applied for *tankhāh jāgīrs*. The reduced pay-scales were calculated by month-ratios.[11] The system went by the Persian name of *tan qarār*, "fixed revenue".[12] There existed 4-, 6-, 8-month ratios, according to which a *jāgīr*-holder was only paid the revenue of four out of twelve months of the harvest year, or six or eight. An example of this is provided by doc. → V.S. 1777, Āśvina ś. 14, ll. 16-19 *verso*. Doc. → V.S. 1797, Māgha b. 5, ll. 9-10, mentions six- and eight-month pay-scales.

---

[7]E.g. for *tan darobast* → rev. y. 1801, Bhādrapada b. 5 for Govindpuro, Sālimpuro and Sekhpuro Baṛo; for *gāṁv darobast*, cp. the document of the same date referring to Gaṅgārāmpur-vās Khijūryā.

[8]For this, cp. the translations of section II 6 of various *parvānaus* issued in rev. y 1801, Bhādrapada b. 5, where the collection of revenue (*hāsil*) is enjoined to be transferred on the grantee.

[9]Cp. e.g. → A.H. 1102, 21 Rabī' II, ll. 6, 43.

[10]For a brief mentioning of *vasūl* as meaning "realized revenue", cp. Siṅgh 1990:149.

[11]For the system of reduction by month-ratios, cp. Habib 1963:264-65.

[12]Gupta 1986: 218 and Singh 1990:149-50.

Assignees could apply for a reduction of the rate of assessment, which was termed *takhfīf(-i dāmī).*[13] This was called for if the actual collection of revenue fell dramatically short of the assessed revenue, such as in times of calamity. If granted, the assignee was entitled to put a claim (*talab*) for an additional assignment, which would be equivalent to the reduction. For an example of *takhfīf*, cp. doc. → V.S. 1777, Āśvina ś. 14, ll. 19-21 *verso*.

The form in which the temple would receive the revenue is stated a few times to be cash, namely, in docs. → A.H. 1078, 30 Jumādā II, l. 32; → A.H. 1106, 12 Jumādā I, l. 19, and → V.S. 1797, Māgha b. 5. For the last-mentioned deed, the nature of the collection procedure required cash payment in any case. The first two documents stipulate that fixed daily allowances out of revenue be paid for the *bhog* of the deities and to the custodian, though it is not stated in what shares.

The revenue collection could be farmed out in *ijārau* (< Pers. *ijāra*).[14] In this volume, there is published one document which represents an *ijārau* lease (→ V.S. 1764, Śrāvaṇa b. 3). The procedures conducive to an *ijārau* lease are reflected by its clauses, namely, that the lessee, here the custodian acting in the stead of the deity GD, had to formally consent (*kabulāti,* < Pers. *qabūliyat,* "consent") to the conditions of the contract. The amount to be remitted by the lessee was given along with the full amount of revenue dues. For his service, the lessee received a commission which was the revenue dues minus the reduced revenue rate to be remitted. In the case of the document in question, the commission was about one fifth of the revenue. The lessee had to produce a surety, called *māl-jāmin* (< Pers. *māl-i ẕāmin*).[15] Normally a banker stood bail for the *ijārau* dues and in return would receive a share of the lessee's profit (Singh 1991:130). In case of the GD temple, GD stood bail, that is, the temple and its wealth vested in the juristic person of the deity. Finally, it had to be stated in the contract at what rates the dues would be remitted at the autumn and spring harvest, respectively.

The *puni* (*punya*) grants[16] were in one case expressly assigned in *jāgīr*, namely, for the grant referring variously to villages Jhujhārpur and Catrapur-vās Khijuryā.[17] Here, the principle that *jāgīrs* were transferable was put into practice, because the assignment shifted to and fro between the two places. From the time of Īśvarsiṅgh,[18] the grant was under the authority of the

---

[13]Gupta 1986:217; for the administrative procedures in case of *takhfīf*, cp. Habib 1963:267.

[14]For the consequences of *ijārau* for the growth of the Kachavāhā State and for the revenue and property system, cp. Gupta 1986:5-37, 223-32; also Singh 1990:129-43, particularly for the subtypes of revenue farming.

[15]Gupta 1986:229 and GJRT, 562.

[16]See presently, pp. 35-37.

[17]*rev. y. 1096, ff., and → V.S. 1767, Āśvina b. 5, ff.

[18]Cp. → rev. y. 1801, Bhādrapada b. 5 (Catrapur-vās Khijuryā) and subsequent deeds.

puni bhog department, which was in charge of religious charities, and assigned in perpetuity.[19] This is evident from section II 7[20] of charity grants, which enjoins that for a charity once granted, the officers must not demand a fresh *parvānau* every year.[21] The title was only to be renewed on the death of the donor or the beneficiary, in which event, the lawful successor of either had to effect or seek the confirmation of the deed. Against this, the *jāgīr* deeds for Jhujhārpur have no such stipulation.

Hence it can be concluded that transferable *jāgīrs* ceased providing religious charities and were gradually converted into grants in perpetuity. This change may have taken place in the regnal period of Jaisiṅgh II, for when Īśvarsiṅgh confirmed his father's deeds, no mention was made of changes and everything was decreed to be executed according to "the hitherto existing regulation".[22]

Types of charities

The charities figuring in the documents were of the following types,

(1) *bhog*
(2) *puni (punya); puni [va/vā] bhog*
(3) *ghās carāī*
(4) *puni (punya) arath*
(5) *puni (punya) ūdik*
(6) *bheṭ, bheṭ ūdik*
(7) *inām*

All these deeds did not provide *ad hoc* benefits but rather established a claim of some kind. To these may be added deeds covering miscellaneous benefits, which were not classified under any of the listed categories.[23]

---

[19]The transfer from the *jāgīr* to the *puni bhog* department is also evidenced by the seals affixed to the deed. While the *jāgīr* department was in charge, the grant had to be sealed by the *baksīs*, who were the Paymasters General and responsible for military tenures of *jāgīr* land, besides the *dīvāns*, the *mustophī* and, of course, the Mahārājā, as is documented by doc. → V.S. 1767, Āśvina b. 5.

[20]This refers to the translations of *parvānaus* in this volume. For *parvānau*, cp. also pp. 49-61.

[21]Cp. Mohiuddin 1971:86-87.

[22]Cp. section II 6 of Īśvarsiṅgh's *parvānaus* of rev. y. 1801, Bhādrapada, b. 5.

[23]Cp. e.g. → V.S. 1773, Bhādrapada ś. 8, a deed for the maintenance of temple-guards and other servants.

(1) *Bhog*

Bhog are the eatables and other consumable ingredients used for worship.[24]

(2) *Puni (punya), puni [va/vā] bhog*

Puni, also *punya*, is a charity to cover non-food expenses, such as garments for the images of deities, festival expenses or the salary of custodians.[25] The term *puni* was also used for charities which were not provided by revenue grants in perpetuity but represented gifts made on special, recurring or singular, occasions.[26] The term *puni bhog* means "charity *(puni)* for *bhog*". A variant of this was *puni bhog vagairah*, "charity *(puni)* for eatables and other worship ingredients, and other perquisites".[27] The type which the *puni bhog* grants represent exhibits numerous terminological modifications because, for example, various kinds of *bhog* might be specified.[28]

If both eatables and non-eatables were covered by a grant, the term used was *puni va* (or *vā*) *bhog*.[29]

(3) *Ghās carāī*

There is a single grant for *ghās carāī*, namely, that of → rev. y. 1801, Bhādrapada b. 5 (pasture) and subsequent deeds. By this type of grant, which falls under the category of revenue grants and therefore needed to be promulgated in the form of a *parvānau*, the right to graze cattle on *khālsā* land was granted free of tax. The cattle grazing tax was called *ghās carāī* (Gupta 1986:226). In principle, this type of grant is an ordinary revenue grant, the difference being that it does not cover the assessed revenue from the crops.

(4) *Puni (punya) arath*

Grants designated *puni arath (punya arath)*, "charity of land property", are, as far as their fiscal treatment is concerned, the equivalents of the *madad-i ma'āś* grants inherited from the Islamic tradition and given to religious people, Muslim or Hindu or other, and to other deserving

---

[24] The current definition of *bhog* as "grant made to meet the expenses of a temple" (RSA. Jaipur, loose leaves. "Definitions of Important Vernacular Terms...", 3 March and 17 December 1938, p. 6) is less precise than the older usage; similarly Singh 1990:208, "grant made for the maintenance of temples".

[25] E.g. → A.H. 1102, 21 Rabī' I; → V.S. 1764, Śrāvaṇa b. 3.

[26] E.g. → V.S. 1859, Pauṣa ś. 10.

[27] E..g. → V.S. 1784, Āśvina b. 11, l. 3 *recto*.

[28] E.g. → V.S. 1773, Āśvina ś. 8, ll. 3-4, *recto*, where the charity is meant for the twilight *bhog*, or → V.S. 1808, Bhādrapada ś. 13, l. 2 *recto*, where the charity is given for "festive *bhog*".

[29] E.g. → A.H. 1078, 30 Jumādā II, of which only the *bhog*-part was renewed by doc. → rev. y. 1801, Bhādrapada b. 5 (Govindpuro).

recipients to ensure their sustenance.[30] In this volume, all *puni arath* grants had brahmin recipients. These grants were made in perpetuity, that is to say, they were transferred to the descendants of the original beneficiary.[31] The religious character of these grants is shown by the oft-occurring stipulation that the recipient bless the grantor or pray for his welfare.[32] They were given for the usufruction of revenue, but they were not alienable. Neither could they be sold nor the land's cultivators be evicted. Kachavāhā *sanads*[33] of grants, though not the *parvānaus*[34] which followed a fixed and in this respect different cliché, often enjoined that the revenue officers must not molest the grantee or meddle with his rights.[35]

It was common for *puni arath* grants to stipulate that the land granted consist half of cultivated and half of fallow, cultivable land. This is in accordance with the "Rule of the Half" of the Mughal administration, as inherited from the Sūr administration and mentioned in the *A'īn* (Habib 1963: 202; Mukherjee and Habib 1988: 246). It seems also to have been a common injunction that the size of the land should be 200 *bīghās*.[36]

(5) *Puni (punya) ūdik*

A *puni ūdik* (< *udak*, "water") is in many respects similar to a *punya arath* grant. There are three of these grants published in this volume. One of them resembles an ordinary *punya arath* deed.[37] Its beneficiary was an individual and not the deity or, in other words, a juristic person. The two remaining *puni ūdiks*[38] are grants in favour of the GD temple and were meant for the maintenance of worship. Two of the documents report the circumstances in which the endowments were made, while the one of rev. y. 1801, being a renewal, does not. The circumstances reported clearly indicate that the grants were the result of a vow, which implied

[30]The term *punya arath* is also found to be used for other items than land property. For example, also robes of honour are found to fall under this category, for which cp. DK 31:528, 567.

[31]In Mughal India *madad-i ma'āś* grants had become hereditary by 1690 (Habib 1963:311).

[32]E.g. → A.H. 1972, 15 Śavvāl, ll. 8-9. Cp. also examples like docs. II, V, VII, XII in Ansari 1984 and Jhaveri 1928, documents, pass.

[33]For which cp. pp. 44-49.

[34]For which cp. pp. 49-61.

[35]Cp. Jhaveri 1928, documents, pass.; also Mohiuddin 1971:70 for the various injunctions.

[36]Cp. → A.H. 1072, 15 Śavvāl, ll. 10-12. Cp. also → V.S. 1769, Jyeṣṭha ś. 13, ll. 37-38, a *puni ūdik* grant, for which cp. presently below.

[37]→ V.S. 1769, Jyeṣṭha, ś. 13. In this grant there appears another characteristic trait of charities of this type, namely, that the 200 *bīghās* granted should yield 1rp. revenue per *bīghā*. Muzaffar Alam (personal communication, July 1995) recalled the same trait as occurring in grants from other regions of northern India. These stipulations were no mere conventions but derived from the endeavour that land given in revenue grant should be brought properly under cultivation, as would be in the interest of an individual drawing income from it on a permanent basis.

[38]→ V.S. 1774, Jyeṣṭha ś. 15, and → rev. y. 1801, Bhādrapada b. 5 (Sekhpuro Baṛo).

an act of religious dedication, *saṃkalp*.[39] This is in accordance with the meaning inherent in the term itself, namely, a charity ensuing from a rite, of which water was a constitutive requirement.[40] A Hindu *saṃkalp(a)* requires that one pronounce one's resolve before the gods "taking in one's hand a copper vessel full of water...".[41]

The difference between a normal *bhog* or *puni bhog* grant and a *puni ūdik* was retained upto this century. When a person became liable to pay *mātamī matalbā*, which were the dues charged to him when, on the death of an estate-holder, he succeeded to his property titles,[42] the regulation was as follows: For *puni ūdik* titles, religious estates were charged half the ordinary rate that had to be paid by holders of secular estates, and for *bhog* land, a quarter of the ordinary rate.[43]

(6) *Bheṭ, bheṭ ūdik*

Bheṭ is basically a "complimentary gift" made to a superior (GJRT), here more specifically a religious donation. It could consist of money or other objects, such as real estate property. A *bheṭ* was not issued on application on the part of the grantee. *Bheṭs* were made for usufruction or consumption of the object granted.[44] *Bheṭ* was not allowed to be alienated or sold.[45]

The single *bheṭ ūdik* which is published in this volume (→ V.S. 1805, Māgha ś. 1) must be a *bheṭ* for which a *saṃkalp* had been made.[46]

(7) *Inām*

The *inām* (< Pers. *in'ām*) grant was made to deserving people in recognition of past services. It provided revenue-free land granted for life.[47]

---

[39]For a discussion of *saṃkalp*, in the sense of "will, testament", cp. Mukherjee and Wright 1979:319-20. – By the 1930s the administrative terminology had become somewhat loose. An *udak* was now defined as "charitable grant to Brahmins etc. Hindus. It is also called Punya" and a *saṃkalp* as "land granted in charity on occasion of a solar or lunar eclipse etc." (RSA. Jaipur, loose leaves, "Definitions of Important Vernacular Terms ...", 3 March and 17 December 1938, p. 5).

[40]This is also clarified by the RSK *s.v. udak*, int. al. "a thing given on making a vow [of which] water [is part]", and *s.v. udakṇau*, "to make a vow to give something while holding water in one's hand", and *s.v. udakī*, "holder of a grant which was bestowed on him by the *udak* rite".

[41]Kane 1974, V:81, quoting from the *Mahābhārata* and giving several more quotations from ritual digests, which enjoin that one take water in one's hand.

[42]For which cp. p. 9, fn. 33.

[43]RSA. Jaipur, loose leaves. "Definitions of Important Vernacular Terms...", 3 March and 17 December 1938, p. 8.

[44]E.g. → V.S. 1840, Āśvina b. 10: [revenue gain from] 13 shops; → V.S. 1797, Māgha b. 5: cash revenue income; → V.S. 1816, Bhādrapada ś. 9: salt.

[45]Docs. → V.S. 1843 a and b and → V.S. 1848, Bhādrapada b. 7.

[46]Cp. above under "(5) *puni ūdik*".

[47]Cp. → V.S. 1860, Māgha b. 7, and → V.S. 1869, Caitra ś. 1.

The procedures of the Kachavāhā revenue administration

The documents issued by the Kachavāhās were prepared in close emulation of the Mughal administrative practice, but they also show particular traits of their own. The study of the formal aspects of the documents provides insight into the consecutive administrative procedures which were required to pass a deed, which is, in fact, tantamount to insight into the fiscal machinery of the Kachavāhās.

An analysis of the procedures of the Kachavāhā revenue administration has to be attempted by way of induction, for so far no administrative manuals relating to Eastern Rajasthan have come to light. Therefore, the available documents have to be examined to discover what procedures they inherently report. These, then, may be compared with the practice of the Mughal chancery.[48] Although manuals contemporary with the deeds published in this book are missing, some help is forthcoming from an Office Note prepared in 1935-36 by the Superintendent Central Records of Jaipur State in the course of preparations for a reform of the chancery procedures.[49] This note must be used with caution, because it sums up procedures followed since the administrative reforms of Rāmsiṅgh II in 1867 and modified in 1921 (Sarkar 1984:354, 381). However, in spite of the intervening changes, many procedures followed in the period under review had been retained until the late 1930s when, on the basis of the traditional administrative regulations, it was sought to ease the procedures involved in the preparation mainly of grants. Even then Jaipur State, although accommodating to the usage the British had introduced, did not really break away from the traditional system.[50] This last reform before Independence took place between 1938 and 1942, and it had as one of its perquisites the information provided by the Central Records Office in 1935-36.

The grants fell under the responsibility of the *dīvānī*, the revenue administration. The Mughal revenue administration has been studied extensively, while Gupta, who studied the revenue system of the Kachavāhās, has given a full description of their "Land Revenue Administration" (1986:163-210), which need not be repeated here. A chart (p. 356) gives an overview of those parts of the administrative machinery that figure in the documents of this volume. It should be emphasized that the chart ignores all other departments besides the revenue

[48]Amongst the many relevant studies, the following have been invaluably helpful for the present discussion: Habib 1963, Ibn Hasan 1936, Khan 1950, Minorsky 1943, Mohiuddin 1971, Siddiqi 1970; in addition to these, studies on Persian diplomatics ante-dating the Mughal period proved extremely useful, especially Busse 1959.

[49]RSA. Jaipur, loose leaves. Office Note, Superintendent Central Records, 7 February and 16 June 1936.

[50]RSA, Jaipur, loose leaves. Council of State, Jaipur, "Resolution No 5", 10 February 1938, and subsequent resolutions taken by the same body.

department, and that within the revenue department, it shows only those which are mentioned in the documents.[51]

The documents allow us to obtain a fairly clear picture of the heads of the fiscal or revenue department, the *dīvāns*,[52] whereas the other officers of the fiscal service appear less clearly, with just a few ministers and *āmil*s being given by their names.[53] It must be borne in mind that on the level of the high offices, there existed considerable mobility. One and the same person could distinguish himself as *āmil, dīvān,* minister[54] or *vakīl*, emissary at the Mughal Court, and also as a high-ranking military officer. The bureaucratic elites in a state like that of the Kachavāhās form a so far nearly totally neglected field of studies, which would be indispensable for an adequate understanding of the social, political and administrative structure of the state.[55] Suffice it to say that from the end of the seventeenth century, the majority of *dīvāns* had been Khaṇḍelvāl Jains, with notable exceptions such as Na/ārāyaṇdās Khatrī or Vidyādhar Cakravartī.[56] The Khaṇḍelvāl Jains had been one of the groups who had been especially supported by Jaisiṅgh II and encouraged to settle in his new capital of Jaipur.[57]

The *dīvānī*[58] was normally headed by two officers, the *dīvān des*, who was in charge of the *khālsā*, the land holdings belonging to the state and directly administered by it, and the *dīvān hajūr(ī),* who was in charge of the assignment of *jāgīrs*. It seems that synonymous designations, namely, *dīvān vatan* (< Persian *vaṭan,* "homeland") for *dīvān des,* and *dīvan tan* for *dīvān hajūr(ī)* were superseded in the course of time. By 1751,[59] the official titles used in the officers' seals had been termed *"dīvān", tout court* for the *dīvān des,* and *"dīvān hajūr"* for

---

[51]The chart represents the structure of the revenue administration up to the administrative reform carried out by Rāmsiṅgh II. The reform affected the entire administration including the administrative divisions of the Jaipur State. For details, cp. Sarkar 1984:354, 381 and Stern 1988:114-64. Out of the documents published in this volume, only one is from the period of Rāmsiṅgh II. (→ V.S. 1930, Phālguṇa ś. 4) and therefore the administrative changes of the latter part of the 19th century hardly surface in this study.

[52]For a list of these, cp. pp. 64-68.

[53]If possible, information on these has been given in the commentaries on the respective documents.

[54]There is some confusion in distinguishing the minister from the *dīvāns*. The Mahārājā's minister was distinct from the heads of the *dīvānī* department. This is evident also from the *parvānaus* in which the grants are often explicitly stated to have been recommended by the minister, who is not mentioned by his title but his name, after which the routine of issuing a deed was set in motion by the *dīvāns*, whose names are given. Cp. e.g. the deeds issued in rev.v. 1801, Bhādrapada b. 5.

[55]Cp. however the information provided by Roy 1978:180-89 and also Ratnavat 1989.

[56]Cp. the table of *dīvāns* for the years 1725 and 1737-38/1739-41, resp., on pp. 65 and 66.

[57]For the fortunes of the Khaṇḍelvāls, cp. Bakhatrām 1964 and Kāslīvāl 1989.

[58]In the period of British paramountcy the revenue department was designated the Mahakmā Dīvānī. It comprised the following branches (*daftars*): Mavājanā (= Daftar Dīvānī Hujūrī), Vakāyā, Sanad-navīs, Nuskhā Punya, Nuskhā Kulli, Nuskhā Kalān, Nuskhā Khurd, Parvānā-navīs. (RSA. Jaipur, loose leaves. Office Note, Superintendent, Central Records, 6 December 1935, p. 3).

[59]For which cp. → V.S. 1808, Bhādrapada ś. 13, ll. 59-60.

the *dīvān* in charge of the assignment of *jāgīrs*. Normally, both acted in tandem, but sometimes a single *dīvān* held both portfolios.

The office of *dīvān sarkār* must have been held by more than one person at the same time, as is indicated by the plural designation used in the documents.[60] He was responsible to the Imperial administration on the level of the district (*sarkār*). It is far from clear how he really related to the central government after the actual breakdown of the Empire. Grover (1962) has produced much useful evidence on this office upto the time of Aurangzeb. In the Mughal administration, it was the *dīvān-i sarkār*'s duty to confirm royal or other decrees. For example, in the case of a *suyūrġāl* (another term for *madad-i ma'āś*) grant entitling its holder to land revenue usually for life but transferable to his heirs, the recipient of its renewal would have to obtain confirmatory *sanads* of various kinds. On the level of the province where his land was located, he had to obtain a confirmatory *sanad* from the provincial revenue officer, the *dīvān-i sarkār,* for

> the *Diwan-i Sarkar* exercised general superintendence and control of the *Parganas* in the *Sarkar,* [and] ...the *Diwan-i Sarkar* was a regular feature of the Mughal administration and was uniformly applicable to the whole Empire. (Grover 1962:68 with fn. 12)[61]

The *baksī* (< Pers. *ba<u>kh</u>śī*) was the Paymaster General who was in charge of *tankhāh jāgīrs* in military tenure; two *baksīs* occur in → V.S. 1767, Āśvina b. 5, but also three of them are found to have endorsed documents.[62]

The *mustauphī/mustophī* (< Pers. *mustaufī*) was the Auditor of Accounts. By his epithet *hajūri/-ī* he is identified as the auditor acting at the Mahārājā's court.

The Kachavāhā State was divided into *parganās*, actually subunits of the larger Mughal administrative units called *sarkārs*, "districts".[63] These again were divided into village clusters, *tapās* (< Pers. *tappa,* "hill", etymology uncertain), and villages, *maujās* (< Pers. *mauza'*). The intermediate subunit "village cluster" could also be missing. The officers on the *parganā* level were addressed as *kamaitī* (< Pers. *qavamat*, pl. of *qā'im*), "administrators, officers", sometimes also as the *mutsadīs* (< Pers. *mutasaddī,* lit. "clerk, accountant", the term usually

60 In the Persian versions, the respective phrase refers unequivocally to the plural, for which cp. → A.H. 1078, 30 Jumādā, ll. 15-16, and → A.H. 1102, 21 Rabī', l. 18. – This office seems not to have figured in the material studied by Gupta (1986), who passes over it in silence.

61 Cp. also Mohiuddin (1971:88, 90-91) for details on the consecutive levels on which confirmatory *sanads* had to be solicited.

62 Doc. of Śrāvaṇa ś. 14, V.S. 1777, Bālānand Pīṭh, Jaipur (courtesy Jagadguru Lakṣmaṇānandjī).

63 For the structure of *parganas*, cp. Gordon and Richards (1985), who analyse the situation of Khandesh.

occurring in the Persian versions of the deeds), "officers, administrators".[64] Certain *sanads* addressed two kinds of officers directly by their office-titles, namely, the *āmils* (< Pers. *'amil*) and perhaps the *amīns* (Pers. *id.*). They were appointed by the *dīvāns* under whose supervision they also worked. The *āmil* was in charge of the revenue collection and supervised the cultivation of arable land. The *amīn* was in charge of the ascertainment and assessment of land under cultivation and the levying of taxes. The *āmil* was sometimes identical with the *amīn* (Gupta 1986:166).

The *potdār* (< Pers. *fuṯadār*) was the *parganā* treasurer, who provided cash payments, and the *modī* was the commissariat, the officer of public provisions, which were stored in the storehouse of the *parganā*.

On the level of the village, *maujā*, we encounter the *paṭels* and the *paṭvārīs* who held hereditary offices. The *paṭel* was responsible for the assessment and collection of revenue and for the measuring of land. He was also to help bringing land under cultivation. The *paṭvārī* was the keeper of the *khasrā* papers, the records containing details of the village's cultivators, their holdings, cultivable land, crops cultivated by season, shares of peasant and the state, respectively, in the holdings (Gupta 1986:184).

Types of documents

Most of the documents of this book were written on paper. Some *puni arath, puni ūdik* and *bheṭ ūdik* grants form an exception, for this type of grants was often incised on copper-plates.[65]

Up to the regnal period of Jaisiṅgh II, the grants were bilingual, Rājasthānī and Persian. Copper-plate grants, however, were only in Rājasthānī, thus carrying on the Indic diplomatic tradition. The Rājasthānī version of bilingual deeds was written first. The versions sometimes differ as to certain factual details, which shows that the Persian version was no mere translation

[64] Some authors retain the literal translation of *mutas̱addī* as "clerk" which is misleading. The officers thus named formed the bureaucratic elite of Rajput states. In the words of Ziegler (1976: 135), who refers especially to the famous chronicler Naiṇsī from Marwar (seventeenth century), "*Mutsaddīs* such as Naiṇsī formed the core of emergent bureaucrats within these small states and were also the most literate men of these courts, trained in business transactions and office routines and holding inherited positions of court service. Such men handled all of the fiscal and administrative details connected with the running of the state, the collection of revenue and the granting of lands."

[65] E.g. → A.H. 1072, 15 Śavvāl; → V.S. 1805, Māgha ś. 1.

of the Indic one, but was drafted independently.[66] Jaisiṅgh II discontinued the practice of issuing bilingual deeds and used only Rājasthānī.[67]

The language designation Rājasthānī is a broad cover-term. There is no single Rājasthānī language, but only a group of Rājasthānī dialects varying greatly with regions and social context. The language used in the Kachavāhā documents is the chancery form of Ḍhūṇḍhāṛī and hence not identical with the spoken Ḍhūṇḍhāṛī, the idiom of the Jaipur region. The deeds issued by the Mārvāṛī administration are in chancery Mārvāṛī.[68]

The documents published in this volume fall under the following categories:

(1) *sanad*
(2) *parvānau*
(3) *yāddāst/yādidāsati*
(4) *dastak (dastag)*
(5) *kāgaj*
(6) letter
(7) office statement
(8) miscellaneous

In the "Calendar of Documents" (pp. 85-111), the documents have been classified according to their type, which was easy if a document text identified its type itself. Where this was not the case, or where the type could not be concluded by analogy, a tentatively chosen English term has been used for classification.

(1) *Sanad*

In the Mughal administration the term *sanad* (Pers. pl. *asnād,* here always *vulgo* "*sanad*s") applied to a wide range of patents, as described in the *Ā'īn* (I, §11:269-70).

> Every written statement of accounts is called a *sanad.* All classes of men adopt such a practice.
> The *sanad* is the voucher which relieves the treasurer of all responsibilities, and on which people receive payment of their claims. Honest experienced officers, upon whose forehead the stamp of

---

[66] E..g. → A.H. 1038, 2 Śavvāl, commentary on ll. 9-10 (Rāj.)/ll. 6-9 (Pers.); → A.H. 1106, 12 Jumādā I, commentary on ll. 41-57 (Rāj.)/l. 20, col. 1 (Pers.).

[67] For a different practice followed in the interregnal period of Vijaisiṅgh, cp.→ A.H. 1123, 19 and 21 Ramaẕān.

[68] Cp. Smith 1975 for a description of the language of the historical documents of Marwar.

> correctness shines, write the agreement upon loose pages and leaves, so that the transaction cannot be forgotten. These loose sheets into which all *sanads* are entered are called the *Daftar* (o.c., 270).

In this wider sense, the copies of *parvānau*s, which were forwarded to the recipients of patents and on which they could establish their claim, are also *sanads*.[69] In the passage quoted from the *Ā'īn*, there is pointed out a characteristic of Mughal and implicitly of Kachavāhā office papers, namely, that all documents and their several copies are kept in loose leave files (*daftar,* "file, records", also "administrative department in charge of a particular kind of records"). In a more specific sense, a *sanad* is what is also called a *sanad-i aẖkām-i dīvānī,* "patent relating to fiscal orders" (Mohiuddin 1971:86). It is this specific kind of *sanad* that appears in this volume. Here, all fiscal decrees not explicitly named otherwise and not falling under the *parvānau* type have been classified as *sanads*. They were issued by Mahārājās, other princes or *dīvāns*.

(2) *Parvānau*

In this volume, the term has remained restricted to one particular type of document, namely, deeds of revenue grant that contain a *résumé* of the office procedures at their different stages.[70] These patents are called *parvānau* (pl. *parvānā*) in the documents themselves.[71] The Kachavāhā *parvānau*s closely follow the Imperial *parvānca*s, which, in turn, were "little miniatures of the *farmāns*" (Mohiuddin 1971:128). They were issued for charities in the form of revenue grants which provided for the expenses of the GD temple and its custodians.

(3) *Yāddāst/yādidāsati*

*Yāddāst*s are memoranda which were prepared on the basis of the court-diary in which all events and all decisions taken throughout the day were entered.[72]

(4) *Dastak/dastag*

These are permits, orders or warrants. In this volume, *dastak*s are directed against defaulters (e.g. → V.S. 1848, Bhādrapada b.7) or addressed to officers at the village level (*paṭel*s and *paṭvārī*s, e.g. [V.S. 1928, Caitra b. 15 (Bicūṇ)]) and several more documents bearing the same date.

---

[69] In the present volume, however, the term *parvānau* has been used in a restricted sense, for which cp. under *"parvānau"* further below on this page.

[70] This is why all revenue deeds that do not contain this section have been classified as *sanads*.

[71] Cp. section II 8 of a *parvānau* discussed on p. 54.

[72] Cp. also p. 55. The only *yāddāst* so named explicitly is → V.S. 1850, Pauṣa ś. 10.

(5) *Kāgaj*

This term occurs twice in the corpus of documents[73] and refers to an office paper dispatched to another office.

(6) Letter

Letters follow conventions in using certain formulas of which the opening and closing ones are especially prominent. Relatively fixed though these appear at superficial reading, they command of great subtlety in following the etiquette applying to the writer and the addressee. In view of this extremely variegated picture, no typology can be attempted here.[74]

There are five letters in the corpus of documents. For epistelographic conventions also evident in *sanad*s authored by *dīvān*s, cp. pp. 46-47.

(7) Office statement

"Office statements", so designated by an English word, belong to the period in which Jaipur State was under British administrative influence.[75]

(8) Miscellaneous

In the "Calendar of Documents"(pp. 85-111), typological classifications other than the aforelisted ones were made *ad hoc* for want of precise terms given in the documents themselves or suggested by analogy.

In the following, the two most clearly characterized and most prominent types of documents published in this volume will be discussed, namely, the *sanad* and the *parvānau.*

Sanad

Given the wide range of documents appropriately termed *sanad*, no attempt can be made to establish subtypes on the basis of a corpus as limited as the present one.[76] However, one well-defined type of Kachavāhā *sanad*s, supplemented by *sanad*s from the Jodhpur chancery, is so prominent that it commends itself to a relatively detailed description, namely, *sanad*s addressed

[73][V.S. 1928, Caitra b. 15 (aggregate grant)] and [V.S. 1929?].

[74]Horstmann [forthcoming] attempts to study just one aspect of letters, namely, their preambles.

[75][V.S. 1995, Āṣāḍha ś. 15].

[76]Also the fact that for many of the documents, photographs were only taken of the *recto* side is a serious obstacle to satisfactory description. Another reason why the establishment of a typology of *sanad*s requires a separate study rather than a sketchy approach is that there exists in them much overlapping in appearance, function and terminology.

by *dīvāns* to *āmils*. They use epistelographic conventions which apply to some extent to the *arajdāsats* (Pers. *'arẕdāśt*, "petitions, letters to a superior"). These latter vary greatly with respect to the formulas they use, whereas the *sanads* in question use a stable stock of formulas. Here, *sanad* → V.S. 1773, Bhādrapada ś. 8 may serve for illustration. A *sanad* of this type can be broken up into the following parts:[77]

I Protocol
- (1) *invocatio*
- (2) *elevatio*
- (3) *salutatio*
- (4) *benedictio*
- (5) addressee
- (6) sender
- (7) salutory formula

II *Dispositio*
- (1) *dispositio* (sometimes with *insertio*)
- (2) *exhortatio* (may be missing)

III Eschatocol
- (1) date
- (2) seals
- (3) endorsements
- (4) addressee

The *sanad* of V.S. 1773 seems to have been written by a single hand, namely, that of the *sanad-navīs* (Pers. *s.-nivīs*), the "*sanad*-writer", who prepares it from a preliminary report, such as a *fard*.[78]

---

[77]In using the mostly Latin diplomatic terms, the standard usage established by Bresslau (1889), and applied *int. al.* by Busse 1959 to the Safavid documents, has been adopted with the necessary modifications.

[78]RSA. Jaipur, looses leaves. Office Note, Superintendent Central Records, "Detailed Note ...", 6 December 1935, p. 14, while describing the procedures obtaining until the 1930s. A *sanad* was not always written by a single hand. In modern times, the date was written by a high-ranking officer. For example, in the regnal period of Rāmsiṅgh II, this had been his minister, by whose family this job was run until the 1930s. As always, the fact that several officers were engaged in preparing a deed reflects how carefully it was sought to safeguard administrative correctness and avoid forgery. – For *fard*, cp. pp. 56-57.

PROTOCOL

(I 1) *Invocatio*

The *invocatio* is *"Śrī Rāmjī"*, written in the middle of the first line.[79] Like in many other *sanads*, the first line has more than one *"Śrī Rāmjī"*. Its number may range from two to four instances. It is not clear who wrote them.[80]

(I 2) *Elevatio*

The *elevatio* consists of the name or the names of the beneficiary of the *sanad* and, if applicable, to the name of the donor, now deceased, who originally promulgated the deed. The *elevatio* is of great practical value in allowing one to ascertain at a glance to which individual or institution a deed refers. It corresponds to the Persian *sar-nāma*. The name given in the *elevatio* is represented by a blank space in the subsequent text of the document.[81] If the *elevatio* consists of several names, these are arranged in the logical sequence of their tacitly assumed insertion in the text.[82]

(I 3) *Salutatio*

The superscribed *salutatio "Rā(ṃ)m-Rā(ṃ)m"* identifies a written communication as a letter, which a *sanad* in fact is in all technical aspects.

(I 4) *Benedictio*

The *benedictio* used by the Kachavāhā chancery is *"sidhi"*, "success". By contrast, *"svasti"* is the *benedictio* appropriate to Jodhpur and several other states, amongst them also Koṭā.[83]

(I 5) Addressee

The addressee is defined by his name, which is prefixed by *"śrī"* and suffixed by *"jī"* and followed by *"jogya liṣataṃ"* (or graphical variants thereof), literally "written as is worthy of [N.N., as precedes]".

---

[79]The *invocatio* of the Jodhpur chancery was, though not invariably, *"śrī parameśvarjī satya chai"*, for which cp. e.g. → V.S. 1835, Māgha b. 10. For another *invocatio*, namely, *"Śrī Jalandharnāthjī satya chai"*, cp. → V.S. 1878, Kārttika ś. 5.

[80]Up to the time of Mādhavsiṅgh II, that is, 1880, on completion of the *sanad* the Mahārājā would write another *invocatio* formula on the left side of the centrally placed one. This applied to *sanads* as much as to all other documents (RSA. Jaipur, loose leaves. Office Note, Superintendent Central Records, "Detailed note...", 6 December 1935, p. 15).

[81]For an exception, cp. p. 51.

[82]In the Jodhpur documents, there occur a few exceptions to this rule, namely, when the name of the deity preceded that of the Mahārāja, although in the text itself, the Mahārājā was mentioned first, for which cp. → *ab* V.S. 1836. In all these documents, a living Mahārājā is referred to.

[83]E.g. docs. → V.S. 1835, Māgha b. 10; → A.H. 1038, 2 Śavvāl.

(I 6) Sender

The sender gives the particulars of his official designation and name, followed by *"kenya"* (or graphical variants thereof), "by".

(I 7) Salutory formula

This is the section where a *sanad* differs considerably from a letter. While in a letter there would now follow an encomium, which would vary as to the rank of both addressee and sender, a *sanad* uses a standardized formula, which, because it is totally fixed and conventional, is often abbreviated, as indicated by a blank space followed by the concluding word of the formula, namely, *"vaṃcyā"* (or graphic variants thereof), "is to be read". The full formula as it occurs in letters would have been *"rām-rām vaṃcyā"*, "Rām-Rām [greetings] are to be read", and, in *parvānau*s, *"suprasād vaṃcyā"*, "benevolence is to be read", "benevolent greetings be [to N.N.]".[84] Sometimes the variant *" – vaṃ juhār vaṃcya"*, "[Rām-Rām] and greetings be read" is used. While in letters there would then follow some sort of more or less elaborate encomium, this has shrunk to the sequence *"aiṭhā kā saṃmācār bhalā chai, thāṃ kā sadā bhalā cāhīje"*, "Here everything is fine, I/we hope that everything is always fine with you".

II MAIN PART

(II 1) *Dispositio*

The *dispositio* contains the actual subject matter and the decree relating to it. .

(II 2) *Exhortatio*

Exhortative phrases enjoining that the officers addressed must desist from interfering with the rights of the beneficiary often follow the *dispositio*. The exhortative phrases are generally styled on the model of the Persian ones.[85] Common exhortations are,

> *tākīd tamām jānījau,* "You must take this to be a complete injunction", thereby enjoining that the addressee must not deviate from the order, either in entirety or in detail (→ A.H. 1038, 2 Śavvāl, l. 37).
>
> *so tākīd rāṣajyau, koi āmi daṣal na karo ke o tumhāro hato,* "This you must observe as an injunction. You must not meddle with [the rights and property of]

[84]Cp. → A.H. 1038, 2 Śavvāl.

[85]Cp. also Mohiuddin 1971:70 for a list of *tā'kīd* and *tahdīd*, "emphasis, injunction" and "threatening", formulas which occur in Mughal *farmān*s and closely resemble the Kachavāhā ones.

the common folk [deeming] that [the property] is yours" (→ A.H. 1108, 22 Rabī' II, ll. 8-9).

mujāhīm matī hau, "There must not occur any interference" (→ A.H. 1123, 19 Ramaẕān, ll. 18-19).

cāhiai ka pravān kāṃ majmun the ṣabardār hoī gāv majkurā the kīsī bhātī vāch va birāṛ vāgai. kulī havujāt the mujāhīm ho matī. ī bāt kī tākīd jāṇijo, "You must in no way tamper with the villages, such as by [extortion of] *vāch* and *virāṛ* etc. and sundry taxes. The injunction on this matter shall be strictly observed" (→ A.H. 1123, 21 Ramaẕān, ll. 10-15).

III ESCHATOCOL

(III 1) Date

(1) The *mitī* portion consists of the word *"mitī"* (or an abbreviation of it), "date" + lunar month + lunar day + Vikrama year.[86] It does not give the place where the *sanad* was prepared.[87]

(III 2) Seals

The seals were affixed below the *mitī,* on the left side that of the *dīvān (des)*, on the right side that of the *dīvān hajūr.*

(III 3) Endorsements

On the left- and right-hand margins, there were written the endorsements of the various departments that took copies of the *sanad.* Each of the departments concerned made a copy for its own records.[88] The *sanad* of V.S. 1773 has two entries running *dā(ṣil) nus(ṣai).* There existed several kinds of *nuskhau* (< Pers. *nuskha*), literally "copy", here designating a "record office".[89] Copies were taken for the records of the *dīvāns*' offices and for several other departments not specified, of which the *sanad-navīs*'s office must have been one.[90] At any rate, copies had to be taken by all the departments dealing with expenses, of which, at least in the 1930s, there were four.[91]

---

[86]In *sanads* from Jodhpur, the Vikrama year follows *"mitī"* and is in its turn followed by the lunar month and day.

[87]Against *sanads* issued by *dīvāns*, those promulgated by Kachavāhā princes do mention the place of promulgation, for which cp. → A.H. 1080, 12 Ramaẕān, and → A.H. 1106, 12 Jumādā II.

[88]For want of relevant administrative studies, one cannot tell precisely what departments and record-offices were involved in issuing a *sanad* and in what sequence.

[89]For *nuskhau*, cp. fn. 91 below.

[90]A study of the endorsements and hence of the administrative routine would also have to take into account the practice followed with other types of papers. Cp. also the discussion of *parvānau*, pp. 49-61.

[91]Nuskhā Punya, N. Kulli, N. Kalān, N. Khurd (RSA. Jaipur, loose leaves. Office Note, Superintendent Central Records, "Detailed note ...", 6 December 1935, p. 3).

The *sanad* of → V.S. 1816, Bhādrapada ś. 9 shows an additional endorsement, a stylized *sarū*, "start" (< Pers. *śurū'*). This is the Mahārājā's endorsement who wrote this when also adding his *"Śrī Rāmjī"* to the *invocatio*. This custom prevailed into this century.[92] The symbol occurs first in the *parvānaus* of V.S. 1801, that is, after the death of Jaisiṅgh II, although the incomplete state of many of the document reproductions does not allow us to determine if the usage started earlier.

Parvānau

Much beyond their practical function and individual contents, the physical appearance of a *parvānau* (< Pers. *parvāna*, "decree") is a symbolic representation of the rank and prestige of a Kachavāhā Mahārājā. Inspired by the Mughal chancery practice, they display the Imperial symbols of regnal power in a modified but nevertheless distinct and self-assertive fashion. They are modelled on the Mughal *farmān* and *parvāna*, the one being the decree of the Emperor himself, the other being a rescript prepared by the Imperial chancery.

The following typological description of *parvānaus* is based on the form these documents had taken by the mid-eighteenth century. Document → V.S. 1801, Bhādrapada b. 5 (Sekhpuro) has been taken as the example for illustration.

The bilingual Rājasthānī and Persian *parvānaus*, which had come to be superseded by monolingual Rājasthānī ones by 1712 (docs. → V.S. 1769 ff.), differ in their physical appearance by the very fact that their text is arranged in two columns, with Rājasthānī in the left- and Persian in the right-hand column, and that their entire text is written on the *recto* page. Unfortunately, the *verso* pages of these were not photographed, although for some of them, it may be suspected that they bore endorsements. In the period of Jaisiṅgh II, the usage to write the commentary and subsequent sections of a *parvānau* (sections III ff.) on the *verso* page became established.[93] It also seems that by the end of the period of Jaisiṅgh II, the elaborate and henceforth stable cliché of *parvānaus* became established, for the deeds confirmed immediately after his death follow this pattern.

---

[92]It fell in disuse after the reforms starting in the late 1930s; cp. RSA, Jaipur, loose leaves, "Copy of Resolution No 5", 10 February 1938, where a sample of the new type of *sanads* is found to be reproduced. Consequent to these changes, the *sanad* superseded all other papers, including *fard, daul, yāddāst* and *parvānau*.

[93]Doc. → V.S. 1784, Āśvina b. 12, ff. This is also why the photographs of documents from that period on are normally of both their *recto* and *verso* sides.

When a *parvānau* had to be renewed, this was effected by a *parvānā sabtī*, "confirmation of the *parvānau*", "confirmatory *parvānau*" (< Pers. [Ar.] *ṣabat*, "steadfastness, argument, proof").[94] The procedure was called *parvānā sabtī kar-*, "to confirm a *parvānau*". The *parvānā sabtī* was made out by the *parganā* authorities, after the chancery had verified and approved of, the applicant's claim.[95]

A *parvānau* of the model type of the mid-eighteenth century can be broken up into six constituent sections, of which some are complex.[96] These are,

I	Protocol
II	Main part
III	Commentary
IV	Eschatocol
V	Seals
VI	Endorsements

I PROTOCOL

(I 1) *Invocatio*

For the *invocatio*, cp. also the discussion of *sanads*, p. 46.

The *invocatio* is written in the middle of the first line, ideally included in double *daṇḍas*. The right-hand *daṇḍa* tends to merge with the *ī-mātrā* of *-jī*. The inclusion of the *invocatio* in double *daṇḍas* is technically termed the *prākāra*, "enclosure", a variant of which is also its underscoring.[97] For the "repetition" of the *invocatio* cp. p. 46.[98] Of these seeming "repetitions", one at least, namely, the one to the left of the central one, has to be taken as the Mahārājā's endorsement, which he applied after the seals of the revenue department had been affixed and the *kaṭār* been drawn.[99]

---

[94]Cp. section III 3 of a *parvānau*.

[95]By the 1930s, any *parvānau* issued by the revenue authorities had come to be called either *parvānā* or *parvānā sabtī* or just *sabtī*, whereas a *parvānau* issued directly by the Mahārājā was named *parvānā khās* (RSA. Jaipur, loose leaves. "Definitions of Important Vernacular Terms...", 3 March 1938, p. 12).

[96]The translated *parvānaus* of these sections have been numbered by bold digits. This has been done for all *parvānaus*, which makes it easy to ascertain in which way earlier *parvānaus* may differ from the cliché of the mid-eighteenth century.

It needs to be borne in mind that the sequence of the sections as they appear in the text was not necessarily identical with the sequence in which they were applied in the course of the preparation of the *parvānau*. This will be discussed in the appropriate places.

[97]For the *prākāra*, cp. Vararuci's *Patrakaumudī* as quoted by Śāstrī 1942:9.

[98]For the *invocatio* being "repeated" once, cp. e.g. → A.H. 1108, 23 Rabīʻ II; twice, → A.H 1123, 21 Ramaẕān.

[99]For which see presently.

(I 2) *Elevatio*

The *elevatio* consists of the name or names raised above the main part (II), for which cp. p. 46. While the general rule is that the *elevatio* contains the names never spelt out in the main part of the *parvānau*, there are a few exceptions to this, namely, in docs. → A.H. 1089, 20 Zī'l-hijja, and A.H. 1102, 21 Rabī' I. These belong to a period when the prevalent "rule of the blank space" had been long-established. Similarly, docs. → A.H. 1038, 2 Śavvāl, and → A.H. 1080, 12 Ramazān, do mention the names, but this seems to have been done for greater clarity, as the texts represent lists of various recipients of charities. In the main part of the text, the blank is prefixed by *ṭhākur śrī*, "deity", and suffixed by *jī*, when talking of a male deity. Sometimes the blank is also prefixed by *ṭhākurdavārā śrī*, "temple of".[100] Sometimes the word *ṭhākur* is missing.[101]

The sequence *śrī — jī* without a corresponding *elevatio* refers to the ruling Mahārājā.[102] If the deed is in confirmation of a grant made by a deceased Mahārājā, he is referred to by "Mahārājā [N.N.], dwelling in Vaikuṇṭha", that is, in the paradise of the Vaiṣṇavas. There seems to linger on an older, not specifically Hindu usage, according to which the late ruler's paradisical abode is not mentioned.[103]

(I 3) Certification

The document was certified as a true copy by the word *sahī*. It means "true, authentic" (< Pers. sahīh) and was written after the completion of the document, although it remains unknown at which stage and by whom exactly.[104]

(I 4) *Kaṭār*

The regnal symbol of the Kachavāhās, as also of other Rajput families, is the double-handled short dagger, the *kaṭār*. It formed part of the attire of the Rajput nobility and was tucked in the cummerband.[105] It seems to have been the *dīvān hajūr*'s privilege to affix on a deed the pictorial symbol of the *kaṭār*. By Rāmsiṅgh II, this job was transferred to his favourite minister and henceforth ran in his family until the custom

---

[100]→ A.H. 1078, 30 Jumādā II.

[101]→ A.H. 1080, 12 Ramazān.

[102]→ A.H. 1072, 15 Śavvāl, l. 5.

[103]Cp. e.g. → A.H. 1078, 30 Jumādā II, l. 11.

[104]RSA. Jaipur, loose leaves. Office Note, Superintendent Central Records, 6 December 1935, p. 13, points to the *dīvān hajūr*, for it says that up to the late nineteenth century, "the figure of dagger and all other signs ... were made by the Dewan, who was in charge of the Dewani Huzuri Daftars". – For the Mewar chancery, Bhaṭnāgar (1987:99) mentions an officer who was especially entitled to certify documents on their completion and was hence called the *sahīvālā*.

[105]Amongst the many illustrations, cp. e.g. Topsfield 1990:68-69, p. 24.

was abandoned in the twentieth century.[106] The certification by the *kaṭār* preceded the Mahārājā's endorsement of the document.[107]

(I 5) Seal

The seal[108] of the ruling Mahārājā was affixed on the right-hand margin of the *recto* page at the beginning of the main part (II) of the document. At what stage and exactly by whom it was affixed remains unknown.[109]

II MAIN PART

(II 1) *Benedictio* and *intitulatio*

For the *benedictio*, cp. p. 46. The *intitulatio* identifies the promulgator by his title and name. If he was a Mahārājā, he would issue the *parvānau* by his "royal order", *devvacanāt*;[110] if he was a prince other than a Mahārājā, he would do so by his "order", *vacanāt.*

(II 2) Addressee

The addressees, the revenue officers, are mentioned by their titles and their administrative territory, that is, the *parganā* in which they collected the revenue. This is completed by the formula ... *dasye/dise/disye suprasād vaṃcya/vaṃcyā,* "with benevolent greetings to [the officers of *parganā* N.N.]" (lit. "benevolence be read"). In older *parvānaus*, there is to be found a mode of addressing the officers which represents a most common Mughal convention, namely, *kamaitī hāl va istakbāl,* "the present and future officers".[111] This is equivalent to the Persian *mutas̱addiyān-i ḥāl va istiqbāl,* a phrase which implies that the injunction remains valid beyond the tenure of the present officers.[112]

(II 3-5) *Narratio*

After II 2, the subject matter (II 3-8) is introduced by the formula *aparaṃca*, literally "furthermore". This has been rendered by "reference". Then follows the *narratio*, the details of the submittal of the application for the grant in question.

---

[106]Cp. p. 49, fn. 92.

[107]Cp. p. 61.

[108]For the individual seals, cp. pp. 73-76.

[109]For the Mughal chancery, cp. *Ā'īn* I:273-74 (para 12); Ibn Hasan 1936: 100-03.

[110]As in similar cases, I have adhered to the Sanskritic transliteration of the grapheme *va* (without diacritical dot in the original) in Indic words, although its phonetic representation was surely [bə]; thus, [dewbəc(ə)nat].

[111]Cp. → A.H. 1123, 19 Ramaẕān, ll. 4-5.

[112]Cp. the Persian version of the document quoted; Mohiuddin 1971:133; also several of the documents published by Jhaveri (1928), e.g. no 4.

The *narratio* contains, (II 3) the *bābati* (Pers. *bābat*), "item", which is covered by the deed and which is identified by the kind of charity, its recipient and the locality from which the charity is drawn, (II 4) the particulars of the application or petition, *araj*, (< Pers. *'arẕ*), namely, by whom it was recommended and when it was submitted. The person who recommended it, or, as the *parvānau* phrased it, "through whom" it was submitted, was, in fact, the Kachavāhā minister, who would pass an order that the application be granted.[113] The date of the petition is the date when it was registered in the court-diary.

By the time of Mādhavsiṅgh I (cp. → V.S. 1808, Bhādrapada ś. 13), a slight modification had been introduced. If the minister was not specifically mentioned, it was reported that the *dīvāns* had endorsed the petition in the *jāgīr* report or the memorandum.[114]

If a *parvānau* was the result of a religious vow of the Mahārājā, as was the case with a *puni ūdik* grant, a recommendation would have been out of place.[115]

Section (II 5) is the *narratio* proper, which gives the contents of the petition. If the petition was for the renewal of a grant, the details of that earlier grant would be related in this paragraph. It must be emphasized that for renewals, the immediately preceding deed was referred to in the *narratio*. Therefore, a renewal often does not allow us to establish the entire history of a grant.[116]

(II 6) *Dispositio*

The *dispositio* is the heart of a *parvānau* because it contains the Mahārājā's order. It is introduced by the phrase *tīh sauṃ/soṃ phurmāmvāṃ chāṃ* ..., "Hereby order is given ..." (literally: "... has been given..."). When *parvānaus* had not yet assumed a totally formalised shape, the *dispositio* was not necessarily introduced by this phrase.[117]

---

[113]To date, applications have not yet been made a research topic. For a specimen, cp., however, Bahura 1996:205-06 for the incompletely reproduced order of Minister Kisanrām Cakravartī which preceded the promulgation of doc. → V.S. 1773, Bhādrapada ś. 8.

[114]E.g. doc. → V.S. 1808, Bhādrapada ś. 13, ll. 3-4, *māphik pharad hakīkati mai dasṣat divāṃnayāṃn;* → rev. y. 1839, Āṣāḍha b. 5, l. 4, *muvāphik yādidāsati maiṃ dīvāṃnyāṃ*. – In principle the entire procedure is a replica of that of the Mughal chancery.

[115]Cp. → V.S. 1769, Jyeṣṭha ś. 13.

[116]Cp. e.g. doc. → rev. y. 1801, Bhādrapada b. 5 (Gaṅgārāmpur-vās Khijūryā). Here the *parvānau* of V.S. 1771, which was issued by Jaisiṅgh II, the immediate antecedent, was mentioned. When this, in its turn, was renewed in V.S. 1808, Kārttika ś. 8 (Gaṅgārāmpur-vās Khijūryā), the deed of Jaisiṅgh's period was no longer referred to.

[117]Cp. e.g. → A.H. 1102, 21 Rabī' II. ll. 5-16).

(II 7) *Exhortatio*

The *exhortatio* contains the injunction that the officers not demand that the beneficiary produce a fresh *parvānau* every year. This command implies that the deed was valid in perpetuity, notwithstanding necessary alterations dictated by circumstances.

(II 8) Account

The concluding paragraph of section II fixes the particulars which had to be carried to account in the account-book. It is introduced by the phrase, *īhīṃ pravānāṃ sauṃ hisāb maiṃ mujrā hoylā,* "Following this *parvānau* there shall be carried to account in the account-book ...". The particulars of the allowances were introduced by *mu(kararā) tanṣāh,* "Fixed allowance of revenue ...". In earlier documents, this phrase might also run *al-mukararā tanṣavāh.*[118] *Tanṣāh,* that is, *tankhāh,* was "income" in a general sense, but referred especially to the notional, and hence variable, revenue income as well as to a fixed allowance.

(III) COMMENTARY

The commentary sets forth the procedures which had to precede the promulgation of a *parvānau.* It is the replica of the *z̲imn* of Mughal documents.[119] The *z̲imn* was written on the *verso* side, a usage which also prevails in the Kachavāhā *parvānaus* from V.S. 1784 onwards. Earlier *parvānaus* would let the commentary follow the *dispositio* on the *recto* side, though normally set off by a new line or at least the sign ":" which marked the beginning of a new paragraph.[120] Part III has been broken up into six subsections.

(III 1) Résumé of administrative procedures

Subsection (III 1) runs "Commentary (*sarah,* < Pers. *śarḫ,* "commentary, explanation") on the memorandum (*yādidāsati*) [based] on the diary-record (*dāṣil vākai*) of (lit. "endorsed, fixed", *karār* < Pers. *qarār*) [date], on report (*ba-risālai*) of Ḍīvāns N.N. and N.N. and the Diarist N.N.".[121]

The commentary is based on the *yāddāst/yādidāsati,* which in its turn, is based on the diary-record. In the words of Khan (1950:XI), the administrative procedure leading to a Mughal *jāgīr parvāna,* which is the exemplar of all *parvānaus,* was the following:

118Cp. → A.H. 1108, 23 Rabī‘ II, line 21.

119For which cp. Mohiuddin 1971:71-73.

120Cp. → A.H. 1078, l. 18.

121This is the exact replica of the phrase used in the Mughal *farmāns,* for which cp. Mohiuddin 1971:71.

When a man appeared at the Imperial court and applied for a *Jāgīr*, the *Dīwān-i-tan* (Minister for salaries) ordered his subordinates to prepare a *Ḥaqīqat* (office statement), stating therein the name of the candidate, his native place, and the date of presentation of his *Nadhr* (offering). Then the *Ḥaqīqat* was placed by the *Dīwān-i-tan* before the *Dīwān-i-A'la* (Prime Minister), who submitted it to the Emperor. If an order was passed for the grant of a *Jāgīr* the Prime Minister endorsed it on the paper. This paper served as a voucher for the chief clerk of the *Dīwān-i-tan* to prepare a *Siyāha-Daul* or an estimate on the basis of it, describing in it the grantee's personal rank, the number of retainers he had to maintain, the salary of himself and that of his retainers, fixed in accordance with the *Dastūru'l-'Amal* of the emoluments of *Manṣabdārs*, and the name of the Pargana from which the grantee had to receive the amount.

The *Daul* was handed over to the *Wāqi'ah-Nawīs* (Diary-writer) who, after making an entry in the *Wāqi'ah* (Diary) drew up an extract called a *Yāddāsht* (Memorandum) for submission to the office of the *'Arḍ-Mukarrar* (Confirmation of orders).

The *Yāddāsht* repeated the details in much the same form as the *Ḥaqīqat* and the *Daul*. On it the *Wazīr* directed that the *Yāddāsht* should be compared with the *Wāqi'ah* (Diary) and verified, and then sent to the *'Arḍ-i-Mukarrar* (confirmation Office). On the margin of the paper, the *Wāqi'ah-Nawīs* (Diary-writer) wrote the text of the *Yāddāsht* according to the *Wāqi'ah*. Next the *Dāroghā* (Superintendent) of the Confirmation Office wrote the date when it was received by that office. Then it was again submitted to the Emperor for approval, after which orders were issued to the officer concerned.

In the Kachavāhā chancery, the procedure was by and large the same. Here, the administrative steps and the papers produced in the course of these, respectively, were the following:

(a) report (*pharad*), with subsequent submission of the petition to the ruler (referred to in section III 1)
(b) statement (*ḍaul/ḍol*) (reproduced in section III 2)
(c) memorandum (referred to in section III 1)
(d) confirmation of the granted petition and passing of the decree (referred to in section III 5)

(a) Report *(pharad)*

The report was called the *hakīkat kī pharad*[122] or *pharad hakīkati*[123], here *fard* (< Pers. *fard-i haqīqat*, GJRT: "statement of circumstances").[124] A *fard* had to be prepared for all new grants, such as *jāgīrs*, cash allowances derived from revenue grants, charities, etc.[125] The *fard* was forwarded to the *dīvān hajūr*'s office. Here, it was verified by the *mavājanā (muvājanā)-navīs* (< Pers. *muvāzana*, "comparative statements, balance sheets," and *nivīs*, "writer"), who wrote a report that the *fard* was in consonance with the *mavājanau (muvājanau)*. In the Mughal administration, and thence adopted by the Kachavāhās, the *muvāzana-yi dah sāla*

> was a consolidated statement of the agrarian conditions obtaining in a *pargana* during the preceding ten years, showing the number of villages, the area of arable land, land under cultivation, waste, forest, gardens, pools, nullah, and the area of *madad maash* land; various crops sown in *rabi* and *kharif* with current prices of every article; *jama* figures, rates of assessments, and particulars of receipts and arrears. (Siddiqi 1970: 38, fn. 76)

In the Kachavāhā system, these records covered a period of either ten or fifteen years each (Gupta 1986:322-23).[126] On this report, the *vākā-navīs* (< Pers. *vāqi'a*, "accidents, events, news"), "diarist, news-writer", wrote the date and sent it to the department, *sīghā* (< Pers. (Ar.) *sīġa*, "section, department"), concerned with orders. Then it was circulated to the various officers who had to sign it. First, the *kaṭārband*, an officer entitled to carry a *kaṭār*,[127] wrote the date; the *vākā-navīs* wrote *raju/ū*, "endorsed, approved" (< Pers. *rujū'*, "returning; reference, answer to a letter" [Steingass][128]), on the right-hand side of the *verso* page. Then the various *daftars*, departments, drew copies of the *fard* for their own records and marked this by the abbreviation *dā.* or *dā:*, for *dāṣil* (< Pers. *dākhil*, "entry"), which is probably an adaptation of Pers. *dākhil śud*, "entered". To this they entered the abbreviated form of the designation of their

---

122 Cp. → V.S. 1782, Mārgaśiras b. 14, ll. 9-10.

123 Cp. → V.S. 1808, Bhādrapada ś. 13, ll. 3-4.

124 Cp. also Mohiuddin 1971:101; Siddiqi 1970: 127.

125 After 1870, the practice of preparing *fards* was reduced; RSA. Jaipur, loose leaves. Office Note, Superintendent Central Records, "Detailed Note ...", 16 December 1935, p. 2. According to the type of grant for which an application had been submitted, the *fards* were prepared by different departments, as can be concluded from the practice prevailing until the late 1930s. *Fards* for *jāgīrs* were prepared by the *mīr baksī*'s office, those for *puni ūdik, inām* and *bhog* by the Nuskhā Punya department.

126 Up to the 1930s, there existed two *muvāzanā* departments which were called the Muvāzanā Kalān and the Choṭā Muvāzanā.

127 For *kaṭār*, cp. pp. 51-52.

128 In the Safavid administration, the word *rujū'* is also used in the term *arbāb-i rujū'*, "legal authorities" (Minorsky 1943:50).

department.[129] Up to 1870, the Mahārājā signed the *fard* before its completion; thereafter only after its completion. The *fard* used to bear *Śrī Rāmjī* as its first line, to which the Mahārājā added another instance of this *invocatio* to the left side thereof. On the back, he wrote the word *sarū/surū*, "start"(< Pers. *śurū'*).

The duty to write *fards* or to add the date on a document was vested in families who had held this office for generations.

(b) Statement (*ḍaul/ḍol*)

The *ḍaul*[130], "statement, estimate", was a prerequisite of the preparation of a *yāddāst.*[131] It was the *ḍaul* which ensured that the personal and financial data, which eventually found their way into the decree, were correct. This is also why the *ḍaul* was repeated in the commentary of the *parvānau.* Thus, although it is an apparent repetition of a portion of the text of the *recto* page, it is actually the basis of what is written there. Like the *fard,* the *ḍaul* passed the department (*sīghā*) of orders, whence it was circulated to the various officers who had to sign it. It was also signed by the Mahārājā.

A *ḍaul* is easily recognizable because it starts with the word *"ḍaul"*, which is followed by the specification of the grant to which it refers.[132] A *ḍaul* bears no seal and it carries two endorsements which are applied between the *elevatio* and the first line of the text. They run, *araj mu[karar] pahocāvau* (or graphic variants thereof), "Let it be submitted again"(literally, "Submit the petition again"). These were written by the minister and the *vākā-navīs.*[133] The back of the *ḍaul* carried the chancery endorsements much like the *parvānau.* The *ḍaul* was retained in the *vākā*-office, called the *vakāyā.*[134]

The *ḍaul* is found to be referred to in the *parvānaus* that have been published in this volume from 1727 onwards (→ V.S. 1784, Āśvina b. 11). This must be due to a reform of the way in which *parvānaus* were prepared. The rule that a *ḍaul* must precede a *parvānau* certainly prevailed before that year, but it was only then that the word *"ḍaul"* came to be added, whereas nothing else was changed in the paragraph concerned.

---

[129]As there appears no *fard* in this volume, the details of the various departments have not been given.

[130]In the Mughal chancery, the term is *daul* (Khan 1950:XI).

[131]Cp. (c) below, p. 58.

[132]For this and the following, cp. Horstmann 1995 with a facsimile of the *ḍaul* published.

[133]RSA. Jaipur, loose leaves. Office Note, Superintendent Central Records, 6 December 1935, p. 10, states that the minister wrote *araj mukarar pahucāvo* while the *vākā navīs* wrote *araj mukarar pahucī*, "It was submitted again.", which is not in consonance with the *ḍaul* published by Horstmann (1995).

[134]RSA. Jaipur, loose leaves. Office Note, Superintendent Central Records, 6 December 1935, p. 10.

(c) Memorandum

The memorandum, *yāddāst/yādidāsati,* was prepared on the basis of the *ḍaul* at the *vākā-navīs*'s department, after the diarist had made a copy of it for his own records. Up to the 1930s, the memorandum was sealed on its back by the Dīvānī, the revenue department, and it was the *vākā-navīs*'s job to write the date and the entries of *raju.*[135] This suggests that in the past, the procedure was similar. A prerequisite of the memorandum was the authentication of the petition after the *fard* had been prepared. It was given by the *dīvāns* and the diarist. This procedure is expressed by the phrase, "on report of Dīvāns N.N. and N.N. and the Diarist N.N.". The report is called *risāla.*

(d) *Risāla*

Different opinions have been expressed on *risāla* (Pers. < *risāla*). Goswamy and Grewal (1967:74, n. 29) sum up the state of the discussion in the late 1960s, namely,

> H.S. Hodivala, keeping in view Abul Fazl's statement that the *risālahdār* was one of the four who signed the *yād-dāsht*, suggests that the word *risālah* in the *ta'līqah*[136] stands for risālahdār (*Studies in Parsi History,* 174 n 44). Abdul Hamid Lāhori states, however, that the prince who was given the power of *risālah* used to write his *rasālatun* on the back of the *farmān* and seal it with his own seal. Below the *risālah*, the *dīwān* wrote his *mā'rifat* or a note of the fact that the *farmān* was being transmitted through his hands (Sarkar, Jadunath, *Mughal Administration,* 224). Sarkar's inference that *rasālatun* indicated the person through whose mediacy the *farmān* was granted appears to be correct. "*Farmāns* granting lands or favours were always issued as the result of suit paid to a minister or other favourite at Court for influencing the Emperor, and the name of such 'intermediary' was entered on the back of the farmān by means of the word *rasalatun* ('through the medium of')". Sarkar goes on to add that some ancient Hindu inscriptions of land-grants conclude with the name of the *dutak* or the intermediary (*ibid.,* 222). S.M. Jaffar takes the *"b'risālati"* in the same sense ("Mughal Farmans in Peshawar", *IHRC,* XVIII, 236-45).

To supplement this, it may be added that *"risālahdār"* is not what the *Ā'īn* really has. The text has *risāla*, which both Blochman and Hodivala, however, interprete as *risāladār* (*Ā'īn*, tr. I:269, n. 2). First of all, *risāla,* "treatise, text", can be taken to be what it literally means, namely, a report. These reports were solicited from the *dīvāns*, who had to endorse the *jāgīr*-reports before they were submitted to the ruler, and from the diarist, who prepared the memorandum. An eighteenth century Persian treatise

---

[135]Similar to the *parvānau* sections IV and V, for which cp. further below.

[136]The abbridged version of the *yāddāśt* (MH).

(Minorsky 1943:52-53) points to a direction which cannot be explored here but which gives an idea of the rank of diarists. Orders given by the king, according to the text, only became operative when the "recorder" *(vāqi'a-nivīs)* had endorsed them with the formula "by the supreme command" *(qayd)*. The text states that, "Reports on the petitions presented to His Majesty belong to the Vāqi'a-nivīs's competence" (*ibid.*, 53). Therefore, it seems likely that the *risāla* represented the authentication and approval on the part of the *dīvān*s and the diarist and was performed after the completion of the *fard*.

(III 2) Statement *(ḍaul/ḍol)*

The text of the *ḍaul* is introduced by the words *atra ḍol* ... (or graphic variants thereof), "Statement as follows:...".

(III 3) *Dispositio*

This section is basically identical with sections II 4-6. It is introduced by *so hukam huvā,* "Therefore the order was passed ...". The conjunction *so* suggests that the order was issued in consequence of the foregoing procedures, for unless a *ḍaul* had been prepared and incorporated in the memorandum, no order could be passed. The difference between the *recto* wording *tīh saum̥ phuramām̥vām̥ chām̥* (II 6) and *so hukam huvā* (III 3) is precisely based on this. The *recto* text is the product of a procedure which states the antecedents and promulgates the decree, while the *verso* text reveals the sequence of the administrative procedures conducive to the result, namely, the promulgation, which is conclusively phrased on the *recto* page. This is not immediately visible as one reads the apparently repetitious phrases of a *parvānau*. The relationship between *recto* as expressing a result and *verso* as expressing the procedure conducive to that result is clearly expressed in Persian *farmān*s, which state that the *résumé* of the order is "recorded *(qalamí shud) ipsissima verba [sic!]* according to the *taṣdíq-i-yád-dásht*" (Mohiuddin 1971:71), that is, the "attestation of the memorandum". To emphasise it once again, it is only due to the described procedures that the intent of a petition can be converted into an order.

Section III 3 orders that the officers effect the "confirmation of the *parvānau*".[137]

---

[137]Cp. also p. 50.

(III 4) *Parvānau*, or several copies of it, issued by the *dīvāns* of the *sarkār*

The paragraph enjoins that the *dīvāns* of the *sarkār*, of which the *parganā* is a subunit, must make out a confirmatory *parvānau* or several copies of it.[138] The details of the procedure are not revealed by this injunction.

(III 5) Confirmation *(araj mukarar)*

This section reflects the last administrative step before a *parvānau* could be issued. After the petition had been granted in principle and all drafting and cross-checking been completed, it had to be submitted once again for the definitive confirmation of the grant. This is stated by the sentence "On [date] the petition was submitted again". Then follows the contents of the petition as checked and granted.

(III 6) Attestation

This section is encountered first in a *parvānau* of 1727 (→ V.S. 1784, Āśvina b. 11). It was written by a scribe different from the one who wrote section II and the preceding portions of section III. The regulation prevailing up to the 1930s was that, while the *parvānau* up to section III 6 was written by the *parvānā-navīs*[139], this part was written by the *mavājanā-navīs.*[140]

Section III 6 states that the *parvānau* was prepared according to the memorandum, which was attested by the appropriate authorities. These were either the minister who had approved of the case or the Mahārājā himself by his endorsement (in writing and/or seal) and, invariably, the *dīvāns*.

(IV) ESCHATOCOL

The eschatocol consisted of the date and the place where the *parvānau* was issued. The word *mitī* was written by the *kaṭārband,*[141] while the date itself and also the place where the document was issued, was written by the officer in charge of signing *fards*, *parvānaus* etc. in this way.

In several documents, the word *liṣau*, "write!", appears twice in the left lower corner of the *verso.*[142] Up to the 1930s, the procedure was the following:[143] After the *kaṭārband* had written

---

[138]The word *parvānau* occurs variously in the singular or plural.

[139]For passages written by other officers, cp. further below on this page and p. 61.

[140]For *mavājanau*, cp. p. 56.

[141]For whom cp. p. 56.

[142]Cp. e.g. → rev. y. 1839, Āṣāḍha b. 5.

[143]RSA. Jaipur, loose leaves. Office Note, Superintendent Central Records, 6 December 1935, p. 12.

mitī, "date", and the officer in charge of signing *fards*, *parvānaus* etc. had completed his part by writing the date and place, the *mīr munśī*, head-clerk, would draw a line in the left corner of the *verso*, on which that officer would write *liṣau*. Only then would the other endorsements (running *raju daphatra*...) be made. The word *liṣau* may thus be interpreted as an imperative to set in motion the further endorsements. The author of the second instance of *liṣau* remains unidentified.

(V) SEALS

The seals of the *dīvāns* and of the *mustauphī* were affixed after the document had been completed up to section IV. Then the deed would be endorsed by the Mahārājā, who wrote the stylised word *sarū/surū*, "start", on the right-hand margin and also *Śrī Rāmjī* on the top of the deed.[144]

Parvānaus would be copied by the *mavājanau* departments, of which there were two up to the 1930s, called the Muvājanā Kalān (Big M.) and the Muvājanā Khurd or Choṭā Muvājanā (Small M.). Only then would the Mahārājā's seal be stamped on the upper right-hand margin of the *recto* page of the *parvānau* and the deed be delivered to the beneficiary, who would have to present it to the revenue officers in order to effect its execution.

---

[144]For which cp. p. 50.

2.1. Appendices

(1) Dīvāns of Amber and Jaipur (1660 to 1812)

(2) The Calendrical System

(3) Seals

(4) Measures, Weights and Currency

(5) *Siyāq* Numerals

Appendix 1

Dīvāns of Amber and Jaipur (1660 to 1812)

The table is based upon the evidence of the documents from the GD temple. Supplementary evidence for the *dīvāns* comes from Gupta 1986. Gupta's transcription has been adapted to the one used here.

Year (A.D.)	Dīvān	References
1660	Nārāiṇdās	→ A.H. 1071, 10 Safar
1662	Madhvandās, Harnāth	→ A.H. 1072, 15 S̄avvāl/V.S. 1719, Āṣāḍha b. 3
1664	Kalyāṇdās	Gupta 1986: 187; Saṃghī Kalyāṇdās Baṛjātyā s/o Dīvān Mohandās, Khaṇḍelvāl Jain (Kāslīvāl 1989: 198-99)
1665	Gajsiṅgh, Kalyāṇsiṅgh	Gupta 1986: 187
1667	Rājā Rām, Tejsiṅgh	Gupta 1986: 187
	Rājā Rām, Harnāth	→ A.H. 1078, 30 Jumādā II
1690	Indraseṇ, Sāh Vijairām	→ A.H. 1102, 21 Rabī'; Vijairām Chābṛā s/o Totārām, Khaṇḍelvāl Jain, *dīvān* also of Jaisiṅgh II (Kāslīvāl 1989: 202)
1692	Kiśordās, Vijairām	Gupta 1986: 187; Kiśordās Mahājan Chābṛā, Khaṇḍelvāl Jain, *dīvān* V.S. 1749-79.
1700	Kisordās, Saṃgahī Likhamīdās	[A.H. 1112, 28 Rabī' II] (doc. not pertaining to GD, hence not treated in this book); Gupta 1986: 187.

Year (A.D.)	Dīvān	References
1705-1706	do.	Gupta 1986: 187
1708	Sāh Phatecand	Phatahcand Chābṛā, Khaṇḍelvāl Jain, *dīvān* V.S. 1765-71 (Kāslīvāl 1989: 200).
1709-1711	Bhikhārīdās, Phatecand	Bhikhārīdās Kāyasth, "Amber's *diwan*" (Bhatnagar 1974, *pass.*, cp. index); for Phatecand, cp. above.
1712	do.	→ V.S. 1769, Jyeṣṭha ś. 13
1713	do.	Gupta 1986: 187
1716	Kisordās, Tārācand	→ V.S. 1773, Āṣādha ś. 8; → V.S. 1773, Bhādrapada ś. 8; for Kisordās, cp. above; Tārācand Bilālā, Khaṇḍelvāl Jain, *dīvān* V.S. 1773-90 (Kāslīvāl 1989: 203)
1717	do., Tārācand, now Sāh Tārācand	→ V.S. 1774, Jyeṣṭha ś., 15
1720	do.	→ V.S. 1777, Āśvina ś. 14
1721	do.	→ V.S. 1778, Āśvina ś. 2
	Tārācand	Gupta 1986: 187
1725	Na/ārāyaṇdās, Kirpārām	Nārāyaṇdās identical with Nārāyaṇdās Khatrī (d. 1748), minister and general of Mādhavsiṅgh (Sarkar 1984: 236)? Kṛpārām Pāṇḍyā s/o Jagrām, Khaṇḍelvāl Jain, *dīvān* V.S. 1780-90; also Amber's *vakīl* at the Mughal Court (Kāslīvāl 1989: 210-02).
1727	do.	→ V.S. 1784, Āśvina b. 11
1728	Rāy Nārāyaṇdās, Kirpārām	Gupta 1986: 187
1730	do.	→ V.S. 1787, Kārttika ś., 3

Year (A.D.)	Dīvān	References
1731	(1) do. (2) Rāy Nārāyaṇdās, Phatecand (3) Rām	Gupta 1986: 187
1732	Nārāyaṇdās, Kirpārām	→ V.S. 1789, Vaiśākha b. 12
1734	do.	→ V.S. 1790, Māgha ś. 4
1737-1738	Rāy Nārāyaṇdās, Vidyādhar	Gupta 1986: 187; for Rāy Nārāyaṇdās, cp. above. Vidyādhar Cakravartī s/o Saṃtoṣrām, Bengali brahmin (DK 16: 155-56), architect of Jaipur; served Jaisiṅgh II in many important functions. "He was promoted to be *Desh Diwan* in 1729 and rewarded in 1734 for the speedy construction of a seven-storeyed palace and in 1735 for bringing the Dravayavati river to Jaipur city" (Sarkar 1984: 216-17). 1734 minister (?), for which cp. → V.S. 1790, Māgha ś. 4. He died in April 1752 (Sarkar 1984: 217).
1739-1741	Vidyādhar, Phaterām	Gupta 1986: 187; for Vidyādhar, cp. above. One Phaterām was the younger brother of Dīvān Kṛpārām, who died in V.S. 1819; Phaterām's identity with the *dīvān* of 1739-41 remains obscure (Kāslīvāl 1989: 201-02).
1742	Rāy Nārāyaṇdās, Bakhatrām	Gupta 1986: 187; for Rāy Nārāyaṇdās cp. above.
1744	Murlīdhar	Gupta 1986: 187
1745	Nārāyaṇdās, Phaterām	→ rev. y. 1801, Bhādrapada b. 5; for the *dīvāns*, cp. above.
1748	Rāy Nārāyaṇdās, Hargovind	Gupta 1986: 187; for Rāy Nārāyaṇdās, cp. above.
1749	Vidyādhar	Gupta 1986: 187; for Vidyādhar, cp. above.

Year (A.D.)	Dīvān	References
1750-1751	Hargovind, Kanhīrām	Gupta 1986: 187; for Hargovind, cp. above. Kanīrām Baid s/o Khemkaraṇ, Khaṇḍelvāl Jain; *dīvān* V.S. 1807-20 (Kāslīvāl 1989: 203-04).
1751	Kanhīrām	→ V.S. 1808, Bhādrapada ś. 13
1759	Kanhīrām, Nandlāl	→ V.S. 1816, Bhādrapada ś. 9; for Kanhīrām, cp. above. Nandlāl Godhā s/o Anūpcand, Khaṇḍelvāl Jain (Kāslīvāl 1989: 205-06).
1773	Saṃgahī Jīvrāj, Saṃgahī Jaicand	uncalendared doc., VRI; S. Jīvrāj, Khaṇḍelvāl Jain, *dīvān* V.S. 1830-40 (Kāslīvāl 1989: 209); S. Jaicand Chābṛā s/o Dīvān Bālcand, Khaṇḍelvāl Jain, *dīvān* V.S. 1829-55 (Kāslīvāl 1989: 211).
1783	Saṃgahī Jīvrāj, Saṃgahī Syojīrām/Sivjīrām	→ rev. y. 1839, Āṣādha b. 5; → V.S. 1840, Āśvina b. 10; for S. Jīvrāj, cp. above. Syojīrām Pāṭnī s/o Ratancand, f/o Dīvān Amarcand, Khaṇḍelvāl Jain, *dīvān* 1824-35, 1835-60, 1860-75 (Kāslīvāl 1989: 213).
1803	Saṃgahī Amarcand, and the *dīvān hajūrī*	→ V.S. 1860, Māgha b. 2; Amarcand Pāṭnī Khindūkā s/o Dīvān Syojīrām, *dīvān* V.S. 1860-92; sentenced to death and executed on British initiative in V.S. 1892 (cp. Stern 1988: 80-1 for the Blake affair; Kāslīvāl 1989: 213-14).
1812	Amarcand, Kṛpārām	→ V.S. 1869, Caitra ś. 1; for Amarcand, cp. above. Kṛpārām (variant spellings) Chābṛā, Khaṇḍelvāl Jain s/o Jaycand, nephew of Dīvān Rāycand, *dīvān* V.S. 1869-75 (Kāslīvāl 1989: 214).

Year (A.D.)	Dīvān	References
	Kirpārām, Likhamīcand	→ V.S. 1869, Jyeṣṭha ś. 13; for Kirpārām, cp. above. Likhamīcand Chābṛā, Khaṇḍelvāl Jain, *dīvān* V.S. 1859-74(Kāslīvāl 1989: 213).

Appendix 2

The Calendrical System

The Islamic calendar was used by the Kachavāhā revenue administration up to, and inclusive of, the period of Mahārājā Bisansiṅgh (d. 1699). The date according to the Islamic calendar could, outside the *eschatocol*, be supplemented by the Vikrama date or the date of the revenue calendar. Jaisiṅgh started using the Vikrama calendar exclusively, although during the interregnum of Vijaisiṅgh, the Islamic calendar was used once again.

Three calendrical systems must be distinguished, namely, the Islamic, the Vikrama and the calendar based on the harvest year, which was identical with the revenue year (abbreviation: rev. y.).

The Islamic calendar

The Islamic year is called *san* (< Pers. *sana*). The year according to the Islamic and the Vikrama calendar occurs often enough side by side in the same document. However, in the material published here, the exact date by year, month and day occurs only once.[1] More instances are available outside this corpus. Often the Islamic and the Vikrama dates of issue of a document differ by several days. This permits the conclusion that the Indic and Persian chancery departments effected their respective versions of the documents on different days.

The Vikrama year

The Vikrama year is called *saṃvat* (abbreviation: V.S.). The beginning of the Kachvāhā Vikrama year is Caitra ś. 1 and follows the system called *pūrṇimānta*, "ending with the full moon". The month starts with the waning half, *bahula* or *kṛṣṇa pakṣa* (abbr. "b"), and its second, waxing half, *śukla pakṣa* (abbr. "ś.") is concluded by the full moon day.[2] The proof that the Kachavāhā calendar follows the *pūrṇimānta* system is provided by document → V.S. 1769, Jyeṣṭha ś. 13. The document was promulgated in the bright half of the month of Jyeṣṭha following the submittal of the application for it on the 14th of the dark half of the same month.

1→ A.H. 1072, 15 Śavvāl/ Āṣāḍha b. 3, V.S. 1719.

2The Gregorian equivalents of Vikrama dates have been derived from the tables in Swamikannu Pillai 1915 and 1922.

The revenue year

The revenue year is called *sāl*. The word *sāl* is prefixed to the Persian word *san* if the calculation is based on the Hijra era, and to the word *saṃvat* if it follows the Vikrama era. The term is, naturally, salient to all revenue grants. It is obviously an abbreviation of *phaslī* (< Pers. *fasl̲ī*) *sāl*, "revenue year" (GJRT, 157).

Under Akbar, the beginning of the revenue year was fixed on the Āśvina, b. 10 of the first year of the Ilāhī era, that is A.H. 963, which, by that day, was equivalent with the Vikrama year 1612 and A.D. 1555. Later in the same year, then equivalent to A.D. 1556, Akbar succeeded to the throne. The beginning of the revenue year is identical with the Hindu Daśaharā festival.

The revenue year thus fixed corresponds in length to the Hindu religious year, which, however, in wide parts of northern India and, for that matter, in Rajasthan starts on Caitra, ś. 1, about March-April. Therefore the Hindu religious year, *saṃvat*, is ahead of the revenue year, *sāl saṃvat,* by about half a year.

The revenue, as calculated in a quasi-Hijra way, is behind the Hijra year because the revenue year follows the Hindu luni-solar calendar and is calculated by the formula *963 + x luni-solar years = current revenue year.* By contrast, the Hijra year of the Islamic calendar remains strictly lunar.

If the quasi-Hijra revenue year based on A.H. 963 is given in a document, its Vikrama equivalent is calculated by adding 649, this being the difference that prevailed in the first revenue year between A.H. 963 and V.S. 1612.

The Kachavāhā revenue year was, however, not identical with the Akbarian one. It rather started on Bhādrapada ś. 2 (Bajekal 1988:585; Bahura 1996:213, fn. 13).[3] Therefore, the revenue year starts five months later than the Vikrama year. This is why when the dates of the Vikrama and revenue years, respectively, differed, both dates were given. This was necessary for the dates from Caitra ś. 1 to Bhādrapada ś. 1.

Harvests and the collection of revenue

Regulations for the collection of revenue are set forth in the *Ā'īn* (tr., II, 48). There are two main harvests, namely the *kharīf* (spelt *ṣarīph*) (< Pers. *k̲h̲arīf*), autumn harvest, and the *rabī* (< Pers. *rabī'*), spring harvest. The autumn crops are gathered about October-November, the spring

[3]It is somewhat misleading to call the Kachavāhā revenue year the "Jayapura Saṃvat" (Bahura 1996:213, fn. 13), for it was restricted to the fiscal sphere.

crops about February-March. The autumn revenue collection was to start approximately from the Daśaharā festival and the spring collection from the Holī festival, that is, the full-moon day of the month of Phālguṇa. The autumn harvest is also called the *sāṣ ūnhālu,* "hot season harvest", and the spring harvest is called the *sāṣ syālu,* "cold season harvest". The terms *ūnhālu* and *syālu* followed by *saṃvat* also mean "hot season harvest" and "cold season harvest", respectively. Therefore, the stipulation that a beneficiary receive a revenue allowance from, say, "the hot season of year so-and-so" means "beginning with the revenue collection from the hot season crop". The documents show a preference for revenue grants to start with the autumn harvest, that is, with the new revenue year.

There also exists an intermediate harvest, which is called the *ādhī* ("half") *phasal.* The intermediate harvest can also form the beginning of a grant's validity (→ A.H. 1108, 23 Rabī‘ II, ll. 1011). This harvest may be identical with the *bhādoṃvī* harvest "... consisting of grains of quick growth, as millet and different sorts of pulse which may be sown at the beginning of the rainy season, and gathered in the month of *Bhādra,* or about September...." (GJRT, 157).

The number of days to a year

The year was calculated variously by 354 or 360 days. For religious purposes, it was calculated by 354 days which is the calculation according to the *cāndra,* the luni-solar year. Each month of that year had an average of 29.5 solar days (12 x 29.5 = 354). However, when calculating the allowance for *bhog,* only 29 days were reckoned for, while 0.5 was neglected.

Doc. → V.S. 1808, Bhādrapada ś. 13, can serve as an illustration. The *bhog* expenses were calculated by 354 days per year (l. 8, *recto*); but from the daily rates, by which certain items were calculated, it is evident that these daily rates had to be multiplied by 29 – and not by 29.5 – to yield the monthly rates. For this cp. ll. 41-46a and 51-53, recto, where 2 1/2 *ser*s of rose-water form the daily allowance; 2 1/2 x 29 = 1 maund, 32 1/2 *ser*s, as given in l. 46a. The same holds good for the provision of ghee granted in that document (ll. 51-53, recto). The daily allowance is half a *ser*; 1/2 x 354 = 177; 177 *sers* = 4 maunds, 17 *ser*s, as given in the document.

The calculation by 354 days is not always made in a straightforward way. In a document of rev. y. 1784, the expenses were calculated by 360 days and then reduced by 1/59 which makes roughly 354 days (Horstmann 1995:142).

The year of 360 days was used for the calculation of salaries, such as those drawn by the custodians of GD.[4]

The months of the year

(a)The names of the lunar months according to the Muslim calendar

(1)Moharram
(2) Safar
(3) Rabī'u'l-avval = Rabī' I
(4) Rabī'u'ṣānī or Rabī'u'l-ākhir = Rabī' II
(5) Jumāda'l-avval = Jumādā I
(6) Jumāda'ṣānī or Jumāda'l-ākhir = Jumādā II
(7) Rajab
(8) Śa'bān
(9) Ramazān
(10) Śavvāl
(11) Zi'l-qa'da or Zī qa'da (also Zū ...)
(12) Zī'l-hijja or Zī hijja (also Zū ...)

(b) The names of the months according to the Hindu calendar

The transcription of the names of the Hindu months has been standardised, because in the documents there prevails a great variety of spellings. The original spelling of the names as they occur in the documents has, however, been retained in the translation. The following list gives the standardised names adopted and, in brackets, some noteworthy equivalents occurring in the documents.

(1) Caitra
(2) Vaiśākha
(3) Jyeṣṭha
(4) Āṣāḍha
(5) Śrāvaṇa
(6} Bhādrapada (Bhādvā)
(7) Āśvina
(8) Kārttika (Kātī)
(9) Mārgaśiras
(10) Pauṣa
(11) Māgha (Mhā)
(12) Phālguṇa

[4]This coincides with Kauṭilya's provision that 30 days make a month for workmen (Kane 1974:658).

Appendix 3

Seals

In the following, there are listed the legends of the seals as they appear in the documents. The arrangement is by the following headings,

Kachavāhā Mahārājās
Kachavāhā Princes
Princes other than Kachavāhās
Dīvāns and *Mustaufī*s of Amber/Jaipur
Dīvāns other than those of Amber/Jaipur
Unidentified
Custodians of the GD Temple

Under these headings, the seals have been arranged chronologically. Slashes in the transcription of legends indicate new lines. Persian seals have been marked by "(Pers.)".

A number of seals have remained illegible, largely or entirely, and were therefore not reproduced. These are the seals of docs. → V.S. 1833, Kārttika b. 4 (with only the name *rāja balvant singh* clearly legible); → V.S. 1835, Māgha b. 10; → *ab* V.S. 1836, and → [V.S. 1878, Kārttika ś. 5].

Kachavāhā Mahārājās

(1) Rāmsiṅgh

(a) (Pers.) *rāja rām/singh banda-yi pād/śāh/'ālamgīr 1078*

"Rāja Rāmsiṅgh, slave of Emperor 'Ālamgīr, 1078"

Document: → A.H. 1078, 30 Jumādā II/17 December 1667.

(b) (Pers.) *mahārāja rām/singh/ibn-i mahārāja/jaī/singh*
1078
"Mahārāja Rāmsingh, son of Mahārāja Jaīsingh, 1078"

Document: → A.H. 1089, 20 Zī'l-hijja/February 1678.

(2) Jaisiṅgh I

(Pers.) *rāja jaī/singh/ibn-i/rāja/mahā singh*
"Rāja Jaī Singh, son of Rāja Mahā Singh"

Document: →V.S. 1700, Kārttika ś. 5/22 September 1643.

(3) Bisansiṅgh

(a) (Pers.) *mahārāja bisan/singh/ibn-i kunvar/kiśan/singh*
"Mahārāja Bisan Singh, son of Prince Kiśan Singh"

Documents: → A.H. 1102, 21 Rabī' I/23 December 1690; → A.H. 1106, 12 Jumādā I/December 1694.

(b) as above but with "1" added

Document: → A.H. 1108, 23 Rabī' II/19 November 1696

(4) Vijaisiṅgh

(Pers.) *mirzā rāja bijaī singh/fidavī śāh 'ālam/pādśāh ġāzī*
1123
"Mirzā Rāja Bijaī Singh, devoted to Śāh 'Ālam, the King [and] Warrior of Faith, 1123"

Documents: → A.H. 1123, 19 Ramazān/31 October 1711; → A.H. 1123, 21 Ramazān/2 November 1711.

(5) Jaisiṅgh II

(a) (Pers.) *rāja jaīsingh/banda-yi śāh 'ālam pād/śāh ġāzī*
"Rāja Jaī Singh, slave of Śāh 'Ālam, the King [and] Warrior of Faith"

Documents: → V.S. 1767, Mārgaśiras b. 2/28 October 1710; → 1769, Jyeṣṭha ś. 13/6 June 1712.

(b) (Pers.) *rāja jaīsingh banda-yi/bahādur śāh/aḫad ġāzī*
"Rāja Jaī Singh, slave of Bahādur Śāh, the Unique, the Defender of Faith"

Document: → V.S. 1769, Mārgaśiras ś. 5/22 November 1712.

(c) (Pers.) *mahārāja dhirāj savāī/jaī singh ibn-i mahārāja/biśan singh*
"Mahārāja dhirāj Savāī Jaī Singh, son of Mahārāja Biśan Singh"

Documents: → V.S. 1773, Āṣāḍha ś. 8/6 June 1716; → V.S. 1774, Jyeṣṭha ś. 15/14 May or 12 June 1717.

(d) (Pers.) *mahārāja dhirāj savāī/jaī singh ibn-i mahārāja/biśan singh*
sanat 5 (added to the left of line 3 – MH)
same as (c) above, but "year 5" added

Documents: → V.S. 1776, Bhādrapada ś. 6/10 August 1719; → V.S. 1776, Mārgaśiras ś. 3/3 December 1719.

(e) (Pers.) *mahārāja dhirāj savāī[jī]/jaī singh ibn-i [mahārāja]/biśan singh*
same as (d) above, but with *[jī]* added after *savāī*

Document: → V.S. 1784, Āśvina b. 11/31 August 1727

(f) *śrī/sītā/rāmo jayati/śrī mahārājādhi/rāja savāī ja/yasiṃhajī*
"Śrī Sītārām are victorious. Śrī Mahārājādhirāj Savāī Jayasiṃhajī"

Documents: → V.S. 1790, Māgha ś. 4/27 January 1734; → V.S. 1797, Māgha b. 5/27 December 1740.

(6) Īśvarsiṅgh

(a) śrīsītārāmo jayati śrī/mahārājādhirāja/śrī savāī īśvara/siṃhajī
cp. Jaisiṅgh II, translation of legend (f)

Documents: All documents published in this volume.

(b) *śrīsītārāmajī/sevakaśreṣṭho himdu[xxxx]/rājyeṣu rājarājeṃdu śrīma/hārājādhirāja savāi/īśvarasiṃhajī*

"The foremost of the servants of Śrī Sītārām, moon amongst the kings of kings in the realms of [...] the Hindus, Śrī Mahārājādhirāj Savāī Īśvarasiṃhajī"

This seal appears on a document of V.S. 1806, Mārgaśiras ś. 12, which refers to the Śyāmsundar temple. It is mentioned here, because it is noteworthy by being different from the Kachavāhā rulers' seals in use since the time of Jaisiṅgh II (cp. Jaisiṅgh II, (f) above) and by its distinctly Hindu ring.

(7) Mādhavsiṅgh I

śrīsītā/rāmo jayati śrī/mahārājādhirā/ja savāī mādha/vasiṃhajī

cp. Jaisiṅgh II, translation of legend (f)

Documents: All documents of his reign.

(8) Pṛthvīsiṅgh

śrīsītārāmo/jayati śrīmahārājādhirāja savāī/pṛthvīsiṃhajī

cp. Jaisiṅgh II, translation of legend (f)

Documents: All documents of his reign.

(9) Pratāpsiṅgh

śrīsītārā/mo jayati śrīma/hārājādhirāja sa/vāī pratāpasiṃ/hajī

cp. Jaisiṅgh II, translation of legend (f)

Documents: All documents of his reign.

(10) Jagatsiṅgh

śrīsītārām/o jayati śrīma/hārājādhirāja sa/vāī jagatasiṃhajī

cp. Jaisiṅgh II, translation of legend (f)

Documents: All documents of his reign.

Kachavāhā Princes

(1) Kīratsiṅgh

(a) (Pers.) *kīrat/singh...*
1062

Document: → A.H. 1071, 10 Safar/15 October 1660.

(b) (Pers.) *kīrat/singh ba[nda-yi]/'ālamgīr/śāh*
1078
"Kīrat Singh, slave of Emperor 'Ālamgīr, 1078"

Document: → A.H. 1080, 12 Ramazān/3 February 1670.

(2) Pahāṛsiṅgh Khaṅgarvat

śrīrāmajī/śrī mahārājadhirā/ja śrī savāī pratāpa/siṃhajī ba[ṃ]dā pahāṛa/syaṃgha ṣaṃgarvata
"Śrī Rāmjī/Śrī Mahārājādhirāj Śrī Savāī Pratāpasiṃha's slave Pahāṛsiṅgh Khaṅgarvat"

Document: → V.S. 1848, Bhādrapada b. 7/ 21 August 1791.

Princes other than Kachavāhās

(1) Sūrajmal of Bharatpur (Jāṭ)

(Pers.) *[...] 1128 (or 1138)/sanat 9/sujān (?)*
8
"[...] 1128 (or 1138), year 9, (?), 8"

Document: → V.S. 1786, Āṣāḍha ś. 3/18 June 1729.

(2) Rāmsiṅgh of Marwar (deposed Mahārājā)

The seal is partly illegible, especially for the legend which encircles the central one. The central legend runs,

mahāmāyā śrī/himgulājaprasādāt [x]/nupati śrīrājarājeśvara mahārājādhirāja mahārājā/śrīrāmaḥ siṃhadeva vijayatejā[xx] jas(?)va/[——————]/[x]rāja[x]
"By the grace of Mahāmāyā Himgulāj, [...] Lord Śrī Rājarājeśvara Mahārājādhirāja Mahārājā Śrī Rāma Siṃhadeva, radiant with victory [...] glorious(?) [...] king [...]"

Document: → V.S. 1822, Pauṣa ś. 14/26 December 1765.

(3) Bakhtāvarsiṅgh of Alvar

śrīsītāramajīsahāya kava/ra baṣatāvarasyaṃgha/rajāvata
"He who is protected by Śrī Sītārām: Prince Bakhtāvarsiṅgh Rajāvat"

Documents: → V.S. 1825, Māgha b. 15/6 February 1769; → V.S. 1825, Māgha ś. 3/9 February 1769.

***Dīvāns* and *Mustaufīs* of Amber/Jaipur**

(1) Dīvān Kiśordās

(Pers.) *kiśordās banda-yi/mahārāja dhirāj savāī/jaī singh*
"Kiśordās, slave of Mahārāja dhirāj Savāī Jaī Singh"

Document: → V.S. 1773, Bhādrapada ś. 8/14 August 1716.

(2) Seals analogous to that of Kiśordās

Dīvān Tārācand, → V.S. 1773, Bhādrapada ś. 8/14 August 1716
Dīvān Nārāyaṇdās, → V.S. 1784, Āśvina b. 11/31 August 1727; → V.S. 1790, Māgha ś. 4/27 January 1734
Dīvān Krapārām/Kripārām, → V.S. 1784, Āśvina b. 11/31 August 1727; → V.S. 1790, Māgha ś. 4/27 January 1734
Mustaufī Vijaisiṅgh, → V.S. 1784, Āśvina b. 11/31 August 1727

(3)Mustaufī Girdhardās

śrīrāmajī/śrīmahārājādhi/rāja savāī jaisyaṃ/ghajī [sevaka][5] *giradhara dāsa*

"Śrī Rāmjī. Girdhardās, servant of Śrī Mahārājādhirāj Savāī Jaisiṅgh"

Document: → V.S. 1790, Māgha ś. 4/27 January 1734.

(4) Dīvāns and Mustaufīs after V.S. 1790/A.D. 1734

After V.S. 1790, the seals had a legend identical to that of Girdhardās's seal, for which cp. above. This was only changed in the period of Rāmsingh, when the seal of the revenue department, and not of an individual officer, was applied.[6]

Dīvāns other than those of Amber/Jaipur

(1) Dīvān Satrasiṅgh (of Mādhosiṅgh Hāṛā of Koṭā)

(Pers.) *satrāsingh/śālī/mādhū/singh gāh*

1019

"Satrā Singh belonging to the Court of Mādho Singh"

Document: → A.H. 1038, 2 Śavvāl/May 1628.

(2) Dīvān of Rāmsiṅgh (deposed Mahārājā of Marwar), name illegible

śrī rājarājeśva/rajī śrī mahārājādhi/rāja śrī savāi rāmasi[ṃ]/hajī

[...]rasira[...]ka/hajī[...]/paṭarā jilā savā/i jaipura

"Śrī Rājrājeśvarjī Śrī Mahārājādhirāj Śrī Savāī Rāmsiṅgh ... district Savāī Jaipur"

Document: → V.S. 1828, Vaiśākha b. 4/3 April 1771.

---

[5] In other legends than that of Girdhardās's seal normally clearly legible.

[6] No documents of this type have been published in this volume.

(3) Dīvān of Jodhpur, Marwar; name illegible

(Pers.) *[dīvān N.N.]/50 (?) rāja[rājeśvara] mahārāj[ā]/[dhi]rāja [mahārājā]/1187 [...]*
"[Dīvān N.N.]/50 (?) Rājrājeśvar Mahārājādhirāj Mahārājā/1187 [...]"

Document: → V.S. 1836, Māgha b. 8/29 January 1779.

(4) Dīvān Gyānmal of Jodhpur, Marwar

(Pers.) *dīvān gyān mal [...]/rāja rājeśvar [mahā]rā[j] /dhirāj [mahārāja]/mān singh 1231* (end of line 2)
"Dīvān Gyān Mal of [...] Rājrājeśvar [Mahārājā] Mān Singh, 1231"

Document: → V.S. 1860, Āṣāḍha ś. 8/27 June 1803.

Unidentified

(1) Rājā Rādhikādās

[...]/vadrā[ṃ]ghrisevakasya/mahīpateḥ rādhikā/dāsadevakasya gauḍe[...]/sya sa mudrikā
"Seal of the servant of the foot [of...], King of Rādhikādāsdev of Gauḍa..."

Document: → *ab* V.S. 1839/1782.

Custodians of the Govinddevjī Temple

(1) Nīlāmbar

śrīgoviṃda/śrīrāmaśaraṇa/caraṇanīlāṃba/raśaraṇa
"Śrī Nīlāmbar takes refuge at the feet of Śrī Govinda and Śrī Rāmśaraṇ[7]"

Document: → V.S. 1833, Śrāvaṇa b. 7/7 July 1776.

[7] Rāmśaraṇ was the predecessor of Nīlāmbar.

(2) Seal used during an interim between two custodians

śrīgoviṃ/dadevo/jayati
"Śrī Govindadeva is victorious"

Document: → V.S. 1863, Kārttika b. 3/30 October 1806.

Appendix 4

Measures, Weights and Currency

Unit	Equivalent in other units of the same system	Metric equivalent
1. Length		
girah[8]		
gaj mukasar (mūkasar)	*16 girah*	c. 68 cm[9]
2. Area		
viśvā		c. 121,40 m^2
bīghā[10]	20 *viśvās*	c. 2428,11 m^2
3. Weight		
māśā	no equivalent given; commonly 8 *rattīs*	
taul/tol[11]	no equivalent given; commonly 1 *tolā* = 12 *māśās*	
chaṭāṃk	no equivalent given; commonly 5 *tolās*	
ser[12]	(1) 28 *tauls*[13] (2) 16 *chaṭāṃks*[14]	

[8]In the Rājasthānī texts, the term is not spelt out, but indicated by fractional numbers.

[9]Pers. *gaz-i mukassar;* for details, cp. → A.H. 1080, 12 Ramaẕān, commentary.

[10]The *bīghā* is taken to be equivalent to the *bīghā-i ilāhī* (Habib 1963:356-62). This was equivalent to about 0.6 acres (1 acre = 4046,86 m^2).

[11]The Mughal *tolā* had a weight of c. 185,5 grains avdp. = 12,057 grams (Hodivala 1923: 224-28). Cp. → V.S. 1773, Āṣāḍha ś. 8 and Bhādrapada ś. 8.

[12]The relation between a *ser* of 28 *tauls* and one of 16 *chaṭāṃks* could not be established.

[13]Calculated by the Mughal standard *tolā*, this would be equivalent to 337,6 grams. For the equivalence of 1 *ser* with 28 *tauls*, cp. the docs. mentioned in fn. 11 above.

[14]For the *ser* = 16 *chaṭāṃks*, cp. → V.S. 1777, Āśvina ś. 14.

Unit	Equivalent in other units of the same system	Metric equivalent
3. Weight		
maṇ (maund)	40 *sers*[15]	
luṇ maṇ (salt maund)[16]		
sirvā (bale?)		
4. Currency		
dām		
ṭakā	50 *dāms*[17]	
ṭakā pakā (standard *ṭakā*)[18]		
paīsā		
ānā (anna)	64 *paīsā*	
rūpayau/-o	16 *ānās*	
Auraṃgśāhī *rūpayau*[19]		

[15]For the equivalence of the maund with 40 *sers*, cp. Gupta 1986:75.

[16]Cp. → V.S. 1816, Bhādrapada ś. 9, and deeds subsequent to it.

[17]Gupta 1986: 72, fn. 2.

[18]Cp. → V.S. 1773, Āṣāḍha ś. 8; in the Amber territory, in that year (A.D. 1716), the silver value of 18 *ṭakās* was 1 rupee (Gupta 1986:315).

[19]Cp. → V.S. 1774, Āśvina b. 11, l. 12. In his sixth regnal year, Aurangzeb increased the weight of the rupee by 6 *cāvals* (rice-grains) of silver, a little less than one percent. However, it seems that the older scales were again in use by the end of the eighteenth century (Habib 1960:6).

Appendix 5

Siyāq Numerals

The Persian versions of the documents make use of the *siyāq* numerals. They are used for rupee amounts, whereas fractions of rupees are rendered by digits. The shape of the *siyāq* numerals varies greatly. The chart shows numerals of the type used in India.[20]

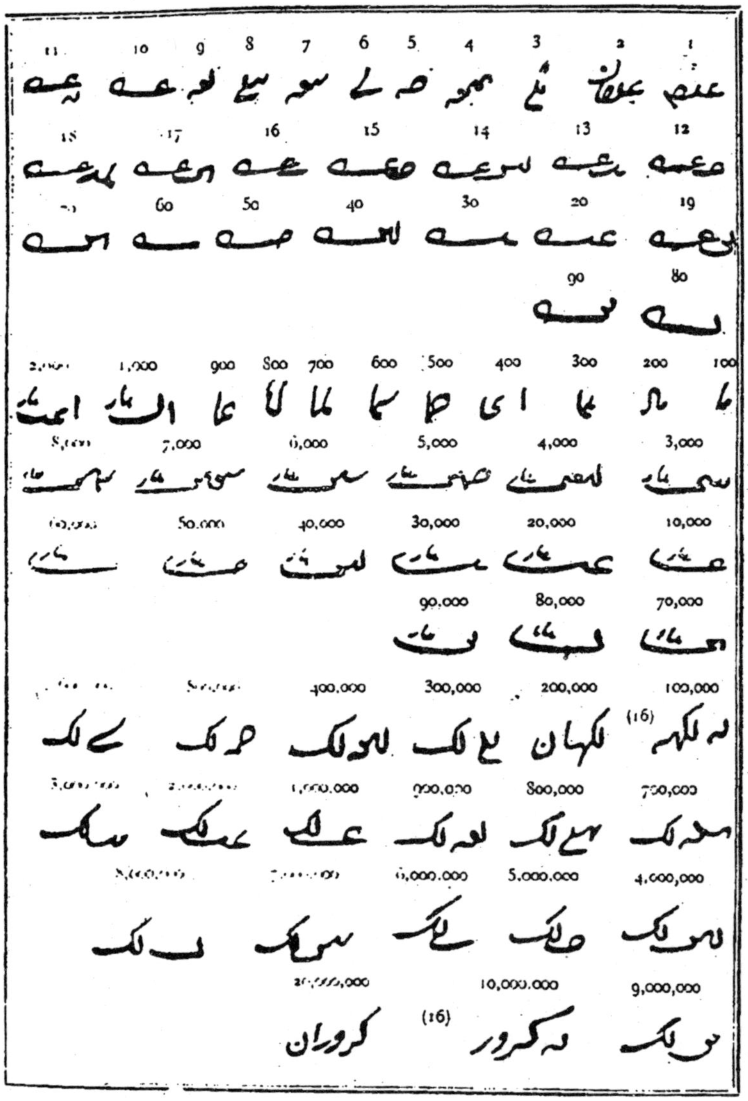

[20]Reproduced from Kazem Zadeh (1915), who in his turn used Stewart 1825.

3. Calendar of Documents

For the years A.D. 1628 (A.H. 1038, 2 Śavvāl) to 1821 (V.S. 1878, Kārttika ś. 5), the origin of the calendared documents can only be given summarily.[1] They were collected and photographed in the course of the Vrindaban Project in the years 1975 to 1978. The Project was carried out under the auspices of the International Association of the Vrindaban Research Institute. The huge collection of filmed documents, which was the fruit thereof, forms part of the holdings of the Vrindaban Research Institute. The Vrindaban Project and its results were described by Mukherjee (1980) in a preliminary report. This study is based on paper prints of those filmed documents, which only by exception bear an indication of their provenance on their back. For their majority, they certainly come from the archives of the GD temple of Jaipur, but some of them were in the 1970s kept in the district court of Mathura, because the GD temple was involved in ongoing litigation concerning its legal titles.

The other documents, that is, those of the years V.S. 1928 ff.,[2] were traced by the present author in 1996. They belong to the holdings of the Rajasthan State Archives, Bikaner. Being office copies of an orthographically not always reliable quality, they have been calendared but not edited. This does not affect the argument of this study, for they form confirmations of deeds known to us by their earlier versions.

The documents calendared are of three kinds, namely,

(1) Documents PUBLISHED in this volume. Throughout the book, reference to them has been made by

→ *date*

(2) Documents digested but NOT PUBLISHED, because they formed mere confirmations of earlier deeds. If confirmed deeds implied noteworthy changes or were remarkable in other ways, these were published in full, however. Reference to unpublished documents has been made by putting their date in square brackets, that is,

---

[1] An exception to this is doc. [rev.y. 1784, Vaiśākha I ś. 15], which belongs to the holdings of the Rajasthan State Archives, Bikaner.

[2] With the exception of → V.S. 1930, Phālguṇa ś. 4, which was also filmed in the course of the Vrindaban Project.

[*date*]

(3) Documents which were UNTRACEABLE but testified to by other deeds. Reference to them has been made by an asterisk preceding the date of the deed, that is,

**date*

All documents which refer to the same grant, with or without change, have been connected by cross-references.

The calendar identifies the deeds by the following identification index, although not all of the categories apply in each case,

DATE, TYPE, PROMULGATOR, ADDRESSEE, GRANTEE, OBJECT, PROVENANCE, EFFECTIVE DATE, PREVIOUS DEED, SUBSEQUENT DEED.

For the identification of document types cp. Chapter 2, pp. 41-44. The term "promulgator" has been used in a purely schematic way and includes also authors of office notes and letters. Names of promulgators have been given in an unequivocal though sometimes abriged form. For full regnal titles and other details, cp. the texts.

The legends of seals have been treated in Appendix 3 to Chapter 2. The edited and translated documents have been marked by "*(seal)*" in the appropriate place of the text.

CALENDAR

DATE: A.H. 1038, 2 Śavvāl/ 25 May 1628
TYPE: *sanad*; bilingual: Rājasthānī and Persian
PROMULGATOR: Dīvān Satrasiṅgh (of Mādhosiṅgh of Koṭā)
ADDRESSEES: *āmils* of *parganā* Bahātarī
GRANTEE: Temples of Mathura and Vrindaban
OBJECT: 1,850rp., revenue realized from two villages
PROVENANCE: Villages Jehuvī, *tapā* Rīnī, and Sāṃhupāṛau, *tapā* Sauhī, both in *parganā* Bahātarī
EFFECTIVE DATE: Autumn harvest V.S. 1685

DATE: V.S. 1700, Kārttika ś. 5/ 22 September 1643
TYPE: *sanad*
PROMULGATOR: Jaisiṅgh I
ADDRESSEE: Mahesdās
GRANTEE: Gosvāmīs Nityānand and Rādhākrisandās Catravaratī (*sic!*; that is, Cakravartī)
OBJECT: Place of Kāśirām's mother (in Vrindaban?)
EFFECTIVE DATE: After relinquishment by present occupant

DATE: A.H. 1071, 10 S̱afar/ 15 October 1660
TYPE: *parvānau*
PROMULGATOR: Prince Kīratsiṅgh
ADDRESSEE: Officers of the Court (*mutasadī hajūrī*)
GRANTEE: GD, his consort, and Vṛndādevī
OBJECT: Garments for the temple images
PROVENANCE: Court
EFFECTIVE DATE: Date of the deed
SUBSEQUENT DEED: → A.H. 1080, 12 Ramaẕān

DATE: A.H. 1072, 15 Śavvāl/ 3 June 1662// Āṣāḍha b.3, V.S. 1719/ 26 May 1662
TYPE: *sanad*, copper-plate grant
PROMULGATOR: Jaisiṅgh I
ADDRESSEES: Officers *(kamaitī)* of *parganā* Amber
GRANTEE: Sivrām, brahmin, s/o Purohit Acalrām
OBJECT: *punya arath* (charitable land), 200 *bīghās*
PROVENANCE: Village Jāhautā, *tapā* Kākaḍ, *parganā* Amber
EFFECTIVE DATE: Autumn harvest V.S. 1719, rev.y. 1070
SUBSEQUENT DEED: *V.S. 1928, Caitra b. 15 (Jāhautā)

DATE: A.H. 1078, 30 Jumādā II/ 17 December 1667
TYPE: *parvānau*; bilingual: Rajasthānī and Persian
PROMULGATOR: Rāmsiṅgh
ADDRESSEES: Officers *(kamaitī)* of *parganā* Amber
GRANTEE: GD (Vrindaban) and Gosvāmī Sevrām
OBJECT: *puni* and *bhog*, annually recoverable amount of 960rp. and 1,200rp., both in cash

PROVENANCE: Cash amount of 960rp.: provenance not specified; cash amount of 1,200rp. from village Govindpur, *tapā* Khoh, *parganā* Amber
EFFECTIVE DATE: Autumn harvest, rev.y. 1075/ V.S. 1724
PRECEDING DEEDS: Not specified; the present deed is, however, specified as a renewal of an earlier one
SUBSEQUENT DEEDS: *A.H. 1112, 1 Jumādā I; → rev.y. 1801/ V.S. 1802, Bhādrapada b. 5 (Govindpuro), partly renewal; [V.S. 1928, Caitra b. 15 (aggregate grant)]
Note: The village appears also as Govindpuro Baṛo or Bujarg and is identical with Raihphoṛā/Rahphoṛā; → V.S. 1764, Śrāvaṇa b. 3

DATE: A.H. 1080, 12 Ramaẕān/ February 1670
TYPE: *sanad*; bilingual: Rājasthānī and Persian
PROMULGATOR: Prince Kīratsiṅgh
ADDRESSEES: Officers *(kamaitī)* of *parganā* Kāmā
GRANTEE: GD, his consort and Vṛndādevī
OBJECT: Garments for the temple images
PROVENANCE: *parganā* Kāmā
EFFECTIVE DATE: A.H. 1079, 29 Jumādā I
PRECEDING DEED: → A.H. 1071, 10 Ṣafar

DATE: A.H. 1089, 20 Ẕī'l-ḥijja/ 2 February 1679
TYPE: *sanad*; bilingual: Rājasthānī and Persian
PROMULGATOR: Rāmsiṅgh
ADDRESSEES: Officers *(kamaitī)* of *parganā* Amber
GRANTEE: GD and his consort
OBJECT: 436rp., formerly a charity of Prince Kisansiṅgh; 200rp. out of these now made a charity of Rāmsiṅgh
PROVENANCE: *parganā* Amber
EFFECTIVE DATE: Rev.y. 1086/ V.S. 1735

UNTRACEABLE
DATE: *rev.y. 1096/ V.S. 1745/c. 1688
SUBSEQUENT DEEDS: *rev.y. 1097/ V.S. 1746, → A.H. 1102, 21 Rabī' I, → A.H. 1106, 12 Jumādā I, → A.H. 1108, 23 Rabī' II

UNTRACEABLE
DATE: *rev.y. 1097/V.S. 1746/c. 1688
PRECEDING DEED: rev.y. 1096/ V.S. 1745
SUBSEQUENT DEEDS: → A.H. 1102, 21 Rabī' I, → A.H. 1106, 12 Jumādā I, → A.H. 1108, 23 Rabī' II

DATE: A.H. 1102, 21 Rabī' I/ 23 December 1690
TYPE: *parvānau*; bilingual: Rājasthānī and Persian
PROMULGATOR: Bisansiṅgh
ADDRESSEES: Officers *(kamaitī)* of *parganā* Amber
GRANTEE: GD, his consort and Vṛndādevī
OBJECT: *jāgīr* for *puni* (charity) for garments etc.; net amount 960rp.
PROVENANCE: Jhujhārpur, *tapā* Khoh, *parganā* Amber

EFFECTIVE DATE: Autumn harvest, rev.y. 1098/ V.S. 1747
PRECEDING DEEDS: *rev.y. 1096/ V.S. 1745 and *rev.y. 1097/ V.S. 1746 (with changes concerning the locality assigned in *jāgīr*)
SUBSEQUENT DEEDS: → A.H. 1106, 12 Jumādā I, → A.H. 1108, 23 Rabī‘ II

DATE: A.H. 1106, 12 Jumādā I/ 29 December 1694
TYPE: *sanad*; bilingual: Rājasthānī and Persian
PROMULGATOR: Bisansiṅgh
ADDRESSEES: Officers *(kamaitī)* of *parganā* Amber
GRANTEE: GD
OBJECT: Cash revenue allowance of 960rp. plus 203rp., 6a.; increment on preceding deed (→ A.H. 1102, 21 Rabī‘ I)
PROVENANCE: *jāgīr* of Jhujhārpur, *tapā* Khoh, *parganā* Amber
EFFECTIVE DATE: Autumn harvest of rev.y. 1103/ V.S. 1752
PRECEDING DEEDS: *rev.y. 1096/ V.S. 1745; *rev.y. 1097/ V.S. 1746; → A.H. 1102, 21 Rabī‘ I
SUBSEQUENT DEED:→ A.H. 1108, 23 Rabī‘ II

DATE: A.H. 1108, 22 [Rabī‘] II/ 18 November 1696
TYPE: *sanad*; bilingual: Rājasthānī and Persian
PROMULGATOR: Bisansiṅgh
ADDRESSEE: Gosvāmī Govindcaran
OBJECT: Charge of 135 *bīghā*s land etc.
LOCALITY: [Dosaich and Dholera near Vrindaban]
EFFECTIVE DATE: as above?
PRECEDING DEEDS: [*farmān*s of Akbar and Śāh Jahān of Ilāhī Year 43 (A.D. 1598/1599) and A.D. 1633, resp.]
SUBSEQUENT DEEDS: → V.S. 1767, Mārgaśiras b. 3, → V.S. 1863, Kārttika ś. 3

DATE: A.H. 1108, 23 Rabī‘ II/ 19 November 1696
TYPE: *parvānau*; bilingual: Rājasthānī and Persian
PROMULGATOR: Bisansiṅgh
ADDRESSEES: Officers *(kamaitī)* of *parganā* Amber
GRANTEE: GD
OBJECT: *jāgīr* for 360rp. personal income of the deity's custodian
PROVENANCE: Jhujhārpur, *tapā* Khoh, *parganā* Amber
EFFECTIVE DATE: Intermediate harvest of rev.y. 1104/ V.S. 1753
PRECEDING DEEDS: *rev.y. 1096/ V.S. 1745, *rev.y. 1097/ V.S. 1746, → A.H. 1102, 21 Rabī‘ I, → A.H. 1106, 12 Jumādā I

UNTRACEABLE
DATE: *A.H. 1112, 1 Jumādā I/ 14 October 1700
PRECEDING DEED: → A.H. 1078, 30 Jumādā II
SUBSEQUENT DEED: → rev.y. 1801/ V.S. 1802, Bhādrapada b. 5 (Govindpuro), [V.S. 1928, Caitra b. 15 (aggregate grant)]

DATE: V.S. 1764, Śrāvaṇa b. 3/ 6 July 1707
TYPE: *sanad*, *ijārau* lease
PROMULGATORS: *dīvān*s of Amber
GRANTEE/*IJĀRAU*-HOLDER: GD and, as *ijārau*-holder, Gosvāmī Govindcaraṇ

OBJECT: *puni* (charity), *ijārau* dues of 401rp. (notional revenue: 503rp. 5a.), in addition to *jāgīr* of 1163rp. 6a. in the same village
LOCALITY: Village Catrapur-vās Khijuryā, *tapā* Khoh [in *parganā* Amber]
EFFECTIVE DATE: rev.y. V.S. 1764
SUBSEQUENT DEEDS: [V.S. 1767, Āśvina b. 5], [rev.y. 1801/V.S. 1802, Bhādrapada b. 5 (Catrapur-vās Khijuryā)], [V.S. 1808, Kārttika ś. 8 (Catrapur-vās Khijuryā)], [V.S. 1818, Mārgaśiras ś. 2]
Note: Catrapur-vās Khijuryā was, for some time, replaced by Jhujhārpur, for which cp. *rev.y. 1096/V.S. 1745 foll.

UNTRACEABLE
DATE: *V.S. 1766/c. 1709
TYPE: *sanad*
PROMULGATORS: *dīvāns*
GRANTEE: not named, either GD, or GD and Rādhāmādhavjī
SUBSEQUENT DEEDS: → V.S. 1777, Āśvina 14; [rev.y. 1784, Vaiśākha I b. 15 (Horstmann 1995)], [V.S. 1928, Caitra b. 15 (Rājsar Phuṭolāv)]

NOT PUBLISHED
DATE: [rev.y. 1767, Āśvina b. 5/ 13 September 1709]
TYPE: *parvānau*
PROMULGATOR: Jaisiṅgh II
GRANTEE: GD
OBJECT: *jāgīr* for *puni bhog*; *jāgīr* covering 503rp., 5a.
PROVENANCE: Catrapur-vās Khijuryā, *tapā* Khoh, *parganā* Amber
EFFECTIVE DATE: Cold season of V.S. 1767
PRECEDING DEED, now altered: → V.S. 1764, Śrāvaṇa b. 3 (*jāgīr* covered 1163rp., 6a.; increment on this amount: 503rp. 5a.)
SUBSEQUENT DEEDS: [rev.y. 1801/ V.S. 1802, Bhādrapada b. 5 (Catrapur-vās Khijuryā)], [V.S. 1808, Kārttika ś. 8 (Catrapur-vās Khijuryā)], [V.S. 1818, Mārgaśiras ś. 2]
Note: This deed replaced the *ijārau* lease of → V.S. 1764, Śrāvaṇa b. 3

DATE: V.S. 1767, Mārgaśiras b. 2/ 28 October 1710
TYPE: *sanad*
PROMULGATOR: Jaisiṅgh II
ADDRESSEE: Gopīraman, custodian of the Rādhādāmodar temple
GRANTEE: Gopīraman (cp. above)
OBJECT: Management of 135 *bīghās kuñj*-land granted to a group of Vaiṣṇava temples
LOCALITY: [Dosaich and Dholera near Vrindaban]
EFFECTIVE DATE: as above?
PRECEDING DEEDS: [*farmāns* of Akbar and Śāh Jahān of Ilāhī Year 43 (A.D. 1598/1599) and 1633, resp.], → A.H. 1108, 22 [Rabī'] II
SUBSEQUENT DEED: → V.S. 1863, Kārttika b. 3

DATE: A.H. 1123, 19 Ramaẕān/ 31 October 1711
TYPE: *sanad*; bilingual: Rājasthānī and Persian
PROMULGATOR: Vijaisiṅgh
ADDRESSEES: Officers *(kamaitī)* of Ṭoḍā Bhīm
GRANTEE: Gosvāmī Jagannāth, custodian of GD

OBJECT: Endowment of 1 mansion and 1 shop
LOCALITY: Ṭoḍā Bhīm, *parganā* Ṭoḍā Bhīm, sarkār *Alvar*
EFFECTIVE DATE: as above?

DATE: A.H. 1123, 21 Ramaẕān/ 2 November 1711
TYPE: *sanad*; bilingual: Rājasthānī and Persian
PROMULGATOR: Vijaisiṅgh
ADDRESSEES: Officers *(kamaitī)* of *parganā* Hiṇḍaun
GRANTEE: GD, Gopīnāth and Śyāmsundarrāy temples
OBJECT: *punī* for *bhog* in the form of revenue *jāgīr*, cp. however subsequent deeds
PROVENANCE: Villages Ḍaharā, Sālampur (in other documents: Sālimpur) and Valhaḍī, *parganā* Hiṇḍaun, *sarkār* Alvar
EFFECTIVE DATE: as above?
SUBSEQUENT DEEDS: (Only for Sālimpur, which out of the three villages was the one granted to GD) *V.S. 1779, Jyeṣṭha b. 10, → rev.y. 1801/V.S. 1802, Bhādrapada b. 5 (Sālimpur), [V.S. 1928, Caitra b. 15 (Sālimpur)]

DATE: V.S. 1769/ rev.y. 1768, Jyeṣṭha ś. 13/ 6 June 1712
TYPE: *parvānau*
PROMULGATOR: Jaisiṅgh II
ADDRESSEES: Officers *(kamaitī)* of *parganā* Amber
GRANTEE: Kisanrām, Bengali brahmin, s/o Govindrām
OBJECT: *punī ūdik,* 200 *bīghās*
LOCALITY: Rājsar Phuṭolāv, *tapā* Rāmgaṛh, *parganā* Amber
EFFECTIVE DATE: Pauṣa b. 15, rev. year 1768 (= V.S. 1768)
Note: Cp. also the deed referring to Rājsar Phuṭolāv, → V.S. 1777, Āśvina ś. 14

DATE: V.S. 1769, Mārgaśiras ś. 5/ 22 November 1712
TYPE: *sanad*
PROMULGATOR: Jaisiṅgh II
ADDRESSEE: Gajsiṅgh
OBJECT: Bhavānīdās Khatrī's orders are to be obeyed
EFFECTIVE DATE: as above

UNTRACEABLE
DATE: *V.S. 1771, Bhādrapada ś.4/ 2 September 1714
SUBSEQUENT DEEDS: → rev.y. 1801/ V.S. 1802, Bhādrapada b. 5 (Gaṅgārāmpuro-vās Khijūryā), [V.S. 1808, Kārttika ś. 8 (Gaṅgārāmpuro-vās Khijūryā)]

UNTRACEABLE
DATE: *V.S. 1771, Āśvina b. 13/ 25 September 1714
SUBSEQUENT DEED: → rev.y. 1801/ V.S. 1802, Bhādrapada b. 5 (pasture), [V.S. 1808, Kārttika ś. 12]

DATE: V.S. 1773, Āṣāḍha ś. 8/ 16 June 1716
TYPE: *parvānau*
PROMULGATOR: Jaisiṅgh II
ADDRESSEES: Officers *(kamaitī)* of *parganā* Amber
GRANTEE: GD

OBJECT: *punya* (charity) in cash and kind for sacrificial feeding; daily allowance of 3 *pakā ṭakās* cash and 1/4 maund and 5 1/2 *sers* kind
PROVENANCE: Treasury of the *modī* of *kasbā* Amber
EFFECTIVE DATE: Caitra b. 1, V.S. 1773/ rev.y. 1772

DATE: V.S. 1773, Bhādrapada ś. 8/ 14 August 1716
TYPE: *sanad*
PROMULGATORS: Dīvāns Kisordās and Tārācand
ADDRESSEES: Sāh Sevārām and Sāh Meghrāj
OBJECT: Maintenance of 9 servants in the service of GD; daily allowance of 13 1/2 *sers* of foodgrains and 18 *paīsās* of oil
PROVENANCE: Treasury of the *modī* of *kasbā* Amber
EFFECTIVE DATE: Āṣāḍha b. 1, rev.y. 1772/ V.S. 1773

UNTRACEABLE
DATE: *V.S. 1774, Jyeṣṭha I, ś. 13/ 14 May 1717
SUBSEQUENT DEEDS: → rev.y. 1801/ V.S. 1802, Bhādrapada b. 5 (Sekhpuro Baṛo), [V.S. 1928, Caitra b. 15 (Sekhpur)]

DATE: V.S. 1774, Jyeṣṭha ś. 15/ 14 May or 12 June 1717
TYPE: *parvānau*
PROMULGATOR: Jaisiṅgh II
ADDRESSEES: Officers *(kamaitī)* of *parganā* Cāṭsū
GRANTEE: GD
OBJECT: *punya udik* of village revenue in entirety
PROVENANCE: Village Dayālpuro, *parganā* Cāṭsū
EFFECTIVE DATE: Caitra b. 13, V.S. 1773/ rev.y. 1772
SUBSEQUENT DEED: [V.S. 1928, Caitra b. 15 (Dayālpuro)]

DATE: V.S. 1776, Bhādrapada ś. 6/ 10 August 1719
TYPE: Order
PROMULGATOR: Jaisiṅgh II
ADDRESSEE: Kisanrām
OBJECT: Order to provide for horsemen and carriers
EFFECTIVE DATE: as above

DATE: V.S. 1776, Mārgaśiras ś. 3/ 3 December 1719
TYPE: Order
PROMULGATOR: Jaisiṅgh II
ADDRESSEE: Jagrām
OBJECT: Order to carry out work on the GD temple and to construct a house for the Gosvāmī; order to give allowance for *bhog* etc.
EFFECTIVE DATE: *bhog* to start on Kārttika ś. 3 [, V.S. 1776]

UNTRACEABLE
DATE: *V.S. 1776/c. 1719
SUBSEQUENT DEEDS: → V.S. 1777, Āśvina ś. 14, [V.S. 1928,Caitra b. 15]

DATE: V.S. 1777, Āśvina ś. 14/ 4 October 1720
TYPE: *parvānau*; incomplete: *invocatio*, *elevatio*, seal missing, two gaps in the commentary
PROMULGATOR: Jaisiṅgh II

ADDRESSEES: Officers *(kamaitī)* of *parganā* [Amber]
GRANTEE: GD and Rādhāmādhavjī, names not given, but mentioned to in RSA, File No 1657-28, 17 December 1952, with reference to preceding deeds
OBJECT: *puni* for *bhog*; allowance of revenue of a village in entirety: 4,239rp., 9a. (GD: 1,956rp. 9a., Rādhāmādhavjī: 2,283rp.)
PROVENANCE: Rājsar Phuṭaulāv, *tapā* Rāmgaṛh, *parganā* Amber
EFFECTIVE DATE: Hot season of V.S. 1776
PRECEDING DEED: *V.S. 1776
SUBSEQUENT DEEDS: [rev.y. 1784, Vaiśākha I ś. 15 (Horstmann 1995)], [V.S. 1928, Caitra b. 15 (Rājsar Phuṭolāv)]
Cp. also doc. → V.S. 1769, Jyeṣṭha ś. 13

DATE: V.S. 1778, Āśvina ś. 1/ 11 September 1721
TYPE: *sanad*
PROMULGATORS: Dīvāns Kisordās and Tārācand
GRANTEE: GD of Vrindaban
ADDRESSEES: Sāh Mohandās and Sāh Sikhānand
OBJECT: Repair work (textiles)
EFFECTIVE DATE: On arrival of an application that expenses for repair work be defrayed and after the work has actually started

UNTRACEABLE
DATE: *V.S. 1779, Jyeṣṭha b. 10/ 29 April 1722
SUBSEQUENT DEEDS: → rev.y. 1801/V.S. 1802, Bhādrapada b. 5 (Sālimpur), [V.S. 1928, Caitra b. 15 (Sālimpur)]

DATE: V.S. 1782, Mārgaśiras b. 14/ 22 November 1725
TYPE: *sanad*
PROMULGATORS: Dīvāns Narāyaṇdās and Kīrpārām
ADDRESSEE: Syāmsiṅgh
GRANTEE: GD of Vrindaban
OBJECT: 70 maunds of coal for the temple plus outstanding claims on coal
PROVENANCE: Vrindaban
EFFECTIVE DATE: Cold season of V.S. 1782
PRECEDING DEED: Refers to a regulation in force
SUBSEQUENT DEED: → V.S. 1787, Kārttika ś. 3

DATE: V.S. 1784, Āśvina b. 11/ 31 August 1727
TYPE: *parvānau*
PROMULGATOR: Jaisiṅgh II
ADDRESSEES: Officers *(kamaitī)* of *parganā* Amber
GRANTEE: GD
OBJECT: *punya* for *bhog* etc.; 1rp. daily allowance for a *sakhī* of GD's consort
PROVENANCE: *parganā* Amber, treasury
EFFECTIVE DATE: Śrāvaṇa b. 7, V.S. 1784/ rev.y. 1783
SUBSEQUENT DEEDS: *rev.y. 1801/ V.S. 1802, Bhādrapada b. 5 (*sakhī*), → V.S. 1808, Bhādrapada ś. 13

NOT PUBLISHED
DATE: [rev. y. 1784, Vaiśākha I ś. 15/13 April 1728]
TYPE: *ḍaul*

GRANTEE: GD and Rādhāmādhavjī
PRECEDING DEED: → V.S. 1777, Āśvina ś. 14
SUBSEQUENT DEEDS: [V.S. 1802, Bhādrapada ś. 8]
Note: The *ḍaul* led to the promulgation of a *parvānau* on Bhādrapada ś. 6, V.S. 1787 (Bahura 1996:207)

DATE: V.S. 1786, Āṣāḍha ś. 3/ 18 June 1729
TYPE: Order
PROMULGATOR: Prince Sūrajmal
ADDRESSEE: Inspectors of trade taxes of villages
OBJECT: Transport of betel-leaves must not be tampered with
LOCALITY: Vrindaban (not explicitly mentioned, but concluded from context)
EFFECTIVE DATE: as above

UNTRACEABLE
DATE: *V.S. 1787, Bhādrapada ś. 6/8 August or 7 September 1730
TYPE: *parvānau*
PROMULGATOR: Jaisiṅgh II
GRANTEE: GD and Rādhāmādhavjī
OBJECT: 4,238rp. 13a. 6p.
PROVENANCE: [Rājsar Phuṭolāv]
PRECEDING DEED: → V.S. 1777, Āśvina ś. 14
SUBSEQUENT DEED: [V.S. 1802, Bhādrapada ś. 8] (Bahura 1996:207)
Note: The document is referred to by Bahura 1996:207. For the, probably incorrectly, calculated amount of 4,238rp. 13a., 6p., against 4,339rp. 9a. in doc. → V.S. 1777, Āśvina ś. 14, cp. Horstmann 1995:141.

DATE: V.S. 1787, Kārttika ś. 3/ 2 November 1730
TYPE: *sanad*
PROMULGATOR: Dīvāns Rāy Narāyaṇdās and Kīrpārām
ADDRESSEES: Officers *(mutasadī)* of Vrindaban
GRANTEE: GD
OBJECT: 70 maunds of coal
PROVENANCE: Vrindaban
EFFECTIVE DATE: V.S. 1787
PRECEDING DEED: → V.S. 1782, Mārgaśiras b. 14

DATE: V.S. 1789, Vaiśākha b. 12/ 10 April 1732
TYPE: *sanad*
PROMULGATORS: Dīvāns Rāy Narāyaṇdās and Kīrpārām
ADDRESSEE: Rāmnāth
GRANTEE: GD of Vrindaban
OBJECT: Authority over watchmen at GD temple transferred on the temple custodian
LOCALITY: Vrindaban
EFFECTIVE DATE: as above

DATE: V.S. 1790, Māgha ś. 4/ 27 January 1734
TYPE: *parvānau*
PROMULGATOR: Jaisiṅgh II
ADDRESSEES: Officers *(kamaitī)* of *parganā* Savāī Jaipur
GRANTEE: GD

OBJECT: Revenue realized from 267 *bīghās*, 2 *viśvās* land for *bhog*
PROVENANCE: *parganā* Savāī Jaipur
EFFECTIVE DATE: Bhādrapada ś. 3, V.S. 1790/ 31 August 1733
PRECEDING DEED: Renewal of an unspecified deed which refers to land now submerged in the Mānsarovar lake; present deed assigns land in compensation for it
SUBSEQUENT DEED: [rev.y. 1801/ V.S. 1802, Bhādrapada b. 5 (267 b., 2 v.)], [V.S. 1928, Caitra b. 15 (aggregate grant); cp. 1.2 of that grant)
Note: The locality is not named in the early grants, but it appears later on as Śrīvrīdavapurā *(sic!)* (RSA, Jaipur, File No 1657-28, Mahakmā Khās, 18 March 1959)

UNTRACEABLE
DATE: *V.S. 1791, Āśvina b. 13/ 14 September 1734
SUBSEQUENT DEEDS: → rev.y. 1801/ V.S. 1802, Bhādrapada b. 5 (pasture), [V.S. 1808, Kārttika ś. 12]

UNTRACEABLE
DATE: *V.S. 1792, Pauṣa b. 5/ 23 November 1735
TYPE: *parvānau*
PROMULGATOR: Jaisiṅgh II
GRANTEE: GD
OBJECT: *bhog* and expenses for festivals; daily allowance: 5rp.; yearly allowance: 1,770rp.
SUBSEQUENT DEED: V.S. 1808, Bhādrapada ś. 13

UNTRACEABLE
DATE: *V.S. 1793, Āṣāḍha b. 14/ 26 June 1736
TYPE: *parvānau*
PROMULGATOR: Jaisiṅgh II
GRANTEE: GD
OBJECT: Yearly allowance of 35rp., 6a. ghee for a lamp
SUBSEQUENT DEED: → V.S. 1808, Bhādrapada ś. 13

DATE: V.S. 1797, Māgha b. 5/ 27 December 1740
TYPE: *sanad*
PROMULGATOR: Jaisiṅgh II
ADDRESSEES: "Officers of the Court and the country"
GRANTEE: GD and Gosvāmī Rāmsaraṇ, custodian of GD
OBJECT: *bheṭ*: 1 1/4rp. to be collected in addition to every 1,000rp. of revenue; 1rp. for GD, 1/4rp. for GD's custodian
PROVENANCE: All *parganās* under the authority of Jaisiṅgh II
EFFECTIVE DATE: Beginning of V.S. 1797
SUBSEQUENT DEEDS: [rev.y. 1801/ V.S. 1802, Bhādrapada b. 5 (1 1/4 rp.)], [V.S. 1802, Āśvina b. 14]; the following two docs. are complementary with regard to the *parganās* to which they refer: [V.S. 1806, Jyeṣṭha ś. 10] and [V.S. 1806, day not identified because the document copy is incomplete]; [V.S. 1809/ rev.y. 1808, Āṣāḍha I ś. 11], [V.S. 1825, Māgha ś. 4], [V.S. 1842, Caitra ś. 8a and b]

UNTRACEABLE
DATE: *V.S. 1798/c. 1741 (reported in RSA, Jaipur, File No 1657-28, 17 December 1952)
GRANTEE: GD
OBJECT: *bhog*; revenue grant of 2,400rp. = 1,600rp. net by the eight-month pay-scale

PROVENANCE: Nīmlā, *tapā* Rāmgaṛh, *parganā* Savāī Jaipur (nowadays in Jamvā Rāmgaṛh Tehsil of Jaipur District; India 1983 [DCH Jaipur]:105, serial/code nos 192/130)
SUBSEQUENT DEEDS: *V.S. 1826, Āśvina s. 8; [V.S. 1928, Caitra b. 15 (Nīmlā)]

NOT PUBLISHED
DATE: [rev.y. 1801/V.S. 1802, Bhādrapada b. 5/ 6 August 1745 (Catrapur-vās Khijuryā)]. The document mentions the name of GD's custodian mistakenly as Govindcaraṇ, who was dead by that time.
OBJECT: *bhog*; village formerly held in *jāgīr*; amount as in preceding deed
PRECEDING DEEDS: → V.S. 1764, Śrāvāna b. 3, [V.S. 1767, Āśvina b. 5]
SUBSEQUENT DEEDS: [V.S. 1808, Kārttika ś. 8 (Catrapur-vās Khijuryā)], [V.S. 1928, Caitra b. 15 (aggregate grant)]

DATE: rev.y. 1801/ V.S. 1802, Bhādrapada b. 5/ 6 August 1745 (Gaṅgārāmpuro-vās Khijūryā)
TYPE: *parvānau*, incomplete
PROMULGATOR: Īśvarsiṅgh
ADDRESSEES: Officers *(kamaitī)* of *parganā* Savāī Jaipur
GRANTEE: GD
OBJECT: *bhog*, 700rp. realized revenue
PROVENANCE: Village Gaṅgārāmpuro-vās Khijūryā, *tapā* Khoh, *parganā* Savāī Jaipur
EFFECTIVE DATE: V.S. 1802
PRECEDING DEED: *V.S. 1771, Bhādrapada ś. 4
SUBSEQUENT DEEDS: [V.S. 1808, Kārttika ś. 8 (Gaṅgārāmpuro-vās Khijūryā)], [V.S. 1928, Caitra b. 15 (aggregate grant)]

DATE: rev.y. 1801/ V.S. 1802, Bhādrapada b. 5/ 6 August 1745 (Govindpuro)
TYPE: *parvānau*
PROMULGATOR: Īśvarsiṅgh
ADDRESSEES: Officers *(kamaitī)* of *parganā* Savāī Jaipur
GRANTEE: GD
OBJECT: Revenue allowance for *bhog*, 1,200 rp.
PROVENANCE: Village Govindpur(o), *tapā* Khoh, *parganā* Savāī Jaipur
EFFECTIVE DATE: V.S. 1802
PRECEDING DEEDS: → A.H. 1078, 30 Jumādā II, *A.H. 1112, 1 Jumādā I
SUBSEQUENT DEED: [V.S. 1928, Caitra b. 15 (aggregate grant)]

DATE: rev.y. 1801/ V.S. 1802, Bhādrapada b. 5/ 6 August 1745 (pasture)
TYPE: *parvānau*
PROMULGATOR: Īśvarsiṅgh
ADDRESSEES: Officers *(kamaitī)* of *parganā* Savāī Jaipur
GRANTEE: GD
OBJECT: Pasture land
LOCALITY: Land on Mānsarovar lake
EFFECTIVE DATE: Bhādrapada ś. 3, V.S. 1802
PRECEDING DEED: *V.S. 1771, Āśvina b. 13
SUBSEQUENT DEED: [V.S. 1808, Kārttika ś. 12]

UNTRACEABLE
DATE: *rev.y. 1801/ V.S. 1802, Bhādrapada b. 5/ 6 August 1745 (*sakhī*)
PRECEDING DEED: → V.S. 1784, Āśvina b. 11
SUBSEQUENT DEED: → V.S. 1808, Bhādrapada ś. 13

DATE: rev.y. 1801/ V.S. 1802, Bhādrapada b. 5/ 6 August 1745 (Sālimpur)
TYPE: *parvānau*
PROMULGATOR: Īśvarsiṅgh
ADDRESSEES: Officers *(kamaitī)* of *parganā* Savāī Jaipur
GRANTEE: GD
OBJECT: Realized revenue for *bhog*
PROVENANCE: Village Sālimpur, *parganā* Hiṇḍaun, and 60 *bīghā*s land in *kasbā* Hiṇḍaun
EFFECTIVE DATE: V.S. 1802
PRECEDING DEED: *V.S. 1779, Jyeṣṭha b. 10
SUBSEQUENT DEED: [V.S. 1928, Caitra b. 15 (Sālimpur)]

DATE: rev.y. 1801/ V.S. 1802, Bhādrapada b. 5/ 6 August 1745 (Sekhpuro Baṛo)
TYPE: *parvānau*
PROMULGATOR: Īśvarsiṅgh
ADDRESSEES: Officers *(kamaitī)* of *parganā* Savāī Jaipur
GRANTEE: GD
OBJECT: *punya ūdik*; 1,808rp. out of the total revenue of a village, for festive robes and butter and cream
PROVENANCE: Sekhpuro Baṛo, *parganā* Hiṇḍaun
EFFECTIVE DATE: V.S. 1802
PRECEDING DEED: *V.S. 1774, Jyeṣṭha I ś. 15
SUBSEQUENT DEED: [V.S. 1928, Caitra b. 15 (Sekhpur)]

NOT PUBLISHED
DATE: [rev.y. 1801/V.S. 1802, Bhādrapada b. 5/ 6 August 1745 (1 1/4rp.)]
PROMULGATOR: Īśvarsiṅgh
EFFECTIVE DATE: V.S. 1802
PRECEDING DEED: → V.S. 1797, Māgha b. 5
SUBSEQUENT DEEDS: [V.S. 1802, Āśvina b. 14]; the following two docs. are complementary with regard to the *parganā*s to which they refer: [V.S. 1806, Jyeṣṭha ś. 10] and [V.S. 1806, day not identified because the document copy is incomplete], [V.S. 1809/ rev.y. 1808, Āṣāḍha I ś. 11], [V.S. 1825, Māgha ś. 4], [V.S. 1842, Caitra ś.8 a and b]

NOT PUBLISHED
DATE: [rev.y. 1801/ V.S. 1802, Bhādrapada b. 5/ 6 August 1745 (267 b., 2 v.)]
PROMULGATOR: Īśvarsiṅgh
EFFECTIVE DATE: V.S. 1802
PRECEDING DEED: → V.S. 1790, Māgha ś. 4
SUBSEQUENT DEED: [V.S.. 1808, Kārttika ś. 8]

NOT PUBLISHED
DATE: [V.S. 1802, Āśvina b. 14/ 13 September 1745 (1 1/4 rp.)]
PROMULGATOR: Īśvarsiṅgh
EFFECTIVE DATE: V.S. 1802
PRECEDING DEED: → V.S. 1797, Māgha b. 5, [rev.y. 1801/ V.S. 1802, Bhādrapada b. 5 (1 1/4 rp.)]

SUBSEQUENT DEEDS: The following two docs. are complementary with regard to the *parganās* to which they refer: [V.S. 1806, Jyeṣṭha ś. 10] and [V.S. 1806, day not identified because the document copy is incomplete], [V.S. 1809/ rev.y. 1808, Āṣāḍha I ś. 11], [V.S. 1825, Māgha ś. 4], [V.S. 1842, Caitra ś. 8a and b]

NOT PUBLISHED
DATE: [V.S. 1802, Bhādrapada ś. 8 (Bahura 1996:207)]
EFFECTIVE DATE: as above
PRECEDING DEEDS: *V.S. 1776; → V.S. 1777, Āśvina ś. 14; [rev.y. 1784, Vaiśākha I ś. 15]; [V.S. 1928, Caitra b. 15 (Rājsar Phuṭolāv)]

DATE: V.S. 1805, Māgha ś. 1/ 8 January 1749
TYPE: *sanad,* copper-plate grant
PROMULGATOR: Vṛndāvandās, Mahārājā of Kha[ṇ]ḍelā, on the strength of an order issued by the Court of Jaipur and (the Chief Minister?) Manrām
GRANTEE: GD
OBJECT: Realized revenue of a village as *bheṭ ūdik* for *bhog*; revenue estimate according to RSA, File No 1657-28, doc. no 144, dt. 17-1-1953: 1,000rp.
PROVENANCE: Gordhanpuro, *parganā* Kha[ṇ]ḍelā
EFFECTIVE DATE: as above?
SUBSEQUENT DEED: [V.S. 1928, Caitra b. 15 (Gordhanpuro)]

NOT PUBLISHED
DATE: [V.S. 1806, Jyeṣṭha ś. 10/ 15 May 1749]
PROMULGATOR: Mādhavsiṅgh
EFFECTIVE DATE: V.S. 1806
PRECEDING DEEDS: → V.S. 1797, Māgha b. 5, [rev.y. 1801/ V.S. 1802, Bhādrapada b. 5 (1 1/4 rp.)], [V.S. 1802, Āśvina b. 14];
SUBSEQUENT DEEDS: The present doc., which refers to *parganā* Rāmpurā, and the next one are complementary with regard to the *parganās* to which they refer; [V.S. 1809/ rev.y. 1808, Āṣāḍha I ś. 11], [V.S. 1825, Māgha ś. 4], [V.S. 1842, Caitra ś. 8a and b]
Note: Rāmpurā had been made a fief of Mādhavsiṅgh upon his birth (Sarkār 1984: 190)

NOT PUBLISHED
DATE: [V.S. 1806/c. 1749], day not identified because the document copy is incomplete
PROMULGATOR: Mādhavsiṅgh
EFFECTIVE DATE: unknown because the document copy is deficient for this part
PRECEDING DEEDS: → V.S. 1797, Māgha b. 5, [rev.y. 1801/ V.S. 1802, Bhādrapada b. 5 (1 1/4 rp.)], [V.S. 1802, Āśvina b. 14];
SUBSEQUENT DEEDS: The present doc., which refers to *parganās* Ṭoḍā Bhīm, Mālpurā, Ṭoṃk and Rāmpurā-Khurad, and doc. [V.S. 1806, Jyeṣṭa ś. 10] are complementary with regard to the *parganās* to which they refer; [V.S. 1809/ rev.y. 1808, Āṣāḍha I ś. 11], [V.S. 1825, Māgha ś. 4], [V.S. 1842, Caitra ś. 8a and b]
Note: Some, if not all of the *parganās* referred to in the document are territories given to Mādhavsiṅgh in a treaty with Īśvarsiṅgh in 1744 (Sarkār 1984: 230)

DATE: V.S. 1808, Bhādrapada ś. 13/ 23 August 1751
TYPE: *parvānau*
PROMULGATOR: Mādhavsiṅgh
ADDRESSEES: Officers *(kamaitī)* of *kasbā* Savāī Jaipur
GRANTEE: GD (Kanak-Vṛndāvan)

OBJECT: *tankhāh punya* (charitable income), entire revenue of a village for festival expenses, *bhog* etc., 2,558rp.
PROVENANCE: Govindpur-vās Hāthyod, *kasbā* Savāī Jaipur
EFFECTIVE DATE: V.S. 1808
PRECEDING DEEDS:*V.S. 1792, Pauṣa b. 5 (1,770rp.), *rev.y. 1801/ V.S. 1802, Bhādrapada b. 5 (*sakhī*) (cp. this one for another further preceding deed), *undated (338rp.,10 a.), *undated (60 rp.), *V.S. 1793, Āṣāḍha b. 14 (35rp., 6a.)
SUBSEQUENT DEED: [V.S. 1928, Caitra b. 15 (aggregate grant)]

NOT PUBLISHED
DATE: [V.S. 1808, Kārttika ś. 8/ 16 October 1751 (Catrapur-vās Khijuryā)]
PROMULGATOR: Mādhavsiṅgh
EFFECTIVE DATE: V.S. 1807
PRECEDING DEEDS: → V.S. 1764, Śrāvaṇa b. 3, [V.S. 1767, Āśvina b. 5], [rev.y. 1801/ V.S. 1802, Bhādrapada b. 5 (Catrapur-vās Khijuryā)]
SUBSEQUENT DEEDS:[V.S. 1928, Caitra b. 15 (aggregate grant)]

NOT PUBLISHED
DATE: [V.S. 1808, Kārttika ś. 8 (Gaṅgārāmpuro-vās Khijūryā)]
PROMULGATOR: Mādhavsiṅgh
PRECEDING DEEDS: *V.S. 1771, Bhādrapada ś.4, → rev.y. 1801/ V.s. 1802, Bhādrapada b. 5
SUBSEQUENT DEED: [V.S. 1928, Caitra b. 15 (aggregate grant)]

NOT PUBLISHED
DATE: [V.S. 1808, Kārttika ś. 8/ 16 October 1751 (Sālimpur)]
PROMULGATOR: Mādhavsiṅgh
EFFECTIVE DATE: V.S. 1807
PRECEDING DEEDS: *V.S. 1779, Jyeṣṭha b. 10, , [rev.y. 1801/ V.S. 1802, Bhādrapada b. 5 (Sālimpur)]
SUBSEQUENT DEED: [V.S. 1928, Caitra b. 15 (Sālimpur)]

NOT PUBLISHED
DATE: [V.S. 1808, Kārttika ś. 12/ 20 October 1751 (pasture)]
EFFECTIVE DATE: V.S. 1807
PRECEDING DEEDS: *V.S. 1771, Āśvina b. 13, → rev.y. 1801/ V.S. 1802, Bhādrapada b. 5 (pasture)

UNTRACEABLE
DATE: *V.S. 1808/ c. 1751
PROMULGATOR: Mādhavsiṅgh
GRANTEE: GD
OBJECT: *bheṭ* of annually 700 maunds of salt
PROVENANCE: Sāmbhar
SUBSEQUENT DEEDS: → V.S. 1816, Bhādrapada ś. 9, [V.S. 1818, Mārgaśiras ś. 2]

NOT PUBLISHED
DATE: [V.S. 1809/ rev.y. 1808, Āṣāḍha I ś. 11/ 11 June 1752]
PROMULGATOR: Mādhavsiṅgh
EFFECTIVE DATE: V.S. 1808
PRECEDING DEEDS: → V.S. 1797, Māgha b. 5, [rev.y. 1801/ V.S. 1802, Bhādrapada b. 5 (1 1/4 rp.)], [V.S. 1802, Āśvina b. 14]; the following two docs. are complementary with

regard to the *parganās* to which they refer: [V.S. 1866, Jyeṣṭha ś. 10] and [V.S. 1806, day not identified because the document copy is incomplete]
SUBSEQUENT DEEDS: [V.S. 1825, Māgha ś. 4], [V.S. 1842, Caitra ś. 8a and b]

DATE: V.S. 1816, Bhādrapada ś. 9/ 1 September 1759
TYPE: *sanad*
PROMULGATORS: Dīvāns Kanhīrām and Nandlāl (Jaipur)
ADDRESSEES: *āmils* of *parganā* Sāmbhar
GRANTEE: GD and GD's custodian
OBJECT: *bheṭ* of 700 maunds of salt
PROVENANCE: Sāmbhar
EFFECTIVE DATE: as above
PRECEDING DEED: *V.S. 1808
SUBSEQUENT DEED: [V.S. 1818, Mārgaśiras ś. 2]

NOT PUBLISHED
DATE: [V.S. 1818, Mārgaśiras ś. 2/ 28 November 1761]
PROMULGATOR: Mādhavsiṅgh
EFFECTIVE DATE: V.S. 1818
PRECEDING DEEDS: *V.S. 1808, → V.S. 1816, Bhādrapada ś. 9

DATE: V.S. 1822, Pauṣa ś. 14/ 26 December 1765
TYPE: Warrant
PROMULGATOR: Rāmsiṅgh (Rāṭhaur)
ADDRESSEE: Kabaṇīga[?]r (?) Mhaimad Sā
GRANTEE: GD
OBJECT: Delivery of salt must not be hindered
PROVENANCE: [Sāmbhar]
EFFECTIVE DATE: as above
Cp. docs. V.S. 1835, Māgha b. 8; *ab* V.S. 1836

DATE: V.S. 1825, Māgha b. 15/ 6 February 1769
TYPE: *sanad*
PROMULGATOR: Prince Bakhtāvarsiṅgh Rajāvat (Alvar)
ADDRESSEE: Gosvāmī Nīlāmbar, custodian of GD
GRANTEE: GD
OBJECT: *bheṭ*, realized revenue of a village for *bhog*
PROVENANCE: Village Rāmsar, *parganā* Livālī
EFFECTIVE DATE: as above
SUBSEQUENT DEEDS: [V.S. 1842, Caitra ś. 8 (b)], [V.S. 1928, Caitra b. 15 (Rāmsar)]
Cp. also doc. [V.S. 1825, Māgha ś. 3].

DATE: V.S. 1825, Māgha ś. 3/ 9 February 1769
TYPE: *sanad*
PROMULGATOR: Prince Bakhtāvarsiṅgh (Alvar)
ADDRESSEE: Gosvāmī Nīlāmbar, custodian of GD
GRANTEE: GD
OBJECT: Village Rāmsar, *parganā* Livālī, assigned for *bhog*; management of revenue collection of this village entrusted to Nīlāmbar
PROVENANCE: Village Rāmsar, *parganā* Livālī
EFFECTIVE DATE: as above?

Cp. also the document of V.S. 1825, Māgha b. 15.

NOT PUBLISHED
DATE: [V.S. 1825, Māgha ś. 4/ 10 February 1769]
PROMULGATOR: Pṛthvīsiṅgh
EFFECTIVE DATE: V.S. 1825
PRECEDING DEEDS: → V.S. 1797, Māgha b. 5, [rev.y. 1801/ V.S. 1802, Bhādrapada b. 5 (1 1/4 rp.)], [V.S. 1802, Āśvina b. 14]; the following two docs. are complementary with regard to the *parganā*s to which they refer: [V.S. 1806, Jyeṣṭha ś. 10] and [V.S. 1806, day not identified because the document copy is incomplete]; [V.S. 1809/ rev.y. 1808, Āṣāḍha I ś. 11]
SUBSEQUENT DEED: [V.S. 1842, Caitra ś. 8a and b]

UNTRACEABLE
DATE: *V.S. 1826, Āśvina ś. 8/ 8 October 1769
GRANTEE: GD
OBJECT: *bhog*; original grant now in *ijārau istamurārī (sic!)*[3]; *ijārau* rate: 1,750rp. for V.S. 1826 and 1,800rp. from 1826 onwards
PROVENANCE: Nīmlā, *tapā* Rāmgaṛh, *parganā* Savāī Jaipur
EFFECTIVE DATE: ?
PRECEDING DEED: *V.S. 1798
SUBSEQUENT DEED: [V.S. 1928, Caitra b. 15 (Nīmlā)]

DATE: V.S. 1828, Vaiśākha b. 4/ 3 April 1771
TYPE: *sanad*
PROMULGATOR: *dīvān* of Rāmsiṅgh (Rāṭhaur)
ADDRESSEES: *paṭel*s and *paṭvārī*s of *kasbā* Savāī Jaipur
GRANTEE: GD
OBJECT: Revenue income from 39 *bīghā*s *khālsā* land for *bhog*
PROVENANCE: Village Atharohī, *kasbā* Savāī Jaipur (the name of the village is normally spelt "Hatharohī")
EFFECTIVE DATE: Hot season harvest of V.S. 1828
SUBSEQUENT DEED: [V.S. 1928, Caitra b. 15 (aggregate grant)]

DATE: V.S. 1833, Kārttika b. 14/ 10 November 1776
TYPE: Order
PROMULGATOR: Rājā Balvantsiṅgh
ADDRESSEE: Not mentioned
GRANTEE: Gosvāmī Nīlāmbar, custodian of GD
OBJECT: Management of the revenue matters entrusted to Nīlāmbar
LOCALITY: Village Karārīyā, *parganā* Gugaur
EFFECTIVE DATE: as above

DATE: V.S. 1835, Māgha b. 10/ 12 January 1779
TYPE: *sanad,* incomplete
PROMULGATOR: Mahārājā Vijaisiṅgh (Jodhpur)
ADDRESSEE: Balrām, custodian of GD
GRANTEE: GD
OBJECT: *bhog*, 100 rp. annual allowance

[3]For *ijārau istamrārī*, cp. Singh 1990:129-34.

EFFECTIVE DATE: ?
SUBSEQUENT DEED: [V.S. 1840, Caitra ś. 8], cp. also → V.S. 1860, Āṣāḍha ś. 9

DATE: *ab* V.S. 1836/ *ab* c. 1779
TYPE: *sanad*
PROMULGATOR: Dīvān Sirdārmal (Jodhpur)
ADDRESSEEs: Upādhyāy Pt. Rāmbagas and Bhaṃ[ḍārī?] Pratāpmal in Sāmbhar
GRANTEE: GD
OBJECT: 750 maunds of salt for GD to be sent to the *dīvān*
PROVENANCE: Sāmbhar
EFFECTIVE DATE: as above
PRECEDING DEEDS: →V.S. 1816, Māgha b. 8, → V.S. 1836, Māgha ś. 8
SUBSEQUENT DEEDS: *V.S. 1856, Jyeṣṭha b. 1, *V.S. 1857, Āśvina b. 1, → V.S. 1860, Āṣāḍha ś. 8, → V.S. 1878, Kārttika ś. 5

DATE: V.S. 1836, Māgha b. 8/ 29 January 1780
TYPE: *sanad*
PROMULGATOR: (from Jodhpur)
ADDRESSEE: Gopīnāth Agarvālau
GRANTEE: GD
OBJECT: 750 maunds of salt
PROVENANCE: Sāmbhar
EFFECTIVE DATE: as above
SUBSEQUENT DEEDS: → *ab* V.S. 1836, *V.S. 1856, Jyeṣṭha ś. 8, *V.S. 1857, Āśvina b. 1, → V.S. 1860, Āṣāḍha ś. 8, → V.S. 1878, Kārttika ś. 5

DATE: V.S. 1839, Jyeṣṭha II b. 15/ 11 June 1782
TYPE: Letter
PROMULGATOR: Written on behalf of Rājā Kisordās
ADDRESSEE: Gosvāmī Kṛṣṇaśaraṇ, custodian of GD
OBJECT: Administration of the land of Kiśordās
LOCALITY: Vrindaban
EFFECTIVE DATE: as above

DATE: *ab* V.S. 1839 (date of year not on photograph), Āṣāḍha ś. 15/ *ab* 1782
TYPE: Letter, incomplete
PROMULGATOR: Written on behalf of Rājā Rādhikādās
ADDRESSEE: Kṛṣṇaśaraṇ, custodian of GD
OBJECT: Confirmation of receipt of a robe of honour

DATE: rev.y. 1839, Āṣāḍha b. 5/ 19 June 1783
TYPE: *parvānau*
PROMULGATOR: Pratāpsiṅgh
ADDRESSEES: Officers *(kamaitī)* of *parganā* Savāī Jaipur
GRANTEE: GD
OBJECT: *sivāy rāhdārī* (toll-tax) assigned for *bhog* etc.
PROVENANCE: *kasbā* Jaitpuro, *parganā* Savāī Jaipur
EFFECTIVE DATE: V.S. 1840
PRECEDING DEED: Referred to but untraceable and undated

NOT PUBLISHED
DATE: [V.S. 1840, Caitra ś. 8/ 10 April 1783]
TYPE: *sanad*
PROMULGATOR: Pratāpsiṅgh
PRECEDING DEED: → V.S. 1835, Māgha b. 10 (of which doc. [V.S. 1840, Caitra ś. 8] is a *verbatim* repetition)
SUBSEQUENT DEED: (Related) → V.S. 1860, Āṣāḍha ś. 9

DATE: V.S. 1840, Āśvina b. 10/ 21 September 1783
TYPE: *parvānau*
PROMULGATOR: Pratāpsiṅgh
ADDRESSEES: Officers *(kamaitī)* of *kasbā* Savāī Jaipur
GRANTEE: GD
OBJECT: *bheṭ*, 13 shops
LOCALITY: *kasbā* Savāī Jaipur
EFFECTIVE DATE: Caitra ś. 3, rev.y. 1839
SUBSEQUENT DEED: [V.S. 2006, Phālguṇa b. 7]

NOT PUBLISHED
DATE: [V.S. 1842, Caitra ś. 8 (a)/ 6 April 1786]
TYPE: *sanad*; bilingual: Rājasthānī and Marāṭhī
PROMULGATOR: *sarkār* of Mādhorāv Sinde, Peśvā (1774-96), since 1784 also Provincial Governor of Delhi and Agra
ADDRESSEES: *āmil*s and officers *(mutasaddiyāṃ)* of the *parganā*s of the territory of Jaipur
PRECEDING DEEDS: → V.S. 1797, Māgha b. 5, [rev.y. 1801/ V.S. 1802, Bhādrapada b. 5 (1 1/4 rp.)], [V.S. 1802, Āśvina b. 14/ 13 September 1745 (1 1/4 rp.)]; the following two documents are complementary with regard to the *parganās* to which they refer: [V.S. 1806, Jyeṣṭha ś. 10] and [V.S. 1806, day not identified because the document copy is incomplete], [V.S. 1809/ rev.y. 1808, Āṣāḍha I ś. 11], [V.S. 1825, Māgha ś. 4]

NOT PUBLISHED
DATE: [V.S. 1842, Caitra ś. 8 (b)/ 6 April 1786]
TYPE: *sanad*; bilingual: Rājasthānī and Marāṭhī
PROMULGATOR: *sarkār* of Mādhorāv Sinde, Peśvā (1774-96), since 1784 also Provincial Governor of Delhi and Agra
ADDRESSEES: *āmils* of the *parganā*s of the territory of Jaipur
GRANTEE: GD
OBJECT: One village for *bhog* (that is, realized revenue of the village concerned)
PROVENANCE: Village Rāmsar, *parganā* Nivālī
EFFECTIVE DATE: as above?
PRECEDING DEED: → V.S. 1825, Māgha b. 15
SUBSEQUENT DEED: [V.S. 1928, Caitra b. 15 (Rāmsar)]

DATE: V.S. 1843a, Śrāvaṇa b. 13/ 23 July 1786
TYPE: Letter
PROMULGATOR: Pratāpsiṅgh
ADDRESSEE: *sarkār* of Mādhorāv Sinde, Peśvā , since 1784 also Provincial Governor of Delhi and Agra
OBJECT: Gosvāmī Dhīrajlāl is trying to sell land given as a religious donation to GD by the Kachavāhās
LOCALITY: Vrindaban

SUBSEQUENT DEED: → V.S. 1848, Bhādrapada b. 7
Cp. the next document.

DATE: V.S. 1843b, Śrāvaṇa b. 13/ 23 July 1786
TYPE: Warrant
PROMULGATOR: [Pratāpsiṅgh]
ADDRESSEES: All the Gosvāmīs of Vrindaban
OBJECT: Gosvāmī Dhīrajlāl is trying to sell land given as a charity to GD by the Kachavāhās; he must be discouraged from tampering with the land
LOCALITY: Vrindaban
SUBSEQUENT DEED: → V.S. 1848, Bhādrapada b. 7
Cp. the preceding document.

NOT PUBLISHED
DATE: [rev.y. 1846, Āṣāḍha I b. 2 (the document is, however, erroneously dated "V.S. 1846"/ 30 May 1790]
TYPE: *sanad*
PROMULGATOR: Dīvāns Bhāgcand and Bhavānīdās
ADDRESSEE: *āmil* of *parganā* Nivāī
GRANTEE: Kuñjbihārī temple
OBJECT: 354rp. for *bhog*
PROVENANCE: Part of the revenue of village Jugalpuro Khurd, *parganā* Nivāī
SUBSEQUENT DEED: [V.S. 1928, Caitra b. 15 (Jugalpuro)]

DATE: V.S. 1848, Bhādrapada b. 7/ 21 August 1791
TYPE: *dastak*
PROMULGATOR: Pahāṛsiṅgh Khangaṛvat, [Chief Minister of Pratāpsiṅgh?]
ADDRESSEES: *jamīndārs* and inhabitants of Vrindaban market
OBJECT: Warning that they must not allow the land of the place to be sold
LOCALITY: Vrindaban
PRECEDING DEEDS: → V.S. 1843a and b, both Śrāvaṇa b. 13

DATE: V.S. 1850, Pauṣa ś. 10/ 11 January 1794
TYPE: *yādidāsati*
PROMULGATOR: [Jaipur Chancery]
GRANTEE: Gosvāmī Kṛṣṇaśaraṇ, custodian of GD
OBJECT: *punya* (charitable gift) of 1,500 rp. on the occasion of the custodian's daughter's wedding
EFFECTIVE DATE: after endorsement

DATE: V.S. 1852, Kārttika ś. 5/ 16 November 1795
TYPE: Report
PROMULGATOR: Mahant Mansārām
OBJECT: Floor of Govind Ghāṭ built by himself and Mathurādās
LOCALITY: Vrindaban

UNTRACEABLE
DATE: *V.S. 1856, Jyeṣṭha b. 1/ 20 May 1799
PRECEDING DEEDS: → V.S. 1836, Māgha b. 8, → *ab* V.S. 1836
SUBSEQUENT DEEDS: *V.S. 1857, Āśvina b. 1, → V.S. 1860, Āṣāḍha ś. 8, → V.S. 1878, Kārttika ś. 5

UNTRACEABLE
DATE: *V.S. 1857, Āśvina b. 1/ 4 September 1800
PRECEDING DEEDS: → V.S. 1836, Māgha b. 8, → *ab* V.S. 1836, *V.S. 1856, Jyeṣṭha b. 1
SUBSEQUENT DEED: → V.S. 1878, Āṣāḍha ś. 8

NOT PUBLISHED
DATE: [V.S. 1860, Āṣāḍha ś. 8/ 27 June 1803]
TYPE: *sanad*
PROMULGATOR: Dīvān Gyānmal (Jodhpur)
ADDRESSEES: Saṃ[gahī] Tejmal and Kuṃ[var] Gulrāj in Sāmbhar
OBJECT: 750 maunds of salt for GD shall be sent to Gyānmal
PROVENANCE: Sāmbhar
EFFECTIVE DATE: as above
PRECEDING DEEDS: →V.S. 1816, Māgha b. 8, → V.S. 1836, Māgha ś. 8, → *ab* V.S. 1836, *V.S. 1856, Jyeṣṭha b. 1
SUBSEQUENT DEED: → V.S. 1878, Kārttika ś. 5

DATE: V.S. 1860, Āṣāḍha ś. 9/ 28 June 1803
TYPE: *sanad*
PROMULGATOR: Dīvān Gyānmal (Jodhpur)
ADDRESSEES: Saṃ[gahī] Tejmal and Kuṃ[var] Gulrāj in Sāmbhar
OBJECT: Annual allowance of 100 rp. for *bhog* of GD to be sent with the brahmin Naval
PROVENANCE: Sāmbhar
EFFECTIVE DATE: as above
PRECEDING DEEDS: (Probably connected) → V.S. 1835, Māgha b. 10 and [V.S. 1840, Caitra ś. 8]

DATE: V.S. 1860, Māgha b. 2/ 30 December 1803
TYPE: *parvānau*
PROMULGATOR: Jagatsiṅgh
ADDRESSEES: Officers *(kamaitī)* of *kasbā* Savāī Jaipur
GRANTEE: GD
OBJECT: *bhog* etc. for a *sakhī* of GD's consort, 379 rp., 8 a.
PROVENANCE: Kalyāṇpur-vās and Jasodānand-vās of village Syosiṅghpurā, *tapā* Khoh, *parganā* Savāī Jaipur
EFFECTIVE DATE: Cold season harvest of V.S. 1860
SUBSEQUENT DEED: [V.S. 1995, Āṣāḍha ś.15]

DATE: V.S. 1860, Māgha b. 7/ 4 January 1804
TYPE: *parvānau*
PROMULGATOR: Jagatsiṅgh
ADDRESSEES: Officers *(kamaitī)* of *parganā* Savāī Jaipur
GRANTEE: Harlāl Gūjar, s/o Cuḍāmaṇi
OBJECT: *inām*, 50 *bīghā*s garden land
LOCALITY: Village Mānpur Saḍho, *kasbā* Jaipur
EFFECTIVE DATE: Hot season harvest of V.S. 1860

DATE: V.S. 1863, Kārttika b. 3/ 30 October 1806
TYPE: Letter
PROMULGATOR: Kṛṣṇaśaraṇdev Śarmā, custodian of GD
ADDRESSEE: Rāy Rāmsiṅgh

OBJECT: Solicits confirmation that 135 *bīghas* land etc. in Vrindaban are under his authority
LOCALITY: [Dosaich and Dholera near Vrindaban]
PRECEDING DEEDS: [*farmāns* of Akbar and Śāh Jahān of Ilāhī Year 43 (A.D. 1598/1599) and A.D. 1633, resp.]; → A.H. 1108, 22 [Rabī'] II/ November(?) 1696, → V.S. 1767, Mārgaśiras b. 3

DATE: V.S. 1868, Mārgaśiras b. 14/ 15 November 1811
TYPE: Message
PROMULGATOR: Jagatsiṅgh
ADDRESSEE: Gosvāmī Rāmnārāyaṇ, custodian of GD
OBJECT: 30,000 rp. borrowed from the addressee will be refunded
LOCALITY: [Jaipur]

DATE: V.S. 1869, Caitra ś. 1/ 14 March 1812
TYPE: *dastak*
PROMULGATOR: *dīvān*(s) of Jaipur, probably Amarcand Pāṭnī and Kṛpārām Chābṛā
ADDRESSEES: *paṭel*s and *paṭvārī*s of *kasbā* Savāī Jaipur etc.
GRANTEE: Candū, Baḍāraṇi
OBJECT: *inām*, 50 *bīghā*s garden land
LOCALITY: On the Amber road and in village Hathrohī
EFFECTIVE DATE: Cold season harvest of V.S. 1869
SUBSEQUENT DEED: → *ab* V.S. 1872
Note: For a grant in Hathrohī cp. also → V.S. 1828, Vaiśākha b. 4

DATE: rev.y. 1869, Jyeṣṭha ś. 13/ 22 June 1812
TYPE: *parvānau*
PROMULGATOR: Jagatsiṅgh
ADDRESSEES: Officers *(kamaitī)* of *parganā* Cāṭsū
GRANTEE: GD
OBJECT: Revenue for *bhog*, 6,288rp.
PROVENANCE: Village Kirpārāmpurā and Ākoḍyā Burakh, affiliate village or villages, of village Śrīkisnapuro, *parganā* Cāṭsū
EFFECTIVE DATE: V.S. 1865 (that is, the *parvānau* is retroactive by 4 years)
SUBSEQUENT DEED: [V.S. 1928, Caitra b. 15 (Srīkīsanpuro) and (Kīrapārāmpuro)]

DATE: *ab* V.S. 1872/ *ab* c. 1815
TYPE: Letter
PROMULGATOR: Candū, Baḍāraṇī
ADDRESSEE: Gosvāmī Rāmnārāyaṇ, custodian of GD
GRANTEE: GD
OBJECT: *bheṭ*, 50 *bīghā*s garden land
LOCALITY: In *kasbā* Savāī Jaipur and in village Hathrohī, *kasbā* Savāī Jaipur
EFFECTIVE DATE: Vaiśākha ś. 15, V.S. 1872
PRECEDING DEEDS: → V.S. 1869, Caitra ś. 1

NOT PUBLISHED
DATE: [V.S. 1878, Kārttika ś. 5/ 31 October 1821]
TYPE: *sanad*
PROMULGATOR: Phaterāj Siṃghvī, official (minister?) of Jaipur
ADDRESSEES: Siṃghvī Sujāṇmal and Uttamrām Āsopā
GRANTEE: GD

OBJECT: 750 maunds of salt; these shall be delivered to the writer
PROVENANCE: Sāmbhar
EFFECTIVE DATE: as above
PRECEDING DEEDS: → V.S. 1836, Māgha b. 8, → *ab* V.S. 1836, *V.S. 1856, Jyeṣṭha b. 1 (*sanad*), *V.S. 1857, Āśvina b. 1, → V.S. 1860, Āṣāḍha ś. 8

UNTRACEABLE
DATE: *V.S. 1928, Vaiśākha b. 4/ 9 April 1871
TYPE: *parvānau*
PROMULGATOR: Collector, Jaipur State
ADDRESSEE: Not mentioned; *parvānau* issued on the strength of a *dastag* issued by Pt. Motīlāl on Kārttika b. 14, V.S. 1928
GRANTEE: GD
OBJECT: 5 *bīghā*s of land [for *bhog*]
LOCALITY: Village Kūkas, *tapā* Havelī, *parganā* Savāī Jaipur. The village lies in the present-day Jamvā Rāmgaṛh Tehsil of Jaipur District (India 1983 (DCH Jaipur): 105, serial code nos 160/59).
EFFECTIVE DATE: Not mentioned
PRECEDING DEED: Not mentioned. The present, untraceable document is referred to in a table of 1953 which lists the villages granted to GD for *bhog* and verified by the State of Rajasthan (RSA, File No 1657-28, Central Record, Dīvānī Hujūrī, 17 January 1953). However, when the grants were verified again in 1959, Kūkas was not verified (RSA, File No 1657-28, Superintendent, Devani Huzuri Daftar and Jaipur Secretariat Records, 18 March 1959).

UNTRACEABLE
DATE: *V.S. 1928, Vaiśākha b. 4/ 9 April 1871
GRANTEE: GD
OBJECT: Village revenue for *bhog*
PROVENANCE: Kūkas, *parganā* Amber *alias* Kūkas, *tapā* Havelī, *parganā* Amber; nowadays in Jamvā Rāmgaṛh Tehsil of Jaipur District (India 1983 (DCH Jaipur): 105, serial/code nos 160/59)

NOT PUBLISHED
DATE: [V.S. 1928, Caitra b. 15/ 7 April 1872 (aggregate grant)]
TYPE: *kāgaj*
PROMULGATOR: Pt. Motilāl
ADDRESSEE: *nāzim* of *zilā* Savāī Jaipur
GRANTEE: GD
OBJECT: Renewal of several grants for *bhog*, namely
(1) In village Hathrohī, *tapā* Hathlī, *kasbā* Savāī Jaipur (in modern times Hathrohī merged with the city of Jaipur)
(1.1) Govindpurā-Khurd-bās Hāthod
(1.2) Hilly land in Śrīvrīdavanpurā
(2) In several villages of *tapā* Khoh, *kasbā* Sāṃgāner
(2.1) Govindpurā Bujarg
(2.2) Gaṅgārāmpurā-bās Khījūrā
(2.3) Catrapurā-vās Khījūrā
(2.4) Sosīghpurā-vās Kīlāṇpurā

PRECEDING DEEDS:
(1.1) → V.S. 1808, Bhādrapada ś. 13
(1.2) Not referred to; supposedly this is the pasture land consisting of 267 *bīghās*, 2 *viśvās* covered by docs. V.S. 1790, Māgha ś. 8 foll., which is classified as "hilly land, low land, etc."
(2.1) → A.H. 1078, 30 Jumādā II, *A.H. 1112, 1 Jumādā I, → rev.y. 1801/V.S. 1802, Bhādrapada b. 5 (Govindpuro)
(2.2) *V.S. 1771, Bhādrapada ś. 4, → rev.y. 1801/V.S. 1802, Bhādrapada b. 5 (Gaṅgārāmpuro-vās Khijuryā), [V.S. 1808, Kārttika ś. 8 (Gaṅgārāmpuro-vās Khijuryā)
(2.3) → V.S. 1764, Śrāvaṇa b. 3, [V.S. 1767, Āśvina b. 5], rev.y. 1801/V.S. 1802, Bhādrapada b. 5 (Catrapur-vās Khijuryā)], [V.S. 1808, Kārttika ś. 8 (Catrapur-vās Khijuryā)](2.4) → V.S. 1860, Māgha b. 2
EFFECTIVE DATE: Hot season harvest of V.S. 1928

NOT PUBLISHED
DATE: [V.S. 1928, Caitra b. 15/ 7 April 1872 (Bicūṇ)]
TYPE: *dastag*
PROMULGATOR: Mahakmā Dīvāṇī, Jaipur State, reign of Rāmsiṅgh II
ADDRESSEES: *paṭel*s and *paṭvārī*s of Bicūṇ
GRANTEE: GD
OBJECT: 1 house
LOCALITY: Village Bicūṇ, *tapā* Bharānā, *parganā* Mojābād (in the present day Phulerā Tehsil of Jaipur District; see India 1983 (DCH Jaipur): 152, serial/code nos 9/65)
EFFECTIVE DATE: Hot season harvest of V.S. 1928
PRECEDING DEEDS: Not referred to, but the document states that it is a renewal of an earlier deed

NOT PUBLISHED
DATE: [V.S. 1928, Caitra b. 15/ 7 April 1872 (Coru)]
TYPE: *dastag*
PROMULGATOR: Mahakmā Dīvāṇī, Jaipur State, reign of Rāmsiṅgh II
ADDRESSEES: *paṭel*s and *paṭvārī*s of village Coru
GRANTEE: GD
OBJECT: Realized revenue of one village for *bhog*
PROVENANCE: Village Coru, *parganā* Phāgī (present-day Cauru in Phāgī Tehsil of Jaipur District; India 1983 (DCH Jaipur): 257, serial/code nos 23/35)
EFFECTIVE DATE: Hot season harvest of V.S. 1928
PRECEDING DEEDS: Not referred to, but the document is stated to be a renewal

NOT PUBLISHED
DATE: [V.S. 1928, Caitra b. 15/ 7 April 1872 (Dayālpuro)]
TYPE: *dastag*
PROMULGATOR: Mahakmā Dīvāṇī, Jaipur State, reign of Rāmsiṅgh II
ADDRESSEES: *paṭel* and *paṭvārī*s of Dayālpuro
EFFECTIVE DATE: Hot season harvest of V.S. 1928
PRECEDING DEED: → V.S. 1774, Jyeṣṭha ś. 15

NOT PUBLISHED
DATE: [V.S. 1928, Caitra b. 15/ 7 April 1872 (Gordhanpuro)]
TYPE: *dastag*

PROMULGATOR: Mahakmā Dīvāṇī, Jaipur State, reign of Rāmsiṅgh II
ADDRESSEES: *paṭel* and *paṭvārīs* of Gordhanpuro, *parganā* Khaṇḍelā
EFFECTIVE DATE: Hot season harvest of V.S. 1928
PRECEDING DEED: → V.S. 1805, Māgha ś. 1

UNTRACEABLE
DATE: *V.S. 1928, Caitra b. 15/ 7 April 1872 (Jāhautā)
TYPE: *kāgaj*
PROMULGATOR: Pt. Motīlāl
PRECEDING DEED: → A.H. 1072, 15 Śavvāl/Āṣāḍha b.3, V.S. 1719

NOT PUBLISHED
DATE: [V.S. 1928, Caitra b. 15/ 7 April 1872 (Jugalpurā)]
TYPE: *dastag*
PROMULGATOR: Mahakmā Dīvāṇī, Jaipur State, reign of Rāmsiṅgh II
ADDRESSEES: *paṭels* and *paṭvārīs* of village Jugalpurā
GRANTEE: GD
OBJECT: Realized revenue of one village for *bhog*
PROVENANCE: Village Jugalpurā, *parganā* Nivāī (in doc. RSA, File No 1657-28, doc. nos 111-112 this is specified as Jugalpurā Khu[rd]; the village lies in Nivāī Tehsil of Tonk District, see India 1983 (DCH Tonk): 25, serial/code nos 97/83)
EFFECTIVE DATE: Hot season harvest of V.S. 1928
PRECEDING DEED: Not referred to, but the document is stated to be a renewal of an earlier deed, which is probably connected with [rev.y. 1846, Āṣāḍha b.2]

NOT PUBLISHED
DATE: [V.S. 1928, Caitra b. 15/ 7 April 1872 (Kīrapārāmpuro)]
TYPE: *dastag*
PROMULGATOR: Mahakmā Dīvāṇī, Jaipur State, reign of Rāmsiṅgh II
ADDRESSEES: *paṭels* and *paṭvārīs* of Kīrapārāmpuro
GRANTEE: GD
EFFECTIVE DATE: Hot season harvest of V.S. 1928
PRECEDING DEED: → rev.y. 1869, Jyeṣṭha ś. 13
Cp. also doc. [V.S. 1928, Caitra b. 15 (Srīkīsanpuro)]

NOT PUBLISHED
DATE: [V.S. 1928, Caitra b. 15/ 7 April 1872 (Maū Khās)]
TYPE: *dastag*
PROMULGATOR: Mahakmā Dīvāṇī, Jaipur State, reign of Rāmsiṅgh II
ADDRESSEES: *paṭels* and *paṭvārīs* of village Maū Khās
GRANTEE: GD
OBJECT: Realized revenue of one village for *bhog*
PROVENANCE: Village Maū Khās, Ghoṃslā Tehsil, *parganā* Hiṇḍaun; the village lies in modern Hiṇḍaun Tehsil of Sawai Madhopur District; see India 1983 (DCH Sawai Mādhopur): 43, serial/code nos 85/17)
EFFECTIVE DATE: Hot season harvest of V.S. 1928
PRECEDING DEED: Not referred to, but the document seems to be connected with a deed of V.S. 1774, Mārgaśiras ś. 1, which was renewed in rev.y. 1801/V.S. 1802, Bhādrapada b. 5. That deed was, however, issued in favour of the Rādhāmādhavjī temple.

NOT PUBLISHED
DATE: [V.S. 1928, Caitra b. 15/ 7 April 1872 (Nīmlā)]
TYPE: *dastag*
PROMULGATOR: Mahakmā Dīvāṇī, Jaipur State, reign of Rāmsiṅgh II
ADDRESSEES: *paṭels* and *paṭvārīs* of village Nīmlā
GRANTEE: GD
OBJECT: Realized revenue of one village for *bhog*
PROVENANCE: Nīmlā, *tapā* Rāmgaṛh, *parganā* Savāī Jaipur; the village lies in the modern Jamvā Rāmgaṛh Tehsil of Jaipur District (India 1983 (DCH Jaipur): 105, serial/code nos 192/130)
EFFECTIVE DATE: Hot season harvest of V.S. 1928
PRECEDING DEEDS: *V.S. 1798; *V.S. 1826, Āśvina ś. 8

NOT PUBLISHED
DATE: [V.S. 1928, Caitra b. 15/ 7 April 1872 (Rājsar Phuṭolāv)]
TYPE: *dastag*
PROMULGATOR: Mahakmā Dīvāṇī, Jaipur State, Rāmsiṅgh II
ADDRESSEES: *paṭels* and *paṭvārīs* of Rājsar Phuṭolāv
GRANTEE: GD
EFFECTIVE DATE: Hot season harvest of V.S. 1928
PRECEDING DEEDS: *V.S. 1776, → V.S. 1777, Āśvina ś. 14, [rev.y. 1784, Vaiśākha I ś. 15 (Horstmann 1995)]

NOT PUBLISHED
DATE: [V.S. 1928, Caitra b. 15/ 7 April 1872 (Rāmsar)]
TYPE: *dastag*
PROMULGATOR: Mīrjā Gūlām Aimad Beg
ADDRESSEES: *paṭels* and *paṭvārīs* of Rāmsar
GRANTEE: GD
EFFECTIVE DATE: Hot season harvest of V.S. 1928
PRECEDING DEEDS: → V.S. 1825, Māgha b. 15, [V.S. 1842, Caitra ś. 8 (b)]

NOT PUBLISHED
DATE: [V.S. 1928, Caitra b. 15/ 7 April 1872 (Sālimpur)]
TYPE: *dastag*
PROMULGATOR: Mahakmā Dīvāṇī, Jaipur State, reign of Rāmsiṅgh II
ADDRESSEES: *paṭels* and *paṭvārīs* of Sālimpur
GRANTEE: GD
EFFECTIVE DATE: Hot season harvest of V.S. 1928
PRECEDING DEEDS: *V.S. 1779, Jyeṣṭha b. 10, →rev.y. 1801/V.S. 1802, Bhādrapada b. 5 (Sālimpur)

NOT PUBLISHED
DATE: [V.S. 1928, Caitra b. 15/7 April 1872 (Sekhpur)]
TYPE: *dastag*
PROMULGATOR: Mahakmā Dīvāṇī, Jaipur State, reign of Rāmsiṅgh II
ADDRESSEES: *paṭels* and *paṭvārīs* of Sekhpur (*alias* Sekhpuro Baṛo)
GRANTEE: GD
EFFECTIVE DATE: Hot season harvest of V.S. 1928
PRECEDING DEEDS: *V.S. 1774, Jyeṣṭha I ś, 15, → rev.y. 1801/V.S. 1802, Bhādrapada b. 5 (Sekhpuro Baṛo)

NOT PUBLISHED
DATE: [V.S. 1928, Caitra b. 15/ 7 April 1872 (Srīkīsanpuro)]
TYPE: *dastag*
PROMULGATOR: Mahakmā Dīvāṇī, Jaipur State, reign of Rāmsiṅgh II
ADDRESSEES: *paṭels* and *paṭvārīs* of Srīkīsanpuro
GRANTEE: GD
EFFECTIVE DATE: Hot season harvest of V.S. 1928
PRECEDING DEED: → rev.y. 1869, Jyeṣṭha ś. 13
Cp. also doc. [V.S. 1928, Caitra b. /15 (Kīrapārāmpuro)]

NOT PUBLISHED
DATE: [V.S. 1929] (? - less likely "1928"; the date is partly illegible)
TYPE: *kāgaj*
PROMULGATOR: Mīrjā Gūlām Aimad Beg
ADDRESSEE: *nāzim* of *zilā* Udehī
GRANTEE: GD
OBJECT: 2,265rp., 8a. for bhog (sacrificial feeding)
PROVENANCE: Villages Gaṇolī (1,441rp., 4a.) and Sahajpur (684rp., 4a.). The grant superseded an earlier grant for village Jaitpuro, *tapā* Kākar, *pargana* Savāī Jaipur.
EFFECTIVE DATE: Hot season harvest of V.S. 1930
PRECEDING DEEDS: Not traceable, for Jaitpuro see however → rev.y. 1839, Āṣāḍha b. 5
SUBSEQUENT DEED: → V.S. 1930, Phālguṇa 4

DATE: V.S. 1930, Phālguṇa ś. 4/ 20 February 1874
TYPE: *kāgaj*
PROMULGATOR: Mirjā Gulām Aimad Beg
ADDRESSEE: *nāzim* of *zilā* Udehī
EFFECTIVE DATE: as above
PRECEDING DEED; [V.S. 1929?]

NOT PUBLISHED
DATE: [V.S. 1995, Āṣāḍha ś. 15/ 12 July 1938]
TYPE: Office statement (thus designated in the document itself)
PROMULGATOR: B.N. Temani (Superintendent Central Records and in-charge Dīvānī Hajūrī and Old Historical Records)
GRANTEE: GD
OBJECT: 759rp. for GD's consort, first deed reported to have been issued in V.S. 1860. The deed of → V.S. 1860, Māgha b. 2 mentions only half that sum which allows for the conclusion that in the same year another deed covering the other half sum was granted
PROVENANCE: Kalyāṇpur-vās and Jasodānand-vās of village Syosiṅghpurā
EFFECTIVE DATE: not mentioned
PRECEDING DEEDS: 1 now untraceable deed, and → V.S. 1860, Māgha b. 2

NOT PUBLISHED
DATE: [V.S. 2006, Phālguṇa b. 7/ 9 February 1950]
TYPE: Report confirming an earlier deed
PROMULGATOR: Gulābcand
PRECEDING DEED: → V.S. 1840, Āśvina b. 10

4. TEXTS AND TRANSLATIONS

Note

(1) If photographs were incomplete, this has been indicated. Missing *verso* pages have only been indicated if they were likely to have been inscribed.

(2) For seals and their translations, cp. Chapter 2, Appendix 3. The translation of Persian seals will be also found separately in each of the Persian text versions.

(3) Regnal and other official titles have not been translated but given in their original form, because they are essential indicators of the provenance of deeds.

(4) The translated versions of documents of the *parvānau* type have been broken up into numbered sections, for which cp. pp.50-61.

(5) Commentaries on details are made by the lines of the original text. Commentaries referring to a document as a whole precede these.

(6) In the edition, the following symbols have been used,

[ ]	addition made by the editor
/ /	insertion made by the scribe
xxx	illegible letters
---	blank
--------------------	line separating *recto* and *verso*
°	following words in the Persian text, marks Indic words

A.H. 1038, 2 Śavvāl/ 25 May 1628

Protocol and *verso* missing.

(१) स्वस्ति श्री महाराज श्री दीवान सत्रसीघजी व-
(२) चनात आमीलान प्र° वहातरी का हाल व़
(३) ईस्तकवाल दीसे सूंप्रसाद वांच्य अत्र
(४) रोजीना वरसौध श्री ठाकूरदुव़ारै श्री मथराजी
(५) व्रदांवनजी मै है तीन कौ फरमाय़ौ है मुव़ाफीक
(६) तेरीष पटा ई° फ° षरीफ सवत १६८५ की थे
(७) मौजे २ तनषुव़ाह कीया है सु मव़ाफीक हाल
(८) हासील की समती करी दस्त वदस्ती व़न कौ प-
(९) हुचै ऐ गाव़ ई कै हव़ाले कीजौ आपनै
(१०) वसाइी लैहीगे तूम कीसही वात का दषल
(११) मत करौ अर जू तुम लीय़ा होई सू फेरी दीजौ
(१२) आगै थे कछु दषल करौगे तौ तूम पास घरा-
(१३) घरु दीवाइी जैगा सालीना १८५०ऽ रू° मौजा
(१४) २

(१५) मौ जेहुवी तपा रीनी श्री ठाकूरदुव़ा-
(१६) र ३ कौ दीनी है ईस मै कछु लीय़ा
(१७) होई सू ईन कौ दीजौ सालीना
(१८) रू° ५४० मौजे १

(१९) श्री गोवीददेव़जी रू°श्री राधावलभजी
(२०) ।।ऽ ऐ° रू रू ।।ऽ
(२१) १८०ऽ १८०ऽ

(२२) श्री मदनमौहनजी द---------------------
(२३) रू° ।।ऽ -----------------------
(२४) १८०ऽ o

(२५) मौ सांहुपाड़ौ तपा सौही साली-
(२६) ना रू° १३१०ऽ मू° मौजे १

(२७) श्री केसौराइीजी दरी	श्री गोवीददेवजी जू रू॰
(२८) रू॰ ।।ऽ	१ऽ वादी रू॰ ।।ऽ हुवी मै
	वाकी ।।ऽ
(२९) १८०ऽ	१८०ऽ
(३०) श्री जुगलकीसोर रू॰ ।।ऽ	श्री वीहारीजी रू॰ ।।ऽ
(३१) रू॰	रू
(३२) १८०ऽ	१८०ऽ
(३३) श्री कीसोरकीसोरीजी	श्री राधारव्रनजी रू॰ ।।ऽ
(३४) रू॰ ।।ऽ रू॰ १८०	रू १८०ऽ
(३५) श्री गोपीनाथजी रू॰ ।।ऽ	श्री ठाकुरदुवारजी गूसा-
(३६) सालीना १८०ऽ	ईजी सालीना रू॰
(३६)	५०ऽ

(३७) ताकीद तमाम जानीजौ तोा २ सावाल
(३८) सन १०३८ मू॰ आगरा

(seal on the right of the Persian text)

[1] Hail! By order of Śrī Mahārāj's Dīvān Satrasiṅghjī, [2-3] with benevolent greetings to the present and future *āmils* of *parganā* Vahātarī. Here: [4] Daily and yearly income. With reference to the temple[s] in Mathura and [5] Vrindaban it has been decreed that, in accordance with [6] the date of the deed, that is, from the autumn harvest of the year [V.S.] 1685, [7] 2 villages have been assigned for income. In accordance with this, the realized [8] revenue income was agreed upon. This must reach them promptly. [9] These villages shall be assigned to them. [9-10] They will populate them themselves. [10-11] You must not take possession of anything, and if you have taken [anything] you must return it. [12] If in future you take anything of it, [13] your own property will be given [to them]. Annual dues: 1,850 rp. Fixed allowance: villages

[14] 2

[15] Village Jehuvī in *tapā* Rīnī has been given to
[16] 3 temples. If any [revenue income] has been taken from these [villages],
[17] it shall be given to them. Annual dues:
[18] 540rp; villages: 1.

[19] Śrī Govinddevjī[1], rp.	Śrī Rādhāvallabhjī
[20] 1/2; equivalent to[2]	1/2rp;
[21] 180rp	180rp

[22] Śrī Madanmohanjī	rate: -------------
[23] 1/2rp.:	--------------------
[24] 180rp.	./.

[25] Village Sāṃhupāḍau in *tapā* Sauhī; annual
[26] dues: 1,310rp.; fixed allowance: 1 village.

[27] Śrī Keśavrāī, rate:	Śrī Govinddevjī,
[28] 1/2rp.:	1rp.; on advanced allowance of 1/2rp., balance of 1/2rp.:
[29] 180rp.	180rp.

[30] Śrī Jugalkiśor, 1/2 rp.:	Śrī Bihārījī, 1/2 rp.:
[31] rupees:	rupees:
[32] 180rp.	180rp.

[33] Śrī Kiśorkiśorījī	Śrī Rādhāramaṇjī, 1/2rp.:
[34] [1/2rp.:] 180rp.	180rp.

[35] Śrī Gopīnāthjī, 1/2rp.;	Temple Gosvāmī,
[36] annual dues: 180rp.	annual dues rupees:
[37]	50rp.

[37] You must take this to be a complete injunction. Date: 2 Śavvāl
[38] A.H. 1038; place: Agra. (seal on the right of the Persian text)

[1] The names of the temples have been given in their standard writing.
[2] The abbreviation *e.* is taken to mean *evaj* "instead of, equivalent". This interpretation remains tentative.

[١] حکمی که متصدیان مهمات پرگنه بهاتر

[٢] حال و استقبال بتوجه امیدوار بوده بدانند که

[٣] چون روزینه سالیانه سری° تهاکردوار° متهرا جی° و بندرابن

[٤] فی اند بموجب تاریخ پروانچه از [...][3] خریف سمبت° ١٦٨٥

[٥] که تنخواه مواضع پرگنه مذکور شده است امر رائج

[٦] از آن دیهای حاصل بوده صحت نموده دست رس خواهد

[٧] رساند و دیهای حواله ایشان نمایند که وارسانند

[٨] رعایا نموده آبادان خواهید ساخت شمایان در آن دیها

[٩] دخل نکنید و اگر چیزی دخل خواهید گرداند از شمایان با تفاوت

[١٠] [...][4] [داده باشد] و آنچه گرفته باشید واپس بدهید

[١١] مقرر س.[5] ١٨٥٠*

[١٢] مواضعات

[١٣] ---

موضع یحوبی تهه° رینی سری° تهاکردوار° گوبند دیو و غیره

[١٤] و آنچه شمایان گرفته باشید واپس بدهید

[١٥] ٥٤٠* [جمع]

[١٦] موضع

[١٧]

سـ ـری°	سـ ـری°	سـ ـری°
گوبند دیو	رادابلبه	مدن موهن
١٨٠*	١٨٠*	١٨٠*

---

[3] Illegible, supposedly a ligature of abbreviations of the words ابتدائی and فصل. The term از ابتدائ فصل خریف occurs in other deeds too. Also in l. 11 the scribe uses an abbreviation, namely .س for سالیانه, whereas in general the Persian versions have abbreviations but rarely. Against this, certain abbreviations are often used in the Rājasthānī versions, cp. "pra." for *parganā*, "i./ī." for *ibtidā*ᶜ, "tā./te./to." for *tārīkh*, "pha." for *faṣl*.

[4] Crossed out in the original.

[5] Abbreviation for سالیانه; written in full in the Rājasthānī version, (l.13).

[۱۸] ______________________________

موضع ساهوپادا تهه° صوهی سالیانه
۱۳۱۰*

[۱۹] موضع

[۲۰]	سـری°	سـری°	سـری°	سـری°
	کسورای	گوبند دیو	جوگل کسور	بهاری جیو°
	۱/۲*	۱*	۱/۲*	۱/۲*
		۱/۲* [وعده]		
		[باقی]		
	۱۸۰*	۱۸۰*	۱۸۰*	۱۸۰*
[۲۱]	سـری°	سـری°	سـری°	سـری°
	کسوکسری	[رادهارون]	گوپیناته	تهاکردوارا°
	۱/۲*	۱/۲*	۱/۲*	جیو° گوسائین°
	۱۸۰*	۱۸۰*	۱۸۰*	۵۰*

[۲۲] در ین باب قدغن لازم دانسته از فرموده تخلف نورزید

[۲۳] تحریر فی التاریخ ۲ شوال سنه ۱۰۳۸

[Seal] (on the right side of the Persian text)

ستراسنگه شالی° مادهو سنگه گاه

(date, left within the rim of the seal)

۱۰۱۹

[1] An order [has been given]! Let it be known to the *mutaṣaddīs*, responsible for the affairs of the *pargana* Bahātrī [2] both present and future, who may be assured of [ruling] benevolence: [3] For the [payment] of the annual daily allowances of the temples situated in Mathura and Vrindaban, [4] in accordance with the date in the *parvānca*, [i.e.] from the beginning of the autumn harvest of the year V.S. 1685, [5] [the revenues from] villages of the aforementioned *pargana* have been declared as payment. That which is obtained from these villages as income shall, in accordance with the applicable directive [6-9], be subject to revision and provided to them. You shall assign to them villages that have been verified as cultivable, and they will

populate.

You shall retain no profits from [the revenues from] these villages, and should you make profit from something, you shall pay the equivalent value as compensation. [10] And that which you have taken you shall give back.

[11] Continued annual allowances: 1,850 [rupees]

[12] [revenues from the] villages:

[13-15] The village of Yehuvī in the *tappā* of Rīnī [for] temple Gobinddev and others. And that which you take you shall give back.

[15] 540 [rupees] in total

[16] [revenues from the] village

[17]	[For] Śrī Gobinddev 180 [rupees]	[For] Śrī Rādhāvallabh 180 [rupees]	[For] Śrī Madanmohan 180 [rupees]

[18] The village of Sāṃhupāḍau in the *tappā* of Sauhī, annually 1,310 [rupees]

[19] [revenues from the] village

[20]	[For] Śrī Keśavrāī 1/2 [rupee]	[For] Śrī Gobinddev 1 [rupee] 1/2 [rupee] agreed [rest]	[For] Śrī Jugalkiśor 1/2 [rupee]	[For] Śrī Bihārī 1/2 [rupee] 180 [rupees]
	180 [rupees]	180 [rupees]	180 [rupees]	

[21]	[For] Śrī Kiśorkiśorī	[For] Śrī [Rādhāramaṇ]	[For] Śrī Gopīnāth	[For] temple Gosvāmī
	1/2 [rupees]	1/2 [rupees]	1/2 [rupees]	
	180 [rupees]	180 [rupees]	180 [rupees]	50 [rupees]

[22] In this matter one must regard strict order as issued [and] not deviate from what has been ordered.

[23] Written on 2nd Śavvāl of the year 1038.

[Seal] Satrāsingh, [servant of the] Court of Mādho Singh

Commentary:

By his seal, the author of the deed, Satrasiṅgh, identifies himself as belonging to the Court of Mādho Singh. The document is clearly not of Kachavāhā origin, for chronological reasons, but also because of the non-Kachavāhā *benedictio*, which is *svasti* and not *sidhi;* because of the position and shape of the *dīvān*'s seal and because of the non-Kachavāhā title of that officer. For the usual seals of *dīvāns* of Amber, albeit from a later period, cp. Chapter 2, Appendix 5. Satrasiṅgh calls himself "Śrī Mahārāj's *dīvān*", a designation which does not occur in the Kachavāhā *sanads*. Most probably, the deed comes from Koṭā. For Mādhosiṅgh Hāṛā of Koṭā s/o Rāv Ratan (d. 1647), cp. MU II: 1-3, also VV 2.2: 1407-10.

As for the villages granted, Vahātarī= Bahātrī, *parganā* of *ṣūba* Agra, *sarkār* Alvar, is not given in the *Ā'īn* (cp. II: 103); see, however, Gupta (1986: 29). For Rīnī, see Gupta (*l.c.*). The village of Jehuvī has not been identified, while Sāṃhupāḍau remains to this day Sāhupāṛā, a village in Basvā Tehsil of Jaipur District (India, 1983 [DCH Jaipur]: 135; serial/code nos 150/108).

In 1628, the GD temple was, for the administration of charities, still grouped with a number of other Vaiṣṇava temples.[6] In some cases, aggregate grants identified the shares of the individual recipients, as would be expected here, where cash income was distributed to several temples. In other cases, no shares are mentioned, which raises the question if the recipients were under the authority of a single manager.[7] The present deed groups the GD temple, which comes first in the list and receives a double share, with eight other temples. A number of these had been founded by or are at least related to, the Caitanya Gosvāmīs of the sixteenth century. These are, apart from Rūp's GD temple, Sanātan's Madanmohan temple, Parmānand's Gopīnāth temple, and Gopālbhaṭṭ's Rādhāramaṇ temple, all at Vrindaban. The other temples are the Rādhāvallabh temple of the deity worshipped by Hit Harivaṃś, also at Vrindaban; the Keśavrāī temple of Mathura, destroyed in 1669; and the Jugalkiśor temple at Vrindaban, said to have been founded in 1628, but perhaps in continuation of an older sanctuary. The Kiśorkiśorī temple remains unidentified, and so does Bihārījī. Maybe, it is the Bāṁke Bihārī temple of Vrindaban. Bāṁke Bihārī was the deity worshipped by Svāmī Haridās under the name of Kuñjbihārī, originally at Nidhiban, a grove in Vrindaban. In the seventeenth century, it was successfully claimed by the Caitanya Gosvāmīs (Entwistle 1987:156, 179-80). Mukherjee and Habib (1988:240, 243) think that Bihārījī, also listed in Akbar's *farmān* of 1598,[8] was probably identical with the Rasik

---

[6] The earliest document of this aggregate type seems to be a *farmān* of Śavvāl 983/January 1576, for which cp. Mukherjee and Habib 1988:237-38.

[7] Cp. for example Mukherjee and Habib 1988:242-43, para 5.9. for a pair of temples to which 100 *bīghās* land were assigned jointly; cp. also → A.H. 1123, 21 Ramaẕān for an aggregate grant for three temples.

[8] This *farmān* lists thirty-five temples of Mathura and its environs (Mukherjee and Habib 1988:238-45).

Bihārī temple of the Nimbārkas at Vrindaban. The present Rasik Bihārī temple of Vrindaban was, however, consecrated much later, namely, in 1814 (Entwistle 1987:221), which does not rule out that there had existed an older temple of Rasik Bihārī.

The shares of 1rp. for GD, and 1/2rp. each for the rest of the deities, were meant for the maintenance of worship, whereas the amount of 50rp. was meant for the salary of the *gosāī*. This seems to refer to a single individual and, therefore, to the manager of several or all of, the temples. The problem of identifying the Gosvāmī would have been facilitated had the *elevatio* of the deed been filmed, for then the beneficiary or beneficiaries of the grant would have been named.

If we go by the hypothesis that the salary was assigned to a single individual and assume that GD headed the group of Vaiṣṇava temples listed in the deed, we may infer that GD's custodian must be identified with the *gosāī*. However, at the time of the deed, the custodianship of GD was disputed. Sanātan, who was the founder of the Madanmohan temple, had transferred his property to his brother, Rūp Gosvāmī, the founder of the GD temple (Habib 1996:156 *s.v.* Sanātan Gosā'in). In 1568, Rūp in his turn transferred the *adhikār* over both Madanmohan and GD to his nephew, Jīv Gosvāmī, the founder of the Rādhādāmodar temple.[9] In his will, Jīv bequeathed his property to Vilāsdās and also stipulated that Vilāsdās pass it on to Kṛṣṇadās (Mukherjee and Wright 1979:316-17). According to Jīv's will and by appointment of Akbar, Kṛṣṇadās became custodian of all the three temples. His term of office is given as 1606 to 1659.[10] However, the Gosvāmīs in the line of Rūp seem to have disapproved of his claim. According to their genealogy, the custodianship of GD was handed down differently and, in 1628, lay in the hands of Govinddās, custodian probably between 1611 and c. 1640.[11] Śāh Jahān's *farmān* of 1644 enjoined that no one interfere with Kṛṣṇadās's rights, which suggests that this had actually happened. The conflict between Jīv's and Rūp's lineages became most embittered in 1659. In that year, Seorām (Śivrām), in the line of Rūp, had been *adhikārī* of GD at least since 1653. In 1659, Jaisiṅgh I confirmed Seorām's right to manage the land and retreats of the GD temple, "despite Krishan Dās's machinations" (Habib 1996:157 *s.v.* Shiv Rām/ Seo Rām).

This, then, suggests that, in 1628, either Kṛṣṇadās, of Jīv's line, or Govinddās, of Rūp's line, was custodian of GD. There remains another problem, namely, over which temples he would

---

9 Mukherjee and Wright 1979:315-16; Habib 1996:156 *s.v.* Jīv Gosvāmī.

10 Habib 1996:132. In 1637 Kṛṣṇadās described himself as having inherited all the property of Vilāsdās Gosvāmī (Mukherjee and Wright 1979:316). In 1644 he was confirmed in his position by Śāh Jahān (Habib 1996:148 *s.v.* Krishan Dās/ Kishan Dās).

11 For which cp. chart "The Custodians of the Govinddevjī Temple", p. 353.

exercise his authority. Several temples mentioned in the deed were not related to the Caitanya Gosvāmīs. This rather suggests that the *gosāī* was not in charge of the management of all the temples listed in the deed.

Rāj. ll. 9-10/ Pers. ll. 6-10: The Persian version adds an injunction, which is missing in the Rājasthānī text, namely, that the land granted be cultivable. This, like comparable instances in other documents, suggests that the Persian version was drafted independently of the Rājasthānī one.

Rāj. l. 37: For *tākīd tamām jānijau* cp. p. 47.

V.S. 1700, Kārttika ś. 5/ 22 September 1643
Verso missing.

।।श्री रांमजी।।

(कटार)

(१) सिधि श्री महाराजाधिराज महारा-
(२) जा श्री जैसिघजी देववचनात म- *(seal)*
(३) हेसंदास दिसे सूप्रसाद वंच्या
(४) अपरंच गूसाइी नित्यानद व
(५) राधाक्रिसनदास चत्र(!)वरती की
(६) अरदासी आई सू पतिसाही फर-
(७) मान व कासीराम की मा सू जैठै
(८) रहै छै ती वेही अरज लिषी थी सू
(९) या की संनद कराइी दीजौ अर जे आ-
(१०) जमषां का मूतसद्या सौ कह्यवा
(११) जाइीगा हाथी आवै तौ ले दीजौ

(१२) मीती काती सू-
(१३) दी ५ सवत
(१४) १७००

Śrī Rāmjī

(dagger)

(seal)

[1] Success! [1-2] By royal order of Śrī Mahārājādhirāj Mahārājā Śrī Jaisiṅghjī, [3] with benevolent greetings to Mahesdās.[12] [4] Reference: By the Gosvāmīs Nityānand and [5] Rādhākrisandās Cakravartī, there [6] was submitted a petition. With reference to an imperial *farmān* [7] and to where Kāsīrām's mother [8] lives, this application was written, and for [9]

[12] The reading of this name remains uncertain.

this a *sanad* shall be made out. [9-11] And when the officers of A'ẓam Khān report that the place has been taken possession of, you shall transfer it.
[12] Date: Kātī ś. [13] 5 [14] V.S. 1700.

Commentary:
The document seems to be related to the incidents alluded to in A'ẓam Khān's *parvāna* of Jumādā I, A.H. 1053 (July-August 1643), which

> Notes that the temple of Gobind Dev Jiu is under the charge of Raja Man Singh *(sic!)*[13] who had appointed Radha Kishandas Chakravarti to supervise worship at the temple. Kashi Ram, who is obstructing the latter, must be prevented from doing so. (Mukherjee and Habib 1989: 296, doc. 26)

l. 3: Mahesdās, an unidentified officer, may have been an *āmil*.

ll. 4-5: Gosvāmī Nityānand Cakravartī, the fourth *adhikārī* of GD, was the father of Rādhākṛṣṇadās, who succeeded him as a custodian. Nityānand seems to have been in office from c. 1640 to c. 1643, and Rādhākṛṣṇadās from c. 1643. His successor Seorām was *adhikārī* from at least 1653 to c. 1689 (Habib 1996: 157). Nothing is known about an interim *adhikārī* between the two.

ll. 9-10: A'ẓam Khān was Governor of Mathura from 1642 to 1645 (Growse 1882: 175-76).

[13] At the time of the deed, the temple was, of course, under the charge of Jaisiṅgh I, as was also duly corrected by Habib 1996: 145 *s.v.* Kāshī Rām.

A.H. 1071, 10 Safar/ 15 October 1660

Invocatio, elevatio and *verso* missing.

(seal)

(१) ॥सिधि श्री महाराजकुंमार कंवर श्री कीरतस्यंघजी देव्रव-
(२) चनात मूतसदी हजूरी दीसे सुप्रसाद वंच्या अप्रंच
(३) पून्यं कपङा श्री ठाकुर गोव्यंददेव्रजी व्रा ठकुरांईीणंजी व्रा
(४) श्री देवी व्रीदाजी साल तंमाम सवागा साल व साल संम-
(५) य्रा ५ का त° जैल दीय्रां जाज्यौ सरैह य्रादीदासती व्राकै
(६) तो॰° १० मा° सफर संन १०७१ मू° साहजंहांनांवाद अत्र पून्यं
(७) कपङा श्री ठाकुर गोव्यंददेव्रजी व्र ठकुरांईीणंजी व्र श्री देवी
(८) व्रीदाजी त° जैल साल व साल पाव्रै संमय्रा पांच कौ हुकंम
(९) हुव्रो वरसालै सं° नराईीणंदास दीव्रांन तो° १० मा° सफर सं-
(१०) न १०७१ मूकरीर अरज पौहची मू° संमय्रा ५

(११)	दसराहौ	दीव्राली	होली
(१२)	१	१	१
(१३)	फुलडोल	राषी	द°
(१४)	१	१	

(१५) मू° साल व साल दीय्रा जाज्यौ थांन साठी

(१६) ६०

(१७)	जांमां	फैटा
(१८)	५	५
(१९)	चीरा	ईजार
(२०)	५	५
(२१)	साङी	घाघरा
(२२)	१०	१०
(२३)	कांचुली	कंनारी
(२४)	१०	१०

(२५)	श्री ठाकुर गोव्यंददेवजी		श्री ठकुरांईणंजी	
(२६)		थांन	थान	
(२७)	२०		२०	
(२८)	जांमां कुरता जरी	फैटा	साडी सालु वुरहां-	घाघरा अत-
(२९)	का		नपूरी	लस का
(३०)	५	५	५	५
(३१)	दरी वागा १	दरी फैटौ १ रू°	द्र° साडी १ गज	दरी घाघरौ १
(३२)	गज ५॥≡	वीस कौ	साढा सात मु-	थांन आधा कौ
(३३)	मुकसर		सांहा (?)	
(३४)	चीरा जरी का	ईजार जरी	कांचुली ताफ-	कंनारी सुंनैहरी
(३५)	५	५	ता की	थांन
(३६)			५	५
(३७)	दरी चीरौ ऐक	द्र° ईजारी ग-	दरी कांचुली १	
(३८)	रू° वाईस कौ	ज २।=॥ मु-	गज १ऽ॥ मुक-	
(३९)		कसर	सर	
(४०)	श्री देवी ब्रीदाजी		द° ---------------------------	
(४१)		थांन		
(४२)	२०			
(४३)	साडी सालु वुर-	घाघरा अतल-		
(४४)	हांनपूरी	स का		
(४५)	५	५		
(४६)	कांचुली ताफता	कंनारी सुनैह-		
(४७)	की	री		
(४८)	५	५		

(४९) दरी स° सदर

(५०) तो° १० मा° सफर संन १०७१ मू° साहजहांनांवाद

(seal)

(II 1) [1-2] Success! By royal order of Śrī Mahārājkumār Prince Śrī Kīratsiṅghjī,

(II 2) [2] with benevolent greetings to the officers of the Court.

(II 3) Reference: [3] Charity (*punya*) of garments for the deity Śrī Govinddevjī and his consort and the goddess Śrī Vrīdā (Vṛndā). [4-5] Five times every year, there shall be given robes, according to the details listed [below].

(III 1) [5] Commentary on the memorandum in the diary of [6] 10 S̱afar A.H. 1071, [written] in Śāhjahānābād,

(III 2) [6-8] namely, the deity Śrī Govinddevjī and his consort and the goddess Śrī Vrīdā shall receive, five times every year, a charity (*punya*) of garments, according to the details listed [below].

(III 3) [8-9] The order was passed on report of Dīvān Saṃ[gahī] Narāīṇdās.

(III 5) [9-10] On 10 S̱afar A.H. 1071, the petition was submitted again. Fixed allowance: Five times

[11] Daśharā	Dīvālī	Holī
[12] 1	1	1
[13] Phulḍol	Rākhī	./.
[14] 1	1	

[15] Fixed allowance: Every year there shall be given 60 items.

[16]	60	
[17]	gowns	sashes
[18]	5	5
[19]	turban pieces	trousers
[20]	5	5
[21]	*sāṛīs*	skirts
[22]	10	10
[23]	blouses	trimmings
[24]	10	10

[25]	God Śrī Govinddevjī		Goddess (Divine Consort)	
[26]		items:		items:
[27]	20		20	
[28-29]	brocaded tunics and *kurtās*	sashes	*sāṛīs* of cotton from Burhanpur	satin skirts
	5	5	5	5
[30-33]	for 1 gown, 5 *gaz-i mukassar*, 11 *girah*	rate: 1 sash at 20rp.	rate: 1 *sāṛī* of 7 1/2 *gaz-i mukassar*	rate: 1 skirt; per item half [of it]
[34-36]	brocaded turban pieces	brocaded trousers	silk (tafetta) blouses	gold trimmings, items:
	5	5	5	5
[37-39]	rate: 1 turban piece at 22rp.	rate: trousers of 2 *gaz-i mukassar*, 6 1/2 *girah*	rate: 1 blouse of 1 1/2 *gaz-i mukassar*	

[40]	Goddess Śrī Vrīdā	
[41]		items:
[42]		20
[43-44]	*sāṛīs* of cotton from Burhanpur	silk skirts
[45]	5	5
[46-48]	silk (tafetta) blouses	gold trimmings
	5	5

[49] Rate as specified above.

(IV) [50] Date: 10 S̲afar A.H. 1071; place: Śāhjahānābād.

Commentary:

Prince Kīratsiṅgh (d. 1673) was the second son of Jaisiṅgh I. In the twenty-third regnal year of Śāh Jahān, the *sarkār*, which comprised "Kāmā, Paharī and Kōh Mujāhid between Āgra and Shāhjahānābād", was assigned to him as fief and residence (MU I: 827). In a document of 1670 (→ A.H. 1080, 12 Ramaẕān), the grant, then renewed, is explicitly reported to relate to Kāmāṁ.

Rāj. ll. 11-14: The deed provides for textiles for certain festive occassions. In the Braj area the festivals in question are observed on the following dates,[14]

Holī	Phālguṇa ś. 15
Phūlḍol	Caitra b. 5
Rākhī	Śrāvaṇa ś. 15
Daśharā	Āśvina ś. 10
Dīvālī	Kārttika b. 15

Rāl. ll. 17ff.: The textiles which the deities received can be identified approximately, and their prices can be also related to the prices given in the *Ā'īn* (tr. I: 98ff.) and by Muṃhto Naiṇsī (1969, II, *pariśiṣṭ* 3), the data of the latter belonging to the middle of the 17th century.

The garments are grouped by pieces and ready-made garments on the one hand, and yardage on the other. Yardage is measured by *gaj mūkasar*, that is, Pers. *gaz-i mukassar*. Habib has carefully discussed the measurement of the *gaz* and established it to be equivalent to 32.242 inches (1963: 359). This, however, holds good of only the standard yard, the *gaz-i ilāhī*. Besides, there were other kinds of yards, the *gaz-i mukassar* being one used for precious cloth. There is, as it seems, no documentary evidence to go by for an exact calculation of it, but it may have come to roughly two thirds of an ordinary yard, although "ordinary" remains a vague notion. In Iran, the *gaz-i mukassar* was equivalent to about two thirds of a *gaz-i śāhī*, and thus 63.12 cm, or, according to a different source, to about 27 inches = 68.68 cm. The Aleppo yard used for measuring cloth is 68 cm long (Hinz 1970: 62[15]). A *gaz* has 16 *girah* (Pers. *girih*), "knots". The word *girah* does not occur in the Rājasthānī text.

[14] Growse 1882: 179-83; Entwistle 1987: 484-91; for the worship as it is carried out in modern times at the GD temple of Jaipur, cp. Singh 1996.

[15] I am grateful to Heike Bill for drawing my attention to this reference.

The various kinds of textiles are,

l.17: *jāṃmau* (< Pers. *jāma*), a gown with "a tight-fitted bodice on the upper part, a skirt for the lower, and full sleeves" (Singh 1979:XXVII). In the successor deed of 1670 (→ A.H. 1080, 12 Ramaẕān, l. 35), the word *colnau* is used instead. – *phaiṭau* is a sash or short turban cloth. Its semantic equivalent is Pers. *fūṭa*, which is basically a strip of cloth, hence (1) loin-band, sash, or (2) turban piece (*Ā'īn*, tr. I, 96, 99).

ll. 19 *pass.*: *cīrau* is a turban piece.
ījār is a pair of trousers (Singh 1979: pl. 40A). In l. 37, column 2, the term *ijārī* occurs.

ll. 23 *pass.*: *kaṃnārī (kinārī)* is a saree trimming. In seventeenth-century Mārvāṛ, golden saree trimmings cost a little less than 2rp. per piece (Muṃhto Naiṇsī 1969, II, *pariśiṣṭ* 3: 457).

ll. 28 *pass.*: The *jāṃmau* is mentioned along with the *kurtau*, shirt. Both were brocaded. – *sālu burhānpurī*; *sālu* is a cotton fabric, often of red colour, and a token of auspiciousness with women. Burhānpur, Khandesh, was a famous centre of cotton and other fabrics (Singh 1979: XXIV; cp. also Tavernier 1925, I: 42). – *atlas* (Pers. *aṭlas*) is a satin fabric.

ll. 32, column 4: The *ghāghrau*, skirt, seems to have measured half the length of a saree, which was 7 1/2 yards long (cp. ll. 31-33, column 3).

l. 33, column 3: One would have expected to read *[mu]kasar*, which, however, is clearly not visible.

ll. 34-35, column 3: *tāftau* (Pers. *tāfta*) is a plain, unbrocaded silk fabric.

A.H. 1072, 15 Śavvāl/ 3 June 1662// **V.S. 1719**, Āṣāḍha b. 3/ 26 May 1662
Copper-plate.

श्री रामजी
सही

(१) सिधि श्री महाराजाधिराज महाराजा श्री ज-
(२) यसिघजी देव़वचनात कमैती प्रगनै आ-
(३) वेर का दिसे सुप्रसाद वाच्या अपरंच २००ऽ
(४) दोइि सै वीघा धरती पुन्य अरथ सिव़राम
(५) प्रोहित अचलराम का वाभण नै मौजै जा-
(६) हौता तपा काकङ इिस तक फसलि षरीफ सं-
(७) वत १७१९ साल १०७० की थे मापि दीजौ जु हा-
(८) सिल लेवो करै अर श्री --- जी नै आसीरवाद
(९) देवो करै वरिसालै परवानगी मधवनदास
(१०) व हरनाथ दीवान धरती वीघा २००ऽ

(११) अवल धरती वीघा दोम धरती वीघा
(१२) १००ऽ १००ऽ

(१३) ते १५ मा : सवाल सन १०७२ मिती असाढ वदि
(१४) ३ संवत १७१९ मूकाम साहजिहानावाद

Śrī Rāmjī

Certified

[1] Success! [1-2] By royal order of Śrī Mahārājādhirāj Mahārājā Śrī Jaysiṅghjī, with benevolent greetings to the officers of *parganā* [3] Amber. Reference: 200 [4] - two hundred - *bīghās* land as charity of land property *(punya arath)* for brahmin Sivrām, [5] son of Purohit Acalrām, [5-6] in village Jāhautā of *tapā* Kākaḍ. [6-7] These shall be measured out and be given [to him] from the autumn harvest of VS 1719, rev. y. 1070, so that [8] he may draw the revenue [8-9] and [in return] bless His Highness. [9-10] As reported in the order *(parvāngī)* of Dīvāns Madhuvandās and Harnāth: 200 *bīghās* land.

[11]	Land of first quality, *bīghās*	Land of second quality, *bīghās*
[12]	100/-	100/-

[13] Date: 15 Śavvāl, A.H. 1072/ Āṣāḍha b. 3, V.S. 1719; place: Śāhjahānābād.

Commentary:

l. 4: Sivrām is not identical with the custodian of GD, Seorām, who was the son of Rādhākṛṣṇadās Cakravartī; cp. → A.H. 1078, 30 Jumādā II and A.H. 1102, 21 Rabī' I, where he is mentioned.

ll. 5-6: Jahautā (modern writing Jāhotā) lies in Amber Tehsil of Jaipur District (India 1983 [DCH Jaipur]: 45, serial/ code nos 105/110).

l. 11: It was common that there was granted for *punya arath* land of which a half was of "first" (*aval* < Pers. *avval*) and the other half of "second" (*dom* < Pers. *dovom*) quality, for which cp. p. 36. "First" quality land was cultivated land, and "second" quality, cultivable waste land (Habib 1963:302). For a comparable case, cp. → V.S. 1769, Jyeṣṭha ś. 13, ll. 35-36, with commentary.

A.H. 1078, 30 Jumādā II/ 17 December 1667

(श्री रामजी)
श्री गोवंददेवजी
श्री जैस्यंघजी

सही

(कटार)

(seal on the right side of the Persian text)

(१) सिधि श्री महाराजाधिराज महारा-
(२) जा श्री रांमसंघजी देव़वचनात
(३) कमोती परगना आंवैर का दीसे सू-
(४) परसाद वंच्या अपरंच रूपया ९६०ऽ
(५) अंके नैव सै साठी वसूली सालीना
(६) व़ मौ° गौवंदपुर तपा षेह परगना
(७) आंवैर का पुंनी व़ भोग ठाकुरदव़ा-
(८) रा श्री --- जी व़गो° जु वीदरा-
(९) वंनजी मौ वीराजमान छै सौ आगै
(१०) मव़ाफक परव़ानै महाराजाधिरा-
(११) ज महाराजा श्री --- जी कै पा-
(१२) व़ता अव ता° ५ जमादील सांनी
(१३) संन १०७८ अरज पौहची सौ दस-
(१४) तूर सावीक वहाल षुद मव़ाफक तफ-
(१५) सील मुकरर कीया सौ परव़ांना का
(१६) मजमून थे षबरदार होई गाव़ व़
(१७) रुपया भोग व़ पुंनी मौ दीजै जू
(१८) लेवै करै : सरैह यादीदासती व़ा-
(१९) का ता° १ रजव संन १०७८ मूकाम
(२०) साहजहांनावाद अत्र पुंनी व़
(२१) भोग ठाकुरदव़ारा श्री --- जी
(२२) जू वीदरावंनजी मौ वीराजमां-
(२३) न छै रुपया ९६०ऽ सालीना व़सू-
(२४) ली व़ मौ° गोव़ंदपुर तपा षेह परग-
(२५) नौ आवैर का पाव़ता अव ता° ५
(२६) जमादील सांनी संन १०७८ अ-

(२७) रज पौहची सौ दसतूर सावीक
(२८) वहाल षुद मव़ाफक तफसील द्रं कम
(२९) द्रव़ा वरीसालौ राजा रांम व़ हर-
(३०) नाथ दीवान तारीष सदर अरज
(३१) मूकरर पौहची
(३२) नकद दसतूर सावीक वहा-
(३३) ल षुद रुपया नौव़ सौ साठी
(३४) सालीना व़सूली
(३५) ९६०ऽ

(३६) कपड़ा व़गो° ठा-	वावती रोजीनै
(३७) कूर श्री गोवंददे-	गुंसाई सौव़रां-
(३८) व़जी व़ ठुकरा-	म अधकारी रो-
(३९) ईणजी व़ वीदा-	जीना रू° १ऽ
(४०) देवीजी रूपया	सालीना
(४१) ६००ऽ वेकसूर	३६०ऽ वसूली

(४२) मौ° गोवंदपुर तपा षैह परग-
(४३) नौ आंवौर का ईवतदाई फसल
(४४) षरीफ साल संन १०७५ संवत
(४५) १७२४ थे वहाल षुद भोग मौ
(४६) मोजा १ रू° १२००ऽ मू° मोजा
(४७) १
(४८) आगौ महाराजाजी की संनद
(४९) मव़ाफक पाव़ता अव वहाल ष-
(५०) द द्रं कम द्रव़ा

(५१) मु : तंनषाह मव़ाफक तफसील जैल

(५२) नकद दसतूर सावीक वहाल षुद
(५३) वेकसूर व़सूली रुपया
(५४) ९६०ऽ सालीना व़-
(५५) सूली

(५६) कपड़ा वगो° ठाकूर	वावती रोजीना
(५७) गोवंददेवजी व़	वे° गुंसाई सौव़रां-
(५८) ठुकराईणजी व़	म अधकारी रोजी-
(५९) वींदादेवीजी सा-	नौ रू° १ मू° साली-
(६०) लीना रु°	ना
(६१) ६००ऽ सालीना वे-	
(६२) कसूर व़सू-	३६०ऽ सालीना
(६३) ली	वसूली

(६४) मौ° गोवंदपूर तपा षेह पर-
(६५) गनै आंवैर का भोग ईवतदाई
(६६) फसल षरीफ साल संन १०७५
(६७) संवत १७२४ थे वहाल षुद रू°
(६८) १२००ऽ मू: मोजा
(६९) १

(७०) ता° ३० जमादील सांनी संन
(७१) १०७८ मूकाम साहजहांनावाद

(I) [Śrī Rāmjī]
Śrī Govinddevjī
Śrī Jaisiṅghjī

Certified

(dagger)

(seal on the right of the Persian text)

(II 1) [1] Success! [1-2] By royal order of Śrī Mahārājādhirāj Mahārājā Śrī Rāmsiṅghjī,

(II 3) [3-4] with benevolent greetings to the officers of *parganā* Amber.

(II 3) [4] Reference: 960rp., [5] in letters: nine hundred and sixty, annually recoverable amount, [6] and, [for] *puni* (charity of non-eatable items) and *bhog*(consumable items), village Govindpur in *tapā* Khoh of *parganā* [7] Amber.

(II 4-5) [7-9] The temples of Śrī [Govinddev]jī etc., which lie in Śrī Vṛndāvanjī, have hitherto [10-12] received these [items] according to a *parvānau* of Mahārājādhirāj Mahārājā Śrī [Jaisiṅgh]jī. [12] Now, on 5 Jumādā II [13] A.H. 1078, there was submitted a petition.
(II 6) [13-14] The hitherto existing regulation has been approved of as automatically renewed, as detailed [below]. [15-16] Taking care of the contents of the *parvānau*, you shall provide a village and money for *bhog* and *puni* [18] so that [the deity] may draw [them as income].

(III 1) [18-19] Commentary on the memorandum [based] on the diary-entry of 1 Rajab A.H. 1078, [written] at [20] Śāhjahānābād.
(III 2) [20] Here: *puni* and [21-25] *bhog*. The deity Śrī [GD]jī, who resides in Śrī Vṛndāvanjī, has been receiving the annually recoverable amount of 960rp. and village Govindpur in *tapā* Khoh of *parganā* Amber. Now, on 5 [26-28] Jumādā II A.H. 1078, there was submitted a petition. The hitherto existing regulation has been approved of as automatically renewed as detailed [below], by rate and [29-30] shares of rate.[16]
(III 1 contd.) On report of Dīvāns Rājā Rām and Harnāth.
(III 5) [30] On the aforementioned date, the application [31] was submitted again[, namely for]:

[32] Cash amount; according to the hitherto existing regulation,
[33] automatically; nine hundred and sixty rupees
[34] annually recoverable dues,
[35] 960rp.

[36] For garments etc., for	Item of daily income
[37] the deity Śrī Govinddev-	for Gosvāmī Sevrām,
[38] jī and his consort	the custodian;
[39] and Vṛndā-	daily 1rp.,
[40] devījī, rupees	annually recoverable dues
[41] 600 net	360rp.

[42] Village Govindpur in *tapā* Khoh of *parganā*
[43] Amber, from the autumn harvest
[44] of rev. y. 1075/V.S.
[45] 1724 renewed automatically; for *bhog*,
[46] 1 village; 1,200rp.; fixed allowance: village
[47] 1

[16] The translation of *dra kam dravā* remains tentative.

[48] Hitherto, according to the *sanad* of the Mahārājājī,
[49] [the deity] has been receiving [this]. Now it is renewed
[50] automatically by rate and shares of rate.[17]

[51] Fixed allowance, as listed in detail [below].

[52-69] (= lines 32-47)

(IV) [70] Date: 30 Jumādā
[71] A.H. 1078; place: Śāhjahānābād.

[17] Cp. fn. 16.

گبند یو جیو°

جی سنگه جیو°

(dagger)

[Seal] (on the right side of the Persian text)

راجه° رام سَنگه بنده پادشاه عالمگیر (۱۰)

[۱] مقرر شد که متصدیان مهمات پرگنه آنبر[18] بعنایت امیدوار

[۲] بوده بدانند که چون مبلغ نهصد و شصت (۹٦۰ *[19]) روپیه وصولی سالیانه

[۳] و موضع گبند پور تپه° کهوه فی العمل پرگنه مذکور در وجه
پون° و بهوگ° تهاکردوارا°

[٤] [...] جیو° و غیره که در بندرابن جیو° براجمان° اند قبل از
این بموجب پروانچه

[٥] مهاراجدهراج° مهاراجه° سری° [...] جیو° می یافت در مواد
بتاریخ پنجم (٥[20])

[٦] جمادی الثانی سنه ۱۰۷۸ بعرض رسید بدستور سابق بحال خود
بموجب تفصیل

[۷] مقرر فرموده ثیم می‌باید که بمضمون پروانچه مطلع گشته موضع و مبلغ
مذکور

[۸] در بهوگ° و پون° واگذارند که میرسیده باشد

[۹] شرح یادداشت واقعه از قرار بتاریخ غرة رجب سنه ۱۰۷۸

[۱۰] مقام شاه جهان آباد انك پون° و بهوگ° تهاکردوارا°

[۱۱] سری° [...] جیو° و غیره که در بندرابن جیو° براجمان° اند

[۱۲] مبلغ نهصد و شصت (۹) روپیه سالیانه وصولی و موضع گبند پور تپه°

[۱۳] کهوه فی العمل پرگنه آنبر مقرر بوده در مواد بتاریخ پنجم (٥)
شهر

[18] Amber. This is the only deed to use two ways of writing the name, namely: آنبر (ll.1,13) and انبر (ll.25,38).

[19] The *siyāq* numbers are written above the numeral in letters.

[20] The digit is written above the numeral in letters, as also in ll.12,13,42.

[١٤] جمادی الثانه سنه ١٠٧٨ بعرض رسید بنابر بدستور سابق

[١٥] بحال خود بموجب تفصیل حکم شد باید که دیوانیان

[١٦] سرکار پروانچه قلمی نمایند برساله زبدة الاقران

[١٧] راجه رام و هرناتهه دیوان بتاریخ صدر بعرض مکرر رسید

[١٨] مقرر

[١٩] نقـــد

بدستور سابق بحال خود

[٢٠] ٩٦٠* سالیانه وصولی

[٢١]

پارچه و غیره تهاکر° سری° گوبند دیو جیو° و تهکرانی جیو° و بندادی جیو°	برای روزینه گوسائین° شورام ادهکاری° مقرر ١* روزینه
٦٠٠* بی قصور	٣٦٠* سالیانه وصولی

[٢٥] موضـــع

گوبند پور تهه° کهوه فی العمل پرگنه انبر از ابتدائی

[٢٦] فصلخریف سالسنه° ١٠٧٥ سمبت° ١٧٢٤ بحال خود در وجه

[٢٧] بهوگ°

[٢٨] موضع

مقرر

١٢٠٠*

مقرر

[٢٩] موضع

[٣٠] سابق بموجب سند مهاراجه° جیو° مقرر بوده در مواد

[٣١] بحال خود حکم شد

[٣٢] مقرر تنخواه بموجب تفصیل ذیل

[٣٣] نقـــد

بدستور سابق بحال خود بی قصور وصولی

[٣٤] ٩٦٠* سالیانه وصولی

[٣٥] پارچه و غیره تهاکر° سری گوبند دیو جیو°
[٣٦] و تهکرانی جیو° و بندادی جیو°
[٣٧] *٦٠٠ بی قصور وصولی

برای روزینه باسم گوسائین° شورام ادهکاری°
مقرر *١ روزینه
*٣٦٠ سالیانه

[٣٨] موضع
گوبند پور تپه° کهوه فی العمل پرگنه انبر در وجه بهوگ° از ابتدائی
[٣٩] فصلخریف سالسنه° ١٠٧٥ سمبت° ١٧٢٤ بحال خود

[٤٠] *١٢٠٠
مقرر

[٤١] موضع

[٤٢] تحریراً فی التاریخ سلخ [٣٠] م جمادی الثانی سنه ١٠٧٨

Gobinddevjīū

Jai Singhjīū

[Seal] Rājā Rām Singh, slave of Emperor ᶜĀlamgīr (10)

[1-2]It has been ordered! Let it be known to the *mutaṣaddīs*, responsible for the affairs of the *pargana* Amber, who may be assured of the [ruling] grace: The sum of 960 (nine hundred and sixty) rupees of annual duties [3] and [the revenues] from the village Govindpur in the *tappā* of Khoh, in the tax collection territory of the aforementioned *pargana*, had hitherto been bestowed [to ensure] *pūn* and *bhog* on the temple [4] [Govinddev]jīū and other [temples] which are situated in Vrindaban[jī], in accordance with a *parvānca* [5] of the Mahārājadhirāj Mahārājā Śrī Jai Singhjīū.

Therefore a petition was presented on the fifth/5 [6] Jumādā II of the year 1078. In conformity with the former decree, [the decree] remains in force without special request in accordance with the list.

[7] We have ordered: Having been informed of the *parvānca* one shall ensure that the temples will [also in future] receive [the revenues from] the village and the aforementioned sum [8] for *bhog* and *pūn*. [9] [According to] the commentary on the memorandum dated first Rajab of the year 1078 [10] in Śāhjahānābād, it has been determined for *pūn* and *bhog* for the temple [11] Śrī [Govinddev]jīū and others which are situated in Vrindabanjīū [12] the sum of nine hundred/9 and sixty rupees of duties annually to be paid and [the revenues from the] village Govindpur in the *tappā* [13] Khoh in the tax collection territory of the *pargana* Amber.

Therefore a petition was presented on the fifth/5 of the month [14-15] Jumādā II of the year 1078. It had been decided that in conformity with the former decree, [the decree] remains in force without special request in accordance with the list. The *dīvān* employees of the [16-17] *sarkār* shall issue a *parvānca*. According to a report by the *dīvān*s Rājā Rām and Harnāth, the best of their kind, the petition was presented once again on the abovementioned date.

[18] Determined

[19] cash amount:

in conformity with the former decree without special request:

[20] 960 [rupees] of duties to be paid annually

[21] [to ensure] fabric etc. for the god Śrī Gobinddevjīū and the goddessjīū and Vṛndādevījīū

600 [rupees] without deduction

for daily allowances for Gosvāmī Seorām, the *adhikārī*

determined: 1 [rupee] daily

360 [rupees] of duties to be paid annually

[25-27] [revenues from the] village

Govindpur in the *tappā* Khoh, in the tax collection territory of the *pargana* Amber, from the beginning of the autumn harvest of the fiscal year 1075/ V.S. 1724 (1167) without special request for *bhog*

[28] village

determined:

1200 [rupees]

determined

[29] village

[30-31] In conformity with the *sanad* of the Mahārājājīū, it had been decreed earlier that [the decree] comes into force without special request.

[32] Determination of payment in accordance with succeeding details:

[33] cash amount:
in conformity with the former [decree], without special request: duties to be paid without deduction
[34] 960 [rupees] of duties to be paid annually

[35]	[to ensure] fabric etc. for the god Gobinddevjīū	for daily allowances for Gosvāmī Seorām the *adhikārī*,
[36]	and the goddessjīū and Vṛndādevījīū	determined: 1 [rupee] daily
[37]	600 [rupees] duties to be paid without reduction	360 [rupees] [of duties to be paid] annually

[38] [revenues from the] village
Govindpur in the *tappā* Khoh, in the tax collection territory of *pargana* Amber, for *bhog*. From the beginning
[39] of the autumn harvest of the fiscal year 1075/ V.S. 1724, without special request

1,200 [rupees]
determined:

[41] village

[46] Written on the last 30. Jumādā II in the year 1078.

Commentary:

The deed refers to Govindpur(o Baṛo/Bujarg) *alias* Raihphoḍā/Rahphoḍā. It is identical with modern Govindpurā *alias* Rohpāṛā in Sanganer Tehsil of Jaipur District (India 1983 [DCH Jaipur]: 169, serial/code nos 70/161). In the beginning of the 18th century, Govindpur was made the site of a new temple for GD, for which cp. pp. 16-17.

ll. 7-8: *ṭhākurdavārā śrī ---jī vagai.*(spelt *vago.*) ...: The deed seems to indicate a change in the administration of GD, although this assumption is based on the Rājasthānī text, which differs partly from its Persian version. The beneficiary of the present deed is GD, but the text refers to "the temples of Śrī [GD]jī etc." as having been the recipients in the past. According to the Indic version, the confirmation is made out for GD alone, the "etc." after the words *śrī----jī* missing (Rāj. l. 22), whereas the Persian version (l. 11) retains "etc.". At any rate, after A.H. 1078/A.D. 1667, GD is always mentioned separately, that is, no longer as the chief of a group of temples.

The deed assigns a cash amount of 960rp. and the assessed revenue of 1,200rp. of Govindpur. In other words, 960rp. would form stable earnings, whereas an assignment of assessed revenue was subject to fluctuation.

A.H. 1080, 12 Ramaẕān/ 3 February 1670

Invocatio and *elevatio* missing.

(कटार)

(seal on the right of the Persian text)

(१) ॥सिधि महाराजाजी श्री
(२) कीरतस्यंघजी देव़वचना-
(३) त कमौती प्रगना कामा का
(४) दीसे सुप्रसाद वंच्या अ-
(५) प्रंची श्री ----- जी
(६) का सेव़ग प्रसाद ले हजुर आ-
(७) य़ा था अर य़ाह मालुम की-
(८) न्ही जो ठाकुर का कपड़ा ई°
(९) ताो २९ जू° अव़ल संन १०७९
(१०) ला° आ° तो २८ जु° अव़ली
(११) संन १०८० व रोज दीव़ाली
(१२) सूधा पछला साल का पा-
(१३) य़ा नही सो हजुर कारषा-
(१४) ना मौ न था थै व़हा सो क-
(१५) पड़ा करि दीजौ त° जौल
(१६) समय़ा ५ का
(१७) होली फुलडोल राषी
(१८) दुसराहा दीव़ाली द°
(१९) मूकरा

(२०) थान गज मूक-
(२१) ५२ सर
(२२) १० ।-ऽ

(२३) श्री ठाकुरजी
(२४) था°
(२५) २२

(२६) या° गुदसता साल
(२७) का वाकी था सो दीजौ

(२८) फौटा द्र° २०ऽ का था°
(२९) २

(३०) हाल का थान
(३१) २०

(३२) चीरा द्र° २२ऽ फौटा द्र° २०ऽ
(३३) थान का था°
(३४) ५ ५

(३५) चोलना था° ईजार था°
(३६) ५ ५
(३७) आसावरी जरी का कुड़ता जरी तथा वा-
(३८) तथा कुड़ता जरी फता वूटादार तथा
(३९) का मसरू

(४०) द्र ४३।।= द्र ३१।।= द्र २५।ऽ द्र १२ऽ
(४१) १ १ १ १
(४२) द्र २६।।= द्र २५।ऽ द्र १८= द्र १३।।≡
(४३) १ २ २ १

(४४) श्री ठुकरानीजी
(४५) था° गज मू°
(४६) १५ ५।=।।ऽ

(४७) साड़ी सालु वू- घाघरा अतलस
(४८) रहानपुरी था° का था°
(४९) ५ ५

(५०) द्र ३।।ऽ द्र° २।।।– द्र° ४ऽ द्र° ३।।ऽ
(५१) ३ २ ३ २

(५२) काचली कौ ता- कीनारी ज° सा-
(५३) फतो तथा दाराई ड़्या नै द्र २।।ऽ
(५४) द्र था° १ कौ गज १ऽ।। का था°
(५५) मू° काचली ५ का मू°
(५६) गज ५

(५७) ५= । ।ऽ

(५८) श्री देवी व्यंदादेवीजी
(५९) था° गज
(६०) १५ ५= । ।ऽ

(६१) साड़ी सालु वुर- घाघरा अतल-
(६२) हानपुरी था° स का था°
(६३) ५ ५

(६४) द्र ३ । ।ऽ द्र° २ । । ।– द्र° ४ऽ द्र° ३ । ।ऽ
(६५) ३ २ ३ २

(६६) काचली कौ दर- कीनारी ज° साड्या
(६७) वाई तथा ताफतौ कौ द्र° २ । ।ऽ मू°
(६८) द्र° १ऽ । । मू° था° था°
(६९) यकौ मू° गज ५
(७०) ५= । ।ऽ

(७१) ताो १२ मा° रमजान सं° १०८०
(७२) मूकाम लंगरकोट

(dagger)

(seal on the right of the Persian text)

[1] Success! [1-2] By royal order of Śrī Mahārājājī Śrī Kīratsiṅghjī, [3-4] with benevolent greetings to the officers of *parganā* Kāmāṁ. [4-7] Reference: The servant of Śrī [Govinddev]jī appeared with consecrated offerings *(prasād)* at Court, and reported [8-13] that the garments for the deity had not been received from 29 Jumādā I A.H. 1079 (4 November 1668) to 28 Jumādā I A.H. 1080 (25 October 1669), and for the Dīvālī day of last year. [13-14] They had not been available at the court factory. [14-15] You shall deliver these garments there (that is, to the temple - MH), according to the details listed, [16] five times[, namely, at]

[17] Holī Phūlḍol Rākhī

[18] Daśharā Dīvālī ./.

[19] [as] a fixed allowance.

[20]	Items:	Yardage *(gaz-i mukassar)*:
[21]	52	
[22]		10 [*gaz*], 5 [*girah*]
[23]		God
[24]		items:
[25]		22
[26]	[According to] the memorandum of last year,	
[27]	there remained a debit. This you shall pay:	
[28]	Sashes, 20 rp. each; items:	
[29]	2	
[30]	Now, items:	
[31]	20	
[32]	turban pieces, 22 rp. each,	sashes, 20 rp. each,
[33]	items:	items:
[34]	5	5
[35]	cloaks, items:	trousers, items:
[36]	5	5
[37]	brocaded *āsāvarī*	brocaded *kuṛtā* and
[38]	and brocaded *kuṛtā*	*bāftā* with floral motifs and
[39]		*maśrū'*
[40]	at 43 rp.10 a.; 31 rp. 2 a.	at 25 rp. 4 a.; 12 rp.
[41]	1 1	1 1
[42]	at 26 rp. 10 a.; 25 rp. 4a.	at 18 rp. 2 a.; 13 rp. 10 a.
[43]	1 2	2 1
[44]		Goddess

[45]	Items:	Yardage *(gaz-i mukassar)*:
[46]	15	5 [*gaz*], 2 1/2 [*girah*]
[47]	*sāṛīs* of cotton	satin skirts,
[48]	from Burhānpur, items:	items:
[49]	5	5
[50]	at 3 rp. 8 a.; 2 rp. 13 a.	at 4 rp.; 3 rp. 8 a.
[51]	3 2	3 2
[52]	[For] blouses silk (tafetta)	brocaded *sāṛī* trimmings,
[53]	and *darvāī*,	each 2 1/2 rp.,
[54]	for each piece 1 [*gaz*], 1/2 [*girah*];	items:
[55]	for 5 blouses	
[56]	*gaz*	
[57]	5 [*gaz*], 2 [*girah*]	5
[58]	Goddess Vṛndādevījī	
[59]	Items:	Yardage *(gaz-i mukassar)*:
[60]	15	5 [*gaz*], 2 1/2 [*girah*]
[61]	*sāṛīs* of cotton	satin skirts,
[62]	from Burhānpur, items:	items:
[63]	5	5
[64]	at 3 rp. 8 a.; 2 rp. 13 a.	at 4 rp.; 3 rp. 8 a.
[65]	3 2	3 2
[66]	[For] blouses *darvāī*	brocaded *sāṛī* trimmings,
[67]	and silk (tafetta),	each 2 1/2 rp.,
[68]	each 1 [*gaz*], 1/2 [*girah*]; for	items:
[69]	1 item *gaz*	
[70]	5 [*gaz*], 2 [*girah*]	5

[71] Date: 12th day of the month of Ramaẕān A.H. 1080,

[72] place: Laṅgarkoṭ.

(dagger)

[Seal] (on the right side of the Persian text)

کیرت سنگه بنده عالمگیر شاه

(date, within the rim of the seal)

۱۰۷۸

[۱] متصدیان مهمات حال و استقبال پرگنه

[۲] کامان بعنایت و التفات امیدوار بوده

[۳] بدانند که سیوك° پرساد° [...] آورده

[٤] اظهار نمود که پارچه تهاکر° از ابتدائی

[٥] ۲۹ جمادی الاول سنه ۱۰۷۹ لغایت ۲۸ شهر جمادی الاول سنه ۱۰۸۰

[٦] و بابت روز دیوالی سال گذشته در سرکار طلب

[۷] است چنانچه که فی الحال در کارخانه موجوده نبود

[۸] بنابر بر پرگنه مذکور تحویل نموده نشد که بموجب تفصیل

[۹] ذیل پارچه برای پوشاکی تهاکر° خواهند رساند

[۱۰] که ثانی الحال مطابق پروانه در حساب مجری و محسوب خواهد شد

[۱۱] در ین باب قدغن تمام دانند

[۱۲] ______ برای روز هولی | ______ برای روز پهول دول | ______ برای روز راکهه

[۱۳] ______ برای روز دسهرا | ______ برای روز دیوالی | [جمع][21]

---

[21] The reading uncertain itself, is corroborated by the Rājasthānī text (l.18): Abbreviation *da* (= *dar* rate, price, tariff etc.). For the *siyāq*-numbers a variant abbreviation of جمع functions as an identification mark, cp. Kazem Zadeh (1915:29). Probably it marks the end of a list of items. Filling an empty space, not only provides for symmetry but also prevents later additions or tampering with the text. However, it is also possible that جمع and *dar* resp. belong to the contents matter of the following line.

[١٤] مقرر

[١٥] *٥٢ تهان°

*١٠ ذرع مكسر
٥ گره

[١٦] ___

برای تهاکر° [...] جیو°

[١٧] *٢٢ تهان°

[١٨] ___

برای سال گذشته که در سرکار طلب است

[١٩] عن فوطه
فی *٢٠ (...[22])
مقرر

[٢٠] *٢ تهان°

[٢١] ___

برای حال

[٢٢] *٢٠ تهان°

[٢٣] چیـــــــــره	فوطـــــــــه
فی *٢٢	فی *٢٠
مقرر	مقرر
*٥ تهان°	*٥ تهان°

[22] Illegible.

[۲٤] جامـــــــــــــــــــــــــــــــــــــه[3]
و کرته° زری و اساوری° زری

*۵ تهان°

پایجامـــــــــــــــــــــــــــــــــــــه[4]
کرته° زری و بافته° بوته دار

*۵ تهان°

[۲۵]

فی *٤۳	فی *۳۱	فی *۲۵	[فی] *۱۲
۱۰ انه	۲ انه	٤ انه	
مقرر	مقرر		
[۱] پوشا	[۱] پوشا	*۱	*۱

[۲٦]

فی *۲٦	فی *۲۵	فی *۱۸	[فی] *۱۳ ۱۰ انه
۱۰ انه	٤ انه	۲ انه	
مقرر	مقرر	مقرر	
[۱] پوشا	پوشایان	*۱ دانه	*۱

[۲۷] ـــ
برای سری تهکرانی° جیو°

[۲۸] *۱۵ تهان°

*۵ ذره [مکسر]
۲ ۰ گره

[۲۹] ســــــــــــــــــــــــــــــــاری°
سالو° برهان پوری

*۵ تهان°

گهاگهـــــــــــــــــــــــــــــــــرا°
اطلس°

*۵ تهان°

[۳۰]

فی *۳	فی *۲	فی *٤	فی *۳
۸ انه	۱۳ انه		۸ انه
*۳	*۲	*۳	*۲

[۳۱]

کانچلــــــــــــــی°
درای° و تافته°

فی *۱ [ذره مکسر]
۱/۲ گره

مقرره
*۵ تهان°

المقرر
*۵ ذره [مکسر]
۲ ۱/۲ گره

کنارــــــــــــــی°
زر ساری°

فی *۱
*۲ ۸ انه
مقرره

*۵ تهان°

[۳۲]

ــ
برای بندرا دیوی جیو°

[۳۳] *۱۵ تهان°

[فی] *۵ ذره [مکسر]
۲ ۱/۲ گره

[۳٤]

سارــــــــــــــی°
سالو° برهان پوری

*۵ تهان°

گهاگهــــــــــــــرا°
اطلس°

*۵ تهان°

[۳۵]

ــــــــــــ	ــــــــــــ	ــــــــــــ	ــــــــــــ
فی *۳ ۸ انه	فی *۲ ۱۳ انه	فی *٤	فی *۳ ۸ انه
*۳	*۲	*۳	*۲

[۳٦]

کانچلــــــــــــــی°
درای° و تافته°

فی تهان°
*۱ ذره م[کسر]

مقرر
*۵ تهان°

المقرره
*۵ ذره [مکسر]
۲ ۱/۲ گره

کنارــــــــــــــی°
زر ساری°

فی تهان°
*۲ ۸ انه
مقرر

*۵ تهان°

[۳۷] تحریر فی التاریخ ۱۲ شهر رمضان سنه ۱۰۸۰ مقام لنگر کوت

[Seal] Kīrat Singh [servant of] the Emperor ᶜĀlamgīr, 1078

[1-3] Let it be known to the *mutaṣaddīs*, [responsible for the] affairs both present and future, of the *pargana* Kāmān, who may be assured of [ruling] grace and favour: The servant, bringing *prasād* of the [Śrī Govinddevjī temple] [4-5], presented [the following petition]: [for the interval] beginning with the 29th Jumādā I of the year 1079 to the 28th of the month Jumādā I of the year 1080 [6] and for the day of *dīvālī* of last year, fabric for garments for the god is outstanding at the *sarkār*. [7] Because at that time nothing had been available at the court factory, [8] nothing had been sent to the aforementioned *pargana*. [Now] in accordance with the succeeding list, [9] fabric for garments for the god shall be delivered. [10] In conformity with the *parvāna* it shall be booked and charged instantly as per account. [11] In this matter one must regard strict order as issued.

[12]	For the day of *Holī*	for the day of *Phulḍol*	for the day of *Rākhī*
[13]	for the day of *Daśaharā*	for the day of *Dīvālī*	[sic!]

[14] determined:

[15] [altogether] 52 items
[of]
10 *ẕirāᶜ-i mukassar*
5 *girih*

[16] **[amount] for the god [Govindevjī]:**

[17] 22 items

[18] outstanding for last year at the *sarkār*:

[19] sashes
at 20 [rupees]
determined:
[20] 2 items

[21] for now:
[22] 20 items

[23]	[for] turban shawls at 22 [rupees] determined: 5 items		[for] sashes at 20 [rupees] determined: 5 items	
[24]	[for] gowns and brocadad *kurtās* and brocaded *āsāvarī* 5 items		[for] trousers and brocaded *kurtās* and *bāfta* with floral motifs 5 items	
[25]	at 43 [rupees] 10 annas	at 31 [rupees] 2 annas	at 25 [rupees] 4 annas	at 12 [rupees]
	determined: [1] set	determined: [1] set	[determined:] 1 [set]	[determined:] 1 [set]
[26]	at 26 [rupees] 10 annas	at 31 [rupees] 4 annas	at 18 [rupees] 2 annas	at 13 [rupees] 10 annas
	determined: [1] set	determined: [2] sets	[determined:] 1 set	[determined:] 1 set

[27] **[amount] for the goddessjīū:**
[28] 15 items
[of]
5 ẕirā^c-i [mukassar]
2 girih

[29]	[for] saris cotton (*sālū*) from Burhanpur [determined:] 5 items		[for] skirts (*ghāghrās*) *aṯlas* [determined:] 5 items	
[30]	at 3 [rupees] 8 annas	at 2 [rupees] 13 annas	at 4 [rupees]	at 3 [rupees] 8 annas
	[determined:] 3 [pieces]	[determined:] 2 [pieces]	[determined:] 3 [pieces]	[determined:] 2 [pieces]
[31]	[for] *kānclīs* *darāī* and *tāfta* [of] 1 *ẕirā* ½ *girih*		[for] brocaded sari trimmings at 2 [rupees] 8 annas	
	determined: 5 items		determined:	
	determined: [altogether] 5 *ẕirāᶜ-i mukassar* 2 ½ *girih*		5 items	

[32] **[amount] for Vṛndādevījīū:**

[33] 15 items

[of]

5 *ẕirāᶜ-i [mukassar]*

2 *girih*

[34]	[for] saris		[for] skirts (*ghāghrās*)	
	cotton (*sālū*) from Burhanpur		*aṯlas*	
	[determined:]		[determined:]	
	5 items		5 items	
[35]	at 3 [rupees]	at 2 [rupees]	at 4 [rupees]	at 3 [rupees]
	8 annas	13 annas		8 annas
	[determined:]	[determined:]	[determined:]	[determined:]
	3 [pieces]	2 [pieces]	3 [pieces]	2 [pieces]
[36]	[for] *kānclīs*		[for] brocaded sari trimmings	
	darāī and *tāfta*		at 2 [rupees]	
			8 annas	
	[of]			
	1 *ẕirā^c-i mukassar*			
	½ *girih*			
	determined:		determined:	
	5 items			
	determined:			
	[altogether]			
	5 *ẕirā^c-i mukassar*			
	2 ½ *girih*		5 items	

[37] Written on the 12th of the month Ramaẕān in the year 1080. Place: Laṃgarkoṭ.

Commentary:

The deed is related to → A.H. 1071, 10 S̱afar, which cp., also for the explanation of textile terms.

ll. 28 *pass.*: *phauṭau* (mod. H. *photā*) = Pers. *fūṭa*, which is basically a strip of cloth, hence (1) loin-band, sash, or (2) turban piece (*Ā'īn*, tr. I, 96, 99). In the deed of → A.H. 1071, l. 17., the word *phaiṭau* is used instead.

l. 35: *colnau*, for which the Persian version has *jāma*, is a gown or cloak, which is complemented by a *kuṛtau*, shirt.

In ll.37-43, the quality and the prices of the suits, that is, *colnau*-cum-*ijār*, are specified. It is not quite clear if the varieties of fabrics described refer to the upper garments alone or comprise the trousers, which form sets with them.

The *āsāvarī* is a gold-brocaded twill (Dhamija and Jain 1989: 121). Famous fabrics of this kind come from Ahmedabad. Gold-thread, *zarī*, used for brocading, is here combined with *āsāvarī* which suggests that *āsāvarī*s were not necessarily gold-brocaded. Especially Surat was renowned for its *zarī* production, and remains so to this day (Dhamija and Jain 1989: 118-19). The *Ā'īn* (tr. I, 98) lists brocade from Gujarat.

Woven mainly in Bharuch, the *bāftā* (Pers. *bāfta*) is a type of precious cotton cloth. It is praised in a text contemporaneous with Mahārājā Mādhavsiṅgh (r. 1750-68), where it is said to come from Navasari near Surat (Singh 1979: XII with notes 21 and 22). Mohanty (1984: 27) describes it as "closely woven in silk, and all or certain portions of the pattern are in gold or silver threads. These fabrics are mostly used for garments and saris. Very often a satin ground weaving is used particularly for garment fabrics". The *bāftā*s have floral or arboreal patterns (Dhamija and Jain 1989: 146), and this is also mentioned in ll. 37-38.

l.39: The *masrū* (Ar. *maśru'*, "permitted") is a mixed cotton and silk fabric. In Islam, pure silk was not allowed to be worn on ritual occasions (for illustrations, cp. Singh 1979: pl. 9C; Dhamija and Jain 1989: 82, 140-1).

ll. 53, 66-67: *dārāī/darvāī* is a plain, unbrocaded silk fabric, for which cp. Singh (1979:XV), who says that it can also be striped. In contemporary Mārvāṛ, the price of this fabric was 1/2rp. per yard (Muṃhto Naiṇsī 1969, II, *pariśiṣṭ* 3: 457). The garments of the goddesses are completed by saree trimmings, *kinārī*s. Brocaded, that is golden saree trimmings cost a little less than 2rp. per piece in Mārvāṛ (Muṃhto Naiṇsī, *l.c.*).

The garments of the deities cost a total of 559rp., 14a. In this connection, cp. doc. → A.H. 1078 and subsequent deeds, which stipulate an annual amount of 600rp. for garments for the deities. The grant coming from Kāmāṁ supplemented this donation.

A.H. 1089, 20 Zī'l-h̠ijja/ 2 February 1679

Invocatio missing.

(कटार)

(seal on the right of the Persian text)

(१) सिधि श्री महाराजाधि-
(२) राज महाराजा श्री रांमसिं-
(३) घजी देव़वचनातु कमैती
(४) प्रगनां आवौरी का दिसे
(५) सुप्रसाद वंच्या अपरंच
(६) आगै रूपया च्यारि सै छ-
(७) तीस सालिनां वावती स-
(८) मै फुलडोल व़ कपड़ा
(९) श्री गोवंददेव़जी व़ ठुकरा-
(१०) नी सरकार कूव़र कीसन-
(११) संघ की थे पावै था अर
(१२) कूव़र नै ईवतदाई साल सं-
(१३) न १०८६ संवत १७३५ थे प्रग-
(१४) नां आंवौरी परी तनषुव़ा-
(१५) ह कीय़ा ईस व़ासतै फुरमाव़-
(१६) ते है जो रूपय़ा २००ऽ
(१७) ---------------- सालिनां ईव-
(१८) तदाई साल संन १०८६ संव-
(१९) त १७३५ थे तौहसील अप-
(२०) णी व़ तौहवील पोतदार की
(२१) थे वा° समै फुलडौल व़ कप-
(२२) ड़ा ठाकुर गोवंददेव़जी
(२३) व़ ठुकराणीजी तनषुवाह
(२४) दिय़ा जाजो सालीनां सा-
(२५) वीक मा° प्रव़ांनां कूव़र ४३६ऽ
(२६) कमी रूपय़ा २३६ऽ व़ाकी बहा-
(२७) ल षुद ई° साल संन १०८६

(२८) संवत १७३५ थे रूपया
(२९) २००ऽ
(३०) तारी २० मा° जील हेज सं-
(३१) न १०८९

(dagger)

(seal on the right margin)

[1] Success! [1-3] By royal order of Śrī Mahārājādhirāj Mahārājā Śrī Rāmsiṅghjī, [3-5] with benevolent greetings to the officers of *parganā* Amber. Reference: [6-11] Hitherto, the deity Śrī Govinddevjī and his consort has received an annual allowance of 436rp. for the event of the Phūlḍol festival and for garments from the *sarkār* of Prince Kisansiṅgh, [11-15] and, starting with rev.y. 1086/V.S. 1735, the Prince has charged the payment [of this] to *parganā* Amber. [15-16] With respect to this, he orders that [16-24], starting with rev.y. 1086/V.S. 1735, 200rp. ------ annually shall be paid as income out of the revenue collected by yourselves and from the treasury of the *parganā* treasurer, for the event of the Phūlḍol festival and for garments for the deity Śrī Govinddevjī and his consort. [24-25] Annual allowance as before, according to the *parvānau* of the Prince: 436rp., [26-28] reduced sum 236rp., balance confirmed automatically, starting with rev.y. 1086/V.S. 1735, rupees

[29] 200rp.

[30-31] Date: 20 Zī'l-hijja A.H. 1089.

(dagger)

[Seal] (on the right side of the Persian text)

مهاراجه رامسنگه ابن مهاراجه جی سنگه

(date, left, within the rim of the seal)

١٠٧٨

[١] مقرر شد که متصدیان مهمات پرگنه انبر

[٢] بعنایت و التفات امیدوار بوده

[٣] بدانند که چون پیشتر مبلغ چهار صد

[٤] و سی و شش روپیه سالیانه بابت

[٥] سمه[23] دهول دول[24] و پارچه سری گوبند یو جیو°

[٦] و تهکرانی° از سرکار اقبال آثار کنور°

[٧] کنور° کشن سنگه می یافتند و کنور° از ابتدائی

[٨] سنه ١٠٨٦ سمبت° ١٧٣٥ بر پرگنه انبر تنخواه

[٩] نموده لهذا امر میفرمائیم که مبلغ [*[25] ٢٠٠]

[١٠] دو صد روپیه [...] سالیانه از ابتدائی

[١١] سنه ١٠٨٦ سمبت° ١٧٣٥ از تحصیل خود و

[١٢] تحویل فوطه دار در وجه سمه دهول دول

[١٣] و پارچه سری° تهاکر° گوبند یو جیو° و تهکرانی°

[١٤] تنخواه میداده باشند

---

[23] Cp. 1.8. Probably a phonetical rendering of the word سمي *samaya*.

[24] Cp. 1.12. Correctly: پهول دول *phūlḍol*.

[25] In the original written above the word *mablaġ*.

[١٥] سالیانه

[١٦] *٤٣٦ سابق بموجب پروانه کنور°
[١٧] *٢٣٦ کمی
[باقی]

[١٨] بحال خود از ابتدائی سنه ١٠٨٦ سمبت° ١٧٣٥
[١٩] *٢٠٠

[٢٠] تحریر فی التاریخ ٢٠ ذوالحجه سنه ١٠٨٩

[Seal] Mahārājā Rām Singh, son of Mahārājā Jai Singh, 1078

[1] It has been ordered! Let it be known to the *mutaṣaddīs*, responsible for the affairs of the *pargana* Amber, [2] who may be assured of [ruling] grace and favour, [3-4]: Formerly the sum of four hundred and thirty-six rupees was given [to the temple] as annual allowances [5] for the occasion of the *Phūlḍol* [festival] and [for provision of] fabric for Śrī Gobinddevjīū [6] and the Goddess by the *sarkār* of Prince Kiśan Singh bearing traces of fortune [7]. Since the beginning [8] of the year 1086/ V.S. 1735 (1678) the Prince had made the payment [for the Temple] incumbent upon the *pargana* Amber.
[9-12] We have therefore ordered the sum of 200[26]/ two hundred rupees in annual allowances [for the Śrī Govinddevjī temple] for the occasion of the *Phūlḍol* [festival] and [for provision of] fabric for Śrī Gobinddevjīū and the Goddess, to be paid from the beginning of the year 1086/ V.S. 1835 from the own [tax] collections and the assets of the *fūṭadār*.

---

[26] written above the word "sum".

[15] Annual allowances:

[16] 436 [rupees] formerly, in accordance with the *parvāna* of the Prince
[17] 236 [rupees] deduction

[18] without special request, from the beginning of the year 1086/ V.S. 1735:
[19] 200 [rupees]

[20] Written on the 20th Ẕū 'l-Ḫijja of the year 1089.

Commentary:

Rāj. l. 9: Documents → A.H. 1071, → A.H. 1078 (only when listing items to be given to the deity) and this one of A.H. 1089 spell out the name of Govinddev instead of substituting a blank for it.

Rāj. ll. 10-11: *Kisansiṅgh*: Rāmsiṅgh's only son, who died in 1682 (Sarkar 1984:150).

A.H. 1102, 21 Rabī'I/ 23 December 1690

[ ]देवजी
श्री गोविंददेवजी

श्री रांमजी

सही

(कटार)

(seal on the right of the Persian text)

(१) सिधि श्री महाराजाधिराज महा-
(२) राजा श्री बिसनसिंघजी देव़-
(३) बचनात कमैती प्रगनां आं-
(४) बैरी का दिसे सुप्रसाद बंच्या
(५) अप्रंच रूपय़ा ९६०ऽ नौ सै
(६) साठि सालियांनां वसुली
(७) वावति पुंनिं कपड़ा व़ागैरह ठा-
(८) कुर श्री गोव्यददेव़जी व़ ठुक-
(९) राय़नजी विदादेवीजी हिसा
(१०) मौ° झुझारपुर तपा षोह
(११) प्रगनां मजकुर ई° फसलि
(१२)षरीफ साल संन १०९८ संव-
(१३) त १७४७ एव़ज महैसव़ास षु-
(१४) रद तपा कांकड़ जो कवुल
(१५) न कीय़ा तंनषुव़ाह फुरमा-
(१६) य़ा है चाहिऐ कि प्रव़ांनां का
(१७) मजमुंन सौं षबरदार होय़
(१८) हासिल लेवा दीज्यौ ज्यौं क-
(१९) पड़ा व़ागैरह का पहुंच्या करै
(२०) ----------- सरह य़ादिदास्ति व़ा-
(२१) कौ ताो १८ मा° र° अवलि सं-
(२२) न ११०२ वरसालै ईंद्रसेणि
(२३) व़ा साह विजैरांम दीव़ांण
(२४) व़ नौवति व़ाकानवीस स-
(२५) दानंद एव़ज मव़ाजा जागीर

(२६) पूंनि कपड़ा व़ागैरह ठाकुर
(२७) श्री गोव्यंददेव़जी जो मौ°
(२८) महैसव़ास षुरद तपा कांक-
(२९) ड़ साल संन १०९७ संवत
(३०) १७४६ थे वमुजिव प्रव़ांनां
(३१) वय़ाजी तंनषुवाह हूव़ा था
(३२) अधिकारी कवुल न कीय़ा
(३३) ईस व़ास्तै अरज पहुंचीं अज-
(३४) रूय़ मिहरव़ांनीं हुकम हुव़ा जो
(३५) जागीर हिसा मौ° झुझारपुर
(३६) तपा षोह प्रगनां आंबैरि
(३७) ई° फ° षरीफ साल संन १०९८
(३८) संवत १७४७ थे एव़ज महैस-
(३९) व़ास षुरद तपा कांकड़ तंन-
(४०) षुव़ाह द्यौह चाहिऐ कि दीव़ां-
(४१) नयांन सरकार परव़ांनां लि-
(४२) षौ तारीष सदर अरज मुकर-
(४३) र पहूंचीं सालीनां व़सुली रू°
(४४) ९६०ऽ

(४५) वा° कपड़ा वा° रोजीनां
(४६) ठाकुर श्री गोव्यं- किसनचरण
(४७) ददेव़जी व़ ठुक- अधिकारी १ऽ रू°
(४८) रांणी विंद्रो- सा°
(४९) देवीजी सा° ३६०ऽ
(५०) ६००ऽ

(५१) मौ° महैसव़ास षुरद एव़ज
(५२) मौ° चतरपुरा प्र° आबैरि
(५३) वमुजिव प्रव़ांनां वय़ाजी
(५४) ई° फ° षरीफ साल संन १०९७
(५५) संवत १७४६ थे तंनषुव़ाह हू-
(५६) व़ा था अधिकारी अमल
(५७) न कीय़ा
(५८) अलमुकररा तंनषुव़ाह जा-
(५९) गीर हिसा मौ° झुझारपूर
(६०) तपा षोह प्र° आंवैरि ई°

(६१) फ° षरीफ साल संन १०९८
(६२) संवत १७४७ मौजा तंन
(६३) रूपय्या १७४५ऽ मु° व़सु-
(६४) ली रूपय्या ११६३ ।=ऽ
(६५) षालसा सरकार २०३ ।=ऽ
(६६) वाकी व़सुली
(६७) ९६०ऽ

(६८) तगीर हरीस्यं- तगीर मुरली-
(६९) घ स्यौव़ प्रं- धर प्रौहत
(७०) मपोता
(७१) ३९१ ।ऽ ३०ऽ

(७२) षालसा सरकार
(७३) ५३८ ।।।ऽ

(७४) ताो २१ मा° र° अव़लि सं-
(७५) न ११०२

(I) [ ]devjī
Śrī Govinddevjī
Śrī Rāmjī

Certified

(dagger)

(seal on the right of the Persian text)

(II 1) [1] Success! [1-3] By royal order of Śrī Mahārājādhirāj Mahārājā Śrī Bisansiṅghjī,
(II 2) [3-4] with benevolent greetings to the officers of *parganā* Amber.
(II 3-6) [5-6] Reference: 960 rupees, [in words] nine hundred and sixty, annually recoverable amount, [7-9] as a charity *(puni)* for garments etc. for the deity Śrī Govinddevjī and his consort and Vrindādevījī, [in terms of a] share [10] of village Jhujhārpur in *tapā* Khoh [11] of the aforementioned *parganā*. [11-16] Instead of Mahaisvās Khurd in *tapā* Kāṃkaṛ, which had not been accepted, these have been assigned for revenue income, starting with the autumn harvest of

rev.y. 1098/V.S. 1747**(II 7)** [16-17] It is necessary that you take care of the contents of the *parvānau*, [18-19] and provide for the receipt of the actual revenue income so that the garments etc. are received properly.

(III 1) [20-22] Commentary on the memorandum [based] on the diary-entry of 18 Rabī'I A.H. 1102, [22] on report of Dīvāns Indraseṇi [23] and Sāh Vijairām [24-25] and the diarist on duty Sadānand.

(III 2) [25] Replacement of villages in *jāgīr*. [26-27] Charity *(puni)* for garments etc. for the deity Śrī GDjī. [27-31] According to the fair copy of a *parvānau*, for this purpose, village Mahaisvās Khurd in *tapā* Kāṃkaṛ had been assigned for revenue income, starting with rev.y. 1097/V.S. 1746. [However,] this was not accepted by the custodian [of the deity]; regarding this, there was submitted a petition.

(III 3) [33-34] Out of benevolence, the order was given that, [35-40] starting with the autumn harvest of rev.y. 1098/V.S. 1747, you shall assign for revenue income the *jāgīr* of a share of village Jhujhārpur in *tapā* Khoḥ of *parganā* Amber, instead of Mahaisvās Khurd in *tapā* Kāṃkaṛ.

(III 4) [40-42] The *dīvāns* of the *sarkār* shall make out *parvānaus*.

(III 5) [42-43] On the aforementioned date, the petition was submitted again [, namely for]: Annually recoverable amount of rupees

[44]	960/--
[45-50] For garments of the deity Govinddevjī and his consort and Vṛndādevījī, annually 600/--	For daily income of Kisancaraṇ, the custodian, 1rp.; annually 360/--

[51] Village Mahaisvās Khurd, instead of [52] village Catarpuro of *parganā* Amber, [53-56] had, according to the fair copy of a *parvānau*, been assigned for revenue income, starting with the autumn harvest of rev.y. 1097/V.S. 1746. [56-57] The custodian[, however,] did not make use of it.

[58-59] Fixed allowance of revenue: *jāgīr* of a share of village Jhujhārpur [60-62], starting with the autumn harvest of rev.y. 1098/V.S. 1747; [62-63] assessed village revenue : 1,745rp.; [63-64] fixed allowance: 1,163rp., 6a.; [65] [revenue from] *khālsā* land of the *sarkār*: 203rp., 6a.; [66] balance : recoverable amount of

[67] 960/--

[68-71] Transferred from Harīsyaṃgh, great-grandson of Syauv:
391rp., 4a.

Transferred from Purohit Murlīdhar:
30rp.

[72-73] [From] the *khālsā* of the *sarkār*:
538rp., 12a..

(IV) [74-75] Date: 21 Rabī' I A.H. 1102.

ا[لله]

(dagger)

[Seal] (on the right side of the Persian text)

مهاراجه بسن سنگه ابن کنور کشن سنگه

[۱] مقرر شد که متصدیان مهمات پرگنه انبر بعنایت و التفات

[۲] امیدوار بوده بدانند که مبلغ نهصد و شصت (۹٦۰*[27]) روپیه سالیانه وصولی

[۳] در وجه بهوگ° و غیره تهاکر° سری° [...] از حصه موضع جوجهارپور تپه° کهوه

[٤] فی العمل پرگنه مذکور از ابتدائی فصلخریف سالسنه° ۱۰۹۸ سمبت° ۱۷٤۷ به

[٥] عیوض[28] موضع مهس واس خورد تپه° کانکر تنخواه فرمودیم

(inserted left-hand side, between ll.5 and 6) قبول و عمل شد

[٦] باید که بمضمون پروانه مطلع گشته واگذارند که در وجه بهوك° و غیره

[۷] ممر تسلیم باشد

[۸] شرح یاداشت واقعه از قرار بتاریخ هشدهم (۱۸[29]) ربیع الاول سنه ۱۱۰۲

[۹] برساله زبدة الاقران اندر سنا و ساهو° بجرام دیوان

[۱۰] و نوبت واقعه نویس بتسلیم درگاه سدانند آنکه به عیوض

[۱۱] معاوضه جاگیر بهوگ° و غیره تهاکر° سری° [...] از آنچه که

[۱۲] موضع مهس واس خورد تپه° کانکر از سالسنه° ۱۰۹۸ سمبت° ۱۷٤٦

[۱۳] از حضور بموجب پروانه بیاضی تنخواه یافته بود ادهکاری°

[۱٤] قبول نکرد و لهذا در باب مناداه بعرض رسید از روی

[۱٥] مهربانی امر شد که جاگیر حصه موضع جوجهارپور تپه° کهوه

[27] In the original written above the word *mablaġ*.

[28] This spelling is used throughout the text. It seems to be phonetical, instead of عوض for which cp. Platts and Steingass, s.v.

[29] The digits are written above the numerals in words.

[١٦] عمله پرگنه انبر از ابتدائی فصلخریف سالسنه° ١٠٩٨ سمبت° ١٧٤٧

[١٧] عیوض موضع مهس واس خورد تپه° کانکر تنخواه دهند

[١٨] باید که دیوانیان سرکار پروانه قلمی نمایند

[١٩] بتاریخ صدر بعرض مکرر رسیده

[٢٠] سالیانه
[٢١] *٩٦٠ وصولی

(note, written in small characters; later addition?)
*٢١٦٠
*١٢٠٠
[باقی]
موضع گوبندپور[30] پروانه نمائیده شد

---

[٢٢]
(crossed out in the original) تهاکر° سری گوبند دیو جیو° و
[٢٣] تهکرانی° دیو° بندا جیو°
رادها جیو°[31]
[٢٤] سالیانه
[٢٥] *٦٠٠

---

[٢٦]
برای روزینه کسن چرن ادهکاری°
*١
[٢٧] سالیانه
[٢٨] *٣٦٠

(oblique, on the left side of the Persian text)

[٢٩] چون موضع مهس واس خورد عیوض موضع چتراپور

[٣٠] عمله پرگنه انبر بموجب پروانه واضع از ابتدائی فصلخریف

[٣١] سالسنه° ١٠٩٧ سمبت° ١٧٤٦ تنخواه تسلیم بود ادهکاری°

[٣٢] عمل نکرد

---

[30] Govindpur. Equivalent note missing in the Rājasthānī version.

[31] Rādhā[jī]. The name misses in the Rājasthānī text.

[٣٣] المقرره تنخواه جاگیر حصه موضع جوجهارپور تهه° کهوه

[٣٤] عمله پرگنه انبر از ابتدائی فصلخریف سالسنه° ١٠٩٨ سمبت° ١٧٤٧

[٣٥] موضع
[٣٦] ١٧٤٥* مشتماهه

[٣٧] مقرره وصولی

[٣٨] ١١٦٣* ٦ انه وصولی
[٣٩] ٢٠٣* ٦ انه خالصه سرکار
[باقی]

[٤٠] ٩٦٠* وصولی

[٤١]	از تغییر هرسنگه سیهو پرم پوته°	از تغییر مرلدهر پروهت°
[٤٢]	٣٩١* ٤ انه	٣٠*
[٤٣]	از خالصه سرکار	[جمع][32]
[٤٤]	٥٣٨* ١٢ انه	

[٤٥] تحریر فی بتاریخ بست یکم ربیع الاول سنه ١١٠٢

[32] Cp. document dated A.H. 1080, 12. Ramaẕān, n.1. The reading is corroborated by the Rājasthānī text, (l.72) abbreviation *da*.

Allāh

[Seal] Mahārājā Biśan Singh, son of Prince Kiśan Singh

[1] It has been ordered! Let it be known to the *mutaṣaddīs*, responsible for the affairs of the *pargana* Amber, who may be assured of [ruling] grace and favour, [2]: We have instructed the sum of nine hundred and sixty rupees of annual duties [3] to be paid [to ensure] *bhog* for the deity Śrī [Govinddevjī], from [the revenues from the] shares of the village Jhujhārpur in the *tappā* of Khoh, [4] in the tax collection territory of the aforementioned *pargana*, from the beginning of the autumn harvest of the fiscal year 1098/ V.S. 1747 (A.D. 1690) in place of [5] [the revenues from the] village of Mahaisvās Khūrad in the *tappā* of Kāmkar (accepted and carried out).

[6-7] After taking notice of the *parvāna*, it shall be ensured that the sum is handed out for *bhog*.

[8-9] [According to] the commentary on the memorandum dated 18/ eighteenth Rabīᶜ I of the year 1102, [the following] was [decreed] in accordance with a report by the *dīvāns* Indra Senā and Śāh Bijairām, the best of their kind, and [10] Sadānand, the *vāqiᶜa-nivīs* in charge, subject of the court: [11-14] [to ensure] *bhog* for the deity Śri [Govinddevjī], [the temple] had been paid a *jāgīr* since the beginning of the fiscal year 1097/ V.S. 1746 (A.D. 1689) by His Highness, in accordance with the lawful *parvāna*, as replacement for [the revenues from the] village of Mahaisvās Khūrad in the *tappā* of Kāṃkar.

The *adhikārī* did not accept [this replacement].

For this reason a petition was presented in respect of this notice.

Through [15-17] [ruling] benevolence it was [subsequently] ruled that payment of a *jāgīr* be instructed, since the beginning of the autumn harvest of the fiscal year 1098/ V.S. 1747 (A.D. 1690), out of shares of the village of Jhujhārpur in the *tappā* of Khoh, in the tax collection territory of the *pargana* Amber, instead [of the revenues from the] village of Mahaisvās Khūrad in the *tappā* of Kāṃkar.

[18] The *divāns* of the *sarkār* shall issue a *parvānca*.

[19] The petition was examined once again on the above-mentioned date.

[20] Annually:

[21] 960 [rupees] of duties to be paid

(2,160 [rupees]
1,200 [rupees] [revenues from the] village of Govindpur; *parvāna* was issued
[rest])

[22] [For] the god Śrī Gobinddevjīū and the [23] goddess and Vṛndājīū and Rādhājīū

[24] Annual allowances:

[25] 600 [rupees]

[26] For daily allowances of Kiśan Caran, the *adhikārī*:
1 [rupee]

[27] Annual allowances:

[28] 360 [rupees]

[29-32] As according to the lawful *parvāna*, [the revenues from the] village of Mahaisvās Khūrad had been approved payment in place of [the revenues from the] village of Catrapurā, in the tax collection territory of the *pargana* Amber, since the beginning of the autumn harvest of the fiscal year 1097/ V.S. 1746 (A.D. 1689), the *adhikārī* had not taken action.

[33] Determination of payment:

a *jāgīr* from the share of the village of Jhujhārpur in the *tappā* of Khoh, [34] in the tax collection territory of the *pargana* Amber, since the beginning of the autumn harvest of the fiscal year 1098/ V.S. 1747 (1690).

[35] [revenues from the] village:

[36] 1,745 [rupees] [at the applicable eight-month rate]

[37] Determination of the duties to be paid:

[38] 1,163 [rupees] 6 annas duties to be paid [*jāgīr*]

[39] 203 [rupees] 6 annas *k͟hālis̱a* of the *sarkār*

[rest]

[40] 960 [rupees] duties to be paid

[41]	transferred from Harisingh, greatgrandchild of Syauv	transferred from Murlīdhar, Purohit 30 [rupees]
[42]	391 [rupees] 4 annas	
[43]	from the *k͟hālis̱a* of the *sarkār* 538 [rupees] 12 annas	

[44] Written on the twenty-first Rabī^{c} I of the year 1102.

Commentary:

The deed refers to three villages, along with which a fourth must be considered while interpreting the deed. The three villages named are

(1)Jhujhārpur, *tapā* Khoh, *parganā* Amber
(2) Mahaisvās Khurd, *tapā* Kāṃkaṛ, *parganā* Amber
(3) Catrapuro, *parganā* Amber.

Jhujhārpur, *alias* Meṃdlā, lies in modern Sanganer Tehsil of Jaipur District (India 1983 [DCH Jaipur]: 169, serial/code nos 95/166). Mahaisvās Khurd lies in Amber Tehsil of Jaipur District (*ibid.*: 46, serial/code nos 146/131). Catrapuro, too, must be sought in modern Sanganer Tehsil with which the ancient *tapā* Khoh merged. There are there three villages by that name. One of these (*ibid.*: 168, serial/code nos 47/162) is a likely candidate, for it neighbours on Jhujhārpur. Together with the fourth village, Govindpuro (→ A.H. 1078, with commentary), Jhujhārpur and Catrapuro form a contiguous tract of land (cp. the map on p. 352). This seems to explain why the custodian did not accept Mahaisvās Khurd in *tapā* Kāṃkaṛ, for that place lies to the south-east of Comu, at quite some distance from those three villages. Revenue to be drawn from isolated places would have implied special administrative efforts, such as a manager to look after the estate.

The deed suggests that the custodian wanted to strengthen his *jāgīr* hold in that contiguous tract of land, which was also ideally situated on the road to Bharatpur and, beyond Bharatpur, to Vrindaban. In pursuit of this aim, the custodian seems to have been quite tenacious. Mahaisvās Khurd had been assigned to him by a *parvānau bayādī* (Pers. *parvāna-yi bayāẕī*). The term literally means "fair copy of a *parvānau*". It seems to represent the finally approved version of it. In DK, many *parvānaus* of this type are reproduced, and they differ in no way from documents just named *parvānaus*. The precise impact of the term *bayādī* remains, therefore, uncertain. In the Mughal Chancellery, a *farmān-i bayāẕī* was an especially urgent and confidential one, which was sealed in such a way that its contents could not be inspected by the unauthorized (Ibn Hasan 1936: 97). The term was also used in the Safavid administration, where a distinction was made between *raqam-i daftarī* and *raqam-i bayāẕī* (Minorsky 1943: 203; transliteration modified - MH). Minorsky thinks that the *raqam-i daftarī* may have been prepared from the *musavadda-yi daftarī,* the draft, whereas the *raqam-i bayāẕī* "directly followed the King's order". Thus, a *parvānau* of the last mentioned variety is likely to have been one authenticated by the Mahārājā.

Mahaisvās Khurd not having appealed to the custodian, "who did not make use of it", Jhujhārpur was assigned to GD and, starting with the autumn harvest of rev.y. 1098/V.S. 1747, came to replace Mahaisvās Khurd. The transfer to Jhujhārpur implied that three shares, amongst these a big *khālsā* portion, were pieced together in order to obtain a *jāgīr* allowing for 960rp. net revenue income. The net income was calculated by the eight-month pay-scale, for which see above, p. 32. The assessed annual revenue was 1,745rp., and 1,163rp., 6a. were equivalent to eight twelfths of this sum. In the case of Jhujhārpur, the reduced allowance was further reduced by the revenue from the *khālsā* portion of the village land. Therefore, that revenue share had to be remitted to the treasury of the *sarkār*. However, the difference between 1,163rp. 6a. and 960rp., that is, 203rp. 6a., were also made a charity for the Phūlḍol festival, as can be concluded from doc. → A.H. 1106, 12 Jumādā I and → V.S. 1764, Śrāvaṇa b. 3, which belong both to a period when the *jāgīr* in Jhujhārpur had been replaced by the *jāgīr* Catrapur-vās Khijuryā.

GD's hold on the revenue resources of the three villages remained unstable over some time. In rev.y. 1097/V.S. 1746 (→ A.H. 1106, ll. 41-52), Catrapur-vās Khijuryā, no doubt the Catrapuro of the present document, which had been replaced first by Mahaisvās Khurd and then by Jhujhārpur, had been transferred to one Kālurām Jāṭ, but was restored to GD later on (→ V.S. 1764, Śrāvaṇa b. 3, foll.).

A.H. 1106, 12 Jumādā I/ 29 December 1694

Invocatio missing.

गोव्यंददेवजी
(कटार)

(seal on the right of the Persian text)

(१) सिधि श्री महाराजाधि-
(२) राज महाराजा श्री विस-
(३) नसिंघजी देव़वचनात
(४) कमैती प्रगनां आंवैरि
(५) का दिसे सुप्रसाद वंच्या
(६) अप्रंच रुपय़ा तींन सै
(७) पांच ३०५ऽ करार अठ-
(८) माहा का मौ° झुझारपुर त-
(९) पा षोह प्रगनां मजकुर
(१०) मैं जव़ाय़द सरकार का
(११) हैं ईस व़ास्तै हुकम फुर-
(१२) माय़ते हैं जो रूपय़ा
(१३) २०३।=ऽ व़सुली तलव
(१४) साविक श्री ---जी त-
(१५) नषुव़ाह देता रहिज्यौ अर
(१६) देह मजकुर जागीर ठाकुर
(१७) श्री ---जी की तंनषुव़ाह
(१८) है व़ास्तै जव़ाय़द कै मुजा-
(१९) हिम मति होह नकद तल-
(२०) व साविक व़ चीठी विदा-
(२१) गी की मैं व़सुल करता र-
(२२) हिज्यौ ईस वात की ताकी-
(२३) द जांणिज्यौ मौजा तंन
(२४) करार अठमाहा १७४५ऽ
(२५) तफाव़त अठमाहा व़ व़-
(२६) सुली रू° ५८१।।=ऽ वा-
(२७) की भोग ठाकुर श्री गोव्यं-
(२८) ददेव़जी रू°९६०ऽ वाकी
(२९) तागीर कालुरांम जा-
(३०) टु षालसा हुवा व़सुली

(३१)   २०३ ।=ऽ
(३२) ई° फ° षरीफ साल संवत ११०३
(३३) संवत १७५२ थे तंनषुव़ाह
(३४) कीय़ा तव तांई सय़े सगला
(३५) रुपय़ा व़सुल न होहि ज-
(३६) व़ाय़द नकद हासिल मौ
(३७) मजकुर का मैं तंनषुव़ाह
(३८) देता रहिज्यौ

(३९) तलव साविक व़ागैरह
(४०)   १२४७ । ।ऽ
(४१) वा° तलव सा-   वा° चीठी वि-
(४२) ल संन १०९७   दागी व़ागैरह
(४३) संवत १७४६ वा° जो कवजन
(४४) भोग ठाकुरजी   प्रगनां आं-
(४५) ऐव़ज चत्रपु-   वैरि परि तंन
(४६) रवास षिजु-   षुव़ाह
(४७)   २८७ । ।ऽ

-- [33]

(४८) ग़्या तपा षो-	कवज	कवज
(४९) ह जो आंण-	करार	करार
(५०) दरांम चौ-	ताो २३	ताो १५
(५१) हांण व़ागै°	मा°	सफर
(५२) तंनषुव़ाह	जील	संन
(५३) हूव़ा ईस व़ा-	हेज	११०४
(५४) स्ते वरात	संन	रू° ८७ । ।ऽ
(५५) करि नक-	११०४	व़सुल
(५६) दी तंनषु-	रू°	१५ऽ वा-
(५७) व़ाह द्यौह	२०ऽ	की
(५८) ९६०ऽ		७२ । ।ऽ
(५९)	कवज	द°---
(६०)	करार	-------
(६१)	ताो [३०][34]	°
(६०)	मा° जुल	

[33] The following text is written on the same *recto* side, turned by 180°, and on the right margin beside the Persian text. Thus the text runs from the bottom of the page upwards.
[34] The Persian version has "30".

(६२)　　　　　　　कदि संन ११०४
(६३)　　　　　　　१९६५

(६४) ताो १२ मा° जु° अव़-
(६५) लि संन ११०६ मू° महा-
(६६) वंन

Govinddevjī
(*dagger*)

(seal on the right of the Persian text)

[1] Success! [1-3] By royal order of Śrī Mahārājādhirāj Mahārājā Śrī Bisansiṅghjī, [4-5] with benevolent greetings to the officers of *parganā* Amber. [6] Reference: Rupees three hundred and [7-11] five, 305/--, fixed according to the eight-month pay-scale, form an additional income of the *sarkār* from village Jhujhārpur in *tapā* Khoh of the aforementioned *parganā*. [11-12] With regard to this, he (the Mahārājā) orders [12-15] that, in conformity with [the deity's] earlier claim, you remit 203rp., 6a. recoverable amount as revenue income of the deity Śrī [Govinddev]jī, [15-18] and that the *jāgīr* of the aforementioned village be made an allowance of the deity Śrī [Govinddev]jī. [18-19] You must not interfere with this additional income. [19-22] You must remit the cash amount, in conformity with the earlier claim and as recorded in the *cīṭhī bidāgī*. [22-23] You must observe the injunction on this matter. [23-24] Assessed village revenue fixed according to the eight-month pay-scale: 1,745rp.; difference by eight-month pay-scale and recoverable amount: 581rp., 10a.; [26-28] [interim] balance: 960rp. for *bhog* of the deity Śrī Govinddevjī; rest, [29-31] transferred from Kālurām Jāṭu to the *khālsā* [income]: 203rp., 6a.

[32-34] The revenue income has been assigned from the autumn harvest of the rev. y. 1103/V.S. 1752. [34-35] If the entire sum is not recovered, [35-38] you shall make a cash payment of the extra allowance, in addition to the realized revenue of the aforementioned village.

[39] Former claim etc.:
[40] 1,247rp., 8a.

[41-57] Item: Earlier claim of rev.y. 1097/ V.S. 1746, covering *bhog* of the deity and replacing Catarpur-vās Khijuryā in *tapā* Khoh, which became allowance of Ānandrām Cauhān and others; [for this] you shall make out a cheque for a cash allowance [of]
[58] 960rp.

[41-46] Item: *cīṭhī bidāgī* etc.; according to receipt, payment charged to *parganā* Amber,
[47] 287rp., 8a.

[48-56] Receipt of 24 Zī'l-hijja A.H. 1104, rp.
[57] 20/--

[48-57] Receipt of 15 Safar A.H. 1104: 87rp., 8a; drawn: 15rp.;

balance:
[58] 72rp., 8a.

[59-62] Receipt of 3[0] Ẕī'l-qa'da A.H. 1104, [63] 195rp.

Rate: ./.

[64-66] Date: 12 Jumādā I A.H. 1106; place: Mahāvan.

گوبند یو جیو

(*dagger*)

[Seal] (on the right side of the Persian text)

مهاراجه° بسن سنگه ابن کنور° کشن سنگه

[۱] مقرر شد که متصدیان مهمات پرگنه انبر بعنایت و التفات

۲[] امیدوار بوده بدانند که چون مبلغ سیصد و پنج روپیه

[۳] برقرار هشتماهه (۸[35]) از موضع جوجهارپور تپه° کهوه عمله پرگنه مذکور

[٤] زواید[36] سرکار است لهذا امر میفرمائیم

[٥] که مبلغ دو صد و سه (۳) روپیه و شش انه وصولی [میشود][37]

[٦] آنرا در طلب سابق سری° [...] تنخواه میدادند

[۷] و دیهه مذکور در جاگیر تهاکر° سری° [...] جیو° تنخواه است

[۸] برای زواید مزاحم نشوند نقد در طلب سابق

[۹] و چتهی بداگی° وصول میدادند باشند در ین باب قدغن بدانند

[۱۰] موضع

[۱۱] *۱۷٤٥ ۸ هشتماهه

[۱۲] *۵۸۱ ۱۰ انه تفاوت هشتماهه و وصولی
[باقی]

[۱۳] *۱۱٦۳ ٦ انه وصولی

[۱٤] *۹٦۰ بهوك° تهاکر° سری گوبند دیو جیو°
[باقی]

[۱۵] برای تغییر کالورام جاتو° که خالصه شد

[۱٦] وصولی

[۱۷] *۲۰۳ ٦ انه

---

[35] The digits are written above the numerals in words, cp. also l.5.

[36] Cp. also ll.8,22: correctly زوائد.

[37] Reading uncertain.

از ابتدای فصلخریف سالسنه ۱۱۰۳ سمبت° ۱۷۵۲
[ما که امر**] وصول نشود
زواید نقد (illegible) موضع مذکور تنخواه دهند[38]

[۱۸] طلب

سابق و غیره
۱۲۴۷* ۸ انه

[۱۹]

برای طلب سالسنه ۱۰۹۷ سمبت° ۱۷۴٦
برای بهوك° تهاکر° جیو°
عوض موضع (illegible)[39]

۹٦۰*

برای چتهی بداگی° و غیره که قبض بر پرگنه
انبر تنخواه شد

۲۸۷* ۸ انه

[38] Written obliquely on the left side of the text. The reconstruction of this portion has only been possible on the basis of its Rājasthānī version.

[39] Probably the forepart of the name Catarpurvās Khijuryā (cp. 1.20).

[۲۰]			
	عوض چترپورمس کهجوریه تهه° کهوه که در جاگیر اندرام چوهان و غیره (illegible) بهاو سنگه[40] [برساله؟] تنخواه شد لهذا برات نموده نقدی تنخواه دهند	قبض قرار بتاریخ ۲۳ ذوالحجه سنه ۱۱۰٤	قبض قرار ۱۵ صفر سنه ۱۱۰٤
		۲۰*	۸۷* ۸ انه وصول ۱۵* [باقی] ۷۲* ۸ انه
		قبض قرار بتاریخ ۳۰ ذوالقعده سنه ۱۱۰۸	
		۱۹۵*	

[۲۱] تحریر فی ۱۲ شهر جمادی الاول سنه ۱۱۰٦ مقام مهابن

[Endorsement of ratification[41]]

[40] Bhāo Singh. No corresponding endorsement in the Rājasthānī version.

[41] Perhaps بيض. Cp. Mohiuddin (1971:128,129); Steingass s.v.

Gobinddevjīū

[Seal] Mahārāja Biśan Singh, son of Prince Kiśan Singh

[1-2] It has been ordered! Let it be known to the *mutaṣaddīs*, responsible for the affairs of the *pargana* Amber, who may be assured of [ruling] grace and favour: The sum of six hundred and thirty-five rupees [3] at the applicable eight-month/ 8 rate of [revenues from the] village Jhujhārpur in the *tappā* Khoh, in the tax collection territory of the aforementioned *pargana* [4] has been realized as surplus by the *sarkār*. Therefore we decree: [5] the sum of two-hundred and three/ 3 rupees and six annas [of the surplus] has to be paid. [6] Hitherto the sum has been given as payment on a former claim of the Śrī [Govinddevjī] temple. [7] [The revenues from the] aforementioned village in form of *jāgīr* is the payment for the Śrī [Govinddev]jīū temple. [8-9] They shall not be disturbed because of the surplus. The cash amount shall be paid on a former claim [of the temple] and a *ciṭṭhī bidā'egī* as before. In this matter one must regard strict order as issued.

[10] [Revenues from the] village

[11] 1,735 [rupees] at the applicable eight-month rate

[12] 581 [rupees] 10 annas difference at the eight-month rate, duties to be paid
[rest]

[13] 1,163 [rupees] 6 annas duties to be paid

[14] 960 [rupees] [to ensure] *bhog* for the god Śrī Gobinddevjīū
[rest]

[15] By transfer, [the share of] Kālurām Jāṭu became *khāliṣa*

[16] duties to be paid

[17] 203 [rupees] 6 annas

The payment is bestowed [on the temple] since the beginning of the autumn harvest of the fiscal year 1103/V.S. 1752. If the sum total cannot be paid, one shall give the payment from the surplus of the cash revenues from the aforementioned village.[42]

[18] Former claim etc.
1,247 [rupees] 8 annas

[19]

[induced] through the claim from the fiscal year 1097/V.S. 1746 [to ensure] *bhog* for the god [Govinddev]jīū, in place of [the revenues from the village [...][43]

960 [rupees]

[induced through] a *ciṭṭhī bidā'egī* etc., payment charged to the account of the *pargana* Amber

287 [rupees] 8 annas

[42] Translated in analogy to the Rājasthānī version; cp.ll.32-37.

[43] This endorsement was completed later, l.20. Supposedly, all entries after l.17 were added later. There occurs the date 1108 at the end of the calculation column. The context of ll.19-20 suggests that also these later additions were made by successive steps.

[20]	in place of [the revenues from the village] Catarpurvās Khijuryā in the *tappā* Khoh, which became *khalisa*, in conformity with the certification directions on behalf of Bhāo Singh instructed as payment. Therefore a cheque shall be filled in and the payment shall be given in cash	revenues dated 23rd Zū'l-Hijja of the year 1104 20 [rupees] revenues dated 30th Ẓū'l-Qi^cda of the year 1104 195 [rupees] 1108	revenues dated 15th Safar of the year 1104 87 [rupees] 8 annas [already] drawn: 15 [rupees] [rest] 72 [rupees] 8 annas

[21] Written on the 12th of the month Jumādā I in the year 1106 in Mahāvan.

[Endorsement of ratification]

Commentary:

The deed belongs to the period of Kṛṣṇacaraṇ's custodianship (1689-96). It refers to Jhujhārpur, which had been made a *jāgīr* allowance in favour of GD in 1690 (→ A.H. 1102). The assessed revenue of the village was 1,745rp., the actual revenue according to the eight-month pay-scale, that is, reduced by four twelfths, was 1,163rp., 6a. In A.H. 1102, 203rp., 6a. (= 305rp. reduced by four twelfths) of this were revenue income of the *khālsā*. The temple received the balance of 960rp.

By A.H. 1106, the assignment of the share of 203rp., 6a. had changed twice. First it had been made an allowance of one Kālurām Jāṭ(u); from whom it was transferred to the *khālsā* land. In A.H. 1106, it was transferred to GD. In a deed of 1694 (Habib 1996: 145 *s.v.* Kishan Charan/Krishan Charan), Kṛṣṇacaraṇ is recorded to have inherited property in Mathura from his predecessor Seorām in 1689. He had succeeded him as custodian, but some time between 1689 and 1692 had left Vrindaban, because of the Jāṭ disturbances, and gone to "the Rājpūta country". He is mentioned to have returned to Kāmāṁ by 1694 (*ibid.*).

The document refers to an earlier claim covering 1,247rp., 8a. It consisted of the long-established yearly allowance to GD and the temple custodian, namely 960rp., and several remittances which amounted to 287rp., 8a. These various amounts were recorded in the "*cīṭhī bidāgī* (Pers. – *bida'egī*) etc.". The term *bidāgī* is a gift to someone taking leave. The *cīṭhī bidāgī* must have been the record-sheets on which receipts of cash gifts of the kind mentioned were entered. The receipts recorded fall in the period between October 1992 and July 1693. They may be connected with Kṛṣṇacaraṇ's above-mentioned travels.

While doc. A.H. 1102 covered the recoverable sum of 960rp, that of A.H. 1106 granted both the amount of 960rp. and that of 203rp., 6a. By the latter share, various earlier occasional payments of a total of 287rp., 8a. (by the eight-month ratio, equivalent to 203rp. 6a.) were superseded and stabilized.

Rāj. ll. 41-47, first col./Pers. l. 20, first col.: The Persian text refers to Bhāvsiṅgh, who is not mentioned in the Indic version.

AH 1108, 22 Rabī‘[44] II/ 18 November 1696

Copy; time and origin unknown.

The Persian version has not been given, because its readings were in many places uncertain; cp., however, the facsimile.

(१) सिधि श्री महाराजाधीराज महाराजाजी श्री वीसनसीं-
(२) घजी देववचनात गुसाइ गोविंदचरनजी दसे सुप-
(३) रसाद वच्या अप्रच्य जमीं वीघा १३५ व वागयत
(४) व कुल व हवेली वा तागीर दयसे(?) महभना (?) वावती
(५) सरकार का वहा है सो बै सरकार की तरफ सो तुम को
(६) सुपरद मुकरर कीया हे वाही एक दस्तूर कदीम ववरदारी
(७) वा नीगहवानी वाहा की तालुक अपने भली
(८) भाती कीया कीज्यो औ सो ताकीद राषज्यो
(९) कोइ आमि दषल न करो के ओ तुम्हारो हतो
(१०) २२ मा° सानी° ११०८[45]

[1] Success! [1-2] By royal order of Śrī Mahārājādhirāj Mahārājā Śrī Bisansiṅghjī, [2-3] with benevolent greetings to Gosvāmī Govindcaraṇjī. Reference; 135 *bīghās* land, gardens, [3-5] *kul* (*kuñj*?), mansions and transferred … (?), items of the *sarkār* there. [5-6] It has been decided that these be entrusted to you by the *sarkār*. [6-8] In connection with that land, you shall exercise yourself the one long-established [administrative] procedure and supervision. [8] This you must observe as an injunction. [9] You must not meddle with [the rights and property of] the common folk, [deeming] these to be yours.
[10] 22 [Rabī‘] II, 1108.

Commentary:

Habib (1996: 138, *s.v.* Gobind Charan) refers to a Persian document in the National Archives of India which is dated A.D. 1696, too. According to this document Govindcaraṇ was "Entrusted also with the charge of 135 *bighas* of imperial grant, retreats (*kunj-ha*), house (*havelī*), and compound, belonging to Maharaja Bishan Singh (Viṣṇu Siṃha), Gobind Charan

44 Inferred from the Persian version.
45 The Persian version reads "1180".

being styled Brah(ma)mūrat Gosā'in. (NAI 2671/17)". The deed mentioned by Habib and the one given here are identical in content. In its Persian version, the year given is 1180. This is certainly a mistake, because Bisansiṅgh was dead by that time.

It is also not explicitly stated that the 135 *bīghā*s referred to are identical with those transferred first in 1633 by Shāh Jahān to Rājā Jaisiṅgh I, and then by Jaisiṅgh I to the group of Vaiṣṇava temples headed by "Gobind Rai"(Mukherjee and Habib 1989: 295), but it is suggested by the document's silence on the location of the land and by the stipulation that it be managed according to the "one long-established [administrative] procedure". In → V.S. 1863 (Kārttika, ś. 3), we come across 135 *bīghā*s, which the authorities of GD feared would be usurped by the *firangī sāhebs*. If the land is identical, as I presume, it consisted of 95 *bīghā*s in Dosaich and 40 *bīghā*s in Dholera (Mukherjee and Habib, *l.c.*). For Dosaich and Dholera, places on the left bank of the Yamuna south of Vrindaban, see the map in Mukherjee and Habib 1989.

A.H. 1108, 23 Rabī‘ II/ 19 November 1696

श्री रांमजी श्री रांमजी
गोव्यांददेव़जी

(कटार)

(seal on the right of the Persian text)

(१) सिधि श्री महाराजाधिराज
(२) महाराजा श्री विसनसिंघजी
(३) देव़वचनात कमैती प्रगनां
(४) आवैरि का दिसे सुप्रसाद
(५) वंच्या अप्रंच रूपय़ा
(६) ३६०ऽ सालीयांनां व़सूली
(७) रोर्जीनां वे॰ गोव्यंदचरण
(८) अधिकारी श्री ---
(९) हिसा मौ॰ झुझारपूर तपा षोह
(१०) प्रगनां मजकुर ई॰ आधी
(११) फ॰ षरीफ साल संन ११०४
(१२) संवत १७५३ थे जागीर
(१३) मैं तंनषुव़ाह फुरमाय़ा है
(१४) चाहिऐ कि प्रव़ांनां का म-
(१५) जमूंन सौं षबरदार होय़
(१६) हिसा मजकुर ई॰ सदर हव़ा-
(१७) लै गूमास्ता मौंर्मी अलेह
(१८) कै कीज्यौ जो हासिल मू-
(१९) तसरफ हूव़ा करै नफर
(२०) सा॰ व़सुली र॰ ३६०ऽ
(२१) अलमूकररा तंनषव़ाह
(२२) जागीर हिसा मौ॰ झुझार-
(२३) पूर तपा षोह प्रगनां आं-
(२४) वैरि ई॰ आधी फ॰ षरीफ
(२५) साल संन ११०४ सं॰ १७५३
(२६) मौजा तंन व़सुली रू॰
(२७) ११६३ ।=ऽ मधे

(२८) ३६०ऽ

(२९) जो हा° सरकार मैं आया
(३०) होय़ सो वाज गिरदांनी-
(३१) द दीज्यौ व़सुली थे
(३२) ज्यादा होय़ सो षाल-
(३३) सा राषिज्यौ

(३४) तारी २३ र° सांनी सं° ११०८

Śrī Rāmjī (2x)
Govinddevjī

(dagger)

(seal on the right of the Persian text)

[1] Success! [1-3] By royal order of Śrī Mahārājādhirāj Mahārājā Śrī Bisansiṅghjī, [3-5] with benevolent greetings to the officers of *parganā* Amber. Reference: [5-13] It has been ordered that, starting with the intermediate harvest of rev.y. 1104/V.S. 1753, a share of village Jhujhārpur in *tapā* Khoh of the aforementioned *parganā* be assigned as revenue income in *jāgīr*, for [the purpose of] 360 rupees to be drawn annually for the daily allowance of the custodian of the deity Śrī [Govinddevjī], named Govindcaraṇ. [14-15] It is necessary that care be taken of the contents of the *parvānau.* [16-18] From the date given above, this share shall be made available to the representative of the aforementioned divine, [16-19] so that he may draw the realized revenue. [19-20] Personal income, recoverable annually: 360rp. [21-25] Fixed allowance of revenue: *jāgīr* of a share of village Jhujhārpur in *tapā* Khoh of *parganā* Amber, starting with the intermediate harvest of rev.y. 1104/V.S. 1753. [26-27] Assessed revenue dues of the village: 1,163rp., 6a.; out of these
[28] 360rp.

[29-31] Realized revenue that has gone to the *sarkār* shall be returned. [31-33] If it exceeds the dues, [the sum in excess] shall be kept by the *khālsā* .

[34] Date: 23 Rabī‘ II, A.H. 1108.

گوبند دیو جیو°

(dagger)

[Seal] (on the right side of the Persian text)

مهاراجه° بسن سنگه ابن کنور° کشن سنگه (۹)

[۱] مقرر شد که متصدیان مهمات پرگنه انبر بعنایت

[۲] و التفات امیدوار بوده بدانند که چون مبلغ

[۳] سیصد و شصت روپیه سالیانه وصولی در وجه روزینه

[٤] باسم گوبند چرن ادهکاری° سری° [...] حصه

[٥] موضع جوجهارپور تپه° کهوه عمله پرگنه مذکور از ابتدائی نصف

[٦] فصلخریف سالسنه ١١٠٤ سمبت° ١٧٥٣ در جاگیر تنخواه

[٧] فرموديم بايد كه بمضمون پروانه مطلع گشته حصه مذکور

[٨] [از] ابتدائی صدر حواله [گماشته][46] او نمایند و واگذارند که

[٩] حاصلات آنرا متصرف می‌شده باشد

[۱۰] [نفری][47] سالیانه

[۱۱] ٣٦٠* وصولی

[۱۲] المقرره تنخواه جاگیر حصه موضع جوجهارپور تپه° کهوه عمله پرگنه انبر

[۱۳] [از] ابتدائی نصف فصلخریف سالسنه ١١٠٤ سمبت° ١٧٥٣

---

[46] Completed on the basis of l.17 of the Rājasthānī text.

[47] Completed on the basis of l.19 of the Rājasthānī text.

[١٤] موضع
[١٥] ١١٦٣* ٦ انه وصولی
[١٦] مسدد داخید

[١٧] آنچه وصول بخالصه خرج شده باشد
[١٨] • باز گردانید دهند و باج از وصولی
[١٩] زیاده باشد بعمل خالصه دادند
[٢٠] ٣٦٠*

[٢١] تحریر فی ٢٣ شهر ربیع الثانی سنه ١١٠٨ [Endorsement[48]]

Gobinddevjīū

[Seal] Mahārājā Biśan Singh, son of Prince Kiśan Singh

[1] It has been ordered! Let it be known to the *mutasaddīs*, responsible for the affairs of the *pargana* Amber, who may be assured of [ruling] grace [2] and favour: We had since the beginning of the autumn harvest of the fiscal year 1104/ V.S. 1753 (A.D. 1696) instructed the sum of [3] 360 rupees of annual duties [4-5] in [the form of a] *jāgīr* [to ensure] payment for Govindcaraṇ, the *adhikārī* of the Śrī [Govinddevjī temple], from [the revenues from a] share of the village Jhujhārpur in the *tappā* of Khoh, in the tax collection territory of the aforementioned *pargana*. [7] Having been informed of the content of the *parvāna* [8] the mentioned share [of the revenues] shall be transferred to his agent and it shall be ensured that the [9] revenues [of the village] are allocated.

[10] Service: annual

[11] 360 [rupees] of duties to be paid

[48] Cp. A.H. 1106, 12 Jumādā I, fn.7.

[12] Determination of payment:
a *jāgīr* from a share of the village of Jhujhārpur in the *tappā* of Khoh, in the tax collection territory of the *pargana* Amber

[13] from the beginning of the middle of the autumn harvest of the fiscal year 1104/ V.S. 1753 (A.D. 1696) onwards:

[14] [revenues from the] village:

[15] 1,163 [rupees] 6 annas duties to be paid

[16] proportionately

[17-19] That which was to be paid out to the *khāliṣa* in duties, shall be returned and the tax duties that [would] exceed the duties to be paid [shall] be paid to the tax collection territory of the *khāliṣa*.

[20] 360 [rupees].

[21] Written on the 23rd of the month Rabī^{c} II of the year 1108. [Endorsement]

Commentary:

Rāj. l. 17: The *gumāstā* (< Pers. *gumāśta*) was in charge of the management of *jāgīr*s and acted as the *jāgīrdār*'s emissary (Mohiuddin 1971: 93; Gupta 1986: 163).

V.S. 1764, Śrāvaṇa b. 3/ 6 July 1707
Verso missing.

श्री रांमजी श्री रांमजी

(कटार)
(illegible Persian seal)

(१) श्री दीव़ांन वचनात मौ° चत्रपुरवास षिजुरचा तपा षोह् तंन व़ं-
(२) सुली रुपय़ा १६६६।।≡ वादि पुनी ठाकूर श्री गोव्यंददेव़जी वि-
(३) राजमांन गोव्यंदपुर ऊरफ रैहफोड़ा रू°११६३।=

(४)	वा° कपड़ा ठाकुर श्री	रोजीनां गुसांई गोव्यं-	फुलड़ौल
(५)	गोव्यंददेव़जी व़गौ°	दचरण	-----------
(६)	६००ऽ	३६०ऽ	२०३।=

(७) वाकी षालसा ऊसुली रू° ५०३।– सो ईजारौ संवत १७६४ का सा-
(८) ल कौ व° गुसांई गोव्यंदचरण नै मुकरिर करि दीय़ौ मुव़ाफीक कवु-
(९) लाति मुसारन अलेह् की थे व़सुली रूपय़ा च्यारि सै ऐक वे ई-
(१०) स वरवसत सरकार पोताषांनै व़सुल करसी ॥8॥
(११) ४०१ऽ
(१२) माल जांमीन ठा° श्री गोब्यंददेव़जी ॥ 8 ॥

(१३)	फसल षरीफ	फसल रव़ी
(१४)	२००।।ऽ	२००।।ऽ

(१५) मीती सांव़ण बदि ३ संबत १७६४

Śrī Rāmjī (2x)

(*dagger*)
(illegible Persian seal)

[1] By order of the *dīvāns*. [1-2] Assessed revenue, to be drawn from village Catrapur-vās Khijuryā of *tapā* Khoh: 1,666rp., 11a. Reduced amount [assigned] as charity *(punī)* to the deity Śrī Govinddevjī [2-3] residing in Govindpur *alias* Raihphoṛā: 1,163rp., 6a.

[4-5] For garments of the deity Śrī Govind-devjī etc.,	Daily allowance of Gusāṃī Govindcaraṇ,	[For the] Phulḍol festival,
[6] 600rp.	360rp.	203rp., 6a.

[7] Rest to be drawn by the *khālsā*: 503 rp., 5a. [7-8] For the revenue year 1764, this has been assigned in *ijārau* to [the person] named[49] Gosvāmī Govindcaraṇ. [8-9] With the assent of the aforementioned person, the recoverable dues of four hundred and one rupees [have been fixed]. [9-10] According to this regulation, he will collect them for the treasury of the *sarkār*:

[11] 401rp.

[12] Surety: the deity Śrī Govinddevjī.

[13] Autumn harvest:	Spring harvest:
[14] 200rp., 8a.	200rp., 8a.

[15] Date: Sāṃvaṇ, b. 3, V.S. 1764.

Commentary::

The custodian of GD, Govindcaraṇ, collected revenue for the *khālsā* in *ijārau* (by a contract of lease; < Pers. *ijāra*). Of 503rp., 5a., he had to pay 401rp. to the *sarkār*, whereas he kept the rest of 102rp., 5a. as a commission. For *ijārau*, cp. p. 33. Holders of *ijārau* had to produce a surety, called *māl-zāmin* (Pers. *māl-ẓāmin*), for which cp. Gupta (1986:229) and GJRT, 562. Normally, a banker stood bail for the *ijārau* dues and, in return, received a share of the *ijāradār*'s profit (Singh 1990: 130). In this case, however, it is the temple and its wealth, impersonated by the deity GD, that stood bail.

---

[49] The abbreviation *va°* of the text is taken to stand for *ba-ism* "named, by the name of" (Pers.).

The document points to the increasing consolidation of GD's hold on the tract of land surrounding the then newly constructed temple. For Catrapur-vās Khijuryā, cp. doc. → A.H. 1102 and → A.H. 1106. In A.H. 1106/A.D. 1696, Catrapur-vās Khijuryā, previously assigned as *jāgīr*, but then replaced by a fresh assignment, figured once again as a *jāgīr*. This assignment is not traceable, but it is mentioned in the present *ijārau* contract. The *jāgīr* assignment provided 1,163rp., 6a., the amount earlier drawn from Jhujhārpur (doc. → A.H. 1108). The entire assessed revenue of village Catrapur-vās Khijuryā was 1,666rp., 11a., but of this, an amount of 503rp., 5a. was the *khālsā* share. When this share was farmed out to GD, the temple collected the entire revenue of the village.

rev.y. 1767, Āśvina b. 5/13 September 1709

Invocatio missing.

गोव्यंददेवजी

सही

(कटार)

(seal)

(१)सिधि श्री महाराजाधिराज महाराजा श्री जैस्यं-
(२) घजी देव्वचनात कमैती परगनां आंवैरि
(३) कां दिसे सुप्रसाद वंच्या अपरंच वावति पुनिं
(४) भोग ठाकुर श्री --- विराजमांन मौ° रह-
(५) फोडा प्रगनां आंवैरि सालीनां रुपया ५०३।–
(६) वसुली मैं जागीर मौ° चत्रपुरवास षिजुर्या
(७) तपा षोह प्रगनां आंवैरि का मैं ईदतदांय
(८) स्यालु संवत १७६७ की सौं मुकरिर फुरमावा
(९) छै सो ईह ईवतदाय सौं हासिल भोग ठाकुरां
(१०) का नैं पहुंचावो कीज्यौ ज्यौं सरवराह भोग की
(११) होवौ करै ----- सरैह यादिदासति दाषिल
(१२) वाकै करार मिंती भादवा सुदि ८ साल संवत
(१३) १७६७ वरिसालै भिषारीदास साह फतेहचंद
(१४) दीवांन व्र निहालचंद वाकानईस अत्र भोग
(१५) ठाकुर श्री --- विराजमांन मौ° रहफोडा
(१६) जो आगैं भोग सालीनां रुपया ११६३।=ऽ की जा-
(१७) गीर मौ° चत्रपुरवास षिजुर्या मैं छी सो ईह
(१८) गांव मैं षालसौ सरकार कौ रुपया ५०३।–
(१९) कौ छौ सो भादवा वदि १४ संवत १७६७ अधि-
(२०) कारी ठाकुर कां अरज पहुंचाई जो मौ गांव
(२१) दरोवसत पुनि भोग मैं होय तौ भोग की स-
(२२) रवराह भली भांति होय़ सो हुकम हुवो व-
(२३) ट रूपया ५०३।– कौ भोग कै सीगै ईवतदा-
(२४) य स्यालु संवत १७६७ की सौं द्योह सो चाहि-
(२५) ऐ दीवांन सरकार का परवांनौ लिषौ मिं-
(२६) ती सदर अरज मुकरिर पहुंची--------------
(२७) अलमुकररा तंनषाह जागीर मौ° चत्रपुर-

(२८) व़ास षिजुर्या तपा षोह् प्रगना आंवैरि ई-
(२९) वतदाय़ स्यालु संवत १७६७ की सौं मुकरिर व
(३०) वहाल जांणि मजवुंन परवांना का सौं वाकि-
(३१) फ होय़ हासिल हवालै करिवो कीज्यौ अर ह-
(३२) रि साल सनंद की तलव मंति कीज्यौ सांनीन
(३३) हाल ईहे (?) परवांना सौं हिसाव मैं मुजरा होयला
(३४) मौजा तंन वसुली रुपया १६६६ ॥≡ मिंनहा आ-
(३५) गैं तंनषाह ठाकुर का भोग वगैरह की वहालं रु-
(३६) पया ११६३ ।= वाकी हाल वावति ईजारा मैं
(३७) रुपया--
(४०) ५०३ ।–

(४१) मिंती आसोज वदि ५ साल संवत १७६७
(४२) मुकांम कसवा आवैर

(verso)

(seal)	*(seal)*	*(seal)*	*(seal)*	*(seal)*
रजु दफत्र भिषारिदास दीव़ान	रजु दफत्र साह फतेचंद दीव़ान	रजु दफत्र ध- रमनराय़ण वकसी	रजु दफत्र महा- चंद वकसी	रजु दफत्र दय़ा- राम मूसतोफी हजुरी

(illegible Persian seal)

(I) Govinddevjī
Certified
(dagger)

(seal)

(II 1) [1] Success! [1-2] By royal order of Śrī Mahārājadhirāj Mahārājā Śrī Jaisiṅghjī,
(II 2) with benevolent greetings to the officers of *parganā* Amber.
(II 3) [2-9] Reference: As an item of charity *(punim)* for *bhog* for the deity Śrī [GD], who resides in village Rahphoṛā in *parganā* Amber, a *jāgīr* covering an annually recoverable amount of 503rp. 5a., in village Catrapur-vās Khijuryā of *tapā* Khoh in *parganā* Amber, has been

assigned, starting with the cold season of V.S. 1767. [9] From that date, you shall deliver the realized revenue for the feeding of the deities so that the management of *bhog* [10-11] can be made.

(III 1) [11] Commentary on the memorandum [based on] the diary-entry of Bhādvā ś. 8, rev. y. [13-14] 1767, on report of Dīvāns Bhikhārīdās and Sāh Phatehcand and Diarist Nihālcand.

(III 2) [1415] Here: *bhog* for the deity Śrī[GD], who resides in village Rahphoṛā. [16] Hitherto, there was [provided] for *bhog* a *jāgīr* of annually 1,163rp. 6a. [17] in village Catrapur-vās Khijuryā. There is in this [18-19] village *khālsā* land which belongs to the *sarkār* [and yields a revenue] of 503rp. 5a. [19-20] On Bhādvā b. 14, V.S. 1767, the custodian submitted a petition that [20-21] the entire village be made a charity *(puni)* for *bhog* [21-22] so that the management of *bhog* can be made properly.

(III 3) [22] Therefore the order was passed that [23-24] you shall give [him] the share of 503rp. 5a. for *bhog*, starting with the cold season of V.S. 1767.

(III 4) [24-25] It is necessary that the *dīvāns* of the *sarkār* make out a *parvānau.*

(III 5) [25-26] On the aforementioned date the petition was submitted again [, namely]:

[27-28] Fixed allowance of revenue. [27-28] You must understand the *jāgīr* of Catrapur-vās Khijuryā of *tapā* Khoh in *parganā* Amber [29-30] to be confirmed, starting with the cold season of V.S. 1767, [30-31] and it may be known to you from the intention of the *parvānau* [31] that you must assign it for the collection of realized revenue. [31-32] And there must not be claimed a *sanad* every year. [32-33] Furthermore, the present state shall be carried to account in the account-book, according to this *parvānau*:[34] Village, assessed revenue dues of 1,666rp. 11a., [34-35] minus assessed revenue income assigned earlier for *bhog* etc. of the deity: [36] 1,163rp. 6a.; balance at present: item in *ijārau* [37] [yielding] rupees

[40] 503rp. 5a.

(IV) [41] Date: Āsoj b. 5, rev. y. 1767; [42] place: *kasbā* Amber.

(seal)	*(seal)*	*(seal)*	*(seal)*	*(seal)*
Endorsed in the records: Bhikhārīdās, Dīvān	Endorsed in the records: Sāh Phatecand, Dīvān	Endorsed in the records: Dharamnārā-yaṇ, Baksī	Endorsed in the records: Mahācand, Baksī	Endorsed in the records: Dayārām, Court-Auditor

(illegible Persian seal)

Commentary:
By this grant, the GD temple consolidated its revenue income from Catrapur-vās Khijuryā conclusively; for the entire village revenue was now transferred to it in *jāgīr*, whereas earlier, the temple had held it partly in *jāgīr* and partly in *ijārau* (→ V.S. 1764, Śrāvaṇa b.3).

V.S. 1767, Mārgaśiras b. 2/ 28 October 1710

॥श्री रांमजी ॥

राधादमोदरजी
गोव्यंददेवजी

(कटार)

(*seal*)

(१) सिधि श्री महाराजाधिराज महाराजा श्री जै-
(२) स्यंघजी देव़वचनात गोपीरमन अधिकारी
(३) ठाकुर श्री --- कां दिसे सुप्रसाद वंच्या अ-
(४) परंच विंरजानंद गुमासतै गुसांई जगनाथ
(५) ठाकुर श्री --- कै अरज पहुंचाई जो विंद-
(६) रावंन मैं कुंज सरकार की तालक धरती वीघा
(७) १३७८ मुवाफीक फुरमांन पातिसाही कै मुक-
(८) रिर सो सरकार सौं तालक म्हां कै छै सो आ-
(९) गैं विर/ज/कुंवार अधिकारी रहतौ सो मुवो अर
(१०) वेटौ वै कै नंही तिह सौं अव वैं की वहु की सला-
(११) ह सौं गोपीरमन भतीजा विरजकुंवार का नैं
(१२) मुवाफीक सलाह गुसांई गोव्यंदचरण की
(१३) सौं मुकरि (!) कीयौ छौ सो वमेदवार छै सरकार
(१४) सौं परवांनौं होय़ ईह वासतै थां नैं लिषां
(१५) छा जो कुंज कौ कांम ऐवज विरजकुंवर की
(१६) तालक थां कै मुकरिर कीयौ छै सो षात्र आ-
(१७) पणीं जमां राषि कांम वैंठा कौ भली भांति
(१८) सौ करि ठाकुर की टहल भली भांति करि-
(१९) वो कीज्यौ मिती मागश्री वदी २ सवत १७६७ मु° आवैर

Śrī Rāmjī
Rādhādāmodarjī
Govinddevjī

(dagger)

(seal)

[1] Success! [1-2] By royal order of Śrī Mahārājādhirāj Mahārājā Śrī Jaisiṅghjī, [2-3] with benevolent greetings to Gopīraman, custodian of the deity Śrī [Rādhādāmodarjī]. [3-5] Reference: Vrijānand, agent of Gusāṃī Jagannāth, [custodian] of the deity Śrī [Govinddev], submitted the petition concerning [5-8] the *kuñj*-land under the authority of the *sarkār* which [measures] 135 *bīghās*. According to an imperial *farmān*, it falls under the authority of the *sarkār*. [8-10] Formerly, Vrijkumār had been entitled to it. He died and left no son. [10-13] Now, on consultation with his wife, Vrijkumār's nephew, Gopīraman, has been decided upon, according to the advice of Gosvāmī Govindcaraṇ, and so he is the candidate. [13-14] A *parvānau* shall be made out by the *sarkār*. [14-16] With reference to this matter, it has been written to you [hereby] that the management of the *kuñj* has been laid upon you by transfer of Vrijkumār's claim. [16-17] On account of this, while sustaining your own responsibilities, [17-18] you shall manage that place properly [18-19] and attend to the deity as it behoves. Date: Māgaśrī, b. 2, V.S. 1767; place: Amber.

Commentary:

Since 1598, the group of Vaiṣṇava temples of Mathura/Vrindaban, which was headed by GD, had enjoyed an imperial grant covering 135 *bīghās* of land, which in 1633 had been transferred by Śāh Jahān to Jaisiṅgh I (Mukherjee and Habib 1989:295 and 293). The copy of a deed promulgated by Mahārājā Bisansiṅgh informs us of the transfer of this land to Govindcaraṇ in 1696 (→ A.H. 1108, 22 Rabī' I).

The Rādhādāmodar temple (RD) had been constructed by, and was therefore the property of, Jīv Gosvāmī (1543-1608; Mukherjee and Habib 1979:315), whereas the GD temple had been founded by Rūp Gosvāmī, the uncle of Jīv Gosvāmī. Thus, the lineages of the custodians of RD and GD are distinct, although the custodianship of both the temples ran for some time in the line of Jīv. This was disputed by those who claimed the custodianship in the line of Rūp, for which cp. → A.H. 1038, 2 Śavvāl, commentary.

The addressee of the deed is Gopīraman. From 1706 to 1725 he was the custodian of RD.[50] He had come to Vrindaban in 1706. In 1698, his uncle (FrBr) Vrijkumār had died. From 1669 until his death, he had been custodian of RD, the fifth one in the line of Jīv Gosvāmī. He was married to Kṛṣṇapriyā and died without issue. It was his widow Kṛṣṇapriyā who, in 1706, asked her nephew Gopīraman to come to Vrindaban and who authorized him to manage the office and property of her late husband. Between 1698 and that year, Kṛṣṇapriyā had been under constant pressure by two Vaiṣṇava monks by the name of Nandkiśor and Bindrāban. They lived in a garden claimed by her, but which they, too, claimed and tried to usurp. Kṛṣṇapriyā's claim was redressed by Nandkiśor, who had become the *vakīl* of Govindcaraṇ, the custodian of GD and, therefore, in the line of Rūp Gosvāmī. Govindcaraṇ is mentioned in the present deed. Both Govindcaraṇ and Nandkiśor tried to oust Kṛṣṇapriyā from the land that she claimed. However, she was able to keep at least the garden in which the cenotaph of Rūp Gosvāmī was located. After long litigation, it was decided in 1707 that Govindcaraṇ's and Nandkiśor's claims were false. Whereas in subsequent years Kṛṣṇapriyā and Gopīraman fell out, the present deed belongs to the period when Gopīraman still sided with his aunt.

Then, there was Jagaṃnāth, custodian of GD from 1710 to 1725. He had succeeded Govindcaraṇ (custodian from 1696 to c. 1710). Through his agent Vrijānand, Jagaṃnāth, in consultation with Kṛṣṇapriyā, pleaded that the management of the 135 *bīgha*s land be transferred to Gopīraman. That land had been entrusted to his own predecessor Govindcaraṇ in 1696 (→ A.H. 1108, 22 Rabī‘ II) as confirmed in 1705 (Habib 1996: 138, *s.v.* Gobind Charan). From the present deed, however, we learn that Vrijkumār had been in charge of the 135 *bīghās* in question. This suggests that, between 1696 and 1698, the year of Vrijkumār's death, there must have taken place a change, which may have been revised by the deed of 1705. In 1710, Jagaṃnāth, being Govindcaraṇ's successor, was certainly entitled to plead for Gopīraman, as the deed states. Nevertheless this plea is a little surprising. It is not readily understandable why Govindcaraṇ did not plead for Jagaṃnāth or Jagaṃnāth not for himself.

[50] For the following, I rely on Habib 1996.

A.H. 1123, 19 Ramaẕān/ 31 October 1711

Invocatio missing.

गोवंददेव़जी

(कटार)

(seal on the right of the Persian text)

(१) सिधि श्री महाराजाधिराज
(२) महाराजाजी श्री मीरजा राजा
(३) वीजौस्यंघजी देव़वचनातु
(४) कमौती हाल व़ा ईसतकवा-
(५) ल प्रगना टोडा भीव़ का दी-
(६) से सुप्रसाद वंच्य अप्रची जौ
(७) कीता ऐेक हव़ेली व ऐेक दुकांन
(८) गौटम महाजन की मुतसल
(९) ऊदौराम सराफ कौ कसवा म-
(१०) जकुर मौ हौ सौ वहू मुसार-
(११) न अलेह की वे° कान्हौ नौ पु-
(१२) नी भेट ठाकुर श्री ---जी
(१३) कौ हव़ेली व़ दुकान मजकुर
(१४) संकलप करी सौ लीषते हौ
(१५) की हव़ेली व़ दुकांन हव़ालौ
(१६) गुसाई जगंनाथ कौ करा-
(१७) ज्यौ व़ा छोडीजौ कीसी भा-
(१८) ती व़ौ हव़ेली व़ा हाटी कौ मुजा-
(१९) हीम मती हौ ज्यौ जौ काम
(२०) वेई गुसाई मजकुर कहौ
(२१) सौ सरंजाम दीज्यौ ता°
(२२) १९ मा° रमजान संन ११२३

Govinddevjī

(*dagger*)

(seal on the right of the Persian text)

[1] Success! [1-3] By royal order of Śrī Mahārājādhirāj Śrī Mirzā Rājā Vijaisiṅghjī, [4-6] with benevolent greetings to the present and future officers of *parganā* Ṭoḍā Bhīm. Reference: [6-7] Share of one mansion, and one shop, [8] [belonging to] Gauṭam Mahājan and [situated] in the vicinity of the money-changer Udairām [9-10] and in the aforementioned township. [10-14] These are a charitable gift *(puni bheṭ)* of the wife of the aforementioned person whose name is Kānhan and who dedicated the aforementioned mansion and shop to the deity Śrī [GD]jī. Therefore, you shall make out an order [15] that the mansion and shop [16-17] be assigned to Gosvāmī Jagamnāth and be relinquished. [17-19] There must not occur any interference with the mansion and shop so that what is [20] ordered by the aforementioned Gosvāmī to be done [21] can be carried out. Date: [22] 19 Ramaẕān A.H. 1123.

سری° گوبند دیو جیو°

(*dagger*)

[Seal] (on the right side of the Persian text)

مرزا راجه° بجی سنگه فدوی شاه عالم پاد شاه غازی

(date, left within the rim of the seal)

۱۱۲۳

[۱] متصدیان حال و استقبال پرگنه توده بهیون

[۲] بعنایت و التفات امیدوار بوده بدانند که

[۳] چون یك قطعه حویلی و یك دکان باسم گتیم مهاجن[51] متصل

[٤] اودیرام صراف در قصبه مذکور واقع است و منکوحه

[٥] مشارکه باسم کانهو بطریق با پون° بهیت° تهاکر° سری° [...]

[٦] حویلی و دوکان مذکور سنکلپ° نموده لهذا قلمی میکنند که

[۷] حویلی و غیره را حواله گسائین° جگناتهه نمایند و واگذارند

[۸] که کسی به هیچ وجه مزاحم نشود و هر کاری که اظهار نمایدند

[۹] سر انجام آن مساعی باشند تحریر فی التاریخ

[۱۰] نوزدهم ۱۹ شهر رمضان المبارك سنه ۱۱۲۳

[51] That is Gautam Mahājan; cp. Rājasthānī version, 1.8.

Śrī Gobinddevjīū

[Seal] Mirzā Rājā Bijai Singh, devoted to Śāh ᶜĀlam, the King and Warrior of faith, 1123

[1] Let it be known to the *mutaṣaddīs*, both present and future, of the *pargana* Ṭoḍā Bhīṃ [2] who may be assured of [ruling] grace and favour: [3] One share of a *ḫavīlī* and one shop on the name Kotīm Mahājan, adjacent to the shop of Udairām Sarāf, are situated in the aforementioned *qaṣaba*. The wife [4] of the [person] concerned named Kānhau has donated as charities [to] the god Śrī [Govinddevjī] [6] the aforementioned [share of a] *ḫavīlī* and shop. Therefore it should be put on record that [7] the [share of a] *ḫavīlī* etc. has been assigned to Gosvāmī Jagannāth. [It shall be] ensured [8-9] that nobody will not on any account interfere in these matters. One shall make every effort to obtain fulfilment of every decreed task. Written on [10] the nineteenth (19) of the blessed month of Ramaẕān in the year 1123.

A.H. 1123, 21 Ramazan/ 2 November 1711

॥श्री रामजी ॥श्री रांमजी ॥श्री रामजी

।

गौवंददेव़जी
गौपीनाथजी
स्यामसुदररायजी

(कटार)

(seal on the right of the Persian text)

(१) सिधि श्री महाराजाधीराज
(२) महाराजाजी श्री मीरजा राजा
(३) वीजौस्यंघजी देव़वचनातु
(४) कमौती हाल व़ा ईसतकवाल
(५) प्रगना हीडोण का दीसे सु-
(६) प्रसाद वंच्य अप्रची मौ° डा-
(७) हरा व़ा सालमपुर व़ वलह-
(८) डी प्रगना मजकुर पुनी भौ-
(९) ग ठाकुर श्री ---जी
(१०) मूकरर हौ[52] चाहीऐ क प्रवान कां
(११) मजमुन थे षबरदार होई गा-
(१२) व़ मजकुरा थे कीसी भाती वाछ
(१३) व़ा वीराड़ वागौ° कुली हवुजात
(१४) थे मुजाहीम हो मती ई वात की
(१५) ताकीद जाणीजो ता २१ रमजान संन ११२३

52 This represents *hai*.

Śrī Rāmjī (3x)

'alif

Govinddevjī
Gopīnāthjī
Śyāmsundarrāyjī

(dagger)

(seal on the right of the Persian text)

[1] Success! [1-3] By royal order of Śrī Mahārājādhirāj Mahārājājī Śrī Mirzā Rājā Vijaisinghjī, [4] with benevolent greetings to the present and future officers [5-6] of *parganā* Hīḍaun (Hiṇḍaun). Reference: [6-10] The villages of Ḍāharā, Sālampur and Valhaḍī of the aforementioned *parganā* are assigned as a charity *(puni)* for *bhog* to the deities Śrī---jī (names as above – MH). [10-11] It is necessary that care be taken of the intention of the *parvānau.* [11-14] You must in no way tamper with the villages, such as by [extortion of] *vāch* and *virāṛ* etc. and sundry taxes. [14-15] The injunction on this matter must be strictly observed. Date: 21 Ramaẕān A.H. 1123.

ا[لله]

گوبند دیو جیو° و گوپی ناتهه دیو جیو° و سیام سندررای جیو°

(dagger)

[Seal] (on the right side of the Persian text)

مرزا راجه° بجی سنگه فدوی شاه عالم پادشاه غازی

(date, left within the rim of the seal)

۱۱۲۳

[۱] متصدیان حال و استقبال پرگنه هندون بعنایت و

[۲] التفات امیدوار بوده بدانند که چون موضع دهرا

[۳] و سالم پور و بلهری پرگنه مذکور در وجه بهوگ° تهاکر° سری

[٤] [...] مقرر است باید که بمضمون پروانه

[٥] مطلع گشته از مواضعات مذکور بهیچ وجه من الوجوه

[٦] از بانچهه° و برار° و غیره کلحوزات مزاحمت و معرض نرسانند

[۷] در ین باب نهایت اکید دانند تحریر بیست یکم ۲۱ رمضان سنه ۱۱۲۳

A[llāh]

Gobinddevjīū

Gopīnāthjīū

Śyāmsūndarrāyjīū

[Seal] Mirzā Rājā Bijai Singh, devoted to Śāh ᶜĀlam, the King and Warrior of the faith, 1123

[1] Let it be known to the *mutaṣaddī*s, both present and future, of the *pargana* Hindaun, who may be assured of [ruling] grace and [2] favour: [The revenues from the] villages Dāhrā [3-4]

and Sālempur and Valahaṛī in the aforementioned *pargana*, are determined [to ensure] *bhog* for the temples Śrī [Govinddevjī, Gopīnāthjī, Śyāmsūndarrāyjī]. Having been informed of the content of the *parvāna*, [4] one should not on any account disturb the aforementioned villages [or] prosecute [6] *bāch*, *barār* and other *kull-i hauzāt*. [7] In this matter one shall exercise proper care. Written twenty-first (21) of Ramazān in the year 1123.

Commentary:

ll. 6-8: Ḍāharā lies in Hiṇḍaun Tehsil of Savāī Mādhopur District (India 1983 [DCH Sawai Madhopur]; 42, serial/code nos 22/24). Sālimpur lies in Toḍā Bhīm Tehsil of Sawai Madhopur (*o.c.*: 27, serial/code nos 124/111). Valhaḍī could not be identified.

ll. 12-13: For *vāch virāṛ*, cp. Singh (1977: 322), who mentions this type of tax as "realized from grain merchants at the time of the sale of grain in the market". The *kulī havujāt* (Pers. *kull-i hauzāt*) were sundry taxes (Singh 1990: 130; for its Persian model, cp. Horst 1955[53]).

[53] I am grateful to Heike Bill for drawing my attention to this article.

V.S. 1769/ rev.y. 1768, Jyeṣṭha ś. 13/ 6 June 1712
Invocatio, elevatio and *verso* missing.

(कटार)

(seal)

(१) सिधि श्री महाराजाधिराज महाराजा श्री जै-
(२) स्यंघजी देव़वचनात कमैती परगनां
(३) आंवैर कां दिसे सुपरसाद वंच्या अपरं-
(४) च वावति पुनिं ऊदिक धरती बीघा २००ऽ
(५) दोय़ सै मौ° राजसर फुटोलाव़ तपा रांमग-
(६) ढ परगनां आंवैर की वंजड लाय़क षेती
(७) किसनरांम गोव्यंदरांम का वांभण वंगाली
(८) नैं मिंती पोस वदि ऽऽ साल संवत १७६८
(९) कै दिन गंगाजी मैं घाट हरदुव़ारजी का मैं
(१०) संकलप करी छै सो थां नैं फुरमांवां छां
(११) जो मतलव परव़ांना का सौं व़ाकिफ हो-
(१२) य़ ईवतदाय़ मिंती संकलप की सौं धरती
(१३) मंपाय़ हवालै कीज्यौ अर परतिवरष
(१४) नवो परव़ांनौ मति मांगिज्यौ ज्यैं हासि-
(१५) ल धरती कौ लें अर आसीरवाद देवौ
(१६) करै[54] ——————————————
(१७) सरेह य़ादिदासति दाषिल व़ाकै करार
(१८) मिंती जेठ सुदि ५ संवत १७६९ साल संवत
(१९) १७६८ वरिसालै भिषारीदास व़ साह फ-
(२०) तेचंद दीव़ांन व़ निहालचंद व़ाकानई-
(२१) स अत्र पुनिं ऊदिक धरती बीघा २००ऽ मौ°
(२२) राजसर फुटोलाव़ तपा रांमगढ परगंन आं-
(२३) वैर की किसनरांम गोव्यंदरांम का वांभण
(२४) नैं मिंती पोस वदि ऽऽ साल संवत १७६८
(२५) गंगाजी घाट हरदुव़ारजी का मैं संकल-
(२६) प हुई सो मिंती जेठ वदि १४ संवत १७६९
(२७) साल संवत १७६८ अरज पहुंची सो हु-
(२८) कम हुवो ईवतदाय़ मिंती संकलप की

[54]The word is corrupt for its last syllable; it may have been corrected from *karau*.

(२९) सौं धरती वंजड लायक षेती कै द्यौह सो
(३०) चाहिजे दीवांन सरकार का परवानौ लि-
(३१) षौ मिंती सदर अरज मुकरिर पहुंची——
(३२) अलमुकररा तंनषाह धरती मौ° राज-
(३३) सर फुटोलाव तपा रांमगढ परगनां
(३४) आंवेर की ईवतदाय मिंती संकलप
(३५) की सौं मुकरिर जांणि धरती वंजड ला-
(३६) यक षेती मंपाय हवालै कीज्यौ————
(३७) धरती वीघा दोय सै——————
(३८) २००ऽ

(३९) मुकरिर याह जो धरती वीघा १ऽ मैं हा-
(४०) सिल ऊनमांन रुपयौ १ऽ वपजै व-
(४१) सी धरती दीज्यौ ॥8॥

(४३) मिंती जेठ सुदि १३ संवत १७६९ साल सं-
(४४) वत १७६८ मुकांम कसवा आंवेर

(I) *(dagger)*
(seal)

(II 1) [1] Success! [1-2] By royal order of Śrī Mahārājādhirāj Mahārājā Śrī Jaisiṅghjī,
(II 2) [2-3] with benevolent greetings to the officers of *parganā* Amber.
(II 3) [3-4] Reference: Item of charitable land *(punim ūdik)*, 200 *bīghās*, [5] [in words:] two hundred, in the village of Rājsar Phuṭolāv in *tapā* Rāmgaṛh [6] of *parganā* Amber, [of the quality of] fallow land suitable for cultivation, [7-8] for Kisanrām, son of Govindrām, Bengali brahmin.
(II 4-5) [8-10] On the day of Pos b. 15 (the *amāvasyā*, new moon day - MH) of rev.y. 1768, I made a vow for this at the *ghāṭ* of the Gaṅgā in Hardvār.
(II 6) [10] Accordingly, order is given [11] that it be known [to you] by the intention of the *parvānau* [12] that the land [13] shall be measured out and transferred, this being effective from the date of the vow.
(II 7) [13-14] And there must not be demanded a fresh *parvānau* every year. In this way, he (Kisanrām - MH) may collect the revenue [15-16] of the land and keep giving his blessings.

(III 1) [17] Commentary on the memorandum [based] on the diary-entry of [18] Jeṭh ś. 5, V.S. 1769/rev.y. [19] 1768, on report of Dīvāns Bhikhārīdās and Sāh [20] Phatecand and Diarist Nihālcand.

(III 2) [21] Here: Charitable land, 200 *bīghās*, in the village of [22] Rājsar Phuṭolāv in *tapā* Rāmgaṛh of *parganā* [23] Amber, for the brahmin Kisanrām, son of Govindrām. [24-26] On Pos b. 15 of rev.y. 1768, a vow for this was made at the *ghāṭ* of the Gaṅgā at Hardvār. [26-27] Accordingly, there was submitted a petition on Jeṭh b. 14, V.S. 1769/ rev.y. 1768.

(III 3) [27-29] The order was passed that you must provide land [of the quality of] fallow land suitable for cultivation, this being effective from the date of the vow.

(III 4) [30] It is necessary that the *dīvāns* of the *sarkār* make out a *parvānau*.

(III 5) [31] On the aforementioned date the petition was submitted again [, namely, for:]

[32] Fixed allowance of revenue: Land in the village of [32-33] Rājsar Phuṭolāv in *tapā* Rāmgaṛh of *parganā* [34-36] Amber. Understanding this to be fixed from the date of the vow, there shall be measured out and provided land [of the quality of] fallow land suitable for cultivation.

[37] Land, two hundred *bīghās*,

[38] 200/-.

[39-41] It has been fixed that there shall be provided land of a kind that yields an estimated revenue of 1rp. per 1 *bīghā*.

[43] Date: Jeṭh ś. 13, V.S. 1769/ rev.y. [44] 1768; place: *kasbā* Amber.

Commentary:

l. 7: One Kisanrām Cakravartī was Minister of Jaisiṅgh II (Roy 1978:44). According to Deb (1947, quoted by Roy, *l.c.*), he was the maternal uncle of Vidyādhar Cakravartī, the Bengali brahmin, who was a high-ranking officer of Jaisiṅgh and the architect of Jaipur. Minister Kisanrām Cakravartī occurs in → V.S. 1773, Bhādrapada ś. 8, l. 8.

l. 10: The grant refers to a *saṃkalp* made by Jaisiṅgh. For *saṃkalp*, cp. pp. 36-37, and, for another incident of a *saṃkalp*, → A.H. 1123, 19 Ramaẕān. The motive for the present dedication was certainly the solar eclipse which took place on the new moon day (17 December 1711). The concluding sentence of the first paragraph, which stipulates that the grantee shall give his blessings in return for the grant, is characteristic of a *puni ūdik* deed, for which cp. p. 36.

ll. 26-27: Although the Mahārājā had decreed the grant of his own accord, the usual administrative procedures, including the "submittal of the petition", were adhered to; for the land to be allocated had to be verified and recorded by the usual administrative procedure.

ll. 29, 35-36: The land to be given consisted entirely of cultivable waste land. Otherwise, often equal shares of cultivated and cultivable land were given in *puni ūdik/arath,* for which cp. also p. 36. The land to be given is called *vaṃjaḍ*. According to the *Ā'īn* (tr., II: 68), this is waste land which has remained uncultivated for five or more years. It was assigned at Rājsar Phuṭolāv, which lies in Jamvā Rāmgaṛh Tehsil of Jaipur District (India 1983 [DCH Jaipur]: 106; serial/code nos 205/176).

V.S. 1769, Mārgaśiras ś. 5/ 22 November 1712
Invocatio missing.

गोव्यंददेव़जी
(कटार)

(seal)

(१) सिधि श्री महाराजाधिराज महाराजा श्री जैस्यं-
(२) घजी देव़वचनात गजस्यंघ दिसे सुपरसा-
(३) द वंच्या अपरंच ठाकुर श्री --- कौ सेव़-
(४) ग भव़ांनीदास षतरी लाहौर में छै सो वैं की
(५) मारफत ठाकुर कै साल में कपडौ व़गैरह रु-
(६) पय़ा सै ग्यारा वारा कौ आव़ै छै सो राह की
(७) दसतग व़गैरह भव़ानीदास का कह्या म-
(८) व़ाफिक कराय़ देवौ कीज्यौ अर कांमकाज वे
(९) ईव़ो कहै सो षसमांनौ राषिज्यौ मिती माग्यश्र सूदी ५ संवत १७६९

Govinddevjī
(dagger)
(seal)

[1] Success! [2-3] By royal order of Śrī Mahārājādhirāj Mahārājā Śrī Jaisiṅghjī, [3-4] with benevolent greetings to Gajsiṅgh. [3] Reference: The servant of the deity Śrī [GD], [4] Bhavānīdās Khatrī, is in Lahore. [4-5] Eleven times a year, the deity has received through him garments etc. [6] worth one hundred rupees. [6-8] You shall issue the road transit permits etc. prepared according to Bhavānīdās's orders. [8-9] And what he orders to be done you must consider binding.
[9] Date: Māgyaśra ś. 5, V.S. 1769.

Commentary:
ll. 2, 4: Bhavānīdās Khatrī and Gajsiṅgh remain unidentified.

ll. 6-7: A road transit permit had to be produced by travellers. "It is issued in the names of the officials of every territory through which the bearer had to pass, and records their name and nature of the business" (Mohiuddin 1971: 97).

V.S. 1773, Āṣāḍha ś. 8/ 16 June 1716
Invocatio and *verso* missing.

गोबिंददेवजी

सही

(कटार)

(seal)

(१) सिधि श्री महाराजाधिराज महाराजा श्री सवा-
(२) ई जैस्यंघजी देववचनात कमैती प्रगनै आवैरि
(३) का दिसे सुप्रसाद वंच्या अप्रंच वावति पुन्य संध्या
(४) भोग ठाकुरजी श्री ––– जी का नै ईस्तक मि-
(५) ती चैत वदि १ संवत १७७३ साल सवत १७७२ थैं त-
(६) हवील मोदीषांना कोठ्यार कसवा आंवैरि का थैं
(७) मुकरर करि था नै फुरमावां छां जो मतलव प्रवा-
(८) ना का थैं वाकिफ होय रोजीना नकद व जिनस
(९) मुवाफिक जैल पहुंचावो कीज्यौं ज्यौं श्री ठाकुरां
(१०) नै भोग लागवो करै अर प्रतवरष नवो प्रवानौं
(११) मति मागिज्यौ थां नै ईही प्रवाना थैं हिसाव मैं मु-
(१२) जरा होसी ––––––––––––––––––––––
(१३) सरह यादिदासत दाषिल वाकै करार मिती जेठ सु-
(१४) दि १५ संवत १७७३ साल संवत १७७२ वरसालै कि-
(१५) सोरदास व ताराचंद दीवान व निहालचंद वाका-
(१६) नवीस अत्र पुन्य संध्या भोग ठाकुर श्री ––– जी
(१७) तहवील मोदीषाना कोठ्यार कसवा आवैरि का
(१८) थैं सो वास्तैं सिध्या भोग के मिती चैत वदि १ संवत
(१९) १७७३ साल संवत १७७२ अरज पहोंची हुकम हु-
(२०) वा नकद जिनसि मु° तपसील जैल ईस्तक मिती
(२१) अरज की थैं मुकरर करि द्योह रोजीना ––––––
(२२) नकद टका जिनसि
(२३) पका ––– –––––
(२४) ३। ।५।।
(२५) नकद –––––––––– जिनस तोल २८ के
(२६) –––––––––––––– ––––––––––––
(२७) ३। ।≤५।।

(२८) चावल सुन- दाल मूंग की
(२९) षर सेर सेर
(३०) ऽ६ ऽ३
(३१) आटा गौहूं घीव़ सेर
(३२) को सेर –– ––––––
(३३) ऽ५ ऽ१।।

(३४) सो चाहिजै दीव़ान सरकार का प्रवानो लिषैं मि-
(३५) ती सदर अरज मुकरर पहूंची ––––––––––––
(३६) मुकररा तनषाह रोक व़ जिनसि तहवील मोदीषां-
(३७) ना कसवा आंवैरि का परि ईस्तक मिती चैत वदि
(३८) १ संवत १७७३ साल संवत १७७२ का थैं रोजीनै
(३९) नकद टका जिनस तोल
(४०) पका तीन २८––––––
(४१) ३। ।ऽ५।।
(४२) नकद –––––––––––– जिनसि ––––––––––
(४३) ––––––––––––––––– ––––––––––––––––
(४४) ३। ।ऽ५।।
(४५) चावल सुन- दाल मूंग की
(४६) षर सेर छ्ह सेर तीन
(४७) ऽ६ ऽ३
(४८) आटा गौहूं घीव़ सेर ड्यो-
(४९) को सेर पांच ढ ––––––––––
(५०) ऽ५ ऽ१।।

(५१) मिती असाढ सुदि ८ संवत १७७३ साल
(५२) [संवत १७७२ मुकाम ----]नावाद

(I) Govinddevjī

Certified
(*dagger*)

(*seal*)

(II 1) [1] Success! [1-2] By order of Śrī Mahārājādhirāj Mahārājā Śrī Savāī Jaisiṅghjī,
(II 2) [2-3] with benevolent greetings to the officers of *parganā* Amber.
(II 3) [3-6] Reference: Regarding an item of charity *(punya)* for the twilight feeding of the deity Śrī [GD]jī, in force from Cait b. 1, V.S. 1773/ rev.y. 1772 [and to be obtained] from the treasury of the *modī*-stores of *kasbā* Amber,
(II 6) [7-8] it has been determined and the order is given to you that it may be known [to you] by the intention of the *parvānau* [8] that you have to provide a daily allowance of cash and kind, [9] according to the details listed [below], [9-10] so that the sacrificial feeding of the deity can take place regularly.
(II 7) [10-11] And there must not be demanded a fresh *parvānau* every year.
(II 8) [11-12] By the present *parvānau*, [the charity] shall be carried to your account in the account-book.
(III 1) [13-14] Commentary on the memorandum [based] on the diary-entry of Jeṭh ś. 15, V.S. 1773/ rev.y. 1772, [14-16] on report of Dīvāns Kīsordās and Tārācand and Diarist Nihālcand:
(III 2) [16-18] Reference: Charity for the twilight feeding of the deity Śrī [GD]jī, from the treasury of the *modī*-stores of *kasbā* Amber. [18-19] On Cait b. 1, V.S. 1773/ rev.y. 1772, there arrived a petition for the twilight feeding.
(III 3) [19-21] There was passed the order that you fix and provide a daily allowance of cash and kind, according to the details listed [below] and in force from the date of the petition.

[22-23]	Cash, *ṭakā pakā*	Kind	
[24]	3/-	1/4 maund, 5 1/2 *sers*	
[25]	cash	kind, 28 *tols* to the *ser*	
[26] ————	————	————	
[27]	3 *ṭakās*	1/4 maund,5 1/2 *sers* [= 15 1/2 *sers*]	
[28]		*sunkhar* rice,	moong pulse,
[29]		*sers*	*sers*
[30]		6/-	3/-
[31]		wheat flour,	ghee, *ser*
[32]		*sers* ————	————
[33]		5/-	1 1/2

(III 4) [34] It is necessary that the *dīvāns* of the *sarkār* make out a *parvānau*.

(III 5) [34-35] On the aforementioned date the petition was submitted again [, namely for:] [36-37] Fixed allowance: Cash and kind, charged to the treasury of the *modī*-office of *kasbā* Amber. [37-38] Starting with Cait b. 1, V.S. 1773/ rev.y. 1772, daily allowance, [namely,]

[39]	cash, *ṭakā pakā*	kind, *tols*	
[40]	three	28 [to the *ser*]	
[41]	3/-	1/4 maund, 5 1/2 *sers*	
[42]	cash ————	kind ————	
[43]	————	————	
[44]	3 *ṭakā*	1/4 maund, 5 1/2 ser	
[45]		*sunkhar* rice,	moong pulse,
[46]		six *sers*	three *sers*
[47]		6/-	3/-
[48]		wheat flour,	ghee, one and a half
[49]		five *sers*	*ser*
[50]		5/-	1 1/2

(IV) [51] Date: Asāḍh ś. 8, V.S. 1773/ rev. [52] [y. 1772; place: Śāhjahān]ābād.

Commentary:

ll. 28-29, 45-46: *sunkhar cāval* is a kind of rice occurring regularly in charitable grants, for which cp. RSA, *Nuskhā punya parvānā sabtī*, Jaipur, *pass.* Despite this, it could not be identified; cp., however, Hindi *sunkharcā*, "a kind of rice which is ripe by the end of Āśvina or the beginning of Kārttika" (HŚS).

V.S. 1773, Bhādrapada ś. 8/ 14 August 1716

श्री रांमजी श्री रांमजी श्री रांमजी

श्री गोवंददेव़जी

रामराम

(१) सिधि श्री साह् श्री सेवारांमजी साह् मेघराजजी
(२) जोग्य लिषतं दीव़ान कीसोरदास ताराचं-
(३) द केन्य ---- वंच्य अैठा का संमाचार भला
(४) छै थां का सदा भला चाहीजे अपरंची ठाकु-
(५) र श्री ---- जी जैनीवास जेता दीन व़ीरा-
(६) जै जेता दीन चोकी राती नै देवा कै वासतै मा-
(७) ली वागौ° नफर ९ राषीवा कै वासतै मारफ-
(८) ती चकरव़ती कीसनरांम की मीती असाढ
(९) वदी १ साल संवत १७७२ अरज पंहौची हुक-
(१०) म हुव़ा जेता दीन ठाकुर श्री ---- जी जैनीवा-
(११) स वीराजै जेतै राती की चौकी कै वासतै माली
(१२) वागौ° नफर ९ राषै ती मै दरी नफर १ नाज
(१३) सेर ऽ१।। तोल २८ मै व़ तेल पईसा दोय भरौ तौ-
(१४) हवील मोदी कसवा आवैरी का सु दौह् सो थां
(१५) नै लिषा छा ई° मी° असाढ वदी १ साल

---

(१) संवत १७७२ का थे जेता दीन ठाकुर श्री ---- जी
(२) जैनीव़ास वीराजै जेता दीन नफर नव़ नै
(३) नाज व़ तेल तौह्वील मोदी कसवा आवैरी
(४) का सु दावौ कीज्यौ थां नै ईही सनदी थे हीसा-
(५) व मै मुजरा होसी दरी नफर नाज सेर डौढ तेल
(६) पईसा दोय भरौ मू° ————————————
(७) ——————————————————
(८) १३।। १८
(९) नफर नव़ चौकी कौ व़ासतै
(१०) मारफ़ती चकरव़ती वीद्याधर
(११) की राषीज्यौ
(१२) नाज जव़ वाजरौ मोठ तेल रोजीना पईसा

(१३) तौल २८ कौ सेर साढा अठारा भरौ
(१४) तेरा रोजीना १८
(१५) १३।।

(१६) मीती भादवा सुदि ८ सवत १७७३

(seal) *(seal)*

दा° नुसषौ

नकल लीषी
दा° नुसषौ
नकल ली

नकल
दफत्र साह सेवाराम

दफत्र साह मेघराज वुतात(?)

॥४॥ साह श्री सेवारांमजी व साह मेघराजजी जोग्य

Śrī Rāmjī (3x)

Śrī Govinddevjī

Rām-Rām

[1] Success! [1-2] Written to Sāh Śrī Sevārāmjī and Sāh Meghrājjī [2] by Dīvāns Kīsordās and Tārācand, [3-4] ... be received. Here, everything is well. We hope that everything is always well with you. Reference: [4-9] For the time that the deity Śrī [GD]jī resides in Jainivās [and] a night guard shall be given to him, there was submitted, on Asāḍh b. 1, rev.y. 1772, through Cakravartī Kīsanrām a petition that 9 servants, such as *mālīs* etc., be maintained. [9-11] The order was passed that, as long as the deity Śrī [GD]jī resides in Jainivās, [11-14] 9 servants, such as *mālīs* etc., be maintained as night guards, and that, for this [purpose], you pay the rate of 1 1/2 *ser* (28 *tauls* per *ser*) of grain and oil for one servant, equivalent to 2 *paīsā*, from the treasury of the *modī* of *kasbā* Amber. [14-*verso* 1] Therefore, we have written to you that, starting with Aṣāḍh, b. 1, rev.y. 1772 [1-4] and as long as the deity Śrī [GD]jī resides in Jainivās, you shall provide regularly grain and oil for 9 servants from the treasury of the *modī*

of *kasbā* Amber. [4-6] By this *sanad*, there shall be booked in the account-book that you provide the rate of 1 1/2 *ser* of grain, and oil for one servant, equivalent to 2 *paīsā*. Fixed allowance:

[7] ---

[8] 13 1/2 18/-

[9-11] Nine servants shall be kept as guards by arrangement of Cakravartī Vidyādhar.

[12] Grain: barley, millet, pulse;
[13-14] thirteen and a half *ser*s
(28 *taul* per *ser*) daily allowance
[15] 13 1/2

Oil: daily allowance, equivalent to
eighteen *paīsā*
18/-

[16] Date: Bhādvā ś. 8, V.S. 1773.

(*seal*) (*seal*)

Entered in the *nuskhau*

Copy written
Entered in the *nuskhau*
Copy written

Copy,
records (*daftar*) of Sāh Sevārām

records (*daftar*) of Sāh Meghrāj [xxxx]

(*addressee*)
Sāh Śri Sevārāmjī and Sāh Meghrājjī

Commentary:

l. 1: In 1716, Sāh Sevārām was *āmil* of *parganā* Āmer (Gupta 1986: 189). Sāh Meghrāj, not mentioned by Gupta, may have been his co-*āmil*. Meghrāj served also as *vakīl* (Rajasthan State Archives 1974, *pass.*).

l. 5: For Jainivās, cp. p. 20.

ll. 8, 10: For Jaisiṅgh's minister, Kisanrām Cakravartī, and for Vidyādhar Cakravartī, cp. → V.S. 1769, Jyeṣṭha ś. 13, commentary.

V.S. 1774, Jyeṣṭha ś. 15/ 14 May or 12 June 1717

Invocatio and *verso* missing.

गोबिंददेव़जी

सही

(कटार)

(seal)

(१) सिधि श्री महाराजाधिराज महाराजा श्री सव़ाई जैस्यं-
(२)घजी देव़वचनात कमैती प्रगनै चाटसू का दिसे सुप्रसा-
(३) द वंच्या अप्रंच वावति पुन्य उदिक गांव़ दयालपुरो प्र-
(४) गनै चाटसू को तन दरोवस्त ठाकुर श्री --- जी
(५) कैं जो मिती चैत वदि १३ सनीचरव़ार संवत १७७३ साल
(६) संवत १७७२ नै महामहावारनी जोग हुव़ो तब संकल-
(७) प करि चढ़ायौ ती स्यौं थां नैं फुरमाव़ां छां जो मतलब प्र-
(८) वाना का थैं व़ाकिफ होय गांव़ दयालपुरो प्रगनै चाट-
(९) सू को ईस्तक मिती चैत वदि १३ साल संवत १७७२ थैं श्री
(१०) ठाकुरां का सेवगां के हव़ाले कीज्यौ प्रतबरष नवो प्रव़ा-
(११) नो मति मांगिज्यौ था नैं ईंही प्रवाना थैं मुजरा हिसाव
(१२) मैं होसी गांव़ दरोबस्त ------------------------------------
(१३) सरह यादिदास्त दाषिल व़ाकै करार मिती असाढ वदि
(१४) ५ संवत १७७३ साल संवत १७७२ वरसालै किसोरदास
(१५) व़ साह ताराचंद दीव़ान निहालचंद वाकानवीस अ-
(१६) त्र गांव़ पुन्य उदिक गांव़ दयालपुरा प्रगनै चाटसू को ठाकु-
(१७) र श्री --- जी कैं मिती चैत वदि १३ संवत १७७३ साल
(१८) संवत १७७२ नै परवी महामहावारणी हुइी तव गांव़ द-
(१९) यालपुरो प्रगनै चाटसू को संकलप करि चढायो थो
(२०) सो व़ास्तैं गांव़ के मिती जेठ वदि ९ संवत १७७३ साल संव-
(२१) त १७७२ अरज पहूंची हुकम हुव़ा गांव़ दयालपुरो प्रगनै
(२२) चाटसू को ईस्तक मिती संकलप की थैं सीगे पुन्य के मु-
(२३) करर करि द्योह गांव़ तन दरोवस्त १ --------------------
(२४) सो चाहिजै दीव़ान सरकार का प्रव़ाना लिषैं मिती सद-
(२५) र अरज मुकरर पहूंची ----------------------------------
(२६) मुकररा तनषाह पुन्य उदिक गांव़ दयालपुरो प्रगनै चा-
(२७) टसू को ईस्तक मिती चैत वदि १३ संवत १७७३ साल सं-

(२८) वत १७७२ थै गाव़ तन दरोवस्त ------------------------

(२९) १

(३०) जो हासिल सरकार मैं आया होइ सो वाज गरदानीद की व-

(३१) रात करि फेरि दीज्यौ --

(३२) मिती जेठ सुदि १५ संवत १७७४

(I) Govinddevjī
Certified
(dagger)
(seal)

(II 1) [1] Success! [1-2] By royal order of Śrī Mahārājādhirāj Mahārājā Śrī Savāī Jaisiṅghjī,
(II 2) [2-3] with benevolent greetings to the officers of *parganā* Cāṭsū.
(II 3) [3] Reference: Item of charitable land *(punya udik)*. [3-4] The entire revenue income of village Dayālpuro in *parganā* Cāṭsū for the deity Śrī [GD]jī. [5] When on Saturday, Cait b. 13, V.S. 1773, rev.y. [6] 1772, there occurred a *mahāmahāvāruṇī* constellation, [6-7] I made a vow to offer [this].
(II 6) [7] Hereby, order is given to you that by the intention [8] of the *parvānau* it shall be understood that village Dayālpuro in *parganā* Cāṭsū [9-10] shall be transferred to the servants of the deities from Cait b. 13, rev.y. 1772.
(II 7) [10-11] There must not be demanded a fresh *parvānau* every year.
(II 8) [11] By this *parvānau*, there shall be carried to your account in the account-book: an entire village.
(III 1) [13] Commentary on the memorandum [based] on the diary-entry of Asāḍh b. [14] 5, V.S. 1773, rev.y. 1772, on report of Dīvāns Kisordās [15] and Sāh Tārācand and Diarist Nihālcand.
(III 2) [16] Here: 1 village as charitable land, [namely,] village Dayālpuro in *parganā* Cāṭsū, for the deity [17] Śrī [GD]jī. On Cait b. 13, [18] V.S. 1773, rev.y. 1772, there occurred a *mahāmahāvāruṇī* day. On that day, the village of [19] Dayālpuro in *parganā* Cāṭsū was vowed to be offered. [20-21] Therefore, relating to this village, there was submitted a petition on Jeṭh ś. 9, V.S. 1773, rev.y. 1772.
(III 3) [21-23] There was passed the order that you assign village Dayālpuro in pargana Cāṭsū as a charity, effective on the date of the vow [23] [, namely]: the entire revenue income of 1 village.

(III 4) [24] It is necessary that the *dīvāns* of the *sarkār* make out *parvānaus*.

(III 5) [24] On the aforementioned date, [25] the petition was submitted again [, namely for:]
[26] Fixed allowance of revenue: Charitable land, village Dayālpuro in *parganā* Cāṭsū. [27] Beginning with Cait b. 13, V.S. 1773, rev. year [28] 1772, village revenue in entirety,

[28] 1

[29] If realized revenue has been paid to the *sarkār*, [30] this shall be returned by cheque remittance.

(IV) [31] Date: Jeṭh ś. 15, V.S. 1774.

Commentary:

l. 3: Dayālpuro: In modern Cāksū Tehsil, there is no village by this name, though there is one called Dayāpurā (India 1983 [DCH Jaipur]: 276, serial/code nos 87/96).

l. 6: The *mahāmahāvāruṇī* is the thirteenth *tithi* of the waning half of the month of Caitra (Caitra b. 13) which falls on a Saturday and has the Śatabhiṣak *nakṣatra* (Kane 1974, V.1: 300; also Kamalākara Bhaṭṭa 1949: 69). In V.S. 1773, this corresponded to Saturday, 10 March 1716.

V.S. 1776, Bhādrapada ś. 6/ 10 August 1719

श्री रामजी
गोविंददेवजी
(कटार)

(seal)

(१) सिधि श्री महाराजाधिराज महाराजा श्री सवाइी जै-
(२) स्यंघजी देव्रवचनात किसनराम दिसे सुप्रसाद वंच्या
(३) अप्रंच ठाकुर श्री --- जी कुरोरी पधारैला सो
(४) तीं स्यौं फुरमांव्रां छां जो सुव्रारी व्र बारबदारी की
(५) सरबराह सिताब करि दीज्यौ मीती भादवा सुदी
(६) १५ संवत १७७६

Śrī Rāmjī
Govinddevjī
(dagger)
(seal)

[1] Success! [1-2] By royal order of Śrī Mahārājādhirāj Mahārājā Śrī Savāī Jaisiṅghjī, [2] with benevolent greetings to Kisanrām. [3] Reference: The deity Śrī [GD]jī will betake himself to Kurorī. Therefore, [4] order is given that horsemen and carriers [5] be provided quickly. Date: Bhādvā ś. [6] 6, V.S. 1776.

Commentary:

<u>l. 2:</u> For Kisanrām, Jaisiṅgh's minister, cp. → V.S. 1769, Jyeṣṭha ś. 13, commentary.

<u>l. 3:</u> Kurorī is taken to be identical with Karaulī in Sawai Madhopur District.

V.S. 1776, Mārgaśiras ś. 3/ 3 December 1719

श्री रांमजी
श्री गोवंददेव़जी
(कटार)

(seal)

(१) सिधि श्री मह़ाराजाधिराज मह़ाराजा श्री सवाई जैस्यंघ-
(२) जी देव़वचनात जगरांम दिसे सुप्रसाद वंच्य अपरं-
(३) ची ठाकुर श्री --- जी का मंदर मै कांम सरु
(४) कीयौ छै सो तय़ार करव़ाय़ दीज्यौ व़ गुसाईजी कै व़ा-
(५) स्तै कोट्ङी ऐक करव़ाय़ दीज्यौ ओर कांम ऊन्हालू
(६) मैं होय़लौ ओर श्री ठाकुरा का भोग व़ सामगरी
(७) की तलव ईवतदाय़ मिती काती सुदि ३ थे चढी होय़
(८) सो दीव़ाई दीज्यौ आगा थे रोजीना दीव़ावौ कीज्यौ
(९) ई वात की ताकीद जाणीज्यौ और य़ा की पाछिली
(१०) देणि छै सो ह़ाल वणै तौक्यै द्याज्यौ नं वणै तौ ऊन्हालू
(११) मैं चुका दीज्यौ मीती मागिश्र सुदि ३ सवत १७७६

----

(१) नकल लिषी   नकल लिषी   वरसालै किसोरदास व़ साह
(२)   ताराचंद दीव़ान

Śrī Rāmjī
Śrī Govinddevjī
(*dagger*)

(seal)

[1] Success! [1-2] By royal order of Śrī Mahārājādhirāj Mahārājā Śrī Savāī Jaisiṅghjī, [2] with benevolent greetings to Jagrām. Reference: [3] In the temple of the deity Śrī [GD]jī work has been started. [4] It shall be completed and for the Gosvāmī a house shall be constructed. And the work [4-5] shall be done in the hot season. [5-7] And if there have accrued arrears on the payment for the deity's *bhog* and worship material since Kārtik, ś. 3., [8] these shall be made good for. In future a daily allowance shall be given. [9] The injunction on this matter must be

observed. And if the arrears [10] due to be settled cannot be cleared at present, [10-11] they shall be payed in the hot season. [11] Date: Māgiśra ś. 3, V.S. 1776.

----

[1] Copy written	Copy written	By report of Dīvāns
[2]		Kisordās and Sāh Tārācand

Commentary:

The document does not identify the temple under construction. Probably, it was that of Kanakvṛndāvan, for which cp. p. 23.

l. 2: Jagrām - officer and *vakīl* of Jaisiṅgh (Bhatnagar 1974: 53; 169, n. 35).

V.S. 1777, Āśvina ś. 14/ 4 October 1720

Invocatio and *elevatio* missing, gaps in the series of photos; seal pasted over in the course of repair work. From the exstant photos it is not clear where the *verso* side of the document begins; it certainly does not start with the commentary (part III of the document, for which cp. the translation). Therefore, the lines of the text are numbered consecutively down to the end. Lines 27-33 and 65-75 of the document have been reconstructed on the basis of the document itself and of a document of rev.y. 1784 (Horstmann 1995). The major portions reconstructed are marked off by *****. Errors in Horstmann 1995 have been tacitly corrected on the evidence of the present document. The graphic peculiarities of the present document have been retained in the reconstruction; thus *ū* prevails in many places where doc. rev.y. 1784 has *u*.

(कटार)

(१) सिधि श्री महाराजाधिराज महाराज[ा श्री सवा]ई जैस्यं-
(२) घजी देव़वचनात कमैती प्रगना [आवैरि] का दिसे सु-
(३) प्रंसाद वंच्या अप्रचिं वावति पुनि भौग व़गैरह् गा-
(४) व़ राजसर फहुटौलाव़ तपा रामगढ प्रगना आबैरि
(५) कौ ठाकर श्री --- जी विराजमांन क-
(६) नकवृदावन जौ हासिल गाव़ कौ ऊन्हालु संवत १७७६
(७) की मै सनदि दिव़ानी सौ पाय़ौं अव व़ास्तै प्रव़ाना सव-
(८) ती कैं मारफति अय़ामल की अरज पहौचाई ती सौ
(९) था नै फूरमाव़ा छा मतलव प्रव़ाना का सौ व़ाकिफ
(१०) हौय़ ईसतग साष स्यालू सवत १७७७ थे गाव़ राजस-
(११) र फूटौलाव़ तपा रांमगढ कौं भौग व़गैरह् की तन-
(१२) षाह् मै मूकरर जाणि हासिल गाव़ दरौवस्त कौ सेव-
(१३) गा के हव़ालै करिवौ कीज्यौ ज्यौं भौग व़गैरह् की सर-
(१४) वराह् करिवौ करैं अर प्रतिवरष नव़ौ प्रव़ानौ मति मागिज्यौं
(१५) था नै ईही प्रवानां सौ हिसाव मै मूजरां हौसी गाव़ दरौवस्त
(१६) सरह् य़ाददिदासति दाष्यल व़ाकै करार मिती आसौज वदि १३
(१७) संवत १७७७ वरिसालै किसौरदास ताराचंद दिव़ांन व़ नि-
(१८) हालचंद व़ाकानईस अत्र पूनि भौग व़गैरह् ठाकर श्री ---
(१९) --- जी विराजमांन कनकविंरदावन तनषाह् दरौव-
(२०) स्त गाव़ राजसर फूटौलाव़ तपा रामगढ प्रगना आवैरि
(२१) जौ हासिल गाव़ कौं सनदि दिव़ानी सौ ऊनहालू सवत १७७६
(२२) ताई पाय़ौं अव वास्तै प्रव़ाना सवती कै अरज पहौची हकं-
(२३) म हूवा ईस्तग स्यालू सवत १७७७ थे प्रव़ानौ सवती करि

(२४) द्यौह पूनि भौग व़गैरह सालीनां रूपयां ४२६९ तन व़सूली
(२५) मुकररा तनषाह गाव़ राजसर फूटौलाव़ तपा रामगढ
(२६) प्रगना आवेरि तन रूपय़ा ७०००ऽ वादि तषफीफ ऊनहालू
****

(२७-३१) [संवत ...- व़सूली] (= ll. 92-96, perhaps followed by [गां])
(३२) व़ रू[पय़ा]
(३३) [४२३९।।–]
****

(३४) पूनि भौग व़गैरह ठांकर श्री ---जी
(३५) सालीनां १९५६।।–

(३६) पूनि भौग रोजीनां रूपय़ा २।।–।।। द्र मा-
(३७) हैं रूपय़ा ७८।·।। मास १२ का रूपय़ा ९३९ ।≡
(३८) वादि तीसा गूणतीसा का तफाव़त का रू° १५ऽ
(३९) वाकी रूपाय़ां ९२४ ।≡

(४०) नकद रौजीना टका २८। द्र° रूप- जिनसि रोजीनां ।५।। की-
(४१) य़ा १ऽ [का टका १८।] रू° मती रूपय़ां
(४२) १।।– १ऽ।।।

(४३) मिश्री मांषण म- त्रकारी संध्या भौग संध्या समै का नै
(४४) लाई भौग नै रोजी- भोग नै रोजी- चाव़ल झीनवा दाली मूग की
(४५) ना टका ना टकां रोजीना ऽ६ द्र° रोजीना ऽ३ द्र°
(४६) ५। ३।· ।१।। मू° रू° ।।।४।।। मू° की°
(४७) दूध रोजीना मण -------------- ।।·।। –।।
(४८) १ऽ द्र° ऽ१ का ।२५ -------------- घीव़ रोजीना ऽ१।। आटौ रोजी-
(४९) २०। द्र ऽ४।।।= की° ना ऽ५ द्र° १ऽ रू°
(५०) ।–ऽ =ऽ

(५१) षूसवौई सालीना व़सूली रूपय़ां
(५२) ४८६ऽ

(५३) अत्र अडगजौ रौजीना तौला
(५४) ३७२।।ऽ २ऽऽ वरस १ का तौला ७२०ऽऽ
(५५) गूलाव कौ रोजी- करणा कौ सां- द्र तौला १ का –।। मू°
(५६) ना मासौ ऽ१ऽ व- लीनां रूपय़ां रूपय़ां
(५७) रस १ का तोला ३०ऽऽ १२।।ऽ ६७।।ऽ

(५८) द्र° तौला १ऽऽ का रू°
(५९) १२ऽ रू°
(६०) ३६०ऽ

(६१) फूलेल सालीना ऊन्मा°   पाणी गूलाव कौ रौजी-
(६२) रूपय़ा ६ऽ   नां ऽ।। मूकररां वरस १ कौ म°
(६३)   ४।।ऽ द्र° रूपय़ा १ऽ कौ सेर ऽ४।।
(६४)   मू° ४०ऽ

****

(६५) वैल वाग का व़गो नगद व़ जीनसी
(६६) मा° १ का रू° ४६।ऽ।। मू° सा° रू° ५५५।=
(६७) वादी तीसा गुणतीसा का रू° ९।ऽ वाकी
(६८) सालीना रूपय़ा पाच सै छीय़ाली-
(६९) स आना दोय़ ५४९=ऽ

(७०) वैल रासी ६ नै मा° १ का रू° अठारा   वागव़ान व़ दरव़ान ११ द्र
(७१) आना डोढ १८–।।ऽ   माहौ नफर १ नै नाज मण ३ऽ
(७२) दाणो रो° सेर साढे   घास रोजीना ट-   मू° मण ३३ऽ द्र रू° १ऽ को मण १।ऽ
(७३) तेरा ।३।। मा° १ का १०ऽ५   का ६। द्र माही का   मू° रूपय़ा छ्हवीस आना छह
(७४) द्र १।ऽ मू° रू°   १८। द्र° १८°। मू° रू°   २६।=
(७५) ८–।।ऽ   १०ऽ

****

(७६) चूगौ मोरा नै रोजीना ऽ३
(७७) मास १ कौ मण २।ऽ द्र १।ऽ
(७८) मू° रू° १।।।–

(७९) ठाकर श्री --- जी कै भोग व़गैरह
(८०) सालीनां रूपय़ा ---------------------
(८१) ------------ २२८३ऽ -----------------

(८२) भौग का रौजीना रूपय़ा ३ऽ   पोसाष का सालीनां
(८३) मास १ का रू° ९०ऽ सालीनां   रूपय़ा --------------
(८४) १०८०ऽ वादी तीसा गुणती-   १२२१ऽ
(८५) सा का रूपयां १८ऽ वाकी
(८६) -------- १०६२ऽ ----------

(८७) सो चाहिजे दिव़ान सरकार का प्रव़ाना लीषौ मि-

(८८) ती आसोज वदि ९ सवत १७७७ अरज मुकरर पहौं-
(८९) ची मूकररा तनषाह पूनि भोग व़गैरह मैं गाव़ रा-
(९०) जसर फूटौलाव़ तपा रांमगढ प्रगना आबेरि त-
(९१) न रूपय़ा ७०००ऽ वादी तषफीफ मूकररी (!) ऊन्हालू
(९२) संवत १७७६ थे रुपय़ा ३००ऽ वाकी ६७००ऽ वादि त-
(९३) फाव़त अठमाहा व़सूली का रूपय़ा २२३३।–।।
(९४) वाकी ४४६६।।– वादी तषफीफ मू॰ य़ादिदास्त व़ा-
(९५) कै करार मिती आसोज वदि ९ संवत १७७७ की स्यां-
(९६) लू थे रूपय़ां २२७।-।। वाकी तन दरौवस्त व़सूली
(९७) रूपय़ा
(९८) -------------------- ४२३९।।– --------------------

(९९) मिती आसौज सुदि १४ संवत १७७७ मू॰ जोधपुर

(dagger)

(II 1) [1] Success! [1-2] By royal order of Śrī Mahārājādhirāj Mahārāj[ā Śrī Savā]ī Jaisiṅghjī,
(II 2) [2-3] with benevolent greetings to the officers of *parganā* [Amber].
(II 3) [3-4] Reference: Item of charity *(puni)* for *bhog* etc., village Rājsar Phuṭolāv in *tapā* Rāmgaṛh of *parganā* Amber. [5-7] According to a *sanad* issued by the *dīvāns*, the deities Śrī [GD and Rādhāmādhav]jī, who reside in Kanakvṛndāvan, received the realized revenue of the village at the hot season harvest[55] of V.S. 1776.
(II 4)[7-8] Through Āyāmal, there has now been submitted a petition for the confirmation of the *parvānau.*
(II 6) [8-9] Hereby, order is given to you that it be known to you by the intention of the *parvānau* [10] that, beginning with the winter harvest of V.S. 1777, village Rājsar [11] Phuṭolāv in *tapā* Rāmgaṛh [11-12] shall be understood to be assigned for revenue income for *bhog* etc., [12] and that the realized revenue of the entire village [13] shall be assigned to the servants [of the deity] [13-14] so that they can make the arrangements for *bhog* etc.
(II 7) [14] And there must not be demanded a fresh *parvānau* every year.
(II 8) [15] Following this *parvānau*, there shall be carried to your account in the account-book: [an] entire village.

---

[55]*ūnhālu* is here feminine and means "hot season harvest", that is Rabī' harvest, whereas the masculine noun *ūnhālu* means "hot season".

(III 1) [16] Commentary on the memorandum [based] on the diary-entry of Āsauj, b. 13, [17] V.S. 1777, on the report of Dīvāns Kisandās [and] Tārācand and [18] Diarist Nihālcand.

(III 2) [18] Here: Charity for *bhog* etc. [for] the deities Śrī [GD and Rādhāmādhav][19]jī, who reside in Kanakvṛndāvan; [19-20] entire revenue income [of] village Rājsar Phuṭolāv in *tapā* Ramgaṛh of *parganā* Amber. [21-22] According to a *sanad* issued by the *dīvāns*, they received the realized revenue of the village up to the hot season [harvest] of V.S. 1776. There has now been submitted a petition for the confirmation of the *parvānau*.

(III 3) [22-23] There was passed the order that, beginning with winter V.S. 1777, you confirm the *parvānau* and provide, [24] as charity for *bhog* etc., an annual allowance of 4,239rp. 9a. [25] Fixed allowance of revenue: Village Rājsar Phuṭolāv in *tapā* Rāmgaṛh [26] of *parganā* Amber, assessed revenue 7,000rp. ./. [26-27] 300rp. reduction by *takhfīf*,

****

[26-27] fixed to begin with the hot season [harvest] of V.S. 1776; balance: 6,700 rp.; [on this,] [28] abatement on the recoverable amount according to the eight-month ratio: 2,233rp. 5a. 2p.; [29] balance: 4,466rp. 9a.; [on this,] reduction by *takhfīf*; in the memorandum [based] on the diary-entry [30] of Āsoj b. 9, V.S. 1777, fixed to begin with the cold season [harvest]: [31] 227rp. 5a. 2 p.; balance: entire revenue, recoverable amount [32] [village?] rupees

[33] 4,239rp. 9a.

****

[34] Charity for *bhog* etc. of the deity Śrī [GD]jī,
[35] annually 1,956rp. 9a.

[36] Charity for *bhog*, per day 2rp. 9a. 3p.; rate per month,
[37] 78rp. 4a. 2p.; for 12 months, 939rp. 7a.;
[38] [thereon] reduction by 1/59 due to [calendrical] discrepancy[56] [=] 15rp.;
[39] balance 924rp. 7a.

[40] Cash, per day 28 *ṭakās* at a rate of [41] [18 *ṭakās*] per rupee;	Food produce, per day 15*sers*, 8 *ch.*; price
[42] 1rp. 9a.	1rp. 12a.

[43] Sugar-candy, butter,	Vegetables for the	For the twilight *bhog*	
[44] cream for *bhog*, per	twilight *bhog*, per	Fine rice,	Moong beans,
[45] day *ṭakā*	day *ṭakā*	per day 6 *sers*, at a	per day 3 *sers*, at a rate

[56] For this, cp. p. 71.

[46]	5	3	rate of 11 *sers*, 8 *ch*., fixed:	of 34 *sers*, 12 *ch*., fixed:
[47] Milk, per day		---------------------	8a. 2p.	1a. 2p.
[48] 1 maund, at a rate of 1 *ser* at 4 *ṭakās*, 25 *dāms*			Ghee, per day 1 *ser*,	wheat flour, per day
[49] 20 *ṭakās*			8 *ch*., at a rate of 4 *sers*, 14 *ch*., price	5 *sers*, at a rate of 1rp.; rupees
[50]			5a.	2a.

[51] Scent, annually recoverable amount: rupees

[52] 486/-

[53] Perfume,		*aṛgjau*, per day 2 *tolās,*
[54] 372rp. 8a.		for 1 year 720 *tolās,*
[55] Rose-scent, per day	lemon [oil?] per year	at a rate of 1 *tolā* for 1a. 2p., fixed:
[56] 1 *māśā*, for 1	rupees	rupees
[57] year 30 *tolās*,	12 1/2	67rp. 8a.
[58] at a rate of 1 *tolā* for		
[59] 12rp.		
[60] 360rp.		

[61] Scented oil, annually approximately	Rosewater, per day
[62] rupees 6	half a *ser*; fixed for 1 year,
[63]	4 maunds, 20 *sers*, at a rate of 1rp. for 4 *sers*, 8 *chaṭāṃks*,
[64]	fixed: 40rp.

****

[65] Cash and food produce for [the maintenance of] cattle, garden etc.;
[66] for 1 month, 46rp. 4a. 2p., fixed: 555rp. 6a.,
[67] [thereon] reduction of 1/59, [i.e.] 9rp. 4a.; balance:
[68] per year, five hundred and fourty-six rupees
[69] and two annas; 546rp., 2a.

[70] For 6 head of cattle, per month 18rp.		For 11 servants, namely, gardeners and gate-keepers, at a rate of
[71] and one and a half annnas; 18rp. 1a. 2p.		3 maunds of wheat per month for 1 servant,
[72] Foodgrains [as fodder], per day thirteen and a half	Grass, per day	fixed: 33 maunds at a rate of 1rp. for 1 maund, 10 *sers*,
[73] *sers*, 13 *sers*, 8 *ch.*, for one month: 10 maunds, 5 *sers*,	6 *ṭakās*, at a rate of	fixed: twenty-six rp., 6a.;
[74] at a rate of 1 maund, 10 *sers* [for 1rp.], fixed:	18 *ṭakās*, 25 *dāms*, per month	26rp. 6a.
[75] 8rp. 1a. 2p.	10rp.	

****

[76] Bird-seed for the peacocks, daily 3 *sers*,
[77] for 1 month 2 1/4 maunds at a rate of 1rp. 4a.,
[78] fixed: 1rp. 13a.

[79] For *bhog* etc. of the deity Śrī [Rādhāmādhav]jī,
[80] annually
[81] 2,283rp.

[82] For *bhog*, daily 3rp.,	For garments, annually
[83] 90rp. per month, annually	rp.
[84] 1,080rp. ./. 1/59,	1,221rp.
[85] [that is,] 18rp., balance:	
[86] 1,062rp.	

(III 4) [87] It is necessary that the *dīvāns* of the *sarkār* make out *parvānaus*.

(III 5) [88] On Āsoj b. 9, V.S. 1777, the petition was submitted again. [89] Fixed allowance of revenue: For a charity for *bhog* etc., village [90] Rājsar Phuṭolāv in *tapā* Rāmgaṛh of *parganā* Amber. [91] Assessed revenue, 7,000rp. [91-92] ./. 300rp. reduction by *ta<u>kh</u>fīf*, fixed to begin with the hot season [harvest] of V.S. 1776; balance: 6,700rp. ./. abatement on the recoverable amount [93] according to the eight-month ratio: 2,233rp. 5a. 2p.; [94] balance: 4,466rp. 9a.; [on this,] reduction by *ta<u>kh</u>fīf*, according to the memorandum [95] [based] on the diary-entry of

Āsoj b. 9, V.S. 1777, fixed to begin with the cold season [harvest]: [96] 227rp. 5a. 2p.; balance: entire revenue, recoverable amount [97] rupees

[98] 4,239 rp., 9 a.

[99] Date: Āsoj ś. 14, V.S. 1777; place: Jodhpur.

Commentary:

The deed refers jointly to the GD and Rādhāmādhavjī temples. The *elevatio* of the deed missing, it does not give a clue to its beneficiaries. However, a *ḍaul* dated rev.y. 1784 and referring to the same grant, mentions in its *elevatio* both GD and Rādhāmādhavjī in successive order. GD received a share of 1,956rp. 9a., and Rādhāmādhavjī one of 2,283rp.

For the first grant, a *puni ūdik*, in Rājsar Phuṭolāv cp. → V.S. 1769, Jyeṣṭha, ś. 13. At a point, the entire revenue income of Rājsar Phuṭolāv was transferred to GD, as is shown by doc. [V.S. 1928, Caitra b. 15 (Rājsar Phuṭolāv)].

l. 8: Āyāmal Khatrī s/o Pañjābrāy was Jaisiṅgh's Minister (DK 3: 473 ff.). In docs. V.S. 1778ff., he bears the title "Rājā". For him, cp. Bhatnagar 1974, *pass.*, especially 179. He was "a master of Persian prose (writing under the pen-name *Agahi*) and the ablest of Jaipur diplomats and administrators", and died on 9 February 1747 (Sarkar 1984: 239).

ll. 43 ff.:

(ll. 43 ff.) The twilight *bhog* is served to the deity at the seventh stage of the eight stages of the *nitya-sevā*, the daily routine of serving and worshipping the deity in the temple. For a description of the *nitya-sevā* in the Vallabhite context, cp. Bennett 1993: 104-07. At that time, the deity receives cooked food and other items for which the ingredients listed are employed.

(l. 44, col. 3) *cāval jhīnvau* is a kind of fine rice (HŚS, s.v. *jhinvā* "fine paddy [*mahīn cāval kā dhān*]").

(l. 53, col. 2) *aṛgjau* is a perfume made of ingredients like saffron, sandalwood, camphor etc. (HŚS *s.v. argjā*).

(l. 55, col. 2) *karṇau* seems to be lemon-scented oil or perfume; *karanā* (H.) is a kind of lemon (HŚS). The substance appears also as *atra karṇā,* "*karṇā*-perfume", for which cp. for example RSA, *Tojī rojnāmā khuśbū-khāna,* V.S. 1782.

(l. 61, col. 1) *phulel,* "aromatic oil" (Bennett 1993: 121, n. 22).

(l. 76) The peacocks at the temple are fed regularly; the theological reason for this is seen in Kṛṣṇa's feeding of animals, such as monkeys, on curd and milk (*Bhāgavatapurāṇa*, X.8.29) or on butter (*ibid.*, X.9.8). Therefore, feeding the peacocks, the birds symbolic of Kṛṣṇa himself, emulates Kṛṣṇa's divine play (Shri Shrivatsa Gosvami, Vrindaban, oral communication, 1994).

ll. 91-98: The calculation contained in lines 91-98 (and in the restored lines 27-33) shows that the balance was rounded off. In the following table, the figures of the deed have been put in brackets if they differed from the arithmetically correct ones.

Assessed revenue	7,000rp.		
reduction by *takhfīf*	300rp.		
		6,700rp.	
abatement by eight-month ratio		2,233rp. 5a. 2p.	
			4,466rp. 10a. 2p. (4,466 rp. 9a.)
reduction by *takhfīf*			227rp. 5a. 2p.
Balance:			4,239rp. 5a. (4,239 rp. 9a.)

The result of 4,239rp. 9a. produced by the document is probably due to a slip of the pen, for I I– is "9a.", which differs only by one missing stroke from "5a.", I–.

For the items of *bhog*, cp. also doc. V.S. 1808, Bhādrapada ś. 13.

V.S. 1778, Āśvina ś. 1/ 11 September 1721

॥श्री रांमजी॥ ॥श्रीरांमजी॥ ॥श्री रांमजी॥ ॥श्री रांमजी॥

गोवंददेव़जी

रामराम

(१) ॥सिधि श्री साह श्री मोहनदासजी व़ा साह सी (?)-
(२) षानंदजी जोग्य लीषतं दीव़ांन किसोर-
(३) दास ताराचंद केन्य --- वं जुहार वंच्य
(४) अैठा का स्माचार भला छै था का स-
(५) दा भला चाहीजे अप्रचि ठाकुर श्री
(६) ---जी कौ मंदिर श्री वीदरावंन-
(७) जी मै छै सो मुव़ाफीक हुकम प्रव़ां-
(८) नगी राजा आय़ामलजी कै था नैं ली-
(९) षां छां जो ठाकुर का मंदीर कै वास्तै
(१०) पङ्दा पंवादार करव़ाय़ दीज्यौ
(११) अरसाय़व़ांन आगै छै सो फाटि गय़ौ
(१२) होय तौ फेर करव़ाय़ दीज्यौ अर मरम-
(१३) ति तलव होय़ अर काम हाल चालतौ
(१४) जाणौ तौ मरमति करव़ाय़ दीज्यौ
(१५) ई वात की ताकीद जांणीज्यौ मिती आ-
(१६) सौज सुदी १ सवत १७७८

Śrī Rāmjī (4x)

Govinddevjī

Rām-Rām

[1] Success! [1-2] Written to Śrī Sāh Śrī Mohandāsjī and Sāh Śrī Sīkhānandjī (?) by Dīvāns Kisordās [3] [and] Tārācand. … greetings. [4] Here all is well. [4-5] We hope that everything is always well with you. [5] Reference: The temple of the deity Śrī [6] [GD]jī, which lies in Śrī Vṛndāvanjī. [7] In accordance with the order of a *parvānau* of Rājā Āyāmal, [8] we have

written to you that [9] for the temple of the deity, [10] there shall be provided a cotton curtain; [11] if the canopy that has been there so far [11-12] is torn, it shall be replaced. [12-13] And if there is an application for repair and you have found the work to be actually in progress, [14] arrange for the repair work to be carried out. [15] The injunction on this matter is to be observed. Date: Āsoj ś. 1, V.S. 1778.

Commentary:

ll. 1-2: Sāh Śrī Mohandās s/o Ṭoirmal, Mahājan, held the post of Superintendent of Building Construction, and had been *āmil* of *parganā* Amber since V.S. 1776 (DK 22: p.?). Sāh Sīkhānand (?) may have been his co-*āmil*.

l. 8: For Rājā Āyāmal, cp. → V.S. 1777, Āśvina ś. 14, commentary on l. 8.

V.S. 1782, Mārgaśiras b. 14/ 22 November 1725

॥श्रीरांमजी॥ ॥श्री रांमजी॥

गोवंददेव्रजी

रांमरांम

(१) ॥सिधि श्री राजी श्री स्यामस्यघजी जोग्य लि-
(२) षतं दीव्रान नराय़णदास व्रा कीरपारांम केन्य
(३) --- वंच्या अैठा का स्माचार भला छै था
(४) का सदा भला चाहजे अप्रची ठाकुर श्री ---
(५) जी कोय़ला जाङा कै स्मै पावै छै त्या मधे मण
(६) सतरी कीतो तनषाह व्रदावन का मुतसद्या
(७) पर करी अर व्रा सिव्राय वाकी रहै सो थे आप-
(८) णा ईह तमाम सो दीव्राजौ अर जाङा मै कैता
(९) मण कोय़ला सरकार सो पाव्रै छै ता की हकीक-
(१०) त की फर/द/ महौर आपणी थे हजुरी भेजीजौ
(११) मिती मागश्र बदि १४ सवत १७८२

रसीद पोस वदी ऽऽ सं-
वत १७८२

Śrī Rāmjī (2x)

Govinddevjī

Rām-Rām

[1] Success! [1-2] Written to officer Syāmsiṅghjī by Dīvāns Narāyaṇdās and Kīrapārām [3] … greetings. Here all is well. [3-4] We hope that everything is always well with you. Reference: The deity Śrī [GD] [5]jī receives coal for the cold season. Of this, [6-7] the share of 70 maunds forms an income which has been charged to the officers of Vrindaban. [7-8] And if there remains an outstanding claim [on the part of the deity], you shall fully settle this yourself. [8-10]

And send the Court a report *(hakīkat kī pharad)* bearing your seal [by which it is stated] how many maunds of coal [the deity] receives from the government during the cold season.
[11] Date: Māgaśra b. 14, V.S. 1782/ 22 December 1725.

(Endorsement on the left margin towards the bottom:)
Received on Pos b. 15, V.S. 1782.

Commentary:
l.1: *śrī rājī śrī syāmsyaṃghjī* is taken to mean "to officer Syāmsiṅghjī", *rājī* being interpreted as "state". Officers could be designated by the institution they represented (cp., for example, KD 951 and 981). Syāmsiṅgh remains unidentified.

V.S. 1784, Āśvina b. 11/ 31 August 1727

॥श्री रामजी॥ ॥श्री रांमजी॥ ॥श्री रामजी॥

गोव्यंददेव़जी

सही

(कटार)

(seal)

(१) सिधि श्री महाराजाधिराज महाराजा श्री सव़ाई जैस्यंघजी
(२) देव़वचनात कमैती प्रगनां आंवैरि का दिसे सुप्रसाद वं-
(३) च्या अप्रंचि वावति पुन्य भोग व़ागैरह रोजीनां ऊसूली
(४) रुपय़ो ऐक १ऽ ठाकुर श्री --- जी की ठकुरांणींजी
(५) की सेव़ा करिवा नैं सषी ऐक पधराई तीं का भोग व़ा वस-
(६) त्र कै व़ास्तै मारफति राजा आय़ामल की मिती सांव़-
(७) ण वदि ७ संवत १७८४ साल संवत १७८३ अरज पहोंची
(८) ती सौं फुरमांव़ां छां मतलव प्रव़ांनां का सौं व़ाकिफ हो-
(९) य़ पुन्य भोग व़ागैरह रुपय़ो ऐक रोजीनां व़सूली ईवत-
(१०) दाय़ मिती अरज की सौं वहाल जांणि तैहव़ील पोतदा-
(११) र प्रगनां आंवैरि का सौं देवो कीज्यो अर प्रतवरष न-
(१२) व़ो प्रव़ांनों मति मांग्यज्यो ईही प्रव़ांनां सौं हिसाव मैं
(१३) मुजरा होय़ला रोजीनां व़सूली रूपय़ो ऐक १ऽ

(१४) भोग नैं रोजीनां आंनां आ- वसत्र नैं रोजीनां आंनां आ-
(१५) ठ ।।ऽ ठ ।।ऽ

(१६) मुकररा तनषाह पुन्य भोग व़ागैरह ईस तक मिती सां-
(१७) व़ण वदि ७ संवत १७८४ साल संवत १७८३ सो वहाल
(१८) जांणिं तैहव़ील पोतदार प्रगनां आवैरि का सौं देवो
(१९) कीज्यो रोजीनां व़सूली रूपय़ो ऐक ओरंगसाही ॥8॥

(२०) १ऽ

(२१) भोग नै रोजीनां आंनां आ- वसत्र नैं रोजीनां आंनां आ-
(२२) ठ ठ

(२३) ।।ऽ ।।ऽ

---

(१) सरह य़ादिदासति दाष्यल व़ाकै करार मिती भादव़ा सुदि १० संवत
(२) १७८४ वरिसालै नरांय़णदास व़ किरपारांम दिव़ांन व़ निहाल-
(३) चंद व़ाकानव़ीस अत्र ङोल पुन्य भोग व़ागैरह ठाकर श्री ---
(४) --- जी की ठकुरांणींजी की सेव़ा कै व़ास्तै ऐक सषी प-
(५) धराई तीं का भोग व़ा वसत्र कै व़ास्तै मारफति राजा आय़ा-
(६) मल की मिती सांवण वदि ७ संवत १७८४ साल संवत १७८३
(७) अरज पहोंची हुकम हूव़ा पुन्य भोग व़ागैरह कै नांय़ रोजी-
(८) नां व़सूली रूपय़ो १ऽ ईवतदाय़ मिती अरज की थे करि त-
(९) नषाह प्रगनां आंवैरि परि करि द्योह सो चाहिज्ये दिवां-
(१०) न सरकार का प्रवांनां लिषैं मिती भादव़ा सुदि १० संव-
(११) त १७८४ अरज मूकरर पहोंची भोग व़ा वसत्र कै व़ास्तै
(१२) रोजीनां ऊसूली ऐक ओरंगसाही ॥8॥

(१३) १ऽ

(१४)	भोग नैं रोजीनां आंनां आठ	वसत्र नैं रोजीनां आंनां आ-
(१५)		ठ
(१६)	।।ऽ	।।ऽ

(१७) मूव़ाफिक य़ादिदासति वमहोर राजा आय़ामाल व़ दस-
(१८) षत दिव़ांनय़ां

(१९) मिती आसोज वदि ११ सवत १७८४ मुकाम आवैर

	(seal)	*(seal)*	*(seal)*
(२०)	रजु दफत्र	रजु दफत्र	रजु दफत्र विजैरांम
(२१)	नराईणदास	क्रपाराम दी-	मुंस्तोफी हजुरि ॥8॥
(२२)	दीवान	व़ान	

(**I**) Śrī Rāmjī (3x)

Govinddevjī

Certified

(dagger)

(seal)

(II 1) [1] Success! [1-2] By royal order of Śrī Mahārājādhirāj Mahārājā Śrī Savāī Jaisinghjī,
(II 2) [2] with benevolent greetings to the officers of *parganā* Amber.
(II 3) [3] Reference: Item of charity *punya)* for *bhog* etc.[, namely], daily allowance [4] [of] one – 1 – rupee. [4-5] There was sent a *sakhī* to attend to the consort of the deity Śrī [GD]jī.
(II 4) [5-7] On Sāvaṇ b. 7, V.S. 1784/ rev. year 1783, a petition for her *bhog* and clothes was submitted through Rājā Āyāmal.
(II 6) [8] Hereby, order is given that it may be known [to you] by the intention of the *parvānau* [9-11] that a charity for *bhog* etc.[, namely], a daily allowance of one rupee, shall be understood to be in force from the date of the petition and that it shall be dispensed from the treasury of the treasurer of *parganā* Amber.
(II 7) [11-12] And there must not be demanded a fresh *parvānau* every year.
(II 8) [12-13] Following this *parvānau*, there shall be carried to account in the account-book the daily allowance of one rupee – 1 –.

[14] For *bhog*, daily annas   For clothes, daily annas
[15] eight – 8 –   eight – 8 –

[16] Fixed revenue allowance: Charity for *bhog* etc. [16-19] Understanding it to be in force from Sāvaṇ b. 7, V.S. 1784/ rev.y. 1783, there shall be given a daily allowance of one Auraṅgśāhī rupee from the treasury of the treasurer of *parganā* Amber,
[20]   – 1rp. –

[21-23]   (= lines 14-15)

(III 1) [1] Commentary on the memorandum [based] on the diary-entry of Bhādvā ś. 10, [2-3] V.S. 1784, by report of Dīvāns Narāyaṇdās and Kirapārām and Diarist Nihālcand.
(III 2) [3] Statement as follows: Charity for *bhog* etc. [3-5] One *sakhī* was sent to attend to the consort of the deity Śrī[GD]jī. [5-7] On Sāvaṇ b. 7, V.S. 1784/ rev. year 1783, a petition for her *bhog* and clothes was submitted through Rājā Āyāmal.

(III 3) [7-9] There was passed the order that, beginning with the date of the petition, you provide a daily allowance of 1rp. as a charity for *bhog* etc. and charge it to *parganā* Amber.

(III 4) [9-10] It is necessary that the *dīvāns* of the *sarkār* make out *parvānaus*.

(III 5) [10-11] On Bhādavā ś. 10, V.S. 1784 the petition was submitted again [, namely:] For *bhog* and clothes, a daily allowance of one Auraṅgśāhī rupee,

[13] – 1rp. –

[14-16] (= *recto*, lines 14-15)

(III 6) [17-18] As endorsed in the memorandum by the seal of Rājā Āyāmal and the signature of the *dīvāns*.

(IV) [19] Date: Āsoj b. 11, V.S. 1784; place: Amber.

(V)

(seal)	*(seal)*	*(seal)*
[20] Endorsed in the record; [21-22] Narāīṇdās, Dīvān	Endorsed in the record; Krapārām, Dīvān	Endorsed in the record; Vijairām, Court-Auditor

V.S. 1786, Āṣāḍha ś. 3/ 18 June 1729

॥श्री रांमजी

(seal)

गोव्यंददेवज़ी के

राम सही

(१) ॥ कंव़रजी श्री सूरजमलजी वचनात
(२) मुसरफ बापार वाजे गांव़न के दिसे
(३) अत्र सिरवे़ २ पानन के श्री ठाकुर
(४) --- महीनें १ मै वार १ आवो करै
(५) सो हासिल राहदारी व़गैर के ते मु-
(६) जाहम मत होवें करौ मिती अ-
(७) साढ सुदी ३ संवत १७८६

Śrī Rāmjī

(seal)

Govinddevjī
Certified [by the name of] Rām

[1] By order of Prince Śrī Sūrajmal. [2] To the inspectors of the trade-taxes of villages. [3] Reference: 2 *sirvā* of betel leaves for the deity Śrī [4] [GD] arrive regularly once a month. [5-6] You must not tamper with this by [imposing] toll-tax etc. [on these goods]. Date: [7] Asāḍh ś. 3, V.S. 1786.

Commentary:

l. 1: Sūrajmal was the son or adopted nephew of the Jāṭ Rājā Badansiṅgh and himself Rājā from 1756 to his death in 1763.

<u>l. 3:</u> The betel leaves for the deity were measured by *sirvā*. This is a weight-unit of goods carried, probably a bale. It differs from the load carried by units of pack-oxen, cart-loads etc. by weighing less than these and hence being charged lower rates of tax. In Eastern Rajasthan, the tax levied on a *sirvā* was twice as much as that on bundles, *bugcau* (Singh 1977: 317).

<u>ll. 5 ff.:</u> The deity's supply of betel leaves was exempted from the "*(hāsil) rāhdārī*, toll-tax, etc.". In Eastern Rajasthan this tax was levied by the state on the carrying of trade goods from the local market (*gañj*) to the *parganā* township, *kasbā*. (Gupta 1986: 103; Singh 1977: 315-18). It was waived in certain cases, of which the deed is an illustration. There was a broad range of sundry taxes, for which cp. Gupta (1986: 106-07). As the present deed refers to the state of affairs under Jāṭ rule, the comparison with Eastern Rajasthan can only serve as a rule of thumb.

V.S. 1787, Kārttika ś. 3/ 2 November 1730

॥श्री रामजी ॥श्री रामजी

श्री गोवंददेव़जी

(१) ॥सिधि श्री मुतसदी श्रीव्रंदावनजी का जोग्य
(२) लिषतं दीवान राय़ नराय़णदास कीरपा-
(३) रांम केन्य --- वंच्या अैठा का स्माचार
(४) भला छै था का सदा भला चाहजै अप्रची
(५) ठाकुर श्री --- जी का भङारी चीनतामणी
(६) जाहर करी जो ठाकुर श्रीजी की सीघङी कै व़ा-
(७) सतै कोईला पोतदार थे पावा छां सो आमी-
(८) ल सनदी हजुरी की तलव करै छै सो ई व़ास-
(९) तै था नै लषिां छां जो सवत १७८६ की सीघङी
(१०) का कोईला पाय़ा होय़ ती माफीक सवत १७८७
(११) की भी सीघङी कै वासतै कोईला दीव़ाय़ दी-
(१२) ज्यो /मण ७०ऽ/ मु° सुदामदी कै मीती काती सुदी ३ संव़-
(१३) त १७८७

Śrī Rāmjī (2x)

Śrī Govinddevjī

[1] Success! [1-3] Written to the officers of Śrī Vrandāvanjī (Vrindaban) by Dīvāns Rāy Narāyaṇdās and Kīrapārām ... greetings. [3-4] Here all is well. We hope that everything is always well with you. Reference: [5] The steward of the deity Śrī [GD]jī, Cīntāmaṇī, [6] reported that [to date] he had received coal for the stove of the deity [7] from the store-house treasurer. [7-8] Therefore, the *āmil* applies for a *sanad* from the Court. [8-9] Accordingly, we are writing this to you: [9-10] For the year V.S. 1786 he must have received the coal for the stove. [10-12] Following the same procedure, you shall provide the coal for the stove also for the year V.S. 1787[, namely,] /70 maunds/, fixed in perpetuity. [12-13] Kātī ś. 3, V.S. 1787.

V.S. 1789, Vaiśākha b. 12/ 10 April 1732

॥श्री रामजी ॥श्रीरांमजी

गोव्यंददेव़जी

रांमरांम

(१) ॥सिधि श्री रांमनाथ जोग्य लिषतं दीवांन
(२) राय़ नरांय़णदास कीरपारांम केन्य --- वं-
(३) च्या अैठा का समाचार भला छै थां का सदा
(४) भला चाहिजे अप्रंच थां कै तालक वरकं-
(५) दाज /श्री/ विदरावनजी मै छै त्या मधे वरकंदा-
(६) ज नफर ५ ठाकर श्री --- जी का गुसाई
(७) तालक रहैला सो थे थां का तालक का मौ-
(८) कूफ करीज्यौ अर वां कीं ऐवज व़ै राषी ले
(९) त्या की हाजरी गुसाई मजकूर की ले करसी तल-
(१०) व व़ां नै देवौ कीज्यौ व़ै व़ां सौ चौकी पैहरा ठा-
(११) करदुव़ारा की चाकरी भली भांती करावो करै-
(१२) ला विद्याधर की त्रफ ठाकरदुव़ारै आदमी
(१३) रहै छै ती का ईतफाक सौ य़े वरकंदाज रहै मीं-
(१४) ती वैसाष वदि १२ सवत १७८९

---

(१) दा° नुसषै नंकल लीषी सरू

(two illegible seals)

Śrī Rāmjī (2x)

Govinddevjī

Rām-Rām

[1] Success! Written to Śrī Rāmnāth by Dīvāns [2] Rāy Narāyaṇdās [and] Kīrapārām. ... [2-3] greetings. Here all is well. [3-4] We hope that everything is always well with you. [4-5] Reference: The watchmen in Vrindaban are under your authority. [5-7] Of these, 5 men shall be kept under the authority of the *gosvāmī* of the deity Śrī [GD]jī. Therefore, your authority [over them] [8] shall be discontinued, and, instead, he shall be in charge of them. [9] Enlist them in the roll of the aforementioned *gosvāmī* and [10] transfer the claim [on them] to him. [10-11] Through these, he will make proper arrangements for the job of guarding the temple. [12-13] In agreement with Vidyādhar, the men posted by him at the temple shall stay there as watchmen. [14] Date: Vaiśākh b. 12, V.S. 1789.

Entered in the *nuskhau* Copy taken Start!

(2 illegible seals)

Commentary:

l. 12: For Vidyādhar, cp. the table "Dīvāns of Amber and Jaipur (1660-1880)", p. 66; → V.S. 1769, Jyeṣṭha ś. 13, commentary on l. 7; → V.S. 1773, Bhādrapada ś. 8, l. 10 *(verso)*, and → V.S. 1790, Māgha ś. 4, ll. 5 *(recto)*, 27 *(verso)*.

V.S. 1790, Māgha ś. 4/ 27 January 1734

Invocatio missing.

गोव्यंददेव़जी

सही

(कटार)

(seal)

(१) सिधि श्री महाराजाधिराज महाराजा श्री सव़ाई जैस्यंघजी देव़वचना-
(२) त कमैती प्रगनां सव़ाई जैपुर का दिस्ये सुप्रसाद वंच्या अप्रंचि वाव-
(३) ति भोग जमी वीघा २६७ऽ २ ठाकर श्री --- जी कै जो वाग घाटी
(४) नींचला व़ागैरह् प्रगनां सव़ाई जैपुर का की जो व़ास्तै जमी कै मारफ-
(५) ति विद्याधर की मिती भादव़ा सुदि १२ संवत १७९० अरज पहौंची आ-
(६) गै कनक वाग व़ गांव़ घाटी की जमीं छी सो मुव़ाफिक तफसील मांन-
(७) सागर तलाव़ मैं आय़ गई वीघा २६७ऽ २

(८)	वाग की धरती वीघा सा-	वाग का पङ्कोटा की	गांव घाटी की धरती
(९)	ढा गुणचास	धरती वीघा वतीस वि-	वीघा ऐक सौं पच्यासी
(१०)	४९।।ऽ	सव़ा वारा	१८५ऽ
(११)		३२।।२	

(१२) तीह् सौं फुरमांव़ां छां मतलव प्रव़ांनां का सौं व़ाकिफ होय़ ऐव़ज क-
(१३) नक वाग व़ागैरह् की जमीं की वाग घाटी नींचला व़ागैरह् प्रगनां स-
(१४) व़ाई जैपुर का की ईस तग मिती भादव़ा सुदि ३ संवत १७९० सौं व-
(१५) हाल जांणिं मांप्यं दीज्यो अर प्रतवरष नव़ो प्रव़ांनौं मति मांग्य-
(१६) ज्यो ईही प्रवांनां सौं हिसाव मैं मुजरा होंयला
(१७) मुकररा तनषाह जमीं वाग घाटी नींचला व़ागैरह प्रगनां सव़ाई
(१८) जैपुर का की ईस तग मिती भादव़ा सुदि ३ सवत १७९० सौं वहाल
(१९) जांणिं मुव़ाफिक तफसील मांप्य दीज्यो वीघा दोय़ सै सतसठि
(२०) विसव़ा दोय़
(२१) २६७ऽ२

(२२)	घाटी नींचलो वाग तीह की जमी	वाग प्रांणनाथ को तींह की जमी	
(२३)	वीघा साढा सात	पङ्कोटा सुधी आंवैरि का की वी-	
(२४)	७।।ऽ	घा गुणचास विसव्ना सतरा	
(२५)		४९।।२	

(२६)		वाग वीघा सोला	पङ्कोटा की वी-
(२७)		१६ऽ	घा तैतीस विस-
(२८)			व्ना स्तरा
(२९)			३३।।२

(३०) कसवा षोह तपा षोह की जो ईना-
(३१) म की जमीं षालसै हुई तींह मांही
(३२) मांप्य दीज्यो वीघा दोय़ सै पोंणा दस
(३३) २०९।।ऽ

---

(१) सरह यादिदासति दाष्यल व्नाकै करार मिती माह वदि ८ संवत १७९० वरिसालै
(२) राय़ नरांय़णदास क्रिपारांम दिव्नांन व्न निहालचंद व्नाकानव्नीस अत्र ङोल
(३) बावति भोग जमीं ठाकर श्री --- जी कै घाटी नींचला वाग व्नागैरह की
(४) प्रगनां सव्नाई जैपुर की जो मारफति विद्याधर की मिती भादव्ना सुदि
(५) १२ संवत १७९० अरज पहौंची आगैं कनक वाग व्न गांव्न घाटी की जमीं
(६) छी सो मांनसागर तलाव्न में मुव्नाफिक तफसील आय़ गई वीघा २६७ऽ२

(७)	वाग की धरती वीघा	वाग का पङ्कोटा की वी-	गांव्न घाटी की वीघा
(८)	साढा गुणचास	घा वतीस विस्व्ना वारा	ऐक सो पचासी
(९)	४९।।ऽ	३२।।२	१८५ऽ

(१०) सो हुकम हुव्ना ऐव्नज वाग की व्न जमीं की वाग घाटी नचिला व्नागैरह प्र-
(११) गनां सव्नाई जैपुर का की ईस तग मिती भादव्ना सुदि ३ संवत १७९० सौं
(१२) द्योह तींह को प्रवांनौं सवती करि द्योह सो चाहिज्ये दिवांन सरकार का प्र-
(१३) व्नांनौं लिषैं मिती माह वदि ८ संवत १७९० अरज मूकरर पहौंची जमी
(१४) मुव्नाफिक तफसील वीघा दोय़ सै सतसठि विस्व्ना दोय़
(१५) २६७ऽ२

(१६) घाटी नींचला वाग तींह् की जमी		वाग प्रांणनाथ को आंवैरि कौ
(१७) वीघा साढा सात		तींह् की जमीं पङकोटा की सुधी वी-
(१८)	७।।ऽ	घा गुणचास विसव़ा सतरा
(१९)		४९।।।२

(२०-२६)) (= *recto*, lines 26-33)

(२७) मूव़ाफिक य़ाददासति वमहोर विद्याधर व़ दसषत दिवांनय़ां
(२८) मिती माह् सुदि ४ संवत १७९० मूकाम सव़ाई जैपूर

(seal)	*(seal)*	*(seal)*
(२९) रजुं दफत्र राई	रजु दफत्र	रजू दफत्र गिरध-
नराय़णदास	क्रपारांम दीवा-	रदास मुस्तोफी हजू-
दीव़ांन	न	रि ॥8 ॥

(I) Govinddevjī
Certified
(dagger)

(seal)

(II 1) [1] Success! By royal order of Śrī Mahārājādhirāj Mahārājā Śrī Savāī Jaisiṅgh,
(II 2) [2] with benevolent greetings to the officers of *parganā* Savāī Jaipur.
(II 3) [2] Reference: Item [3] of *bhog*[, namely,] the 267 *bīghās*, 2 *viśvās* land for the deity Śrī [GD]jī, which consisted of garden-land, hilly land, [4] low-land etc. in *parganā* Savāī Jaipur.
(II 4) [4-5] On Bhādvā ś. 12, V.S. 1790, there was submitted a petition for this land through Vidyādhar.
(II 5) [6] Formerly, it consisted of the Kanak garden and village slopes.
As specified [below], [7] this [land, namely,] 267 *bīghās*, 2 *viśvās* has submerged in Lake Mānsāgar.

[8] Garden-land, *bīghās*	Land of garden-enclosures,	Village slopes,
[9] forty-nine and a half	*bīghās* thirty-two and	*bīghās* one hundred and eighty-five
[10] 49 1/2b.	*viśvās* twelve	185b.
[11]	32b., 12v.	

[8] Garden-land, *bīghās*	Land of garden-enclosures,	Village slopes,
[9] forty-nine and a half	*bīghās* thirty-two and	*bīghās* one hundred and
		eighty-five
[10] 49 1/2b.	*viśvās* twelve	185b.
[11]	32b., 12v.	

(II 6) [12] Hereby, order is given that it be known [to you] by the intention of the *parvanau* that [12-15] instead of the land consisting of gardens etc. of Kanak, [an assignment of] land consisting of gardens, slopes and low land etc. in *parganā* Savāī Jaipur shall be understood to be in force from Bhādvā ś. 3, V.S. 1790, and [the land] be measured out and transferred.

(II 7) [15-16] And there must not be demanded a fresh *parvānau* every year.

(II 8) [16] Following this *parvānau*, there shall be carried to account in the account-book:

[17] Fixed allowance: [17-20] Understanding [the assignment] to be in force from Bhādvā ś. 3, V.S. 1790, sloping and low garden-land etc. in *parganā* Savāī Jaipur shall be measured out according to the [following] details and be transferred: *bīghās* two hundred and seventy-six and *viśvās* two,

[21] 267b., 2v.

[22] Sloping and low garden-land, of this,	Garden of Prāṇnāth in Amber;
	of this land,
[23] *bīghās* seven and a half	comprising enclosures,
[24] 7 1/2b.	*bīghās* forty-nine and 17 *viśvās*
[25 I	49b., 17v.

[26]	Gardens, *bīghās* sixteen	Enclosures,
[27]	16b.	*bīghās* thirty-three
[28]		and *viśvās* seventeen
[29]		33b., 17v.

[30] *Inām* land in *kasbā* Khoh, *tapā* Khoh,

[31] which became *khālsā*-land, out of this

[32] there shall be measured out *bīghās* two hundred and nine and three quarters

[33] 209 3/4b.

(III 1) [1] Commentary on the memorandum [based] on the diary-entry of Māh b. 8, V.S. 1790, by report of [2] Dīvāns Rāy Narāyaṇdās and Kripārām and Diarist Nihālcand.

(III 5) [13] On Māh b. 8, V.S. 1790, the petition was submitted again [, namely for] [14] *bīghās* two hundred and sixty-seven , *viśvās* two of land, according to the [following] details ,
[15] 267b., 2v.
[16-23] (= *recto*, lines 22-33)

(III 6) [27] As endorsed in the memorandum by the seal of Vidyādhar and the signature of the *dīvāns*.
(IV) [28] Date: Māh ś. 4, V.S. 1790; place: Savāī Jaipur.

(V)

(seal)	*(seal)*	*(seal)*
[29] Endorsed in the record, Rāī [30] Narāyaṇdās, [31] Dīvān	Endorsed in the record, Krapārām, Dī- vān	Endorsed in the record, Gir- dhardās, Court- Auditor

Commentary:
For the rise of the level of Lake Mānsarovar (Mānsāgar), cp. pp. 20-21.

ll. 5 *(recto)*, 27 *(verso)*: The fact that Vidyādhar recommended the *bhog* grant and endorsed it by his seal suggests that in 1734 he served as Minister. For Vidyādhar, cp. also the commentary on the preceding document.

V.S. 1797, Māgha b. 5/ 27 December 1740

॥श्री रांमजी

गोव्यंददेव़जी
सही

(कटार)

(seal)

(१) ॥सिधि श्री महाराजाधिराज महाराजा श्री सव़ाई जैस्यंघजी
(२) देव़वचनात मुतसदी हजूरि व़ा देस कां दिसे सुप्रसाद वंच्या
(३) अप्रंचि सरकार मैं माल व़ साय़र राहदारी व़ पेसकस षाल-
(४) सा व़ जागीरदार ठाकरलोग व़ ईजारा का प्रगनां व़ागैरह दरो-
(५) वस्त जमां की लार रुपय़ो ऐक हजार परि रुपय़ा ऐक १ऽ भेट ठा-
(६) कर श्री ---जी व़ा आंनां च्यारि भेट गुसांई रांमस-
(७) रणजी अधिकारी श्रीजी का की ईवतदाय़ संवत १७९७ थे मु-
(८) करर करी छै सो सिव़ाय़ जमां सरकार तैहसील श्रीजी कै
(९) भंडार पौंचावो करौ अर ठाकर लोगों सौं अठमाहौ पाव़तौ
(१०) होय़ ती सौं अठमाहा कै हिसाव ल्यौह अर जो छमाहौ पाव़तौ
(११) होय़ ती सौं छमाहा कै हिसाव भोमि की लार तैहसील करि पौ-
(१२) हचाय़ द्यौह मिती वदि ५ संवत १७९७ मुकाम षाटु

Śrī Rāmjī

Govinddevjī

Certified

(dagger)

(seal)

[1] Success! [1-2] By royal order of Śrī Mahārājādhirāj Mahārājā Śrī Savāī Jaisiṅghjī, [2] with benevolent greetings to the officers of the Court and the country.[57] [3-5] Reference: For the entire revenue of the state, [namely,] the land revenue and toll-tax and *peskas* [levied on] the

[57]Cp. pp. 39-40 for the revenue officers of "the Court and the country".

khālsā and on the *jāgīr*-holding nobles and on the *ijārau parganās*, [5-8] there has been fixed on every thousand rupees 1 rupee religious donation *(bheṭ)* for the deity Śrī [GD]jī, and four annas for Gosvāmī Rāmsaraṇ, custodian of the deity. [8-9] Therefore, you shall collect these as extra-revenue of the state and deliver them to the treasury of the deity. [9] And if a noble receives [his emoluments] by the eight-month pay-scale, [10] you shall calculate [this extra-revenue] by the eight-month pay-scale, and if he receives them by the six-month pay-scale, you shall calculate it by the six-month pay-scale. [11-12] You shall collect and deliver it together with the *bhom*. Date: Māh b. 5, V.S. 1797; place: Khāṭu.

Commentary:

The temple and its custodian are granted 1rp. and 4a., respectively, levied on the taxes, according to the various categories of taxed land and tax-payers.

<u>ll. 3-5:</u> The taxes comprise the "entire revenue", *darobast jamā*; *jamā* (Pers. *jama'*) is, technically, the assessed or notional revenue (Gupta 1986: 216). In the present context, however, the items comprised by *jamā* are of the categories of both land revenue and other taxes. That "entire revenue" comprised the following categories of taxation:

(1) *māl*, the tax on crop, that is, the land revenue as such (Gupta 1986: 145).

(2) *sāyar rāhdārī* (Pers. *sāīr* –); *sāyar* are the remaining taxes besides the revenue raised on the crop inclusive of perquisites *(māl o jihāt)*. The term *sāyar rāhdārī* is equivocal, because the toll-tax (*hāsil rāhdārī kau*, for which cp. doc. → V.S. 1839, Āṣāḍha b.5) is just one out of many kinds of *sāyar* taxes. However, a related term, namely *sivāy rāhdārī*, occurs in doc. → V.S. 1839 (cp. above) where it seems to point explicitly to the toll-tax. Therefore, *sāyar rāhdārī* is tentatively taken to mean only "toll-tax", the tax levied by the state on commodities carried through its territory (Singh 1977: 315-18). Gupta (1986: 157) draws attention to the fact that *rāhdārī* appears variously under the heading of *sāīr jihāt* and/or *sivāy jamābandī*.

(3) *peskas* (Pers. *pīśkaś*) comprises a variety of tributes paid by officials to the ruler on appointment to an office and other occasions. Especially relevant in connection with the revenue administration seems to be the tribute which *ijārau*-holders would have to pay (Singh 1990: 133 for the special case of *ijārau* in perpetuitiy). Cp. also Gupta 1986:181.

ll. 3-4: The taxation covered the crown-land (*khālsā*) and the land held in *jāgīr* as well as in *ijārau*. Hence the state itself, the *jāgīr*-holding nobility and the *parganās* held in *ijārau* had to pay the new tax. By acquiring *parganās* in *ijārau*, Jaisiṅgh II had been able to vastly extend his territory (Gupta 1986: 14-37; Wills 1933: app. E and G). The term *ijārau parganā* is thus practically synonymous with the then relatively recently acquired territory of the Kachavāhā state.

ll. 6-12: The "religious donation" (*bheṭ*) was styled an "extra-revenue of the state" (*sivāy jamāṃ sarkār*). The revenue officers were to collect it at the same time as they would collect the *bhomi*, but they were to send it directly to the treasury of GD. The levying of the extra-tax took place by the pay-scales calculated by month-ratios applying to the individual nobles (ll. 9ff.); for the pay-scales cp. p. 32. The *bhom(i)* (l. 11), also *bhom-bāb*, was paid by *bhūmiās* (or *bhomiās*), "those who held right over the *bhūm/bhom*". Basically this type of landlords belonged to clans dominant in an area, and these were mostly Rajput. There were two types of *bhūmiās*. One held hereditary right over the renevue of the land, including non-agricultural taxes; the other held hereditary proprietary right over the land as such and can be identified with *zamīndārs*, a difference being that these *bhūmiās* were not allowed to sell the land under their control. They were entitled to unpaid service of labour, had a share in the surplus income of the village, and the right to levy a number of taxes, both on the trade traffic, and thus including *rāhdārī*, and on village affairs and ceremonies, such as marriages.

> The major source of his (the *bhūmiā's* - MH) income, it appears, should have been from his personal holding which was nominally assessed and exempted from other agricultural cesses. It is also likely that a substantial part of his holding was devoted to the cultivation of cash crops as he was in a position to provide the necessary inputs. However it appears from the Khasra (field book of a village - MH) documents that the cropping pattern of the holdings of many bhomias was also dominated by extensive cultivation of foodgrains. Part of his liquid capital was also invested in usury. The bhom right was keenly vied for, and there seems to have been an ever growing tendency on the part of several members of the dominant clans to create new bhom rights in hitherto exclusively raiyati villages (villages populated by ordinary cultivators - MH). (Singh 1990: 45)

The *bhom* tax seems to have been more or less nominal (Bhadani 1978-80; Gupta and Moosvi 1970). No *bhom* cesses were levied on charitable land (*punya udik, punya arath, inām*).

l. 12: Khāṭu lies in Sīkar District of Rājasthān.

rev. y. 1801/ V.S. 1802, Bhādrapada b. 5 / 6 August 1745 (Gaṅgārāmpur-vās Khijūryā)

Invocatio, elevatio and *verso* missing; date inferred from the other petitions submitted on Āṣāḍha b. 5 and ratified on Bhādrapada b. 5 of the same year.

(कटार)

(seal)

(१) सिधि श्री महाराजाधिराज महाराजा श्री सव़ाई ईश्वरस्यंघजी दे-
(२) व़वचनात कमैती प्रगनां सव़ाई जैपुर का दिस्य़े सुप्रसाद वंच्या अ-
(३) प्रंचि वावति भोग ठाकर श्री ---जी का मै गांव़ गंगारांमपुरो
(४) वास षिजूरच्या तपा षोह प्रगनां सव़ाई जैपुर को जो व़ासतै गांव़
(५) कै मारफति राजा आय़ामल की मिती असाढ वदि ५ साल संव-
(६) त १८०१ अरज पहौंची आगै गांव़ मजकूर उपेजा रुपय़ा सात सै को
(७) मुव़ाफिक प्रवांनै सवती महाराजा वैकुंटवासीजी श्री ---जी
(८) का करार मिती भादव़ा सुदि ४ संवत १७७१ का सौं पाव़ै छा सो साष ऊ-
(९) न्हालू संवत १८०१ ताई हासिल पाय़ो अव ईस तग संवत १८०२ सौं
(१०) हाल को प्रवांनौं कराय़ो चाहै तीह सौं फुरमांव़ां छां मतलव प्रव़ांना का
(११) सौं व़ाकिफ होय़ गांव़ गंगारांमपुरो वास षिजूरच्या तपा षोह प्रगनां
(१२) सव़ाई जैपुर को साविक दसतूर वहाल जांणिं ईस तग संवत १८०२
(१३) सौं हासिल हव़ालै करिवो कीज्यौ अर प्रतवरष नव़ो प्रवांनौं मति मा-
(१४) ग्यज्यो ईही प्रव़ांनां सौं हिसाव मै मुजरा होय़ला
(१५) मुकररा तनषाह गांव़ गंगारांमपुरो वास षिजूरच्या तपा षोह प्रगनां
(१६) सव़ाई जैपुर को साविक दसतूर वहाल जांणिं ईस तग संवत १८०२
(१७) सौं हासिल हव़ालै करिवो कीज्यो ऊपेजा रुपय़ा ७००ऽ को गाव़ दरोवस्त

(I) (*dagger*)

(seal)

(II 1) [1] Success! [1-2] By royal order of Śrī Mahārājādhirāj Mahārājā Śrī Savāī Īśvarsiṅghjī,

(II 2) with benevolent greetings to the officers of *parganā* Savāī Jaipur.

(II 3) [2-4] Reference: Item of *bhog* of the deity Śrī [GD]jī, [namely,] village Gaṅgārāmpuro-vās Khijūryā in *tapā* Khoh of *parganā* Savāī Jaipur.

(II 4) [4-6] For this, there was submitted a petition through Rājā Āyāmal on Āṣāḍha b. 5, V.S. 1802/rev. y. 1801[, as follows]:

(II 5) [6-8] To date, [the deity] has received the aforementioned village yielding 700rp. [of realized revenue], according to a confirmatory *parvānau* promulgated by the late Mahārājā Śrī [Jaisiṅgh]jī on Bhādvā ś. 4, V.S. 1771.[58] [8-9] By this, he received the realized revenue up to the hot season harvest of V.S. 1801. [9-10] Now he wishes that the *parvānau* be renewed from V.S. 1802.

(II 6) [10] Hereby, order is given that [10-11] it be known [to you] by the intention of the *parvānau* [11-13] that the hitherto existing regulation shall be understood to be in force and village Gaṅgārāmpuro-vās Khijūryā be assigned for [income of] realized revenue from V.S. 1802.

(II 7) [13-14] And there must not be demanded a fresh *parvānau* every year.

(II 8) [14] Following this *parvānau*, there shall be carried to account in the account-book:

[15] Fixed allowance of revenue: [15-17] Understanding the hitherto existing regulation to be in force, there shall be assigned, beginning with V.S. 1802, village Gaṅgārāmpuro-vās Khijūryā in *tapā* Khoh of *parganā* Savāī Jaipur, for [income of] realized revenue. An entire village yielding 700 rp.

Commentary:

ll. 3-4: In modern Bassī Tehsil of Jaipur District, there is a village by the name of Gaṅgārāmpurā (India 1983 [DCH Jaipur]: 195, serial/code nos 74/48). It neighbours on three villages by the name of Khijūriyā, namely, Khijūriyā Ahīrvān, – Brāhmaṇ and – Jāṭān (*ibid.*, serial/code nos 116/49, 117/42, 118/50).

l. 5: For Rājā Āyāmal cp. → V.S. 1777, Āśvina ś. 14, commentary on l. 8.

[58] For *upejau*, cp. p.32.

rev. y. 1801/V.S. 1802, Bhādrapada b. 5 (Govindpuro)/ 6 August 1745

॥श्री रांमजी ॥ ॥श्री रांमजी ॥ ॥श्री रांमजी

गोव्यंददेव़जी

सवाई जैस्यंघजी

सही
(कटार)

(seal)

(१) सिधि श्री महाराजाधिराज महाराजा श्री सवाई ईश्वरस्यंघजी
(२) देव़वचनात कमैती प्रगनां सव़ाई जैपुर का दिस्ये सुप्रसाद वंच्या
(३) अप्रंचि वावति भोग ठाकुर श्री --- जी कै सालीनां ऊसू-
(४) ली रुपय़ा १२००ऽ मैं गांव़ गोव्यंदपुरो तपा षोह प्रगनां सवाई जैपु-
(५) र को जो वासतै गांव़ कै मारफति राजा आय़ामल की मिती असा-
(६) ढ वदि ५ साल संवत १८०१ अरज पहौंची जो गांव़ मजकूर मुव़ा-
(७) फिक प्रव़ांनैं सवती महाराजा वैकुंटवासी श्री --- जी का
(८) करार तारीष १ जुमादलि अव़ल सन ११११२ का सौं पाव़ै छा सो हा-
(९) सिल संवत १८०१ तांई पाय़ो अव हाल को प्रव़ांनौं कराय़ो चाहै
(१०) तींह सौं फुरमांव़ां छां मतलव प्रव़ांनां का सौं व़ाकिफ होंय़ सालीनां
(११) व़सूली रुपय़ा वारा सै मैं गांव़ गोव्यंदपुरो तपा षोह प्रगनां सव़ा-
(१२) ई जैपुर को साविक दसतूर वहाल जांणि ईस तग संवत १८०२ सौं
(१३) हासिल हव़ालै करिवो कीज्यो अर प्रतवरष नव़ो प्रव़ांनौं मति मां-
(१४) ग्यज्यो ईही प्रव़ांनां सौं हिसाव मैं मुजरा होय़ला
(१५) मुकररा तनषाह गांव़ गोव्यंदपुरो तपा षोह प्रगनां सव़ाई जैपुर
(१६) को साविक दसतूर वहाल जांणि ईस तग संवत १८०२ सौं हासिल
(१७) हव़ालै करिवो कीज्यो तन दरोवस्त मै सालीनां ऊसूली रूपय़ा वारा सै

(१८) १२००ऽ

----

(१) सरह य़ादिदासति दाषिल व़ाकै करार मिती सांव़ण वदि ११ संवत १८०२ साल सं-
(२) वत १८०१ वरिसालै राय़ नराय़ंणदास फतेरांम दिव़ांन निहालचंद व़ाकान-
(३) व़ीस अत्र डौल भोग ठाकुर श्री ---जी जो व़ास्तै भोग कै मारफति राजा
(४) आय़ामल की मिती असाढ वदि ५ साल संवत १८०१ अरज पहौंची जो साली-
(५) नां ऊसूली रूपय़ा १२००ऽ मैं गांव़ गोव्यंदपुरो तपा षोह प्रगनां सव़ाई जैपुर

(६) को मूव़ाफिक प्रव़ांनैं सवती महाराजा वैकुंटवासीजी श्री ---जी करार ता-
(७) रीष १ जुमादलि अव़ल सन ११११२ का सौं पाव़ै छा सो संवत १८०१ ताई पायो
(८) अव हाल को प्रव़ांनौं करायो चाहै सो हुकम हुव़ा ईस तग संवत १८०२ सौ प्र-
(९) व़ानौं सवती हाल को करो सो चाहिज्ये दिव़ांन सरकार का प्रव़ांनां लिषै मिती
(१०) साव़ण वदि ११ संवत १८०२ साल संवत १८०१ अरज मूकरर पहौंची गांव़ मजकू-
(११) र तन दरोबस्त ऊसूली रुपया वारा सै
(१२) १२००८
(१३) मूव़ाफिक यादिसति मै दसषत राजा आयामल व़ दिंनयांन

(१४) मिती भादव़ा वदि ५ सा° सं° १८०१ मूकाम सव़ाई जैपुर

(seal) *(seal)* *(seal)*

(१५) रजु दफत्र राय न-	रजु दफत्र	रजू दफत्र फतेरां-
(१६) रायणदास दीवान	फतेराम दी-	म मुंस्तोफी हजूरि
(१७)	व़ान	

सरू
दा° मव़ाजनै

दा° मव़ाजनै

लिषौ लिषौ

(I) Śrī Rāmjī (3x)

Govinddevjī
Savāī Jaisiṅghjī

Certified
(dagger)

(seal)

(II 1) [1] Success! [1-2] By royal order of Śrī Mahārājādhirāj Mahārājā Śrī Savāī Īśvarsiṅghjī,
(II 2) with benevolent greetings to the officers of *parganā* Savāī Jaipur.
(II 3) [3-5] Reference: Item of *bhog* of the deity Śrī [GD]jī, [namely,] village Govindpuro of *tapā* Khoh in *parganā* Savāī Jaipur, for an annually recoverable amount of 1,200 rp.
(II 4) [5-6] For this village, there was submitted a petition through Rājā Āyāmal on Āṣāḍha b. 5, rev. y. 1801[, as follows]:
(II 5) [6-8] To date, [the deity] has received the aforementioned village according to a confirmatory *parvānau* promulgated by the late Mahārājā Śrī [Jaisiṅgh]jī on 1 Jumādā I, A.H. 1112. [8-9] By this, he received the realized revenue until V.S. 1801. [9] Now he wishes that the *parvānau* be renewed.
(II 6) [10] Hereby, order is given that [10-11] it be known [to you] by the intention of the *parvānau* [10-13] that the hitherto existing regulation shall be understood to be in force and that from V.S. 1802 village Govindpuro of *tapā* Khoh in *parganā* Savāī Jaipur shall be assigned for [income of] realized revenue, which covers the annually recoverable amount of 1200 rp.
(II 7) [13-14] And there must not be demanded a fresh *parvānau* every year.
(II 8) [14] Following this *parvānau,* there shall be carried to account in the account-book:
[15-17] Fixed allowance of revenue: Understanding the hitherto existing regulation to be in force, from V.S. 1802, there shall be assigned for [income of] realized revenue,village Govindpuro in *tapā* Khoh of *parganā* Savāī Jaipur: Entire revenue; annually recoverable amount of twelve hundred rupees.
[18] 1,200/- rp.

(III 1) [1] Commentary on the memorandum [based] on the diary-entry of Sāvaṇ b. 11, V.S. 1802/ [2-3] rev. y. 1801, on report of Dīvāns Rāy Narāyaṇdās and Phaterām and Diarist Nihālcand.
(III 2) [3] Statement as follows: *bhog* of the deity Śrī [GD]jī. [3-4] For [this] *bhog*, there was submitted ... rev.y.1801 (= *recto*, lines 3-4), [namely,] [4-8] that he has received village Govindpuro in *tapā* Khoh of *parganā* Savāī Jaipur according to... renewed. (= *recto*, lines 6-9).

(III 3) [8-9] Therefore, the order was passed that you renew the confirmatory *parvānau* from V.S. 1802.

(III 4) [9] It is necessary that the *dīvāns* of the *sarkār* make out *parvānaus*.

(III 5) [9-12] On Sāvaṇ b. 11, V.S. 1802/ rev.y. 1801, the petition was submitted again [, namely for]: The aforementioned village, entire revenue; annually recoverable amount, twelve hundred rupees,

1,200/- rp.

(III 6) [13] As endorsed in the memorandum by Rājā Āyāmal and the *dīvāns*.

(IV) [14] Date: Bhādvā b. 5, rev.y. 1801; place: Savāī Jaipur.

(V) *(seal)*	*(seal)*	*(seal)*
[15-17]		
Endorsed in the record; Rāy Narāyaṇdās, Dīvān	Endorsed in the record; Phaterām, Dīvān	Endorsed in the record; Phaterām, Court-Auditor

Start!

Entered in the *mavājanau*　　Entered in the *mavājanau*

Write! Write!

rev.y. 1801/ V.S. 1802, Bhādrapada b. 5 (Sālimpur)/ 6 August 1745

Invocatio missing.

गोव्यददेवजी

सवाई जैस्यंघजी

सही

(कटार)

(seal)

(१) सिधि श्री महाराजाधिराज महाराजा श्री सवाई ईश्वरस्यंघजी देवव-
(२) चनात कमैती प्रगनां हिङौंण का दिस्ये सुप्रसाद वंच्या अप्रंचि वा-
(३) वति भोग ठाकर श्री --- जी कै गाव सालिमपुर व धरती वी-
(४) घा ६०८ प्रगनां हिङौंण का सो वासतै गांव वागैरह कै मारफति
(५) राजा आयामल की मिती असाढ वदि ५ संवत १८०२ साल संव-
(६) त १८०१ अरज पहौंची आगैं गांव मजकूर वागैरह प्रगनां हिङौंण
(७) का मुवाफिक प्रवांनैं सवती महाराजा वैकुंटवासीजी श्री --- जी
(८) करार मिती जेठ वदि १० संवत १७७९ का सौं पावै छा सो हासिल सा-
(९) ष ऊन्हालू संवत १८०१ ताई पायो अव हाल को प्रवांनौं सवती क-
(१०) रायो चाहै छै तीह सौं फुरमांवां छां मतलव प्रवांनां का सौं वा-
(११) किफ होय गांव सालिमपुर दरोवसत वा धरती वीघा साठि
(१२) प्रगनां हिङौंण का ईस तग संवत १८०२ सौं साविक दसतूर
(१३) वहाल जांणि हासिल हवालै करिवो कीज्यो अर प्रतवरष न-
(१४) वो प्रवांनौं मति मांग्यज्यो ईही प्रवांनां सौं हिसाव मैं मुजरा होयला
(१५) मुकररा तनषाह गांव वागैरह प्रगनां हिङौंण का ईस तग संव-
(१६) त १८०२ सौं साविक दसतूर वहाल जांणिं हासिल हवालै क-
(१७) रिवो कीज्यो गांव वागैरह
(१८) गांव सालिमपुर प्रगनां हिङौं- धरती कसवा हिङौंण की वी-
(१९) ण को तन दरोवस्त ऐक घा साठि
(२०) १ ६०८

---

(१) सरह यादिदासति दाषिल वाकै करार मिती सांवण वदि ११ संवत १८०२ साल
(२) संवत १८०१ वरिसालै राय नरांयणदास फतेरांम दिवांन व निहालचंद वाकान-
(३) वीस अत्र ङोल भोग गांव वागैरह ठाकुर श्री --- जी का कै वास्तै मार-
(४) फति राजा आयामल की मिती असाढ वदि ५ संवत १८०२ साल संवत १८०१
(५) अरज पहौंची जो गांव सालिमपुर दरोवसत व धरती वीघा साठि कसवा
(६) हिङौंण की मुवाफिक प्रवांनैं सवती महाराजा वैकुंटवासीजी श्री --- जी

(७) करार मिती जेठ वदि १० संवत १७७९ का सौ पाव़ै छा सो साष ऊन्हालू संवत
(८) १९०१ ताई हासिल पाय़ो अव वहाल को प्रवांनौ सवती कराय़ो चाहै सो
(९) हुकम हुव़ा संवत १८०२ का साल सौं प्रवांनौं सवती करि द्योह सो चाहि-
(१०) ज्ये दिव़ांन सरकार का प्रवांनां लिषैं मिती सांव़ण वदि ११ संवत १८०२
(११) साल संवत १८०१ अरज मूकरर पहौंची गांव़ व़ागैरह
(१२) गांव़ सालिमपुर प्रगनां हिङौंण धरती कसवा हिङौंण की वीघा साठि
(१३) को तन दरोवसत
(१४) १ ६०ऽ

(१५) मूव़ाफिक य़ादिदासति मैं दसषत राजा आय़ामल व़ा दिव़ानय़ांन

(१६) मिती भादव़ा वदी ५ सा° सं° १८०१ मूकाम सवाई जैपूर

(seal)	*(seal)*	*(seal)*
(१७) रजू दफत्र राय़ नरां-	रजु दफत्र फ-	रजू दफत्र फतेरां-
(१८) य़णदास दीव़ान	तेरांम दीव़ान	म मुंसतोफी हजूरि

सरू
दा° मव़ाजनै

दा° मव़ाजनै

(I) Govinddevjī

Savāī Jaisiṅghjī

Certified

(*dagger*)

(*seal*)

(II 1) [1] Success! [1-2] By royal order of Śrī Mahārājādhirāj Mahārājā Śrī Savāī Īśvarsiṅghjī,
(II 2) with benevolent greetings to the officers of *parganā* Hiṇḍauṇ.
(II 3) [2-4] Reference: Item of *bhog* of the deity Śrī [GD]jī, [namely,] village Sālimpur and 60 *bīghā*s land in *parganā* Hiṇḍauṇ.
(II 4) [4-6] For this, there was submitted a petition through Rājā Āyāmal on Āṣāḍha b. 5, V.S. 1802/ rev. y. 1801[, as follows]:

(II 5) [6-8] To date, [the deity] has received the aforementioned village etc. of *parganā* Hiṇḍauṇ, according to a *parvānau* promulgated by the late Mahārājā Śrī [Jaisiṅgh]jī on Jyeṣṭha b. 10, V.S. 1779. [8-9] By this, he received the realized revenue up to the hot season harvest of V.S. 1801. [9-10] Now he wishes that the confirmatory *parvānau* be renewed.

(II 6) [10] Hereby, order is given that [10-11] it be known [to you] by the intention of the *parvānau* [11-13] that the hitherto existing regulation shall be understood to be in force and that the entire village Sālimpur and 60 *bīghās* land in *parganā* Hiṇḍauṇ shall be assigned for [income of] realized revenue from V.S. 1802.

(II 7) [13-14] And there must not be demanded a fresh *parvānau* every year.

(II 8) [14] Following this *parvānau*, there shall be carried to account in the account-book:

[15-17] Fixed allowance of revenue: Understanding the hitherto existing regulation to be in force, there shall be assigned for [income of] realized revenue a village etc. in *parganā* Hiṇḍauṇ, from V.S. 1802: A village etc.

[18-19] The entire revenue of village Sālimpur in *parganā* Hiṇḍauṇ: one	Land in *kasbā* Hiṇḍauṇ, sixty *bīghās*
- 1 -	60/-

(III 1) [1] Commentary on the memorandum [based] on the diary-entry of Sāvaṇ b. 11, V.S. 1802/ [2] rev. y. 1801, on report of Dīvāns Rāy Narāyaṇdās and Phaterām and Diarist Nihālcand.

(III 2) [3-5] Statement as follows: For a village etc. for *bhog* of the deity Śrī [GD]jī, there was submitted ... rev. year 1801 (= *recto*, lines 4-6), [namely,] [5-8] that he has received ... renewed. (= *recto*, lines 6-10).

(III 3) [8-9] Therefore, the order was passed that you renew the confirmatory *parvānau* and provide [the village and land] from V.S. 1802.

(III 4) [9-10] It is necessary that the *dīvāns* of the *sarkār* make out *parvānaus*.

(III 5) [10-11] On Śrāvaṇa b. 11, V.S. 1802/ rev. y. 1801, the petition was submitted again [, namely for]: A village etc.

[12-14] (= *recto*, lines 18-19)

(III 6) [15] As endorsed in the memorandum by Rājā Āyāmal and the *dīvāns*.

(IV) [16] Date: Bhādvā b. 5, rev.y. 1801; place: Savāī Jaipur.

(V) [17-18]

(seal)	*(seal)*	*(seal)*
Endorsed in the record; Rāy Narāyaṇdās, Dīvān	Endorsed in the record; Phaterām, Dīvān	Endorsed in the record; Phaterām, Court-Auditor

Start!

Entered in the *mavājanau* Entered in the *mavājanau*

Commentary:

l. 3: For Sālimpur cp. → A.H. 1123, 21 Ramaẕān, with commentary.

l. 5: For Rājā Āyāmal cp. → V.S. 1777, Āśvina ś. 14, *recto*, l. 8, with commentary.

rev.y. 1801/ V.S. 1802, Bhādrapada b. 5 (Sekhpur(o) Baṛo)/ 6 August 1745

॥श्री रांमजी

गोव्यंददेवजी

सवाई जैस्यंघजी

सही

(कटार)

(seal)

(१) सिधि श्री महाराजाधिराज महाराजा श्री सवाई ईश्वरस्यंघजी देव़-
(२) वचनात कमैती प्रगनां हिंङौण दिस्ये सुप्रसाद वंच्या अप्रंचि
(३) वावति पुन्य ऊदिक षास पोसाक व़ागैरह ठाकर श्री --- जी कै
(४) गांव़ सेषपुर वङो प्रगनां हिंङौण को सो मारफति राजा आय़ामल
(५) की मिती असाढ वदि ५ साल संवत १८०१ अरज पहौंची जो गांव़ म-
(६) जकूर षास पोसाक व़ मांषन मलाई मैं मुव़ाफिक प्रवांनैं महाराजा
(७) वैकुंटवासीजी श्री --- जी करार मिती प्रथम जेठ सुदि १५ सं-
(८) वत १७७४ का सौं पाव़ै छा सौ हासिल साष ऊन्हालू संवत १८०१ ता-
(९) ई पाय़ो अव हाल को प्रवांनौं संवत १८०२ सौं कराय़ो चाहै तीह सौं
(१०) फुरमांव़ां छां मतलव प्रव़ांनां का सौं व़ाकिफ होय़ षास पोसाक
(११) व़ागैरह मैं गांव़ सेषपुरो वङो प्रगनां हिंङौण को साविक दसतूर
(१२) वहाल जांणि ईस तग संवत १८०२ सौं हासिल हव़ालै करिवो की-
(१३) ज्यो अर प्रतवरष नव़ो प्रवांनौं मति मांग्यज्यो ईही प्रव़ांनां सौं
(१४) हिसाव मैं मुजरा होय़लां
(१५) मुकररा तनषाह गांव़ सेषपुरो वङो प्रगनां हिङौंण को साविक
(१६) दसतूर वहाल जांणि ईस तग संवत १८०२ सौं हासिल हव़ालै क-
(१७) रिवो कीज्यो तन दरोवसत ऊसूली रूपय़ा

(१८) १८०८

(१९) षास पोसाक का रुंपय़ा पंदरा सै	मांषन मलाई का रुपय़ा दोय़ सै
(२०) ऊगणीस	निव़ासी
(२१) १५१९८	२८९८

---

(१) सरह य़ादिदासति दाषिल व़ाकै करार मिती साव़ण वदि ११ संवत १८०१ वरिसालै

(२) राय़ नराय़णदास फतेरांम दिवांन व़ निहालचंद व़ाकानव़ीस अत्र ङोल पुन्य ऊदिक व़ागै-
(३) रह ठाकुर श्री --- जी कै वास्तै मारफति राजा आय़ामल की मिती असाढ वदि ५
(४) साल संवत १८०१ अरज पहौंची गांव़ सेषपुरो वङो प्रगनां हिङौण सो षास पो-
(५) साक व़ माषन मलाई मैं मूव़ाफिक प्रव़ानैं महाराजा वैकुंटवासीजी श्री --- जी
(६) करार मिती प्रथम जेठ सुदि १५ संवत १७७४ की सौं पाव़ै छा सो हासिल साष ऊ-
(७) न्हालू सवत १८०१ ताई पाय़ो अव हाल को प्रव़ांनौं संवत १८०२ सौं कराय़ो चा-
(८) है सो हुकम हुव़ा प्रव़ानौं हाल को करि द्योह सो चाहिज्ये दिव़ांन सरकार का प्रव़ां-
(९) नां लिषैं मिती साव़ण वदि ११ साल सवत १८०१ अरज मूकरर पहौंची गाव़ मज-
(१०) कूर तंन दरोवस्त ऊसूली रूपय़ा
(११) १८०८८

(१२) षास पोसाक का रुपय़ा पंदरा सै ऊगणी- माषन मलाई का रुपय़ा दोय़ सै निव़ासी
(१३) स
(१४) १५१९८ २८९८

(१५) मूव़ाफिक य़ादिदासति मैं दसषत राजा आय़ामल व़ा दिव़ानय़ांन

(१६) मिती भादव़ा वदि ५ सा° सं° १८०१ मूकाम सव़ाई जैपूर

(seal) *(seal)* *(seal)*

(१७) रजु दफत्र राय़ न-	रजु दफत्र फ-	रजू दफत्र फतेरां-
(१८) राय़णदास दीव़ान	तेराम दीव़ा-	म मुंस्तोफी हजूरि
(१९)	न	

सरू
दा° मव़ाजनै

दा° मव़ाजनै

(I) Śrī Rāmjī

Govinddevjī

Savāī Jaisiṅghjī

Certified

(*dagger*)

(*seal*)

(II 1) [1] Success! [1-2] By royal order of Śrī Mahārājādhirāj Mahārājā Śrī Savāī Īśvarsiṅghjī,
(II 2) with benevolent greetings to the officers of *parganā* Hiṇḍauṇ.
(II 3) [2-3] Reference: Item of charitable land *(punya ūdik)* for [the purpose of] festive robes etc. for the deity Śrī [GD]jī; [4] village Sekhpur Baṛo of *parganā* Hiṇḍauṇ.
(II 4) [4-5] For this, there was submitted a petition through Rājā Āyāmal on Asāḍh b. 5, V.S. 1802/ rev.y. 1801[, as follows]:
(II 5) [5-8] According to a *parvānau* promulgated by the late Mahārājā Śrī [Jaisiṅgh]jī on Jeṭh I ś. 15, V.S. 1774, the deity has received the aforementioned village for festive robes as well as for butter and cream. [8-9] He received the realized revenue up to the hot season harvest of V.S. 1801. Now he wishes that the *parvānau* be renewed from V.S. 1802.
(II 6) [9-10] Hereby, order is given that [10-11] it be known [to you] by the intention of the *parvānau* [11-13] that the hitherto existing regulation shall be understood to be in force and that for [the purpose of] festive robes etc. village Sekhpur Baṛo of *parganā* Hiṇḍauṇ shall be assigned for [income of] realized revenue from V.S. 1802.
(II 7) [13] And there must not be demanded a fresh *parvānau* every year.
(II 8) [13-14] Following this *parvānau*, there shall be carried to account in the account-book:
[15] Fixed allowance of revenue: [15-17] Understanding the hitherto existing regulation to be in force, from V.S. 1802 there shall be assigned for [income of] realized revenue Sekhpuro Baṛo of *parganā* Hiṇḍauṇ: Entire assessed revenue; recoverable amount, rupees

[18]	1,808/-
[19-21] For festive robes, fifteen hundred and nineteen rupees	For butter and cream, two hundred and eighty-nine rupees
1,519/-	289/-

(III 1) [1] Commentary on the memorandum [based] on the diary-entry of Sāvaṇ b. 11, V.S. 1802/ [2] rev.y.1801, on report of Dīvāns Rāy Narāyaṇdās and Phaterām and Diarist Nihālcand.

(III 2) [2-3] Statement as follows: For a a charity etc. [3-5] for the deity Śrī [GD]jī, there was submitted a petition through Rājā Āyāmal on Asāḍh b. 5, rev. year 1801[, as follows:] [4-8] ... be renewed (= *recto*, lines 5-9).

(III 3) [8] Therefore, the order was passed that you renew the *parvānau* and provide [the granted amount] from V.S. 1802.

(III 4) [8-9] It is necessary that the *dīvāns* of the *sarkār* make out *parvānaus*.

(III 5) [9] On Sāvaṇ b. 11, rev. y. 1801, the petition was submitted again [, namely for]: [9-10] The aforementioned village; entire assessed revenue; recoverable amount, rupees

[11] 1,808/-

[12-14] (= *recto*, lines 19-21)

(III 6) [15] As endorsed in the memorandum by Rājā Āyāmal and the *dīvāns*.

(IV) [16] Date: Bhādvā b. 5, rev.y. 1801; place: Savāī Jaipur.

(V) *(seal)*	*(seal)*	*(seal)*
[17-18]		
Endorsed in the record; Rāy Narāyaṇdās, Dīvān	Endorsed in the record; Phaterām, Dīvān	Endorsed in the record; Phaterām, Court-Auditor

Start!	
Entered in the *mavājanau*	Entered in the *mavājanau*

Commentary:

l. 4: Sekhpur(o) Baṛo cannot be identified unequivocally. In present-day Ṭoḍābhīm Tehsil of Sawai Madhopur District, there are two neighbouring villages of that name, viz., Paṭṭī Śekhpurā and Śekhpurā proper (India 1983 [DCH Sawai Madhopur]: 27, serial/code nos 105/26 and 131/131). They lie a few miles across the western border of Hiṇḍaun Tehsil. For Rājā Āyāmal cp. → V.S. 1777, Āśvina ś. 14, *recto*, l. 8, with commentary.

rev.y. 1801/ V.S. 1802, Bhādrapada b. 5 (pasture)/ 6 August 1745
Invocatio missing.

गोव्यंददेवजी
सवाई जैस्यंघजी
सही
(कटार)

(seal)

(१) सिधि श्री महाराजाधिराज महाराजा श्री सवाई ईश्वरस्यंघजी देव़-
(२) वचनात कमैती प्रगनां सव़ाई जैपुर का दिस्ये सुप्रसाद वंच्या अ-
(३) प्रंचि वावति घास चराई ठाकर श्री --- जी की गाय़ घास च-
(४) रै सो मारफति राजा आय़ामल की मिती असाढ वदि ५ साल
(५) संवत १८०१ अरज पहौंची जो गांय़ां का चरवा कै व़ासतै मांगथ-
(६) ला व़ पांणीढाल गिरद तलाव़ मांनसरोव़र को मुव़ाफिक प्रव़ां-
(७) नैं सवती महाराजा वैकुंटवासीजी श्री --- जी करार मिती
(८) आसोज व़दि १३ संवत १७७१ का सौ पाव़ै छा सो मिती भादव़ा
(९) सुदि २ साल संवत १८०१ ताई गाय़ चरी अव हाल को प्रवांनौ क-
(१०) राय़ो चाहै तीह सौं फुरमांव़ां छां मतलव प्रव़ांनां का सौं व़ाकि-
(११) फ होय़ गाय़ चरवा नैं मांगथला व़ पांणीढाल गिरद तलाव़
(१२) मांनसरोव़र की साविक दसतूर वहाल जांणिं ईस तग मिती
(१३) भादव़ा सुदि ३ संवत १८०२ सौं गाय़ चरवा दीज्यौ अर प्रतवर-
(१४) ष नव़ो प्रव़ांनौं मति मांग्यज्यो
(१५) मूकररा तनषाह मागथला व़ पांणीढाल गिरद तलाव़ मांन-
(१६) सरोव़र को साविक दसतूर वहाल जांणि ई तग मिती भादव़ा
(१७) सुदि ३ संवत १८०१ सौं गाय़ चरवा दीज्यौ

---

(१) सरह य़ादिदासति दाषिल व़ाकै करार मिती साव़ण वदि ११ साल संवत १८०१ वरि-
(२) सालै राय़ नराय़णदास फतेरांम दिव़ांन व़ निहालचंद व़ाकानव़ीस अत्र ङोल घास
(३) चराई ठाकर श्री --- जी का कै व़ास्तै मारफति राजा आय़ामल की मिती असाढ
(४) वदि ५ साल संवत १८०१ अरज पहौंची जो गांय़ां का चरावा कै व़ास्तै मांगथला व़
(५) पांणींढाल गिरद तलाव़ मानसरोव़र का मूव़ाफिक प्रव़ानै सवती महाराजा वै-
(६) कुंटवासीजी श्री --- जी करार मीती आसोज वदि १३ संवत १७७१ का सौ पाव़ै
(७) छै सो भादव़ा सुदि २ साल संवत १८०१ ताई गाय़ चराई अब हाल को प्रव़ांनौ स-
(८) वती कराय़ो चाहै सो हुकम हुव़ा साविक दसतूर प्रव़ांनौं हाल को लिषो सो चाहि-
(९) ज्ये दिव़ांन सरकार का प्रव़ांनां लिषै मीती साव़ण वदि ११ साल संवत १८०१ अर-
(१०) ज मुकरर पहौची मागथला पांणीढाल गिरद तलाव़ मानसरोव़र का
(११) ।

(१२) मू° य़ादिासति मैं दसषत राजा आय़ामल व़ दिव़ांनय़ान

(१३) मिती भादव़ा वदि ५ सा° सं° १८०१ मूकाम सव़ाई जैपूर

	(seal)	*(seal)*	*(seal)*
(१४)	रजु दफत्र राय़ नरां-	रजु दफत्र	रजू दफत्र फतेरां-
(१५)	य़णदास दीव़ान	फतेरांम दीव़ा-	म मुंस्तोफी हजूरि
(१६)		न	

सरू

(I) Govinddevjī
Savāī Jaisiṅghjī

Certified
(*dagger*)

(*seal*)

(II 1) [1] Success! [1-2] By royal order of Śrī Mahārājādhirāj Mahārājā Śrī Savāī Īśvarsiṅghjī,

(II 2) with benevolent greetings to the officers of *parganā* Savāī Jaipur.

(II 3) [2-4] Reference: Pasture, where the cows of the deity Śrī [GD]jī graze.

(II 4) [4-5] For this, there was submitted a petition through Rājā Āyāmal on Āṣāḍha b. 5, rev.y. 1801[, as follows]:

(II 5) [5-8] To date, [the deity] has received for grazing cows, the land of Māgthalā and Pāṇīḍhāl by Lake Mānsarovar, according to a confirmatory *parvānau* promulgated by the late Mahārājā Śrī [Jaisiṅgh]jī on Āsoj b. 13, V.S. 1771. [8-9] By this, the cows grazed [there] until Bhādvā ś. 2, rev.y. 1801. [9-10] Now he wishes that the *parvānau* be renewed.

(II 6) [10] Hereby, order is given that [10-11] it be known [to you] by the intention of the *parvānau* [11-13] that the hitherto existing regulation shall be understood to be in force and that the land of Māgthalā and Pāṇīḍhāl by Lake Mānsarovar shall be granted for the purpose of grazing cows from Bhādvā ś. 3, V.S. 1802.

(II 7) [13-14] And there must not be demanded a fresh *parvānau* every year.

(II 8) [15-17] Fixed allowance: [15-17] Understanding the hitherto existing regulation to be in force, from Bhādvā s. 3, rev.y. 1801 there shall be granted the land of Māgthalā and Pāṇīḍhāl by Lake Mānsarovar.

(III 1) [1] Commentary on the memorandum [based] on the diary-entry of Sāvaṇ b. 11, V.S. 1802/ [2] rev.y. 1801, on report of Dīvāns Rāy Narāyaṇdās and Phaterām and Diarist Nihālcand.

(III 2) [2-6] Statement as follows: For pasture for [the use of] the deity Śrī [GD]jī, there was submitted ... on Āsoj b. 13, V.S. 1771 (= *recto*, lines 3-8). [7-8] By this, the cows were grazed [there] until ... be renewed (= *recto*, lines 9-10).

(III 3) [8] Therefore, the order was passed that you make out a renewed *parvānau* according to the hitherto existing regulations.

(III 4) [8-9] It is necessary that the *dīvāns* of the *sarkār* make out *parvānaus*.

(III 5) [9-10] On Sāvaṇ b. 11, rev.y. 1801, the petition was submitted again [, namely for]: Māgthalā and Pāṇīḍhāl by Lake Mānsarovar.

[11] |

(III 6) [12] As endorsed in the memorandum by Rājā Āyāmal and the *dīvāns*.

(IV) [13] Date: Bhādvā b. 5, rev.y. 1801; place: Savāī Jaipur.

(V) *(seal)*	*(seal)*	*(seal)*
[14-16]		
Endorsed in the record; Rāy Narāyaṇdās, Dīvān	Endorsed in the record; Phaterām, Dīvān	Endorsed in the record; Phaterām, Court-Auditor

Start!

Commentary:

ll. 5-6: For Mānsarovar (Mānsāgar) Lake, cp. pp. 19-21.

Mā(ṃ)gthalā and Pā(ṃ)ṇīḍhāl are toponyms. The maps, which belong to the holdings of the Jaipur City Palace and show these places, are not readily accessible, but in their catalogue of these maps, Bahura and Singh mention Māṃgthalā as being given on one of them (1990: 39. 101, map no 205 "Coloured map of Sawai Jaipur ... early 18th century").

V.S. 1805, Māgha ś. 1/ 8 January 1749

Copper-plate.

॥श्री रांमजी

गोव्यंददेव़जी

सही

(१) ॥सिधि श्री महाराजि श्री व्रंदावनदासजी
(२) वचनातु मो° गोरधनपुरो प्र° षडेला श्री-
(३) जी का भोग व़ासतै भेट ऊदिक श्री क्रसना
(४) अरपण करी दीयो सो हासील गांव़ मै होसी
(५) सो श्रीजी कै पहोचीसी मीती माह सुदी १
(६) संवत १८०५ का हुकम हजुरी मुकाम सव़ाइ
(७) जैपुर दसकत मनराम का इथ सीर लोक :
(८) अपदतं प्रदतं जे मेटतं वीसधरा ते नरा न-
(९) रक जोइ ततो लौ चंद दीव़ाकरा

Śrī Rāmjī

Govinddevjī

Certified

[1] Success! [1-2] By order of Śrī Mahārāj Śrī Vrandāvandāsjī (Vṛndāvandās): [2-4] The village of Gordhanpuro in *parganā* Khaḍelā was given in dedication to Śrī Kṛṣṇa, as a religious donation of charitable land *(bheṭ ūdik)* for *bhog* of the deity. [4-5] Therefore, the realized revenue of the village shall be delivered to the deity. [5-6] On Māh ś. 1, V.S. 1805, [there was issued] in Savāī Jaipur a Court order endorsed by Manrām. Such moral [prevails in the] world: [8-9] He who takes away land given by me or by someone else will go to hell, [this holds true] as long as moon and sun exist.

Commentary:

l. 1: Vṛndāvandās, Mahārājā of Kha(ṇ)ḍelā, was the son of Savāī Siṅgh of Śekhāvāṭī (Tod 1829-32, II: 324). Vṛndāvandās refers to a Court order issued in Jaipur (line 6), that is, an order issued by the central Kachavāhā chancery and not by himself. Khaṇḍelā, which in Akbar's time belonged to the *sarkār* of Narnaul in *s̲ūba* Agra, was obtained in *ijāra* by Jaisiṅgh in 1723 (Wills 1933: 76; App. G, p. II gives 1734). The town of Khaṇḍelā with its hinterland belongs to Śrīmādhopur Tehsil of Sikar District; Gordhanpuro cannot be traced, having probably merged with the town.

l. 7: One Manrām, designated *"baid cākar sirkār kā"*, is mentioned in DK (16: 193) for the year V.S. 1778. Supposedly, the Manrām of the present deed was a Minister.

ll. 7-9: The words *ith sīr lok* is the corrupt form of Skt. *ittham śīlo loke*. This phrase and the sentence following in lines 8 and 9 form a punitive formula, which occurs often at the end of land-grants. It is a corrupt descendant of a Sanskrit formula, which occurs in many variations (Sircar 1965: 196, stanza 132 with fn. 2). For Rājasthānī counterparts, cp. also the patents published by Bhāṭnagar (1987: 23, 25 [lines 9-10], 27 [lines 6-7], 29 [lines 5-6], 32 [lines 5-6], 33 [lines 6-7]).

V.S. 1808, Bhādrapada ś. 13/ 23 August 1751

Invocatio, elevatio and fag-end missing.

सही

(कटार)

(seal)

(१) सिधि श्री महाराजाधिराज महाराजा श्री सवाई माधवस्यंघजी देववचनात कमैती कसवा सवाई जै-
(२) पुर का दिस्ये सुप्रसाद वंच्या अप्रंचि वावति तनषाह पुन्य वतछव भोग वागैरह ठाकर श्री ---
(३) जी विराजमांन श्री कनकव्रिदावन मै त्या का वतछव भोग वागैरह कै वास्तै माफिक फरद हकीक-
(४)ति मै दसषत दिवांनयांन करार मिती भादवा सुदि ३ संवत १८०८ अरज पहौंची जो आगैं भोग वतछ-
(५) व वागैरह कारषांनां पुन्य का सौं मुवाफिक सनदि दिवांनी व प्रवांनां थे पावै छै मुवाफिक तफ-
(६) सील सालनिां वसूली रुपया पचीसैं अठांवन २५५८ऽ

(७) भोग वतछव मुवाफिक सनदि दिवांनी करार मिती पोस वदि ५ संवत १७९२ का
(८) सौं रोजीनां वसूली रुपया ५ ऽ ती का वरस १ का दिन ३५४ का रुपया सतरा सै सतरि
(९) १७७०ऽ

(१०)	सांवण भादवा का रुपया दोय सै नवै	आसोज काती का रुपया ऐक सो तीस
(११)	२९०ऽ	१३०ऽ
(१२)	पोसाष रंगीन का रुपया दोय सै	पोसाष सरद की ऐक का रुपया चा-
(१३)	२००ऽ	लीस ४०ऽ
(१४)	भोग नैं रुपया निवै	भोग नै रुपया निवै
(१५)	९०ऽ	९०ऽ

(१६)	मोतीचुर का रु-	सालूंणी का रु-	मेवा का रुपया	दही मांठी का रु-	मोतीचुर का रुपया	सलूंणी का रुपया	मेवा का रुपया पैंता-
(१७)	पया तीस	पया पंदरा	पदरा	पया तीस	तीस	पदरा	लीस
(१८)	३०ऽ	१५ऽ	१५ऽ	३०ऽ	३०ऽ	१५ऽ	४५ऽ

(१९)	माग्रश्र पोस का रुपया च्यारि सै पैंतीस	माह फागण का रुपया पांच सै छतीस	
(२०)	४३५ऽ	५३६ऽ	
(२१)	पोसाष ४ का रुपया तीन सै	पोसाष का रुपया च्यारि सै छह	
(२२)	३००ऽ	४०६ऽ	
(२३)		वसंती का रुपया एक सो	होली की का रुपया तीन सै छह
(२४)		१००ऽ	३०६ऽ
(२५)	भोग नै रुपया ऐक सो पैतीस	भोग नै रुपया ऐक सो तीस	
(२६)	१३५ऽ	१३०ऽ	

(२७) षीचड्डी का रुपय़ा मोतीचुर का रु- सलूंणी का रुप- धुप का रुपय़ा गुलाव का पां- मोतीचुर का रु- सलूंणी का रुप- तिल चांव़ली का

(२८) साठि पय़ा तीस य़ा पदरा तीस णी षसवोई का पय़ा तीस पय़ा तीस रुपय़ा वीस

(२९) ६०ऽ ३०ऽ १५ऽ ३०ऽ ५०ऽ ३०ऽ ३०ऽ २०ऽ

(३०) चैत व़ैसाष मै रुपय़ा एक सो दस जेठ असाढ मै रुपय़ा दोय़ सै गुणहत्रि

(३१) ११०ऽ २६९ऽ

(३२) गुलाव का पांणी मोतीचुर का रु- सलूंणी का रुपय़ा मेव़ा का रुपय़ा पोसाष ३ का रुपय़ा एक सो वीस

(३३) चंदण षसवोई पय़ा तीस पदरा पदरा १२०ऽ

(३४) ५०ऽ ३०ऽ १५ऽ १५ऽ भोग का रुपय़ा ऐक सो गुणचास

(३५) १४९ऽ

(३६) मोती-चू- सलूंणी का मेव़ा का मिश्री का कचा मे- गुलाव का मसालो

(३७) र का रुपय़ा रुपय़ा रुपय़ा रुपय़ा व़ा का रुपय़ा पांणी का रु- पय़ा रुपय़ा

(३८) ३०ऽ १५ऽ १५ऽ २०ऽ २५ऽ ४०ऽ ४ऽ

(३९) सषी १ ठाकर श्री --- जी व़ा ठूकरांणीजी की सेव़ा करिवा नै पधराई छी ती का माफि-

(४०) क प्रवांनैं करार मिती भादव़ा वदि ५ साल संवत १८०१ का सौं रोजीनां व़सूली रुपय़ा ऐक १ऽ

(४१) भोग नै आंनां आठ ।।ऽ वसत्रां नैं आंनां आठ ।।ऽ

(४२) मुकररा वरस १ का दिन ३५४ का रुपय़ा तीन सौ चोव़न

(४३) ३५४ऽ

(४४) समय़े होली कै माफिक सनदि सुदामदि पाव़ै रुपय़ा व़सूली तीन सै अढतीस आंनां दस

(४५) ३३८।।=

(४६) भोग महीनां एक का रुपय़ा पोसाष कपड्डा व़ागैरह नै रुपय़ा गुलाव अवीर अड्गजा फु- गुलाव का पांणी रोजीनां सेर ऽ२।।

(४६a) ती का महीना १ का मण १।।।२।।

(४७) १९।।= १००ऽ लेल चंदन केसरि नै रुपय़ा मुकररा रुपय़ा

(४८) १८२।।ऽ ३६ऽ

(४९) समय़े स्याल कै कोय़ला सिघड्डी नै सदामदि पाव़ै माफिक सनदि मण १२०ऽ ती का रुपय़ा

(५०) ६०ऽ

(५१) घिरत दीव़ो श्री --- जी की हजूरि हमेस जुय़ै सो पाव़ै माफिक सनदि करार मिती असाढ व-

(५२) दि १४ संवत १७९४ की थे रोजीनां सेर ऽ।। मुकररा वरस १ का मण ४।७ ती का रुपय़ा

(५३) ३५।=

(५४) सो संवत १८०७ ताई पाय़ो अव व़तछव़ भोग वागैरह मै गांव़ गोव्यंदपुर वास हाथ्योद तालक कासवा सव़ाई जै-

(५५) पुर तन भोमि व़ागैरह सुधां व़सूली रुपय़ा २५५८ऽ को दरोवस्त कराय़ो चाहै तीह सौं फुरमांव़ां छां मतलव प्रव़ांनां

(५६) का सौं व़ाकिफ होय़ गांव़ गोव्यंदपुर वास हाथ्योद तालक कसवा सव़ाई जैपुर को तन भोमि व़ागैरह सुधां व-

(५७) हाल जांणि ईस तग संवत १८०८ सौं हवाले कीज्यो अर प्रतवरष नवो प्रवांनौं मति मांग्यज्यो ईही प्रवांनां
(५८) सौं हिसाव मै मुजरा होयला
(५९) मुकररा तनषाह गांव गोव्यंदपुर वास हाथ्योद तालक कसवा सवाई जैपुर को वहाल जांणि ईस तग सं-
(६०) वत १८०८ सौं हवाले कीज्यो मुकररा गांव मजकूर तन दरोवस्त भोमि वागैरह सुधां वसूली रुपया पचीसैं अठांवन
(६१) २५५८

---

(१) सरह यादिसति दाष्यल वाकै मिती भादवा सुदि १० संवत १८०८ वरिसालै कन्हीरांम दिवांन व --- वाकानवीस अ-
(२-५१) त्र ङौल तनषाह पुन्य वतछ्व भौग वागैरह ... (= *recto*, lines 2-51)

(५२) सो संवत १८०७ तांई पाया अव वतछ्व भोग वागैरह मै गांव गोव्यंदपुरं वास हाथ्योद तालक कसवा सवाई जैपुर
(५३) तन भोमि वागैरह सुधां वसूली रुपया २५५८ को दरोवस्त ईस तग संवत १८०८ थे कराग्रो चाहै सो दसषत षास हू-
(५४) कम हूवा माफिक तफसील प्रवांनौं सवती लिषो सो चाहिज्ये दिवांन सरकार का प्रवांनां लिषै मिती भादवा सु-
(५५) दि १० संवत १८०८ अरज मुकरर पहौंची गांव मजकूर तन दरोवस्त भोमि वागैरह सुधां वसूली रुपया पचीसै अठांवन

(५६) २५५८

(५७) मुवाफिक यादिदासति फरद हकीकति मै दसषत षास व दिवांनयांन

(५८) मिती भादवा सुदि १३ संवत १८०८ मुकाम सवाई जैपुर

	(seal)	*(seal)*
(५९) रजू दफत्र क-	रजु दफत्र दीवा-	रजू दफत्र वषत-
(६०) न्हीरांम दीवांन	न हजूर	रांम मस्तौफी हजूरि

दा° मवाजनै
लिषौ

(I) Certified

(*dagger*)

(*seal*)

(II 1) [1-2] Success! By royal order of Śrī Mahārājādhirāj Mahārājā Śrī Savāī Mādhavsiṅghjī,

(II 2) [1-2]with benevolent greetings to the officers of *kasbā* Savāī Jaipur.

(II 3) [2] Reference: Item of income; charitable income *(tankhāh punya)* for festivals, *bhog* etc. for the deity Śrī [3] [GD]jī residing in Śrī Kanakvrīdāvan (-vṛndāvan).

(II 4) [3-4] On Bhādvā s. 3, V.S. 1808, there was submitted a petition for his festivals, *bhog* etc., which was endorsed by the *dīvāns* in the report (*pharad hakīkati*) [, as follows]:

(II 5) [4-5] To date, [the deity] has received *bhog*, festival [expenses] etc. from the factories concerned with religious charities, [as] was in accordance with a *sanad* of the *dīvāns* and a *parvānau*. [5-6] According to the [following] detailed specification, [this amounts to] an annually recoverable amount of two thousand five hundred and fifty-eight rupees — 2,558/-.

[7] *bhog* and festival [expenses] according to the *sanad* of the *dīvāns*, endorsed on Pos b. 5, V.S. 1792: [8] daily recoverable amount 5 rupees; for 1 year of 354 days, this [amounts to] seventeen hundred and seventy rupees

[9] 1,770/-

[10] For Sāvaṇ and Bhādvā, two hundred and ninety rupees	For Āsoj and Kātī, one hundred and thirty rupees
[11] 290/-	130/-
[12] For coloured suits, two hundred rupees	For one suit for the cold season, forty rupees
[13] 200/-	40/-
[14] For *bhog*, ninety rupees	For *bhog*, ninety rupees
[15] 90/-	90/-

[16]	For motīcur,	For salt,	For dried fruit,	For yoghurt	For motīcur,	For salt,	For dried fruit,
[- 17]	thirty rp.	fifteen rp.	fifteen rp.	and buttermilk, thirty rp.	thirty rp.	fifteen rp.	forty-five rp.
[18]	30/-	15/-	15/-	30/-	30/-	15/-	45/-

[19] For Māgyaśra and Pos, four hundred and thirty-five rupees	For Māh and Phāgaṇ, five hundred and thirty-six rupees

[20] 435/-	536/-
[21] For 4 suits, three hundred rupees	For suits, four hundred and six rupees
[22] 300/-	406/-
	[23] For Vasantī, one hundred rp. — For suits for Holī, three hundred and six rp.
	[24] 100/- — 306/-
[25] For *bhog*, one hundred and thirty-five rp.	For *bhog*, one hundred and thirty rupees
[26] 135/-	130/-
[27] For *khicṛī*, For motīcur, For salt, For incense,	For rosewater, For *motīcur*, For salt, For sesame *khicrī*,
[28] sixty rp. thirty rp. fifteen rp. thirty rp.	fifty rp. thirty rp. thirty rp. twenty rp.
[29] 60/- 30/- 15/- 30/-	50/- 30/- 30/- 20/-
[30 In Cait and Vaisākh, one hundred and ten rupees	In Jeṭh and Asāḍh, two hundred and sixty-nine rupees
[31] 110/-	269/-
[32] Rosewater, and For *motīcūr*, For salt, For dried fruit,	For 3 suits, one hundred and twenty rupees
[33] sandalwood perfume, thirty rp. fifteen rp. fifteen rp.	120/-
[34] 50/- 30/- 15/- 15/-	For *bhog*, one hundred and forty-nine rupees
	[35] 149/-

[36] (→ to column 2:)	For *motīcūr*,	For salt,	For dried fruit,	For sugar-candy,	For *kaccā* dried fruit,	For rosewater,	Other items,
[37] (→ to column 2:)	rupees	rp.	rupees	rupees	rupees	rupees	rupees
[38] (→ to column 2:)	30/-	15/-	15/-	20/-	25/-	40/-	4/-

[39] There had been sent 1 *sakhī* to serve the deity Śrī [GD]jī and his consort; for her, [40] according to a *parvānau* endorsed on Bhādvā b. 5, rev.y. 1801, the daily recoverable amount of one rupee,

[41] For *bhog*, eight annas — 8/-   For garments, eight annas — 8/-

[42] Fixed allowance for 1 year of 354 days: three hundred and fifty-four rupees

[43] 354/-

[44] According to a *sanad*, he always receives for the Holī season the recoverable amount of three hundred and thirty-eight rupees, 10 annas

[45] 338rp., 10a.

[46]	For *bhog* for one month, rupees	For suits, cloth etc. rupees	For rose-scent, coloured powder, *aṛgjau* perfume,	For rosewater, daily 2 1/2 *sers*
[46a]				for one month 1 maund and 32 1/2 *sers*;
[47]	19rp., 14a.	100/-	scented oil, sandalwood, saffron colour; rupees	fixed: rupees
[48]			182rp., 12a.	36/-

[49] According to the *sanad*, he always receives for the cold season, for 120 maunds of coal, rupees

[50] 60/-

[51-52] According to a *sanad* endorsed on Asāḍh b. 14, V.S. 1793, [the deity] receives for a butter-lamp, which is always burning in the presence of the deity Śrī [GD]jī, a daily allowance of a half *ser*; fixed allowance for 1 year: 4 maunds, 17 *sers*; for this rupees

[53] 35rp., 6a.

[54] This he received until V.S. 1807.

(II 5) [54-55] Now he wishes that village Govindpur-vās Hāthyod, part of *kasbā* Savāī Jaipur, of which the assessed revenue dues inclusive of *bhomi* etc. are 2,558rp., be transferred to him in its entirety.

(II 6) [55-56] Hereby, order is given that it be known [to you] by the intention of the *parvānau* [56-57] that the hitherto existing regulation shall be understood to be in force and village Govindpur-vās Hāthyod, part of *kasbā* Savāī Jaipur, with its assessed revenue dues inclusive of *bhomi* etc. be assigned from V.S. 1808.

(II 7) [57] And there must not be demanded a fresh *parvānau* every year.

(II 8) [57-58] Following this *parvānau*, there shall be carried to account in the account-book:

[59-60] Fixed allowance of revenue: Starting with V.S. 1808, village Govindpur-vās Hāthyod, part of *kasbā* Savāī Jaipur, shall be assigned anew. Fixed allowance: The aforementioned village; entire assessed revenue income, inclusive of *bhomi* etc.; recoverable amount: two thousand five hundred and fifty-eight rupees

[61] 2,558/-

(III 1) [1] Commentary on the memorandum [based] on the diary-entry of Bhādvā ś. 10, V.S. 1808, on report of Dīvān Kanhīrām and Diarist ---.

(III 2) [2-53] Statement as follows: Income, charitable income for festivals, *bhog* etc. ... be transferred to him in its entirety (= *recto*, lines 2-55).

(III 3) [53-54] Therefore, an order, endorsed by His Highness, was passed that you shall make out a confirmatory *parvānau* according to the detailed specification.

(III 4) [54] It is necessary that the *dīvāns* of the *sarkār* make out *parvānaus*.

(III 5) [54-55] On Bhādvā s. 10, V.S. 1808 the petition was submitted again [, namely for]: The aforementioned village, entire assessed revenue income, inclusive of *bhomi* etc.; recoverable amount: two thousand five hundred and fifty-eight rupees,

[56] 2,558/–

(III 6) [57] As endorsed by His Highness and the *dīvāns* in the memorandum [based on] the report (*pharad hakīkati*).

(IV) [58] Date: Bhādvā ś. 23, V.S. 1808; place: Savāī Jaipur.

(V) *(seal)*		*(seal)*
[59-60] Endorsed in the record; Kanhīrām, Dīvān	Endorsed in the record, *dīvān hajūr*	Endorsed in the record; Bakhatrām, Court-Auditor

Entered in the *mavājanau*

Write!

Commentary:

Several of the grants mentioned in the deed could not be traced.

The document states that GD "resides at Kanakvṛndāvan"; for Kanakvṛndāvan cp. pp. 19-21, 23.

<u>ll. 3-4 *(recto)*:</u> For *pharad hakīkatī*, cp. p. 56.

ll. 7 *(recto)* ff.: As for the items that the temple needed, cp. also doc. → A.H. 1080, 12 Ramaẕān for the garments, and doc. → V.S. 1777, Āśvina ś. 14 for the eatables. Only for a few items, the prices can be related to prices given elsewhere. For most items, the deed gives only lump-sums unrelated to quantities. The quantified items are rosewater (*recto*, ll. 46-47), coal (*recto*, ll. 49-50), and ghee (*recto*, ll. 51-53).

Rosewater was now more expensive than in V.S. 1777 (and also in rev.y. 1784; Horstmann 1995). While according to the present deed 1rp. would fetch a little more than 2 *sers* (2 *sers*, 1 *tolā*, 1 *māśā* and nearly 2 *rattīs*), according to the documents of V.S. 1777 and rev.y. 1784, 1rp. would fetch 4 *sers*, 8 *chaṭāṃks*.

Coal cost 1rp. per 2 maunds (120 maunds cost 60rp.).

The yearly provision of 4 maunds, 17 *sers* (= 177 *sers*) of ghee for the lamp cost 35rp., 6a. Accordingly, 1rp. would fetch a little more than 5 *sers*. This is a lower price than that of V.S. 1777 and rev.y. 1784, when 1 rp. would fetch 4 *sers*, 14 *chaṭāṃks*. It would have been helpful to know if ghee for fuel was of the same quality as that used for cooking.

Two more items of *bhog*, which were not commented on for doc. → V.S. 1777, Āśvina ś. 14, call for explanation, namely, *motīcur/motīcūr* and *kacau mevau* (*recto*, ll. 16 *pass.*; *recto*, ll. 26 *pass.*). For *motīcur*, cp. BPL 354: "a sweetmeat made up of very fine *buniyā̃* shaped like pearls"; *buniyā̃* is "a small round hollow sweetmeat of gram-*besan* (chickpea meal - MH), fried in clarified butter or oil and covered with sugar" (BPL 353); *kacau mevau*, is unpeeled dried fruit, such as nuts.

l. 54 *(recto)*: The revenue source, village Govindpur-vās Hāthyod, can be related to the modern Hāthod in Jaipur Tehsil of Jaipur District (India 1983[DCH Jaipur]: 90, serial/code nos 42/63).

l. 55 *(recto)*: For *bhomi*, cp. doc. → V.S. 1797, l. 11, with commentary.

V.S. 1816, Bhādrapada ś. 9/ 1 September 1759

॥श्री रांमजी ॥ ॥श्री रांमजी ॥श्री रांमजी ॥
गोबिंददेव्जी

रांमरांम

(१) ॥सिधि श्री आंमिलांन प्रगनां सांभरि का जो-
(२) ग्य लिषतं दीवांन कन्हीरांम नंदलाल केनि
(३) --- बंच्या अैठा का स्माचार भला छै थां का
(४) सदा भला चाहिज्ये अप्रंचि ठाकुर श्री ---
(५) जी व्रा गूसांईजी की भेट सलूणी लुण म्ण सात
(६) सै ७००ऽ सालीनां श्री हजूरि सौं कीयो छै तीह
(७) सौं थां नै मा° प्रव्रानगी राजा हरसहाय की सौ
(८) लिषां छां जो ई° संवत १८१६ थे सालीनां लू-
(९) ण म्ण सात सै ७००ऽ प्रगनां मजकूर सौं दै-
(१०) वो कीज्यो हर साल संनदि तलव मति कीज्यो
(११) मिती भादव्रा सूदि ९ संवत १८१६

(seal) *(seal)*

दा° नुसषै
नकल लिषी
नकल लिषी [xx]

सरू
दा° नुसषै
नकल लषी

Śrī Rāmjī (3x)
Govinddevjī

Rām-Rām

[1] Success! [1-2] Written to the *āmil*s of *parganā* Sāmbhar by Dīvāns Kanhīrām and Nandlāl [3]... with greetings. Here all is well. [3-4] We hope that all is always well with you. [4-6]

Reference: The Court has made a religious donation *(bheṭ)* of annually seven hundred — 700 — salt maunds of salt to the deity Śrī [GD]jī and to the Gosvāmī. [6-8] Hereby, we are writing to you in accordance with an order of Rājā Harsahāy that [8-10] you shall forward annually 700 salt maund of salt from the aforementioned *parganā*. You must not claim a [fresh] *sanad* every year. [11] Date: Bhādvā s. 9, V.S. 1816.

(seal) *(seal)*

Entered in the *nuskhau*
Copy written
Copy written [xx]

Start!
Entered in the *nuskhau*
Copy written

Commentary:

l. 7: Rājā Harsahāy Khatrī s/o Ṭhākurdās was *musāhib* (< Pers. *muṣāhib*), "royal companion", at the Court of Jaipur (DK 3: 726-33). The present document suggests that he also served as Minister. In V.S. 1813, he received a *mans̱ab* of 5,000 (*l.c.*: 726-27).

ll. 8-9: Salt was measured by "salt maunds", which the documents do not allow us to relate to other measures of capacity called *maṇ* (cp. also p. 305, transl. ll. 7-9).

V.S. 1822, Pauṣa ś. 14/ 26 December 1761

॥श्री परमेश्वर सत्य छै

(seal)
(कटार)

(१) ॥स्वस्ति श्री श्री राजराजैश्वर म्हाराजाधिराज माहा-
(२) राजा श्री रांमसिघजी देवबचनांत कबणीग[?]-
(३) र म्हैमद सा दीसे सूप्रसाद बांचजे
(४) । तथा ठाकुर श्री गोमददेवजी री सलूणी अ-
(५) टकी हुवै सो उठाय दीजो टील मत कीजो हु-
(६) कम छै
(६) । सं° 1822री मी° पोस सूद १४ मू° जैपूर

Śrī Parameśvar is the Truth

(seal)
(dagger)

[1-2] By royal order of Śrī Śrī Rājrājeśvar Mahārājādhirāj Mahārājā Śrī Rāmsiṅghjī, [2-3] with benevolent greetings to Kabaṇīga[?]r Mhaịmad Sā.
[4-5] Reference: The [delivery of] salt to the deity Śrī Govinddevjī has been hindered. [5-6] Stop this and do not obstruct [the delivery]. [6-7] This is an order.
[8] V.S. 1822, Pos ś. 14; place: Jaipur.

Commentary:
Rāmsiṅgh, who was the deposed Mahārājā of Marwar and ruled nominally from 1746-72, had lost his throne to Bakhatsiṅgh. From 1751 his territory remained reduced to Marwar's portion of the salt-lake of Sāmbhar (Tod 1829-32: II, 594; Gahlot 1925: 132-33).

V.S. 1825, Māgha b. 15/ 6 February 1769
Seal on the wrapper.

॥श्री गोबिंददेव़जी (श्री र)ामजी

नीलांबरजी

(१) ॥प्रंमपूज्यं गूसाईजी श्री ---जी सूकव़रजी
(२) श्री बषताव़रस्यंघजी की धोक बचीजौजी अप्रंचि
(३) श्री ---जी की भेट प्रगना लिव़ाली कौ गा-
(४) व़ मो° रामसर कीय़ौ छै सोई गाव़ कौ व़पेजौ हौय
(५) सो श्री कै भोग व़ागरै(!) का षरच मै लगाजो
(६) मिती म्हा वदी ऽऽ संवत १८२५

(address:)

प्रंमपूज्य गुसाईजी श्री नीलांबरजी जौग्यं

Śrī Gobinddevjī [Śrī R]āmjī

Nīlāmbarjī

[1-2] To the most venerable Gosvāmījī Śrī [Nīlāmbar]jī, most humble greetings from Prince Śrī Bakhtāvarsiṅghjī. Reference: [2-4] Village Rāmsar in *parganā* Livālī has been made a religious donation *(bheṭ)* to Śrī [GD]jī. Whatever revenue is realized from this village [5] shall be spent on *bhog* etc. for the deity.
[6] Date: Mhā b. 15, V.S. 1825.

(address:)
To the most venerable Gosvāmījī Śrī Nīlāmbarjī

Commentary:
The deed is connected with doc. → V.S. 1825, Māgha ś. 13.

l. 2: Bakhtāvarsiṅgh of Alvar, Mahārājā from 1790 to 1815 (Nath 1996: 171). The ruling family of Alvar belonged to the Narūkā clan of the Kachavāhās. They claimed to have housed GD on his way to Amber, GD being their tutelary deity (cp. p. 15). Nath (1996: 171-72) argues convincingly that Bakhtāvarsiṅgh, who in 1806 built a GD temple at the fort of Rājgaṛh, took over an existing Kachavāhā temple, which had been dedicated to GD and which he restored and endowed with grants for *bhog*. Nath's argument is modified by the present deed in so far as it shows that the Narūkās evinced interest in GD as early as the latter part of the eighteenth century. This may go to indicate that they vied with the Jaipur Kachavāhās for the religious legitimation of their independent regnal status. They eventually established a separate state of their own in 1775, that is, six years after the date of the present deed.

ll. 3-4: Rāmsar lies in Lālsoṭ Tehsil of Jaipur District (India 1983 [DCH Jaipur]: 306, serial/code nos 221/273). There is another village by the same name in that tehsil, but it lies outside of what would formerly have been *tapā* Khoh.

l. 4: *vapejau* (*upejau/ūpejaủ*) is the realized revenue, *hāsil*, for which cp. p. 32.

V.S. 1825, Māgha ś. 3/ 9 February 1769

॥श्री रांमजी ॥

॥श्री गोबंददेव़जी ॥

रांम सही

(seal)

(१) ॥सिंधिं श्री कव़रजी श्री बषताव़रस्यंघजी बचनातं प्रगनां-
(२) तं लिव़ाली का औहद्यादारा दसे सूप्रसाद बंचा अप्रंचि मो-
(३) जे मजकूर कौ गांव़ रामसर श्री --- जी कै भोग व़ास्तै
(४) चढायौ छै सो श्रीजी का हव़ालदार आवै छै जा नै अमल
(५) कराय़ दीजौ अर य़ी गाव़ सू कही बात की षेचल करौ मती
(६) मिती महा सूदि ३ संवत १८२५

Śrī Rāmjī

Śrī Govinddevjī

Certified [in the name of] Rām

(seal)

[1] Success! By order of Prince Bakhtāvarsiṅghjī, [1-2] with benevolent greetings to the officers of *parganā* Livālī. Reference: [3-4] Village Rāmsar of the aforementioned group of villages has been offered to the deity Śrī [GD]jī for *bhog*. [4] Now the agent of the deity is going there (lit: "comes" - MH). Allow him to collect the revenue, and do not tamper with the affairs of that village. [6] Date: Mahā ś. 3, V.S. 1825.

Commentary:

Cp. the commentary on the preceding document.

The present document uses a terminology conspicuous in two respects. One is *parganātaṃ*, Pers. pl. *parganāt*, for *parganā*. The other is the term *moje majkūr*, where *maujā* must be taken to refer to a group of villages, which suggests that the *parganā* was identical in extension with a single group of villages.

V.S. 1828, Vaiśākha b. 4/ 3 April 1771

॥श्री रांमजी ॥

श्री गोव्यददेवजी

(seal)

(१) श्री दीवान वचनात मो° अथरोही कस्वा स्वाई ज्पुर की का पटल पटवार(ी)
(२) दस्ये अत्र गांव मज्कूर म ज्मी वीघा ३९ऽ भोग ठा° श्री --- जी
(३) की षालस छी सो मा° कफियत पंडित मौतीलालजी करार मिती
(४) चत वु १४ स १८२८ के वदसतूर वाहम हूई छे सो अमै दर हासल
(५) ई° साष ऊन्हाल स १८२८ थे देवौ कीजो मीती बसाष वुदी ४ संब-
(६) त १८२८

Śrī Rāmjī

Śrī Govinddevjī

(seal)

[1] By order of the *dīvān* to the *paṭel*s and *paṭvārī*s of village Athrohī in *kasbā* Savāī Jaipur. [2-3] Reference: In the aforementioned village, 39 *bīghā*s land for *bhog* of the deity Śrī [GD]jī are *khālsā* land. [3] According to the report of Paṇḍit Motīlālji of Cait b. 14, V.S. 1828, these, according to the regulations [of revenue collection], belong together (?). [4-5] You shall now give it [to GD] for revenue collection, [that is,] from the hot season harvest of V.S. 1828. Date: Vaiśākha b. 4, V.S. [6] 1828.

Commentary:
The bearer of the seal, a *dīvān* whose name is illegible, pays allegiance to Rāmsiṅgh, the son of Mahārājā Abhaisiṅgh of Marwar, who succeeded his father in 1749, but was soon dislodged and died in exile in Jaipur in 1773 (Sarkar 1984: 244). It seems worth noticing that the *dīvān* uses an *invocatio* current with the Kachavāhās, though not with the Rāṭhaurs, who use mostly *śrī parameśvar satya chai.*

l. 4: The text of this line is not quite clear to me. I read ... *badastūr bāham*... and interpret *bāham* as Persian *bā-ham*, "together".

V.S. 1833, Kārttika b. 14/ 10 November 1776

श्री रामजी १

श्री गोविंददेव़जी

(seal)

(१) श्री महाराजधिराज श्री राजाजी
(२) श्री वलव़ंतसिंहजी देव़वचना-
(३) तं श्री गुसाई नीलांवरजी आ-
(४) गै श्री --- जी कै प्रगनै गुगौ-
(५) र कौ गाव़ मौ° करारीय़ा चढा-
(६) य़ौ है सो हमेसा य़ा गांव़ कौ अ-
(७) मल पहुंचवौ करैगौ मिती कु-
(८) व़ार वदि १४ संवत १८३३

Śrī Rāmjī 1

Śrī Govinddevjī

(seal)

[1] By royal order of Śrī Mahārājādhirāj Śrī Rājājī [2] Śrī Balvantsiṅghjī. Śrī Gusāī Nīlāmbarjī. Earlier, [4-6] village Karārīyā of *parganā* Gugaur has been made an offering to the deity Śrī [GD]jī. [6-7] He (Nīlāmbar) will always obtain the revenue of this village. [7-8] Date: Kuvār b. 14, V.S. 1833.

Commentary:
Both, Balvantsiṅgh and the locality, cannot be identified conclusively. One Balvantsiṅgh, who was a contemporary of Nīlāmbar, was Rājā of Kānaudā, now Mahendragaṛh in Hisar District, Haryana (AME: Kānauda/Mohindargarh, 4A, 6A, 28+, 76+). He "usurped many villages in

Hansi-Hisar district during the late eclipse of the (Moghul - MH) government" (Sarkar 1984: 263). "Gugaur" is perhaps a variant writing of "Gurgāv" (Gurgaon).

ll. 6-7: *so hamesā... amal pahuṃcvau karaigau*, "He will always obtain the revenue..."; also, "He will always have access to the revenue matters...".

V.S. 1835, Māgha b. 10/ 12 January 1779
Verso missing.

॥श्री परमेश्वरजी सत्य छै

ठाकुरजी श्री गोविंददेवजी

(seal)

(१) ॥स्वस्ति श्री जैपुर सुथांने श्री वलरामजी जोग्य
(२) राजराजेश्वर महाराजाधिराज महाराजा श्री विजै-
(३) सिंघजी लिषावतं श्री रामराम वाचजो ---
(४) ।अप्रंच महाप्रसाद वस्त्र मेलीया सो माथै चढा-
(५) य लीया नै --- रै भोग रा रुपी-
(६) या एक सो री वरसोद रो प्रवांनो कर मेल्यो है सो पों-
(७) चसी --- ।संबत १८३५ रा माहा वद १०

Śrī Parameśvarjī is the Truth

Deity Śrī Govinddevjī

[1] Hail! [1-3] To Śrī Balrāmjī in Jaipur, written on behalf of Rājrājeśvar Mahārājādhirāj Mahārājā Śrī Vijaisiṅghjī. Rām-Rām! —
[4] Reference: You sent [me] *mahāprasād* (consecrated food) and a robe; [4-5] I received it most humbly (lit. "raising it to my forehead" - MH), and for [GD] I have issued and dispatched a *parvānau* covering 100rp. annual allowance. [6-7] This will reach [you]. — V.S. 1835, Māhā b. 10.

Commentary:
Vijaisiṅgh (r. 1752-1793) was the son and successor of the Rāṭhaur Mahārājā Bakhatsiṅgh of Marwar (Gahlot 1925: 136, 145).

When the deed was renewed in V.S. 1840, Caitra ś. 8, the present deed was not referred to.

***ab* V.S. 1836/ *ab* c. 1779**

Verso missing.

।श्री परमेश्वरजी सत्य छै
।श्री ठाकुरजी श्री गोविददेवजी
।श्री महाराजाजी

(seal)

(१) ॥स्वस्ति श्री सांभर सूथाने ऊपाधी पं॰ श्री रांम-
(२) वगसजी भं॰ परतापमलजी जोग्य जोधपूर था
(३) दीवांण श्री सिरदारमल जी लिषावतं पगे लागंणे
(४) जूहार वाचजो अठा रा संमाचार श्री ---जी
(५) रै तेज प्रंताप सूं भला छै थां रा सदा भला चाहीजै
(६) ।तथा --- जैपुर विराजै जिंणां
(७) रै सलुंणी रो लुंण मंण ७५०ऽ अषरे साढा सात
(८) सो पधरावंण री संनद संबत १८३६ रा म्हा बूद ८
(९) री है जिंण माफक हमैंही पधरावां कीजो श्री ह[जूर रो
(१०) हुकम छै ...]

Śrī Parameśvarjī is the Truth
Deity Śrī Govinddevjī
Śrī Mahārājājī

(seal)

[1] Hail! [1-2] To Upādhyāy Pt. Śrī Rāmbagasjī and Bhaṃ[ḍārī] Pratāpmaljī at Sāmbhar, written from Jodhpur [3] on behalf of Dīvān Śrī Sirdārmaljī, with humble greetings! [4-5] Here all is well thanks to the glory and prowess of Śrī [Mahārājā]jī. I hope that all is always well with you.

[6] Reference: The [deity GD], who resides in Jaipur. [7-9] There exists a *sanad* of V.S. 1836, Māgha b. 8, according to which 750 salt maunds of salt — in words: seven hundred and fifty — shall be sent for him. [9] According to this, send them only to me. [9-10] [This is an order issued by the] Court.

Commentary:

In the latter part of the 18th century, Sāmbhar was variously under the control of Jodhpur and the Marāṭhās (Bhattacharya 1972: 18, 36).

V.S. 1836, Māgha b. 8/ 29 January 1780

श्री परमेश्वरजी सत्य छै

ठाकुरजी श्री गोविंददेवजी

(seal)

(१) ॥स्वस्ति श्री सांभर सुथांने अगरवाला गोपीन(T)-
(२) थजी जोग्य जोधपुर था [...लिषाव-]
(३) तं रांमरांम वाचजो । तथा --- सवा-
(४) ई जैपुर विराजै जिंणां रै सलूंणी रो लूंण मंण ७५०ऽ
(५) अषरे साढी सात सो पधरावंण रो हूकंम हूवो है
(६) सु वरसावरस पधरायां कीजो श्री हजूर रो हूकंम छै
(७) संबत १८३६ रा माहा बूद ८

(left margin:)

। संनद री नकल दफतर मै उतराय पा-
छी सूंप देजो

Śrī Parameśvarjī is the Truth

Deity Śrī Govinddevjī

(seal)

[1] Hail! [1-3] To Agarvālau Gopīcand at Sāmbhar, written from Jodhpur [on behalf of...]. Rām-Rām! — Reference: [The deity GD], who resides in Savāī Jaipur. There has been given order that 750 salt maunds of salt — in words: seven hundred and fifty — shall be sent to him.
[6] Send them every year. This is an order issued by the Court.
[7] Māhā b. 8, V.S. 1836.

(endorsement, left margin:)

Forward the *sanad* after making a copy for the record.

V.S. 1839, Jyeṣṭha II b. 15/ 11 June 1782

॥श्री ब्रजचंदजी ॥

कृष्णशर्णजी

(१) ॥सिधि श्री सरब उपंमा जोग्य महाराज गो-
(२) ॥स्वामिजी श्री ---जी जोग्य
(३) ॥लीषायतं राजा किशोरदासजी केन्य दं-
(४) डवत वंच्या अठा का समाचार श्री ---जी की कृपा
(५) सु भला हे आप का भला चाहजे कृपा अनूग्रह राषो
(६) हो ती सु बीसेष राषोगा अपरंच श्री धाम मे म्हा की
(७) धरती हे जी का काम वास्तें अधकारी हंसदास
(८) बुलाय्यो छो सो जी येवा लीषी श्री गुंसांइी-
(९) जी का पत्र बीना आबो न होसी सो अ-
(१०) ब आप वां के नाव ताकीत पत्र लीषाय अ-
(११) ठे भेजोगा सो च्यार दिन के वास्तें अठे आ-
(१२) य म्हा को जवाब सुनज्याय अठे सारो ब्यो-
(१३) हार आप की आग्याही को जानोगा क्रपा
(१४) कर कागद स्माचार लीषाबु करोगा मीती
(१५) द° जेष्ट बदि ऽऽ स° १८३९

Śrī Brajcandjī

Kṛṣṇaśaraṇjī

[1] Success! [1-2] To Mahārāj Gosvāmī Śrī [Kṛṣṇaśaraṇ]jī, worthy of all epithets, [3] written on behalf of Rājā Kiśordāsjī, [4-5] with humble greetings. Here all is well thanks to your grace. [5] I hope all is well with you. [5-6] Keep me in your grace and favour, especially in connection with the present matter. Reference: [6-7] I possess land in Vrindaban (Śrīdhām, "The [blessed] Abode" - MH), [7-8] for the management of which I have asked *adhikārī* Haṃsdās to come. [8] He [, however,] wrote [8-9] that he would not come without a letter [entitling him to this job] by Śrī Gosvāmījī (that is, Kṛṣṇaśaraṇ - MH). [9-11] Therefore, please have a letter of confirmation written now and send it here [11-12] so that, when he comes here for a while, he

may give me his reply. [12-13] Remain assured that matters here are entirely at your disposal. [13-14] Kindly keep writing to me. [14-15] Date: Jeṣṭ II b. 15, V.S. 1839.

Commentary:

l. 3: Rājā Kiśordās remains unidentified. He must belong to the same family as Rājā Rādhikādās, for whom cp. → *ab* V.S. 1839. The *invocationes* of both deeds are identical, and so are the scribes of the forepart of the present deed and of the post-V.S. 1839 deed.

l.7: Haṃsdās was supposedly the *adhikārī* of Vrindaban's GD temple. Cp. also p. 24.

***ab* V.S. 1839/** 1782

॥श्री ब्रजचंदजी ॥

कृष्णशर्णजी

(१) ॥सिधि श्री सरब उपंमा जोग्य महाराज गोस्वामिजी श्री--
(२) ॥---जी ज्योग्य लीषायतं राजा राधिकादासजी के-
(३) ॥न्य दंडवंत बंच्या अठा का समाचार श्री ---जी की कृपा सु भ-
(४) ला हे आप का सदा भला चाहजे कृपा अनुग्रग राषो हो ती सु ज्यादा राषोगा अप-
(५) रंच कागद आय्यो महाप्रसाद प्रसादी सीरपाव भेज्यो सो माथे चढाय लीयो
(६) अठे तो सारो व्योहार आपही को जानोगा म्हा के तो आग्या सीवाय दुसरी वा-
(७) त छे न्ही क्रपा कर कागद समाचार लीषावु करोगा मीती असाढ सुद १५ संवत १८...

(on the wrapper:)

(seal)
...मिजी श्री कृष्णशर्ण...

Śrī Brajcandjī

Kṛṣṇaśaraṇjī

[1] Success! [2-3] To Mahārāj Gosvāmījī Śrī [Kṛṣṇaśaraṇ]jī, worthy of all epithets, written on behalf of Rājā Rādhikādāsjī, [3] with humble greetings. [3-4] Here all is well thanks to your grace. I hope that all is always well with you. [4-5] Keep me in your grace and favour, especially in connection with the following matter. Reference: [5] There arrived a letter [from you], and you sent me *mahāprasād* (consecrated food) and a robe of honour, which I most humbly received (lit. "raising it to my forehead" - MH). [6] You may be assured (lit.: "please know" - MH) that all that is done here is at your disposal. [6-7] For me, nothing exists but your command. [7] Kindly keep writing [to me]. Date: Asāḍh ś. 15, V.S. 18[...]

(on the wrapper:)

(seal)

[... Gosvā]mijī Śrī Kṛṣṇaśaraṇ...

Commentary:
The document belongs to the period of A.D. 1782-1806, the term of Kṛṣṇaśaraṇ's office. Rājā Rādhikādās Bahādur must belong to the same family as the author of the preceding letter; cp. the commentary thereon.

rev.y. 1839, Āṣāḍha b. 5/ 19 June 1783

॥श्री रामजी॥ ॥श्री रामजी

गोव्यंददेव़जी

सही

(कटार)

(seal)

(१) सिधि श्री महाराजाधिराज महाराजा श्री सव़ाई प्रतापसिंह-
(२) जी देव़वचनात कमैती प्रगनां सव़ाई जैपुर का दसे सुप्रसाद
(३) वंच्या अपरंच वावति भोग व़गैरह गांव़ ठाकुर श्री ---जी
(४) नैं जो मुव़ाफिक यादिदासति मैं दसषत दीव़ांनयांन करार
(५) मिती जेठ सुदि १० साल संवत १८३९ अरज पहौंची कसवो
(६) जैतपुरो तालका प्रगनां सव़ाई जैपुर को सिव़ाय राहदारी
(७) भोग व़गैरह व़ास्तै संवत १८४० थे ओर चढायो सो प्रवांनूं
(८) सवती का दसषत करायो चाहै तींह सू फुरमांव़ां छां मतल-
(९) व प्रवांनां का सूं व़ाकिफ होय कसवो जैतपुरो तालका प्रग-
(१०) नां सव़ाई जैपुर को सिव़ाय राहदारी संवत १८४० थे सीगै भो-
(११) ग व़गैरह कै जांणि हासिल हव़ालै करिवो कीज्यो अर प्र-
(१२) तवरष नव़ो प्रव़ांनूं मति मांग्यज्यो ईही प्रवांनां सूं हिसाव मै
(१३) मुजरा होयला
(१४) मुकररा तनषा कसवो जैतिपुरो तालका प्रगनां सव़ाई
(१५) जैपुर को सिव़ाय राहदारी संवत १८४० थे सीगै भोग व़गैरह
(१६) कै जांणि हासिल हव़ालै करिवो कीज्यो ऐक

(१७) १

---

(१) सरह यादिदासति दाषिल व़ाकै करार मिती असाढ वदि १ सा-
(२) ल संवत १८३९ वरसालै संगही जीवराज संगही स्योजीराम दी-
(३) व़ांन व़ नौवति व़कायानव़ीस वंदे सरकार जैतराम अत्र डोल
(४) भोग व़गैरह गांव़ ठाकुर श्री ---जी कै व़ास्तै मुव़ाफिक
(५) यादिदासति मैं दसषत दीवांनयांन करार मिती जेठ सुदि १०
(६) साल संवत १८३९ अरज पहौंची कसवो जैतपुरो तालका प्र-
(७) गनां सव़ाई जैपुर को सिव़ाय राहदारी भोग व़गैरह कै वास्तै सं-
(८) वत १८४० थे ओर चढायो सो प्रवांनूं सवती का दसषत करा-
(९) यो चाहै सो दसषत षास हुकम हूव़ा मुव़ाफिक लिषे द्यो
(१०) ती को प्रवांनूं सवती लिषो सो चाहिज्ये दीवांन सरकार का प्र-

(११) वांनां लिषै मिती असाढ वदि १ साल संवत १८३९ अरज मुक-
(१२) रर पहौंची मुकररा कसवो जैतपुरो सिव़ाय राहदारी तालका
(१३) प्रगनां सव़ाई जैपुर को ऐक

(१४) १
(१५) मुव़ाफिक यादिदासति मै दसषत षास व़ दीवांनयांन

(१६) मिती असाढ वदी ५ साल संवत १८३९ मूकाम स्व़ाई जैपूर

(seal)	*(seal)*	*(seal)*
(१७) रजू दफत्र दीव़ा-	रजु दफत्र दीवांन सं-	रजू दफत्र काजी छीत्र
(१८) न संगही जीव़राज	गही स्योजीरांम	महमद मुसतोफी हजूरी

(left margin:)
लिषौ नकल लीषी रजु
लिषौ दफत्र साहजी जीवण-
रांम आमिल दा° मव़ाजनै

(right margin:)
दा° मवजनै

(I) Śrī Rāmjī (2x)

Govinddevjī

Certified

(dagger)

(seal)

(II 1) [1] Success! [1-2] By royal order of Śrī Mahārājādhirāj Mahārājā Śrī Savāī Pratāpsiṃhjī,
(II 2) [2-3] with benevolent greetings to the officers of *parganā* Savāī Jaipur.
(II 3) [3] Reference: As item of *bhog* etc.; a village for the deity Śrī [GD]jī.
(II 4) [4-5] As endorsed by the *dīvāns* in the memorandum of Jeṭh ś. 10, rev.y. 1839, there was submitted a petition that,
(II 5) [5-7] starting with V.S. 1840, the toll-tax of *kasbā* Jaitpuro, part of *parganā* Savāī Jaipur, be granted again for *bhog* etc. [7-8] Therefore, he wishes that the confirmatory *parvānau* be attested to be in force.

(II 6) [8-9] Hereby, order is given that it be known [to you] by the intention of the *parvānau* [9-11] that, starting with V.S. 1840, the toll-tax of *kasbā* Jaitpuro, part of *parganā* Savāī Jaipur, shall be transferred for the purpose of *bhog*.

(II 7) [11-12] And there must not be demanded a fresh *parvānau* every year.

(II 8) [12-13] Following this *parvānau*, there shall be carried to account in the account-book:

[14] Fixed allowance of revenue: [14-16] From V.S. 1840 ... of *bhog* (= *recto*, lines 9-11): One [locality]

[17] 1

(III 1) [1-3] Commentary on the memorandum [based] on the diary-entry of Asāḍh b. 1, rev.y. 1839, on report of Dīvāns Saṃgahī Jīvrāj and Saṃgahī Syojīrām and the diarist on duty, servant of the government, Jaitrām.

(III 2) [3-4] Statement as follows: For *bhog* etc., a village for the deity Śri [GD]jī, [4-9] according ... to be in force (= *recto*, lines 4-8).

(III 3) [9] Therefore, an order endorsed by His Highness was passed. [9-10] Transfer it according to what is written [here]. Make out a confirmatory *parvānau* for it.

(III 4) [10-11] It is necessary that the *dīvāns* of the *sarkār* make out *parvānaus*.

(III 5) [11-13] On Asāḍh b. 1, rev.y. 1839 the petition was submitted again.

Fixed allowance: The toll-tax of *kasbā* Jaitpuro, part of *parganā* Savāī Jaipur: One [locality]

[14] 1

(III 6) [15] As endorsed in the memorandum by His Highness and the *dīvāns*.

(IV) [16] Date: Asāḍh b. 5, rev.y. 1839; place: Savāī Jaipur.

(V) *(seal)*	*(seal)*	*(seal)*
[17-18]		
Endorsed in the record; Dīvān Saṃgahī Jīvrāj	Endorsed in the record; Dīvān Saṃgahī Syojīrām	Endorsed in the record; Qāzī Chītra Mahmad, Court-Auditor

(left margin:)		*(right margin:)*
Write!	Copy written and endorsed in the	Entered in the *mavājanau*
Write!	record, Sāhjī Jīvaṇrāj, Āmil	
	Entered in the *mavājanau*	

Commentary:

Jaitpuro, headquarters of the earlier *parganā* of that name. At least until V.S. 1786/A.D. 1729, Jaitpuro figured as a *parganā* (Bahura and Singh 1988, no. 1468). Subsequently, it was incorporated in Savāī Jaipur, which, since its foundation in A.D. 1726, had come to absorb several former *parganās* (Gupta 1986: 36-37). Jaitpuro, modern Jetpurā, lies in Amber Tehsil of Jaipur District (India 1983 [DCH Jaipur]: 45, serial/code nos 113/154).

For *sivāy-rāhdārī*, cp. the commentary on → V.S. 1797, Māgha b.5 ll. 3-5.

V.S. 1840, Āśvina b. 10/ 21 September 1783

Fag-end of *verso* missing.

॥श्री रामजी
गोविंददेवजी

सही
(कटार)

(seal)

(१) सिधि श्री महाराजाधिराज महाराजा श्री सवाई प्रतापसिंहजी देववचनात
(२) कमैती कसवा सवाई जैपुर का दसे सुप्रसाद वंच्या अपरंच वावति भेट
(३) हाट्यां वागैरह ठाकुर श्री ---जी नैं जो मारफति राय रतनला-
(४) ल की मिती चैत सुदि ५ साल संवत १८३९ अरज पहौंची गुसांई किस्न-
(५) सरणजी की हवेली कसवा सवाई जैपुर मैं ती कै मुतसिल वाजार
(६) की हाट्या वागैरह १३ सरकार की सो भेट करी सो दसषत करायो चा-
(७) हे तींह सूं फुरमांवां छां मतलव प्रवांनां का सूं वाकिफ होय हाट्या वा-
(८) गैरह तेरा हवेली कसवा सवाई जैपुर मैं गुसाई किस्नसरणजी की
(९) ती कै मुतसिल वाजार की सरकार की इवतदाय मिती चैत सुदि ३
(१०) साल संवत १८३९ थे सीगै भेट कै जांणि हवाले कीज्यो अर प्रतवर-
(११) ष नवो प्रवांनूं मति माग्यज्यो ईही प्रवांनां सूं हिसाव मैं मुजरा होयला
(१२) मुकररा तनषाह हाट्या वागैरह हवेली कसवा सवाई जैपुर मैं गुसां-
(१३) ई किस्नसरणजी की ती कै मुतसिल वाजार की सरकार की इवत-
(१४) दाय मिती चैत सुदि ३ साल संवत १८३९ थे सीगै भेट कै जांणि हवाले
(१५) कीज्यो तेरा

(१६)	१३
(१४) हाटि ग्यारा	थडी दोय
(१५) ११	२

---

(१) सरह यादिदासति दाषिल वाके करार मिती आसोज वदि ७ संवत १८४० वरसाले
(२) संगही जीवराज संगही सिवजीराम दीवान नोवति वाकानवीस वंदे सरकार जैत-
(३) राम अत्र डोल भेट हाट्यां वागैरह ठाकुर श्री ---जी कै वास्तै मारफति
(४) राय रतनलाल की मिती चैत सुदि ५ साल संवत १८३९ अरज पहौंची गुसांई कि-
(५) स्नसरणजी की हवेली कसवा सवाई जैपुर मैं ती कै मुतसिल वाजार की हाट्या वागै-
(६) रह १३ सरकार की सो भेट करी सो दसषत करायो चाहै सो हुकम हूवा मुवाफिक

(७) लिषे सीगै भेट कै द्यो ती को प्रवांनूं सवती लिषो इवतादाय मिती चैत सुदि ३ सा-
(८) ल संवत १८३९ थे सो चाहिजे दीवान सरकार का प्रवांनां लिषै मिती आसोज वदि ७
(९) संवत १८४० अरज मुकरर पहौंची मुकररा हाट्या वगैरह तेरा

(१०) १३
(११) हाटि ग्यारा थडी दोय
(१२) ११ २

(१३) मुवाफिक यादिदासति मैं दसषत राय रतनलाल वा दीवांनयान
(१४) मिती आसोज वदी १० संवत १८४० मुकाम सवाई जैपुर

(seal)	*(seal)*	*(seal)*
(१५) रजू दफत्र दीवान	रजू दफत्र दीवान सं-	रजू दफत्र काजी छीत्र
(१६) संगही मोहनराम	गही स्योजीरांम	महमद मुसतोफी हंजूरी

(I) Śrī Rāmjī
Govinddevjī

Certified

(dagger)
(seal)

(II 1) [1] Success! By royal order of Śrī Mahārājādhirāj Mahārājā Śrī Savāī Pratāpsiṃhjī,

(II 2) [2] with benevolent greetings to the officers of *kasbā* Savāī Jaipur.

(II 3) [2-3] Reference: Item of religious donation of shops etc. to the deity Śrī [GD]jī.

(II 4) [3-4] For this, there was submitted a petition through Rāy Ratanlāl on Cait ś. 5, rev.y. 1839 [, as follows]:

(II 5) [4-6] Neighbouring upon Gosvāmī Kisnasaraṇ's mansion in *kasbā* Savāī Jaipur, there are 13 shops etc., which belong to the government. These were made a religious donation [in favour of GD]. [6-7] This he wishes to be endorsed.

(II 6) [7] Hereby, order is given that it be known [to you] by the intention of the *parvānau* that [7-9] 13 shops, neighbouring upon the mansion of Gosvāmī Kisnasaraṇ in *kasbā* Savāī Jaipur and forming part of the bazaar of the government, [10] shall be transferred [to GD] from Cait ś. 3, rev.y. 1839, under the category of "religious donation (*bheṭ*)".

(II 7) [10-11] And there must not be demanded a fresh *parvānau* every year.

(II 8) [11] Following this *parvānau*, there shall be carried to account in the account-book:

[12-15] Fixed allowance: Shops etc., neighbouring upon the mansion of Gosvāmī Kisnasaraṇ ... category of "religious donation" (= lines 7-10): thirteen

[16] 13

[17-18] shops: 11 shops with sitting platforms: 2

(III 1) [1-3] Commentary on the memorandum [based] on the diary-entry of Āsoj b. 7, V.S. 1840, on report of Dīvāns Saṃgahī Jīvrāj and Saṃgahī Sivjīrām and the diarist on duty, servant of the government, Jaitrām.

(III 2) [3] Statement as follows: For a religious donation of shops etc. to the deity Śrī [GD]jī, [3-4] there was submitted a petition through Rāy Ratanlāl on Cait ś. 5, rev.y. 1839 [, as follows]: [4-6] (= *recto*, lines 4-7).

(III 3) [6-7] Therefore, the order was passed that, according [7] to what has been written [here], you transfer these under the category of "religious donation".

(III 4) [7] Make out a confirmatory *parvānau* for it, effective from Cait ś. 3, rev.y. 1839. [8] It is necessary that the *dīvāns* of the *sarkār* make out *parvānaus*.

(III 5) [8-9] On Āsoj b. 7, rev.y. 1840, the petition was submitted again [, namely for]: Fixed allowance of thirteen shops etc.

[10] 13

[11] shops: eleven shops with sitting platforms: two

[12] 11 2

(III 6) [13] As endorsed in the memorandum by Rāy Ratanlāl and the *dīvāns*.

(IV) [14] Date: Āsoj b. 10, V.S. 1840; place: Savāī Jaipur.

(V) *(seal)*	*(seal)*	*(seal)*
[15-16]		
Endorsed in the record;	Endorsed in the record;	Endorsed in the record;
Dīvān Saṃgahī Mohanrām	Dīvān Saṃgahī Syojīrām	Chītra Mahmad, Court-Auditor

Commentary:

<u>ll. 3-4 *(recto)*, 13 *(verso)*:</u> Rāy Ratanlāl, Minister and Mahārājā Pratāpsiṅgh's *vakīl* to the British (Bahura and Singh 1988, *s.v.* Rai Ratanlal).

V.S. 1843a, Śrāvaṇa b. 13/ 23 July 1786

॥श्री रामजी ॥

सीतारामजी

गोविंदजी

(१) ॥ सिधि श्री महाराजाधिराज आलीजांह माहाराजा श्री सूवे-
(२) दार माधोरावजी सींदे जोग्य लिषतं महाराजाधिराज महारा-
(३) जा श्री सवाई प्रतापसिंहजी केन श्री --- वंच्या अैंठा
(४) का समाचार श्री ---जी की कृपा सूं भला छै राज्य का
(५) सदा भला चाहिज्ये अपरंच श्री वडा महाराज बृंदावानजी मै
(६) व्यासां की जमी मोलि ले र जायगां वणाय गंज वसाय श्री ---
(७) जी की भेट करी अब जाहिर हुई जो धीरजलाल गुंसांई वै धरती
(८) की उठा का अधिकार्यां सूं षेचल करि राषी छै सो मुतसद्यां नै
(९) ताकीद करि द्योला जो धरिजलाल गुंसांई नं वै धरती सूं मु-

(continued on left margin:)
(१) जाहिम न होवा द्यो
(२) ओर कागद समाचा-
(३) र लिषावता रहोला
(४) मिती श्रावण वदि
(५) १३ संवत १८४३

Śrī Rāmjī

Sītā-Rāmjī

Govindjī

[1] Success! [1-3] Written to His Excellency the Provincial Governor Śrī Mahārājādhirāj Mahārājā Mādhorāvjī Sinde by Mahārājādhirāj Mahārājā Śrī Savāī Pratāpsiṃhjī … greetings. Here [4] all is well thanks to your grace. [4-5] I hope that all is well with [your] realm. Reference: My ancestor bought the land of the Vyāses in Vrindaban, constructed the places there, founded the market, and [6-7] made these a religious donation *(bheṭ)* to the deity Śrī [GD]jī. [7-8] Now it has been reported that Gosvāmī Dhīrajlāl keeps bothering the *adhikārīs* of

that place for the land. [8 - margin, l. 1] Therefore, you must give a strict order to the officers that they not tolerate that Gosvāmī Dhīrajlāl tamper with that land. [margin, ll. 2-3] And keep me informed by correspondence. [margin 4-5] Date: Śrāvaṇa b. 13, V.S. 1843.

Commentary:

ll. 1-2: Mādhorāv Śinde, the Marāṭhā Peśvā (r. 1774-96), had been appointed Provincial Governor of Delhi and Agra and vice-regent of the Empire in 1784 (CHI V. 364).

ll. 6: The *vyās* proprietors, from whom the Kachavāhās had bought land in Vrindaban, remain unidentified. Śrīvatsa Gosvāmī, Director, Śrī Caitanya Prema Saṃsthāna, and junior *gosvāmī* of the Rādhāramaṇ temple of Vrindaban, asserts that they are identical with Harirām Vyās's family, to whom much of the land in Vrindaban belonged (personal communication, September 1997; for Harirām Vyās, cp. Pauwels 1996:2-10).

l. 7: Gosvāmī Dhīrajlāl remains unidentified.

V.S. 1843b, Śrāvaṇa b. 13/ 23 July 1786
Verso missing.

॥श्री रामजी ॥

गोविंदजी

(१) वृंदाबनजी का श्री समस्त गुंसांयां संम्हां को नमस्कार बंच्या
(२) अपरंच श्री वडा महाराज बृंदावनजी में ब्यासां की धरती मोलि ले
(३) र गंज बसाय वा जायगां बणाय श्री ---जी की भेट करी छी
(४) सो अब मालूम हुई जो धीरजलाल गुंसांई वै जमीनें ओरां नें बेच्यो
(५) चाहै छै सो वै नै समझाय द्योला जो ई जायगां स्यूं मुजाहिम न होय
(६) मिती श्रावण वदि १३ संवत १८४३

Śrī Rāmjī
Govindjī

[1] Greetings to all the Gosvāmīs of Vṛndābanjī. [2-3] Reference: My ancestor bought the land of the Vyāses in Vrindaban, founded the market, constructed the places there, and made these a religious donation *(bheṭ)* to the deity Śrī [GD]jī. [4-5] Now it has been reported that Gosvāmī Dhīrajlāl intends to sell this land to others. [5] So please make it clear to him that he must not tamper with these places. [6] Date: Śrāvaṇ b. 13, V.S. 1843.

Commentary:
The author of this warrant was certainly Mahārājā Pratāpsiṅgh, for the document deals with the same matter and is written by the same scribe and on the same day as the preceding one.

V.S. 1848, Bhādrapada b. 7/ 21 August 1791

Verso missing.

श्री ॥श्री रामजी ॥

(seal)

(१) दस्तक श्री बृंदावनजी का गंज सरकार का
(२) जमीदारां वा वास्यंदा दसे अत्र जाहरि हु-
(३) ई जो गंज की जमी गुंसांई वागैर है वेचै छै
(४) सो उठा की जमी कही नें वेचवा वा लेवा दी-
(५) ज्यो मति उठा की हकीकति होय सो लिष-
(६) बो कीज्यो मिती भादवा बदी ७ सबत
(७) १८४८

Śrī Śrī Rāmjī

(seal)

[1-2] Warrant: To the *zamīndārs* of the *sarkār* and the inhabitants of the market of Bṛndāvan. Reference: It has been reported [3] that the Gosvāmīs and others are selling land of the market. [4-5] You must not allow that land to be either sold or bought. [5-6] If there is anything to report regarding that locality, write [to me]. [6-7] Date: Bhādvā b. 7, V.S. 1848.

Commentary:

In the early 1790s, Ṭhākur Pahāṛsiṅgh Khaṅgarvat was one of Mahārājā Pratāpsiṅgh's emissaries in the negotiations with the Marāṭhās, who had invaded the Jaipur territory. His seal (cp. p. 77) styles him "the slave of ... Pratāpsiṅgh", thus suggesting that in 1791 he also formally served him as a minister, for which cp. Bayley 1894: 78. A branch of the Khaṅgarvats, a Kachavāhā clan, held the estate of Dūdū, which had been given to Ānandsiṅgh, Pahāṛsiṅgh's father *(l.c.)*.

For the alienation of charitable land in Vrindaban, cp. also → V.S. 1843 a and b.

V.S. 1850, Pauṣa ś. 10/ 11 January 1794

Verso missing.

॥श्री रांमजी ॥श्री रांमजी

रु° १५००ऽ सी° पुन्य
के द्यो

(endorsements:)

मा° दसषत करो   मा° द°/षत/ करौ

(text:)

(१) यादिदासति गुसाई किस्नसरणजी
(२) कै बेटी को व्याह सो हुकम हूवो सौ
(३) दसषत होय ती माफिक पावै मिती
(४) पोंस सूदि १० संवत १८५०

Śrī Rāmjī (2x)

1,500rp., these you shall give under the category of "charitable gift *(punya)*".

(endorsements:)

Proceed according to endorsement!   Proceed according to endorsement!

(text:)

[1] Memorandum: Wedding of Gosvāmī Kisnasaraṇ's (Kṛṣṇaśaraṇ) [2] daughter. The order was passed and [3] shall be signed. Accordingly, he will receive [the money]. Date: [4] Poṃs ś. 10, V.S. 1850.

V.S. 1852, Kārttika ś. 5/ 16 November 1795

श्री गोबंजी

(१) श्री बंदाबनजी म घाट परस बनाइी गोबद
(२) घाट परस बनाइी म्हंत मनसाराम न व्रा
(३) मुथरादास न परमारथजी के जा की लागते
(४) लगाई रुपीया ११४ऽ येक सो चोद लगे
(५) ईट चुना बङी मजुरा कु लगे सो रुपीया
(६) श्री गोबंदजी का (?) भंडार सु लगे रुपीया
(७) ११४ऽ येक सो चोदा भंडार सु पुजारीजी नं-
(८) दनदनजी के मारफते रुपीया भरे
(९) पाये दसषत म्हंत मनसाराम के : मती
(१०) कुंवार सदी ५ समत १८५२

Śrī Govindjī

[1] In Bandābanjī (Vrindaban), there was constructed the floor of a bathing place (*ghāṭ*). The Govind [2] *ghāṭ* floor was constructed by Mahant Mansārām and [3] Mathurādās. On the place of the Lord, [4] they spent the sum of 114rp., [in words:] one hundred and fourteen, [5] spent on brick-work, plastering and daily wages. This money [6] was spent by the treasury of Śrī Govindjī. [6-9] 114rp., [in words:] one hundred and fourteen, were paid from the treasury by Pujārī Nandnandanjī. The money was paid, [as testified by the] signature of Mahant Mansārām. Date: [10] Kuṃvār ś. 5, V.S. 1852.

Commentary:
The identity of Mahant Mansārām and Mathurādās remains obscure. It is also not clear if Mathurādās was also a *mahant.*

For Govind *ghāṭ*, cp. Entwistle (1987: 314): "A Goswami of the temple of Govind Dev at Vrindaban constructed a flight of steps leading down to the river that is understood to incorporate or lie adjacent to the original Tindukatirtha. It has become known as Bengali or

Govind Ghat, and is referred to as such in more recent itineraries (that is, pilgrimage itineraries of Vrindaban - MH)."

V.S. 1860, Māgha b. 2/ 30 December 1803

॥श्री रामजी

सवाई प्रतापसिंहजी गोव्यंददेवजी

सही
(कटार)

(seal)

(१) सिधि श्री महाराजाधिराज महाराजा श्री सवाई जगतसिंहजी देवव-
(२) चनात कमैती प्रगनां सवाई जैपुर का दसे सुप्रसाद वंच्या अपरंच
(३) बावति भोग वागैरह गांव ठाकुर श्री ---जी की ठकुराणी-
(४) जी की सेवा कै वास्तै सषी एक आगै छै अव सषी दुसरी महाराजा वै-
(५) कुंठबासीजी श्री ---जी मिती वैसाष सुदि ६ साल संवत
(६) १८५८ नै पधराई छी त्यां कै वास्तै मुवाफिक यादिदासति में दसष-
(७) त दीवांनयांन करार मिती पोस वदि १४ संवत १८६० अरज पहौची
(८) भोग वागैरह नै गांव स्योस्यंघपुरा मै वास कल्याणपुरा वास जसोधा-
(९) नंदपुरा मौजा २ तपा षोह प्रगनां सवाई जैपुर तन भोमि वागैरह सुधां
(१०) रुपया ९८२ऽ म्धे तन ७५९ऽ ती का वसूली ३७९।ाऽ को इवतदाय साष
(११) स्यालू संवत १८६० थे करि देवा को हुकम हूवो सो दसषत करायो
(१२) चाहे तींह सूं फुरमांवां छां मतलव प्रवांनां का सूं वाकिफ होय गांव
(१३) स्योस्यंघपुरा मैं वास कल्याणपुरा वास जसोधानंदपुरा मौजा २ त-
(१४) पा षोह प्रगनां सवाई जैपुर तन भोमि वागैरह सुधां रुपया नौ सै वी-
(१५) यासी म्धे तन सात सै गुणसठि ती का उसूली तीन सै घुण्यासी आ-
(१६) नां आठ को इवतदाय साष स्यालू संवत १८६० थे सीगै भोग वागैर-
(१७) ह कै जांणि हांसिल हवालै करिवो कीज्यो अरज प्रतवरष नवो प्रवां-
(१८) नूं मति मांग्यज्यो ईही प्रवांनां सूं हिसाव मै मुजरा होयला
(१९) मुकररा तनषाह गांव स्योस्यंघपुरा मैं वास काल्याणपुरा वास जसो-
(२०) धानंदपुरा मोजा २ तपा षोह प्रगनां सवाई जैपुर को इवतदाय साष स्या-
(२१) लू संवत १८६० थे सीगै भोग वागैरह कै जांणि हासिल हवालै करिवो
(२२) कीज्यो तन भोमि वागैरह सुधां रुपया ९८२ऽ म्धे तन ७५९ऽ ती का वसू-
(२३) ली तीन सै घुण्यासी आनां आठ

(२४) ३७९।ाऽ

(२५) भोग नै रुपया एक सौ निवासी आ- वस्त्र नै रुपया एक सो निवासी आ-
(२६) नां वारा नां वारा

(२७) १८९।।ऽ १८९।।ऽ

---

(१) सरह् यादिदासति दाषिल वाकै करार मिती पोस सुदि १२ संवत १८६० व-
(२) रसालै संगही अमरचंद दीवांन व नौवति वकायानवीस वंदे सरकार
(३-११) किरपाराम अत्र डोल भोग वागैरह् गांव... चाहै (= *recto*, lines 3 - 12) सो दस-
(१२) षत षास हुकम हुवा मुवाफिक लिष्ये द्यो ती को प्रवांनू सवती लिषो
(१३) सो चाहिज्ये दीवांन सरकार का प्रवांनां लिषै मिती पोस सुदि १२ संव-
(१४-२१) त १८६० अरज मुकरर पहौंची मुकररा गांव स्योस्यंघपुरा मै... (= *recto*, lines 19 - 27)

(२२) मुवाफिक यादिदासति मै दसषत षास वै दीवांनयांन

(२३) मिती माह बुदि २ संबत १८६० मुकाम सवाइ जपुरै

(seal) *(seal)*

(२४) रजू दफत्र दीवा- रजु दफत्र दीवांन रजू दफत्र सदासूष
(२५) न संगही अमरचंद हजूरि ॥8 ॥ मसतोफी हजूरि

(left margin:)
दा° मवाजनै

(right margin:)
दा° मवाजनै

(I) Śrī Rāmjī
Savāī Pratāpsiṃhjī Govinddevjī

Certified
(*dagger*)

(*seal*)

(II 1) [1] Success! [1-2] By royal order of Śrī Mahārājādhirāj Mahārājā Śrī Savāī Jagatsiṃhjī,
(II 2) with benevolent greetings to the officers of *parganā* Savāī Jaipur.
(II 3) [2-4] Reference: Item of *bhog*; a village. For the purpose of serving the consort of the deity Śrī [GD]jī, one *sakhī* (icon representing the confidante of the deity's consort - MH) had been here since before. [4-6] Later on, the late Mahārājā Śrī [Savāī Pratāpsiṃh]jī sent another *sakhī* on Vaisākh ś. 6, rev.y. 1858 (27 April 1803).
(II 4) [6-7] For this, there was submitted a petition endorsed by the *dīvāns* in the memorandum of Pos b. 14, V.S. 1860.

(II 5) [8-11] There was passed an order that for the purpose of *bhog* etc. there be given, starting with the cold season harvest of V.S. 1860, a recoverable amount of 379rp., 8a. out of the assessed revenue of 749rp., which forms part of the assessed revenue, inclusive of *bhomi* etc., of 982rp. of two affiliate villages of village Syosiṅghpurā in *tapā* Khoh of *parganā* Savāī Jaipur, [namely,] Kalyāṇpurā-vās and Jasodhānandpurā-vās. [11-12] [The deity] wishes that this be endorsed.

(II 6) [12-17] Hereby, order is given that it be known [to you] by the intention of the *parvānau* that, starting with the cold season harvest of V.S. 1860, there shall be assigned, under the category of "*bhog* etc.", for [income of] realized revenue, two affiliate villages ... Jasodhānandpurā-vās (= lines 7-11; numerals not in figures but in words).

(II 7) [17-18] And there must not be demanded a fresh *parvānau* every year.

(II 8) [18] Following this *parvānau*, there shall be carried to account in the account-book:
[19-22] Fixed allowance of revenue: Starting with the cold season harvest of V.S. 1860, there shall be assigned, under the category of "*bhog* etc.", realized revenue of ... (there follow the names of the village and the villages affiliated to it with their exact location - MH). [22-23] Recoverable amount of three hundred and seventy-nine rupees, eight annas out of the assessed revenue of 759rp., which form part of the assessed revenue, inclusive of *bhomi* etc., of 982rp.

[24]	379rp., 8a.
[25-26] For *bhog*, one hundred and eighty-nine rupees and twelve annas	For garments, one hundred and eighty-nine rupees and twelve annas
[27] 189rp., 12a.	189rp., 12a.

(III 1) [1-3] Commentary on the memorandum [based] on the diary-entry of Pos ś. 12, V.S. 1860, on report of Dīvān Saṃgahī Amarcand and the diarist on duty, servant of the government, Kirpārām.

(III 2) [3-11] Statement as follows: *bhog* etc.; a village ... that this be endorsed (= *recto*, lines 3-12).

(III 3) [11-12] There was passed an order endorsed by His Highness. You shall pay as is written [here].

(III 4) [12] Make out a confirmatory *parvānau*. [13] It is necessary that the *dīvāns* of the *sarkār* make out *parvānaus*.

(III 5) [13-14] On Pos ś. 12, v.S. 1860, the petition was submitted again [, namely for]: [14-21] Fixed allowance of revenue: Recoverable amount of ... 982rp. (= *recto*, lines 14-27).

(III 6) [22] As endorsed in the memorandum by His Highness and the *dīvāns*.

(IV) [23] Date: Māh b. 2, V.S. 1860; place: Savāī Jaipur.

(V) *(seal)* *(seal)*

[24-25]

Endorsed in the record;	Endorsed in the record;	Endorsed in the record;
Dīvān Amarcand	*dīvān hajūr*	Sadāsukh, Court-Auditor

(left margin:)	*(right margin:)*
Entered in the *mavājanau*	Entered in the *mavājanau*

Commentary:

Syosiṅghpurā, now Śyosiṃhpurā *alias* Kallāvālā, and Jasodhānandpurā-vās, now Yaśodānandanpurā *alias* Āśābālā, lie in Saṅgāner Tehsil of Jaipur District (India 1983 [DCH Jaipur]: 171, serial/code nos 188/118 and 211/184). Kalyāṇpurā(-vās) is not traceable, though its name may have survived with some modification in the *alias* "Kallāvālā".

Besides the present deed, there must have existed another one made out for another 379rp. 8a. and providing *bhog* for GD's consort. This can be concluded from document [V.S. 1995, Āṣāḍha ś. 15] which reports the following: The revenue of Syosiṅghpurā, calculated by the six-month scale, was 982rp. Of these, 759 rp. were granted for *bhog* of the deity GD's consort. This goes to say that besides the share of 379rp. 8a., which the *sakhī* received and which is covered by the present deed, another 379rp. 8a. were the share of Rādhājī.

<u>l. 9 *(recto)*:</u> For *bhomi*, cp. the commentary on doc → V.S. 1797, Māgha b.5, ll. 6-12.

V.S. 1860, Māgha b. 7/ 4 January 1804

Invocatio, elevatio and fag-end of *verso* missing.

सही

(कटार)

(seal)

(१) सिधि श्री महाराजाधिराज महाराजा श्री सवाई जगतसिंहजी देववचना-
(२) त कमैती कसवा सवाई जैपुर का दसे सुप्रसाद वंच्या अपरंच वावति इ-
(३) नांम धरती वीघा ५०ऽ वाग वा वाग का षरच नैं हरलाल चुडामणि का गू-
(४) जर धाभाई महाराजा वैकुंठवासीजी श्री ---जी का नैं जो मु-
(५) वाफिक यादिदासति मैं दसषत दीवांनयांन करार मिती पोस सुदि १४
(६) संवत १८६० अरज पहौंची जो इनांम धरती गांव मांनपुर सढा तालिक
(७) कसवा सवाई जैपुर की वीघा ५०ऽ क्यार्‌या की वाग वणावा नै वा वाग का
(८) षरच नैं इवतदाय साष ऊन्हालू संवत १८६० थे करि देवा को हुकम हूवो
(९) सो दसषतां को उमेदवार तींह सूं फुरमांवां छां मतलव प्रवांनां का सूं वा-
(१०) किफ होय धरती वीघा पचास क्यार्‌या की गांव मांनपुर सढा तालिक
(११) कसवा सवाई जैपुर की वाग वणावा नै वा वाग का षरच नैं इवतदाय सा-
(१२) ष ऊन्हालू संवत १८६०ऽ थे सीगै इनांम कै जांणि मांप्य हवालै कीज्यो अर
(१३) प्रतवरष नवो प्रवांनूं मति मांग्यज्यो ईही प्रवांनां सूं हिसाव मै मुजरा हो-
(१४) यला
(१५) मुकररा तनषाह धरती गांव मांनपुर सढा तालिक कसवा सवाई जैपुर
(१६) की वाग वणावा नै वा वाग का षरच नै इवतदाय साष ऊन्हालू संवत १८६०
(१७) थे सीगै इनांम कै जांणि मांप्य हवालै कीज्यो क्यार्‌या की वीघा पचास

(१८)	५०ऽ	
(१९)	वाग वास्तै भारमल डोर्‌या की कोठी	वाग का षरच नै सूरिजमल गोपाल
(२०)	नीचै वीघा ग्यारा विस्वा आठ	कायथ की वावडी कोठी नीचै वीघा
(२१)		अडतास (!) विस्वा वारा
(२२)	११।३	३८।।२

---

(१) सरह यादिदासति दाषिल वाकै करार मिती माह वदि ५ संवत १८६० वरसा-
(२) लै संगही अमरचंद दीवांन व नौवतिं वकायानवीस वंदे सरकार किरपा-
(३) राम अत्र डोल इनांम धरती वाग वा वाग का षरच नैं हरलाल चूडामणि
(४) का गूजर धाभाई महाराजा वैकुंठवासीजी श्री ---जी का कै वास्तै
(५) मुवाफिक यादिदासति मैं दसषत दीवांनयांन करार मिती पोस सुदि १४ सं-

(६) वत १८६० अरज पहौंची जो इनांम धरती गांव मांनपुर सढा तालिक कस-
(७) वा सवाई जैपुर की वीघा ५०ऽ क्यार्‌या की वाग वणावा नै वा वाग का षरच नै
(८) इवतदाय साष उन्हालू संवत १८६० थे करि देवा को हुकम हूवो सो दसष-
(९) तां को उमेदवार सो दसषत षास हुकम हूवा मुवाफिक लिष्ये द्यो ती को प्र-
(१०) वांनूं सवती लिषो सो चाहिज्ये दीवांन सरकार का प्रवांनां लिषै मिती माह
(११) वदि ५ संवत १८६० अरज मुकरर पहौंची मुकररा वाग वा वाग का षरच नै ध-
(१२) रती क्यार्‌यां की वीघा पचास

(१३) ५०ऽ
(१४) वाग वास्तै भारमल डोर्‌या की कोठी नीचै — वाग का षरच नै सूंरिजमल गोपाल
(१५) वीघा ग्यारा विस्वा आठ — कायथ की वावडी कोठी नीचै वीघा अ-
(१६) ११।३ — डतीस विस्वा वारा
३८।।२

(१७) मुवाफिक यादिदासति मै दसषत षास व दीवांनयांन

(१८) मिती माह बुदि ७ संबत १८६० मुकाम सवाइ जपुर

(seal) *(seal)*

(१९) रजू दफत्र दीवान — रजु दफत्र दीवां- — रजू दफत्र सदासूष
(२०) संगही अमरचंद — न हजूरि ॥8॥ — मसतोफी हजूरि

(I) Certified
(dagger)

(seal)

(II 1) [1-2] Success! By royal order of Śrī Mahārājādhirāj Mahārājā Śrī Savāī Jagatsiṃhjī,
(II 2) with benevolent greetings to the officers of *kasbā* Savāī Jaipur.
(II 3) [2] Reference: Item of [3-4] land exempted from taxation *(inām)*. 50 *bīghā*s land for the purpose of [laying out] a garden and for purchasing a garden, for Harlāl, son of Cuḍāmaṇi, Gūjar, *dhābhāī* (foster-brother, that is, a wet-nurse's son - MH) of the late Mahārājā Śrī [Pratāpsiṃh]jī.

(II 4) [4-6] For this, there was submitted a petition endorsed by the *dīvāns* in the memorandum of Pos ś. 14, V.S. 1860[, as follows]:

(II 5) [6-9] He applies that it be attested that there was passed an order that, from the hot season harvest of V.S. 1860, there be assigned [to him] in *inām* 50 *bīghās* land in village Mānpur Saḍho, which is part of *kasbā* Savāī Jaipur, for the purpose of laying out a garden with irrigation banks and for purchasing a garden.

(II 6) [9-10] Hereby, order is given that it be known [to you] by the intention of the *parvānau* [10-12] that there shall be measured out and assigned, from the hot season harvest of V.S. 1860, under the category of "*inām*", fifty *bīghās* land in village Mānpur Saḍho, which is part of *kasbā* Savāī Jaipur, for the purpose of laying out a garden with irrigation banks and for purchasing a garden.

(II 7) [12-13] And there must not be demanded a fresh *parvānau* every year.

(II 8) [13-14] Following this *parvānau*, there shall be carried to account in the account-book:

[15-17] Fixed allowance: There shall be measured out and assigned, under the category of "*inām*", from the hot season harvest of V.S. 1860, land in village Mānpur Saḍho, part of *kasbā* Savāī Jaipur, for laying out a garden and for purchasing a garden: Fifty *bīghās* land with irrigation banks

[18]	50/-
[19-21] For a garden: Below the house of Bharmāl Ḍoryau, eleven *bīghās* and eight *viśvās*	For purchasing a garden: Below the stepwell and house of Sūrijmal Gopāl Kāyasth, thirty-eight [*bīghās*] and twelve *viśvās*
[22] 11b., 8v.	38b., 12v.

(III 1) [1-3] Commentary on the memorandum [based] on the diary-entry of Māh b. 5, V.S. 1860, on report of Dīvān Saṃgahī Amarcand and the diarist on duty, servant of the government, Kirpārām.

(III 2) [3-9] Statement as follows: *inām* for the purpose ... purchasing a garden (= *recto*, lines 3-9).

(III 3) [9] Therefore, there was passed an order endorsed by His Highness that you transfer the land according to what is written [here].

(III 4) [9-10] Make out a confirmatory *parvānau*. It is necessary that the *dīvāns* of the *sarkār* make out *parvānaus*.

(III 5) [10-12] On Māh b. 5, V.S. 1860, the petition was submitted again [, namely for]: Fixed allowance: Fifty *bīghā*s land with irrigation banks for [laying out] a garden and for purchasing a garden.
[13-16] (= *recto*, lines 18-22)
(III 6) [17] As endorsed in the memorandum by His Highness and the *dīvān*s.

(IV) [18] Date: Māh b. 7, V.S. 1860; place: Savāī Jaipur.

(V)

(seal)		*(seal)*
[19-20]		
Endorsed in the record,	Endorsed in the record,	Endorsed in the record;
Dīvān Saṃgahī Amarcand	*dīvān hajūr*	Sadāsukh, Court-Auditor

Commentary:
The village, which is nowadays called Mānpurā Saṛvā, lies in Jaipur Tehsil of Jaipur District (India 1983 [DCH Jaipur]: 91, serial/code nos 68/91). It is situated on the western side of the road from Jaipur to Amber.

V.S. 1863, Kārttika b. 3/ 30 October 1806

॥श्री राधागोविंददेवजी ॥

गोस्वामिश्रीश्रीकृष्णशरणदेव-
शर्मण :

(seal)
वृंदावनधांम

(१) ॥स्वस्ति श्रीमद्राधागोविंददेवचरणा-
(२) रविंदसेवापरायण राय श्री रामसिंह-
(३) जी जोग्येषु --- परमसुभासीर्वाद प्रयो-
(४) जन च विशेष : एषां नै श्री श्री ---जी प-
(५) रमानंदपूर्वकविराजिते छे नताह्राते
(६) अत्रानंद परंतु ईहां के वडे म्हाराजि
(७) के श्री श्री --- मैं जमी वीघा १३५६ एवं
(८) कुंज महैल वाग हाटि हवेली और गौड-
(९) देश सूं जात्री आवैं ता का [xx]ल माल चूं-
(१०) गी ए सव वडे महाराजि नै श्रीजी की भेट
(११) चढाय दिये है सो सदा सूं श्रीजी कौ
(१२) इन मैं अमल चल्यो आवैं हैं और अ-
(१३) व कोई कोई षेचल करैं हैं और वडे महा-
(१४) राजि नै ए सव वस्तुन के पातसाही पर-
(१५) वानां करां दिये है सो आपने घर मैं मौ-
(१६) जूद है और अव मथुरा वृंदावन मै सा-
(१७) हेव कौ अमल भयो है ता सूं तुम कूंलि-

---

(१) नांम कौ लिषाय भेजोगे जा मैं ई-
(२) न सव वस्तुन मैं श्री जी कौ अमल
(३) रहै और फिरंगी कौ जव ताई अमल
(४) रहै तव ताई षेचल नही होय सो करौ-
(५) गे और (?) समंचार श्री लाल मुनसी के काग-
(६) द सूं जांनौगे और तुम श्रीजी के अनन्य
(७) सेवक हौ तुमारौ नांम करि कैं सदा श्री
(८) श्री जी के चरणारविंद मैं तुलसी चंदन
(९) चढावै हैं सो श्री जी तुम्हारौ कल्याण

(१०) करैंगें मंगलादि समांचार हमेंस लि-
(११)षोगे मिती कात्तिक वदि ३ सं १८६३ के

(verso, bottom line, fold bearing address:)
...सिंहजी जोग्य

Śrī Rādhā-Govinddevjī

From him whose well-being lies in
Gosvāmī Śrī Śrī Kṛṣṇaśaraṇdev

(seal)

Abode of Vrindaban

[1] Hail! [1-3] To Rāy Śrī Rāmsiṅghjī, devoutly engaged in the service of the feet of Śrīmad-Rādhā-Govinddevjī, blessings [of ...] for his (Rāmsiṅgh's) supreme welfare. [3-4] The special purpose [of writing this letter] [4-5] is the following: Śrī Śrī [Kṛṣṇaśaraṇdev] resides in the Supreme Bliss. [6] Here all is well. [6-11] However, here, at the late Mahārāj's (that is, Kṛṣṇaśaraṇ's MH) place, there are 135 *bīghās* land and retreats *(kuñj)*, estates, gardens, market-stalls, mansions, and the ... *(a crease in the paper makes of the line illegible* - MH) tax and toll charged on pilgrims, who come from Bengal, [all of] which had been given to the late Mahārāj as His Highness's religious offering *(bheṭ)*. [11-12] That is to say, His Highness's right to collect revenue had always been vested in him. But now, [13] there are people who interfere with this. However, [13-15] the Imperial *parvānaus*, which were issued to the late Mahārāj for all these items, [15-16] are with me, [16-17] whereas now the Sāhib exercises the right to collect revenue in Mathura and Vrindaban. [17 - *verso* 1] Therefore, send a bond [1-3] confirming that the right to collect revenue on all these items lies with His Highness, [3-4] and that as long as the foreigners exercise the revenue authority, [4] there must not be interfered [with that right]. [4-5] Please act accordingly; [5-6] you will gather additional news from the letter of Śrī Lāl Munśī. [6-7] You are an entirely devoted servant of the Lord. [7-9] In your name, I always offer Tulsī leaves and sandalwood [paste] to the lotus-feet of the Lord. [9-10] Therefore, the Lord will work your well-being. [10-11] Please keep writing to me in all matters. Date: Kāttik b. 3, V.S. 1863.

(verso, *bottom line, fold bearing address:*)
... letter to [Rāy Śrī Rām]siṅghjī

Commentary:

In 1830, Mathura and Vrindaban passed under British rule (Growse 1979: 44). In the document, the British are called *sāhib* and *firangī*. The letter was written by a caretaker in the office of custodian of GD, perhaps by Rāmnārāyaṇ, the son and designated successor of Gosvāmī Kṛṣṇaśaraṇ. Kṛṣṇaśaraṇ had died on Āṣāḍha b. 7, V.S. 1863/22 June 1806. His son succeeded him as late as Kārttika ś. 7, V.S. 1864/6 November 1807 (cp. chart "The Custodians of the Govinddevjī Temple", n. 18, 19). The seal, which the writer of the letter used, was not that of an appointed custodian, whose name it would have borne, but rather points to that caretaker.

ll. 2-3: Rāy Rāmsiṅgh, though not identified, must be taken to have been Jaipur's Minister.

ll. 4-5: The words *eṣāṃ nai* and ...*virājite* ... *natāhāte* are corrupt Sanskrit and somewhat obscure. The sentence conveys that Kṛṣṇaśaraṇ is dead, "resides in the Supreme Bliss".

V.S. 1868, Mārgaśiras b. 14/ 15 November 1811

॥श्री रामजी

(१) गुंसांईजी श्री रांमनारायणजी सूं
(२) म्हारो नमस्कार बंच्या अपरंच रुप-
(३) या तीस हजार आयका ३००००ऽ जमी-
(४) यत षरच नें देवा वास्तै लीया सो मु-
(५) तसद्यां नैं कहि दीयो छै सो आप कै
(६) पहुंचाय देसी मीती मागश्र वदी
(७) १४ सं° १८६८

(seal of Mahārājā Jagatsiṅgh)

Śrī Rāmjī

[1-2] I pay respect to Gosvāmī Śrī Rāmnārāyaṇjī. Reference: [2-3] With regard to the thirty thousand rupees income — 30,000rp. — , [4] which had been borrowed to be spent on troops, [5] the officers have been instructed, [5-6] and they will forward these to you. [6-7] Date: Māgaśra b. 14, V.S. 1868.

(seal of Mahārājā Jagatsiṅgh)

V.S. 1869, Caitra ś. 1/ 14 March 1812

॥श्री रांमजी ॥श्री रामजी ॥श्री रांमजी

(seals of the *dīvāns*, first name: [x]*m*[x]*cand*[59], second name : *–rām*[60])

(१) श्री दीवान बचनात कसवा स्वाई जैपूर वागैरह् का पटैल पटवा-
(२) र्‌या दस्ये अत्र वावति ईनाम धरती वीघा ५०ऽ वाग वणावा नै वा वा-
(३) ग का षरच नै चंदु वडारणि नै जौ मा° प्रवान सवती करार मिती फाग-
(४) ण सूदि ११ संवत १८६९ ईनाम धरती वीघा पचास कसवा स्वा-
(५) ई जैपूर वागैरह् की वाग वणावा नै वा वाग का षरच नै ई° साष स्या-
(६) लु संवत १८६९ थे सीग ईनाम कै जांणि माप्य हवाले कीज्यो
(७) वीघा पचास ॥8॥

(८) ५०ऽ

(९) वाग वणावा नै कसवा मजकुर की	वाग का षरच नै गांव्र हथरोही
(१०) आवैरि का गला मै मुतसलि भ-	तालिक कसवा मजकुर की वीघा
(११) टजी का वाग कै वीघा सतरा	तेतीस
(१२) १७ऽ	३३ऽ

(१३) मिती चेत सूदि १ संवत १८६९

[59]Probably, Amarcand Pāṭnī (cp. "Table of Dīvāns").
[60]Probably, Kṛpārām (cp. "Table of Dīvāns").

Śrī Rāmjī (3x)

(seals)

[1-2] By order of the *dīvāns*, to the *paṭel*s and *paṭvārīs* of *kasbā* Savāī Jaipur etc. [2-3] Reference: Item of land exempt from taxation *(inām)*; 50 *bīghās* land for Baḍāraṇi Candu, for a garden to be laid out and [another] one to be purchased. [3-5] In accordance with a confirmatory *parvānau*, ratified on Phāgaṇ ś. 11, V.S. 1869, [there has been granted] an *inām* of 50 *bīghās* land — fifty — in *kasbā* Savāī Jaipur etc., for a garden to be laid out and one to be purchased. [5-6] There shall be measured out and assigned, from the cold season harvest of V.S. 1869, under the category of "*inām*", [7] fifty *bīghās*,

[8] 50/-

[9-11] For a garden to be laid out on the Amber road of the aforementioned *kasbā* and neighbouring upon the garden of Bhaṭjī, seventeen *bīghās*	For a garden to be purchased in village Hathrohī, part of the aforementioned *kasbā*, thirty-three *bīghās*
[12] 17/-	33/-

[13] Date: Cet ś.1, V.S. 1869.

Commentary:

l. 1-2: More than one *paṭel* and *paṭvārī*, respectively, are addressed. While it has been documented that there could exist more than one *paṭel* for a single village (Singh 1970 and Gupta 1986: 182-83), this must be at least inferred also for the *paṭvārī*.

l. 3: Candu/-ū was the household manager *(baḍāraṇi)* of Bhaṭ(ṭi)yānī, wife of Mahārājā Pratāpsiṅgh. In DK (25: 901-03), she is mentioned between V.S. 1860 and V.S. 1898, the year of her death. On *baḍāraṇīs*, see Bahura and Singh 1988: XXVII (fn.).

l. 9: Village Hathrohī now forms part of Jaipur.

V.S. 1869, Jyeṣṭha ś. 13/ 22 June 1812

॥श्री रामजी

गोविंददेवजी

सही
(कटार)

(seal)

(१) सिधि श्री महाराजाधिराज महाराजा श्री सवाई जगतसिंहजी देववचनात कमैती प्रगनां चाटसू का
(२) दसे सुप्रसाद वंच्या अपरंच वावति भोग गांव तन भोमि वागैरह सुधां रुपया ६२८८ऽ का ठाकुर
(३) श्री ---जी कै वास्तै मुवाफिक यादिदासति मैं दसषत दीवांनयांन करार मिती जेठ सु-
(४) दि १२ साल संवत १८६९ अरज पहौंची भोग मैं गांव किरपारामपुरा वागैरह प्रगनां चाटसू तन
(५) भोमि वागैरह सुधां रुपया ६२८८ऽ का ईवतदाय संवत १८६५ थे करि देवा को हुकम हूवो सो दसष-
(६) त करायो चाहैं तीह सूं फुरमांवां छां मतलव प्रवांनां का सूं वाकिफ होय गांव किरपारामपुर वागैर-
(७) ह प्रगनां चाटसू तन भोमि वागैरह सुधां रुपया वासठि सै अठ्यासी का ईवतदाय संवत १८६५ थे
(८) सीगै भोग कै जांणि हासिल हवालै करिवो कीज्यो अर प्रतवरष नवो प्रवांनूं मति मांग्यज्यो
(९) ईही प्रवांनां सूं हिसाव मैं मुजरा होयला
(१०) मुकररा तनषाह गांव किरपारामपुरा वागैरह प्रगनां चाटसू का ईवतदाय संवत १८६५ थे सीगै भो-
(११) ग कै जांणि हासिल हवालै करिवो कीज्यो तन भोमि वागैरह सुधां रुपया वासठि सै अठ्यासी ॥8॥

(१२)	६२८८ऽ	
(१३)	गांव किरपारामपुरा तन भोमि वागैरह सुधां रुप-	गांव श्रीकिस्नपुरो वास आकोड्या बुजरष त-
(१४)	या अठाईसै तेतीस	न भोमि वागैरह सुधां रुपया चौतीसै पचावन
(१५)	२८३३ऽ	३४५५ऽ

---

(१) सरह यादिदासति दाषिल वाकै करार मिती जेठ सुदि १२ साल संवत १८६९ वरसालै किरपाराम लिषमीचंद दी-
(२-५) वांन व नौवति वकायानवीस वंदे सरकार किरपाराम अत्र डोल भोग गांव ठाकुर... करायो चाहै (= *recto*, lines 3 - 6) सो दसषत षास हुकम हूवा मुवाफिक लिषे सीगै भोग कै
(६) द्यों ती को प्रवांनूं सवती लिषो सो चाहिज्ये दीवांन सरकार का प्रवांनां लिषै मिती जेठ सुदि १२ साल संवत १८६९
(७) अरज मुकरर पहौंची मुकररा गांव मजकूर वागैरह तन भोमि वागैरह सुधां रुपया वासठि सै अट्यासी ॥8॥

(८-११) (= *recto*, lines 12 - 15)

(१२) मुवाफिक यादिदासति मैं दसषत षास व दीवांनयांन

(१३) मिती जेठ सुदि १३ साल स्वत १८६९ मु° स° जपुर

(seal)	*(seal)*	*(seal)*
(१४) रजू दफत्र दीवान	रजु दफत्र दीवान	रजु दफत्र राम-
(१५) किरपाराम	लिषमिचंद	सूर मसतौफी हुजुर

(endorsements on left and right margin:)

दा° मवाजनै सरू दा° मवाजन

(I) Śrī Rāmjī

Govinddevjī

Certified

(*dagger*)

(*seal*)

(II 1) [1] Success! By royal order of Śrī Mahārājādhirāj Mahārājā Śrī Savāī Jagatsiṃhjī,

(II 2) [1-2] with benevolent greetings to the officers of *parganā* Cāṭsū.

(II 3) [2-3] Reference: Item of *bhog* of the deity Śrī [GD]jī; a village yielding an assessed revenue, inclusive of *bhomi* etc., of 6,288rp.

(II 4) [3-4] For this, there was submitted a petition endorsed by the *dīvāns* in the memorandum of Jeṭh s. 12, rev. y. 1869 [, as follows]:

(II 5) [4-6] [The deity] wishes that it be attested that there was passed an order that from V.S. 1865 villages Kirpārāmpurā etc. of *parganā* Cāṭsū, which yield an assessed revenue, inclusive of *bhomi* etc., of 6,288rp., be given [to him] for *bhog*.

(II 6) [6-8] Hereby, order is given that it be known [to you] by the intention of the *parvānau* that villages Kirpārāmpurā etc. of *parganā* Cāṭsū, which yield an assessed revenue, inclusive of *bhomi* etc., of 6,288rp., shall under the category of "*bhog*", be assigned for [income of] realized revenue.

(II 7) [8] And there must not be demanded a fresh *parvānau* every year.

(II 8) [9] Following this *parvānau*, there shall be carried to account in the account-book:

[10-11] Fixed allowance of revenue: Villages Kirpārāmpurā etc. … realized revenue (= *recto*, lines 6-8; numerals not in figures but in words).

[12] 6,288/-

[13-14]

Village Kirpārāmpurā; assessed revenue, inclusive of *bhomi* etc., two thousand eight hundred and thirty-three rupees

Village Śrīkisnapuro, hamlet Ākoḍyā Bujrakh; assessed revenue, inclusive of *bhomi* etc., three thousand four hundred and fifty-five rupees

[15] 2,833/- 3,455/-

(III 1) [1-2] Commentary on the memorandum [based] on the diary-entry of Jeṭh ś. 12, rev. y. 1869, on report of Dīvāns Kirpārām and Likhamīdās and the diarist on duty, servant of the government, Kirpārām.

(III 2) [2-5] Statement as follows: *bhog* of the deity … shall be given [to him] for *bhog* (= *recto*, lines 3-6).

(III 3) [5-6] Therefore, there was passed an order endorsed by His Highness that you give it [to him] under the category of "*bhog*", according to what is written [here].

(III 4) [6] Make out a confirmatory *parvānau*. It is necessary that the *dīvāns* of the *sarkār* make out *parvānaus*.

(III 5) [6-7] On Jeṭh ś. 12, rev. y. 1869, the petition was submitted again [, namely for]:
Fixed allowance of revenue: The aforementioned village etc.; assessed revenue, inclusive of *bhomi* etc., six thousand two hundred and eighty-eight rupees.
[8-11] (= *recto*, lines 12-15)

(III 6) [12] As endorsed in the memorandum by His Highness and the *dīvāns*.

(IV) [13] Date: Jeṭh ś. 13, rev. y. 1869; place: Savāī Jaipur.

(V) *(seal)* *(seal)* *(seal)*

[14-15]

Endorsed in the record, Dīvān Kirpārām

Endorsed in the record, Dīvān Likhamicand

Endorsed in the record; Rāmsūr, Court-Auditor

(left margin:)	*(right margin:)*	
		Start!
Entered in the *mavājanau*	Entered in the *mavājanau*	

Commentary:

ll. 4, 13: Village Kirpārāmpurā (now written "Kṛpā-") lies in Cāksū Tehsil of Jaipur District. In the same tehsil, there lie four villages by the name of Śrīkiśanpurā, three of which are contiguous. Ākoḍiyā cannot be identified in that area. In the same tehsil, but far from these villages and, therefore, hardly a suitable candidate, there is, in fact, a village by that name (India 1983 [DCH Jaipur]: 275-79; Kirpārāmpurā: serial/code nos: 156/145; Śrīkiśanpurā: serial/code nos: 249/133, 250/54, 251/53, 252/55; Ākoḍiyā: serial/code nos: 5/80).

l. 2 *(recto)*: For *bhomi*, cp. the commentary on doc. → V.S. 1797, Māgha b. 5, ll. 6-12.

***ab* V.S. 1872/** c. 1815

Incomplete.

॥श्री रामजी
गोव्यंददेवजी

सवाई प्रतापसिंहजी
हजूरि

(१) ॥सिधि श्री सर्वोपमां विराजमान पुज्य श्री गौस्वांमीजी
(२) श्री ५ रामनारायणजी जोग्य लिषतं सेवग राज वडा-
(३) रणि चंदू सरकार माजी श्री भट्यांणीजी म्हल महा-
(४) राजा वैकुंठवासीजी श्री ---जी का की की
(५) डंडवत मालूंम होय आप कै सदैव आनंद चाहि-
(६) ज्ये अैंठा का समाचार श्री ---जी की कृपा
(७) सूं भला छै अपरंच म्हारै रामजी वाग कसवा सवाई
(८) जैपुर मै आंवैरि कै गलै मुतसलि भटजी का वाग कै
(९) मुरतव वणायो तीं मै धरती मुवाफिक प्रवांनैं सवती क-
(१०) रार मिती फागण सुदि ११ संवत १८६९ थे वीघा पचा-
(११) स तफसील जैल ॥8 ॥

(१२)	५०ऽ	
(१३)	वाग नीचै वा वाग सुधां ध-	वाग का षरच नै गांव हथरो-
(१४)	रती कसवा मजकूर की वी-	ही की तालिक कसवा मज-
(१५)	घा	कूर की वीघा
(१६)	१७ऽ	३३ऽ

(१७) सो मुवाफिक हुकम श्री --- कै ठाकुर श्री --
(१८) ---जी की भेट मिती वैसाष सुदि १५ साल संवत
(१९) १८७२ थे प्रवांनां सवती सुधां चढायो सो हासिल वागै-
(२०) रह आवै सो श्री ---जी कै भोग लगाय द्रवार को पु-
...

ab V.S. 1872/c. 1815

Śrī Rāmjī
Govinddevjī

Savāī Pratāpsiṃhjī
Court

[1-2] Success! To the venerable Śrī Gosvāmījī Śrī 5 Rāmnārāyaṇjī, worthy of all epithets, [2-4] written by the servant of the State, Candū, Manager of the Household of the Queen *(sirkār mājī)* Bhaṭyāṇī of the Palace of the late Mahārājā Śrī [Pratāpsiṃh]jī [5] [whose] humble greetings may be accepted. [5-6] May you always enjoy bliss. [6-7] Here all is well thanks to the grace of Śrī [Gosvāmī]jī. [7-9] Reference: The Rāmjī Garden, which belongs to me and lies on the Amber road in *kasbā* Savāī Jaipur and neighbours upon the garden of Bhaṭjī, has been laid out. [9-11] 50 *bīghā*s land of this are, according to a confirmatory *parvānau* ratified on Phāgaṇ ś. 11, V.S. 1869, of a kind detailed [below]:

[12] 50/-

[13-16] Land below a garden and land with a garden in the aforementioned *kasbā*, *bīghā*s	For a garden to be purchased, of village Hathrohī, which belongs to the aforementioned *kasbā*, *bīghā*s
17/-	33/-

[17-18] According to an order of the Court, [in force] from Vaiśākh s. 15, V.S. 1872, this land had been given as a religious donation to the deity Śrī [GD]jī along with a confirmatory *parvānau*. [19-20]. The revenue collected etc. being spent on the *bhog* of the deity Śrī [GD]jī, the Court's ...

Commentary:

ll. 2-3: For Candū, cp. → V.S. 1869, Caitra ś. 1, l. 3, with commentary.

l. 2: According to epistelographic manuals, "Śrī" put five times is appropriate when writing to a *svāmī*; cp. *Lekhapaddhati* 58, l. 14.

V.S. 1930, Phālguṇa ś. 4/ 20 February 1874
Verso missing.

॥श्री रांमजी

हजूर गौविददेवजी

[xxx] दा° करो

(१) नाजिम जिला उदेही श्री गंगापुर का जौग्य लिषतं मिरजा गुलाम अैमद वेग के-
(२) नि --- वंच्या अप्रचि माफिक हुकम श्री --- कै कैफियत म्हैकमै म्होतस्मै आ-
(३) लिये रायल कोनसल की वैमजमुन ठाकुरजी श्री ---जी का भौग मै
(४) गाव ति म्धे मौ° जैतपुरा तपा काकङ प्रगना सवाई जैपुर तैहसील कालष का ज-
(५) मा सरासरी सालिना रू° २२६५॥ऽ ती की ऐवज मौ[°] गणोली रू° १४४९।–ऽ वा मौ[°] स्हज-
(६) पुर रू° ७८४।ऽ मू° मौ° २ निजांमत मजकुर का ज्मा सरासरी
रू°२२२५॥–ऽ का निकाल
(७) देणे वास्तै आई ति सू लिषा छा मौ° गणोली वगैर° मौ° २ भौग श्रीजी का मै ज्मा सरा-
(८) सरी सालिना रू°२२६५॥ऽ अक्ये रूपया दौय हजार दौय सै पैस्ट आना आठ मै तप-
(९) सील जैल भुगत्या छै ---
(१०) मौ° मजकुर मौ° स्हजपुर
(११) -------------------------------------- --------------------------------------
(१२) सो अमल दीवाय हासिल डी° साष उन्हालू संवत १९३० थे लेवा दीज्यो मि-
(१३) ती फागण सुदि ४ स° १९३०

Śrī Rāmjī

To Govinddevjī

[xxx] Enter in the records!

[1] Written to the Nāzim of Udehī and Śrī Gaṅgāpur by Mirzā Gulām Ahmad Beg, [2-3] … greetings. Reference: There has been received a report from the Noble High Court, [that is,] the Royal Council, which is in accordance with an order of His Highness and has the following intention: [3-4] Village for *bhog* of the deity Śrī [---]jī. [4-5] For this purpose, [there has served to date] the estimated annual revenue of 2,265rp. 8a. from village Jaitpuro of *tapā* Kākaṛ in *parganā* Savāī Jaipur, *tehsīl* Kālakh. [5] Instead of this, village Gaṇolī, with 1,449rp. 5a., and village Sahajpur, with 784rp. 4a. [yield of revenue, have been assigned]. [6-7] Fixed: There

shall be allocated 2 villages of the aforementioned *nizāmat,* estimated revenue 2,225rp. 9a. [7] Therefore, I am writing [to you] that village Gaṇolī etc., [that is,] 2 villages, [8-9] bear the estimated annual revenue expenses of 2,265rp. 8a. – in words: two thousand two hundred and sixty-five rupees [and] eight annas – for *bhog* of the deity, as detailed [below]:

[10] The aforementioned village Village Sahajpur

[11] --

[12] You shall assign and make available the realized revenue from the hot season harvest of V.S. 1930.

[12-13] Date: Phāgaṇ ś. 4, V.S. 1930.

Commentary:

ll. 4-6: Gaṇolī is the name of a cluster of villages lying in Bāmanvās Tehsil of Sawai Madhopur District (India 1983 [DCH Sawai Madhopur]: 70-71, serial/code nos 15/73, 16/69 and 58/70). This village cluster is contiguous to Sahajpur, which lies in the Gaṅgāpur Tehsil of the same district (*o.c.*: 89, serial/code nos 100/66).

For village Jaitpuro, cp. → rev. y. 1839, Āṣāḍha b. 5

CHARTS

The Mahārājās of Amber and Jaipur (1621-1880)

Name	Regnal period	Exact dates and references[1]
Jaisiṅgh I	1621-1667	Pauṣa ś. 10, V.S. 1678/13 December 1621 - Śrāvaṇa b. 14, V.S. 1724/10 July 1667; V.V. 2.2.: 1287, 1294; Sarkar 1984: 111; death of Jaisiṅgh's father Bhāvsiṅgh on 13 December 1621, succession of Jaisiṅgh on 18 December 1621; *ibid.*142: d. 28 August 1667.
Rāmsiṅgh I	1667-1689	Āśvina b. 6, V.S. 1724/29 August 1667 - Āśvina ś. 5, V.S. 1746/8 September 1689;VV 2.2: 1295-96; Sarkar 1984: 145, 154: 10 September 1667 - April 1689.
Bisansiṅgh (Viṣṇusiṅgh)	1689-1699	Āśvina ś. 5, V.S. 1746/8 September 1689 - Māgha b. 5, V.S. 1756/30 December 1699; VV 2.2: 1296-97; Bhatnagar 1974: 19; Sarkar 1984: 151: 30 April 1689; *ibid.*: 155, n. 16: 31 December 1699.
Jaisiṅgh II	1700-1743 (cp. however under Vijaisiṅgh for an interregnal period)	Phālguna b. 1, V.S. 1756/24 January 1700 - Āśvina ś. 14, V.S. 1800/21 September 1743; VV 2.2: 1297, 1299; Sarkar 1984: 157: 20 February 1700 - 21 September 1743.
Vijaisiṅgh	1708-171?	Sarkar 1984: 161, 193: c. 10 January 1708 - 171?; d. 1729; in confinement from 1713 (Bhatnagar 1974: 87).
Īśvarsiṅgh	1743-1750	V.S.1800/1743-Pauṣa b. 12, V.S. 1807/14 December 1750; VV 2.2: 1301; Sarkar 1984: 240: d. 13 December 1750.
Mādhavsiṅgh I	1750-1768[2]	Pauṣa ś. 14, V.S. 1807/30 December 1750 - Phālguṇa (c.) ś. 15, V.S. 1824/3 March 1768; VV 2.2: 1301, 1306; Sarkar 1984: 256, 259 (giving as the date of his death 5 and 6 March 1768, resp.).

[1] Conversion of dates according to Swamikannu Pillai 1915 and 1922.

[2] As early as 1749, however, Mādhavsiṅgh promulgated *parvānaus*, which referred to his own territory, in which he used the regnal title of the Kachavāhās (docs. [V.S. 1806, Jyeṣṭha ś. 10] and [V.S. 1806]).

Name	Regnal period	Exact dates and references
Pṛthvīsiṅgh	1768-1778	Phālguṇa ś. 15 or Caitra b. 3, V.S. 1824/3 or 6 March 1768 - Vaiśākha b. 3, V.S. 1835/15 April 1778; VV 2.2: 1306; Sarkar 1984: 260, 269, n. 1: 7 March 1768 - 13 April 1778.
Pratāpsiṅgh	1778-1803	Vaiśākha b. 4, V.S. 1835/16 April 1778 - Śrāvana ś. 13, V.S. 1860/1 August 1803; VV 2.2: 1307-08.
Jagatsiṅgh	1803-1818	Śrāvana ś. 14, V.S. 1860/2 August 1803 - Pauṣa b. 9, V.S. 1875/22 December 1818; VV 2.2: 1316-17.
Jaisiṅgh III	b. 1819- d. 1835 (minority rule)	Vaiśākha ś. 1, V.S. 1876/25 April 1819 - Māgha ś. 8, V.S. 1891/6 February 1835; VV 2.2: 1320; Sarkar 1984: 334.
Rāmsiṅgh II	[1835-1851 minority rule] r. 1851-1880	b. Bhādrapada II, ś. 14, V.S. 1890/28 September 1833; d. Bhādrapada ś. 14, V.S. 1937/17 September 1888 (VV 2.2: 1320, 1337); proclaimed king on 6 February 1835 (VV 2.2: 1320); installed as ruling king in September 1851 (Stern 1988: 97; Bahura and Singh 1988: XXXII).

Grants in favour of the Govinddevjī temple as verified by the State of Rajasthan in the 1950s

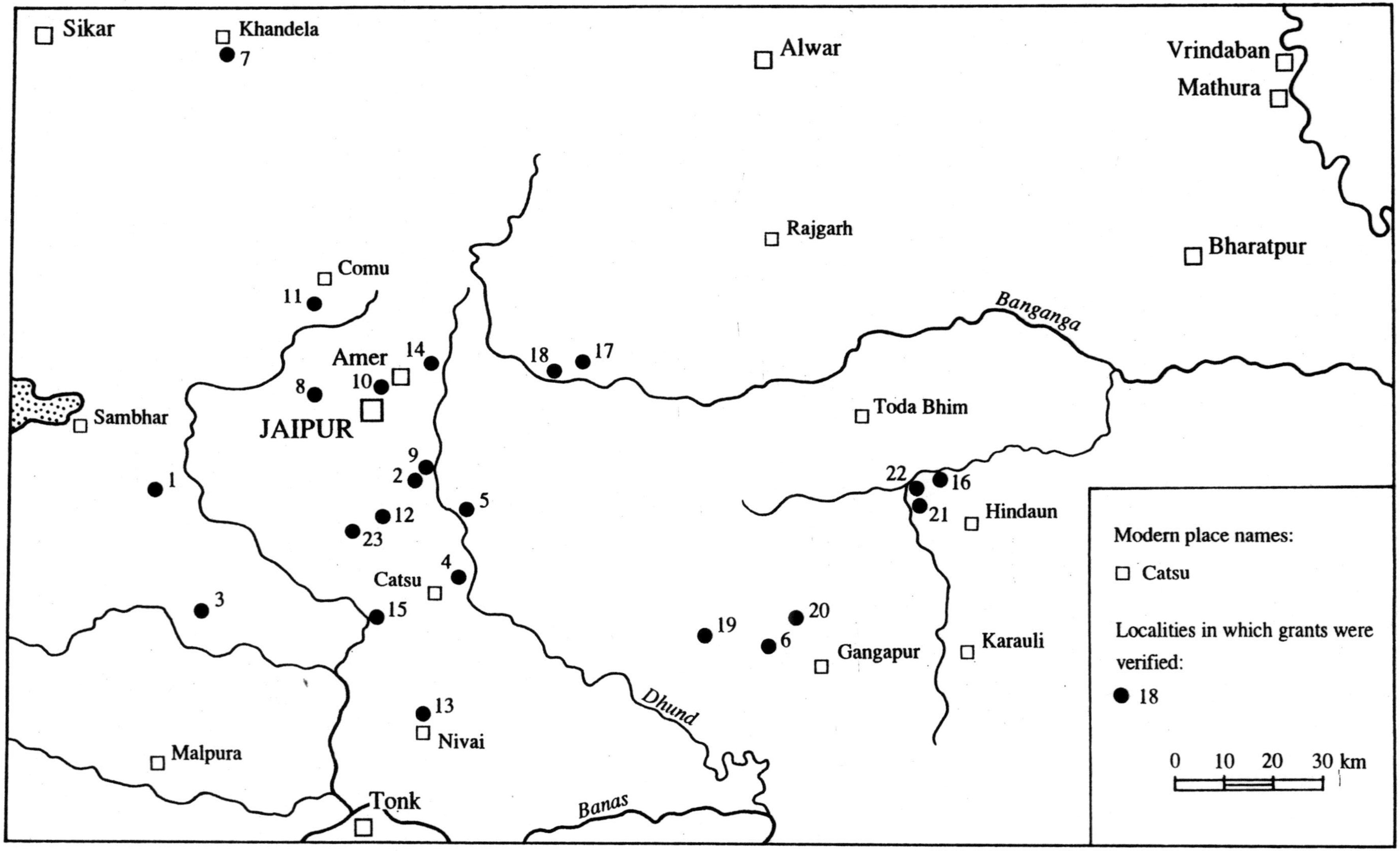

1 Bicūṇ
2 CatrapurvāsKhijurā
3 Coru
4 Dayālpuro
5 Gaṅgārāmpuro
6 Gaṇolīx
7 Gordhanpuro
8 Govindpur-vās-Hāthyod
9 Govindpuro (Baṛo)
10 Hathrohī (including: Śrīvrīdāvanpurā)
11 Jāhautā
12 Jasod(h)ānand-vās
13 Jugalpuro Khurd
14 Kūkas
15 Kirapārāmpurā-vas of Śrīkisnapuro
16 Maū Khās
17 Nīmlā
18 Rājsar Phuṭolāv
19 Rāmsar
20 Sahajpur
21 Sālimpur
22 Sekhpuro Baṛo (geographical identification uncertain)
23 Syosiṅghpurā

The Custodians of the Govinddevjī Temple

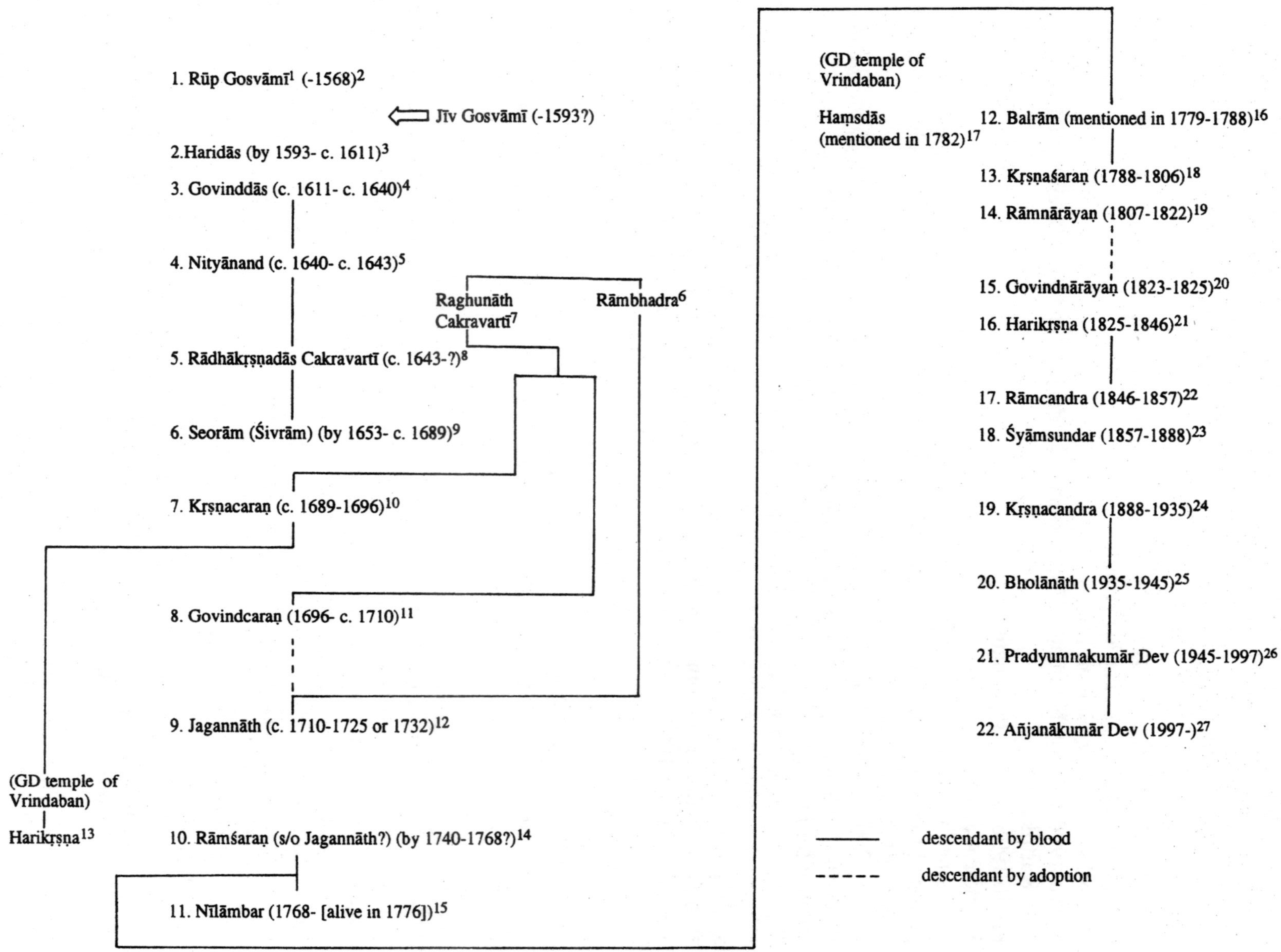

Notes to Chart

[1]Because of the great diversity of their spellings, names have been standardized in a Sanskritic Hindi way, unless they always occurred in a Non-Sanskritic spelling. For a chart of custodians up to the 1760s, cp. also Horstmann 1996:187-88. That chart has been modified here for a few points.

[2]Cp. Habib 1996:132 and 142-43, 144 *s.v.* Haridās/Hardās, Jīv Gosā'in/Jīva Gosvāmī (1568).

[3]Habib 1996:142-43, *s.v.* Haridās/Hardās.

[4]Habib 1996:139 *s.v.* Gobind Dās.

[5]Habib 1996:152 *s.v.* Nitānand Dās; designated *adhikārī* in 1641/42, alive in 1643 (→ V.S. 1700, Kārttika ś. 5).

[6]Habib 1996:143 *s.v.* Jagannāth.

[7]See note 4 above.

[8]Mentioned in 1643 (→ V.S. 1700,Kārttika ś. 5); in the same year, he is reported to have been appointed to conduct the worship at the GD temple (Habib 1996:153 *s.v.* Rādhā-Kishan Dās Chakravartī, s/o Nitānand).

[9]Habib 1996:156-57 *s.v.* Shiv Rām/Seo Rām; designated Gosāī Shiv Rām in 1648; *"pujārī"* of GD in 1652. The term *pujārī* was perhaps used synonymously with *adhikārī*, a designation in evidence for him in 1653.

[10]Cp. Habib 1996:145 *s.v.* Kishan Charan/Krishan Charan, and 143 *s.v.* Har Kishan.

[11]Younger brother of Kṛṣṇacaraṇ; cp. Habib 1996:138-39 *s.v.* Govind Charan; also 143 *s.v.* Jagannāth.

[12]S/o Rāmbhadra and adopted s/o his predecessor Govindcaraṇ; cp. Habib 1996:143-44 *s.v.* Jagannāth. Habib 1996:132 gives 1725 as the final office-year of Jagannāth. Roy 1985 gives 1732 on the strength of the pedigree produced by Pradyumnakumār, the then *adhikārī* of GD. Jagannāth was alive in 1729, but in 1725 he had gifted all his property to Harikṛṣṇa (Habib 1996:143-44). Harikṛṣṇa is probably identical with the *adhikārī* of GD in Vrindaban, who is in evidence in 1731, for which cp. Bahura and Singh 1988:no 1414.

[13]"S/o Kishan Charan s/o Raghunāth Chakravartī" (Habib 1996:143 *s.v.* Har Kishan). In 1731, he is mentioned as *adhikārī* of GD in Vrindaban, for which cp. Bahura and Singh 1988:no 1414.

[14]In the corpus of documents published here, Rāmśaraṇ appears first in 1740 (→ V.S. 1797, Māgha b. 5). Roy (1978:164) reports that the then *adhikārī*, Pradyumnakumār, claimed that Jagannāth was the first married custodian of GD. Though this is incorrect, the custodian's allegiation seems to implicate that Jagannāth started a lineage of blood descendence. Roy (1985) gives the years 1732-62 as the term of office of Rāmśaraṇ.

[15]In the corpus published in this volume, Nīlāmbar appears first on 6 February 1769 (→ V.S. 1825, Māgha b. 15). However, from doc. [V.S. 1825, Māgha ś. 4], the confirmation of an earlier grant, it can be concluded that his predecessor had died before Bhādrapada b. 8, V.S. 1825/4 September 1768, for this was the day when he had applied for the confirmation of the grant in question.

Nīlāmbar was the beneficiary of a deed of 10 November 1776 (→ V.S. 1833, Kārttika b. 14), hence presumably alive. Pradyumnakumār, custodian from 1945 to 1997, reported that both Nīlāmbar and his successor Balrām were the sons of the tenth *adhikārī,* Rāmśaraṇ (Roy 1978:165).

[16]→ V.S. 1835, Māgha b. 10, and also note 15 above.

[17]→ V.S. 1839, Jyeṣṭha II b. 15.

[18]Kṛṣṇaśaraṇ was designated junior *gosvāmī (choṭā gusāṃī)* on Phālguṇa ś. 3, V.S. 1837/26 February 1781. He married three years later so that he was probably very young at the time of his designation. His father died in 1788, and the Mahārājā paid his condolence visit to him on

Caitra ś. 11, V.S. 1845/2 April 1788 (DK 5:284). Kṛṣṇaśaraṇ himself died on Āṣāḍha b. 7, V.S. 1863/22 June 1806. For Kṛṣṇaśaraṇ cp. DK 5:283-98.

[19]Rāmnārāyaṇ was the disciple of Kṛṣṇaśaraṇ. The *mātamī* ceremony (the condolence ceremony which also implied the investiture of Rāmnārāyaṇ) after Kṛṣṇaśaraṇ's death took place on Kārttika ś. 7, V.S. 1864/6 November 1807 (DK 5:540). Cp. also note 18 for the surprisingly long interval between Kṛṣṇaśaraṇ' s death and the installation of Rāmnārāyaṇ. Rāmnārāyaṇ died on Friday, Jyeṣṭha b. 12, V.S. 1879/17 May 1822 (DK 5:542).

[20]Govindnārāyaṇ was Rāmnārāyaṇ's disciple and was adopted by Rāmnārāyaṇ's widow. He succeeded to the office on Monday, Pauṣa b. 5, V.S. 1880/22 December 1823 (DK 5:326-27 and 587-88).

[21]Harikṛṣṇa (Harikisan); the *mātamī* (for which cp. note 19 above) for Govindnārāyaṇ was celebrated on Friday, Āṣāḍha b. 11, V.S. 1882 (DK 5:587-88), which is not in accordance with the date given by Svamikannu Pillai, according to whom this *tithi* ended on Sunday, 12 June 1825.

Govindnārāyaṇ's own son had died of smallpox and therefore the succession was transferred to Harikṛṣṇa (DK 5:387-88). It is not reported if Harikṛṣṇa was related to him by blood.

[22]He succeeded to the custodianship on Monday, Kārttika b. 1, V.S. 1903/5 October 1846 (DK 5:536, where the name of his father and predecessor is rendered incorrectly as "Harkisoran"). He was dead by the end of 1857, for which cp. note 23 below.

[23]Disciple of Rāmcandra. He succeeded to the custodianship on Pauṣa b. 13, V.S. 1914/14 December 1857 (DK 5:582).In DK (5:584), he appears last in V.S. 1921. The date of his death is given by Roy 1978:165. He was the father of Kṛṣṇacandra, who succeeded him (RSA. Jaipur, File No 1657-28, pedigree produced by Pradyumnakumār on 21 January 1949).

[24]RSA. Jaipur, File No 1657-28; also Roy 1978:165-66.

[25]Roy 1978:165; RSA. Jaipur, File No 1657-28, 6 December 1956.

[26]Expired on 3 December 1997.

[27]S/o Pradyumnakumār, succeeded his father on 14 December 1997.

Kachavāhā Revenue Administration

(Departments concerned with charitable grants)

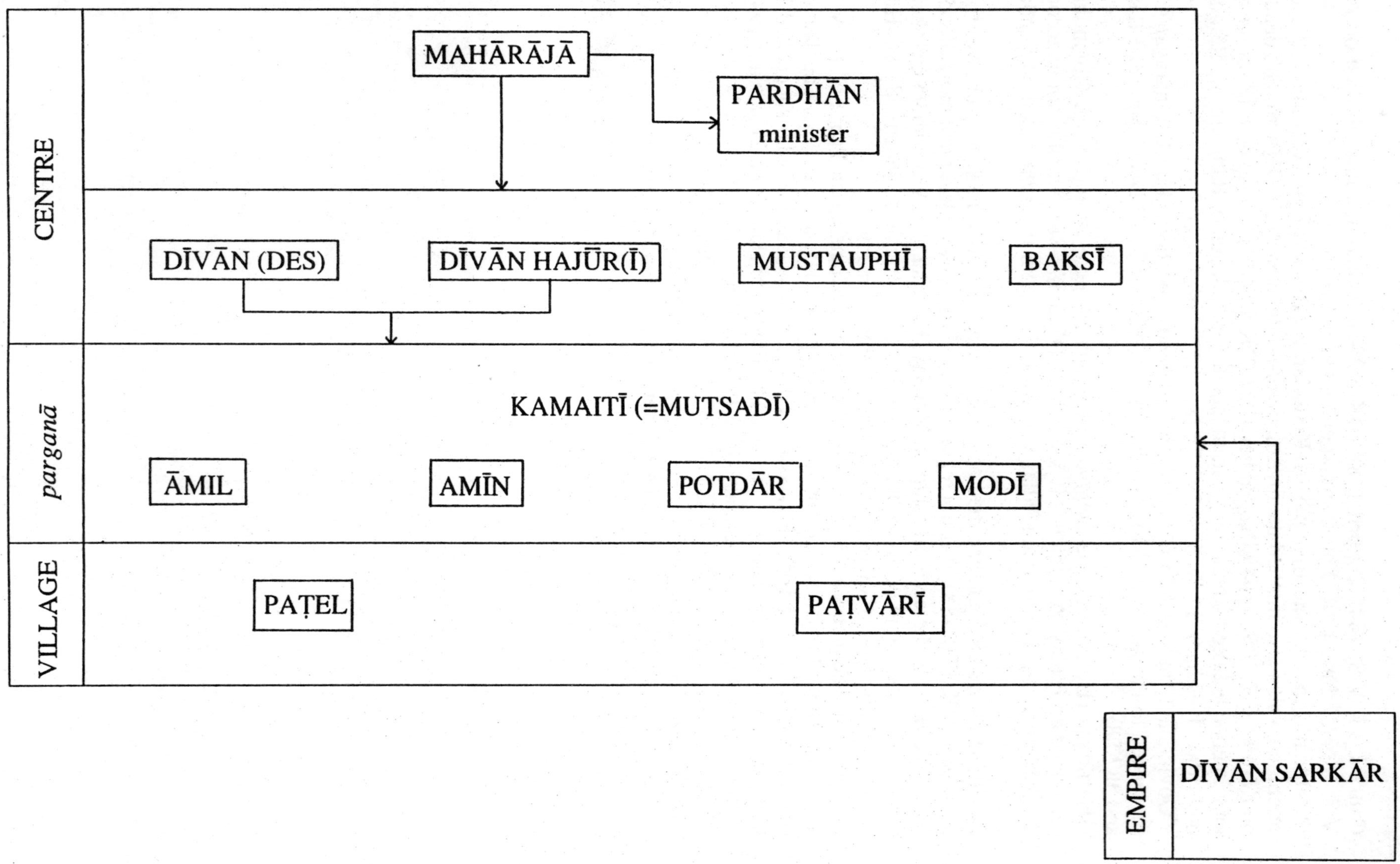

Bibliography

Unpublished sources

Dastūr komvār, Jaipur. 32 vols. (1718-1918). Rajasthan State Archives, Bikaner. (MS., transcripts of *taujīs*, 1718-1918.)

Rajasthan State Archives, Bikaner. Jaipur. File no 1657-28.

Rajasthan State Archives, Bikaner. Jaipur, loose leaves. Office note, Superintendent Central Records and in-charge Diwani Huzuri Office, 6 December, 7 February and 16 June 1936. – Council of State, Jaipur. "Resolution No 5", 10 February 1938. – "Definitions of important vernacular terms", 3 March and 17 December 1938.

Rajasthan State Archives, Bikaner. Jaipur. *Nuskhā kalān.*

Rajasthan State Archives, Bikaner. Jaipur. *Nuskhā punya parvānā sabtī.*

Rajasthan State Archives, Bikaner. Jaipur. *Tojī rojnāmā khuśbū-khānā, V.S. 1782.*

Vrindaban Research Institute. Microfilms, Vaiṣṇava Temples. Reel One: Govinddevji Mandir. VRI: T/1.

Published material

Abū'l-Fazl 'Allāmī. 1927-49.
The Ā'īn-i Akbarī. Vol. 1: Transl. by H. Blochman. 2d ed. rev. and ed. by D.C. Phillott (1927). Vols. 2-3: Transl. by H.S. Jarrett. 2d ed. rev. by Jadunath Sarkar (1949, 1948). 3 vols. Repr. Calcutta, 1977.

Asher, Catherine B. 1996.
"Kacchavāha pride and prestige: The temple patronage of Rājā Māna Siṃha". In: Case 1996: 215-30.

Ātmārām. 1979.
Savāī Jayasiṃh caritra. Ed. Gopāl Nārāyaṇ Bahurā. Jaipur.

Aziz, Abdul. 1945.
The Mansabdari system and the Mughal army. Lahore.

Bahura, Gopal Narayan. 1996.
"*Śrī Govinda gāthā*: Service rendered to Govinda by the rulers of Āmera and Jayapura". Case 1996: 195-213.

Bahura, Gopal Narayan, and Candramani Singh. 1988.
Catalogue of historical documents in the Kapad Dwara, Jaipur [Pt. 1]. Jaipur.

——— 1990.
Catalogue of historical documents in the Kapad Dwara, Jaipur. Pt. II: Maps and plans. Jaipur.

Bajekal, Madhavi. 1988.
"The state and the rural grain market in eighteenth century eastern Rajasthan". *Ind. Ec. and Soc. Hist. Rev.* 25.4: 443-73.

Bakhatrām Sāh. 1964.
Buddhi-vilās. Ed. Padmadhar Pāṭhak. Jodhpur.

Bayley, C.S. 1894.
Chiefs and leading families in Rajputana. Repr. Gurgaon, 1992.

Bennett, Peter. 1993.
The path of grace: Social organisation and temple worship in a Vaishnava sect. Delhi.

Bhadani, B.L. 1978-80.
"The allodial proprietors" (?): The bhūmias *(sic!)* of Marwar". *Indian Historical Review* 5/6.1-2: 141-53.

Bhaṭnāgar, Rājendraprakāś. 1987.
Mevāṛ kā rājya-prabandh evam Mahārānā Rājsiṃhakālīn do bahiyāṃ. Udaypur.

Bhatnagar, V.S. 1974.
Life and times of Sawai Jai Singh, 1688-1743. Delhi.

Bhattacharya, Sukumar. 1972.
The Rajput states and the East India Company, from the close of the 18th century to 1820. New Delhi.

Bill, Heike. 1995.
"Persische Urkunden aus Rajasthan (Indien)". Unpubl. M.A. thesis. University of Bamberg.

Bresslau, Harry. 1889.
Handbuch der Urkundenlehre für Deutschland und Italien. 1. Band. Leipzig.

Busse, Heribert. 1959.
Untersuchungen zum islamischen Kanzleiwesen an Hand turkmenischer und safawidischer Urkunden (Abh. d. Dt. Arch. Inst. Kairo, Islam. Reihe, Bd. 1). Kairo.

Case, Margaret H. (ed.). 1996.
Govindadeva: A dialogue in stone, photographs by Robyn Beeche. New Delhi.

Clémentin-Ojha, Catherine. 1997.
"L'affaire des tilaka: Procès des vishnouïtes à Jaipur 1863-1867". Thèse d'habilitation, Ecole des Hautes Etudes en Sciences Sociales . Paris (unpubl. MS.).

Dhamija, Jasleen, and Jyotindra Jain (ed.). 1989.
Handwoven fabrics of India. Ahmedabad.

Dodwell, H.H. (ed.). 1929.
British India, 1497-1858 (= *The Cambridge History of India,* vol. V). 3rd Ind. repr. New Delhi, n.d.

Entwistle, Alan W. 1987.
Braj: Centre of Krishna pilgrimage. Groningen.

Gahlot, Jagdīścandra. 1925.
Mārvāṛ rājya kā itihās. Repr. Jodhpur, 1991.

Gordon, Stewart. 1996.
"Robes of honour: A 'transactional' kingly ceremony". *Ind. Ec. and Soc. Hist. Rev.* 33.3: 225-42.

Gordon, Stewart, and John F. Richards. 1985.
"Kinship and pargana in eighteenth century Khandesh". *Ind. Ec. and Soc. Hist. Rev.* 22.4: 371-97.

Goswamy, B.N. and J.S. Grewal. 1967.
The Mughals and the Jogis of Jakhbar: Some madad-i-ma'āsh *and other documents.* Simla.

Grierson, George A. 1885.
Bihar peasant life, being a discursive catalogue of the surroundings of the people of that province ...Repr. Delhi, 1975.

Grover, B.R. 1962.
"Diwan-i Sarkar in the Mughal administration". *Ind. Historical Records Commission,* Proceedings 37.2: 65-71.

Growse, Frederick S. 1882.
Mathurá: A district memoir. Repr. New Delhi, 1979.

Gupta, Satya Prakash, and Shireen Moosvi. 1970.
"Bhomi in the territories of Amber (c. 1650-1750)". *PIHC,* 32d session, Jabalpur: 353-59.

Gupta, Satya Prakash. 1986.
The agrarian system of eastern Rajasthan (c. 1650 - c. 1750). Delhi.

Habib, Irfan. 1960.
"The currency system of the Mughal empire (1556-1707)". *Medieval India Quarterly* 4.1-2: 1-21.

Habib. Irfan. 1963.
The agrarian system of Mughal India (1556-1707). London.

——— 1982.
An atlas of the Mughal empire. Delhi.

——— 1996.
"A documentary history of the Gosā'ins (gosvāmīs) of the Caitanya sect at Vṛndāvana". In: Case 1996: 131-59.

Hinz, Walther.
Islamische Masse und Gewichte, umgerechnet ins metrische System (= Handbuch der Orientalistik, Erste Abtlg., Ergänzungsbd. I.1*).* Leiden and Köln.

Hodivala, Shahpurshah Hormasji.1923.
"The weight of the Mughal *tola*". In: *Historical studies in Mughal numismatics* (Occasional Memoirs of the Numismatic Society of India, II). Repr. Bombay, 1976: 224-34.

Horst, Heribert. 1955.
"Ein Immunitätsdiplom Schah Muḥammad Hudābandäs vom Jahre 989/1581". *ZDMG* 105: 289-97.

Horstmann, Monika. 1994a.
"Govinddevjī of Vrindaban and Jaipur and its Kachavāhā patrons from the mid-seventeenth to the mid-eighteenth century". In: Entwistle, Alan W., and Françoise Mallison (ed.). *Studies in South Asian devotional literature.* New Delhi and Paris: 82-93.

——— 1994b.
"Ein Kapitel nordindischer Religionspolitik im 18. Jahrhundert: Jaisingh II. und die religiösen Orden". *Zeitschrift für Religionswissenschaft* 2.1: 49-67.

——— 1995.
"An annual budget of Govinddevjī: A document of V.S. 1784". *ZDMG* 145.1: 125-47.

——— 1996.
"Śrī Govindadeva and his custodians from 1643 through the time of Jaya Siṃha II (1700-1743)". In: Case 1996: 185-93.

——— 1998
"Religious dignitaries in the court protocol of Jaipur (mid-eighteenth to early nineteenth century)". In: Berkemer, Georg – Tilmann Frasch – Hermann Kulke (ed.), *Explorations in South-Aian History* [Festschrift for Dietmar Rothermund]. Delhi.

——— [forthcoming].
"The preambles of official letters from Rajasthan: Towards a stylistic typology."

Ibn Hasan. 1936.
The central structure of the Mughal empire. Repr. New Delhi, 1980.

India. 1983.
Census of India 1981. Ser. 18. Rajasthan. Pts. XIII-A&B: District Census Handbook...: Jaipur District. Jaipur.

idem: Sawai Madhopur District. Jaipur.

idem: Tonk District. Jaipur.

Jhaveri, Krishnalal Mohanlal (ed., transl.). 1928.
Imperial farmans *(A.D. 1577 to A.D. 1805) granted to the ancestors of His Holiness the Tikayat Maharaj.* Bombay.

Kamalākara Bhaṭṭa. 1949.
Nirṇayasindhu. 5th ed. Bombay.

Kane, Pandurang Vaman. 1974.
History of Dharmaśāstra 5.1. 2d ed. Poona.

Kāslīvāl, Kastūrcand. 1989.
Khaṇḍelvāl Jain samāj ka vṛhad itihās. Pt. 1. Jaipur.

Kazem Zadeh. 1915.
"Les chiffres *siyāk* et la comptabilité Persane". *Revue du Monde Musulman* 30: 1-51.

Keśavdatt. 1944.
Kīrti-sudhāsāgar. Prayāg.

Khan, M. Naseer-ud-Din (ed.). 1950.
Selected documents of Shāh Jahān's reign. Hyderabad.

Kṛṣṇabhaṭṭa. 1958.
Īśvaravilāsamahākāvya. Ed. Devarṣibhaṭṭa Śrīmathurādās. Jodhpur.

Kṛṣṇadās Kavirāj. 1977-81.
Śrīgovindlīlāmṛtam (with *Sadānandavidhāyiṇīṭīkā* of Vṛndāvan Cakravartī), ed. and publ. by Śrī Haridās Śastrī. Vrindaban.

Lāḷas. Sītārām. V.S. 2018-35.
Rājasthānī sabad kos. 4 vols. in 9 pts. Jodhpur.

Lekhapaddhati. 1925.
Ed. Chimanlal D. Dalal with preface ... by Gajanan K. Shrigondekar. Baroda.

Michell, George. 1996.
"The missing sanctuary." In: Case 1996: 115-22.

Minorsky, V. (tr.). 1943.
Tadhkirat al-mulūk: *A manual of Ṣafavid administration (circa 1137/1725)*...(E.J.W. Gibb Memorial Series, n.s. 16). London.

Mohanty. Bijoy C. 1984.
Brocaded fabrics of India. 2 vols. Ahmedabad.

Mohiuddin, Momin. 1971.
The chancellery and Persian epistelography under the Mughals. From Bábur to Sháh Jahán (1526-1658). Calcutta.

Mukherjee, T[arapada]. 1980.
"Manuscripts and documents in Gauḍīya temples of Vrindaban and Rajasthan". *IAVRI Bulletin* 8: 9-17.

Mukherjee, Tarapada, and Irfan Habib. 1988.
"Akbar and the temples of Mathura and its environs", *PIHC*, 48th session, Dabolim, Goa University: 234-50.

——— 1989.
"The Mughal administration and the temples of Vrindavan during the reigns of Jahangir and Shajahan". *PIHC,* 49th session, Dharwad: 287-300.

——— 1990.
"Land rights in the reign of Akbar". *PIHC,* Golden Jubilee Session, Gorakhpur University: 236-55.

Mukherjee, Tarapada, and J.C. Wright.1979.
"An early testamentary document in Sanskrit". *BSOAS* 42.2: 297-320.

Muṃhto Naiṇsī. 1969.
Mārvāṛ rā parganāṃ rī vigat. Ed. Nārāyaṇsiṃh Bhāṭī. Pt. 2. Jodhpur.

Nābhādās. 1977.
Nābhājī [Nābhādās]. *Bhaktamāl*, with the commentary of Priyādās, ed. with a subcommentary by Sītārāmśaraṇ Bhagavānprasād Rūpkalā. 6th printing. Lucknow.

Nath, R. 1996.
"Śrī Govindadeva's itinerary from Vṛndāvana to Jayapura, c. 1534-1727". In: Case 1996: 161-83.

Pauwels, Heidi Rika Maria. 1996.
Kṛṣṇa's round dance reconsidered: Harirām Vyās' Hindī Rās-pañcādhyāyī. Richmond, Surrey.

Platts, John T. 1884.
A dictionary of Urdū, classical Hindī, and English. Repr. of the 5th ed. 1930. London, 1974.

Rajasthan State Archives. 1974.
A descriptive list of the vakil *reports addressed to the rulers of Jaipur (Rajasthani).* Bikaner.

Ranavat, S. Singh. 1989.
Rajput nobility (with special reference to the Kacchavaha nobility of Jaipur 1700-1858 A.D.). Jaipur.

Roy, Ashim Kumar. 1978.
History of the Jaipur city. New Delhi.

Śāh Navāz Khān. 1941.
The Maāthir-ul-umara [*Ma'āṣir-al umarā'*], *being biographies of the Muḥammadan and Hindu officers of the Timurid sovereigns of India from 1500 to about 1780 A.D.*, by Nawwāb Ṣamṣām-ud-daula Shāh Nawāz Khān and his son 'Abdul Ḥayy, transl. by H. Beveridge. 2d ed. rev. ... by Baini Prashad. 2 vols. in 3 pts. Patna. Repr. Patna, 1979.

Sāqī Musta'idd Khān. 1870-73.
Ma'āṣir-i 'Ālamgirī. Calcutta.

Sarkar, Jadunath. 1984.
A history of Jaipur, c. 1503-1938. Hyderabad etc.

Śastri *(sic!)*, Hirananda. 1942.
Ancient vijñaptipatras (= *Śrī-Pratāpasiṃha Mahārāja Rājyābhiṣekha Granthamālā,* Memoir No. I). Baroda.

Shakeb, M. Zia A. 1995.
"Aspects of Golconda-Iran commercial contacts". *Islamic Culture,* 69.2 (April 1995): 1-39.

Sharma, Sri Ram. 1940.
The religious policy of the Mughal emperors. 3rd ed. New Delhi, 1988.

Showers, H.L. 1916.
Notes on Jaipur. 2d ed. 1st ed. 1909. [Jaipur.]

Siddiqi, Noman Ahmad. 1970.
Land revenue administration under the Mughals (1700-1750). Repr. New Delhi, 1989.

Singh, Candramani. 1979.
Textiles and costumes from the Maharaja Sawai Man Singh II Museum, Jaipur. Jaipur.

Singh, Dilbagh. 1970.
"Position of *patel* in eastern Rajasthan during the eighteenth century". *PIHC,* 32d session, Jabalpur: 360-66.

——— 1977.
"Nature and incidence of taxes levied on inland trade in eastern Rajasthan during the 17th and 18th centuries". *PIHC,* 38th session, Utkal University (Bhubaneswar): 311-26.

——— 1990.
The state, landlords and peasants: Rajasthan in the 18th century. New Delhi.

Sircar, Dinesh Chandra. 1965.
Indian epigraphy. Delhi.

Smith, John D. 1975.
"An introduction to the language of the historical documents from Rājasthān". *Modern Asian Studies* 9.4: 433-64.

Steingass, F. 1892.
A comprehensive Persian-English dictionary. Repr. Beirut, 1975.

Stern, Robert W.
The cat and the lion: Jaipur State in the British raj. Leiden 1988.

Stewart, Charles. 1825.
Original Persian letters and other documents, with fac-similes. London.

Swamikannu Pillai, L.D. 1915.
An Indian ephemeris, A.D. 1800 to A.D. 2000. Repr. New Delhi, 1987.

——— 1922.
An Indian ephemeris, A.D. 700 to A.D. 1799. 7 vols. Repr. Delhi, 1982.

Śyāmaldās. 1886.
Vīrvinod: Mevāṛ kā itihās. 2 vols. in 3 pts. Repr. Delhi, 1986.

Śyāmsundardās. 1986.
Hindī śabd sāgar. 11 vols. Rev. and enlarged 2d ed. Banaras.

Tavernier, Jean-Baptiste. 1925.
Travels in India, transl. and ed. by V.Ball. 2d rev. ed. by William Crooke. 2 vols. New Delhi, 1977.

Thakur, Nalini. 1996.
"The building of Govindadeva". Photographs by Robyn Beeche. In: Case 1996: 11-68.

Tod, James. 1829-32.
Annals and antiquities of Rajast'han, or the central and western Rajpoot states of India. Repr. of the 2d ed. 1914. 2 vols. New Delhi, 1978.

Topsfield, Andrew. 1990.
The City Palace Museum Udaipur: Paintings of Mewar court life. Photographs by Pankaj Shah. Ahmedabad.

Tsybulsky, V.V. 1979.
Calendars of Middle East countries: Conversion tables and explanatory notes. Moscow.

Vashishtha, Vijay Kumar. 1978.
Rajputana Agency, 1832-1858. Jaipur.

Wills, C.U. 1933.
A report on the land-tenures and special powers of certain thikanedars *of the Jaipur State (= The Jaipur Gazette, extraordinary* 51.4605: 18th November, 1933). Jaipur.

Wilson, H[orace] H[ayman]. 1855.
A glossary of the judicial and revenue terms and of useful words occurring in official documents relating to the administration of the government of British India ... 2d ed. Delhi, 1968.

Ziegler, Norman. 1976.
"The seventeenth century chronicles of Mārvāṛa: A study in the evolution and use of oral traditions in western India". *History in Africa* 3: 127-53.

Index

of Names and Administrative Terms

(In the Index, the grapheme *ṣ*, which in the documents represents [kh] and [x], has been rendered by *kh*.)

FACSIMILES

Note

Consecutive photographs of a single document often overlap. The text junctures have been marked by ● on the margin of consecutive facsimiles.

Abbreviations Used in the Rājasthānī Text

(Grammatical variants represented by the abbreviations have been ignored.)

ई°	ईवतदाय
ई° फ°	ईवतदाय फसल
ए°	ऐवज (?)
ऊनमा°	ऊन्मान (ऊनमान)
की°	कीमती
ज°	जरी
जु°, जू°	जुमादा, जूमादा
ठा°	ठाकुर
त°	तफसील
ता°, तो°, तोा°	तारीष
था°	थान
द°	दर, दरी; दुतीय, द्वितीय
दा°	दाषिल
द्र°	दर, दरी
प्र°	प्रगना,परगना
म°	मण
मा°	माफिक; माह
मु°, मू°	मुकरर(ा), मूकरर(ा); मुकसर,मूकसर; मुकाम, मूकाम
मौ°	मौजा
या°	यादिदासति
र°	रबी
रु°, रू°	रुपयौ, रूपयौ
रो°	रोजीना
ला° आ°	equivalent of Pers. (Ar.) *li-ġāyat*, "until"
व°	वइसम
व़गै°,वगौ°, व़ागै°	वगैरह, वागैरह
वा°	वावति
वे°	वेइसम (वइसम)
सं°	संन; संवत
स°	सरैह; सवाई;
सा°	साल; सालीना
सी°	सीगै

A.H. 1038, 2 Śavvāl / 25 May 1628

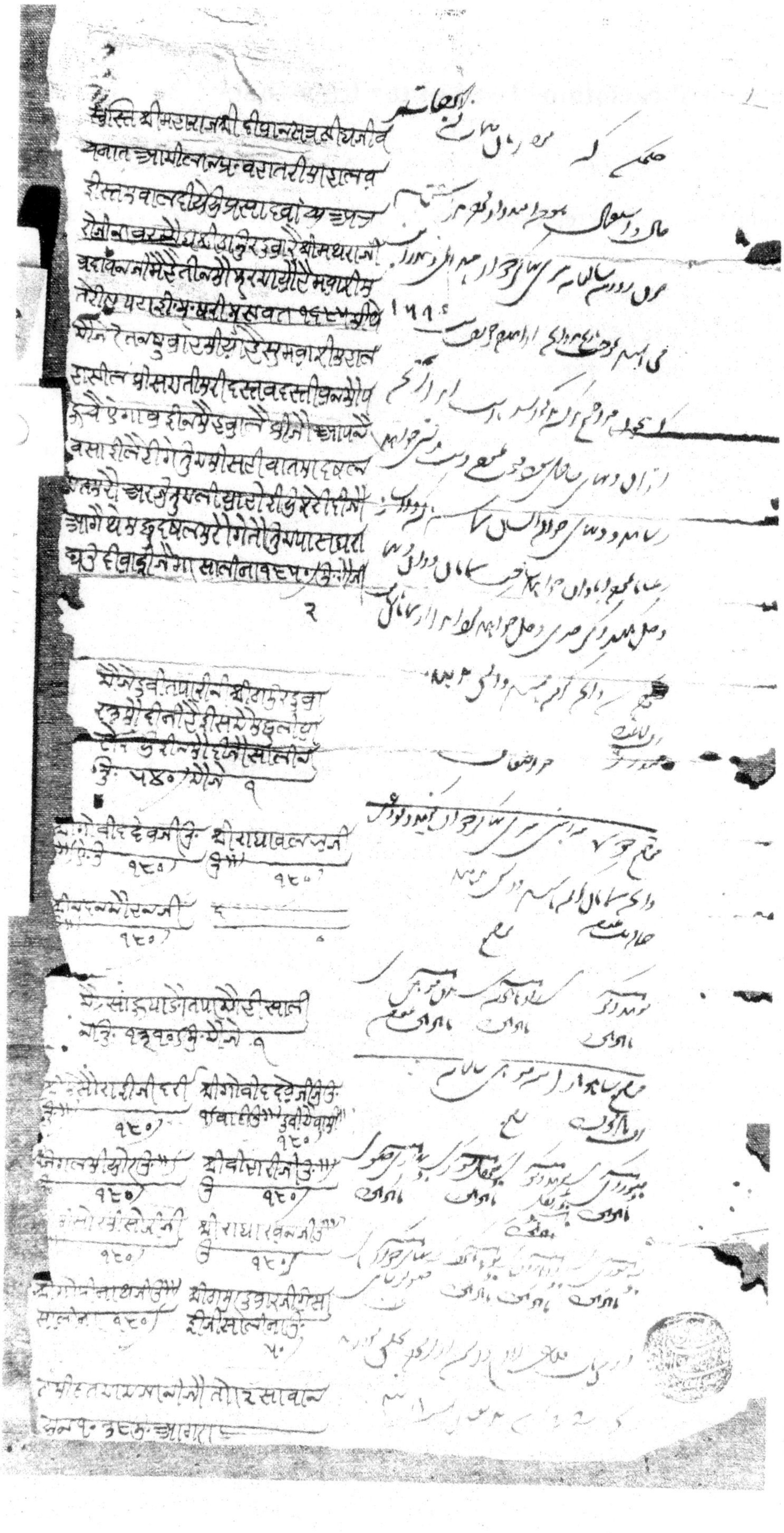

V.S. 1700, Kārttika ś. 5 / 22 September 1643

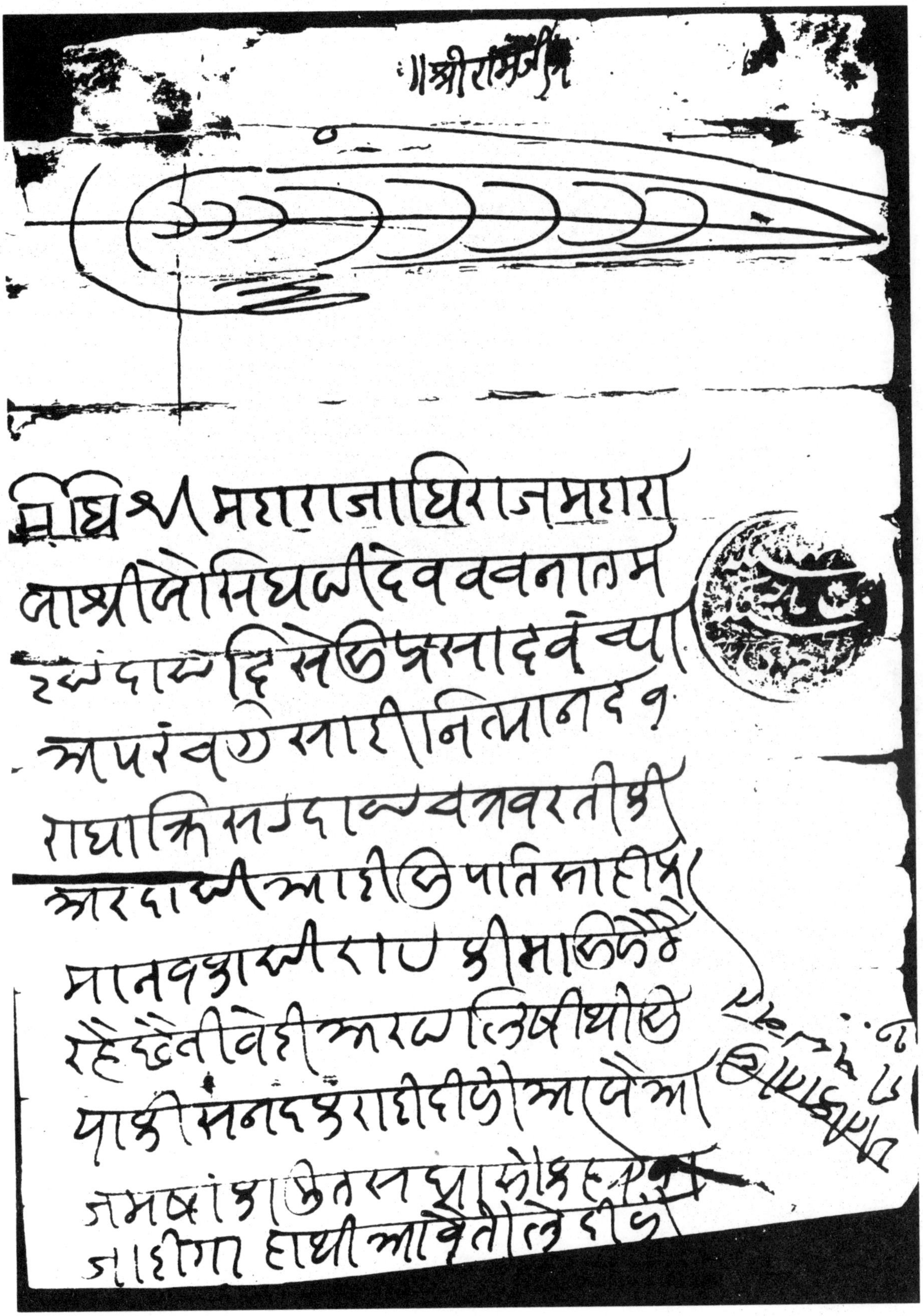
॥श्रीरामजी॥

सिधश्री महाराजाधिराज महारा

जाश्रीजैसिंघजीदेववचनात म

A.H. 1071, 10 Safar / 15 October 1660

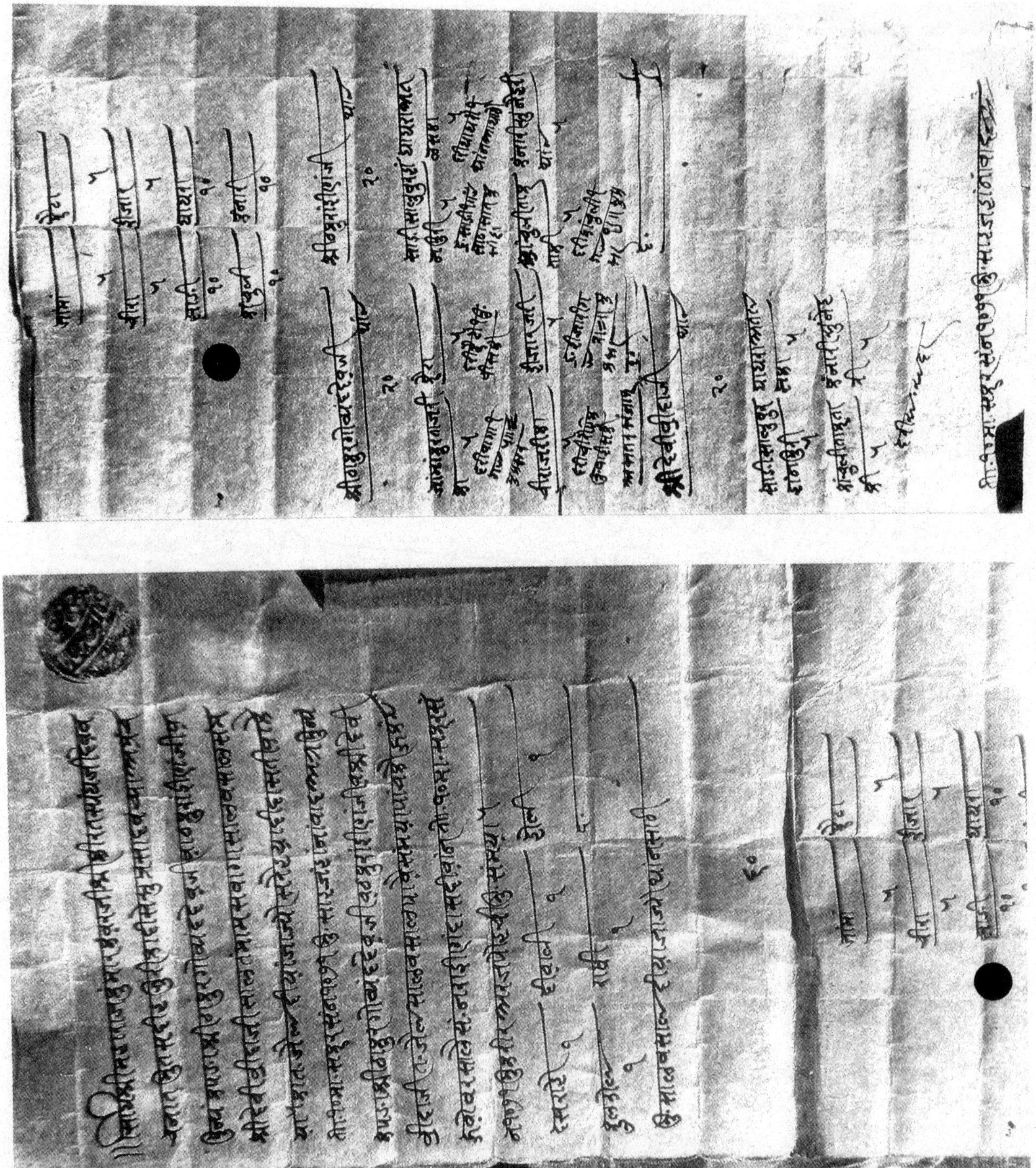

A.H. 1072, 15 Śavvāl / 3 June 1662 // Āṣāḍha b. 3, V.S. 1719 / 26 May 1662

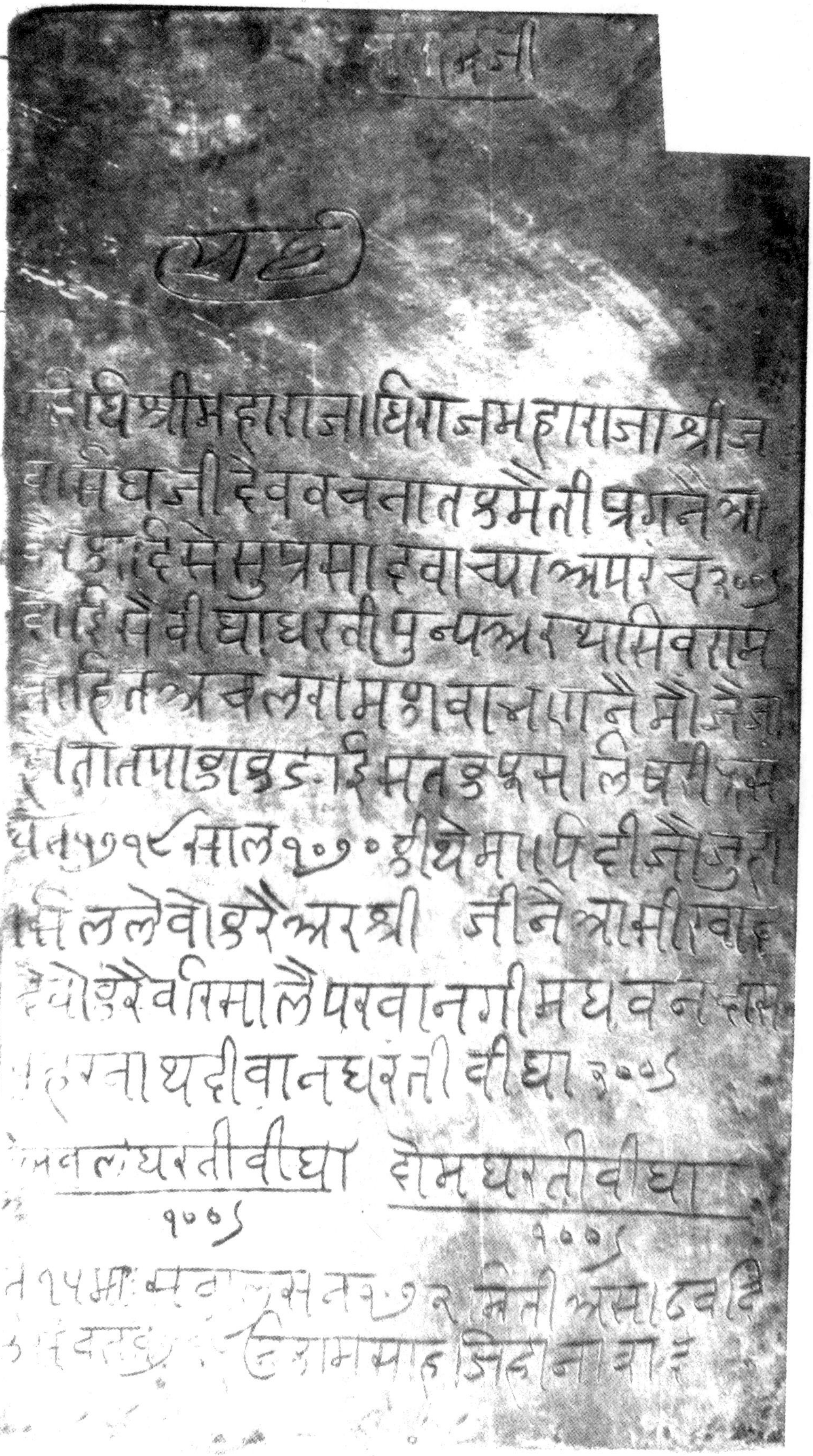

A.H. 1078, 30 Jumādā II / 17 December 1667

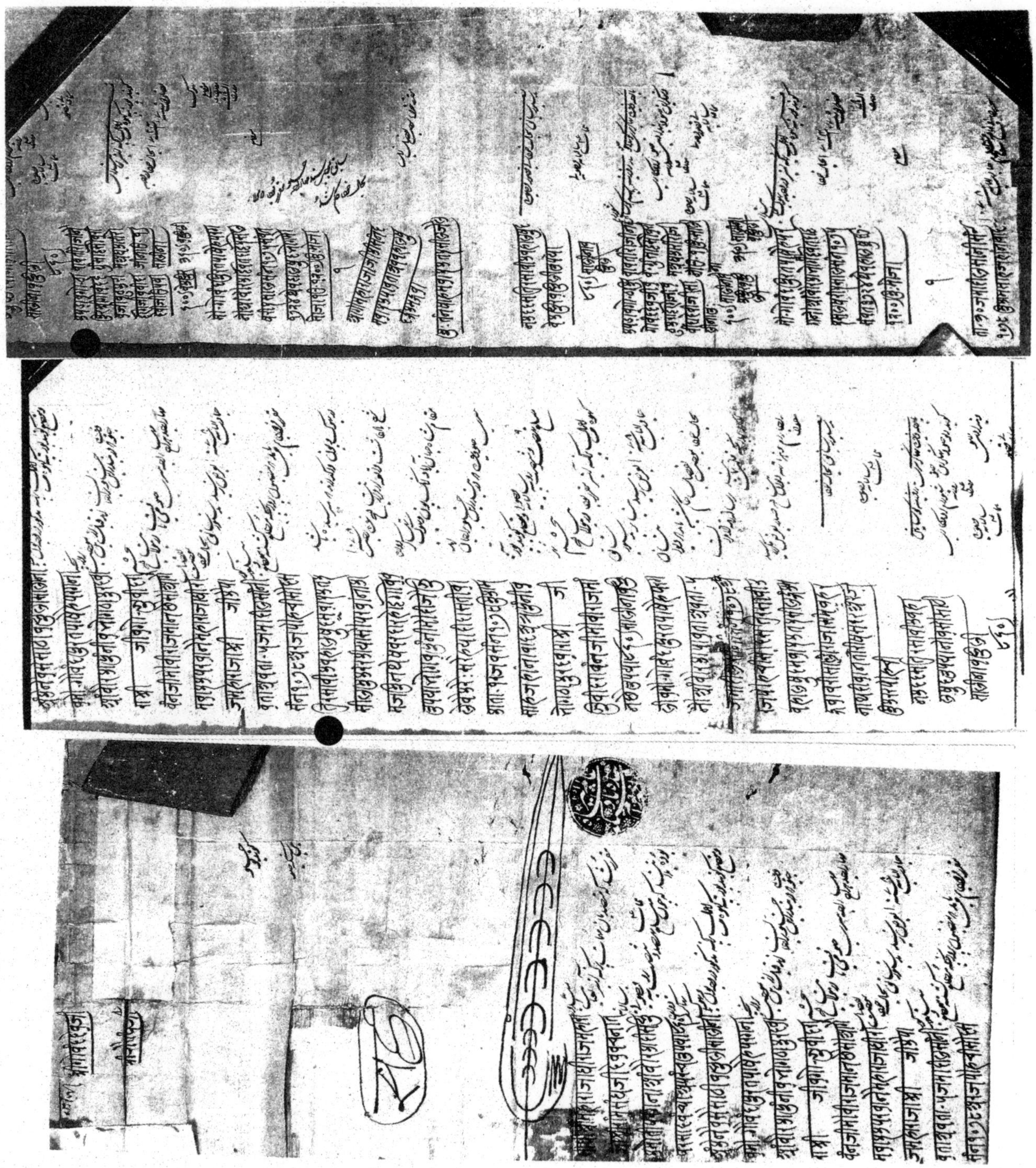

A.H. 1080, 12 Ramaz̲ān / 3 February 1670

A.H. 1089, 20 Zī'l-ḥijja / 2 February 1679

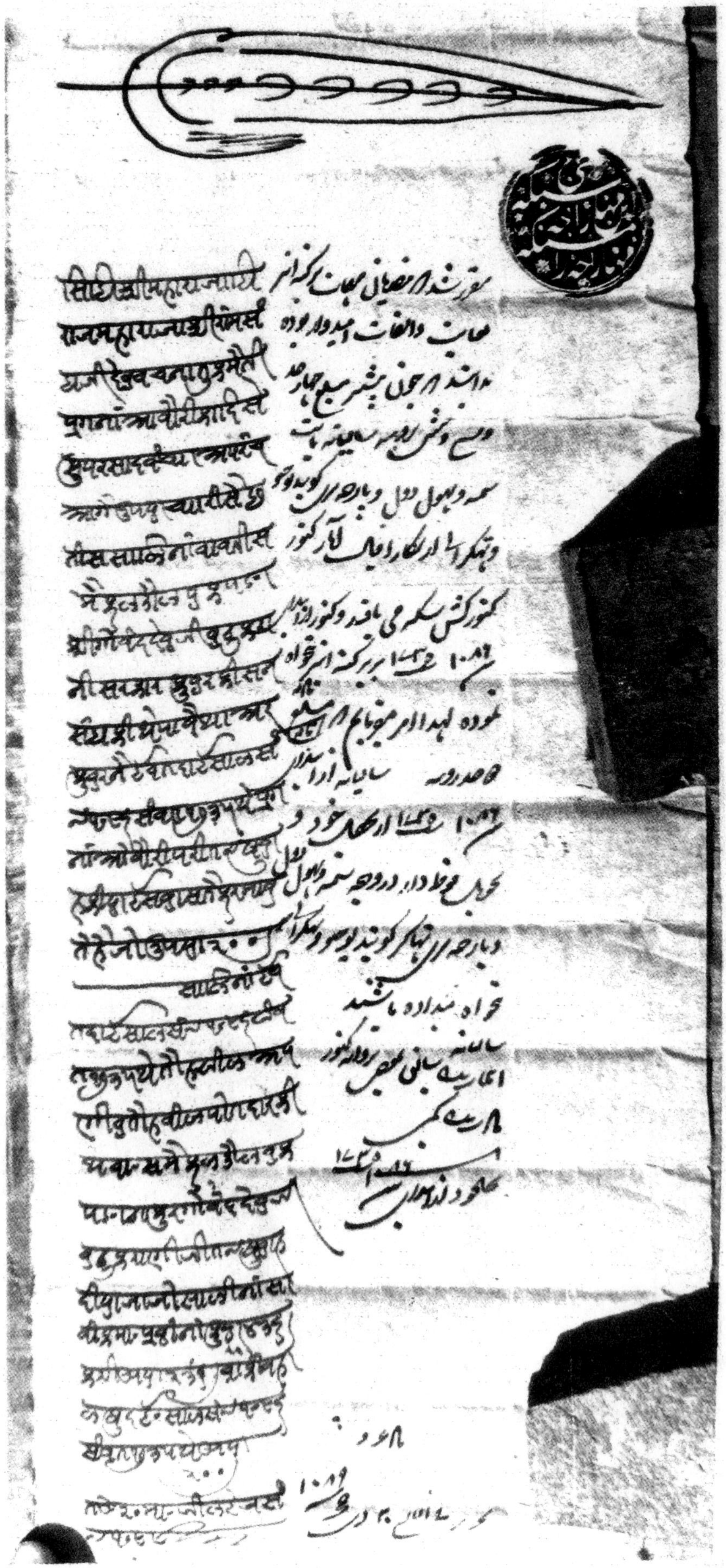

A.H. 1102, 21 Rabī‘ I / 23 December 1690

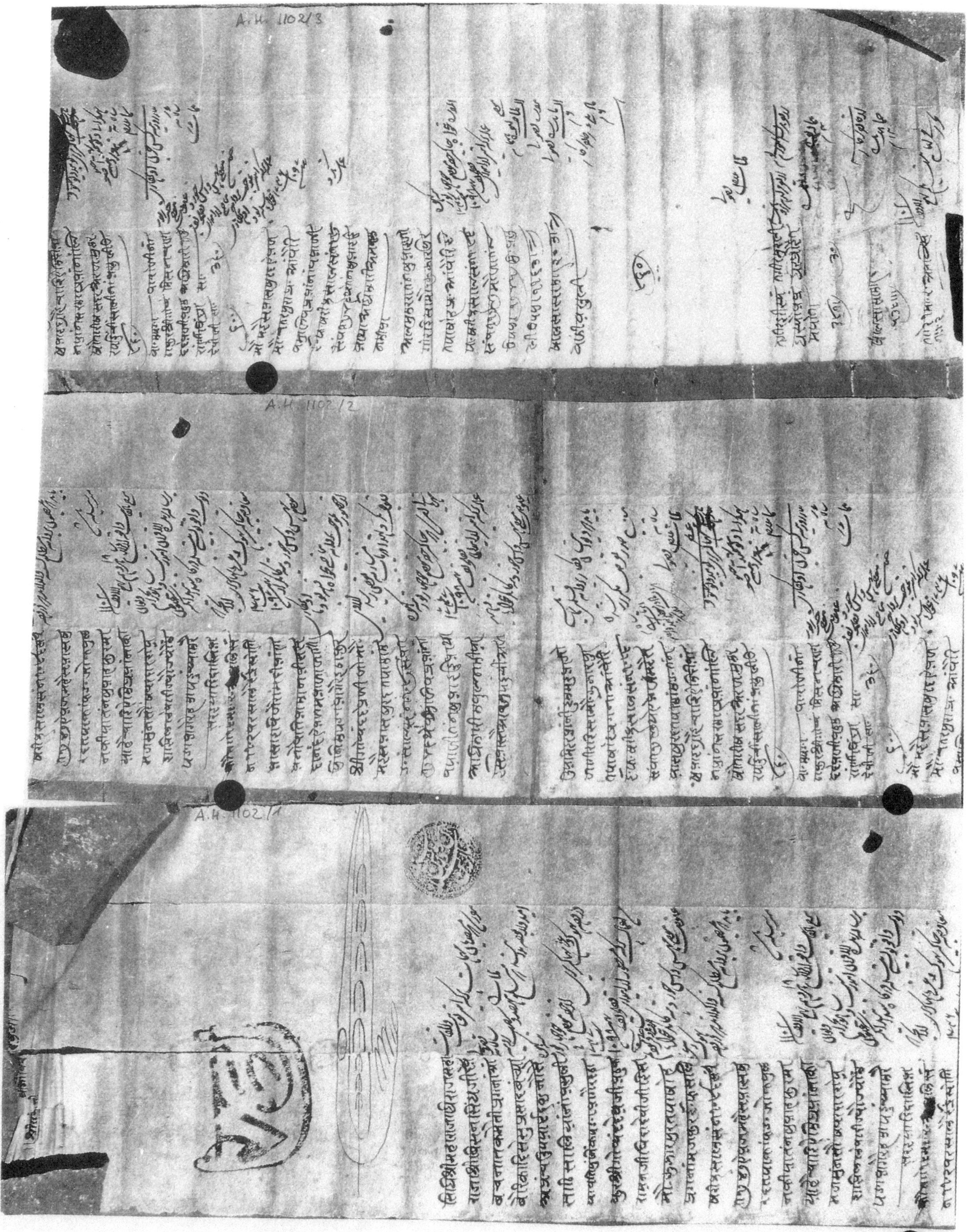

A.H. 1106, 12 Jumādā I / 29 December 1694

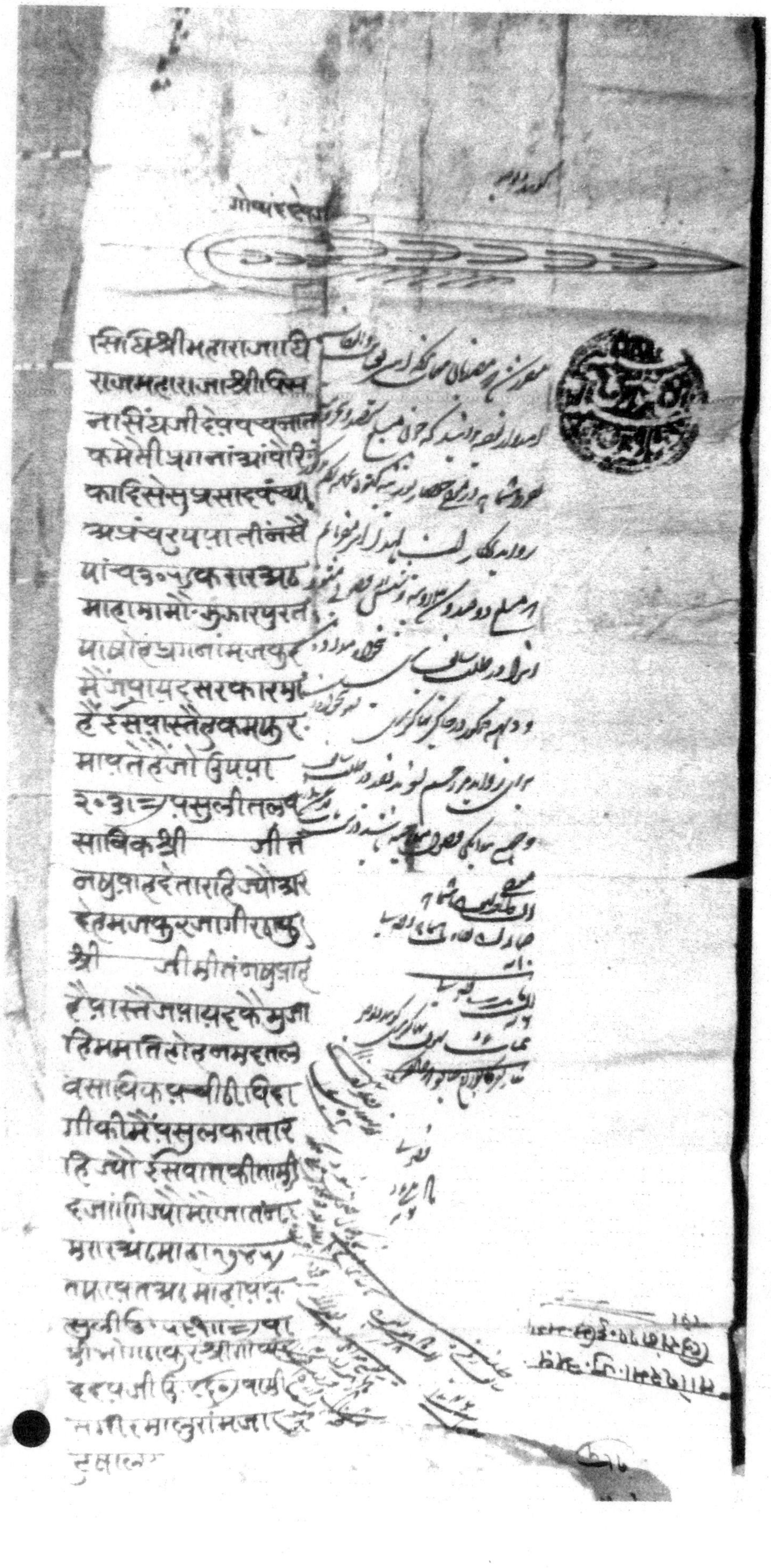

सिध श्री मतारा जा [illegible]
राजमतारा जा श्री [illegible]
नासिंघ जी [illegible]
कमैमी [illegible]
कादिसमु प्रसाद [illegible]
[illegible] तीजमैं
[illegible] कसार अठ
मातामामो [illegible] पुरतै
[illegible]
मैं [illegible] सरकारमां
तैं रसपास्तै लकमफर
मापतत जो [illegible]
२०३।=/ पसुलीतलव
साबिक श्री जीतै
नखुसाल देतारहि ज्यां अर
हतमजाकुरजागीरहां
श्री जी मोतं नखुसाल
हैपास्तै जपायरहकै मुजा
तिममातिलोलनमरतल
वसाबिक पस्वीठीपिदा
गीकीमैं पसुलकरतार
हिज्यो रसवातकीलामी
दजागिज्यां मोपातनर
मरार अठमाता [illegible]
तफरपत अठमाता पस
सुलीडि पहौ।।=/पा
श्री जोगनाकुर श्री गो [illegible]
दरपजी डि [illegible]
नगीरमाल्हुरांमजा
टुखालसा रुपाप सुली
२०३।=
[illegible] सालसंतामा २
संघान [illegible] परथे [illegible]
कीपातधतां इसपेसगल
उपय पसुलनलोलिज
पायदलमरहतासिलमो
मलपुरमम्मैं तंमखुसाल
देता रहिज्या
नरलवसाबिकपागरल
[illegible]
[illegible] वसा [illegible]
[illegible] दागीपागर
[illegible] जोमुचपु
जोगनाकुरजी [illegible]
[illegible] पोरपरितर्व
रपासाबिजु [illegible]

A.H. 1108, 22 [Rabī'] II / 18 November 1696

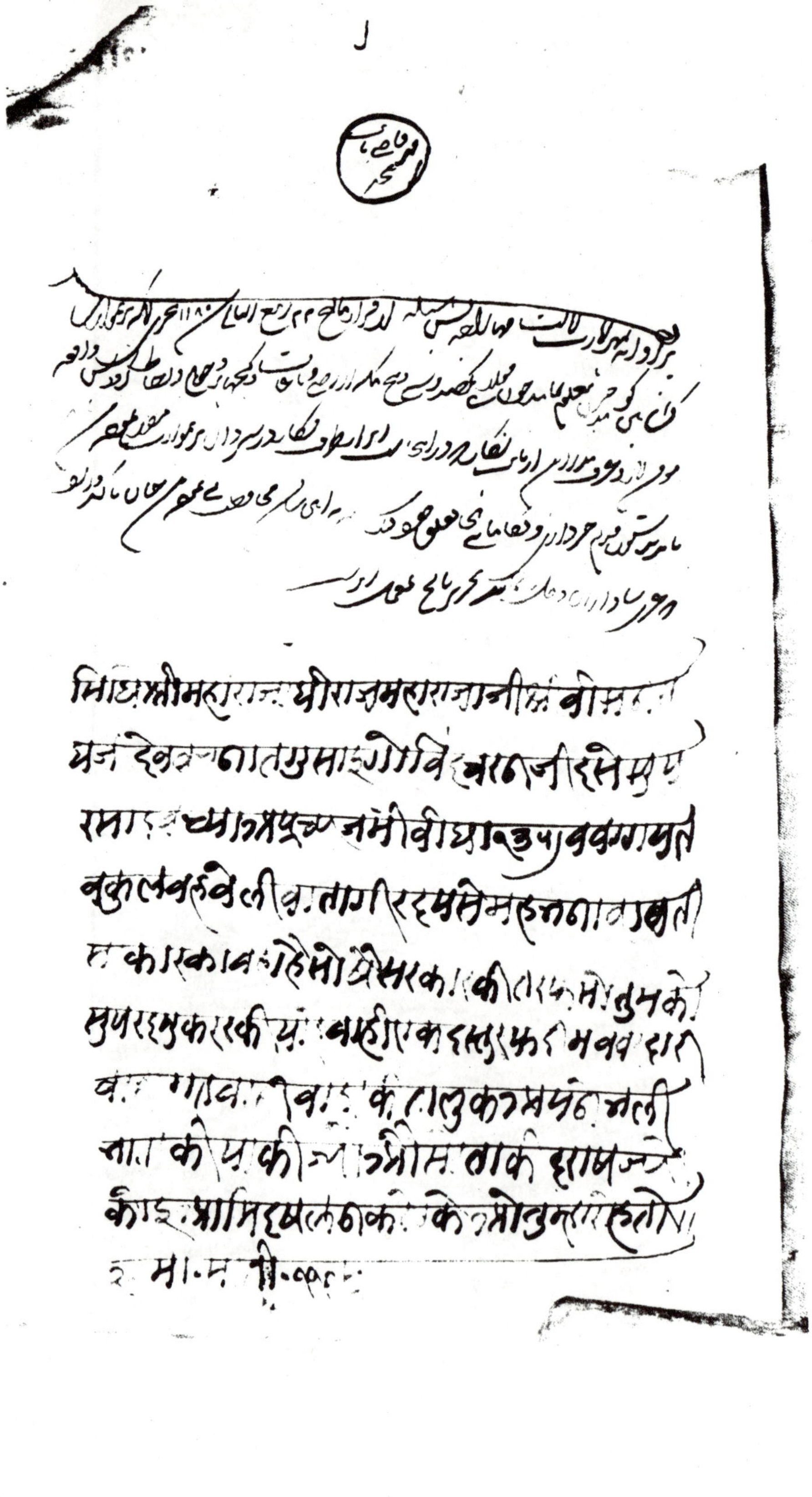

A.H. 1108, 23 Rabī‘ II / 19 November 1696

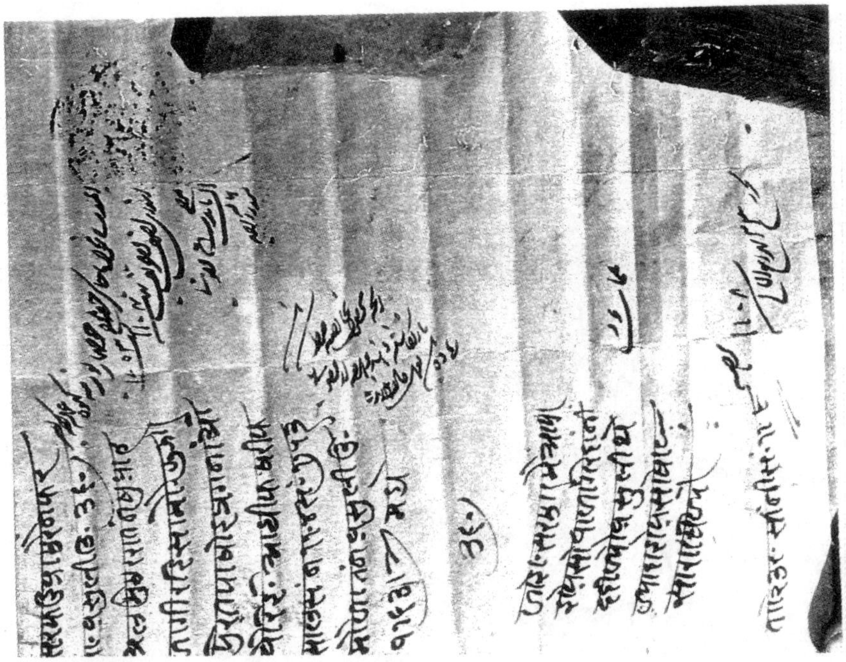

V.S. 1764, Śrāvaṇa b. 3 / 6 July 1707

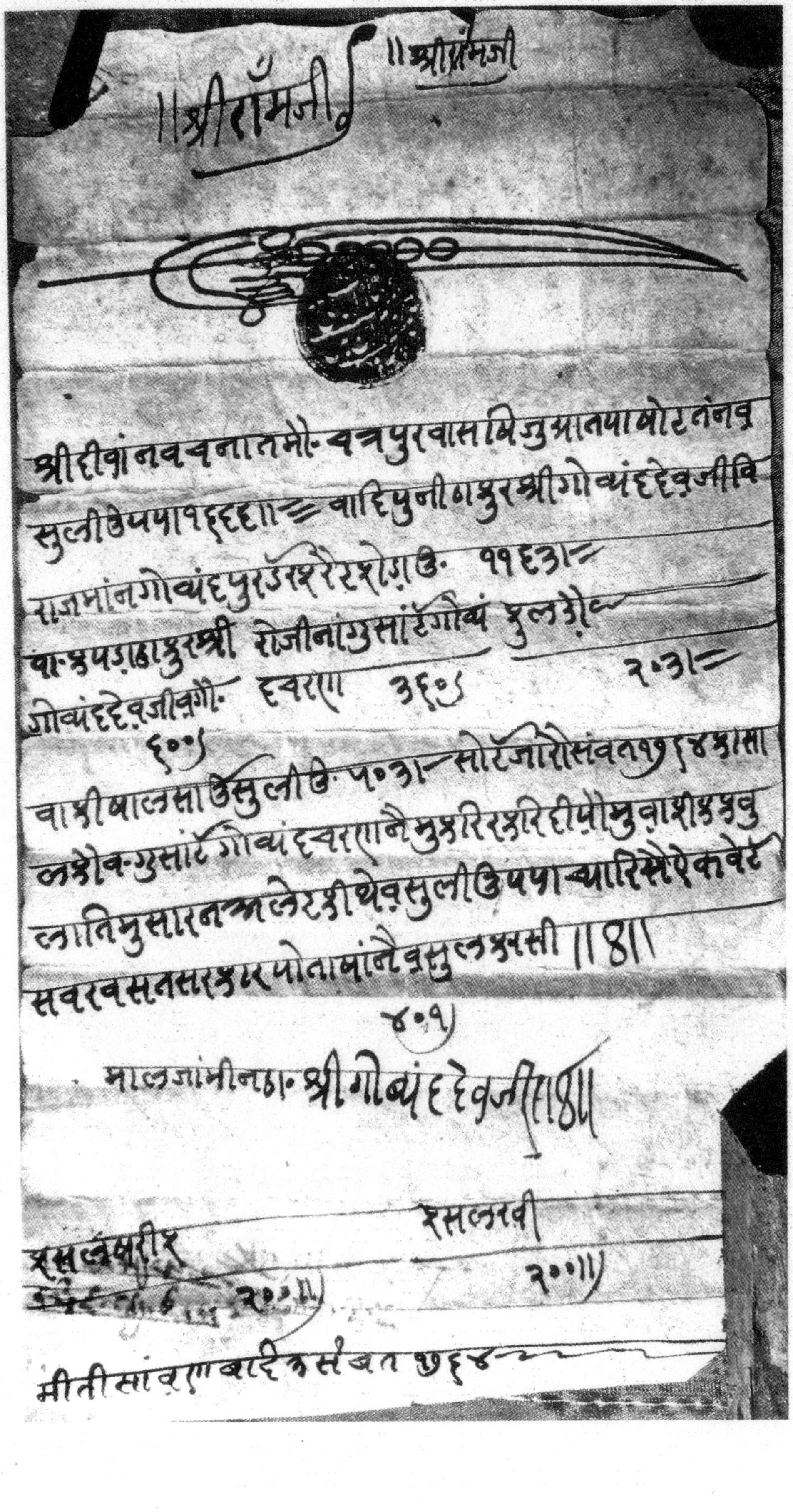

V.S. 1767, Mārgaśiras b. 2 / 28 October 1710

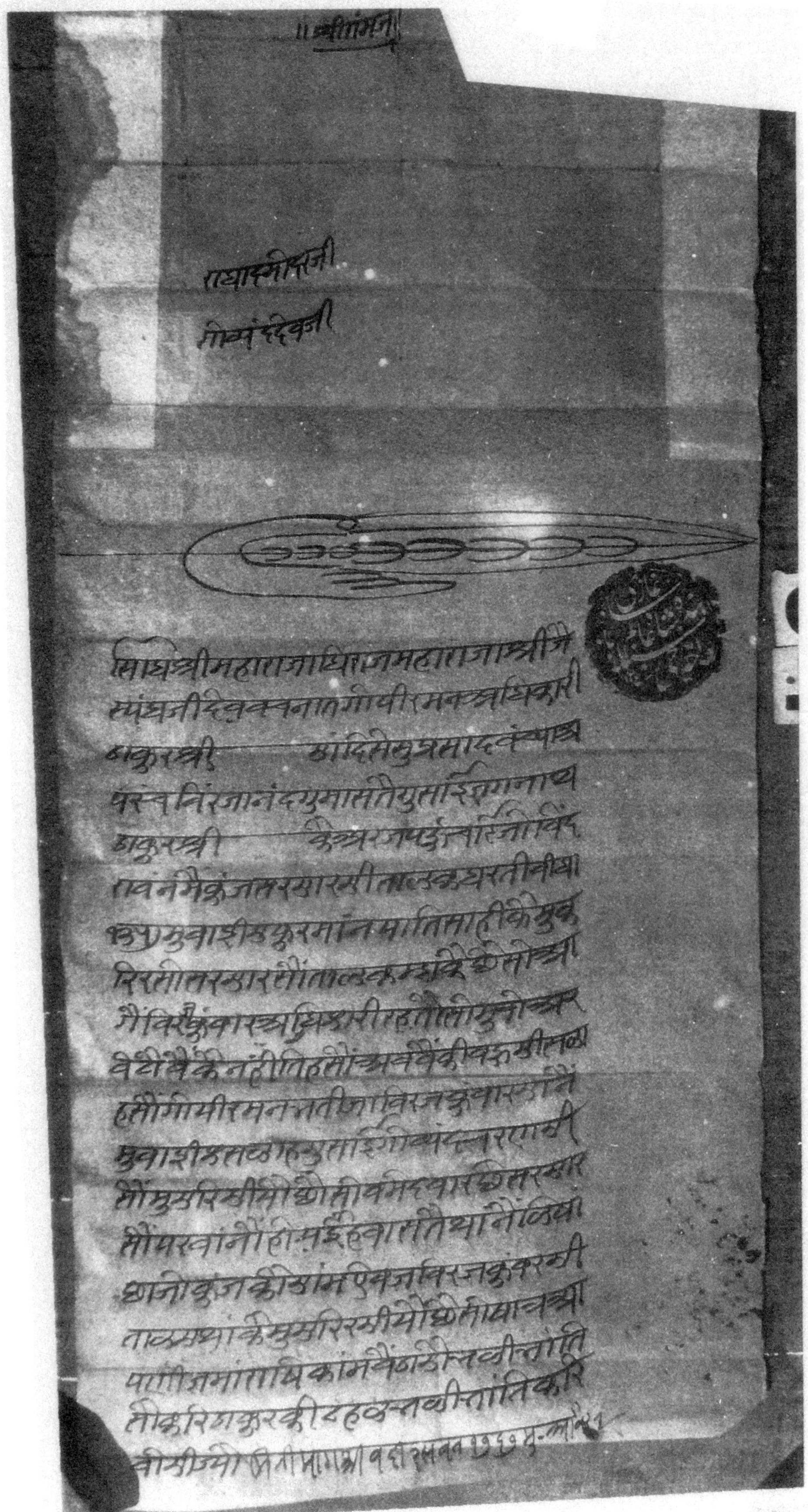

A.H. 1123, 19 Ramazān / 31 October 1711

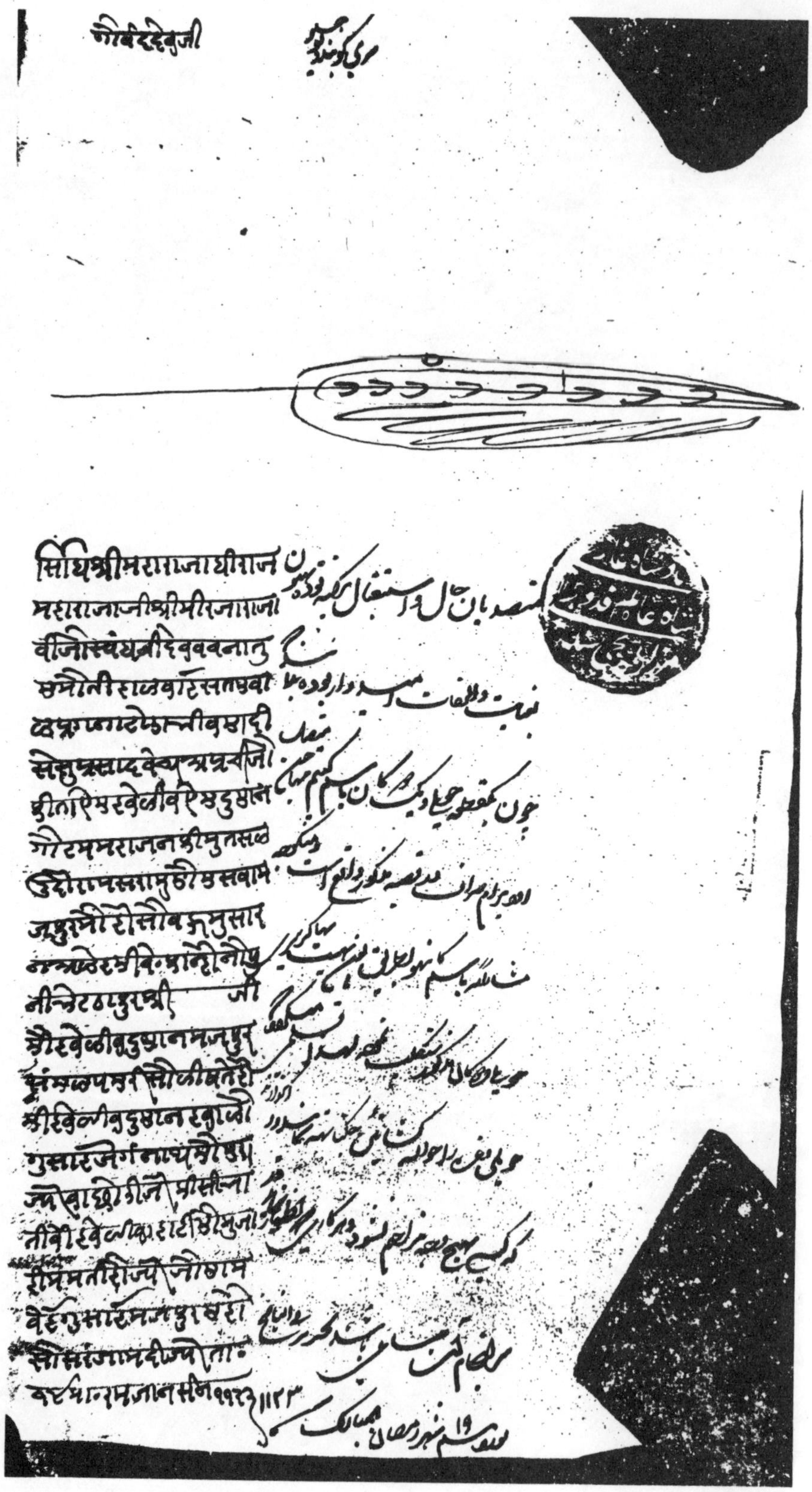

A.H. 1123, 21 Ramazān / 2 November 1711

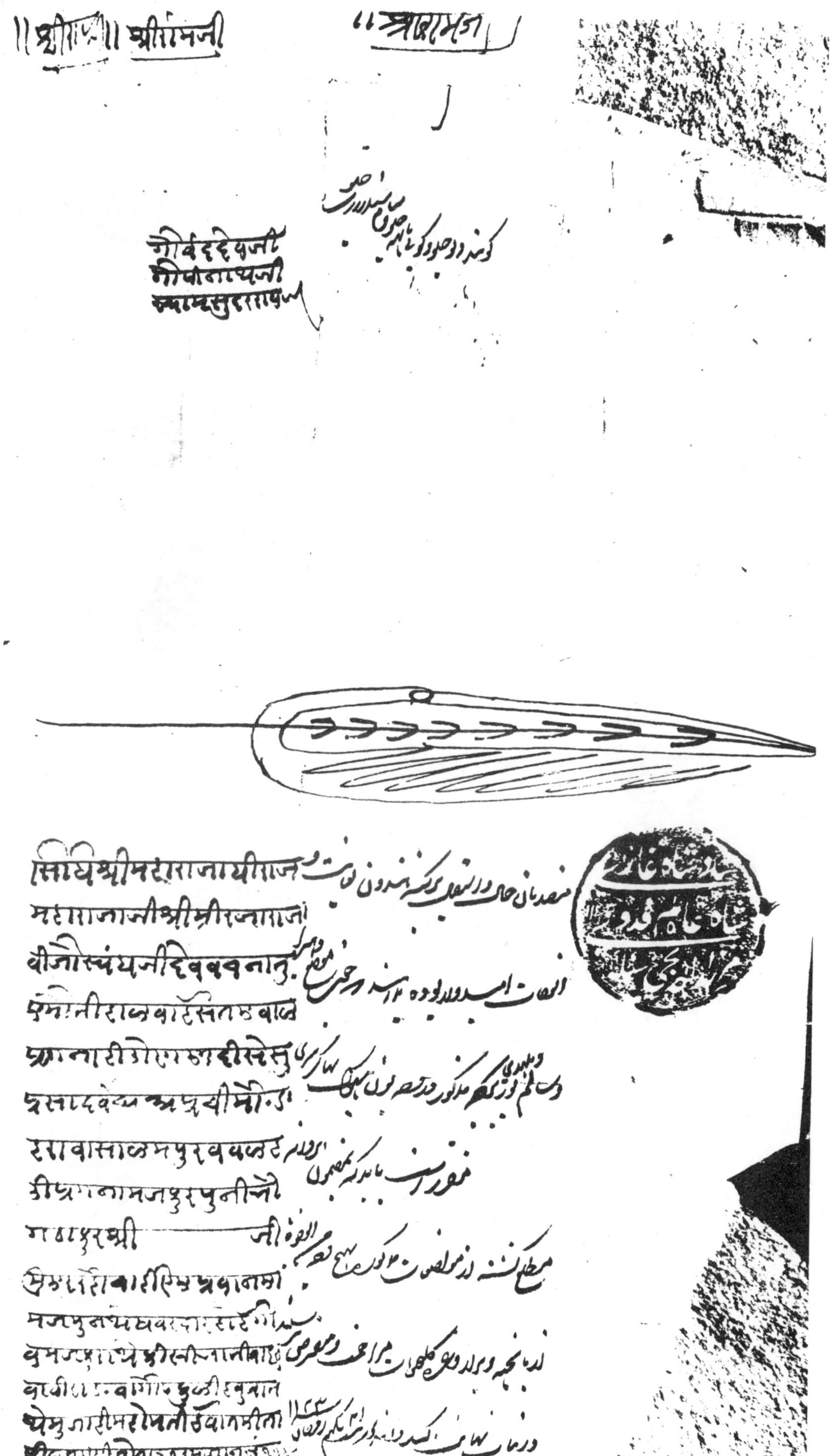

V.S. 1769 / rev.y. 1768, Jyeṣṭha ś. 13 / 6 June 1712

V.S. 1769, Mārgaśiras ś. 5 / 22 November 1712

गोव्यंददेवजी

सिधश्रीमहाराजाधिराजमहाराजाश्रीजैस्यं
घजीदेववचनातगजरूपंथदिसेसुपरसा
[illegible] श्रीपरसंठाकुरश्री डोसेव
गलवांनीदासयतरीलाहोरमैंछैसोदेवेंसी
मारफतठाकुरकैसाळमैंफपडीवगेरहु
[illegible]गिराराबारामैंआवेछैसोराहमी
दसतगवगेरहलवांनीदासफाकेलाम
ल्यापिरमुरायदेवीसीजोआरकांमकाजवे
[illegible]

V.S. 1773, Āṣāḍha ś. 8 / 16 June 1716

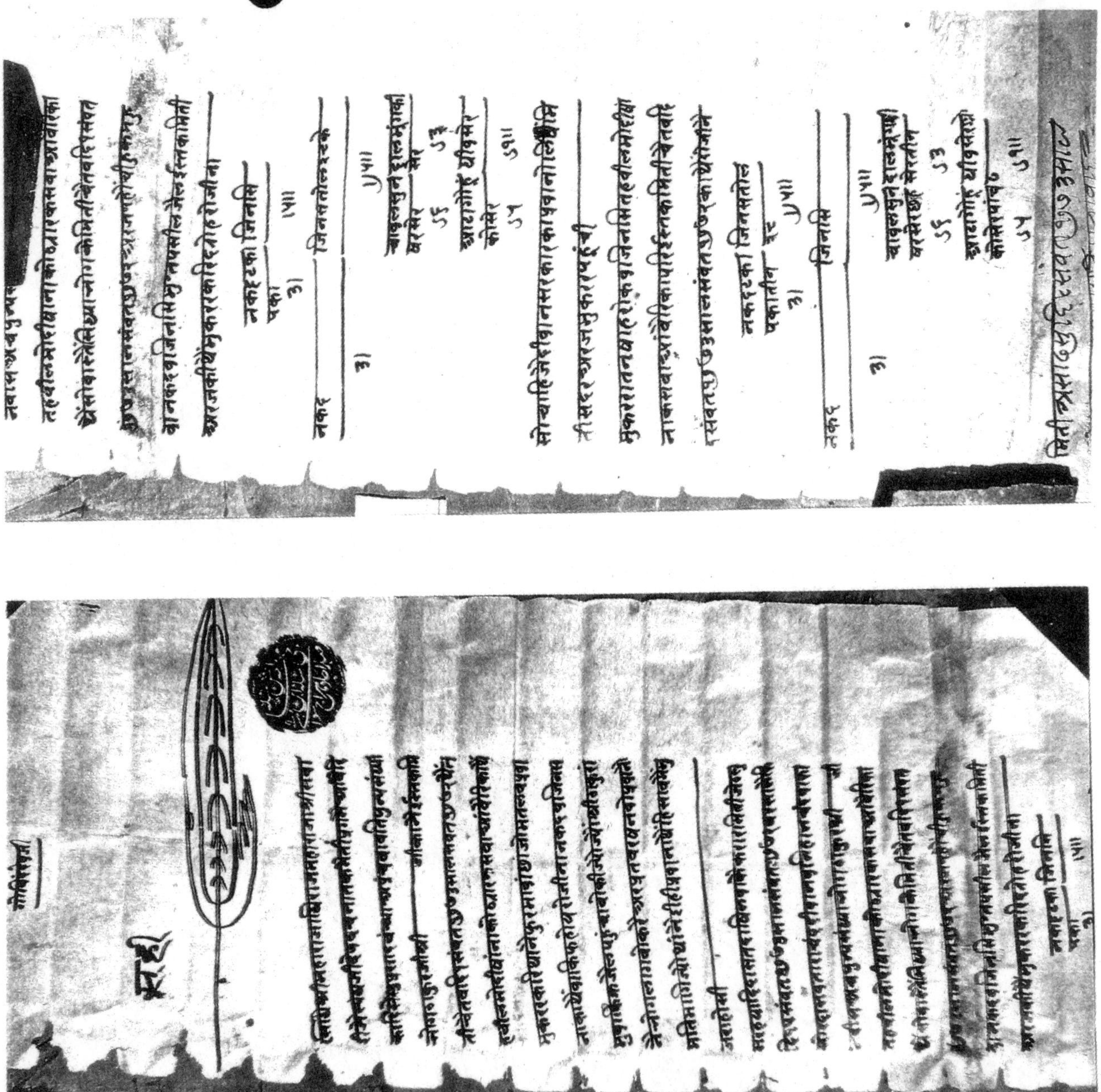

V.S. 1773, Bhādrapada ś. 8 / 14 August 1716

V.S. 1774, Jyeṣṭha ś. 15 / 14 May or 12 June 1717

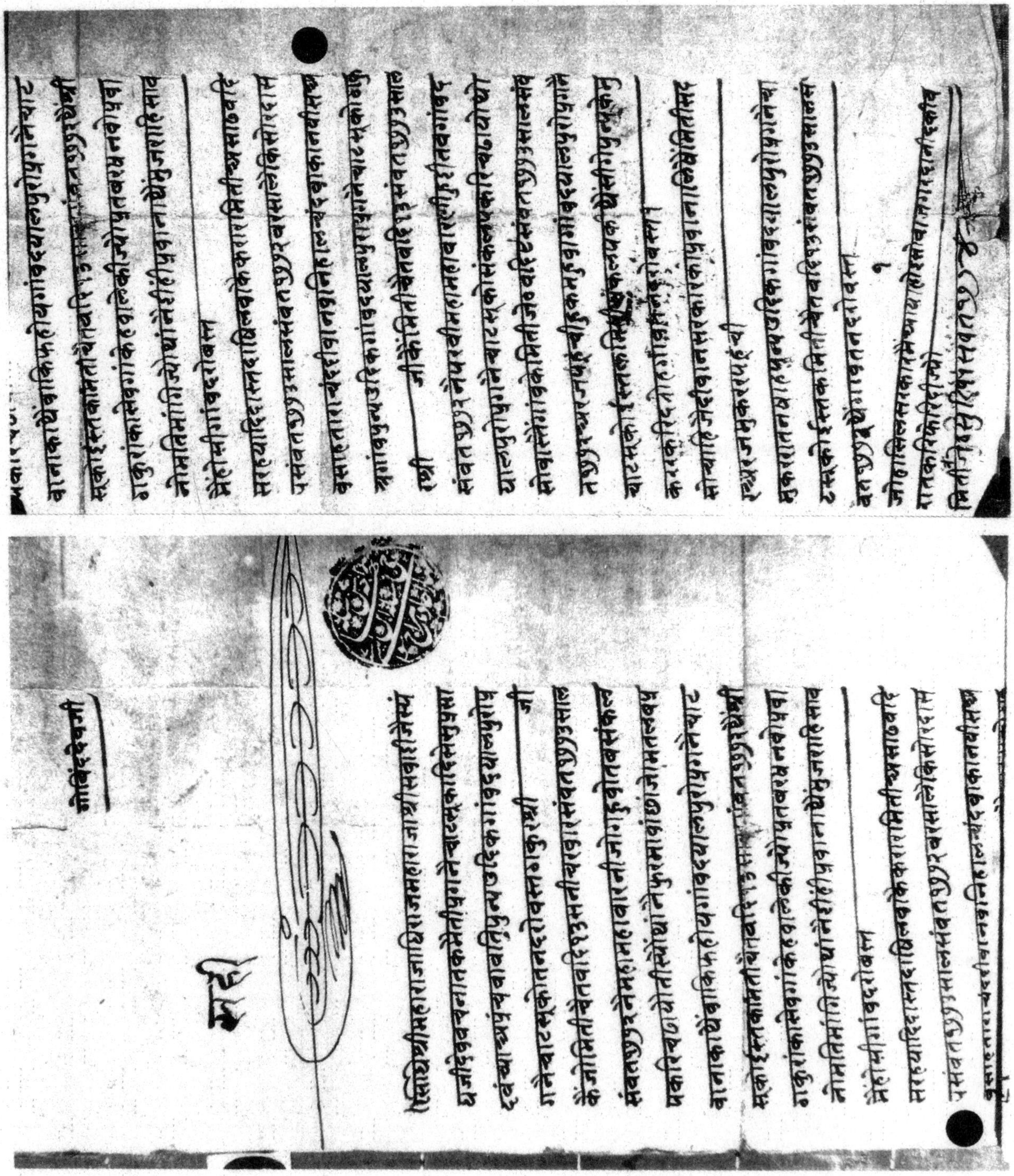

॥श्रीरामजी॥

गोविंददेवजी

।स्वस्ति श्री महाराजाधिराज महाराजा श्री सवाई जै
स्यंघजी देव वचनात किसनराम दिसे सुप्रसाद वंचै
अप्रंच ठाकुर श्री जीकुरो रीपयाहैं ल्गासो
तीस्यों कुरमां वांधां जो सुवारी व वार वरदारी की
सरवराह सेताव करि दीज्यो मीती भादवा सुदी
१५ संवत १७७६

V.S. 1776, Mārgaśiras ś. 3 / 3 December 1719

V.S. 1777, Āśvina ś. 14 / 4 October 1720

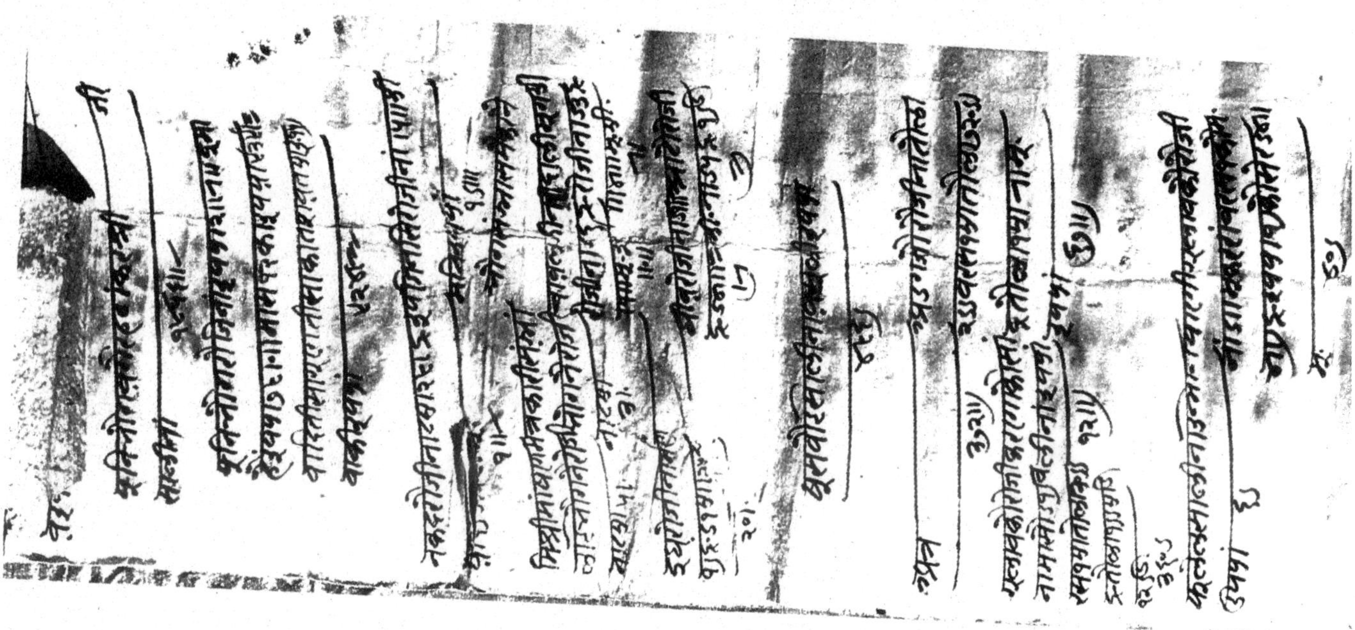

V.S. 1778, Āśvina ś. 1 / 11 September 1721

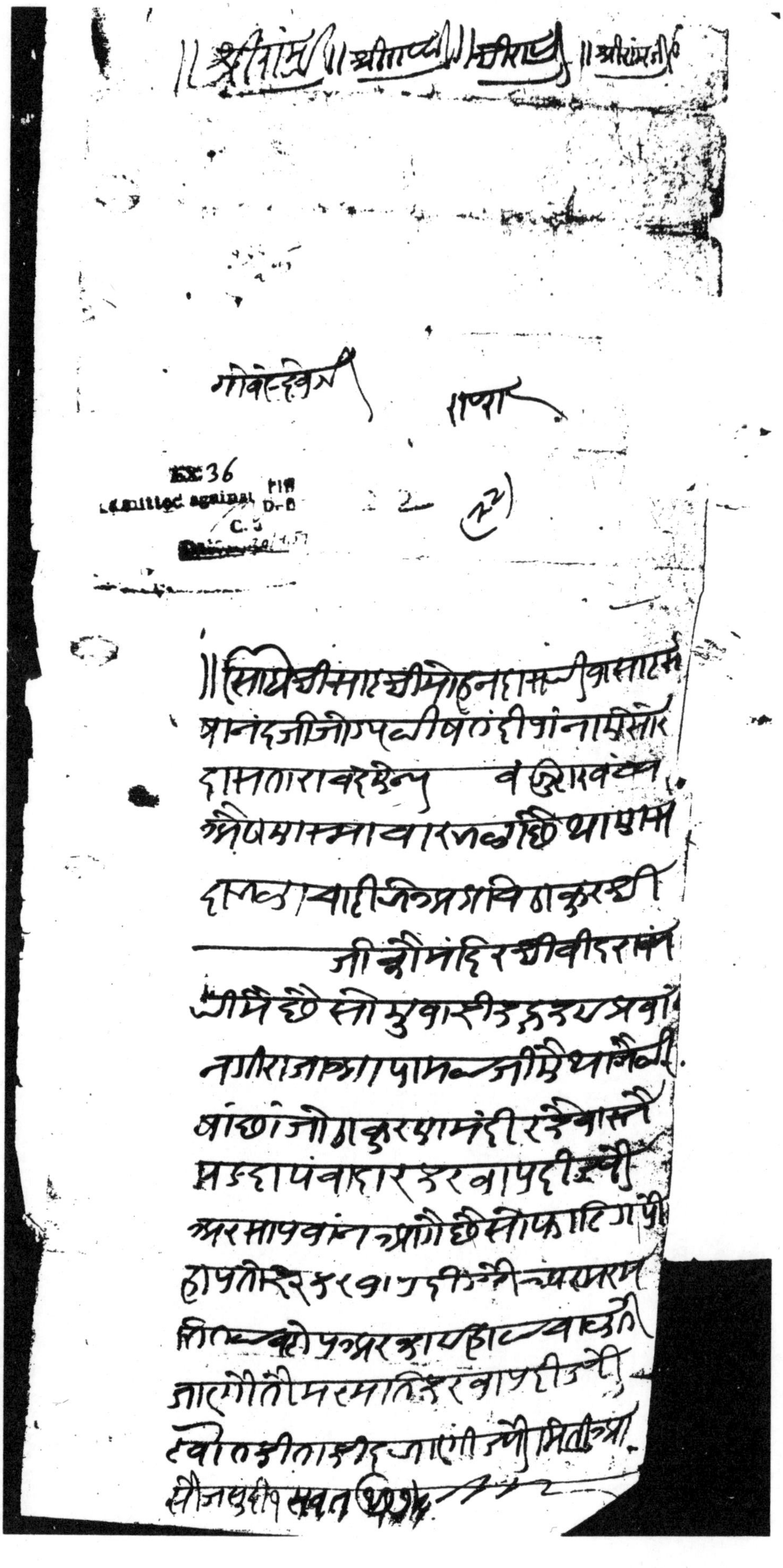

V.S. 1782, Mārgaśiras b. 14 / 22 November 1725

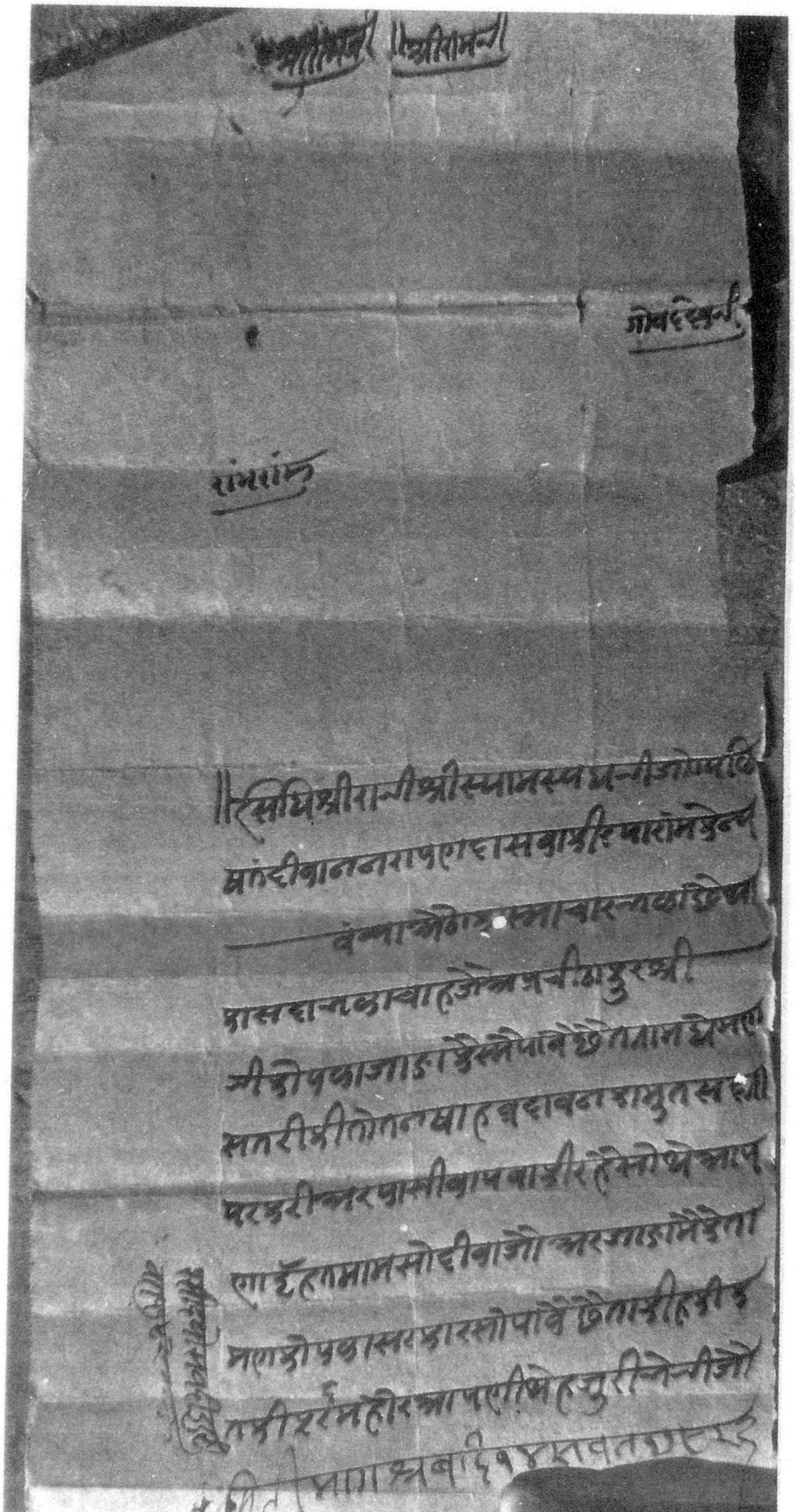

V.S. 1784, Āśvina b. 11 / 31 August 1727

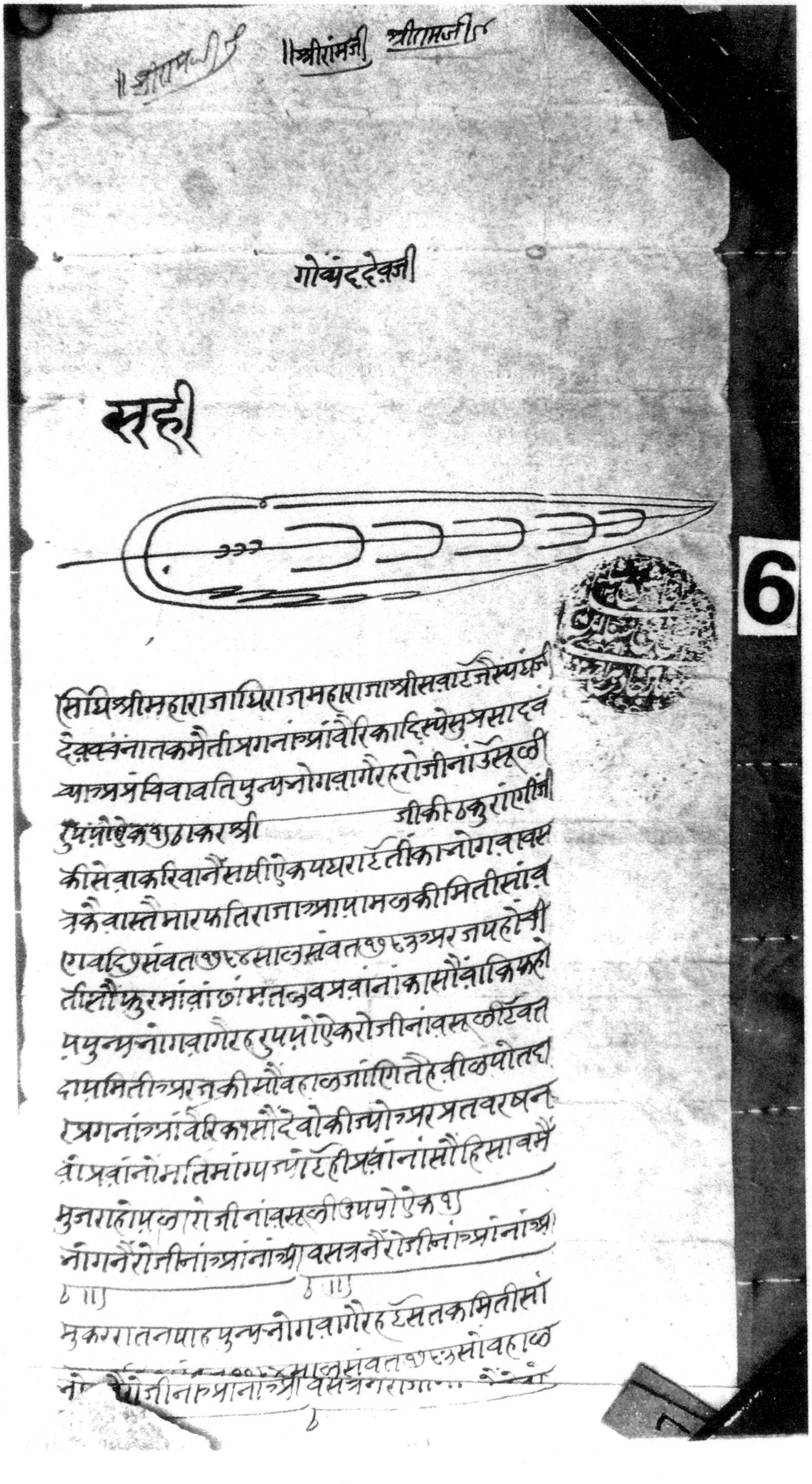

॥श्रीरामजी ॥श्रीरामजी श्रीरामजी

गोव्यंददेवजी

सही

6

सिधिश्रीमहाराजाधिराजमहाराजाश्रीसवाईजैस्यंघजी
देववनातकमैंतीप्रगनांआंबेरिकादिस्येसुप्रसादव
व्यासश्रीसिवावतिपुन्यजोगवागेरहरोजीनांउसूळी
दुंपयोएक १ ठाकरश्री जीकीठकुराणीजी
कीसेवाकरिवानैसम्पीएकपयरारतीकाजोगवाव
त्रकैवास्तैमारफतिराजाश्रीआपामळकीमितीसाव
णवदि संवत १७८४ सालसंवत १७८३ अरजपहोंचीं
तीसौंफुरमावांछांमतलबपरवानाकासौंवाकिफहो
पपुन्यजोगवागेरहरुपयोएकरोजीनांवसूळीदवत
दापमितीअरजकीसौंवहाळजांणितेहवीलपोतदा
रप्रगनांआंबेरिकासौंदेवोकीज्योअरसतवरषनं
वंपरवानोमतिमांगयज्योरहीपरवानांसौंहिसावमैं
मुजराहोपरवारोजीनांवसूळीउपयोएक १
जोगनैरोजीनांआंनाश्री वसत्रनैरोजीनांआंनाश्री
८ ॥ ८ ॥
मुकरराततपाहपुन्यजोगवागेरहरसतकमितीसां
[illegible] सालसंवत १७८३ सौंवहाळ
[illegible] रोजीनांआंनाश्री वसत्रगरा [illegible]
८

6

[illegible]

कीसेवाकरिवानैंसम्ही एकपयरा टतीकान्नोगनसर

त्रकैवास्तेमारफतिराजान्याप्रामककीमितीसांव

णवदि ७ संवत १७६४ सालसंवत १७६३ अरजपहोंनी

तीस्तैभुरमांवांछांमतलबम्रवानांकासौंवाकिफहो

प्रमुन्मुन्नोगवागेरह रुपयो एकरोजीनांवसल्कीरवत

दाप्रमितीअरजकीसोवहाळजांणितेहवीलपोतदा

रप्रगनांआंवेरिकासौंदेवोकीज्योअरसतवरषनं

वांप्रवांनोंमतिमांगपज्यौ रहीप्रवांनांसौंहिसावमैं

मुजराहोयछै रोजीनांवसल्कीरुपयो एक १

नोगनैंरोजीनांआंनांआ वसत्रनैंरोजीनांआंनांआ

० ॥ ० ॥

मुकररातनगाह मुन्मुन्नोगवागेरह दसतकमितीसां

वणवदि ७ संवत १७६४ सालसंवत १७६३ सोवहाळ

जांणिंतेहवीलपोतदाररप्रगनांआंवेरिकासौंदेवो

कीज्यो रोजीनांवसल्कीरुपयो एकअोरंगसाहीगी

(१)

नोगनैंरोजीनांआंनांआ वसत्रनैंरोजीनांआंनांआ

० ० ॥ ॥

स्वस्ति श्री माहाराजाधिराज माहाराजा श्री दरबार सु दि संवत
१८२४ पारीक नरायणदास किरपाराम दीवान वनिहाळ
नें सवाउवान श्रीसथ [illegible] पुन्य जोगवा गैरह ठाकर श्री
जीकी ठकुराणी जी की सेवा के वास्तै एक सबीप
घरा दत्ती [illegible] जोगवा वसन्त के वास्तै मारफत राजा श्री
[illegible] की मिती सावण वदि ५ संवत १८२४ सा [illegible] संवत १८२३
[illegible] महोत्सी कुम [illegible] पुन्य जोगवा गैरह के नां परोजी
नां [illegible] उपपो [illegible] मिती अरज कीधे करि
[illegible] आवेरी पारिक करि [illegible] सो [illegible] दिवा
न सरकार का परवांना लिखे मिती भादवा सुदि १० संवत
१८२४ अरज करार प होजी जोगवा वसन्त के वास्तै
रोजीनां उस [illegible] उपपो ऐ [illegible] रंगसाही ॥छ॥

१)

जोगनै रोजीनां आनां आठ ८ वसन्त नै रोजीनां आना [illegible]

॥) ॥)

[illegible] दिदासांति वमहोरराजा श्री [illegible]
सयतादिवांनसा

मिती आसोज वदि ११ संवत [illegible] श्री [illegible] वरेन्द्र

[illegible] विनैरांम
[illegible] [illegible] कृपारांम दी [illegible] मुस्तोफी हजुरी ॥छ॥
दीवान [illegible] वान [illegible]

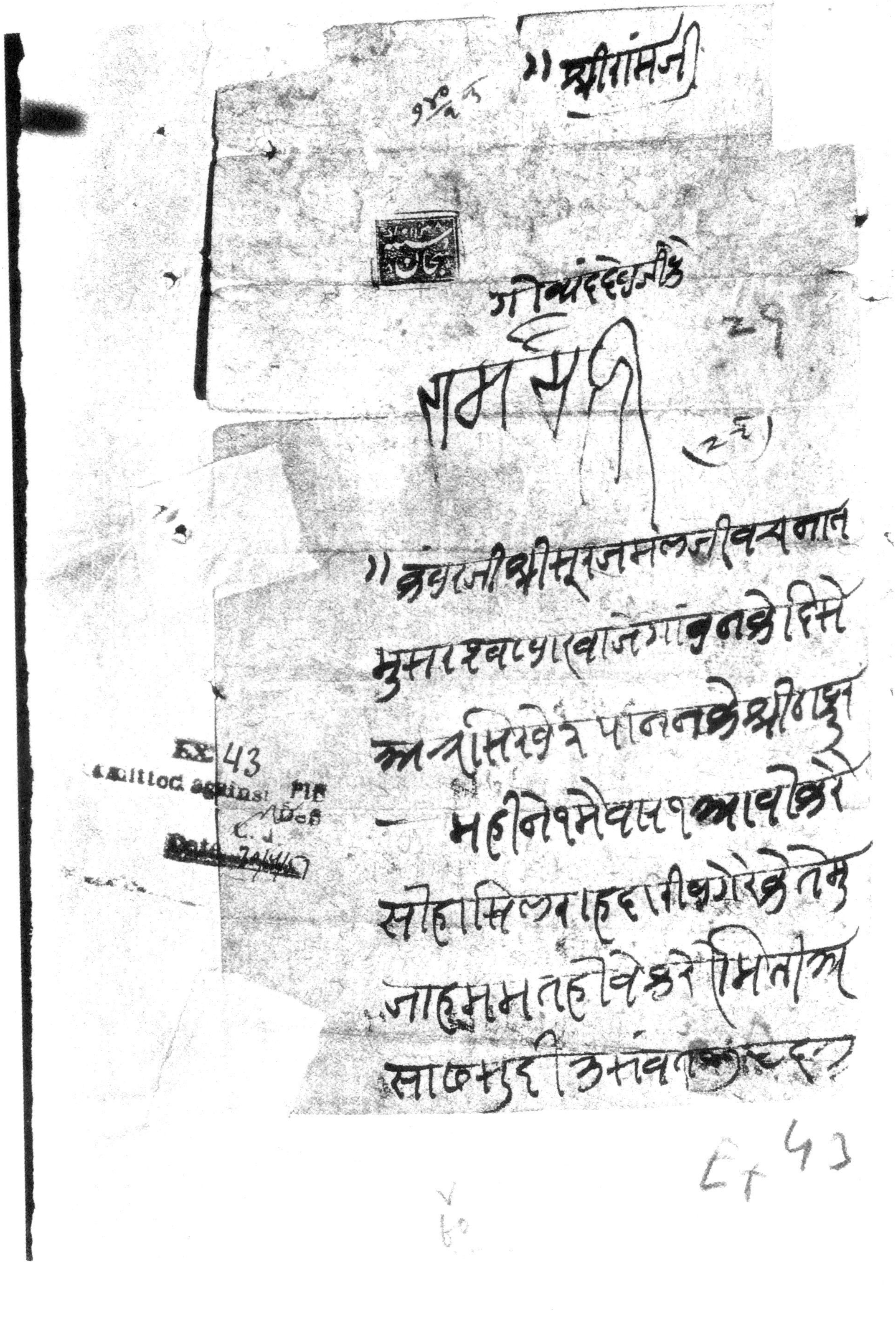

V.S. 1787, Kārttika ś. 3 / 2 November 1730

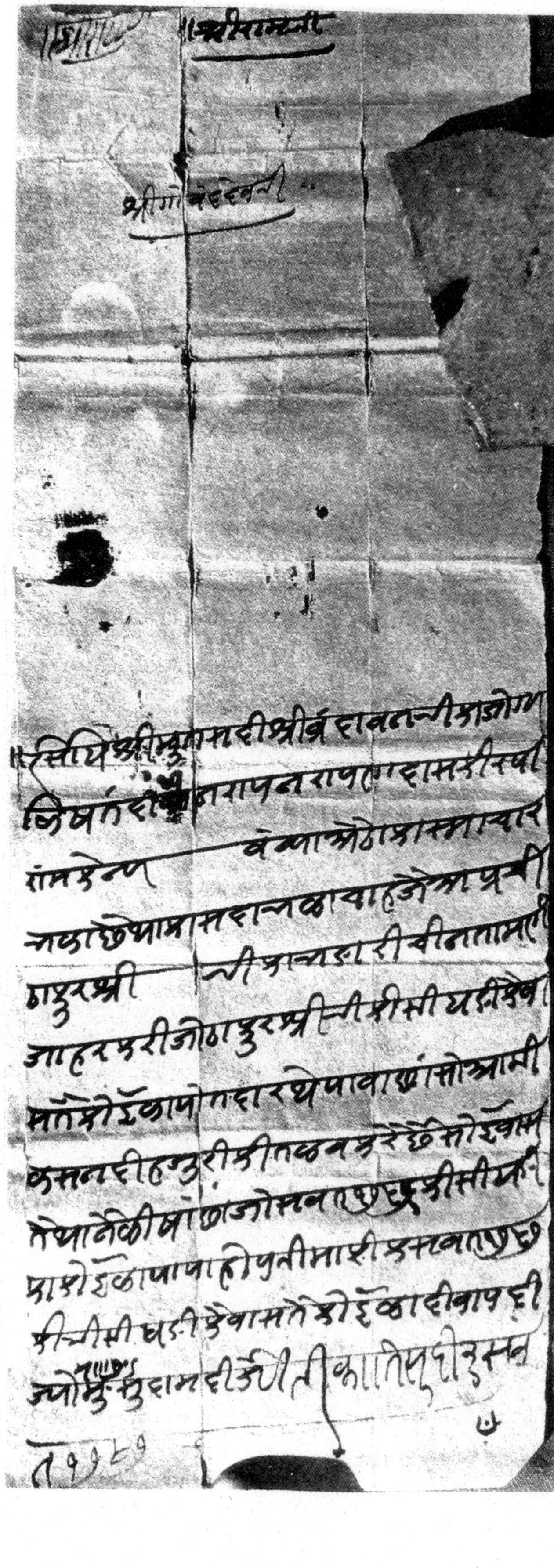

V.S. 1789, Vaiśākha b. 12 / 10 April 1732

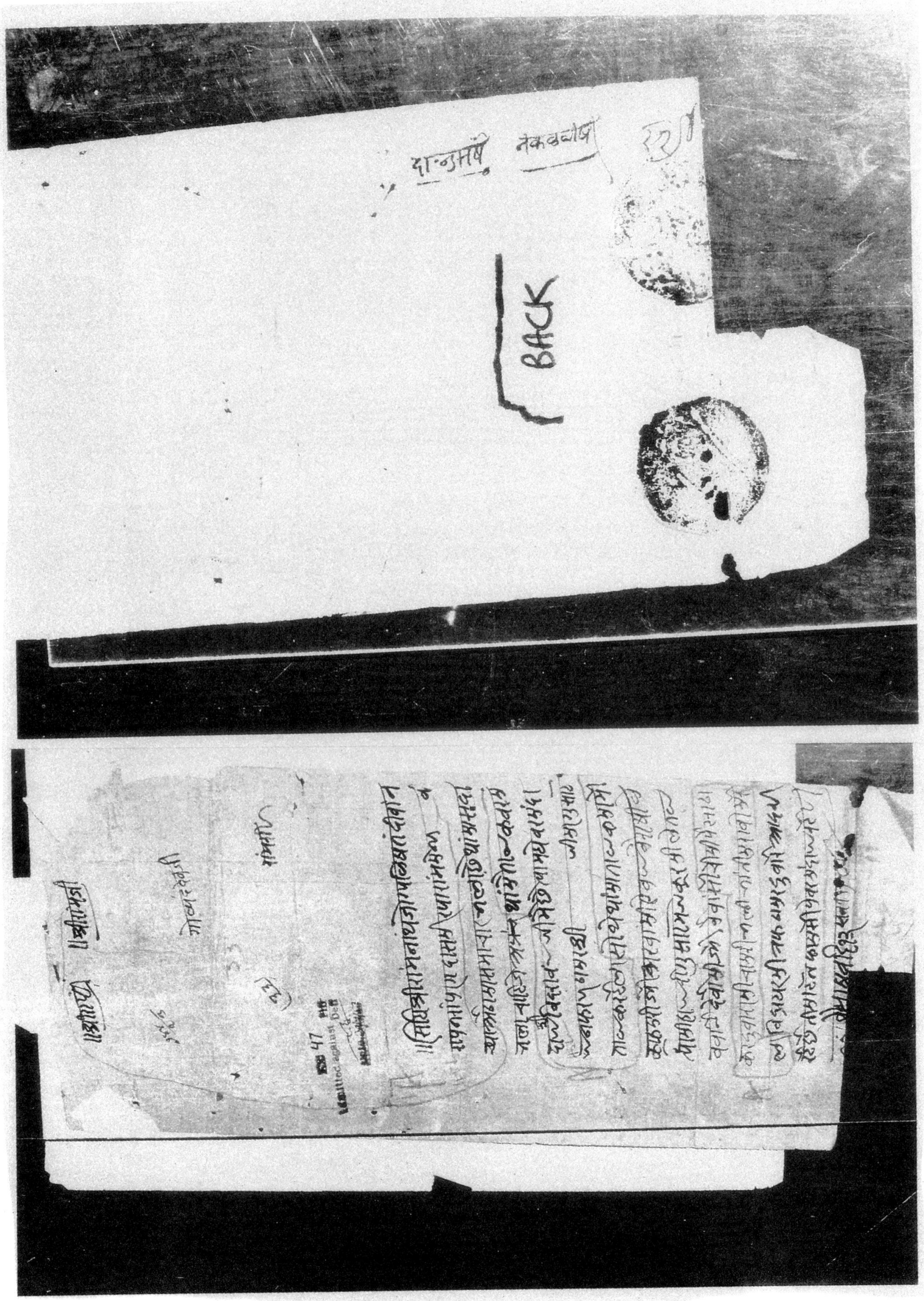

V.S. 1790, Māgha ś. 4 / 27 January 1734

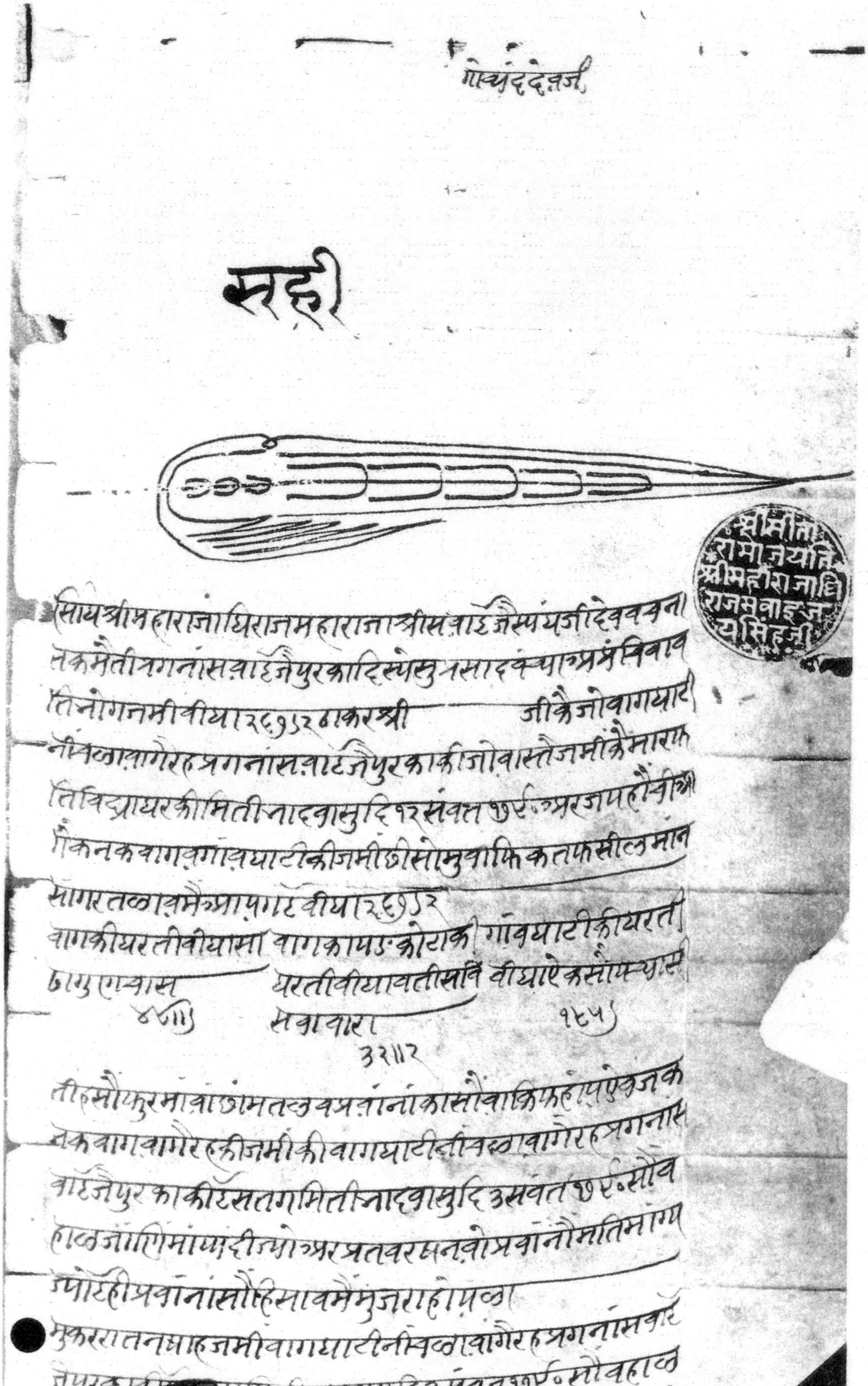

गोव्यंददेवजी

सही

श्री सीता रामो जयति श्री महाराजाधिराज सवाई जयसिंहजी

सिधश्री महाराजाधिराज महाराजा श्री सवाई जैस्यंघजी देववचना
त कमैती अगनां सवाई जैपुर का दिस्यै सुप्रसाद वंच्या अप्रंच विवाव
ति नो गनमी वीघा २६॥२ ठाकर श्री जी कै जो बाग घाटी
नी मिख्वा वगेरह अगनां सवाई जैपुर का कै जो वास्तै जमी कै भाराम
ति विद्याधर की मिती भादवा सुदि १२ संवत १७९० अरज पहौंची श्री
जी कै नकबाग वगाव घाटी की जमी छी सो मुवाफिक तफसील मान
सागर तळाव मैं आपगार वीघा २६॥२

बाग की धरती वीघा सा ढागु ग्यास	बाग का पड कोटा का धरती वीघा वतीसा वि	गांव घाटी की धरती वीघा एक सो प्च्यासी
४७॥	सवा वारा	१८५

३२॥२

तीहसौ फुरमावा छा मतवव अगनां का सो वाकिफ हाय एवज क
त कबाग वगेरह की जमी की बाग घाटी की मिख्वा वगेरह अगनां स
वाई जैपुर का कीरसतग मिती भादवा सुदि ३ संवत १७९० सौ व
हाळ जांणि मांपरदी अब अर प्रतवरसन वो अवांनौ मति मांग
ज्यो रही अवांनां सो हिसाव मैं मुजरा होयला
मुकररा तन मा ह जमी बाग घाटी नी मिख्वा वागेरह अगनां सवाई
जैपुर का [illegible] गामिती भादवा सुदि ३ संवत १७९० सौ वहाळ

सिध श्री महाराजाधिराज महाराजा श्री सवाई जैस्यंघजी देव वचनात
तकमैं तीत्र गनांस वाई जेपुर का दिसं सुप्रसाद पत्र प्रमाणे
तिनां गनमीनी बीघा २६।।२ ठाकर श्री जीकै जो बाग घाटी
[illegible] गेरह प्रगना सवाई जेपुर का कांजांवास्ते जमीं कै मारा
[illegible] मती भादवा सुदि ९ संवत १७९८ [illegible]
[illegible] जमीं छीसां मुवाफिक तफसील मान

[illegible] बीघा २६।।२
[illegible] बाग का [illegible] गांव घाटी [illegible]

[illegible] धरती बीघा [illegible] बीघा [illegible]

४७।।। सम्रावारा १८५।

३२।।२

[illegible] जमीं की बाग घाटी [illegible] गेरह प्रगना
[illegible] जेपुर का [illegible] मिती भादवा सुदि ३ संवत १७९९ सो
[illegible] मांगदीजो [illegible]
[illegible] मुजरा है [illegible]
[illegible] जमी बाग घाटी [illegible] गेरह प्रगना सवाई
जेपुर का [illegible] मिती भादवा सुदि ३ संवत १७९९ सो [illegible]
[illegible] मुवाफिक तफसील मांगदीजो बीघा दो [illegible]
[illegible]

२६।।२

घाटी [illegible] बाग [illegible] की जमीं बाग [illegible] की [illegible] की जमी
बीघा [illegible] पड कोटा [illegible] की
धागु [illegible]

७।। ४९।।।२

बाग बीघा सोला पड कोटा की
१६। बतीस [illegible]
[illegible]
३३।।।२

[illegible] की जा [illegible]
[illegible] की जमी [illegible]
[illegible] बीघा दो [illegible]
[illegible]

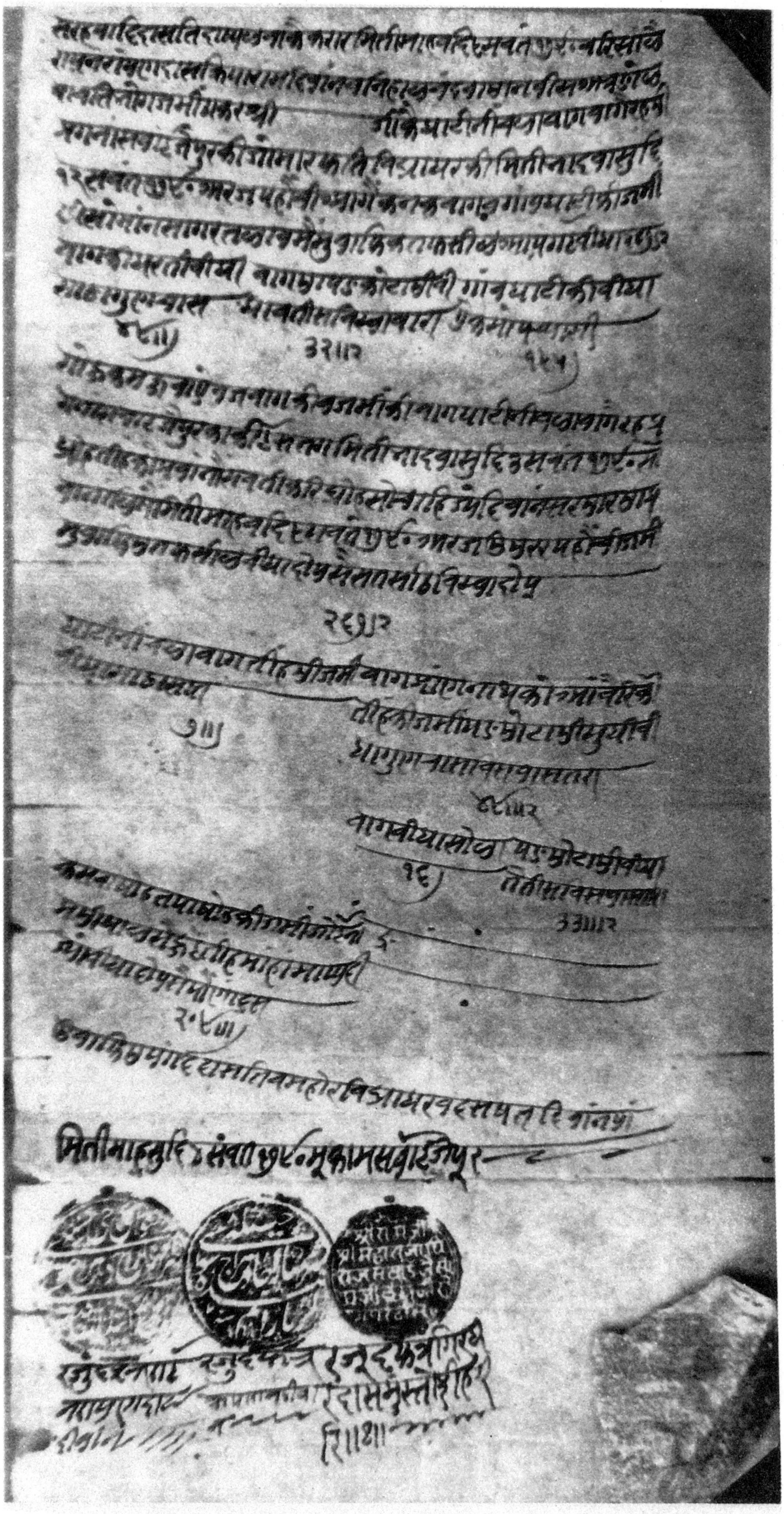

मिती माह सुदि ३ संवत १७९० मुकाम सवाई जैपुर

॥श्रीरांमजी

गोव्यंददेवजी

सही

श्रीसीता
रामो जयति
श्रीमहाराजाधि
राज सवाई ज
यसिंह नी

॥सिधिश्रीमहाराजाधिराजमहाराजाश्रीसवाईजैस्यंघजी
देववचनातमुतसदीहजूरिवादेसकांदिसेसुप्रसादवंच्या
अप्रंचिसरकारमैंमालवसाएरराहदारीवपेसकसषाल
सावजागीरदारांवकरलोगवइजाराकाप्रगनांवागैरहदरो
बस्तजमांकीज्योरुपयाएकहजारपरिरुपयोएक१)नेरा
करश्री जीकाआंनांच्यारिजैरगुसांईरांमस
रणजीअधिकारीश्रीजीकाकीईवतदायसंवत१७९६थेमु
कररकरीछैसोसिवायजमांसरकारतैहसीलकरिश्रीजीकै
भंडारपोंहचावोकरौअरवकरलोगांसौंअठमाहाहोपावतौ
होयतौसौंअठमाहाकैहिसावलीजोअरजोछमाहाहोपावतौ
होयतौसौंछमाहाकैहिसावजोमिकीज्यातैहसीलकरिपो
हचायद्यौहमितीमाहवदि५संवत१७९७मुकामअदे

rev.y. 1801 / V.S. 1802, Bhādrapada b. 5 / 6 August 1745
(Gaṅgārāmpuro-vās Khijūryā)

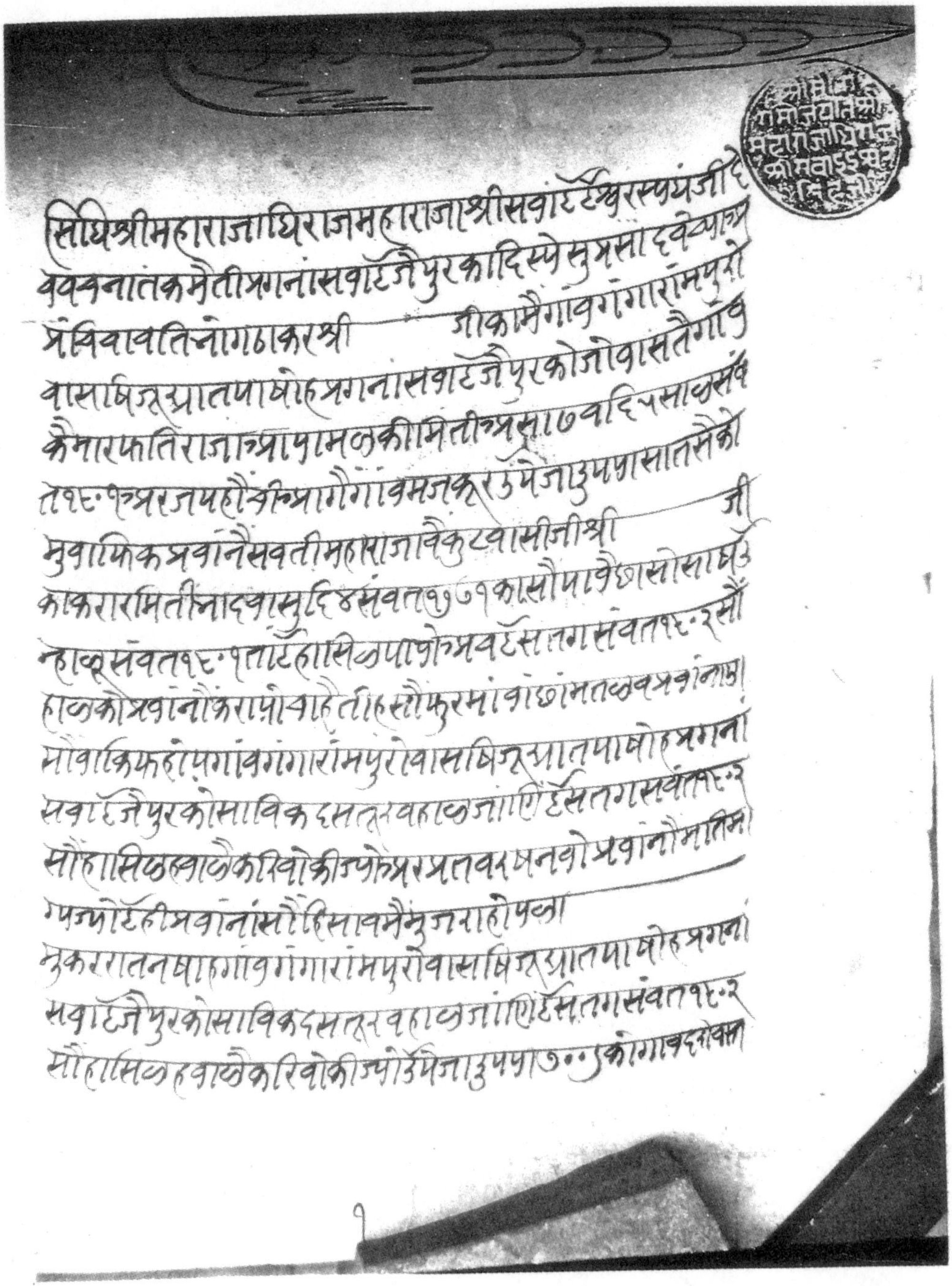
सिधिश्रीमहाराजाधिराजमहाराजाश्रीसवाईईश्वरसिंघजीदे
ववचनातकमेतीम्रगनांसवाईजैपुरकादिस्पेसुप्रसादवंच्यात्र
प्रंखिवावतिन्नागठाकरश्री जीकामैंगांवगंगारांमपुरो
वासाबिज्रमातपाबोहम्रगनांसवाईजैपुरकोजोवासतैगांव
कैमारफातिराजाप्रापामलकीमितीम्रसा७वदि५सावसं
त१८०५प्ररजयहौंश्रीप्रागैगांवमजकूरउपैजाउपपासातसैको जी
मुवाफिकप्रवानैसवतीमहाराजावैकुंठवासीजीश्री
काकरारमितीभादवासुदि४संवत१७७१कासोपावैछासोसाधेउ
न्हाकसंवत१८०१ताईहासिलपापोम्रवईसतगसंवत१८०२सौं
हालकोप्रवानोकरापोवाहेतीहसोफुरमांवोछांमतलवप्रवांनाउ
मोवाफिकहांपगांवगंगारांमपुरोवासबिज्रमातपाबोहम्रगनां
सवाईजैपुरकोसाविकदसतूरवहालजांणिईसतगसंवत१८०२
सौंहासिलबहालकरिवोकीज्योप्रसतवरसनवोप्रवानोमांतीम
गपज्योईहीप्रवांनांसौंहिसावमैंमुजराहोयला
न्हकरसतनघाहगांवगंगारांमपुरोवासबिज्रमातपाबोहम्रगनां
सवाईजैपुरकोसाविकदसतूरवहालजांणिईसतगसंवत१८०२
सौंहासिलबहालकरिवोकीज्योउपैजाउपपा७००)कोगांवदनोवस

rev.y. 1801 / V.S. 1802, Bhādrapada b. 5 / 6 August 1745 (Govindpuro)

॥श्रीरामजी॥ ॥श्रीरामजी ॥श्रीरामजी

गोव्यंददेवजी

सवाईजैस्यघजी

सही

सिधिश्रीमहाराजाधिराजमहाराजाश्रीसवाईईश्वरस्यघजी
देववचनात कमेतीप्रगनांसवाईजैपुरकादिस्येसुप्रसादवच्या
श्रीप्रसिवाबातिजोगठाकरश्री जीकेसाकीनांउर्स
कीरुपया१२००)मैंगांवगोव्यंदपुरोतपाषोहप्रगनासवाईजैपु
रकोजोवासतैगांवकेमारफतिराजाआयामलकीमितीअसा
ढवदि५साकसंवत१८०१अरजपहोंचीजोगांवमजकूरमुवा
फिकप्रवांनैसवतीमहाराजावैकुंठवासीजीश्री जीका
करारतारीष१जुमादलअवलसन११९२कासोंयाछैछासोहा
सिलसंवत१८०१तांईपायोअववहालकोप्रवांनौकरापोस्याहै
तीहसौहजूरमांवाछोमतलबप्रवांनाकासौवाकिमहोयसाकीना
वसूकीरुपयाबारासैमैगांवगोव्यंदपुरोतपाषोहप्रगनासवा
ईजैपुरकोसाविकदसतूरबहालजांणिईसतगसंवत१८०२सौं
हासिलहवाकैकरिबोकीज्योअरप्रतबरषनवोप्रवांनौमतिमा
गज्योटहीप्रवांनासौंहिसाबमैंमुजराहोयच्या
मुकररतनषाहगांवगोव्यंदपुरोतपाषोहप्रगनासवाईजैपुर
कोसाविकदसतूरबहालजांणिईसतगसंवत१८०२सौंहासिल
हवाकैकरिबोकीज्योतनदरोवस्तमैसाकीनांउर्सकीउपभगवानसी

१२००)

सरहपादिदासाति दाखिल पाछे मुरारा मिती सावण वदि १ संवात १८०२ रसाव्हसे
वत १८० १ पारिमाखै रापनवां पुरादास फतेराम दिवान वनिहाल चंद खा जान
वीसरूप त्रडीक जोग गढ़ रसी — श्री गोपाल सोतेल छेम न फतिराम
आपापम श्री मिती मसाढ वदि पसाव्ह संवत १८०१ आरज पहों बीजो साथी
नांउ सूखी छिपा ₹२००) में गांव गरेस्यू दं पुरोत पाखो ह्मगनां सभ छेजेउर
सोख्या पिछमयां नै सेवा तीम्हराज साबे मूटे पासी गीत्री — श्री ठराव्ही
लेस गुमादा छि सम्य छान ११२ मासों पाछे छासो संवत १८०१ ताहैमाछे
मवहाव्ह सो भरानी मराणे गाहे सो कृष्णमका गाटे सातग संवत १८०२ रसोत्र
पैसो सम्पती हाख्य भोमरसो स्वा हिपे दिवान सरमार भाभ वानां पीवे मिती
सावण वदि ११ सवत १८०२ साव्ह संवत १८०१ भराजा भरर पहें बांगा वमज्ज
रतानद मेवच राउ हस्ती डुपपा वारानै

१२००)

६ वाकिम पादि दसाति मेद मधतराजा करणा भामवच दिवानेपा —

मिती भादवा वदि ५ मा० सं० १८०१ मुकाम मवाह जैपूर

रजुसूत्राल रजुहस्त | सूरफत फती
सहदाल दीवान | शोगाम ही | मनुसा हरिसी
वान

गोवर्द्धनदेवजी

सवाईजैस्यंघजी

सही

श्री सित
रामजयति श्री
महाराजाधिराज
श्री सवाई ईसर
सिंह जी

सिधिश्रीमहाराजाधिराजमहाराजाश्रीसवाईईसरस्यंघजीदेव
वचनातकमैतीप्रगनांसवाईजैपुरकादिस्येसुप्रसादवच्याअप्र
प्रंविवावातियासवराईठाकरश्री जीकीगायपयासव
रैसांमारफातिराजाप्राप्रामककीमित्तीअसाढवदि५साल
संवत१८०१अप्रजयहौबीजेरेगांपांचखरवाकैवासतैमांगष
लावपांणीढोलगिरदत्तलावमांनसरोवरकोमुवाफिकप्रवां
नैसवतीमहाराजावैकुंटवासीजीश्री जीकरारमिती
आसोजवदि१३संवत१७८०कासौपावैछासोमितीभादवा
सुदि२साल्संवत१८०१ताईगायपवरीअवहालकोप्रवांनोक
रापाहलैहीहसोंकुरनांवाछांमनखवप्रवानांकासौवाकि
फहांयगायखरवानैमांगधलावपांणीढालगिरदत्तलाव
मांनसरोवरकीसाविकदस्तूरवहालजांणिरैसतगामिती
भादवासुदि३संवत१८०२सौगायपखरवादीज्योअरसप्रतवर
प्रवांप्रवांनौमातिमांगपज्यो
ऊमरांतनघाहमागधलावपांणीढालगिरदत्तलावमांन
सरोवरकोसाविकदस्तूरवहालजांणिरैसतगामितीभादवा
सुदि३संवत१८०२सौगायपखरवादीज्यो

सरहपादिदासतिदाबिच्छम्हे म्हरा मिती सावण वदि १ संवत १८०४ वरी
सावे रापुनराप णदास फते राम दिवान [illegible] दवा [illegible] नवी सगत्र [illegible]
वराठ ठामस्थी जीरा क्षेत्र स्तोमाद फतिराज [illegible] मिती सा[illegible]
वदि १ साव्छ संवत १८०० [illegible] पा [illegible] राव [illegible] भागधव
पाणी छावगिरदत्वा भूमान् [illegible] भवाने सवती महाराजा [illegible]
कुट्या सतीथी जी [illegible] वदि ३ संवत १८०१ [illegible]
[illegible] सोनाद भासु [illegible] साव्छ संवत १८०१ [illegible] वहा [illegible]
वतीभ्रराणे [illegible] नौहा [illegible] पो सोवाहि
ज्यो दिगावसुरभातमा [illegible] मीती सावण वदि १ साव्छ संवत १८०
गछिमरदपटो श्री भागपव्छा पाणी छावागिरदत्वा भूमान करो [illegible]

१ पूा दि दासाती मैं [illegible] गपरणा अदि वांनगाान
मिती भादवा वदि ५ सा० सं० १८०१ मुकाम सव ई ज्जूर

श्री रामजी
श्री महाराजाधिरा
ज श्री सवाई ईश्व
र[illegible]जी सेवक कराप
तेराम दास

श्री रामजी
श्री महाराजाधि
राज श्री सवाई ईश्व
रसिंहजी सेवक
फतेराम

श्री रामजी
श्री महाराजाधि
राज श्री ईश्वर सि
घजी सेवक फ
तेराम

नजुदकु त्रापनां [illegible] — नजुहकत्रु फतेरा
पणेद्रासदीवान [illegible] गोगामदीवा — ममुसोरी हिजरा
ना

[illegible]

rev.y. 1801 / V.S. 1802, Bhādrapada b. 5 / 6 August 1745 (Sālimpur)

गोव्यंददेवजी

सवाईजैस्यंघजी

सही

सिधिश्रीमहाराजाधिराजमहाराजाश्रीसवाईजैस्यंघजीदेव
वचनात कमैतीप्रगनांहिंडौणकादिस्येसुप्रसादवंच्याअप्रंचविचा
वतिलोगलकरश्री जीकेगांवसालिमपुरअघरतीवी
याद प्रगनांहिंडौणकासोवासतेगांववागेरहकेमारफाति
राजअपापामलकीमितीअसाढवदि५संवत१८०२सालसंव
त१८०१अरजपहोंचीआगेगांवमजकूरवागेरहप्रगनांहिंडौण जी
कामुवाफिकपरवांनैसवतीमहाराजावैकुंठवासीजीश्री
करारमितीजेठवदि१०संवत१७७९कासौंपावेछैसोहासिलसा
षडउन्हालूसंवत१८०१तांईपापोअवहालकोप्रयांनौंसवतीकै
रापांवाहेछैतीहसौंफुरमांवांछांमतलवपरवानांकासौंवा
किफहोपगांवसालिमपुरदरोवसतवायरतीवीयासाठि
प्रगनांहिंडौणकाईसतगसंवत१८०२सौंसाविकदसतूर
वहालजांणिहासिलहवालेकरिवोकीज्योअरप्रतवरषन
वोप्रवांनौंमतिमांगज्योईहीप्रवानासौंहिसावमैमुजराहोयछै
मुकररातनषाहगांववागेरहप्रगनांहिंडौणकाईसतगसंव
त१८०२सौंसाविकदसतूरवहालजांणिहासिलहवालेके
रिवोकीज्योगांववागेरह
गांवसालिमपुरप्रगनांहिंडौं घरतीकसवाहिंडौणकीवी
णकांतनदरोवसतऐन यासाठि

१०

१

सही पादिदासतिहासिन्नकाकेरानमितीसांवणमवदि १ संवत १८०२ साछ

सेपात १८० पखिसाछैरापनरां पणदास फतेरांमदिवांन मिहाकुनदेवाजान

वीसमनदङोछलोगगांववागेर हकम स्त्री जीमाके गासुतमार

फातिराजाकाप्रामछ जीमितीमासाछवदि ५ सवत १८० २ साछमनात १८

चमरजापहोपीजिजोगांवसाछिमपुरदरोगनसातन अरतीबीमासमाठिमसत

हिङौणमजीमुवाफिमुप्रवानेसेवतीमहाराजाधिकुटवासीतीवी

करायमितीजिठवादि १० संवत १७७४ मासोपाविछ्मातो मछउन्हाकेसपात

१८० पताईहासिछपापोगमबहछमोगवांनोसेवातीअरापोजहैसो

कुप्रमकु गासवत १८० २ मासाछसोप्रवांनोसेवतीम रिछोहसोस्वाहि

ज्पेदिवानसिरमारअपजगतांविपेमितीसावणवदि २ सवंत १८० २

साछमनात १८० चेगमरजछिमासरपहोमी गांववागेरह

गांवसाछिमपुर परगनांहिङोण परतीकम पाहिङौ णमीवीयासाठि

मोतनदासेविसात

१ . . ६०

खवाफिमपादिदासातिमैदे [illegible] राजाकाप्रामछवादिवानकान

मितीभादवावदी ५ सा० सं० १८० मुकाम मनोहरपुर

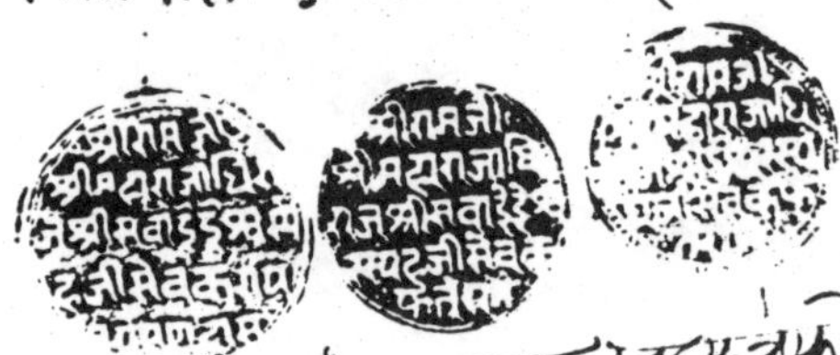

रजूहदफ्तरापनोर ३ दस्तनपु रजूहदफ्तर फतेरां

पणदासदीवान जीरांमदीवान मुमुसतापीहरजूरी

rev.y. 1801 / V.S. 1802, Bhādrapada b. 5 / 6 August 1745 (Sekhpuro Baṛo)

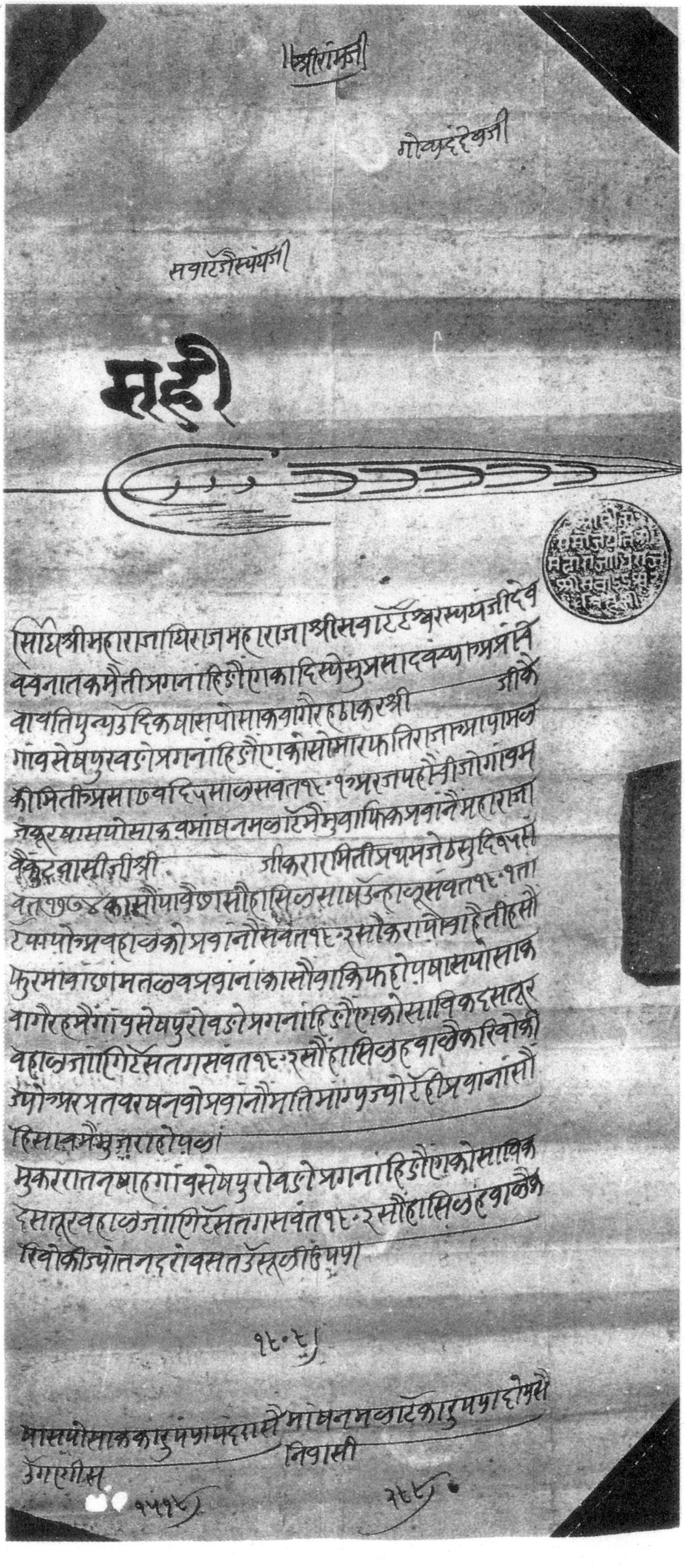

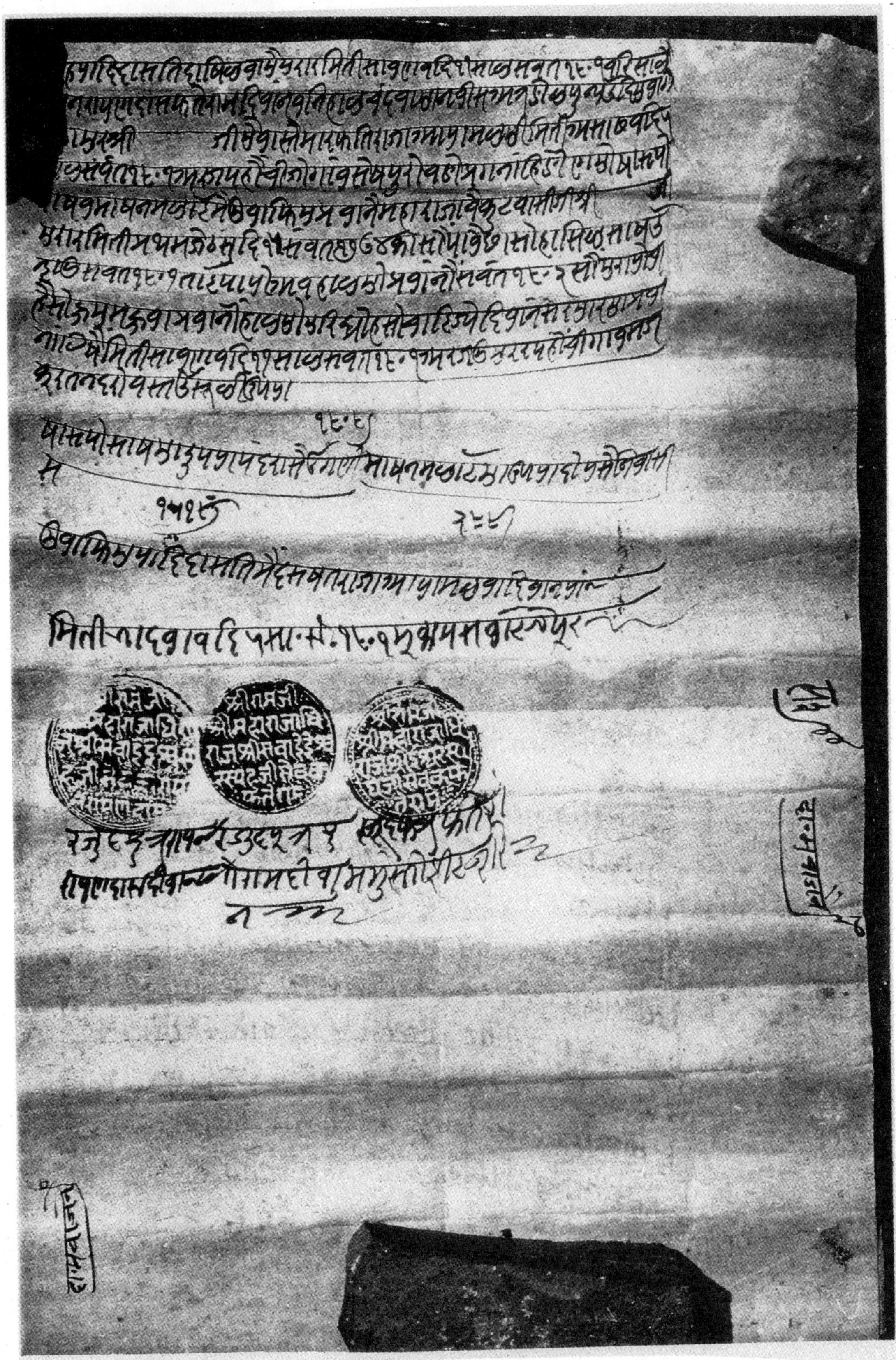

V.S. 1805, Māgha ś. 1 / 8 January 1749

V.S. 1808, Bhādrapada ś. 13 / 23 August 1751

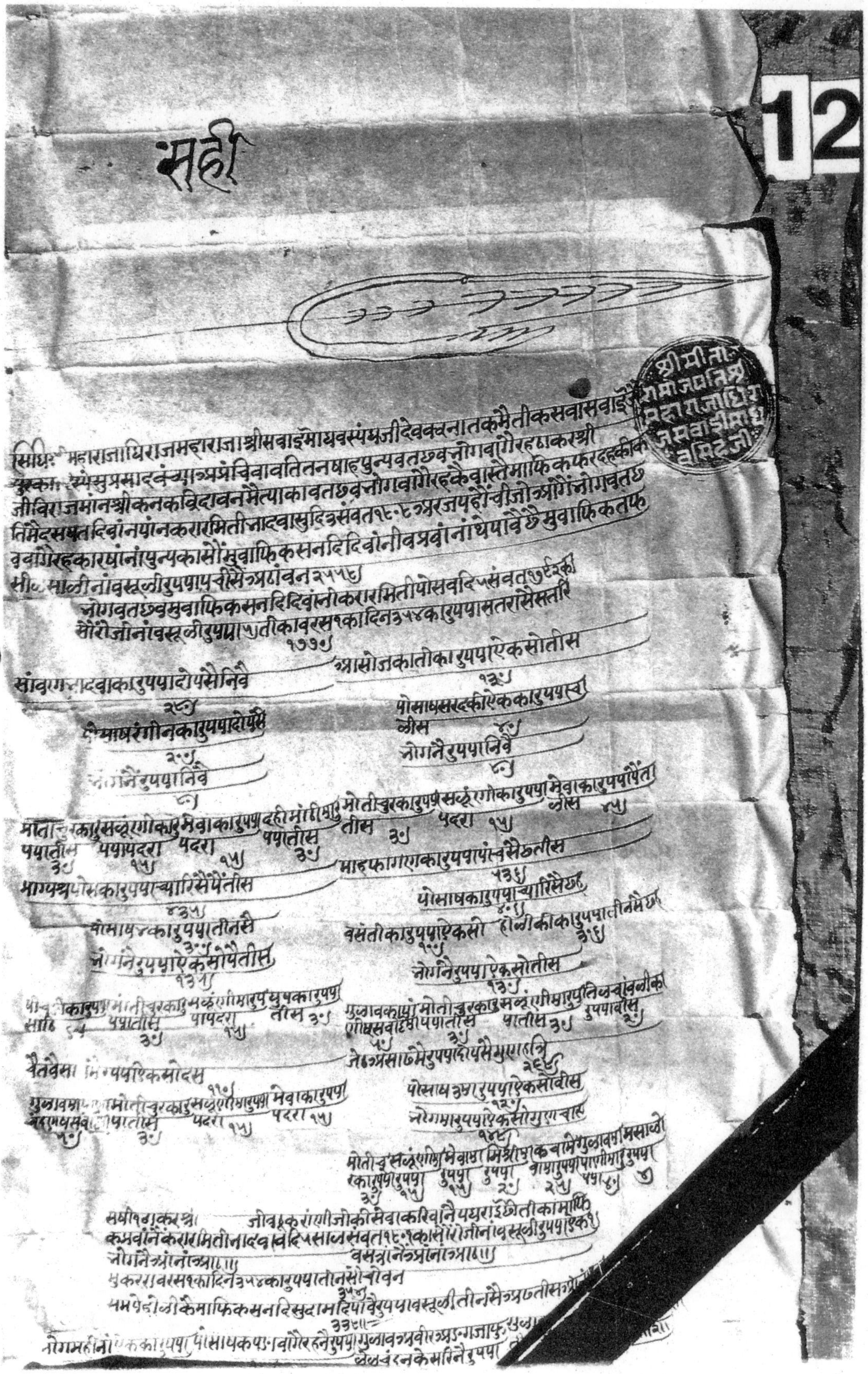

[illegible] सुप्रसादव्या [illegible] स्ते माफक [illegible]
जीविराजमानश्रीकनकविद [illegible] वीजोआगेजोगवतछ
तिमिदसपत दिवानपांनकरार [illegible] पावैछै मुवाफिकतफ
ववागेरहकारषांनांपुन्यकासे [illegible]
सीळमाळीनांवस्तलीरुपया [illegible] वदि संवत [illegible] की
जोगवतछवुमुवाफिकसन [illegible] कारुपयासतरासैसतर
सैरोजीनांवस्तलीरुपया [illegible] तीकावरसएकादिन [illegible] कारुपयासतरासैसतर
१७७०

आसोजकातीकारुपयाएकसोतीस
१३०
सांवणभादवाकारुपयादोयसैनिवै
२९०
पोसाषसरदकीएककारुपया
तीस ४०
पोसाषरेगोनकारुपयादोयसै
२०
जोगनैरुपयानिवै
९०
जोगनैरुपयानिवै
९०

मोतीचुरकारुसळूणोकारुमेवाकारुपया दहीमाटीमारु पयातीस पयापदरा पदरा १५ पयातीस ३० ३० १५
मोतीचुरकारुपया सळूणोकारुपया मेवाकारुपया पैंता तीस ३० पदरा १५ लीस ४५
माहफागणएकारुपयापांचसैछतीस
१३६
माघश्रणोमकारुपयाच्यारिसैपैंतीस
४३५
पोसाषकारुपयाच्यारिसैछ
४०
पोसाषकारुपयातीनसै
३००
वसंतीकारुपयाएकसो
१००
होळीकीकारुपयातीनसैछ
३०६
जोगनैरुपयाएकसोपैंतीस
१३५
जोगनैरुपयाएकसोतीस
१३०

[illegible] कारुपया मोतीचुरकारु सळूणोमारुपया धुपकारुपया [illegible] पयातीस पयपदरा तीस ३० ३० १५
मुळावकापां मोतीचुरकारुसळूणोमारुपुतिकवांळीका [illegible] पयातीस पातीस ३० रुपयावीस २० ३०
जेठअसाढमेरुपयादोयसैगुणहत्रि
२६९
चैतवैसाषमेरुपयाएकसोदस
११०
मुळावकापां मोतीचुरकारुसळूणोमारुपया मेवाकारुपया [illegible] पातीस पदरा १५ पदरा १५ ३०
पोसाषउपारुपयाएकसोवीस
१२०
जोगमारुपयाएकसोगुणचास
१४९
मोतीचुरसळूणोमेवामिश्रीपाकवालोगुळावसमसाबी कारुपयारुपया रुपया रुपया [illegible] ३० १५ १५ २० २५ ५

मयीएतकरश्री जीवाहूकुरांणीजीकीसेवाकरिवानेपयराईछैतीकामाफि
कसवांनेकरारमितीनादवावदिपसावसंवत१९०१कासेरोजीनांवस्तलीरुपयाएक
जोगनैश्रांनांश्रा॥ वसत्रांनेश्रांनांश्रा॥
मुकररावरसएकादिनै [illegible] कारुपयातीनसैनीवन
३५९
मपेडीजीकेमाफिकसनदिसुदामदिपावैरुपयावस्तूलीतीनसैश्रछतीसश्रनिरस
३३६॥
जोगमहिनांएककारुपया पोसाषकपडावागैरहनैरुपया गुळावश्रवीरश्रतरगजाफु सुळावकापांणीरोजीनांसेर१॥ तीमामहीनाश्रामरणा॥॥
खेळवंदनकेसरिनैरुपया मुकररारुपया
१९॥ १०० १९२॥ ३॥
मनपस्याळीकेकीपळासियरजीनेसदामदिपावैमाफिकसनरिमण१९०१तीकारुपया
६०
धितदीवीश्री जीकाहजरिहमेसनुपेसापावैमाफिकसनरिकरारमितीश्रसाढव
दि संवत१९१ की पेरोजीनांसेरश्रामुकरावरसएकामणजातीकारुपया
३५॥
सोसंव[illegible]तीइपापोश्र वतछवजोगवागेरहमेगांवगोव्यंदपुरवासहाथ्योदताळकसवासवाईजै
[illegible] मिवागेरहसुयांवस्तलीरुपया [illegible] कोदरोवस्तकरायोवाहेतीहसौंकुरमांवांछांमत[illegible]
[illegible] तेगांवगोव्यंदपुरवासहाथ्योदताळककसवासवाईजैपुरको तन जो मिवागे[illegible]
[illegible] मतासंवत१९०९मेंहवालेकीज्योश्ररसतवरषनवोप्रवांनोमतिमांगमज्योहैली[illegible]
सौं [illegible] वेमुजराहोय ॥
मुकर[illegible]षांहगांवगोव्यंदपुरवासहाथ्योदताळककसवासवाईजैपुरकोवहाळजाणगिईसत [illegible]
वत१९०९ मेंहवालेकीज्योमुकररागांवमजकूरतनदरोवस्तजोमिवागेरहसुयांवस्तलीरुपया [illegible]

सरूपा॰ ... मनिदाघ्यलनाकेकरारमितीनादवासुदि१०संवत१९००परमाकैकनहींरामदिवांनन्न वीकानवीसत्री
ऋऊरुतमषाहपुन्यवतछव नोगवागेरहवाकरश्री जीविराजमांनश्रीकनकेविंदावनमित्याकावत
छवनोगवागेरहकेवास्तेमाफिकफरदहकीकातिमैदसषतदिवांनपानकरारमितीनादवासुदिसंवत१९०६
अरजपहोंचीजीश्रीमेंवतछव नोगवागेरहकारपांनांपुन्यकासेंसुवाफिकसनदिदिवीनोवुअवांनांथपविछेमा
फिकनफसीलसाळीनोवसलीरुपयापचीसेअठावन२५५८॥
नोगवतछवमुवाफिकेसनदिकरारमितीपोसवदि५संवत१७९२कीसीरोजीनांवसलीरुप
पानुतीकावरस१कादिनतीन३५४कारुपयासतरासेसतरि
१७७०॥
सांवणसुदवाकारुपयादोयसैनिवे
२९०॥
आसोजकातीकारुपयाऐकसोतीस
१३०॥
पोसमाघरंगोनकारुपयादोयसै
२००॥
पोसमाघसरदमोषकारुपयाचालीस
४०॥
नोगनैंरुपयानिवे
९०॥
नोगकारुपयानिवे
९०॥
मोतीचुरकारुपयासलुंणीकारुपया मेवाकारुपयादहीमांडीकारुपयातीस पंदरा पंदरा
३०॥ १५॥ १५॥ ३०॥
मोतीचुरकारुपयासलुंणीकारुपयामेवाकारुपयापैंताळीस तीस दरा
३०॥ १५॥ ४५॥
मांगसरपोसकारुपयाच्यारिसैपैंतीस
४३५॥
माहफागणकारुपयापांचसैछतीस
५३६॥
पोसमाघकारुपयातीनसै
३००॥
पोसमाघकारुपयाच्यारिसैछ
४०६॥
नोगाकारुपयाऐकसोपैंतीस
१३५॥
वसंतीकारुपयाऐकसो
१००॥
होळीकीकारुपयातीनसैछह
३०६॥
...तिकारुपयामोतीचुरकारु सलुंणीकारुपयामेवाकारुपयापाती पांतीस पांपदरा
६०॥ ३०॥ १५॥ ३०॥
नोगनैरुपयाऐकसोतीस
१३०॥
चैतवैसाषकारुपयाऐकसोदस
११०॥
गुलाबकापांणीमोतीचुरकारुसलुंणीकारुपयातिळवांवनीकी पसवोकारुपयापैंतीस तीस रुपयावीस
३५॥ ३०॥ २०॥
गुलाबकापांणीमोतीचुरकारुसलुंणीकारुप मेवाकारुपया वरणजनवाईकोरुपया रुपया पा दरा
१५॥ ३०॥ १५॥ १५॥
जेठअसाढमैंरुपयादोयसैगुणहत्रि
२६९॥
पोसमाघकारुपयाऐकसोवीस
१२०॥
नोगकारुपयाऐकसोगुणन्यासी
१७९॥
मोतीचुरसलुंणीमेवाकामिश्रीकाकवासेवागुलावमगांमसाला कारुपयारुपयारुपयारुपयाकारुपयापीसारुपयाकारुपया
३०॥ १५॥ १५॥ २०॥ २५॥ ४०॥
सबीपालकरश्री जीवहूकरांणीजीकीमेवाकरिवानेपथराईछीतीमाफिकप्रवांने
कगरमितीनादवावदि५सांवसंवत१९०१कासीरोजीनांवसलीरुपयाऐकस
नोगनेंआंनांआठ॥ वसतनेंआंनाआठ॥
मुकरावरस१कादिन३५४कारुपयातीनसैचोवन
३५४॥
मपहोळीकेमाफिकसनदिसदामदियाविवसलीरुपयातीनसैअठतीसआंनांदस
नो॰ ...कारुपया पोसामघकप...वागेरहनेरुपया
१४॥ ३३८॥
समपेस्पालाकेकोपवासियानेंसदामदियावैमाफिकसनरिमगणरतीकारुपया गुलाबअबीरआगजाफुलेगुलावकोपांणीछीतीनांसेरा
अंबरनकेसारिनेरुपया तीकामहीनाकोमण
१२॥ ९०॥
घिरतदीवोश्री कारुपया
३६॥
वदि संवत१९०३काथेरोजीनोसेर आमुकेरावरस१कामण२तीकारुपया
सोसंवत छतांईपापाअववूतछवनोगवागेरहमेगोवगोवांपुरवासदाध्योदतादनककसवासव ईजेपुर
३५॥
तननोग ...गेरहसुधांवसलीरुपया२५५८कोदरोवस्तईमतग संवत१९०६मेकरापोचाहेसोंदसषतषासह
कमध्वामाफिकतफसीलप्रवांनोसंवतीलिषासोनाहिजुपेरिवीनेसरकारकामवांनांलिषेमितीनादवासु
दिसं॰ ११८०६अरजमुकररपहोनोगावमजकरतनदरोवस्तनोमिवागेरहसुधांवसलीरुपयापचीसेअठावन
माफिककयादिदासतिफरदहकीकातिमैदसषतषासवदिवांनपांन
२५५८॥
मिती ... वासुदि २ संवत१९०६ मु॰ कामसवाईजैपुर
... रामसनेहीकीहस्ते

V.S. 1816, Bhādrapada ś. 9 / 1 September 1759

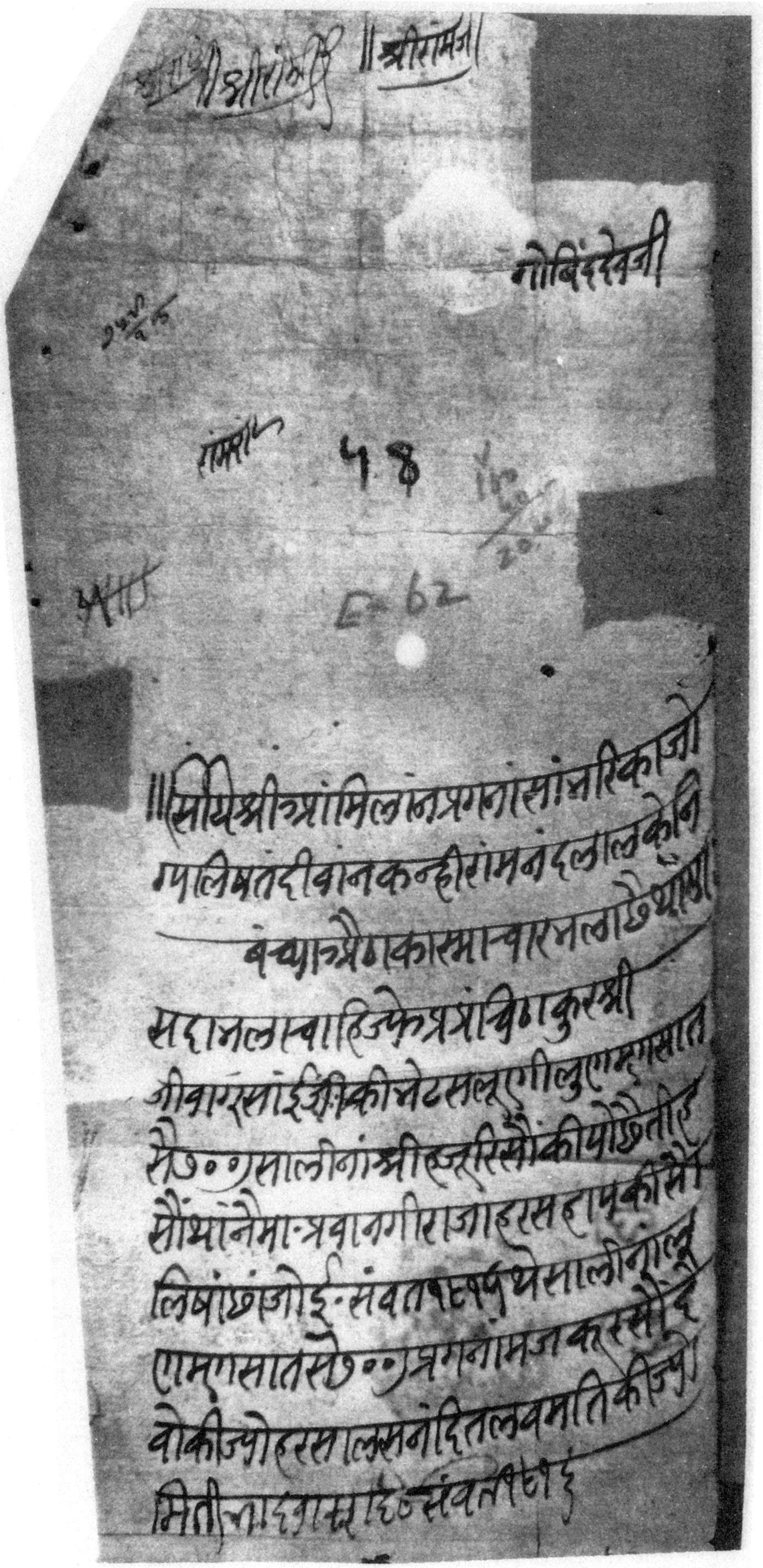

॥श्रीरामजी॥

श्रीगोविंददेवजी

॥सीधश्री ग्रांमिलांनप्रगनासांगानेरिकाजो
गपालिषतदीवानकन्हीरांमनंदलालकेनि
बंच्याश्रीठाकरआंनचारमलाछेथांथा
सदामलाखाहिज्केप्रांचीठाकुरश्री
जीवारसांईजीकीजेटमलूणीलुणमगसात
सै७००सालीनांश्रीहजरिसौकीयाछैतीह
सौंश्रानेमान्प्रवानगीराजाहरसहायकीसै
लिषीछैजोई संवत१८१५पैसालीनालू
णमगसातसै७००प्रगनामजकुरसौंद
वोकीज्योहरसालसनदितलबमातिकीज्यो
मितीभादवासुदि९संवत१८१६

V.S. 1822, Pauṣa ś. 14 / 26 December 1765

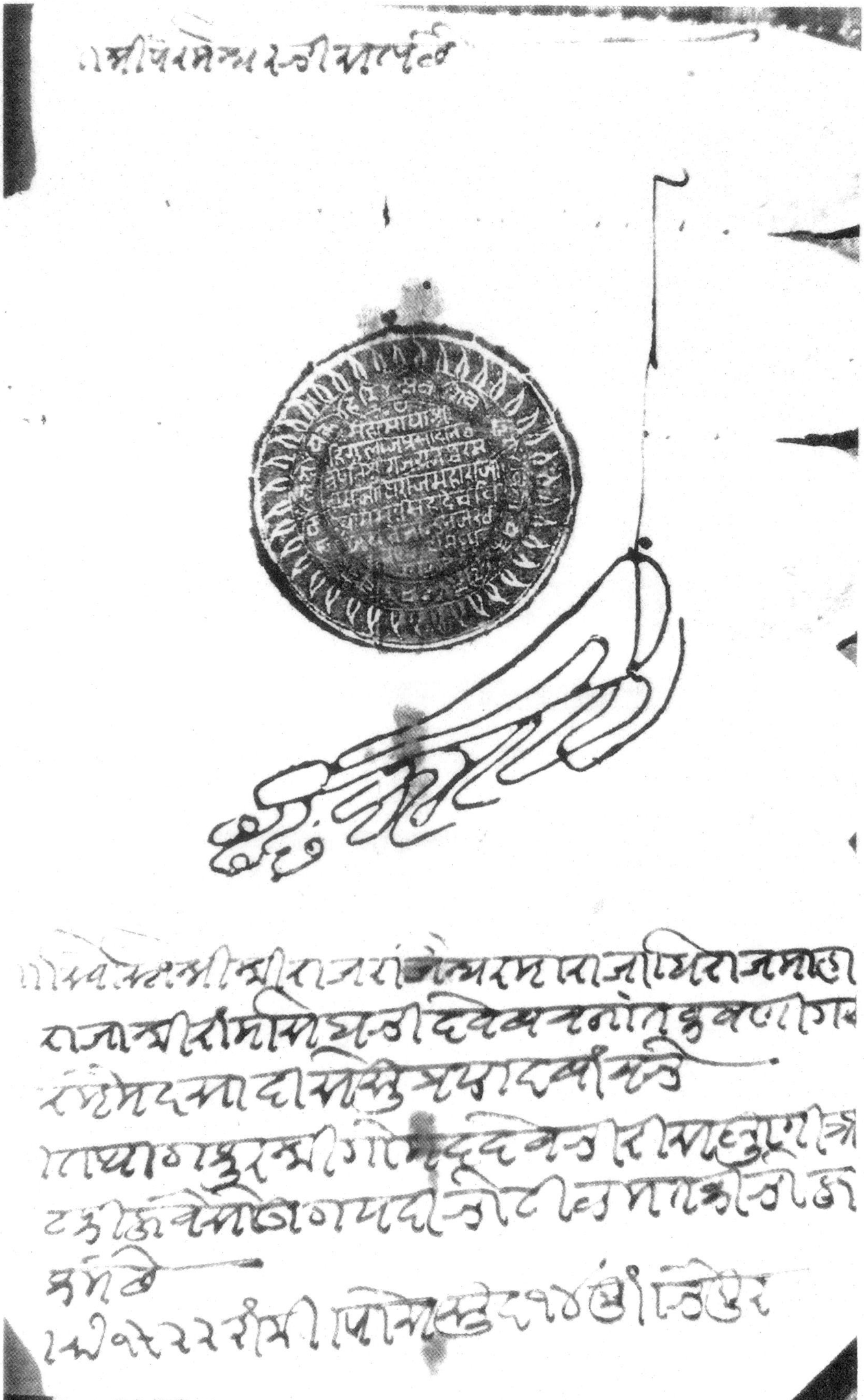

V.S. 1825, Māgha b. 15 / 6 February 1769

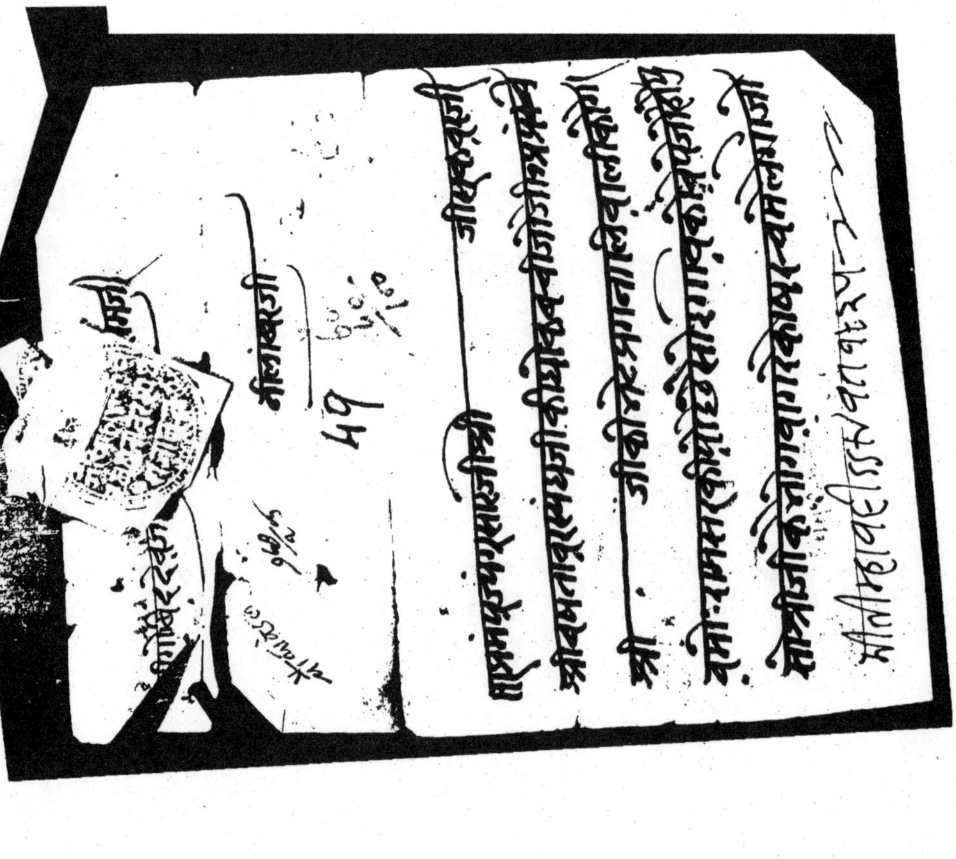

V.S. 1825, Māgha ś. 3 / 9 February 1769

॥श्रीरामजी

॥श्रीगोबंददेवजी

रामसही

॥सिधश्रीकछजीश्रीबषतावरस्यंघजीबचनातंभगना
नंखंडेलवालीकानंश्रीहयादारादसेसुप्रसादबंचाजप्रंबेमो
जेमजकुरकोगावरामसरश्री जीकेभोगवास्ते
चढायोछैसोश्रीजीकाहवालदारआवैछैजानेअमल
करायदीजोअरपीगावसुकहीबातकीखेचलकरोमती
मितीमहासुद ३ संवत १८२५

V.S. 1828, Vaiśākha b. 4 / 3 April 1771

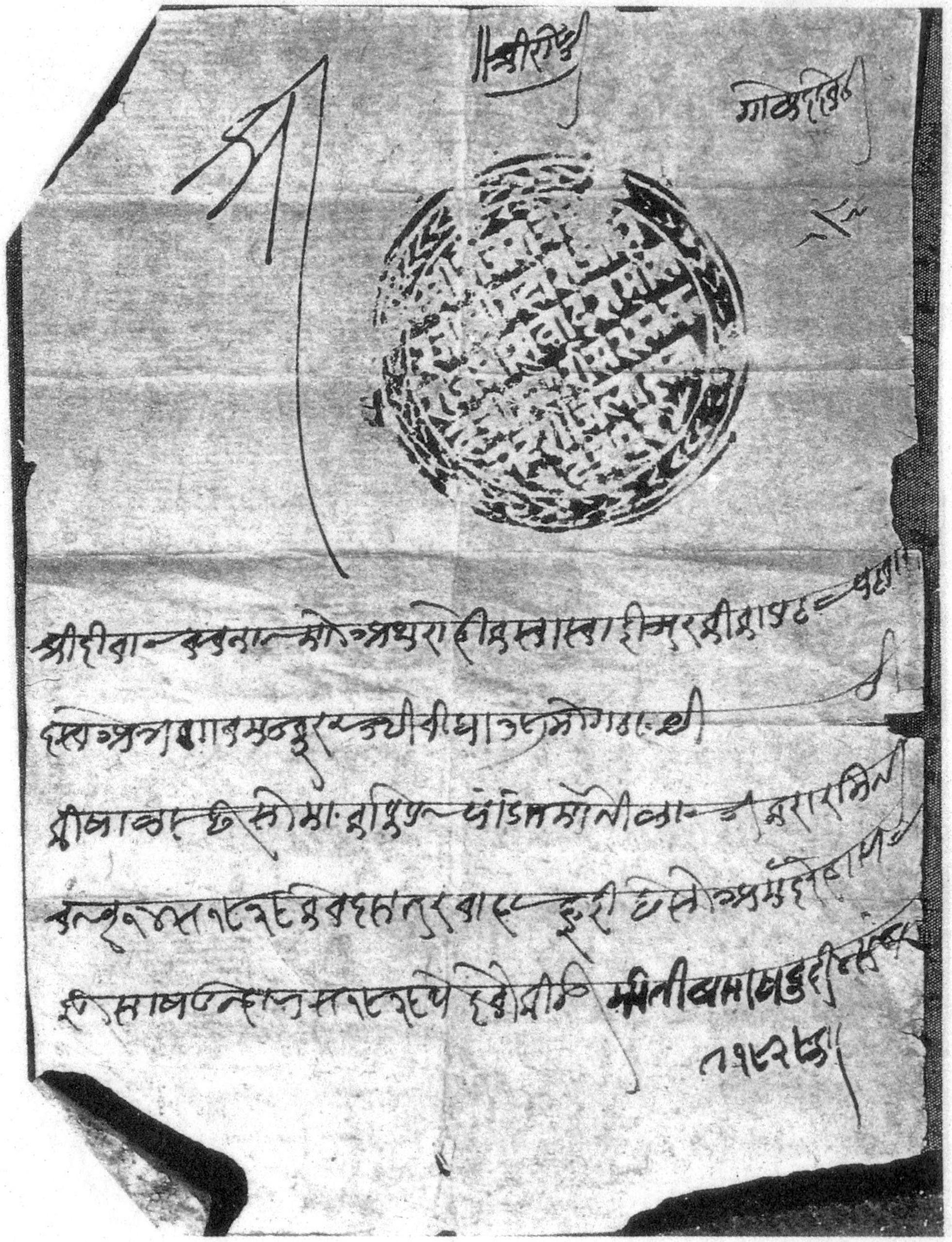

V.S. 1833, Kārttika b. 14 / 10 November 1776

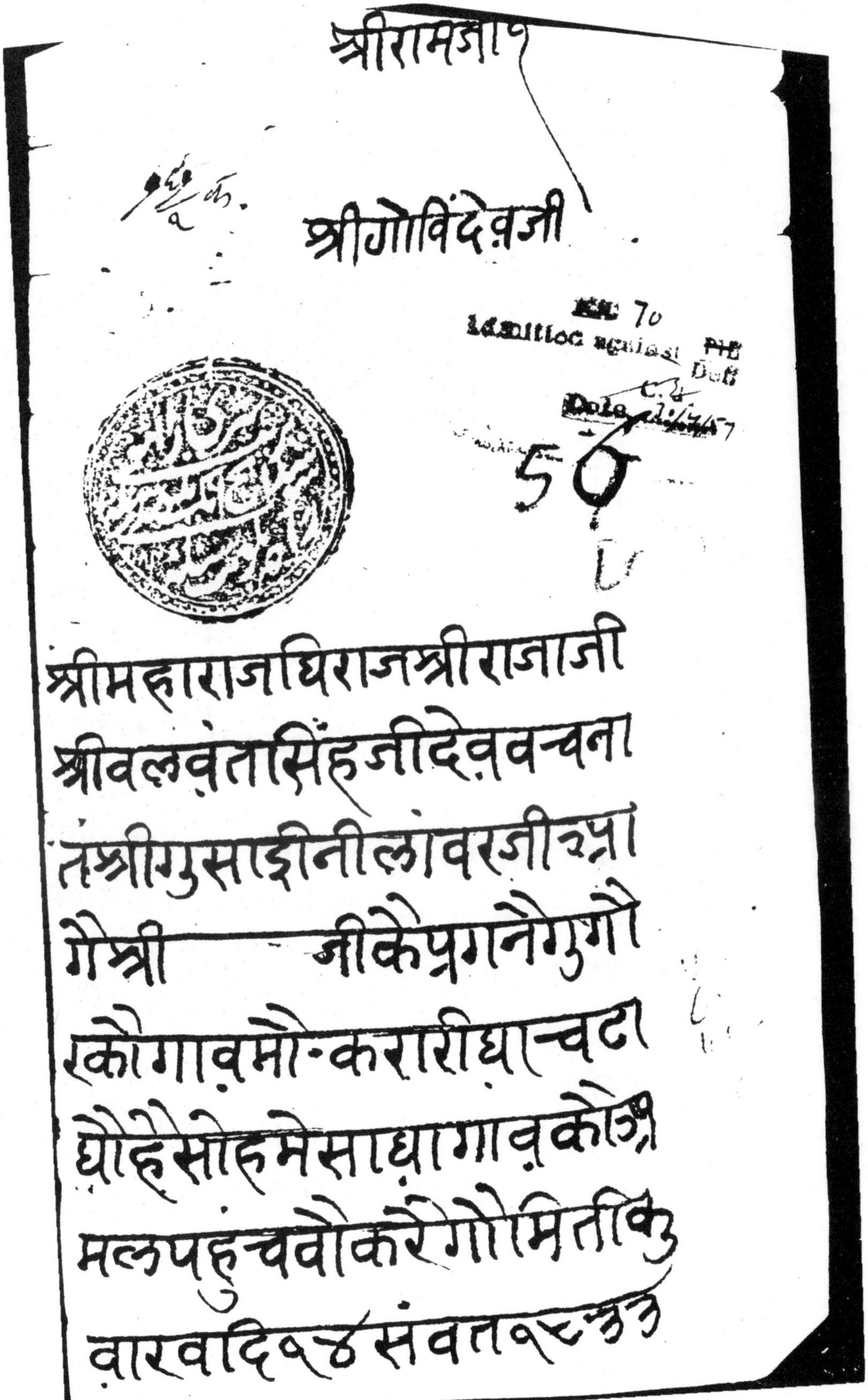

श्रीरामजी

श्रीगोविंदेवजी

श्रीमहाराजधिराजश्रीराजाजी
श्रीवलवंतसिंहजीदेववचना
तश्रीगुसाईनीलांवरजीरूप्रा
गेश्री जीकेप्रगनेगुगो
रकौगावमौ॰करारीघाच्वटा
घोहेसोहमेसाधागावकोअ
मलपहुंचवौकरेगोमितीकु
वारवदि१४संवत१८३३

V.S. 1835, Māgha b. 10 / 12 January 1779

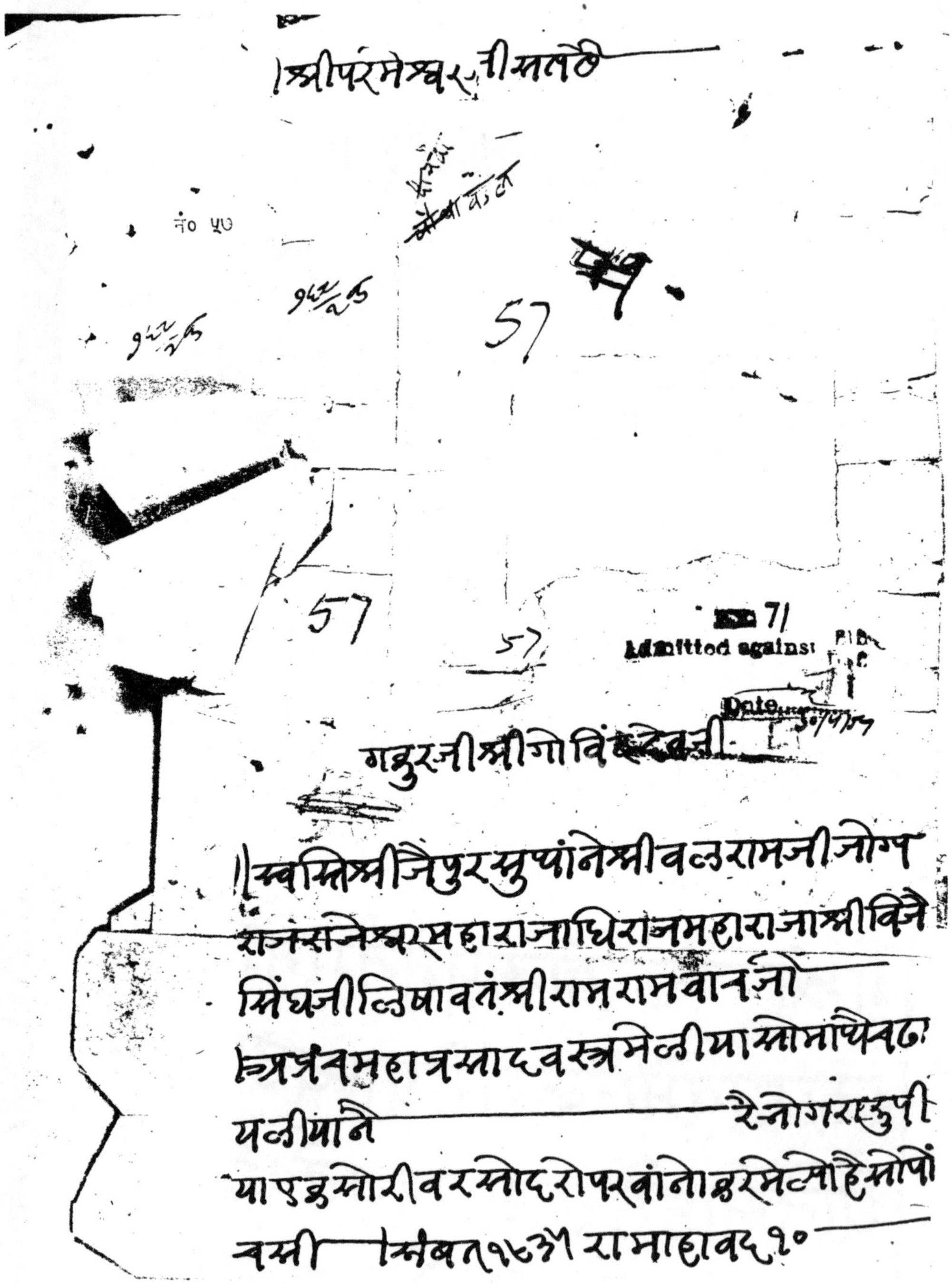

।श्रीपरमेश्वरजीसतछै

नं० ५७

57

57

गडुरजीश्रीगोविंददेवजी

।स्वस्तिश्रीजैपुरसुथांनेश्रीवलरामजीजोग्य
राजश्रीमहाराजाधिराजमहाराजाश्रीविजै
सिंघजीलिषावतंश्रीरामरामवांचजो
अप्रंचमहाप्रसादवस्त्रमेलीयासोमाथेचढा
यलीयाछै रैजोगरहुपी
याएकअमोरीचरचोदरोपरवांनोकरमेल्योहैसोपो
चसी संवत१८३५रामाहावद१०

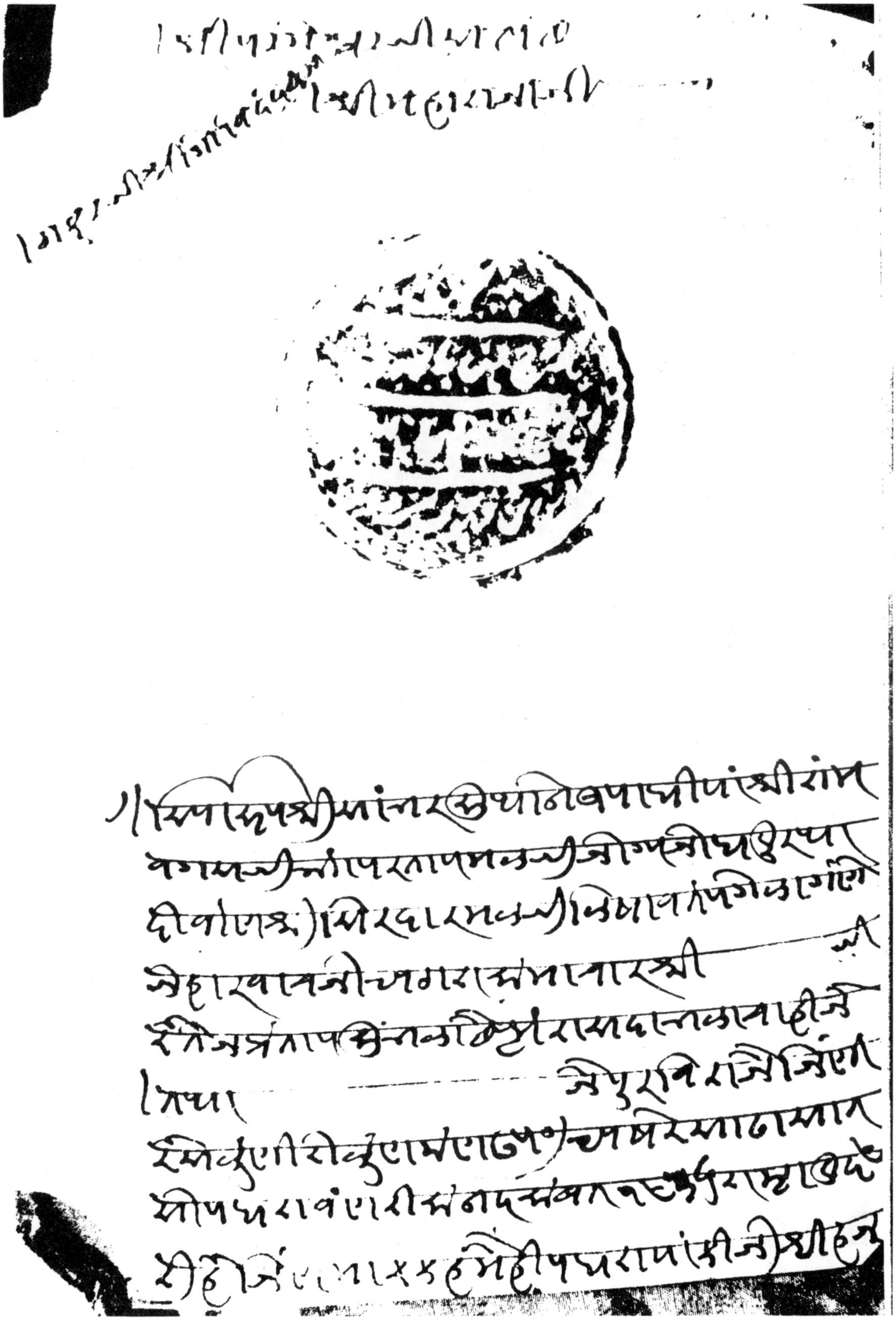

V.S. 1836, Māgha b. 8 / 29 January 1780

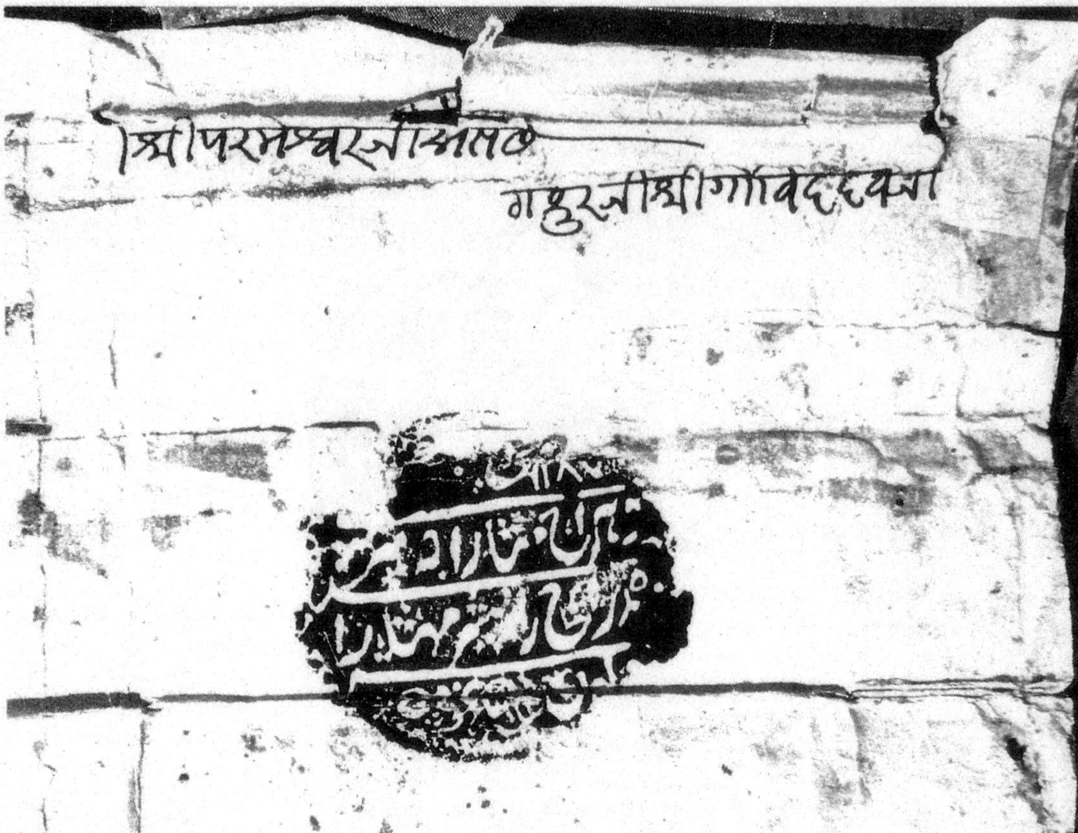

V.S. 1839, Jyeṣṭha II b. 15 / 11 June 1782

।।श्रीरामजी।।

लसवाणीजी

।।स्वस्ति श्री सरब उपमा जोग महाराज गो

।।स्वामिजी श्री - - - - - - - जी जोग

।।लीयायतं राजा किसोरदासजी केन्य दं

डवत बंचाजो अठाका समाचार श्री - - जी की कृपा

सु भला छै आपका भला चाहिजे सपाजी न्गर हरामो

हातीसुबीसियर रावां गावा अपरंच श्री धाम मे म्हा की

घर तीरा जो [illegible] काम न्हारूो सेचा [illegible]

बुलाया छो सो जी येवाली [illegible]

जी का पत्र बीना आवो न होसी सो आ

[illegible] बांके नाव [illegible] ग पत्र [illegible]

[illegible] च्यार दिन के वास्ते [illegible]

यहां का जवाब सुना [illegible]

हर आप की [illegible] जानोगा [illegible]

[illegible] दी [illegible]

[illegible] जेष्ठ [illegible] १८३९

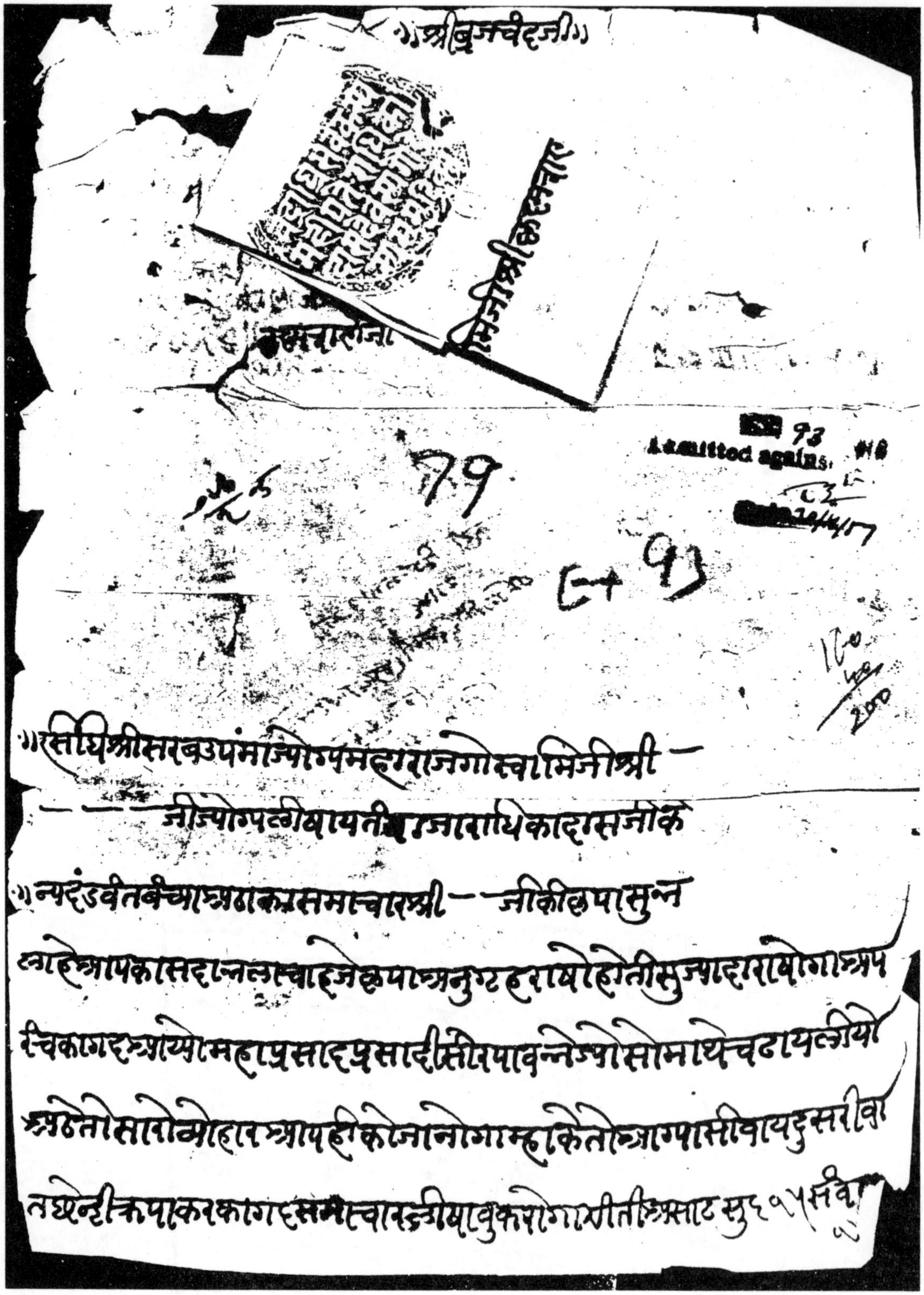

॥श्रीव्रजचंद्रजी॥

॥स्तिश्रीसरबउपमांजोगमहाराजगोस्वामिजीश्री —

— — — जीजोगपत्रीबायती [illegible] जाराधिकादासजीके

॥न्यदंडवतबंच्याअठाकासमाचारश्री — जीकीक्रपासुभ्र

लाहेआपकासदाभलाचाहजेक्रपाअनुग्रहराखेहोतीसुज्यादाराखोगाअप

चिकागरआयोमहाप्रसादप्रसादीतीरपावन्नप्योसोमाथेचढायलीयो

अठेतोसारोमोहारआपहीकोजानोगाम्हाकैतोआगपासीवायदुसरीवा

तछेन्हीक्रपाकरकागदसमाचारदीयाबुकरोगामीतिआसाढसुद१५संवत

rev.y. 1839, Āṣāḍha b. 5 / 19 June 1783

॥श्रीरामजी ॥श्रीरामजी

गोव्यंददेवजी

सही

सिधिश्रीमहाराजाधिराजमहाराजाश्रीसवाईप्रतापसिंह
जीदेववचनातकैमतीप्रगनांसवाईजैपुरकादसेसुप्रसाद
वंच्याउपरंचवावतिनोगवैगेरहगांवठाकुरश्री जी
नैंजामुवाफिकयादिदासतिमैंदसषतदीवांनयांनकरार
मितीजेठसुदि१०सालसंवत१८३९उपरजपहोंचीकसवो
जैतपुरातालकाप्रगनांसवाईजैपुरकोसिवायराहदारी
नोगवैगेरहकैवास्तैसंवत१८४०थेउपरचढायोसोपवांनै
सवतीकादसषतकरायोचाहैतीहसूफुरमांवांछांमतल
वप्रवांनांकासूंवाकिफहोयकसवोजैतपुरोतालकाप्रग
नांसवाईजैपुरकोसिवायराहदारीसंवत१८४०थेसीगेनो
गवैगेरहकेजांणिदासिलहवालेकरिवोकीज्योउपरप्रु
तवरषनवोप्रवांनूंमतिमांगपज्योईहीप्रवांनांसूंदिसावर्भ
मुजराहोयला
मुकररातनषाहकसवोजैतपुरोतालकाप्रगनांसवाई
जैपुरकोसिवायराहदारीसंवत१८४०थेसीगेनोगवैगेरह
केजांणिदासिलहवालेकरिवोकीज्योएक

सरूपादिदासतिदाषिलवाकिकरारमितीआसाढवदि१सा
लसंवत्१८३८वरसालिसंगढ़ीजीवराजसंगढ़ीरूपोजीरामदी
वांनवनेवातिवकायानवीसवंदेसरकारजैतरामअत्रडील
जोगवगैरहगांवठाकुरश्री जीकैवास्तैमुवाफिक
पादिदासतिमिंदसषतदीवांनपांनकरारमितीजेठसुदि१०
सालसंवत१८३८आरजपहोंचीकसबोजैतपुरीतालकाअ
गनांसवाईजैपुरकोसिवापराहदारीजोगवगैरहकैवास्तैसं
वत१८४०थीओरचलायोसोअवांनूंसवतीकादसषतकूरा
योचाहैसोदसषतषासरूकमरूवामुवाफिकलिषदीजो
तीकोअवांनूंसवतीलिषोसोचाहिजेदीवांनसरकारकाअ
वांनालिषेमितीआसाढवदि१सालसंवत१८३८आरजमुक
रपहोंचीमुकररकसबोजैतपुरोसिवापराहदारीतालका
अगनांसवाईजैपुरकोएक

मुवाफिकपादिदासतिमिंदसषतषासदीवांनपांन

मिती असाढ वदी १ साल संवत १८३८

V.S. 1840, Āśvina b. 10 / 21 September 1783

॥श्रीरामजी॥

गोविंददेवजी

सिधिश्रीमहाराजाधिराजमहाराजाश्रीसवाईप्रतापसिंहजीदेववचनात
कमेतीकसवासवाईजैपुरकादसमुप्रसादवंच्याअपरंचववातिजेट
हाद्यांवागैरहठाकुरश्री जीनेंजोमारफतिरायरतनला
लकीमितीचैतसुदि१सालसंवत१८३९रेअरजपहोंचीगुसांईकिस्न
सरणजीकीहवेलीकसवासवाईजैपुरमेंतीकिमुतासिलवाजार
कीहाद्यावागैरह१३सरकारकीसोजेटकरीसोदसषतकरायोछा
हैतींहस्तकरमावांछामतलववप्रवानांकासंवा।किफहोयहाद्यावा
गैरहतेराहवेलीकसवासवाईजैपुरमेंगुसांईकिस्नसरणजीकी
तीकिमुतासिलवाजारकीसरकारकीदस्वतदाय।मितीचैतसुदि३
सालसंवत१८३९रेथेसीगैजेटकैजांणिहवालेकीज्यो।अरप्रतवर
षनवोप्रवानोंमातिमागपज्योईंहीप्रवानांसंहिसाबमेंमुजराहोयल्ला
मुकररातनमालहाद्यावागैरहहवेलीकसवासवाईजैपुरमेंगुसां
ईकिस्नसरणजीकीतीकेमुतासिलवाजारकीसरकारकीदस्वत
दायमितीचैतसुदि३सालसंवत१८३९रेथेसीगैजेटकेजांणिहवाले
कीज्योतेरा।

१३

हाटिग्यारा थडीदोय

सरहपादिदासतिदाखिळवाके.करारमितीआसोजवदि६संवत१९४०वरसाळे
संगहीजीवराजसंगहीसिवजीरामदीवानवानोवतिवाकानबीसवंदेसरकारजेत
रामअत्रजोळनेटहाझांवागैरहठाकुरश्री —— जीकेवास्तेमारफति
रापरतनळाळकीमितीचैतसुदि७साळसंवत१९३९अरजपहोंचीगुसांईकि
सनसरणजीकीहवेळीकसबासवाईजेपुरमेंतीकेमुतासिळबाजारकीहाझावागै
रह१उसरकारकीसोनोटकरीसोदसपतकरापोंचाहेसोहुकममहरवाममुवाफिक
ळिखेसीगैनेटकेओतीकोप्रवांनसवतीळिखोइवतदापमितीचैतसुदिआ
ठसंवत१९३९थेसोनाहिजेदीवानसरकारकापरवानोळिखेमितीआसोजवदि
संवत१९४०अरजमुकररपहोंचीमुकरराहाझावागैरहतेरा

१३

हाटिगपारा —— घडीदोय

११ २

मुवाफिकपादिदासतिमेंदसखतराप्ररतनळाळवादीवानपान

मिती ...... संवत१९४०मुकामसवाईजेपुर

हजूरदफ्तरदी... हजूर... दीवानतीहजूरदफतरकाजीछीत्र
संगहीमोहनरा... संगहीमोजीराम महमदमुसतोफीहजूरी

॥श्रीरामजी

सीतारामजी गोविंदजी

॥सिधिश्री महाराजाधिराज श्री आलीजाह महाराजा श्री सूबे
दार माधोराव जी सींदे जोग्य पालिषतं महाराजाधिराज महारा
जा श्री सवाई प्रितापसिंहजी के न श्री वंच्या अठा
का समाचार श्री जी की कृपा सूं भला छे राज्य का
सदा भला चाहिजे अपरंच श्री वडा महाराज वृंदावनजी में
व्यासां की जमी मोकलि लेर जाय गांव गाय गंज वसाय श्री
जी की भेट करी अब जा हरि कुई जोधीरज लाल गुसांई विधे रत्ती
कीन वाका आधिका स्यां सूं पेचल करि राषी छै सो मुतसद्यां ने
ताकीद करि दीछा जोधीरज लाल गुसांई ने विधे रती सूं स्व

ज्याहि मन होवा छे
और कागद समाचा
र लिखावता रहोला
मिती श्रावण वदि
१३ संवत १८४३

V.S. 1843b, Śrāvaṇa b. 13 / 23 July 1786

॥श्रीरामजी

गोविंदजी

Ex. 81

Ex 81

वृंदाबनजीकाश्रीसमस्तगुसांयांम्हांकोनमस्कारबंच्या
अपरंचश्रीवडामहाराजवृंदावनजीमेंब्यासांकीधरतीमोलिले
रगंजबसायवाजायगांवबणायश्री जीकीभेटकरीछी
सोअबमालमहुईजोधीजलालगुसांईवेजमीनेंअोरांनेंबेच्या
चाहेछेसोवेनेंसमझायदीजोलाजोईजायगांस्तुंमुजाहिमनहोय
मितीश्रावणवदि१३संवत१८४३

V.S. 1848, Bhādrapada b. 7 / 21 August 1791

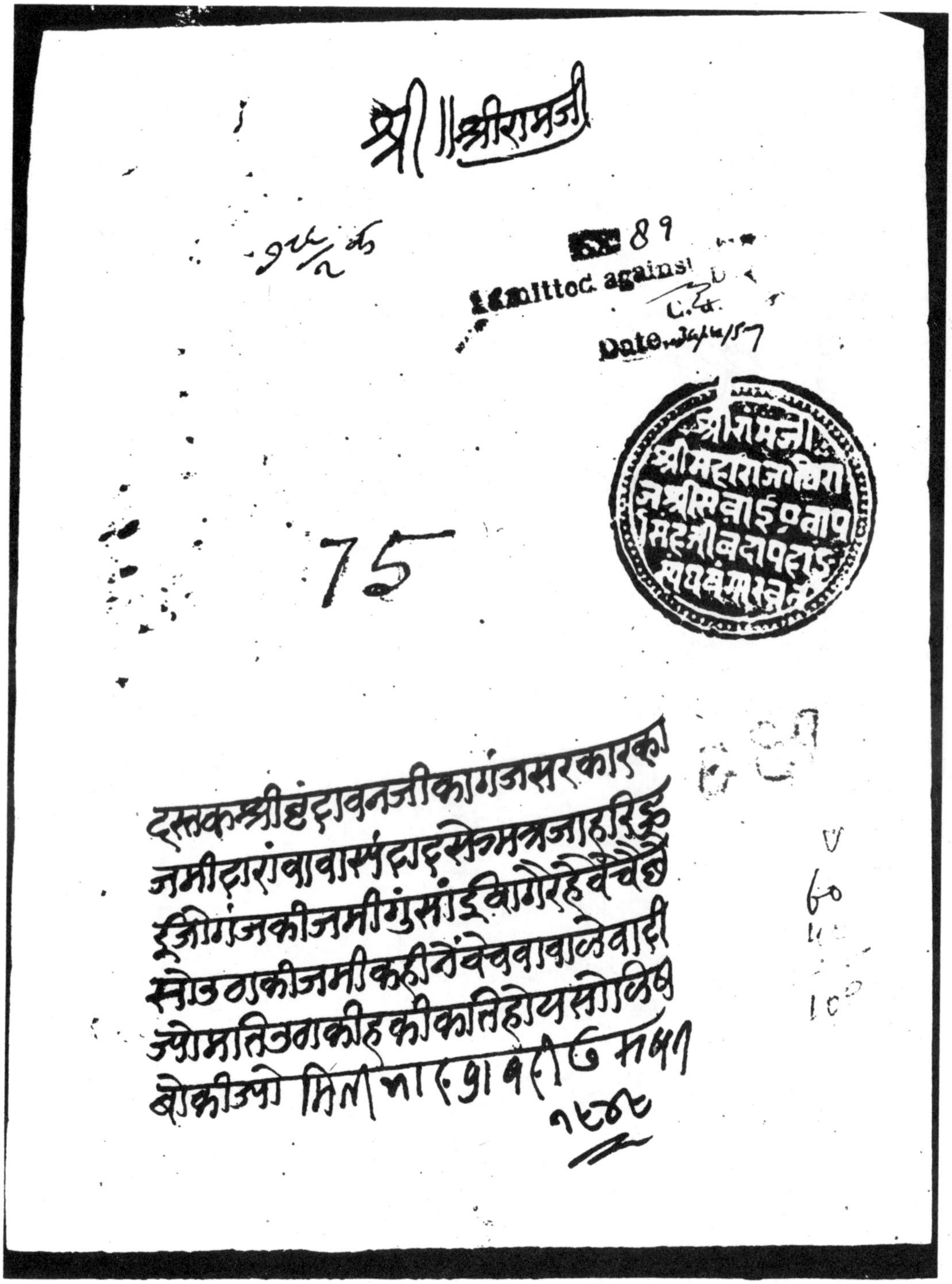
श्री ||श्रीरामजी

89

Admitted against

75

श्रीरामजी

दस्तकश्रीबृंदावनजीकागंजसरकारका
जमीदारांबाबास्यंदादसेगमत्रजाहरिकु
दूजीगंजकीजमीगुसांईवागेरहे वेचैछे
सोउणाकीजमीकहीनेंबेचवावालेवादी
ज्योमातिउणकीहकीकातिहोयसोलिख
बोकीज्यो मिति भा॰ ब॰ ७ संवत
१८४८

V.S. 1850, Pauṣa ś. 10 / 11 January 1794

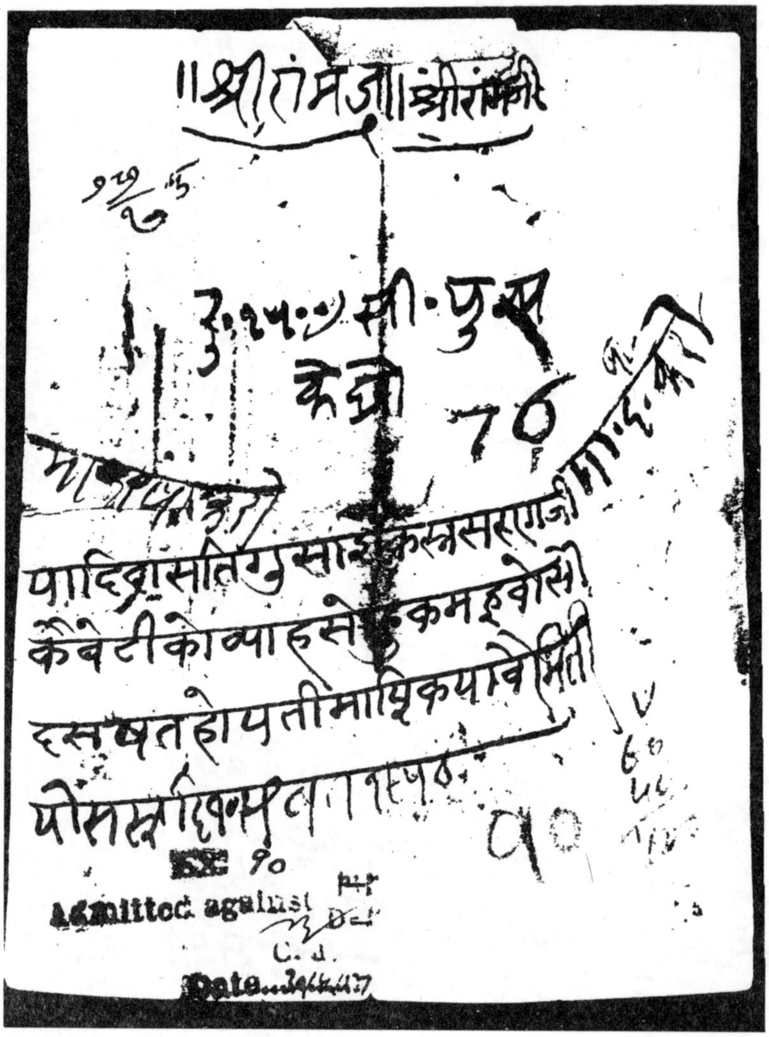
॥श्रीरामजी॥ श्रीरामजी

पादिशासतिगुसाईं केसवसरणजी
कैबेटीको व्याहसे हुकम हवोसी
दसषत होयती माफिक यावे मिती
पोससुदि१०सं१८५०

Admitted against
C.J.

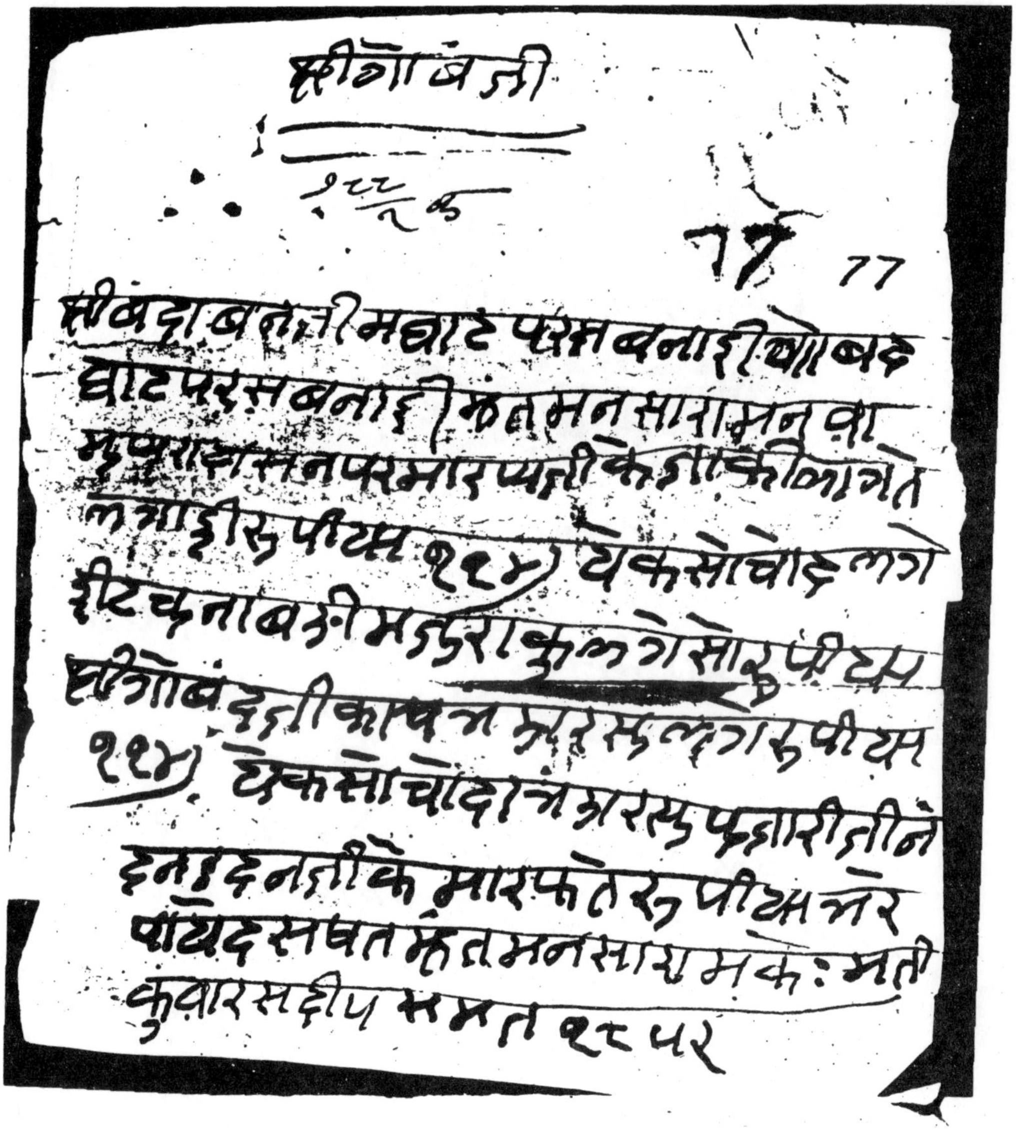

श्रीगोबंदजी

१८५२

77

श्रीबंद्राबनजी म घाट परस बनाई गोबंद
घाट परस बनाई मीत मनसाराम न वा
मुणराइसमनपरमार प्यजी के हाकी लागे ते
लगाई रुपीयस ११४) येकसो चोद लगे
ईट चुना बजी मजुरा कुल गे सो रुपीयस
श्रीगोबंदजी का पत्र अरस लगा रुपीयस
११४) येकसो चोदा नेअरस फुहारीजीने
इनाइदनजी के मारफत रुपीया ओर
पांचदसषत मीत मनसाराम के : मती
कुवार सदीप समत १८५२

V.S. 1860, Āṣāḍha ś. 9 / 28 June 1803

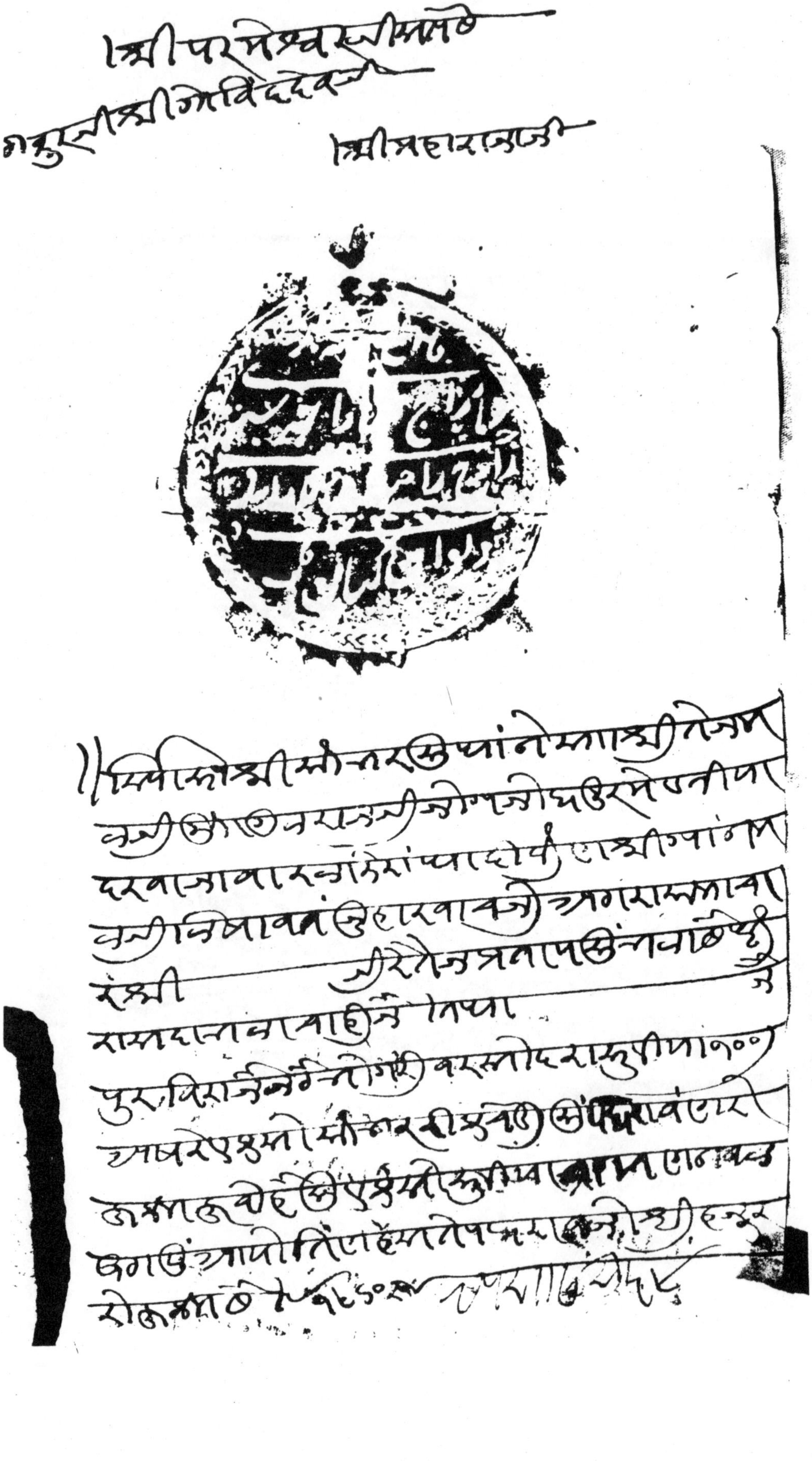

श्री परमेश्वरजी सहाय छै

प्रभुजी श्री गोविंददेवजी

श्री महाराजाजी

V.S. 1860, Māgha b. 2 / 30 December 1803

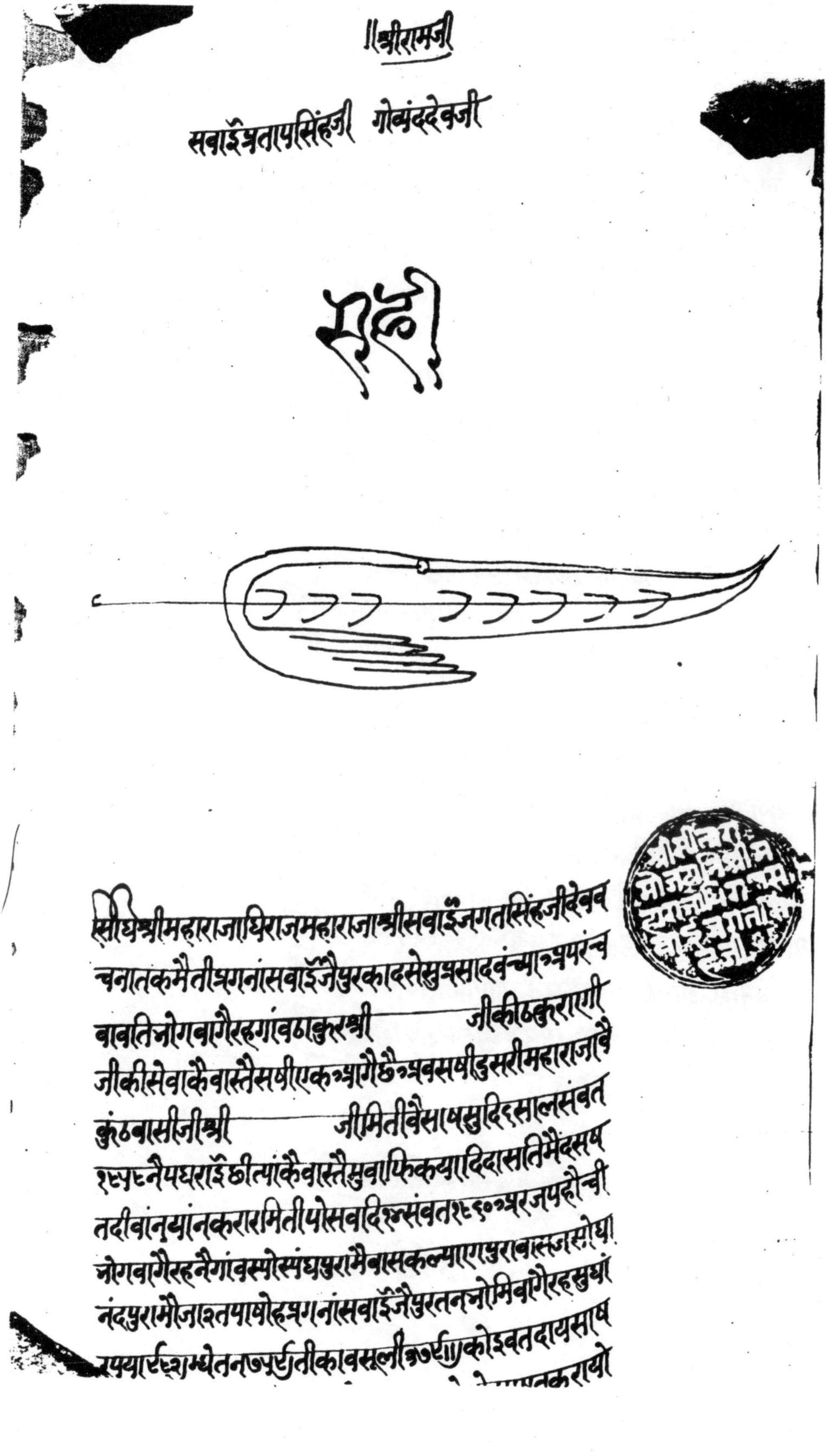

॥श्रीरामजी॥

सवाईप्रतापसिंहजी गोव्यंददेवजी

सही

सीधश्रीमहाराजाधिराजमहाराजाश्रीसवाईजगतसिंहजीदेववचनातकमैतीअगनांसवाईजैपुरकादसेसुप्रसादवंच्याअपरंच

बावतिजोगबागैरहगांवठाकुरश्री जीकीठकुराणी

जीकीसेवाकैवास्तैसषीएकआगैछैअवसषीदुसरीमहाराजावै

कुंठवासीजीश्री जीमितीवैसाषसुदि६सालसंवत

१८५९नैपधराईछीत्यांकैवास्तैसुवाफिकव्यादिदासतिमैदसष

तदीवांनुयांनकरारमितीपोसवदि॥संवत१८६०अरजपहोंची

जोगवागैरहनैगांवस्पोस्यंघपुरामैबासकल्यांणपुराबास्जसोधा

नंदपुरामौजाश्तपाषोहअगनांसवाईजैपुरतनजोमिवागैरहसुधां

रुपयार्र्ह्श्मधेतनअपूर्ईतीकावसूलीक्ऽ७र्ई॥कोइवतदायसाष

नकरायो

श्रीसीतारा
मो जयति श्री म
हाराजाधिराज स
वाई जगतसिं
हजी

श्री

सीधश्रीमहाराजाधिराजमहाराजाश्रीसवाईजगतसिंहजीदेवव
चनातकमैतीश्रगनांसवाईजैपुरकादसेसुश्रसादवंच्याअपरंच
बावतिजोगवागैरहगांवठाकुरश्री जीकीठकुराणी
जीकीसेवाकैवास्तैसषीएकआगैछैअवसषीदुसरीमहाराजावै
कुंठवासीजीश्री जीमितीवैसाषसुदि९सालसंवत
१८५८नैपधराई छीत्यांकैवास्तैसुवाफिकयादिदासातिमैंदसष
तदीवांनूयांनकरारमितीपोसवदि३संवत१८६०अरजपहोंची
जोगवागैरहनैगांवस्योस्यंघपुरामैवासकल्याणपुरावासजसोधा
नंदपुरामौजा२तपाषोहअगनांसवाईजैपुरतनजोमिवागैरहसुधां
दुपयार१९३अधेतन७५९तीकावसूलीअ७९॥कोइवतदायसाष
स्यालूसंवत१८६०थेकरिदेवाकोहुकमहूवोसोदसषतकरायो
चाहैतीहसूंहुरमांवाछांमतलबअवांनाकासूवाकिफहोयगांव
स्योस्यंघपुरामैंवासकल्याणपुरावासजसोधानंदपुरामौजा२त
पाषोहअगनांसवाईजैपुरतनजोमिवागैरहसुधांदुपयानौसेबी
यासीअधेतनसातसैगुणसठितीकाउसूलीतीनसैछुएपासीआ
नांआठकोइवतदायसाषस्यालूसंवत१८६०थेसीगैजोगवागैर
हकैजांणिहासिलहवालैकरिवोकीज्योअरअतवरषनवोअवा
नूंमतिमांगज्योईहीअवांनांसूंहिसावमैमुजराहोयला
मुकररातनषाहगांवस्योस्यंघपुरामैवासकल्याणपुरावासजसो
धानंदपुरामोजा२तपाषोहअगनांसवाईजैपुरकोइवतदायसाषस्या
लूसंवत१८६०थेसीगैजोगवागैरहकैजांणिहासिलहवालैकरिबो
कीज्योतनजोमिवागैरहसुधांदुपयार१९३अधेतन७५९तीकावसू
लीतीनसैछुएपासीआनांआठ

३७९॥

जोगनैदुपयाएकसौनिवासीआवरवनैदुपयाएकसोनिवासीआ
नांवारा नांवारा
१८९॥ १८९॥

सरहयादिदासातिदाषिलवाकैकरारामितीपोससुदि१२संवत१९९०व
रसालैसंगहीअमरचंददीवांनवनोवातिवकायानवीसवंदेसरकार
किरपारामअन्नडोलजोगवागैरहगांवठाकुरश्री —————— जीकी
ठकुराणीजीकीसेवाकैवास्तैसषीएकआगैछैअवसषीदुसरीमहा
राजावैकुंठवासीजीश्री —————— जीमितीवैसाषसुदि६सालसं
वत१९५९नैपधराईछीत्यांकैवास्तैमुवाफिकयादिदासातिमैंदसषत
दीवांनयानकरारमितीपोसवदि१४संवत१९९०अरजपहोंचीजोगवा
गैरहनैगांवस्पोस्पंद्यपुरामैवासकल्याणपुरावासजसोधानंदपुरा
मौजा२तपाषोहअगनांसवाईजैपुरतनजोमिवागैरहसुधांरुपया
९९३मधेतन७४९तीकाउसूली३७४॥कोइवतदायसाषस्पावसं
वत१९९०थेकरिदेवाकोहुकमहुवोसोदसषतकरायोचाहेसोदस
षतषासहुकमहुवासुवाफिकलिष्येद्योतीकोअवांनूसवतीलिषो
सोचाहिज्येदीवांनसरकारकाअवांनांलिषोमितीपोससुदि१२संव
त१९९०अरजमुकररपहोंचीमुकररागांवस्पोस्पंद्यपुरामैवासकल्या
णपुरावासजसोधानंदपुरामोजा२तपाषोहअगनांसवाईजैपुरतन
जोमिवागैरहसुधांरुपया९९३मधेतन७४९तीकाउसूलीतीनसैचु
मालीसआंनांआठ

३७४॥

जोगनैरुपयाएकसोनिवासीआवस्थानैरुपयाएकसोनिवासीआ
नांवारा —————— नांवार

१८७॥ १८७॥

मुवाफिकयादिदासातिमैदसषतषासवैदीवांनयांन

मिती माहवुदि२संवत१९९०मुकामसवाईजैपुर

श्रीरामजी
श्रीमहाराजाधिरा
जश्रीसवाईमानसिं
घजीसेवकसं
अमरचंद

श्रीरामजी
श्रीमहाराजाधिरा
जश्रीमाधोसिंघजीसेवक
सदासुष

दसषतदीवा
नसंगहीअमरचंद

हुकमहजूरदीवांन
हजूरिआठ॥

दसषतसदासुष
मसतोफीहजूरि

सिधश्रीमहाराजाधिराजमहाराजाश्रीसवाईजगतसिंहजीदेववचनात
तकमैतीकसबासवाईजैपुरकादसेसुप्रसादवंच्याअपरंचबातीर
नामधरतीवीघा१०बागवावागकाखरचनैहस्तलालजुउमाणिकरा
जरधानाईमहाराजावैकुंठवासीजीश्री जीकानैजोष
वाफिकयादिदासतिमैदसषतदीवांनयांनकरारमितीपोससुदि१०
संवत१८६०अरजपरदीवीजोइनांमधरतीगांवमानपुरसट्ठतालिक
कसबासवाईजैपुरकीवीघा१०कयाध्याकीबागवणावानैवाबागका
खरचनैइनतदायसाषउन्हालूसंवत१८६०थेकरिदेवाकोहुकमहूवो
सोदसषतांकोउमेदवारतीहसखुरमांवाठामतलबभवानांकासूबा
किफहोयधरतीवीघापचासक्याध्याकीगांवमानपुरसट्ठतालिक
कसबासवाईजैपुरकीबागवणावानैबावागकाखरचनैइनतदायसा
षउन्हालूसंवत१८६०थेसीगैइनांमकेजाणिमांप्पहवालेकीजोअर
प्रतवखनवोभवानांनुमतिमांप्पजोईहीभवानांसूरिसाकमैमुजराहो
यला

मुकररातनषाहधरतीगांवमानपुरसट्ठतालिककसबासवाईजैपुर
कीवागवणावानैबावागकाखरचनैइनतदायसाषउन्हालूसंवत१८६०
थेसीगैइनामकेजाणिमांप्पहवालेकीजेोल्याध्याकीवीघापचास

१०।

बागवास्तैजारमलडोध्याकीकोठीबागकाखरचनैसूरिजमलगोपाल
नीन्चैवीघागपाराबिस्वा काययकीबाउडीकांठीनीन्चैवीघा
उतालसबिस्वाबारा

११।३ ३८॥२

सरह्वा।देदासातिदाषिलवाकैंकरारामितीमाहवदिपसंवत१९८०व१९
लैसंगहीअमरचंददीवानवनौवातिवंकायांनवीसवरेसरकाराकैरपा
रामअत्रडोलइनांमघरतीवागवावागकाषसनेहैरलालचूअमाएी
कागजरघायाइमहाराजावैकुंठवासीजीश्री जीकाकैवास्ते
मुवाफिकक्यादिदासातिमैंदसषतदीवानयानकरारामितीपोससुदि१५सं
वत१९८०अपरजपहौंचीनोइनांमघरतीगांवमानपुरसठानालिककस
वासवाईजैपुरकीवीघा१५अष्याकीवागवणगवानैवावागकाषरचने
इवतरायसाषउन्हालूसंवत१९८०थेकरीदेवाकोहुकमकूवोसोदसष
तांकोउमेदवारसोदसषतषासहुकमदूवासुवाफिककालिष्योछोतीकोघ
वानूंसवतीविषोसोन्वाहिजेदीवानसरकारकापरवानाकिषैमितीमाह
वदिपसंवत१९८०अपरजमुकररपहौंचीमुकरराबागवावागकाषरचनेघ
रतीआयांकीवीघापचास

पुन

बागवास्तेनारमलओझाकीकोठीनीचैवागकाषरचनेसूंरिजमलगोपाल
वीघाअथाराविस्वाअाठ कायथकीवावडीकोठीनीचेवीघाअठ
उतीसविस्वावारा
१३।३ ३४।१२

मुवाफिकक्यादिदासातिमैंदसषतषासकरीवानयान
मितीमाहबुदि६संवत१९८०मुकामसवाइजपुर

श्रीरामजी
श्रीमहाराजाधिरा
जश्रीसवाईजगत
सिंहजीसेवकसं
अमरचंद

श्रीरामजी
श्रीमहाराजाधिरा
जश्रीसवाईजगत
सिंहजीसेवक
सदासुष

रजूदफतरदीवान संगहीअमरचंद
रजूदफतरदीवां महजूरि
रजूदफतरसदासुष मसतौफीदफ्तरि

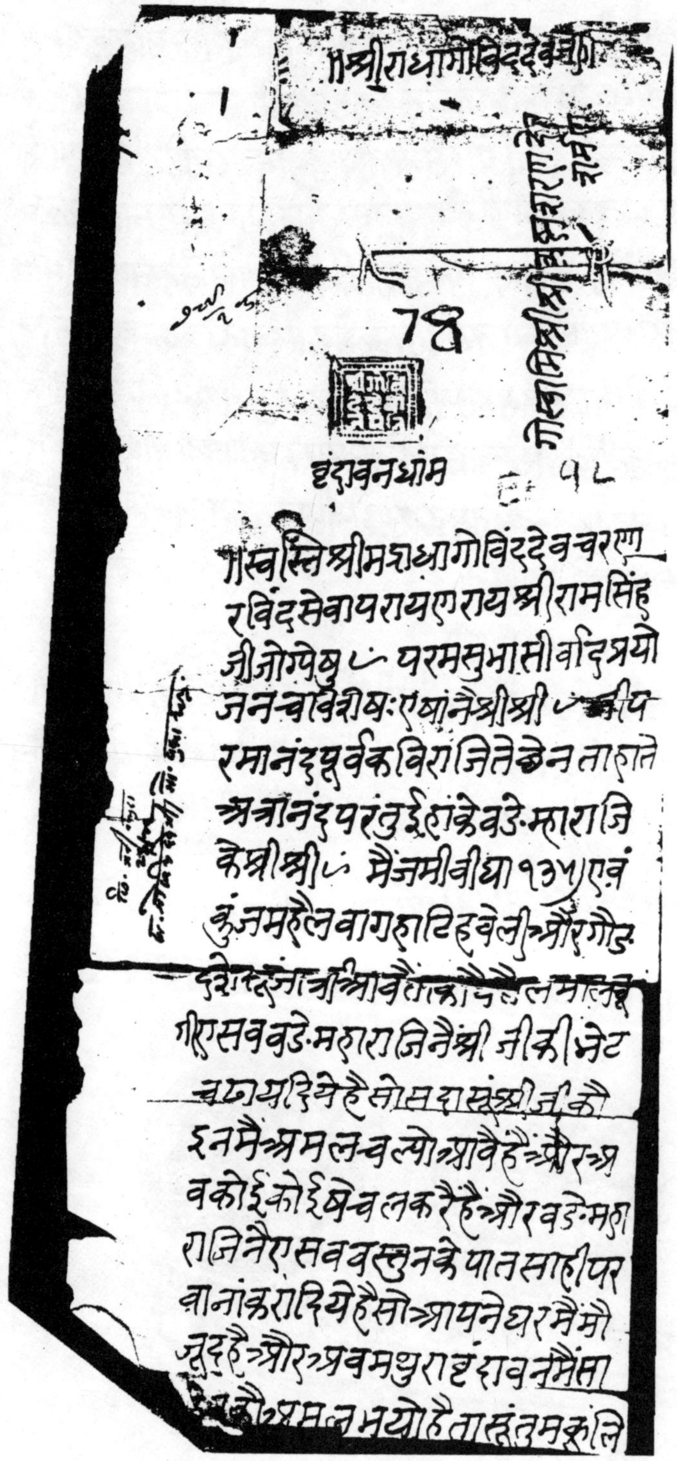

॥श्रीराधागोविंददेवजी॥

78

वृंदावनधाम 58

॥स्वस्तिश्रीमद्राधागोविंददेवचरणा
रविंदसेवापरायण राय श्रीरामसिंह
जीजोग्येषु ॥ परमसुभासीर्वादप्रयो
जनं च विशेषः एथांनै श्रीश्री ॥ [illegible]प
रमानंदपूर्वक विराजिते छेन ताहाते
अत्रानंद परंतु ईहांके बडे म्हाराजि
के श्रीश्री ॥ मैं जमी बीघा १३५ एवं
कुंजमहैल बाग हाटि हवेली और गौड़
[illegible]
गीए सब बडे महाराजिनै श्रीजी की भेट
चढाय दिये है सो सदा सं श्रीजी कौ
इन मैं अमल चल्यो आवै है और अ
ब कोई कोई षेचलक रै है और बडे महा
राजिनै ए सब वस्तुनके पातसाही पर
वानां क्रा दिये है सो आपने घर मैं मौ
जूद है और अब मथुरा वृंदावन मैं सा
[illegible] अमल भयो है तासूं तुम कुलि

नांमकौलिषायभेजोगेजामैंई
नसववस्तुनमैश्री जीकौअमल
रहैऔरफिरंगीकौजवताईअमल
रहैतवताईअचलनहीहोयसोकरौ
गेऔरसमचारश्रीलालमुनसीकेकाग
दसंजांनौगेऔरतुमश्रीजीकेअनन्य
सेवकहोतुमारौनामकरिकैसदाश्री
श्री जीकेचरणारविंदमैंतुलसीचंदन
चढवैहैसोश्री जीतुम्हारोकल्याण
करैगेंमंगलादिसमाचारहमैंसलि
षोगेमितीकात्तिकवदि३सं१८९३के

सिहजीजोग

BACK

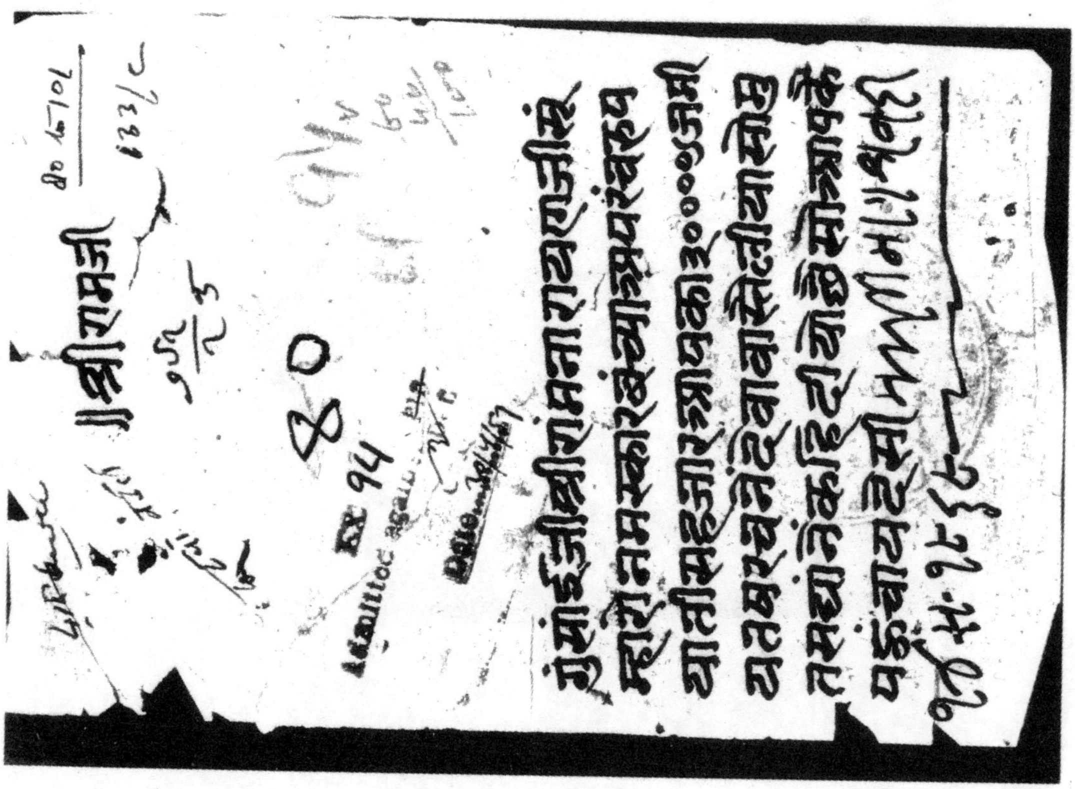

॥श्रीरामजी

गुसांईजी श्री रांमनारायणजी सूं
म्हारो नमस्कार बंच्या अपरंच रुप
या तीस हजार आपका ३०००० जमी
यत खरच नें देवा वास्तै लीया सो मु
तसद्यां नें कहि दीयो है सो आपकै
पहुंचाय देसी [illegible]
१९ सं. १८६८

V.S. 1869, Caitra ś. 1 / 14 March 1812

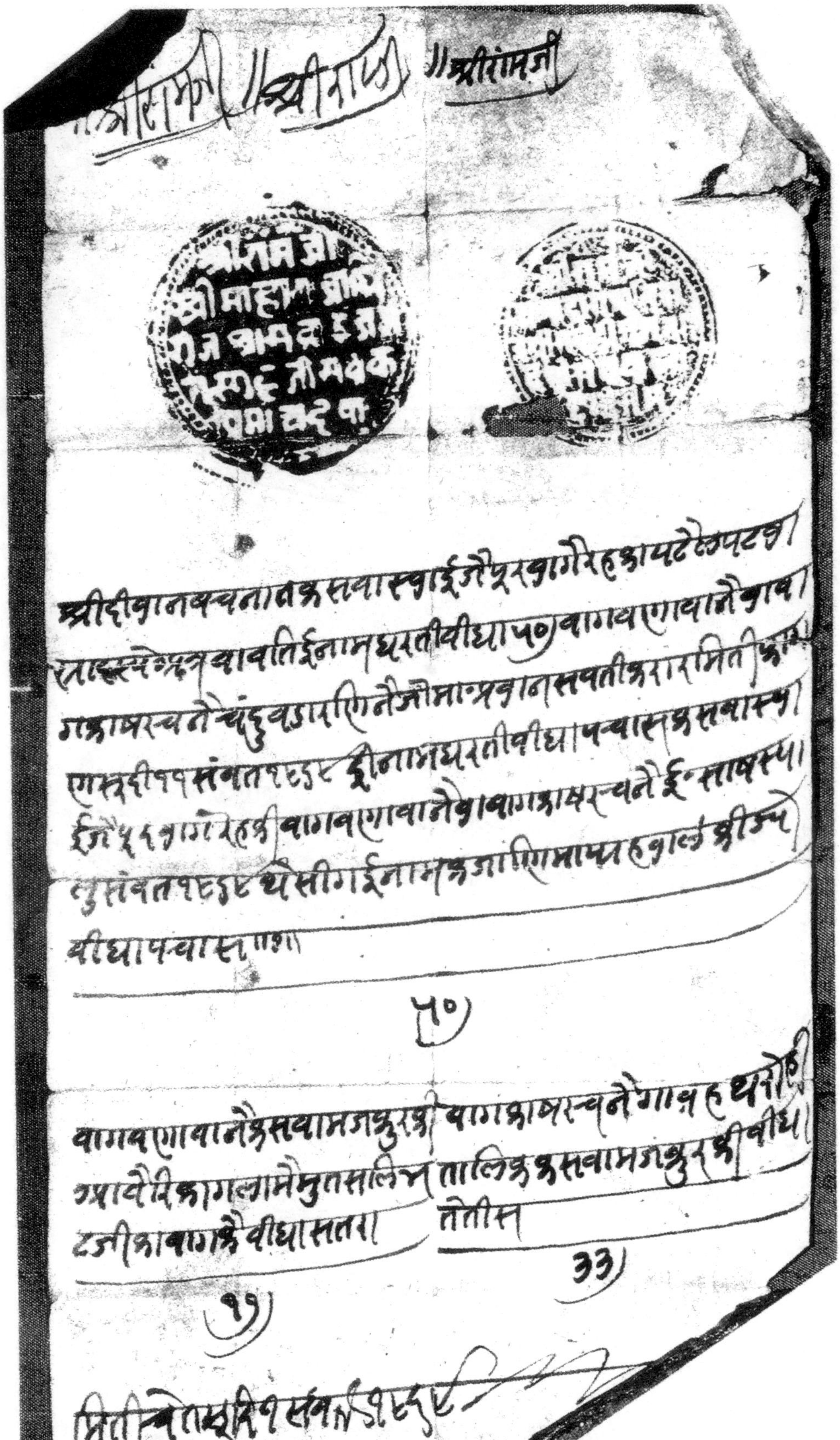

॥श्रीरामजी

गोविंददेवजी

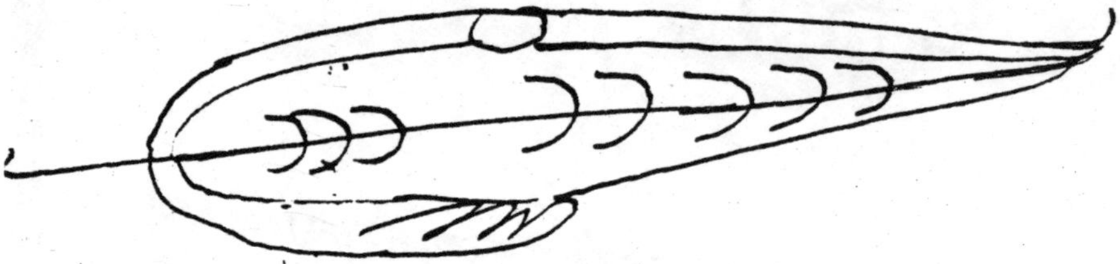

स्वस्ति श्री महाराजाधिराज महाराजा श्री सवाई जगतसिंहजी देव वचनात कमैती अगनां चाटस्सू
दसेसु प्रसाद वंच्या अपरंच बवानि भोगगांव तन जो मिवागेरह सुधां उपया १२९७) का ठाकुर
श्री जीकै अस्तै मुवाफिक ग्यादि दास निमैं दसखत दीवांनयांन करार मितीजिख सु
दि १२ साल संवत १८ ९९ कृ अस जप दोंची जो भोग मैं गांव किरपारामपुरा वागेरह अगनां चाटस्सू तन
जो मिवागेरह सुधां उपया १२९७) का ईवनदाय संवत १८ ९५ थे करि देवा कोई हुकम छो मोदसख
नकरायो थो तै नीद सूफुरमां गांठां मनलव अवांनां का असंवाकि फुहोयगांव किसमारामपुरा वागेर
ह अगनां चाटस्सू तन जो मिवागेरह सुधां उपया वासठि सै अठ्यासी का ईवनदाय संवत १८ ९५ थे
सीगी भोगकै नांगो दासिलद वाल्लै करिवो कीज्यो अरअन करवन बोअवां दूमति मांगपज्यो
ईदीधवांनां सूं दिमान मैं सुजरा होयला
मुकरगांन नयादगांव किरपारामपुरा वागेरह अगनां चाटस्सू का ईवनदाय संवत १८ ९५ थे सीगी भो
गकै नांगो दासिलद वाल्लै करिवो कीज्यो तन जो मिनागेरह सुधां उपया वासठि सै अठ्यासी गांव

१२९७)

गांव किरपारामपुरा तन जो मिवागेरह सुधां उपगांव श्री किसनपुरी वासभ्या को आधु जरखन
तन जो मिवागेरह सुधां उपपाचौतीसै पचावन
चाल्यरडईमैनेनीम

२८३३) ३४५५)

सरहयादिरासनिदाषिलबाकेकरारमितीजेठसुदि१२ मालसंवत१८९९वरसपालैकिरपारामलिषमीचंददी
वांनवनौवातिवङ्कापानवीसवंदेसरकारकिरपारामअत्रडोलजोगगांवठाकुरस्री जीकैवासतैमु
वाफिक यादिरासातिमैंदसषतदीवांनथांनकरारमितीजेठसुदि१२सालसंवत१८९९अरजपरैचीजोजोगमे
गांवकिरपारामपुरावागैरहप्रथनांचात्स्तनजोमिवागैरहसुधांउपपा१२९७काईवतदायसंवत१८९५थे
करीरेथाजोऊकमफवोसोदसषतकरायोचाहेसोदसषतषासकुकमफनामुवाफिककलिषेसीगैजोगके
दोतीवेअवानसवतीलिषीसोचाहिज्येदीवांनसरकारकाअवांनालियेमितीजेठसुदि१२सालसंवत१८९९
अरजमुकरसपहैंचीमुकररागांवमजकूरवागैरहतनजोमिवागैरहसुधांउपपावासकैसैअठासी॥छ॥

१२९७

गांवकिरपारामपुरातनजोमिवागैरहसुधांउपपाअठगांवश्रीकिसनपुरोवासअआकोडा[illegible]रषतनजोमिवा
ईसैतेतीस गैरहसुधांउपपाचौतीसैपचावन

२८३३ ३४५५

मुवाफिकयादिदासातिमैंदसषतषासवरीवांनपांन ४

मिताजेठसुदि१३ मालसंवत१८९९ [illegible]

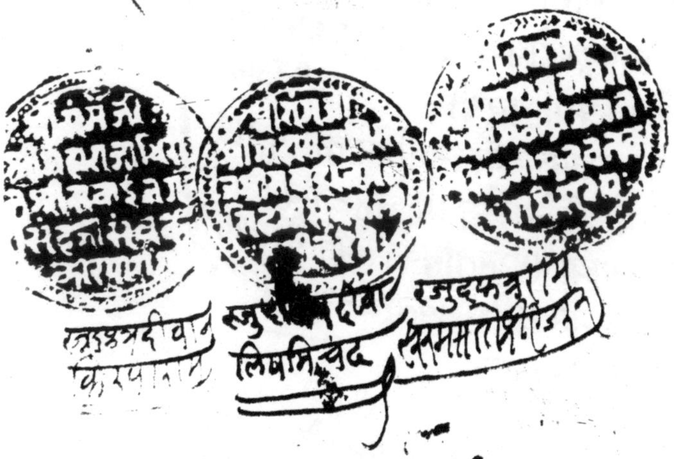

॥श्रीरामजी॥

गोव्यंददेवजी

सवाईप्रतापसिंहजी

हजूरि

॥स्विस्त श्रीसर्वोपमांविराजमानपुज्यश्रीगोस्वांमीजी
श्रीपरामनारायणजीजोग्यलिषतसेवगराजवड
राणिचंदूसरकारमाजीश्रीनद्यांणीजीम्हलमहा
राजावैकुंठवासीजीश्री ——— जीकाकी
ऊवतमाल्ूमहोयआपकैसदैवआनंदचाहि
ज्येअठैठाकुसमाचारश्री ——— जीकीक्रिपा
सूंनलाछेअपरंचम्हारैरामजीबागकसवासवाई
जैपुरमैआंवेरिकैगलैसुतमालिनूटजीकानागकै
मुरतववणायोतैमिंधरतीसुवाफिअवानैसवतीक
रारमितीफागणसुदि१२संवत१८६९थेवीयापचा
सतफसीलजेल॥८॥

५०/

बागनीचैवावागसुधांय बागकाषरचनैगांवहरगरी
रतीकसद!मजकरकीवीहीकीत॥लिकुकसन!मजा
करकीवीया
या
३३/

१७/

मोमुवाफिकहुकमश्री ——— कैठाकुरश्री
जीकानंद मितीवैसाषसुदि१५मालसंवत
१८७२थेअवानांमवतीसुधांचा!सोहासिलवागे
नहचांनेमांश्री ——— जीकैनोगालगु!यडवारको!पू

V.S. 1930, Phālguṇa ś. 4 / 20 February 1874

॥श्रीरामजी हजूर गोविंददेवजी

नाजिम जिला नंदेहै श्री गंगापुर का जो मपलिषत मिरजा गुलाम हेमदवेग कि
नि कव्या अत्र विमाफिक हुकम श्री केकेफिपत म्हेहेकमे म्होतमेजी
लिषे रापल कोनसल की वेमजमुन ठाकुरजी श्री जीका गोगमे
गाव तिम्ये मौजे तनपुरा तपा काक ऽ आना सवाई जेपुर मौजे सील का लष का ज
मासमास्सरी सालिना रु. २२६५॥।) ती की ऐवज मौगाणोली रु. १४७॥) वा मौ स्हजे
पुर रु. ७८७॥) म्ह मौ २ निजामत मजकुर का जमा आसरा मरी रु. २२२५॥) कानिकाल
देणे वास्ते आदी तिम्ह लिषा छा मौ गाणोली कोर मौ. २ नीग श्री जीका मे जमा सरा
सरी सालिना रु. २२६५॥।) अकने रु पपादीपह हजार दोय से पैस ठ आना आठ मे तप
सील जेल म्हगात्या छै
मौ मजकुर मौ स्हजपुर

सो अमल दीवा पहासिल ईस्षाषत नहाल संवत १९३० थेले वादीज्यो सि
तीफागण सुद ४ सं १९३०